DATE DUE

JY 1 6 '98			
NO 4 0l			
MY 9 '02			
FE 5 0			

DEMCO 38-296

THE TRANSFORMING
HAND OF REVOLUTION

Reconsidering the American

Revolution as a Social Movement

UNITED STATES CAPITOL HISTORICAL SOCIETY
Clarence J. Brown, President

PERSPECTIVES ON THE AMERICAN REVOLUTION
Ronald Hoffman and Peter J. Albert, Editors

Diplomacy and Revolution: The Franco-American Alliance of 1778

Sovereign States in an Age of Uncertainty

Slavery and Freedom in the Age of the American Revolution

Arms and Independence: The Military Character of the American Revolution

An Uncivil War: The Southern Backcountry during the American Revolution

Peace and the Peacemakers: The Treaty of 1783

The Economy of Early America: The Revolutionary Period, 1763–1790

Women in the Age of the American Revolution

To Form a More Perfect Union: The Critical Ideas of the Constitution

Religion in a Revolutionary Age

Of Consuming Interests: The Style of Life in the Eighteenth Century

The Transforming Hand of Revolution: Reconsidering the American Revolution as a Social Movement

The Transforming
Hand of Revolution

Reconsidering the American

Revolution as a Social Movement

Edited by RONALD HOFFMAN
and PETER J. ALBERT

Published for the

UNITED STATES CAPITOL HISTORICAL SOCIETY

BY THE UNIVERSITY PRESS OF VIRGINIA

Charlottesville and London

THE UNIVERSITY PRESS OF VIRGINIA
Copyright © 1995 by the Rector and Visitors
of the University of Virginia

First Published 1996

Printed in the United States of America

Library of Congress Cataloging-in-Publication Data

The transforming hand of revolution : reconsidering the American Revolution as a
social movement / edited by Ronald Hoffman and Peter J. Albert.
    p. cm. — (Perspectives on the American Revolution)
    Includes index.
    ISBN 0–8139–1561–9 (alk. paper)
    1. United States—History—Revolution, 1775–1783—Social aspects.
I. Hoffman, Ronald, 1941– . II. Albert, Peter J. III. Series.
E209.T835 1995
973.3′1—dc20   95–20320
                                    CIP

Contents

CONTENTS

Preface

THE THEME of this volume is one that has engaged my interest since my days as a graduate student at the University of Wisconsin. My serious consideration of the topic began in the late 1960s when, in the course of research for my dissertation on Revolutionary Maryland, I examined the correspondence of Charles Carroll of Carrollton, one of Maryland's signers of the Declaration of Independence. These letters, particularly those between Carroll and his father, Charles Carroll of Annapolis, introduced me to a world that no one knew existed in 1967. At that time, the reigning orthodoxy governing interpretations of the American Revolution saw its coming as primarily an affair of the mind. As exemplified in the writings of Bernard Bailyn, Jack P. Greene, Edmund S. Morgan, and Gordon S. Wood, this rich body of scholarly thought portrayed a Revolutionary movement led by impassioned, disinterested idealists bent on creating a new nation committed to the grand republican principle of liberty. I had, I must confess, been exposed to an alternate interpretation at Wisconsin, but even the line of reasoning propounded by Merrill Jensen—and Carl Becker before him—that the Revolutionaries had been motivated by opportunism, self-interest, and a desire for power in addition to their ideological convictions—did not prepare me for what the Carrolls had to say.

Depending on one's sensibilities, the Carrolls' role in the coming of the Revolution could be interpreted as falling within the ken of either historiographical school—at least up until August 2, 1776, when Charles Carroll of Carrollton signed the Declaration of Independence. But when Carroll left Philadelphia to return to Maryland, he went home to some stark Revolutionary realities. Confronted by what he believed to be a threat of anarchy from a sorely disaffected populace, he recanted his signing of the Declaration and urged reconciliation with the mother country lest all be lost—*all* being one of colonial America's most considerable fortunes. Realizing over the next few months that rejoining the empire was impossible, he worked with his colleagues in Maryland's leadership elite to establish the most conservative of all the new state constitutions as a means of securing their control of the government. Equally important, Carroll and his associates moved to popularize the Revolution by enacting a radical economic program designed to curry favor with the citizens of a debt-ridden society at the expense of creditors—the Carrolls chief among them. Although there was virtually no disagreement among Maryland's Revolutionary leaders about the critical need for this policy, Charles Carroll of Carrollton's father opposed it vociferously. From 1777 through 1780, father and son argued vigorously with each other, and through their letters there emerges a vivid portrayal of what the Revolution meant both for the planter class, whose wealth and position placed it at risk, and the "lesser sort," who were expected to do most of the fighting and the dying.

The image of the American Revolution revealed in the Carroll correspondence presented a dimension of that experience that contrasted sharply with what I had read in the literature as a graduate student. Clearly, the Carrolls perceived in the lesser sort's challenge to their class's privileged status and notions of proper social order dangers that equalled those posed by the military might of the British empire. The turmoil of war and its attendant social dislocation unleashed resentments long suppressed by the structural framework of colonial society, and when invigorated by the "leveling" tendencies inherent in the "contagion" of Revolutionary rhetoric, this rancor threatened the leadership's social and political position, as well as its wealth.[1] To survive the Revolution, the aristocracy had to bend with the times. As Carroll bluntly told his father: "There is a time when it is wisdom to yield to injustice, and to popular frensies & delusions: many wise and good men have acted so. When public bodies

---

[1] Bernard Bailyn, *The Ideological Origins of the American Revolution* (Cambridge, Mass., 1967), chap. 7.

commit injustice, and are exposed to the public & can not vindicate themselves by reasoning, they commonly have recourse to violence & greater injustice towards all such as have the temerity to oppose them, particularly when their unjust proceedings are popular."[2]

It seemed to me then, as it seems to me now, that Charles Carroll of Carrollton and his associates were talking about and trying to deal with class conflict. Carroll recognized, as did his colleagues, that support for the Revolution was uncertain. Beyond their dislike for arbitrary British policy, the people had limited interest in backing a war effort that they quickly realized would demand far more of them than imperial rule ever had. To give the debtor majority a stake in the successful outcome of the war, the leadership elite devised legislation that voided the bulk of internal credit obligations by making paper currency legal tender for the payment of sterling debts and shifted the tax base from polls to land and slaves. I suppose that these sacrifices could be interpreted as virtuous acts on the part of a disinterested elite to save the patriot cause, but I believe the aristocracy took these steps in order to *save themselves* and to *contain* the Revolution.

A few years later, I turned my attention to the South during the American Revolution and found striking parallels between what occurred there and the situation Carroll and his colleagues faced in Maryland. Indeed, what Carroll feared would happen in Maryland did in fact take place in North Carolina. By the late 1770s, North Carolina's Revolutionary leaders believed they were fighting a civil war as much as a war of independence. Urged by militia officers to make greater efforts to secure the domestic front, the beleaguered officials of the government in Hillsborough had no idea where the domestic front was located. The capture of the governor, Thomas Burke, by a raiding party of disaffected partisans, and his imprisonment on James Island with persons who were disenchanted with *both* sides, vividly depicts the desperate character of the situation.

Similarly, my work on Nathanael Greene, the general in

[2] Charles Carroll of Carrollton to Charles Carroll of Annapolis, Nov. 13, 1777, Carroll Papers, MS 206, no. 444, Maryland Historical Society, Baltimore.

charge of the southern theater from 1780 to 1783, confirmed the perilous position of the patriot cause within a disordered society so rent with economic and social division that its members had little incentive to swear allegiance to it. Like Carroll, Greene understood that the clash of class interests permeated the wartime situation and that these interests were far more complex and ran much deeper than the issues of imperial dispute. The broad context of the war provided a framework within which old scores could be settled and other agendas pursued, and it was Greene's recognition of and acute sensitivity to these divisive undercurrents that allowed him to develop the policies that held the South together until the final treaty of peace could be negotiated.[3]

These reflections suggest a few of the insights that can be gained from pursuing J. Franklin Jameson's perceptive suggestion that scholars pay serious attention to the social character of the American Revolution. Moreover, the compelling image of Revolutionary transformation that he proposed more than fifty years ago remains, as the richly imaginative essays in this volume attest, a tellingly accurate description of the effect of the seminal event in our nation's history.

RONALD HOFFMAN

[3] Returning to these themes in 1992, in a paper entitled "The American Revolution as a Civil War" presented at the University of Barcelona, gave me an opportunity to resurvey the fine studies that have, during the last quarter-century, increased our understanding of the southern experience during the war years. Among these are Ronald Hoffman, Thad W. Tate, and Peter J. Albert, eds., *An Uncivil War: The Southern Backcountry during the American Revolution* (Charlottesville, Va., 1985), and Rachel N. Klein, *Unification of a Slave State: The Rise of the Planter Class in the South Carolina Backcountry, 1760–1808* (Chapel Hill, 1990).

Acknowledgments

THE EDITORS WISH to acknowledge the contributions of the other participants at the U.S. Capitol Historical Society's symposium "'The Transforming Hand of Revolution': Reconsidering the American Revolution as a Social Movement," Edward Countryman, Nathan O. Hatch, James A. Henretta, John M. Murrin, Mechal Sobel, and Sean Wilentz. We would also like to acknowledge the help of Diane Koch, Mary C. Jeske, and Aileen Arnold in the preparation of this manuscript.

THE TRANSFORMING
HAND OF REVOLUTION

Reconsidering the American

Revolution as a Social Movement

MOREY ROTHBERG

John Franklin Jameson and the Creation of *The American Revolution Considered as a Social Movement*

IMMEDIATELY UPON ITS publication in 1926, John Franklin Jameson's *The American Revolution Considered as a Social Movement* was recognized as a significant contribution to American historical scholarship. In his consideration of the book for the *American Historical Review,* Allan Nevins observed that "the scholarship is impeccable, the style is polished, and that, above all, the outlook is broad and thoughtful."[1] As Nevins pointed out, the volume is remarkable for the great variety and detail of information concisely expressed and for its uniformly positive tone, the latter justified, in Nevins's view, "on the ground that the idea held in view throughout is that of progress."[2] The lectures that comprise the book reinforce the public image that Jameson cultivated of an urbane, tolerant,

---

[1] Allan Nevins, review of *The American Revolution Considered as a Social Movement, American Historical Review* 32 (1926): 167–68. Jameson thanked Nevins for his "very amiable review of my little book." He added that "it was a dubious procedure to print any notice of my book in a journal edited by me, but on the whole I thought I owed it to the Princeton University Press to not have it ignored in the *American Historical Review*" ([John Franklin Jameson] to Nevins, Aug. 27, 1926, American Historical Association Records, Box 305, Manuscript Division, Library of Congress). Still, Jameson buried the review in the "Minor Notices" section.

[2] Nevins review, p. 168.

1

detached man of letters, which to a large extent he was. As they were originally delivered in 1895 at Barnard College, these lectures, titled *The American Revolution as a Social Movement,* reveal a highly opinionated, politically engaged individual for whom the American Revolution and its consequences created problems that his own very turbulent society had been unable to resolve. It is the genesis of these lectures, and a related series of largely unpublished writings leading up to them, that this essay for the most part addresses, for in these works Jameson displayed both the acuity and cosmopolitanism for which he was nearly legendary and the difficulties he encountered as a patrician scholar who felt obligated to think and write about people with whom he had little empathy.

The success of Jameson's book was the capstone of a career marked by significant achievements. Born in a suburb of Boston, Jameson was first and foremost a New Englander whose Calvinist ancestors stood as monuments along the path he knew he must follow. Educated at Roxbury Latin School and then at Amherst College, from which he graduated in 1879, Jameson received from schooling and parental guidance a steady reinforcement of the commitment to service that seemed to him the essence of Puritan thought. However traditional Jameson's upbringing, the post–Civil War development of the American university, symbolized most impressively by the founding of the Johns Hopkins University in 1876, made college teaching a much more attractive focus for his reformist energies than did the more commonly accepted professions of law, medicine, or the ministry. Jameson enrolled as a graduate student at Johns Hopkins in the fall of 1880, and with the awarding of his doctorate in history in 1882, the first given at the university in that field, Jameson joined the growing ranks of urban professionals who proposed to substitute expertise for political partisanship as the source of authority and power in modern America.

A distinguished professor of history for over twenty years at Johns Hopkins, Brown University, and the University of Chicago, Jameson in 1905 assumed the directorship of the Department of Historical Research at the Carnegie Institution of Washington. In this position, which he held for twenty-three years, he initiated or continued a breathtaking array of projects—editorship of the *American Historical Review,* campaigns for a national historical publications commission and a national archives, publication of guides to foreign archives, documentary histories of the slave trade and slave laws, and an annual bibliographical guide, *Writings on American History.* Jameson incorporated the American Council of Learned Societies (ACLS), produced an atlas of American history, and provided guidance for the *Dictionary of American Biography.* He took on, furthermore, numerous influential assignments within the American Historical Association, the presidency of which he held in 1907. These many activities were but a partial realization of his vision of a great national historical enterprise emanating from Washington under his leadership. His singular achievement at the department of historical research, particularly through his editing of the *American Historical Review,* was to lift American historical scholarship out of the parochialism encouraged by geographical isolation. In 1928 he became chief of the division of manuscripts at the Library of Congress and the first incumbent at the library of its endowed chair in American history. Whether he was editing the *Review,* chairing the Historical Manuscripts Commission of the American Historical Association, encouraging the ACLS, lobbying bureaucrats and politicians for a national archives building, or increasing the manuscript treasures of the Library of Congress, Jameson displayed an intellectual cosmopolitanism few could match. Within the ACLS in particular, Jameson proved the perfect interlocutor in drawing out the common interests of philologists, historians, archaeologists, and others whose thoughts rarely intersected.[3]

Although Jameson grew up within a family of modest

[3] For further information on Jameson's background and career, see Morey D. Rothberg, "Servant to History: A Study of John Franklin Jameson, 1859–1937," Ph.D. diss., Brown University, 1982; idem, "'To Set a Standard of Workmanship and Compel Men to Conform to It': John Franklin Jameson as Editor of the *American Historical Review,*" *American Historical Review* 89 (1984):957–75; and idem, "The Brahmin as Bureaucrat: J. Franklin Jameson at the Carnegie Institution of Washington, 1905–1928," *Public Historian* 8 (1986):47–60. See also the introduction to Morey Rothberg and Jacqueline Goggin, eds., *John Franklin Jameson and the Development of Humanistic Scholarship in America,* vol. 1, *Selected Essays* (Athens, Ga., 1993).

means—he lived with his parents throughout his four years as an undergraduate at Amherst College and supported the family while teaching at Johns Hopkins—he learned early to regard himself as a member of a social and intellectual elite. His mother, Mariette Thompson Jameson, was descended from a founder of Woburn, Massachusetts, and she admonished her son while he was still a youth to "associate with those not our equals to benefit them if possible." Frank Jameson's unease at socializing with different classes of people distressed her, "for sometimes it is really one's duty to associate with inferiors."[4] As valedictorian of the class of 1879 at Amherst, Jameson reminded the graduating seniors of their responsibility to resolve the great issues of their day, not thinking themselves superior in this work, "but we must feel that we are under stronger obligations to attempt it."[5]

When Jameson enrolled at Johns Hopkins, he entered an environment that encouraged budding scholars to view their work in relation to current political issues. Jameson took up the challenge in the first major paper he wrote as a student in the Johns Hopkins Seminary of Historical and Political Science, an essay titled "The Disturbances in Barbados in 1876." Noting the violent response of poor blacks on the island to the apparent indifference of the planter class to their misery, Jameson considered various modes of governance that might resolve the island's problems and settled on what he termed "an impartial administrative despotism" in which "the two races, each restrained from oppression of the other, may most quickly and happily arrive at the condition in which the establishment of a constitutional government is not only possible, but wise."[6]

[4] Mariette Thompson Jameson to John Franklin Jameson, Jan. 12, 1880, John Franklin Jameson Papers, box 5, Manuscript Division, Library of Congress. See also Rothberg, "Servant to History," chap. 1.

[5] [Jameson], "Buddha," July 1, 1879, Jameson Papers, box 25.

[6] Jameson, "The Disturbances in Barbados in 1876," in Rothberg and Goggin, eds., Selected Essays, pp. 11–12. Jameson's scholarly interest in the West Indies was probably encouraged by a trip his family made there in 1867 when he was seven years old. See Jameson, diary, [1867], Jameson Papers, box 1.

The guiding principle upon which historical study proceeded in the Johns Hopkins Seminary was the village community theory, which later became known as the germ theory. According to this hypothesis, the beginnings of American political institutions could be found in the structure of English parish assemblies and, beyond the parish assemblies, in the procedures for land distribution followed by "Teutonic farmers" in the forests of medieval Germany.[7] Study of the history of local institutions, according to Herbert Baxter Adams, the head of the Seminary, would stimulate "the expansion of the local consciousness into a fuller sense of its historic worth and dignity, of the cosmopolitan relations of modern local life, and of its own wholesome conservative power in these days of growing centralization." Moreover, institutional history drew a line of continuous development from local attachments to national citizenship, and from national citizenship to membership in the international community, eliminating any need for the political parties so disliked by the mugwump reformers who found safe refuge in the Hopkins Seminary and in other American universities.[8] Finally, the history of the locality proved that Americans had England far more than Germany to thank for the beneficent combination of national sovereignty and local self-government.[9]

The appreciation expressed by historians for British influence in American history heralded what one scholar has termed "the great rapprochement" between elites in Great-Britain and the United States in the late nineteenth century.[10] Enemies and then rivals since the American Revolution, Brit-

---

[7] Herbert Baxter Adams, *The Germanic Origin of New England Towns*, Johns Hopkins University Studies in Historical and Political Science, 1st ser., no. 2 (1882):48, 58; see also Rothberg, "Servant to History," pp. 45–46.

[8] Herbert Baxter Adams, *Co-operation in University Work*, Johns Hopkins University Studies in Historical and Political Science, 1st ser., no. 2 (1882):89. See also Rothberg, "'To Set a Standard of Workmanship and Compel Men to Conform to It,'" p. 958.

[9] Rothberg, "Servant to History," p. 46.

[10] See Bradford Perkins, *The Great Rapprochement: England and the United States, 1894–1914* (New York, 1968).

ain and America found reason for accord as imperialism took hold in both countries. In particular, influential New Englanders who found themselves competing for position and prestige with more recent immigrant stock from eastern Europe and the Mediterranean sympathized with the imperial designs of their Anglo-Saxon brethren overseas. American patricians idealized England as a model of national purpose, ethnic homogeneity, and aristocratic control that they might hope to emulate.[11]

As a graduate student and later as an instructor at Johns Hopkins, Jameson made light of the Seminary's obsession with local institutions. "Our men have received from Adams altogether too one-sided an impulse to study the local institutions under the Anglo-Saxons," he confided to his diary. "I am going to get over that period in two meetings."[12] Yet Jameson never publicly disavowed the village community theory, and his own writings reflected the same desire to recreate the sturdy spirit of Anglo-Saxon democracy in a society far too ethnically diverse to support such a notion.[13]

The idea of a democratic but deferential society evolving over centuries became, if anything, even more appealing to Jameson as class and ethnic differences made themselves increasingly visible to him. On one occasion in the fall of 1882,

[11] Ibid., pp. 8, 64, 66, 68, 74; John Higham, *Strangers in the Land: Patterns of American Nativism 1860–1925* (New Brunswick, N.J., 1955), pp. 108–9, 137–39; Barbara Miller Solomon, *Ancestors and Immigrants: A Changing New England Tradition* (Cambridge, Mass., 1956), pp. 59–61; Cushing Strout, *The American Image of the Old World* (New York, 1963), pp. 134, 140–41, 144; A. S. Eisenstadt, *Charles McLean Andrews: A Study in American Historical Writing* (New York, 1956), pp. 206–7.

[12] Jameson, diary, Sept. 28, [1883], Jameson Papers, box 3. See also John Higham, *History: Professional Scholarship in America* (1965; reprint ed., Baltimore, 1983), pp. 160–62; and the introduction to Marvin E. Gettleman, ed., *The Johns Hopkins University Seminary of History and Politics: The Records of an American Educational Institution, 1877–1912*, 5 vols. (New York, 1987–90), 1:14–24.

[13] I have found instructive, in considering Jameson's intellectual and political beliefs, the remarks made by John Higham at a ceremony at the National Archives on Sept. 28, 1987, the fiftieth anniversary of Jameson's death.

Adams adjourned the weekly meeting of the Seminary to permit its members to observe a political rally. Jameson left the rally disgusted at what appeared to him the low aptitude of the masses, "but every political meeting I have attended has had the same effect, to shatter my rising respect for the people, in their political capacity, and make me despise them." In 1886, he described Isidor Rayner, a congressional candidate in Baltimore, as "a vulgar, loudly-dressed, dirty young Jew."[14]

Such attitudes made Jameson an unlikely candidate to view with insight the role of common people in history, but a social historian he meant to become. When James Bryce suggested to him on a visit to Baltimore in November 1883 that determining the social aspect of politics would prove most challenging, Jameson assured himself that this would be his greatest achievement.[15] Before this discussion, his extensive reading schedule had led Jameson to discover the works of Henry Thomas Buckle and Hippolyte Taine, scholars who in different ways stimulated the study of social history. For Taine, the author of a study on the ancien régime, understanding French history before the Revolution meant exploring that history from every perspective, immersing oneself in its social texture.[16]

While Taine was passionately engaged with his subject, Henry Buckle, in his *History of Civilization in England*, stood at a distance from the people and events he discussed. He was at pains to show how "scientific" history could be, citing an impressive number of works in anthropology, geography, biology, botany, and chemistry. Physical and social influences stood far behind intellect, however, as the prime mover in his

[14] Jameson, diary, Oct. 27, [1882], Oct. 18, [1886], Jameson Papers, boxes 2, 4. See also Rothberg, "The Brahmin as Bureaucrat," p. 49, and Edward N. Saveth, *American Historians and European Immigrants, 1875–1925* (New York, 1948), p. 14.

[15] Jameson, diary, Nov. 26, [1883], Jameson Papers, box 3.

[16] Hippolyte Taine, *The Ancient Regime*, trans. John Durand (1881; reprint ed., Freeport, N.Y., 1972), pp. viii–x, 179–80; Rothberg, "Servant to History," p. 52.

grand scheme. Around the world, nature and mind were at war with each other, and in Europe alone the mind had triumphed.[17]

Taine was far superior to Buckle, Jameson concluded, because "he understands and can set forth the course and origins of a popular movement, and the social condition of a whole nation," but it was Henry Buckle whom Jameson more closely resembled in his writings.[18] As Buckle remained an intellectual historian while professing to write social history, so Jameson saw the realm of ideas as a restraining influence on the unpredictable and often undesirable consequences of social movements.

A series of lectures on state constitutional and political history that he delivered at the Seminary in January 1885 and later published in the Johns Hopkins University Studies in Historical and Political Science provided Jameson his first extended foray into social history. He began provocatively by commenting that "our political histories have for the most part been Iliads; they are filled with the deeds of the chieftains 'wise in council,' 'fertile in devices,' 'kings of men,' . . . while the rest of the well-greaved Achaians stand in their ranks unnoticed and unsung." John Bach McMaster's *History of the People of the United States*, if flawed, represented a healthy departure from this practice, Jameson acknowledged, "but the true history of our nation will not be written until we can obtain a correct and exhaustive knowledge of the history of public opinion upon politics, the history of the political views and actions of the average voter."[19] Politics still provided Jameson the essential frame of reference, and the "voter," a statistical entity, was the center of attention rather than the tradespeople, merchants, farmers, and lawyers that Taine embraced.

It was this constitutional history of the individual states on which Jameson focused as the subject of what he modestly

[17] Henry Thomas Buckle, *History of Civilization in England*, 2 vols. (New York, 1860), 1:109–13.

[18] Jameson, diary, Oct. 19, [1881], Jameson Papers, box 2.

[19] Jameson, *An Introduction to the Study of the Constitutional and Political History of the States*, in Rothberg and Goggin, eds., *Selected Essays*, vol. 1, p. 18.

decided would be his "magnum opus" many years hence.[20]
While still an instructor at Johns Hopkins, he began to sketch
the outline of this project, focusing first on the American
South. A number of reasons may have encouraged him in this
direction. Residents of Baltimore, a southern city, understandably made up a sizable proportion of both the undergraduate and graduate students in the early years of the
university, and the history of slavery became a subject for investigation in the Johns Hopkins Seminary.[21] Also, the problem of elite rule over a multiracial society, which Jameson had
examined in his essay on Barbados, appeared to extend to
the post-Reconstruction South.[22] Undoubtedly, the South as
an area for research appealed to Jameson because of its prox-
imity to Baltimore, where he hoped to remain permanently
as a professor at Johns Hopkins. An unusual further incentive
in this direction came from his close relationship to a board-
inghouse owner in Baltimore, Martha Ward Carey—a Virginian, a friend to many of the Hopkins graduate students, and a
real-life Scarlett O'Hara, who had lifted herself and her family
from destitution following the Civil War.[23] While Jameson had

[20] Jameson, diary, Mar. 15, [1883], Jameson Papers, box 2.

[21] John David Smith, *An Old Creed for the New South: Proslavery Ideology and Historiography, 1865–1918* (Westport, Conn., 1985), chap. 5. In the fall of 1884, thirteen of the thirty graduate students in history at Johns Hopkins came from Maryland, twelve of these from Baltimore. The subject of slavery in the antebellum North stimulated a lively debate in the Seminary in the spring of 1885, and a paper on the subject by Jameson. (*Johns Hopkins University Circulars* 4 [1884]:8–10; Jameson, "What Became of the Northern Slaves?" May 22, 1885, Jameson Papers, box 25. See also Hugh Hawkins, *Pioneer: A History of the Johns Hopkins University, 1874–1889* [Ithaca, N.Y., 1960], p. 271; and James Curtis Ballagh, "The Johns Hopkins University and the South," *Johns Hopkins University Circulars* 20 [1901]:23.) For this and other related information, I acknowledge the research assistance of Jacqueline Goggin.

[22] Jameson explicitly compared the problems Great Britain experienced in governing Barbadian blacks to those encountered by Radical Republicans during Reconstruction, although he later regretted introducing this sensitive issue in the Seminary (Jameson, "Disturbances in Barbados," p. 11; idem, diary, Nov. 19, [1880], Jameson Papers, box 1).

[23] Peter Matthiessen, "Homegoing," in Evelyn Ward, *The Children of Bladensfield: With an Essay by Peter Matthiessen* (New York, 1978), pp. 120–21.

grown up in an atmosphere that left no room for doubt that slavery had been an unmitigated evil, an intense exchange of views with Martha Carey in 1885 provoked him to "feel more distinctly how awful a thing the war was, until I begin to doubt whether it would not have been better to let them go."[24]

When Jameson left Baltimore in the fall of 1888 for a professorship at Brown University, he took with him his plans for the investigation of southern history—at different times he envisaged an edition of the Virginia Company records and biographies of John C. Calhoun and Richard Henry Lee— even though he was now considerably farther away from his sources.[25] Invited to return to Johns Hopkins in the spring of 1891, Jameson used the occasion to lecture at the Seminary on the constitutional and political history of the South and subsequently to travel through the eastern half of Virginia, examining private and public collections of documents.[26]

In these lectures Jameson again found that it was easier to talk about abstractions than about people. How did it happen, for example, that highly aristocratic Virginia produced a Declaration of Rights, the abolition of entail and primogeniture, and the disestablishment of the Anglican Church? The solution to this apparently contradictory situation was the influence of the Enlightenment, embodied in the words and deeds of Thomas Jefferson.[27] Ideas moved history, and at least in Virginia they were strong enough "to cast off the shackles of oligarchical privilege and base the new government upon the broad foundations of popular support."[28] Speaking the fol-

[24] Jameson, diary, May 5, [1885], Jameson Papers, box 3.

[25] Ibid., July 6, [1885], Sept. 30, [1889], ibid., boxes 3, 4; J. Franklin Jameson to John Jameson, Apr. 1, 1888, ibid., box 8.

[26] Herbert B. Adams to J. Franklin Jameson, July 3, 14, 1890, ibid., box 46; [Jameson], "A Little Journey of Historical Research in Eastern Virginia. Read before the [Rhode Island] Historical Society on February 23, 1892," ibid., box 28.

[27] Jameson, "Lectures on the Constitutional and Political History of the South," in Rothberg and Goggin, eds., Selected Essays, p. 96; see also Rothberg, "Servant to History," pp. 123–24.

[28] Jameson, "Lectures on the Constitutional and Political History of the South," p. 84.

lowing year on the colonial history of Virginia, first at the Peabody Institute in Baltimore and then before a meeting of the Rhode Island Historical Society, Jameson made plain his belief that, even more than Jefferson's statecraft, the secret to success in Virginia politics rested with the existence of a largely rural, homogeneous society of Anglo-Saxon heritage in which mobility between classes coexisted with clearly understood traditions of deference to education and position: "Towns and trade had little place in Virginia, and the vast majority of the great middle class consisted of yeomen, small planters and farmers. They were a vigorous class of genuine English stock, sturdy and manly, sharing the independent spirit of the richer planters, yet naturally following the lead of the latter in political, as well as in social matters. They were considerably more ignorant than their social superiors, but they had the same generous and hospitable dispositions."[29]

The farther west and south one moved from Virginia, the more turbulent and politically troubling was the history of the region; reason and a common ancestry could not contain the struggle between opposing economic interests. It was actually in the Old Southwest of Alabama, Mississippi, Kentucky, and Tennessee that democracy would be most firmly anchored, Jameson found. Here was the birthplace of Jacksonian democracy, and, anticipating Frederick Jackson Turner's discussion of the frontier, the reason was economic: "In these regions a new type of American humanity was being developed, destined in time to force upon the older portions of the south a democracy more complete than their own, because based upon economic conditions more favorable to pure democracy, and an Americanism more fervent because more perfectly free from economic and mental dependence upon Europe."[30] Left to themselves, the masses displayed both a marvelous zest for democracy and an appalling ignorance of

[29] [Jameson], "Virginia History, 1763–1812, Lectures Delivered at the Peabody Institute, Baltimore, Jan. 26, 28, Feb. 2, 4, 1892: I. Virginia and the Revolution, 1763–1783," Jameson Papers, box 28, p. 11; see also [Jameson], "A Little Journey of Historical Research," p. 38.

[30] Jameson, "Lectures on the Constitutional and Political History of the South," p. 144.

the restraints necessary to prevent freedom from dissolving first into anarchy and then into tyranny. This was the lesson Jameson found in the history of Jacksonian democracy and, more recently, in the amazing growth of Populism, "a movement on the part of masses hitherto but slightly engaged in politics, which threatens to put the conduct of our public affairs into the hands of a vast horde of unintelligent farmers, whose ardency and inexperience combine to put them in the power of loud demagogues and skillful wire-pullers."[31]

The role of race and class in history could not be ignored, but it could be downplayed. The economics of cotton production and the expansion of slavery led inevitably to the outbreak of the Civil War, Jameson acknowledged, but he added,

> Probably historians of the future will look back upon the history of the slavery question, as an episode in our national history,— an episode of enormous consequence, indeed, but still, properly speaking, an episode. It interrupted rather than essentially modified the development of this great Democratic republic. A foreign body had been lodged in our political system and increased and festered until the acute surgery of Civil War was necessary to remove it. But then the natural evolution of American politics is resumed and it becomes possible for us to link our studies of the present time with studies of that remoter period before slavery became a dominant political force in the South.[32]

Along with his explorations in southern history, Jameson examined the colonial and Revolutionary history of the North. Here the results were even more distressing to this Brahmin scholar, for the middle colonies especially compelled a recognition of ethnic as well as economic diversity as contributing factors to political development. Reassuringly, he concluded in an 1890 lecture, "The Origin of Political Parties in the United States," that party disputes were minimal in his native Massachusetts, which was "unified by severe measures

[31] Jameson, ibid., p. 160; see also Rothberg, "Servant to History," pp. 125–26; and idem, "'To Set a Standard of Workmanship and Compel Men to Conform to It,'" p. 973.

[32] Jameson, "Lectures on the Constitutional and Political History of the South," p. 165.

based on the conviction that the interests and wills of individuals must be strictly subordinated to the interest and will of the community." Political conflict was greatest in the colonies of New York and Pennsylvania, both populated heavily by Germans. The Germans in Pennsylvania, "not having inherited traditions of self-government and of Anglo-Saxon modes of political action, were largely indifferent to public affairs, desiring only to be undisturbed and to be prosperous." In colonial New York, Jameson found the same propensity to individual aggrandizement and "a similar dead-weight of non-English population indifferent to large political questions and therefore at the disposal of energetic politicians."[33]

The Revolution stimulated the creation of political parties throughout the seaboard colonies, loyalists among the old, wealthier, mercantile elite, and whigs largely from the debtor and yeoman class, along with the anomalous Virginian aristocracy attracted to the Revolutionary cause out of a fierce spirit of local independence. When Jameson presented his thoughts on the social history of the American Revolution as part of the Lowell Institute lectures in 1920, the *Boston Evening Transcript* headlined his assertion that the loyalist cause was worthy of much greater appreciation than it had been accorded in the past.[34] Indeed, Jameson's discussion in his public lectures on party development in the Revolutionary era was predominately an endorsement of loyalism. "It has for a century been customary in America to speak of the Tories with aversion and even hostility, as of persons who were not only enemies but traitors," he pointed out in "The Origin of Political Parties" and again in the Barnard lectures on the Revolution:

> It is time that all this should cease. Can men become traitors to a nation which does not yet exist by remaining faithful to a government which has long existed? Why is it customary among us to eulogize the faithfulness of the Union men of West Virginia, of eastern Tennessee and of North Carolina during the late civil

[33] Jameson, "The Origin of Political Parties in the United States," in Rothberg and Goggin, eds., *Selected Essays*, pp. 47, 49–50.

[34] "Tories Not as Painted," *Boston Evening Transcript,* Nov. 10, 1920.

war? Is it not because, against the strong opposition of communities determined to secure independence and set up a new government, they remained firm in allegiance to the old government to which they had long been attached and in devotion to the old flag? But this is precisely what the Tories did.[35]

Jameson's loyalist leanings in the 1890s accorded well with the emerging "imperial school," represented by the Columbia University historian Herbert L. Osgood and his student George Louis Beer, and then later by Charles M. Andrews of Yale. His *The Colonial Background of the American Revolution*, published in 1924, and his four-volume *The Colonial Period in American History* (1934–38), like the works of Osgood and Beer, had their intellectual and political roots in the 1890s, although most of the books these men wrote were published later. The imperial school historians uniformly shared an appreciation of England's global dominion and a corresponding suspicion of the American colonial claims of injustice supported by the democratic nationalist historians George Bancroft and John Fiske. "It is easily conceivable," Beer wrote in 1907, "and not at all improbable that the political evolution of the next centuries may take such a course that the American Revolution will lose the great significance that is now attached to it, and will appear merely as the temporary separation of two kindred peoples whose inherent similarity was obscured by superficial differences, resulting from dissimilar economic and social conditions."[36]

---

[35] Jameson, "Origin of Political Parties," pp. 51–52. See also [Jameson], "The American Revolution as a Social Movement. I. Whigs and Tories" (1895), Jameson Papers, box 25. The surviving copy of this lecture is fragmentary, making pagination here impractical. For a similar assessment of loyalist motives, see Moses Coit Tyler, "The Part of the Loyalists in the American Revolution," *American Historical Review* 1 (1895):24–45.

[36] George Louis Beer, *British Colonial Policy, 1754–1765* (New York, 1907), p. 316. See also idem, *The Commercial Policy of England Toward the American Colonies* (New York, 1893), pp. 8–9; Herbert L. Osgood, *The American Colonies in the Seventeenth Century*, 2 vols. (New York, 1904), 1:xxx–xxxi; Charles M. Andrews, *The Colonial Background of the American Revolution: Four Essays in American Colonial History* (New Haven, 1924), pp. 160–61; idem, *The Colonial Period of American History*, 4 vols. (New Haven, 1934–38), 4:ix; George Ban-

Jameson's expansionist and internationalist commitments, as well as his innate conservatism, led him to embrace the loyalist cause with fervor. "The desire to keep all branches of the Anglo-Saxon race in union," he declared in the Barnard lectures, "the vision of a mighty English empire securely founded upon the parent island and the vast American continent, and ruling India and the islands of the sea, the vision which had kindled to its greatest warmth the imaginative genius of Pitt, was apt to seem most attractive to the most full and cultivated minds."[37] It was perhaps this very willingness to view the loyalist position sympathetically that provoked Jameson's conclusion that the American Revolution was "a civil war as well as a war against England," adding that "if the American Revolution was in large measure a conflict between internal parties, its result was a party triumph." It was a man very ill at ease with the subject of revolution who informed his audience that the patriotism of combatants in the Civil War was far more admirable than that of the founding generation, "with its brilliant story of ardent enthusiasm and its less familiar but not less veracious tale of widespread apathy, indifference, and disaffection." The period of national union since the Revolution had engendered, "even in these piping times of peace, a public spirit more ardent and active than was to be found in the civil life of America a hundred years ago."[38] This in a lecture sponsored by the Daughters of the American Revolution!

Repeatedly in his explorations of the Revolutionary period, Jameson's intelligence and powers of investigation led him toward conclusions that were profoundly disturbing to his conservative instincts and probably upsetting to a large segment

---

croft, *History of the United States from the Discovery of the American Continent*, 6 vols. (New York, 1883–85), 4:3–5; John Fiske, *The American Revolution* (Boston, 1891), pp. 33–35, 44–45; and Peter Novick, *That Noble Dream: The "Objectivity Question" and the American Historical Profession* (Cambridge, 1988), pp. 80–84.

[37] [Jameson], "The American Revolution as a Social Movement. I. Whigs and Tories."

[38] Ibid.

of the reading public he might address. How could the American Revolution be considered a "social movement," he asked in the Barnard lectures. This had been the fate of the French Revolution, where rebellion against a savagely unjust political and social system had ended in a new era of political tyranny, but the "Anglo-Saxon" who made the American Revolution "had no mind to destroy or recast his social system. He sought for political freedom, but he had no mind to allow revolution to extend itself beyond that limited sphere. As Burke said, he was 'taught to look with horror on those children of their country who are prompted rashly to hack that aged parent to pieces and put him into the kettle of magicians, in hopes that by their poisonous weeds and wild incantations they may regenerate the paternal constitution.'" Whatever their designs, the leaders of the American Revolution unleashed powerful forces that transformed both the social and political spheres of American life. Echoes of Hippolyte Taine surfaced in Jameson's observation that "the various fibres of a nation's life are knit together in great complexity. It is impossible to sever some without also loosening others, and setting them free to combine anew in widely different forms."[39]

Once again, Jameson confronted a contradiction he could not easily remove: a peaceful and conservative society of Anglo-Saxon yeomen had generated a revolution that threatened to tear that society apart. The egalitarianism of which Americans boasted, it seemed, had been born initially of violent conflict. What did such a discovery reveal about the American past? What did it portend about the future? Perhaps the Populists, that "vast horde of unintelligent farmers," had their own revolutionary tradition to draw upon. What indeed had happened to that "social movement" that there should be such strife in the land now? Jameson did not answer these troubling questions directly, but his reluctance to publish the lectures for over thirty years, and then only when their political implications and personal consequences for him were diminished, suggests a conviction on his part that what the conservative canons of scientific history and his own politi-

[39] Ibid.

cal beliefs did not permit him to say, he might better refrain from acknowledging in print.[40]

The most noteworthy feature of Jameson's lectures on the Revolution, apart from his willingness to view it as a social conflict, was the broad scope he gave to his presentation, considering religion, intellect, slavery, commerce and industry, land policy, and the West, all at a time when the study of these subjects by professional scholars was still a novelty. Much of this material from the Barnard lectures has not survived, but we have newspaper accounts of later versions. We also can glean from the manuscripts we do have an indication of why and how these subjects found their way into his discussion, and even the stimulus behind the entire series of lectures.

America in the 1890s made its military presence felt in the world with newfound vigor, and while Jameson applauded the expansion of American and, to his mind, Anglo-Saxon power, the patrician spirit in him felt a twinge of uneasiness over its domestic political consequences. "We are undergoing, or entering upon, one of those revivals of militant, not to say bellicose, patriotism which periodically recur in the history of all masculine nations," he observed at the conclusion of his 1895 lectures at Barnard: "We hope to annex territory. We build a great navy, and are secretly desirous that it shall do something striking. We wish for a spirited foreign policy. We revive the memory of wars. We talk of subjecting our schoolboys to military drill. We grow suspicious of foreign immigration, and talk hysterically of protecting American institutions from a foreign church. We exalt the flag." The expression of pride in national purpose was admirable, but, he warned, "it behooves us to be on our guard against the excesses of that spirit, to see to it that our strength does not tempt us to injustice, that our inevitable expansion is carried on peacefully and

[40] See Rothberg, "Servant to History," pp. 128–29. Jameson's ambivalence toward the idea of the American Revolution as a social movement is further indicated by his comment in 1936 that he published these lectures only because the Vanuxem Foundation, which sponsored their presentation at Princeton in 1925, required it. See J. Franklin Jameson to Merle E. Curti, Nov. 18, 1936, Merle Curti Papers, box 21, State Historical Society of Wisconsin, Madison.

righteously." Thus it gratified Jameson, while acknowledging the element of blood and carnage, to emphasize those accomplishments in American history that "have been chiefly the results of peaceful endeavor and of innocent social progress."[41] His discussion of the Revolution and slavery focused on the role of both evangelical religion and Enlightenment thought in stimulating the creation of antislavery societies and the manumission of slaves.[42] Personally skeptical of the value of religious organizations, if not the validity of religious belief, Jameson in his earlier lectures on Virginia commented approvingly on the related growth in the early nineteenth century of romanticism, religious belief, and political conservatism: "That love of all that is venerable, that reverent conservatism which Burke was teaching the world of thoughtful men to prefer, was sure to stimulate religion." Religion and romanticism both "called men back to the admiration of the heroic, the marvellous, the supernatural, and the imaginative, and therefore powerfully attracted the attention of the age to a renewed interest in religion, and especially to the Christian religion, so full of heroic, marvellous, supernatural and imaginative elements, and so venerable with that antiquity in which romantic feeling took delight."[43] An innovative methodology had evolved from a conservative political purpose. Jameson moved beyond the realm of politics, which appeared to be an arena of irrational behavior, even violence. He emphasized instead social endeavors where reason prevailed: literature, business, religious thought. In these public lectures, if not in what he published, Jameson attempted to channel political dialogue along avenues that the patrician intellect and the professional scholar could control.

In the years between Jameson's 1895 lectures at Barnard and the publication of his book in 1926, the study of the American Revolution and its consequences was transformed.

[41] J. Franklin Jameson, "The Revolution as a Social Movement: Lectures on Slavery and the West," in Rothberg and Goggin, eds., *Selected Essays*, pp. 229–30.

[42] Ibid., pp. 205–19.

[43] [Jameson], "Virginia History, 1763–1812. IV. Virginia in Power, 1801–1812," pp. 22–23.

Younger scholars around the country, unshackled by Jameson's devotion to Brahmin New England, embraced the diversity of American society as they examined its social and political conflicts. In 1894 Orin G. Libby analyzed state by state the ratification vote on the Constitution and discovered political divisions along economic and geographic lines, with upland opposing Tidewater, commerce confronting agriculture.[44] In a 1907 essay, *The Spirit of American Government,* J. Allen Smith, a professor of political science at the University of Washington, startled the nation by announcing that, contrary to popular belief, "constitutional government is not necessarily democratic." In fact, democracy, representing the striving many, and the Constitution, representing the wealthy few, were often opposed, an assertion that provoked even greater controversy when put forward by Charles Beard in his *Economic Interpretation of the Constitution,* published in 1913.[45]

The theme of class conflict and struggle against privilege, which resonated throughout the Progressive era, animated the most significant historical studies of the American Revolution. Divisions within colonies over race, class, and economic and geographical differences, to which Jameson had alluded in his lectures, formed the core of arguments presented in a number of monographs. Charles Henry Lincoln, in his 1901 study of Revolutionary Pennsylvania, pointed to strife between the English Quakers in eastern Pennsylvania and the German and Irish communities to the west.[46] Carl L. Becker, in his study of provincial New York, found that a political struggle between freemen and aristocracy predated the conflict between the colony and the Crown; it was a question, he

[44] Orin G. Libby, *The Geographical Distribution of the Vote of the Thirteen States on the Federal Constitution, 1787–88* (Madison, Wis., 1894), pp. 5, 29, 44, 48–49, 69.

[45] J. Allen Smith, *The Spirit of American Government: A Study of the Constitution: Its Origin, Influence, and Relation to Democracy* (New York, 1907), pp. 3, 31–32; Charles A. Beard, *An Economic Interpretation of the Constitution of the United States* (New York, 1913), pp. 17–18, 63, 188, 290–91, 324–25.

[46] Charles Henry Lincoln, *The Revolutionary Movement in Pennsylvania, 1760–1776* (1901; reprint ed., Cos Cob, Conn., 1968), pp. 13, 40–41.

said, both of "home rule" and "who should rule at home."[47] Charles H. Ambler and H. J. Eckenrode determined class and geography to be crucial in determining political alignments in Revolutionary Virginia, while R. D. W. Connor discovered a cleavage between "Radicals" and "Conservatives" within the patriot cause in North Carolina.[48]

Arthur M. Schlesinger, Sr., provided a sweeping overview of intracolonial political conflict. Building on Becker's revelation of a whig merchant class struggling simultaneously against Great Britain abroad and proletarian revolt at home, Schlesinger found the same dynamic at work throughout the northern commercial colonies. "To carry on their propaganda successfully," Schlesinger wrote, "the merchants had found it necessary to form alliances with their natural enemies in society—with the intelligent, hopeful radicals who dreamed of a semi-independent American nation or something better, and with the innumerable and nameless individuals whose brains were in their biceps, men who were useful as long as they could be held in leash."[49]

As a new generation of scholars revealed a Revolutionary society filled with conflict, Jameson remained caught between his desire to explore the social aspects of American political history and his conservative political instincts that appeared to frustrate that desire. He oscillated in his public statements between an emphasis on the significance of historical study as a nation-building device and on the necessity to represent the diversity of American culture. Upon arriving in Washington in the fall of 1905, Jameson made clear his commitment to

[47] Carl L. Becker, *The History of Political Parties in the Province of New York, 1760–1776* (Madison, Wis., 1909), pp. 8, 10–11, 22.

[48] Charles H. Ambler, *Sectionalism in Virginia from 1776 to 1861* (1910; reprint ed., New York, 1964), pp. 30–31; H. J. Eckenrode, *The Revolution in Virginia* (Boston, 1916), pp. 6–7; R. D. W. Connor, *History of North Carolina* (Chicago, 1919), pp. 402, 411, 423–24.

[49] Arthur M. Schlesinger, Sr., *The Colonial Merchants and the American Revolution, 1763–1776* (New York, 1918), pp. 306–7. See also James Truslow Adams, *Revolutionary New England, 1691–1775* (Boston, 1923), pp. vii, 88, 100, 109, 114, 288–89, 397, 405; Arthur M. Schlesinger, Sr., *New Viewpoints in American History* (New York, 1928), pp. 165–67, 172, 178–80.

documenting constitutional and political history. "Even after the tide has set in the direction of economic and social history strongly," he insisted, "even violently, as is the manner of American currents, even in that socialistic millennium toward which we are no doubt advancing, it is to be hoped that students, however fascinated with the narrative and the theory of social movement, however penetrated with the conviction that economic forces have controlled all human destinies, will yet remember that for the last four hundred years the actual form in which human life has mainly run its course has been that of the nation."[50]

As strenuously as Jameson asserted the primacy of national politics, however, he could be equally eloquent in reminding both scholars and the public how intellectually impoverished this perspective had become. He used the occasion of his presidential address in 1907 to the American Historical Association to focus the attention of his colleagues on the social implications of American religious history, at that point a topic almost completely neglected by scholars. Religion, more than any other single element, permeated the lives of Americans generation after generation, Jameson observed. While the statistics of economic growth gave substance to the structure upon which American social history would be built, "no view is truthful that leaves out of account the ideals which animated these toiling millions, the thoughts concerning the universe and man which informed their minds."[51] Jameson recognized that a dramatically transformed political environment worldwide demanded the investigation of historical subjects previously ignored. "What sort of histories will a socialized and internationalized Europe desire?" Jameson asked in a 1912 address titled "The Future Uses of History." "What information regarding the past will be demanded by a socialized, probably in some sense socialistic, America?" While political and constitutional history would not lose their sig-

[50] Jameson, "Gaps in the Published Records of the United States," *American Historical Review* 11 (1906):819.

[51] Jameson, "The American Acta Sanctorum," in Rothberg and Goggin, eds., *Selected Essays,* p. 179.

nificance, social and economic history would rise in importance because these elements of past societies most nearly
correlated with the salient features of the industrial age.[52]

In the end, though, Jameson's conservatism triumphed
over his intellectual ambition. "I have always thought it much
more difficult to document, with any sense of security, the social and economic history of the United States than the political or constitutional," he confessed to Frederick Jackson
Turner in 1927. "You do not have definitely limited bodies of
materials, handed down by authority, like statutes or other
manageable series, but a vast lot of miscellaneous material
from which the historian picks out what he wants, and so the
effort to document must often be by a process of selection,
and if selection, always open to the suspicion of being a bi-
assed selection, or one made to sustain a set of views."[53] He
clearly felt most comfortable emphasizing the value of ethnic
homogeneity and unity of purpose, wherever these elements
could be found in American history. A lecture he delivered at
Brown University in 1915 titled "American Blood in 1775"
stressed "the good fortune which left this American people
substantially unchanged in composition during the first sixty
years of its existence as a separate nation." At the conclusion
of this "period of adolescence and education," Jameson observed, "our institutions were fully formed, and no influx of
newcomers thereafter could essentially alter them."[54]

[52] Jameson, "The Future Uses of History," ibid., p. 314.

[53] [J. Franklin Jameson] to Frederick Jackson Turner, Nov. 25, 1927,
Jameson Papers, box 132. When the Committee on Research of the American Historical Association decided to award a grant from its newly established Beveridge Fund to Richard Shryock for a history of the public health
movement in America, Jameson was disappointed. He thought a grant in
the field of political history was more appropriate from a fund established
in memory of Sen. Albert J. Beveridge, but, he added, "with the general
proposition that the emphasis may well hereafter be placed on social and
economic history I should not feel able to dissent. Those aspects of history
may well have their innings" ([J. Franklin Jameson] to Worthington C.
Ford, May 10, 1928, Jameson Papers, box 48).

[54] Jameson, "American Blood in 1775," in Rothberg and Goggin, eds.,
Selected Essays, pp. 186–87.

When the United States entered the First World War in April 1917, Jameson sought to align the historical profession solidly behind the war effort. "How can public opinion in America be enlightened, homogeneous, and powerful," he asked, "in a crisis which is in the plainest way the product of historic forces, if it is not informed in the facts and lessons of history?"[55] The tricentennial celebration in November 1920 of the landing of the Pilgrims provided Jameson the opportunity to remind Americans once more that the foundation of American democracy, symbolized by the signing of the Mayflower Compact, was the individual and societal discipline that supported political consensus and social harmony.[56]

Given his steadfast political and social commitments, it comes as no surprise that when Jameson published *The American Revolution Considered as a Social Movement* in 1926, he largely restated the arguments put forward in his lectures at Barnard over thirty years earlier. As a result of his being invited to deliver this discussion in 1925 as the Vanuxem lecturer at Princeton, Jameson reduced the original six lectures to four.[57] The result, when compared to the original manuscript, is a model of compression and literary grace. The concision with which Jameson wrote in fact highlighted his major theme: the tensions experienced by a conservative society grappling with revolutionary forces. Language provided Jameson the instrument through which he muted this tension, as he sought simultaneously to explain the American Revolution while he controlled its implications.

The first lecture, originally titled "Whigs and Tories" and in a subsequent version "Parties and Participants," became "The Revolution and the Status of Persons" in the book. Although the book is dense with detail, the thrust and parry of Revolutionary politics, so much a part of the younger generation's historiography, is largely missing from his account. The ex-

[55] Jameson, "Historical Scholars in War-Time," ibid., p. 328.

[56] Jameson, "The Arrival of the Pilgrims," ibid., p. 245.

[57] [J. Franklin Jameson] to Dana Munro, Oct. 22, 27, 1925, Jameson Papers, box 114; "Dr. Jameson to Lecture," *New York Times*, Nov. 3, 1925, p. 16.

tended defense of loyalism is gone, as is the enumeration of Anglo-Saxon virtues; but in place of these is the pointed observation that the vigor of the Revolution resided largely "not in the mob or rabble, for American society was overwhelmingly rural and not urban, and had no sufficient amount of mob or rabble to control the movement, but in the peasantry, substantial and energetic though poor, in the small farmers and frontiersmen."[58] Indeed, the title of *The American Revolution Considered as a Social Movement,* altered from that of the original lectures, indicates an additional layer of detachment from the suggestion of widespread upheaval; this is simply one way, we are reminded, of examining the conflict.

Following Becker and Schlesinger, Jameson refined his argument to place the merchants on the side of the whigs rather than the loyalists.[59] But his larger purpose remained that of demonstrating how conservative the American Revolution truly was, even to the point of contradicting assertions made in earlier writings. Previously, in his "American Blood in 1775," Jameson noted the socially disruptive effects of the "transmarine" colonial migration; now he observed that "American society in the colonial period had a more definite and stable organization than it ever has had since the Revolution."[60] He explained once more how, with the abolition of entail and primogeniture, economic democracy laid the groundwork for political democracy. But if new economic relationships did emerge, and with them new political relationships, the vehicle for change was an all-encompassing idea rather than boisterous agitation: "The hot sun of revolution withered whatever was not deeply rooted in the soil. There was no violent outbreak against the land-system, for there had been no grinding oppressions or exactions connected with it. No maddened and blood-stained peasants rushed furiously from château to château, burning court-rolls and shedding

[58] Jameson, *The American Revolution Considered as a Social Movement* (1926; reprint ed., Princeton, 1967), p. 18.

[59] Ibid., p. 13.

[60] [Jameson], "American Blood in 1775," p. 186; Jameson, *American Revolution as a Social Movement,* p. 19.

the blood of seigneurs and châtelains. But in a quiet, sober, Anglo-Saxon way a great change was effected in the land-system of America between the years 1775 and 1795."[61] As with politics and land, so too with commerce and manufacturing. "Ardently as many thousands were engaged in the actual work of fighting," Jameson explained, "for most men in the thirteen American states industrial life went on during these seven years, not without disturbance, to be sure, but without cessation in its development."[62] The commercial break with England caused undoubted hardships while it simultaneously liberated Americans from artificial restrictions.[63] The removal of royal support for the Anglican church stimulated the disestablishment of state-supported religion in New York and in the South.[64] The effect of Jameson's eloquent prose and skillful organization of material is to present the Revolution as an intricate tapestry of events, rather than the hodgepodge captured in the 1895 lectures, stability and gradual progress in the midst of violent upheaval. It is the American Revolution and the nation as Jameson preferred to see them.

The American Revolution Considered as a Social Movement holds a special place of honor among historians, regardless of the ultimate judgment placed upon the argument it presents. Notwithstanding its shortcomings, Jameson's discussion of the Revolution remains an admirable attempt to view the conflict as an event that permeated society in all its endeavors. For some scholars, the book's combination of intellectual refinement, understanding, wit, and literary skill convinced them at a formative point in their lives to take up the study of history; for many more, the value of the book as an accessible introduction to the American Revolution for undergraduate and graduate students has kept it on reading lists for seventy years; and for the students themselves, especially the individuals whose contact with American history is a solitary survey

---

[61] Jameson, *American Revolution as a Social Movement*, p. 32.

[62] Ibid., p. 49.

[63] Ibid., p. 53.

[64] Ibid., pp. 85–90.

course, it is a lasting reminder that history can have meaning in a society that willfully ignores it. It is not the volume Jameson intended to write as a young instructor at Johns Hopkins, but it is a work we will be grateful he did write for many years to come.

BARBARA CLARK SMITH

Social Visions of the
American Resistance
Movement

J. FRANKLIN JAMESON surveyed a host of social changes that
followed from the achievement of American Independence,
charting the transformation wrought by this eighteenth-
century Revolution.[1] Colonists who began by thinking about
political representation and the location of sovereignty, he argued, ended by rethinking familiar social arrangements ranging from landholding to inheritance to relationships between
church and state. Most strikingly, perhaps, "liberty," at first
understood in terms of the political rights of free, white
American men, soon came to bear on the status of enslaved
African-Americans. All this occurred as new actors took the
helm of the Revolution and unanticipated ramifications of Independence worked themselves out. In this formulation,
what had been political changed into something social, what
had been narrowly constructed became broadly felt. Following Jameson, other historians have similarly suggested that
the Revolution was in the first instance a political matter, and
that it became over time—through "the transforming hand
of revolution" or "the contagion of liberty"—a process with
social consequences.[2] In Jameson's metaphor, "The stream of

I am grateful to James A. Henretta, Edmund S. Morgan, and Alfred F.
Young for their helpful comments on early drafts of this article.

[1] J. Franklin Jameson, *The American Revolution Considered as a Social Movement* (1926; reprint ed., Boston, 1956).

[2] Ibid., p. 9; "the contagion of liberty" is Bernard Bailyn's phrase, in *The
Ideological Origins of the American Revolution* (Cambridge, Mass., 1967),
chap. 6.

revolution, once started, could not be confined within narrow banks, but spread abroad upon the land"; that is, the process of revolution escaped control, it exceeded its authors' original intent.[3] In this view, the Revolution's social characteristics were significant, but they were acquired rather than innate.

Yet there was an additional, alternative way in which the Revolution was social in nature—not in consequence, but in intention; not eventually, but from the first years of resistance. As described by Arthur M. Schlesinger, Sr., nonimportation and nonconsumption movements were critical to the patriot cause.[4] First devised by a handful of Boston merchants in 1764, agreements not to consume, then not to import, foreign luxuries quickly formed in urban centers and later spread to rural villages. These pacts figured prominently in colonial resistance against the Stamp Act of 1765, the Townshend Acts of 1767, and the Tea Act of 1773. Massachusetts towns responded to the Coercive Acts with "a solemn league and covenant" to end trade over the summer of 1774, and it surprised few patriots when the first Continental Congress instituted a broad-based "Association" to end consumption and importation that fall. However common and plausible it may be to identify the patriot movement with the petitions and resolves of assemblies and conventions or with the pamphlets and newspapers that dissected British colonial policies, it is vital to remember that most Americans who became engaged in the resistance movement became engaged in one or another nonimportation, nonconsumption pact. Becoming a patriot no doubt meant adopting certain views regarding political repre-

[3] Jameson, *American Revolution as a Social Movement*, p. 9. Jameson spoke of "the social *consequences*" of revolution (emphasis mine) and Arthur M. Schlesinger, Sr., introducing the 1956 reprint of Jameson's essays, noted that Jameson traced "the effects of Independence" (ibid., pp. 10–11, xi). I am drawing here on the insights of James A. Henretta, whose commentary at the 1989 U.S. Capitol Historical Society symposium, "The Transforming Hand of Revolution": Reconsidering the American Revolution as a Social Movement, underscored Jameson's slighting of human intention and agency.

[4] Arthur M. Schlesinger, Sr., *The Colonial Merchants and the American Revolution, 1763–1776* (1918; reprint ed., New York, 1968).

sentation and the nature of the empire, but in pragmatic and immediate terms it meant enlisting in a boycott of trade.

In adopting boycotts, colonists welded together economic and political tactics. Patriots hoped to squeeze English manufacturers and merchants who, in turn, might lobby Parliament to revise an objectionable colonial policy. Yet when Edmund S. Morgan closely examined American arguments for fidelity to trade boycotts, he found that patriot writers did not generally stress the effect such measures would have across the Atlantic.[5] Instead they emphasized the crucial effects boycotts would have at home, profound benefits to American society and culture that would follow if colonists would suspend the purchase and use of imported goods. A trade boycott would inculcate the virtues of industry and thrift while combatting the idleness, sloth, and taste for luxury that led to slavery. There were assumptions here about such basic matters as work, leisure, and material success that informed the colonists' adoption of the nonimportation, nonconsumption tactic and hence many Americans' entry into the resistance movement. If we take seriously such ideas, Morgan argued, we will conclude that the American Revolution was, in some measure, "an ethical movement."[6] Between them, Schlesinger and Morgan established that important aspects of the resistance movement elude characterization as narrowly "political" in nature.

This essay builds on the work of Schlesinger and Morgan, revisiting the nonimportation and nonconsumption movements with particular attention to the social and cultural changes that they embodied. My purpose is less to revise than to supplement Morgan's point: the boycotts did express and enforce ethical commitments. Yet every system of ethics is

[5] Edmund S. Morgan, "The Puritan Ethic and the American Revolution," in idem, *The Challenge of the American Revolution* (New York, 1976), pp. 88–138.

[6] Ibid., p. 89. On the morality embodied in one significant clause of the Continental Association, see Anne Fairfax Withington, "Morality and American Identity: 1774–1776: A Discussion of Article 8 of the Association of 1774," Ph.D. diss., Yale University, 1983.

grounded in social structure and experience. In seeking to purify themselves and their society, in shifting relationships onto a more ethical footing, patriots expressed social ideals and sought social change. Indeed, trade boycotts reshaped relations among neighbors, among different social classes, and between the genders. They embodied notions of what was fair and virtuous that we can understand only in light of social and cultural developments of the eighteenth century. To illuminate the nature of the patriots' nonimportation non-consumption pacts, then, we must begin by attending to social and cultural change.

Two lines of recent work clarify the ground on which eighteenth-century colonists formulated their desire to change relationships within American societies. First, re-search and analysis by Michael Merrill, James A. Henretta, Christopher Clark, and others has fundamentally altered our understanding of rural life and rural exchange in the north-ern colonies in the eighteenth century.[7] These historians have argued that many, perhaps most, households produced goods for their own use, for the use of others in their locality, and only in the last instance for exchange in a wider Atlantic mar-ket. The bulk of exchange took place locally among neigh-bors, brethren, and kin—people who might or might not hold one another particularly dear but who did expect to con-

[7] Michael Merrill, "Cash Is Good to Eat: Self-Sufficiency and Exchange in the Rural Economy of the United States," *Radical History Review* 4 (1977):42–71; James A. Henretta, "Families and Farms: *Mentalité* in Pre-Industrial America," *William and Mary Quarterly*, 3d ser. 35 (1978):3–32; Christopher Clark, "The Household Economy, Market Exchange, and the Rise of Capitalism in the Connecticut Valley, 1800–1860," *Journal of Social History* 13 (1979):169–89; idem, *The Roots of Rural Capitalism: Western Massa-chusetts, 1780–1860* (Ithaca, N.Y., 1990). Also of interest are Robert E. Mutch, "Yeoman and Merchant in Pre-Industrial America: Eighteenth-Century Massachusetts as a Case Study," *Societas* 7 (1977):279–307, and Winifred B. Rothenberg, "The Market and Massachusetts Farmers, 1750–1855," *Journal of Economic History* 41 (1981):288–314. For a valuable bibliog-raphy, see Edwin G. Burroughs, "The Transition Question in Early American History: A Checklist of Recent Books, Articles, and Dissertations," *Radical History Review* 18 (1978):173–90. More recent work is cited in Clark, *Roots of Rural Capital*, chap. 1.

tinue dealing with one another again and again.[8] Local transactions involved various members of different households:
wives, daughters, and sons as well as husbands and fathers
swapped labor, farm produce, and manufactured goods with
members of neighboring households. Moreover, transactions
sometimes took months or even years to accomplish. It was
perfectly routine for a rural craftsman to give a farm family
shoes in the fall and take a calf in return come the spring. At
any given moment, a rural household would be owing some
neighbors and owed by others; households took part in—they
existed within—a complex network of local trade relationships.

Such exchange did not occur in an insulated or separate
realm where "the rules of the market" reigned supreme. Instead it was firmly embedded in society. These local transactions, in other words, were not merely economic, for people
had yet to accept the fragmentation of life and consciousness
inherent in that category.[9] One Delaware farmer of the early
nineteenth century expressed the social nature of local transactions when he called them "neighboring." He also spoke of
local exchange as "borrowing and lending," a form of trade
and a concomitant series of ideals and assumptions distinct
from "buying and selling" in the wider marketplace.[10] In the

[8] Tom R. Burns has emphasized the defining influence of expectations
for continued transactions in making such transactions "social" ones, in
which participants privilege the establishment and maintenance of reciprocal ties over the achievement of maximum profit (Burns, "Models of Social
and Market Exchange: Toward a Sociological Theory of Games and Social
Behavior," in Craig Calhoun, Marshall W. Meyer, and W. Richard Scott,
eds., *Structures of Power and Constraint: Papers in Honor of Peter M. Blau* [New
York, 1990], pp. 129–35).

[9] The implications of these historians' revision of rural history for understanding eighteenth-century farm families' conscious ideals are described
clearly in Clark, *Roots of Rural Capitalism*, chap. 1. See also idem, "Economics
and Culture: Opening Up the Rural History of the Early American Northeast," *American Quarterly* 43 (1991):279–301.

[10] James Ball of Mill Creek Hundred, Delaware, in *Andrew Griffin* v. *John
Ball*, January 1804, New Castle Co. Court of Chancery Records 1806–7,
case G-4, Delaware Hall of Records, Dover. I have treated one Delaware
farm family's experiences in *After the Revolution: The Smithsonian History of
Everyday Life in the Eighteenth Century* (New York, 1985), chap. 2.

context of ongoing neighborly transactions, it made sense to understand the purpose of trade as "mutual" benefit for all parties, and not—as a minister stressed in the 1770s—the advantage of one party over others.[11] Other colonists shared some of the parson's assumptions—that people both would and should be accountable for their dealings, that rules other than profit-maximization applied to exchange. At the least, it was necessary for people to walk away from a transaction with a sense of having been equitably treated in order for the parties to deal again. At times, and even routinely, people subordinated immediate, maximum gain to the maintenance of relationships in which economic benefit formed only one part.

Of course rural people did "buy and sell" as well as "borrow and lend." Many farm families dealt with nearby storekeepers, merchants who might participate in exchange according to local rules for the same but who might also introduce new rules and practices—the charging of interest on debts, for example. Farm families welcomed the imported cloth, crockery, hardware, and other items that stocked storekeepers' shelves. Moreover, a growing number of farm households produced with an eye to the commercial market. Facing declining soil fertility, farmers in the Connecticut River Valley, for example, began to specialize in livestock production for the plantation economies of the West Indies. Elsewhere, too, farmers engaged with the marketplace. How deeply they did so varied from community to community and within towns from household to household.[12] Henretta, Clark, and Merrill do not ar-

---

[11] Jonathan French, *A Practical Discourse against Extortion* (Boston, 1777). Other sermons also treated the ethics of exchange, including Jeremiah Condy, *The Godly and Faithful Man* (Boston 1747). Richard B. Morris, *Government and Labor in Early America* (New York, 1946), chap. 1, attests to the persistence of Americans' expectations that government regulation should ensure equity in exchange.

[12] On the Connecticut River Valley, see Clark, *Roots of Rural Capitalism*, and Margaret E. Martin, *Merchants and Traders of the Connecticut River Valley* (Northampton, Mass., 1939). An overview is James A. Henretta, *The Evolution of American Society, 1700–1815: An Interdisciplinary Analysis* (Lexington, Mass., 1973), pp. 22–23 and chap. 1.

gue that "the market" was unknown or the profit motive unheard of in rural America. They do insist on the presence and, at times, the priority of other, powerful processes and motives.

Indeed, even in centers of commercial exchange, ideals of neighboring still demonstrably carried weight in people's lives. When Bostonians opposed the construction of a centralized marketplace in the early decades of the century, many did so because they preferred to deal with country people whom they knew and trusted rather than with the large retailers who would dominate a central market.[13] Surveying the major port cities of eighteenth-century America, Gary B. Nash has noted the persistence of ideals upholding fairness in exchange, ideals that bespoke a certain, continued inhospitality to market values.[14] Even in the face of the corrosive power of the Atlantic trade, then, notions of neighboring sometimes held their own. Indeed, neither vestigial nor archaic, such notions might appear the more valuable to some inhabitants precisely as others, increasingly engaged in long-range "buying and selling," seemed to abandon them. As colonists' dependence on distant markets grew greater, so might insistence on neighbors' obligations within local trade networks.[15] Conflicts within and between communities took shape as different forms and conceptions of exchange clashed with one another. Thus we must understand the economy and society of the northern colonies of eighteenth-century America as, in Allan Kulikoff's term, "transitional," that is, subject to the influence of conflicting expectations, ideals, and

[13] Benjamin Colman, *Some Reasons and Arguments . . . for Setting Up Markets in Boston* (Boston, 1719), p. 5. See also Barbara Clark Smith, "Markets, Streets, and Stores: Contested Terrain in Pre-industrial Boston," in Elise Marienstras and Barbara Karsky, eds., *Autre temps, autre espace: Etudes sur l'Amérique pré-industrielle* (Nancy, France, 1986), pp. 181–97.

[14] Gary B. Nash, *The Urban Crucible: Social Change, Political Consciousness, and the Origins of the American Revolution* (Cambridge, Mass., 1979).

[15] Thus the occasional riot and the more endemic tensions within cities as explored by Nash, *Urban Crucible*. See also my "Food Rioters and the American Revolution," *William and Mary Quarterly*, 3d ser. 51 (1994):3–38.

practices.[16] Colonists who adopted nonimportation and non-consumption pacts in the 1760s and 1770s did so in that transitional context.

Equally, other broad developments influenced resistance tactics as well. Historians have recently delineated several streams of culture that ran through eighteenth-century British-American society. Many elite Americans took on a new ideal of life in the course of the 1700s, an ideal analyzed by Richard L. Bushman as the ideal of "cultivation," or "gentility."[17] Gentility was, as Bushman describes it, an imported ideal, and its proponents deliberately modeled their deportment, manners, and practices on those of English gentlepeople. On its most intangible level, the pursuit of gentility constituted a new way of constructing one's identity, a striving after a social and aesthetic ideal of personal "grace," "polish," or "refinement." This ideal also involved the growth of new social forms or occasions—tea ceremonies, balls, and elegant dinners. It involved, too, the construction of new spaces to accommodate such forms—parlors, ballrooms, and dining rooms in elegant Georgian mansions built by well-to-do Americans beginning in the early 1700s. In these places, on these occasions, select companies of social equals or near-equals gathered together to demonstrate and exercise their genteel accomplishments. The "select" or "exclusive" quality of such groups was important. Bushman sets such gatherings midway, as it were, between the inclusive community gatherings of the Middle Ages and the tight family unit of the nineteenth century. Inherent in the quest for gentility, too, was a particular relationship to material culture, for goods—teapots, card tables, and a host of other fashionable and often expensive items—were necessary props in the pursuit of this cultural ideal. Aspiring to gentility thus entailed a new and

[16] Allan Kulikoff, "The Transition to Capitalism in Rural America," *William and Mary Quarterly*, 3d ser. 46 (1989):120–44.

[17] Richard L. Bushman, "American High-Style and Vernacular Cultures," in Jack P. Greene and J. R. Pole, eds., *Colonial British America: Essays in the New History of the Early Modern Era* (Baltimore, 1984), pp. 345–83. Bushman, *The Refinement of America* (New York, 1990), pp. 3–180.

close relationship to the Atlantic market that provided those necessary goods.

It illuminates the nature and meaning of gentility as a social ideal to compare it with a second stream of culture—a popular or plebeian American culture. Plebeian culture too was imported, at least in its first instance. There were many waves of immigration into the American colonies and hence, as Alfred F. Young has argued, a "massive carryover" of popular cultural forms, parallel to the more fully documented cultural baggage carried by the literate elite.[18] Once in America, popular forms and beliefs might be suppressed, forgotten, or muddled, but far from all were totally lost. When ships' carpenters marched an interloper around Boston on a pole, when rural men gathered to discipline husbands known for mistreating their wives, when petty artisans and laborers marched effigies of the pope around the seaports on the anniversary of Guy Fawkes, they were showing familiarity with the repertoire of the English plebeian public. And when Cotton Mather lamented "that the Minds and Manners of Many People about the Countrey are much corrupted, by foolish Songs and Ballads, which the Hawkers and Pedlars carry into all parts of the Countrey," he was acknowledging that there persisted a stream of culture that was simply outside elite control.[19]

As yet historians have uncovered only some elements of that cultural stream, but we can say that, like genteel culture, plebeian culture had its occasions. They ranged from annual Pope's Days and Christmas maskings to the rather more frequent public hangings and other public punishments at which crowds of men and women of various social classes attended as representations of the community or "town." Participants were significantly more than observers at these times; often people added their insults and condemnation to the sentence inflicted by magistrates or, alternatively, mitigated

---

[18] Alfred F. Young, "English Plebeian Culture and Eighteenth-Century American Radicalism," in Margaret Jacob and James Jacob, eds., *The Origins of Anglo-American Radicalism* (London, 1984), pp. 185–212.

[19] *Diary of Cotton Mather, 1709–1724*, Massachusetts Historical Society *Collections*, 7th ser. 8 (1912):242.

that sentence by offering the criminal sympathy and support. Occasions of plebeian cultural expression were not exclusive or select, then, but they sometimes did (like genteel occasions) involve the marking of social boundaries. This was true not only for popular involvement in public punishments ordered by the state but also on the myriad occasions when people of humble social status assumed the right to initiate punishment against nonindicted and nonconvicted offenders—gathering in crowds and acting against violators of the community's (or at least the crowd's) sense of morality, equity, or the common good. This culture also had its venues, including streets, taverns, and marketplaces.[20]

It highlights some of the differences between genteel and popular cultures to compare tea drinking, a ceremony central to the gentility, with rum drinking, as it was practiced on a broader social basis. Briefly put, elite tea drinking often took place in private parlors among a select group of people of similar social class. The company included women as well as men; indeed, a woman might preside over the party, and some tea gatherings were all-female affairs. Tea parties in genteel parlors required an elaborate material culture—some if not all of the following items: teapots and their rests, teacups and saucers, tea cannisters, teakettles or urns, teaspoons and spoon dishes, sugar bowls, sugar tongs, cream jugs, slop bowls, strainers, tea trays, and tea tables—plus plates and utensils for any food consumed with the tea. By contrast, much rum drinking took place in a different physical, social, and cultural context. The site was often public: taverns, streets, or militia mustering fields. The occasion was generally hospitable to wide participation, although sometimes rum drinking enlivened all-male gatherings. Rum drinking re-

[20] Alfred F. Young, "Pope's Day, Tar and Feathers, and Coronet George Joyce, Jun.: From Ritual to Rebellion in Boston, 1745–1775," *Bulletin of the Society for the Study of Labour History* 27 (1973):25–29. W. W. Newell, "Christmas Maskings in Boston," *Journal of American Folklore* 9 (1896):178. In connecting crowds with traditions and practices of public punishment, I am building on, but also departing from, Pauline Maier, *From Resistance to Revolution: Colonial Radicals and the Development of American Opposition to Britain, 1765–1776* (New York, 1972), chap. 1.

quired little or no material culture; it was possible and common merely to pass the bottle.[21]

In at least two respects, we must recognize that this comparison is overneat. First, colonists of most ranks might consume either tea or rum; neither beverage held a single, fixed social meaning, and far from every sip or tipple was taken in so ritualized a social frame. As Peter Thompson has shown, in Philadelphia elite men drank rum and wine "within the territory of genteel manners," in private or semiprivate ceremonies that used china bowls and silver spoons.[22] Similarly, middling and lesser colonists might consume tea, either emulating the gentry or, as T. H. Breen has suggested, simply for the sake of the hot stimulant.[23] Second, genteel and plebeian streams of culture were not symmetrically opposed to each other or always even directly engaged. Other powerful streams of culture, after all, flourished in colonial America; within Euro-American society alone, artisanal republicanism and evangelical religion had profound effects. Far from being simply counterposed, then, genteel culture and popular culture stood in complex relationship to each other. It was perfectly possible, for example, for adherents of popular culture to admire gentility among their social betters. Although the genteel ideal was inherently invidious, it may have been felt as such more keenly by those socially closest to the elite than by those farther away from them. Thus, plebeian culture was not particularly critical of consumption, as republicanism and evangelicalism could be. For its part, gentility seems to have had a two-sided relationship to plebeian culture. There was a certain amount of cooperation: The American elite, genteel or

[21] Rodris Roth, *Tea Drinking in Eighteenth-Century America: Its Etiquette and Equipage,* U.S. National Museum Bulletin 225 (Washington, D.C., 1961). Rhys Isaac, *The Transformation of Virginia, 1740–1790* (Chapel Hill, 1982), pp. 94–98, 107–8, 111, 132, 253–54, 260.

[22] Peter Thompson, "'The Friendly Glass': Drink and Gentility in Colonial Philadelphia," *Pennsylvania Magazine of History and Biography* 113 (1989):549–73.

[23] T. H. Breen, "'Baubles of Britain': The American and Consumer Revolutions of the Eighteenth Century," *Past and Present* 119 (1988):83–84.

not, did supply their social inferiors with rum or money for rum on numerous occasions—election days, militia musters, Pope's Days, and others.[24] Yet the truly genteel gentleman or lady must have felt discomfort with aspects of plebeian life— its vulgarity, its manifest lack of polish or order. If some members of the American elite felt as comfortable swilling rum in the taverns as sipping tea in the parlor, in its essence, surely, gentility entailed a certain removal, a distancing of self from the common and the vulgar.[25]

Nonimportation, nonconsumption movements placed both relationships with the market and, less obviously, interactions between genteel and common, on a new footing. To detail how they did so, let us focus on the Association of 1774, the Continental Congress's nonimportation, nonexportation, nonconsumption scheme. People who joined the Association had often participated in similar agreements before, and the social ideals inherent in the Association had been part of the resistance for nearly a decade. Although they varied in their details, earlier pacts were also "associations" or "leagues," organizations outside of legislative doors, embracing but also separate from such existing bodies as local governments or "the crowd." All these pacts conferred political significance on ordinary events and mundane parts of life; a patriot was one who did not import, consume, or raise prices on scarce imported goods or the domestic products that replaced them. A patriot, then, clearly fulfilled neighborly ideals, privileging bonds with fellows over immediate, narrow self-interest.

Moreover, like earlier pacts, the Association called on Americans to participate in and submit to an extensive system of local surveillance. It called on all men qualified to vote for the lower house of their colonial assembly to meet together in their town, county, or city and elect from their own number a committee to be in charge of enforcement. Marblehead, Massachusetts, for example, elected a Committee of Observation to oversee the trade boycott and, as the town put it, "to

[24] In addition to Isaac, *Transformation of Virginia*, see Charles S. Sydnor, *Gentlemen Freeholders: Political Practices in Washington's Virginia* (Westport, Conn., 1950), chap. 4.

[25] Bushman, *Refinement of America*, esp. pp. 182–87.

attend to the Conduct of ministerial Tools and Jacobites in the Town."[26] Other towns also elected committees, usually called Committees of Inspection, or else turned enforcement over to preexisting committees that had been set up to enforce earlier plans for nonimportation and nonconsumption.

How many men served on the committees and how often they met depended on the situation of the town or county. In seaports such as Boston and Salem, where trade was extensive and sizable merchant communities might conceivably raise prices on scarce imported goods, surveillance posed a substantial task, and committees of 50 to 60 were chosen.[27] At the other extreme, the little town of Warwick, Massachusetts, did not elect a committee, not out of lack of fervor for the cause but because of a lack of retailers offering British goods in the village. For agricultural settlements such as Warwick, towns that were small and isolated enough not to have access to British goods, little surveillance was needed. In between the two extremes of Boston and Warwick were the great majority of New England towns. Most towns did elect committees, with an average of 9 or 10 men serving on them. Outside New England, counties chose committees. In Maryland these bodies ranged from 20 men, the committee in one county, to 200 men in another. One historian has estimated that, throughout the colonies, at least seven thousand men served on committees established to enforce the Association in 1774. Not surprisingly, many of those elected to committees of inspection had been local leaders, men who had served in an important local office before. Yet often newer men were also included, for the task of enforcement required substantial numbers and a unity among classes, so towns drew on some outside the ranks of their established and experienced leadership.[28]

Many committees' first task entailed gathering the signatures of people who agreed to support the Association, sometimes requiring individuals to swear an oath that they would

---

[26] *Boston Gazette,* Jan. 16, 1775.

[27] David L. Ammerman, *In the Common Cause: American Response to the Coercive Acts of 1774* (New York, 1975), pp. 105–6; the Boston committee was listed in the *Boston Gazette,* Dec. 12, 1774.

[28] Ammerman, *Common Cause,* pp. 106–7, 109–10.

support the compact. The committees aimed at getting the signatures of heads of households, who would in turn take responsibility for ensuring that their slaves, servants, children, and other dependents complied. This meant that in some places women, who—as widows—were often household heads, signed the Association. Indeed, women's involvement in the nonimportation and nonconsumption movements was vital, and it marked those movements as creating a significantly new type of politics. Women appeared in resistance rhetoric as helpless victims of insolent British soldiers stationed in Boston or as symbols of such abstract ideals as liberty and wisdom, but in trade boycotts they appeared as participants and, to a degree, political actors.[29] The Association was one of the first American political documents to use the feminine pronoun, not in reference to entities such as "the mother country" or "liberty," but in reference to real female human beings. It did so, sadly, only when laying out how violators of the boycott should be treated, what punishment should be meted out to "him or her."[30] But the fact remained that, as the Continental Congress itself realized, women's participation mattered. Although few women were involved in importing and exporting goods, they did own retail shops and taverns, where they often marketed items besides the basics of food and alcohol. Urban women shopped for their families' home consumption, and women were as able and as likely to consume foreign goods as were men. Women had the power to break the provisions of the Association. As a result, the success of nonimportation and nonconsumption required female participation to an unprecedented degree. By the same token, free men who did not fulfill the voting requirements and

[29] Ibid., p. 118, "Ladies of the Association," *William and Mary Quarterly*, 1st ser. 8 (1899):36. For women as victims, see Oliver Morton Dickerson, comp., *Boston under Military Rule, (1768–1769), as Revealed in a Journal of the Times* (1936; reprint ed., New York, 1970). On women's activities in trade boycotts, see Mary Beth Norton, *Liberty's Daughters: The Revolutionary Experience of American Women, 1750–1800* (Boston, 1980), pp. 156–77, Elizabeth Cometti, "Women in the American Revolution," *New England Quarterly* 20 (1947):329–46, and Schlesinger, *Colonial Merchants*.

[30] Samuel Eliot Morison, ed., *Sources and Documents Illustrating the American Revolution, 1764–1788* (1923; reprint ed., New York, 1977), p. 124.

who could not therefore either serve on committees or elect committeemen also had to be included in some ways. Indeed, the only people safely left out of the Association in some form were slaves and, perhaps, indentured servants—people who had no difficulty limiting the extent to which they imported, exported, or consumed.[31]

Participation involved—or could involve—a great deal more than subscribing a signature to an agreement. Some people outside committees took pains to make other people sign up. In September 1774, for example, forty-one blacksmiths who lived in Worcester County met together and agreed "not to do any work for anyone we esteem an enemy to the country," meaning all who failed to subscribe to the Association and especially those who flouted its nonconsumption provisions. Any one of their members who broke this boycott, they decided, would also qualify as an "enemy," due to face social and economic ostracism from his fellows. William Aitchenson, a merchant who would not sign the Association in Norfolk, Virginia, described the method used there to pressure colonists into compliance. The mob, he said, erected a pole near the capitol, where the committee met, and attached a bag of feathers to the top of the pole, and put a barrel of tar underneath. Those accused of loyalism were forced to stand next to the pole in front of the committee and retract anything they had previously said about how treasonous the Association seemed to them, or about the limitations of the mental capacities of those who sat on committees. According to Aitchenson, two men who imported tea contrary to the nonimportation agreement were almost tarred and feathered by the mob, and were saved only when a "gentleman" intervened on their behalf. In the end they had only to promise to deliver the tea to be burned. This incident sug-

[31] In Weymouth, copies of the Association were printed and distributed to all household heads, leading Boston to urge other towns to do likewise, so "every Master of a Family in each Town ... will then have his Duty plainly before him, & ... assist the several Committees that might be appointed" (*Boston Gazette* Dec. 12, 1774). On women as retailers, shoppers, and marketers, see Norton, *Liberty's Daughters*, pp. 138, 142–45, and Karen J. Friedmann, "Victualling Colonial Boston," *Agricultural History* 47 (1973):189–205.

gests a certain amount of cooperation between committees and the mob working outside committees; it also suggests that sometimes onlookers wanted to act more harshly toward violators of the Association than did gentlemen among the local leadership. The Worcester blacksmiths and the Norfolk mob provide two particularly dramatic and visible cases, but surely there were many instances when more private and informal influence within households and within communities brought individuals into compliance with the Association.[32]

The propensity of Americans to pressure others into signing copies of the Association should not hide the fact that, in one sense, it did not really matter whether or not individuals subscribed. Refusal to sign did not mean, in the eyes of committees and other patriots, that an individual was not obligated to follow all of the agreement's provisions. Once the community acted to endorse the Association by electing a committee of inspection, individual choice about the matter ended. Participants took the lack of voluntarism so much for granted that in various places committees dispensed with the process of gathering signatures altogether. Instead they simply assumed that the Association would be binding on everyone.

Most committees enforced the Association by calling suspects to committee meetings and requiring them to explain their conduct. The Northampton committee, for example, asked one "Mr. Adams" to appear and answer charges that he had imported a barrel of tea contrary to the agreement. Many committees depended on receiving information against alleged violators from private citizens. Thus, a Colonel Tuper complained to the Hadley committee against Phineas Lyman, and Northampton "voted [that] Deacon Clark wait on Benjamin Edwards junr. and satisfy himself whether sd Benjn will appear before the committee on Wednesday 24th at 5 p.m. to answer to Philip Young."[33] If the suspect failed to satisfy the

---

[32] *Boston Gazette,* Nov. 28, 1774; Ammerman, *Common Cause,* pp. 120–21.

[33] Committee of Northampton to the Committee of Inspection at Leverel, Jan. 1, 1776, Joseph Hawley Papers, 1774–77 folder, New York Public Library; committee of Hadley to committee of Northampton, Jan. 5, 1776,

committee of his or her compliance, or at least of sincere repentance and intention of following the regulations in the future, the committees generally responded by publishing the name of the violator in the local press. This publication of violators' names served as a signal to everyone else to end all trade and socializing with the offender until she or he reformed. Like the Worcester blacksmiths, other supporters of nonimportation and nonconsumption effectively treated violators as "enemies"—that is, in the manner in which Americans were treating citizens of Great Britain, by cutting them off from all trade. As a result, the newspapers became filled with the publications of committees, with accusations, denials and justifications, claims and counterclaims.[34]

The *Boston Gazette*, for example, showed the activities of numerous committees in support of the Association. In January 1775 the committee of Petersham published the names of several men they called "incorrigible enemies of America," because "after all the friendly Expostulations and Intreaties which we have been able to make Use of" the committee found them firmly opposed to the trade boycott. Until they repented, the report concluded, they should be considered "traitorous Parricides to the Cause of Freedom."[35]

Similarly, the Dartmouth committee enforced the price ceilings required by the Association. The committee had examined the case of one Isaac Howland, accused of raising the price of salt from 3 shillings, the usual price in the town, to 4 shillings. Questioned about the matter, Howland had admitted to the markup and, to compound matters, refused to promise the committee either that he would lower the price or that he would recompense the buyers from whom he had

---

ibid.; Northampton Committee of Safety meeting, Aug. 9, 1776, ibid.; *Boston Gazette*, Oct. 16, 1775, records the Rutland committee's dependence on an informer.

[34] In addition to the incidents detailed below, occasions when violators of the Association were published in the *Boston Gazette* were legion, including Oct. 24, 1774, July 3 and 24, Aug. 14, Sept. 4, 11, and 16, Oct. 30, and Dec. 4, 1775. Other "enemies" appeared in other newspapers as well.

[35] Ibid., Jan. 16, 1775.

extorted the extra shilling. The Dartmouth committee therefore resolved to publish Howland's name, with the hope that
"he shall return to a sense of his misconduct."[36]

About the same time, the committee of Waltham published
Eleazer Bradshaw, a hatter who, the committee charged, had
made a practice of traveling back and forth from Albany, ostensibly engaged in the fur trade but actually smuggling tea.
Bradshaw found a Waltham baker, David Townshend, a willing partner to retail the tea. The committee published both
men's names and concluded with the hope that "these TEA
MERCHANTS get what they deserve." As a resident of Waltham,
Townshend felt the impact of his neighbors' displeasure;
within a few weeks he published an apology for his behavior.
Bradshaw, a transient, was less vulnerable to censure, promising the combined committees of Weston, Waltham, Newtown,
Waterbury, and Sudbury that he would "be the death of any
person that should molest him" in his trade.[37]

As this last newspaper entry suggests, publishing the name
of a violator of the Association may have been intended at
times to do more than inform the public to cut off all trade
and social intercourse with the offender. Whatever committees intended, they surely knew that publication of people's
names might spark broader community action against them.
In Wrentham, for example, a crowd of four to five hundred
people gathered outside the house of Mr. N. Alldis, published
for buying tea. Alldis and four of his friends publicly promised to desist from all further purchases of that commodity;
they apologized to the crowd for making "exasperating
speeches which have justly inflamed the minds of all friends
of American liberty, in that we have heretofore paid no attention to any convention or congress, but have boldly opposed
them." The *Boston Gazette* published an account of this whole
affair, and presumably this public recantation restored the
five men to the good graces of their patriot neighbors.[38]

These examples make clear that the Association's participa-
tory politics reached well beyond committee members to in-

[36] Ibid., Nov. 13, 1775.

[37] Ibid., Oct. 2, 16, 1775.

[38] Ibid., Dec. 21, 1774.

clude a much broader public. Indeed, on some occasions individuals bypassed committees to publish direct accusations against one another. Thomas Lillie of Marblehead, for example, caught with two barrels of tea, publicly apologized to neighbors and saw his tea burned as well. Lillie claimed in the *Essex Gazette* that he had bought the tea from Simon Tufts, a Boston merchant. Tufts replied by assuring all readers that it was his hired help who had sold the tea, that he himself had not been present at or concerned in the sale, and that it would not happen again. Might he have a "Restoration of their Favour and Confidence?"[39] A similar protestation of innocence came from the leather-dressers of Boston, responding to a rumor impugning their patriotism with accusations of avarice. "To the Public: Whereas, it has been reported that the Leather-Dressers are endeavoring to increase their Stocks of Wool, and when they have got what will be taken off this Season in their own Hands, intend to raise the Price; it is so far from the Truth, that they are determined strictly to adhear to their former [price]." The leather-dressers took the opportunity to warn butchers not to advance the price they asked for skins, then concluded stirringly, "Let the demand be ever so great, the Leather-Dressers are determined not to raise the Price."[40]

Essential to the politics of nonimportation, then, was the use of publicity and public adjudication of various claims and counterclaims. Accusations, denials, and confessions all appeared in the public newspapers, and readers could pass judgment on the conduct and patriotism of their neighbors.[41] Moreover, people of most ranks could make accusations that would require the accused to make some sort of public response in self-defense. Many whose names were never published in the press no doubt appeared before committees to

[39] *Essex Gazette*, Mar. 28, 1775. Tufts's reply is in the *Boston Gazette*, Apr. 3, 1775.

[40] *Boston Gazette*, Jan. 16, 1775.

[41] The York County Congress recommended posting of names of violators in all public houses as well as in the press (*Boston Gazette*, Nov. 28, Dec. 5, 1774). Examples of denials and apologies are found ibid., Oct. 3, 1774, Aug. 14, Dec. 25, 1775.

rebut someone's accusation against them.[42] In some places, too, crowds of people not on the committee attended the committee meetings to witness (and thereby influence) all proceedings. In fact, crowds could command public apologies without going through the intermediary of the official committee at all.

One final example of this public process. In January 1775, Portsmouth, New Hampshire, reported these proceedings: "About 60 pounds of TEA was publicly burnt on the Parade in the Town at 8 o'clock in the Evening, last Wednesday, belonging to a person who bro't it from Salem, who was so far convicted of his own Error in attempting the Sale of that condemn'd Commodity, that he put it in the Fire himself in presence of a large Number of Spectators."[43] This account reveals several elements essential to Americans' experience of and involvement in nonconsumption and nonimportation pacts. The scene was a drama, a spectacle, a public humiliation in which the offender against the community's values and practices acted out his repentance and submission to those norms. The offender, in other words, publicly accepted the authority of the local patriot leadership on the committee and the authority of the whole community to engage in surveillance over many aspects of the individual's day-to-day behavior.

The use of surveillance, the boycott, and publicity proved potent against merchants, for traders depended for a livelihood almost entirely on "commerce" with their neighbors. Haverhill merchant Enachy Bartlett admitted as much when he apologized to fellow townspeople for his earlier political opinions and for having imported tea. He begged forgiveness for past errors in both judgment and conduct and promised never to repeat his mistakes, for "my Comfort in life does so much depend on the regard and good will of those among whom I live."[44] People used merchants' dependence on trade

[42] Ammerman, *Common Cause*, pp. 120–21.

[43] *Boston Gazette*, Jan. 23, 1775. Breen emphasizes the significance of tea burnings in "'Baubles of Britain,'" pp. 99–100.

[44] Enachy Bartlett, Sept. 9, 1774, Miscellaneous Bound Collection, Massachusetts Historical Society, Boston. (None of his actions had ever pro-

to counteract their growing independence from local standards and practices of exchange. Of course, leverage against nonmerchants also came from their dependence on their neighbors. It was a hard thing, the committee of Pownalborough admitted, to "deprive a man of the benefits of society." Even if threatening crowds never materialized and one could get along outside the traffic of neighborhood exchange, it still took nerve, we can imagine, for a man to enter into a tavern where his name was posted, or to appear at church on Sunday when a gazette had listed him as an "enemy" a few days before. One's "Comfort in life" depended on far more than economic well-being. Many colonists must have agreed with the Rev. Asa Dunbar, of Weston and Sudbury, that it was best to remain "in good fellowship with every friend to American liberty."[45]

Not surprisingly, some Americans complained about the tyranny of committees and crowds. One Virginian, who styled himself a patriot, nonetheless noted that immense powers were "lodged with Men whom I should think must themselves be surprised at the great authority they have stepd. into."[46] Even patriots might justly fear and resent that state of affairs, he suggested. A New Yorker who chose loyalty to Britain wrote about the nonimportation, nonconsumption movement in 1774: "The resolves of the Continental Congress are now executing in the several Provinces and political inquisitors are appointed in each town to pry into the conduct of individuals."[47] It was a fair description of the situation, and matters were surely more outrageous when the inquisitors were not appointed committee members but self-appointed crowds. Indeed, the nonimportation movement presumed that what seemed individual business to some was actually

---

ceeded "for the sake of preferment," he assured his neighbors, but always from concern for his country.)

[45] *Boston Gazette*, Sept. 11, Dec. 18, 1775.

[46] Ammerman, *Common Cause*, p. 121.

[47] Henry Hilton to Robert Nicholson, Feb. 21, 1775, in Catherine S. Crary, comp. and ed., *The Price of Loyalty: Tory Writings from the Revolutionary Era* (New York, 1973), pp. 29–30.

public (which was to say, social) business. Activities that some considered individual and private affairs—what one bought, what one sold, what one consumed, what one paid for it—all became matters of public knowledge, public discussion, and, on occasion, public discipline. The public in question, moreover, was a broad one, embracing some inhabitants unqualified to serve on or even vote for committees. A host of transactions became liable to the scrutiny and jurisdiction of those who qualified merely as neighbors.

The patriot movement thus contained ideas and practices that had long been part of a world that asserted neighborliness, mutuality, and accountability as central values. Moreover, despite the important use of publicity, only some cases made it into the newspapers. The committee of Petersham, for one, clearly expressed a preference for private and friendly admonition to the use of publicity, justifying their decision to publish someone's name by recounting their futile attempts at private "Expostulations." Similarly, the committee of Rehoboth articulated its understanding of its role: "The great end of discipline," they said, was "to take away the sin and save the sinner." They tried private discussion before public action, and we can well imagine that private individuals used admonitions (not to say threats) before public indictment.[48] The accounts in the press were just the tip of the iceberg, then, and we need to assume much more widespread informal participation. Equally important was the clear expectation that *accusers* were supposed to act like neighbors too.

As trade boycotts instituted changes in neighborly relations, they also altered relations of class. When the Worcester blacksmiths agreed to boycott non-Associators, they consciously redefined their relationship with the fifty-two members of the prominent Chandler family who refused to support the plan. The Chandlers had long dominated Worcester with their wealth, receiving many appointments to local political positions. Blacksmiths who voted to boycott non-Associators were therefore setting up a conflict, courting a confrontation with

[48] For committee of Petersham, see note 35 above. The committee of Rehoboth published its sentiments in *Boston Gazette*, Sept. 11, 1775.

members of the upper class in their area. They were willing—perhaps in some cases anxious—to define members of the elite as enemies, and to do so to their faces. The patriot movement allowed mechanics to refuse to shoe the horse of a county squire. Wherever well-to-do Americans hung back from the cause, they found themselves vulnerable to the oversight and discipline of their social inferiors.[49]

In addition, nonconsumption elements of the resistance movement had particularly notable effects on class relations in the colonies. The eighth article of the Association spelled out the necessary change:

> We will, in our several stations, encourage frugality, economy, and industry, and promote agriculture, arts and the manufactures of this country, especially that of wool; and will discountenance and discourage every species of extravagance and dissipation, especially all horse-racing, and all kinds of gaming, cock-fighting, exhibitions of shews, plays, and other expensive diversions and entertainments; and on the death of any relation or friend, none of us . . . will go into any further mourning-dress, than a black crape or ribbon on the arm or hat, for gentlemen, and a black ribbon and necklace for ladies, and we will discontinue the giving of scarves and gloves at funerals.[50]

Few of these provisions were new to the movement in 1774. A full ten years earlier, Boston merchants had first agreed on sartorial restraint, especially at funerals, and other parts of this nonconsumption clause were familiar to patriots as well.[51] Although this clause explicitly addressed different ranks of Americans in their "several stations," its provisions affected elite and genteel Americans in a particular way, for a good many of the banned occasions constituted occasions when class differences were particularly visible. Gentlemen pre-

[49] Edward M. Cook, Jr., *The Fathers of the Towns: Leadership and Community Structure in Eighteenth-Century New England* (Baltimore, 1976), pp. 189–90. Not all blacksmiths were necessarily of humble social status. The group in Worcester County included prosperous landed men as well as the less well-to-do.

[50] Morison, ed., *Sources and Documents*, p. 124.

[51] Schlesinger, *Colonial Merchants*, pp. 63–64, 107–14.

sided at horseraces in the middle and southern colonies, for example; in Virginia, racing and its inevitable companion, gambling, underscored gentry superiority, setting common planters and others who attended firmly into the position of spectators.[52] Similarly, outside New England, the theater provided elite colonists with an opportunity to see and be seen, dressed in expensive clothing, alighting from expensive carriages, and in the midst of expensive company. Especially within New England, funerals provided an occasion for the well-to-do to wear expensive mourning clothes, ride in expensive carriages, and give out expensive tokens (imported gloves and scarves) to mourners of high social status. The theater, balls and entertainments, and lavish funerals all were occasions for what a later age would call "conspicuous consumption."[53] Thus the nonconsumption aspect of the resistance movement limited or banned occasions on which members of the colonial elite most conspicuously set themselves off from those of their neighbors who were less well-to-do.

Yet, as indicated by the Continental Congress's endorsement of nonconsumption, the movement did not constitute a frontal attack on the wealthy or on social distinctions in American society. We can read the Association and earlier nonconsumption schemes as defenses of the American elite: trade boycotts were not explicitly critical of the wealthy, and although for the elite to buy from American rather than English artisans and manufacturers would have an economic effect, still the Association did not call for a redistribution of wealth. Instead, it gave the relatively well-to-do opportunities to dem-

---

[52] Isaac, *Transformation of Virginia*, pp. 98–101, and T. H. Breen, "Horses and Gentlemen: The Cultural Significance of Gambling among the Gentry of Virginia," *William and Mary Quarterly* 3d ser. 34 (1977):239–57.

[53] On the theater, see Withington, "Morality and American Identity," chaps. 4 and 5. On funerals, ibid., chap. 6; Arthur M. Schlesinger, Sr., *The Birth of the Nation: A Portrait of the American People on the Eve of Independence* (Boston, 1968), pp. 135–36 and chap. 9; David E. Stannard, *The Puritan Way of Death: A Study in Religion, Culture, and Social Change* (New York, 1977), pp. 103–34. On English aristocrats' and merchants' use of funerals, see Lawrence Stone, *The Crisis of the Aristocracy, 1558–1641* (Oxford, 1965), pp. 572–81.

onstrate publicly that they could be patriots too. It gave the upper classes ways to make clear to neighbors that their wealth—unlike the wealth of the British upper classes—was not corrupting, and that, indeed, differences in wealth and status in American society were not significant.

The elite could not only refrain from importing and consuming, they could publicly appear at new occasions—committee meetings, tea-burnings, and simple, unostentatious funerals, now transformed into occasions of conspicuous *non*consumption. They could exhibit their virtue. How important this function was to the elite appears in the coverage that such funerals received in the colonial press. The *South Carolina Gazette* reported one case: "Few had more friends than this amiable and excellent LADY, yet the latter clause of the eighth article of the Association was strictly adhered to at this funeral." When a Philadelphia alderman died in early 1775, Hugh Gaine's *New-York Gazette, and the Weekly Mercury* stressed both the virtue of the deceased and the virtue of the mourners at the funeral, which was "conducted agreeable to the resolves of the Continental Congress."[54] Similarly, the press made a point of reporting the decision of the student body at Harvard to have their degrees printed on locally manufactured paper and to wear homespun suits at graduation ceremonies.[55] Individuals did not have to publicize their patriotism and virtue in so many words, as Thomas Lillie, Enachy Bartlett, and the leather-dressers of Boston had done. They could publicize them in so many actions.

If the upper classes in the patriot movement used nonconsumption to their own advantage, that they needed to do so reflects something of the power and disposition of more ordinary participants. Occasions on which the elite demonstrated their virtue both encouraged the participation of ordinary people (indeed, they may have been a requirement for that participation) and worked to channel it. If they avoided wide-

[54] *South Carolina Gazette,* quoted in Ammerman, *Common Cause,* p. 117. *New York Gazette, and the Weekly Mercury,* Jan. 30, 1775, reprinted in Frank Moore, comp. and ed., *Diary of the American Revolution: From Newspapers and Original Documents,* 2 vols. (1860; reprint ed., New York, 1969), 1:16–17.

[55] Schlesinger, *Colonial Merchants,* p. 110.

scale class hostility such as that which appeared in the attack on Gov. Thomas Hutchinson's house, they paid a price by deferring to the standards and values of those beneath them in the social scale. The genteel had to renounce aspects of gentility.

For their part, ordinary participants accepted differences in wealth and social status. They did not deny that it was possible to be both wealthy and a patriot. They did insist, however, that the rich should not use their money and status against other members of the community. They insisted that the well-to-do renounce efforts to set themselves apart from or above their less fortunate neighbors. They did not accord to prosperous people freedom to use their wealth just as they chose. Here was a social vision in which the uses of wealth were regulated or contained within limits.

Finally, nonconsumption pacts prohibited a social occasion particularly central to gentility—the ceremony of tea drinking. Notably, patriot criticisms of tea appeared before Lord Townshend laid a duty on that item, a fact that underscores that tea drinking held significance in American society prior to and apart from its status as a taxed import. It is significant, too, that as occasions of tea drinking were suppressed, occasions of rum drinking were multiplied by the resistance movement. Not only did patriots enter into militia exercises more often than previously, they also celebrated events and anniversaries—such as the repeal of the Stamp Act—with ceremonies that included the drinking of numerous patriotic toasts by the assembled company.[56] Consumption of rum—like tea, an imported beverage—did not come under attack within the resistance movement, a fact that underscores the essential nature of the movement as an alliance across lines of class. As dictated by nonconsumption, occasions that supported the solidarity of men of different ranks replaced those sometimes invidious events, tea parties.

The ban on tea also carried significant consequences for relationships of gender in American society, as was evident in

[56] Newspaper articles denounced tea in the New York and Philadelphia press in 1765 and 1766. Schlesinger, *Colonial Merchants,* p. 108, 111–12. Richard J. Hooker, "The American Revolution Seen through a Wine Glass," *William and Mary Quarterly,* 3d ser. 11 (1954):52–77.

various expressions of Americans' antitea fervor. In 1775, for example, the *Pennsylvania Journal* ran a satirical petition, ostensibly from "divers OLD WOMEN of the city." "Your petitioners," the article read, "fear it will be utterly impossible for them to exhibit so much patriotism as to totally disuse [tea]." As a substitute, the petitioners alleged, chocolate was too heavy a drink, which "must destroy that brilliancy of fancy, and fluency of expression, usually found at tea tables, when they are handling the conduct or character of their absent acquaintances." The petition asked "an indulgence," permission to continue drinking tea for "those spinsters, whom age and ugliness have rendered desperate in the expectation of husbands; those of the married, where infirmities and ill behavior have made their husbands long since tired of them, and those *old women* of the *male gender* who will most naturally be found in such company."[57]

Here, clearly, was hostility toward men who drank tea with the women instead of rum with the men. Here was hostility toward gentility, including the "brilliancy" and "fluency" of conversation associated with it. The conversation satirized was malicious gossip—a surprising target for patriots who busied themselves tirelessly with the "conduct and character" of their neighbors. What was under attack was not nosing into others' private affairs but the *private* nosing into others' affairs, adjudication within the closed company of tea drinkers instead of a more public and less select arena. Clearly, too, the *Journal*'s article expressed a vicious hostility toward women, and although it is a particularly venomous example, it was far from the only expression that linked tea drinking, females, and dependence in a derogatory manner. Indeed, some people associated women closely with consumption in general and genteel consumption in particular along with its allegedly debilitating effects. Benjamin Franklin was one of a number of figures who blamed his wife for introducing aspects of gentility into his household regimen.[58]

[57] *Pennsylvania Journal*, Mar. 1, 1775, reprinted in Moore, comp. and ed., *Diary of the American Revolution*, 1:30–31.

[58] Benjamin Franklin, "Autobiography," in Benjamin Franklin, *Writings*, ed. J. A. Leo Lemay (New York, 1987), p. 1382. Cotton Mather had claimed

How did misogyny work in a cause that required and promoted women's participation? Vigorous denunciations of women who drank tea took on further meaning in light of a contrast, often explicitly drawn. When Franklin bought his sister Jane a wedding present in the 1760s, he told her that he had thought about choosing a tea table but had decided instead on a spinning wheel.[59] It was a highly symbolic choice. What the Association did not say, but what everyone in colonial society knew, was that to stop importing cloth meant a steep rise in the number of women-hours that needed to be put in on the wheel. The attack on tea parties was matched by the promotion and celebration of spinning parties in their stead. The denunciation of idle tea sippers found its counterpart in the high praise patriots provided for women as producers. Widely publicized spinning parties provided women with occasions for exhibiting their capacities for patriotism through conspicuous production. Eschewing tea parties and promoting spinning and other home manufactures, the Association disparaged women only as they stood outside the context of a household economy.[60]

Practically speaking, then, trade boycotts and nonconsumption agreements moved women who had begun to enter the realm of consumption back into the realm of household production. Many colonists hailed the switch from tea drinking to spinning as a reaffirmation of tradition and moral strength, expressing a belief in the superiority of production within the relatively self-sufficient community unit. These adjustments of gender role formed one aspect of the trade boy-

---

in the 1690s that woman's role was "to Spend (or . . . Save) what others *Get*," quoted in Nancy F. Cott, *The Bonds of Womanhood: "Woman's Sphere" in New England, 1780–1835* (New Haven, 1977), p. 20. Compare Jan Lewis, "The Republican Wife," *William and Mary Quarterly*, 3d ser. 44 (1987):698, who notes that consumption was also associated with men in the late eighteenth century. Ruth H. Bloch explores the male nature of notions of republican virtue in "The Gendered Meanings of Virtue in Revolutionary America," *Signs* 13 (1987):37–58.

[59] Norton, *Liberty's Daughters*, p. 18.

[60] Ibid., pp. 156–70, recounts public celebration of spinning parties and women's productivity.

cotts' overall thrust: the boycotts rejected integration into and dependence upon the world market for women and men alike. As Edmund Morgan noted, proponents of nonconsumption asserted that the wider market was not necessary, that all the Atlantic market had to offer were "trifles" and "baubles"—a sure thrust against genteel ideals that rendered many imports essential.[61] The movement for home manufacturing promoted local forms and standards of exchange over commerce with England and Europe. This was a reassertion of rural values against the encroachments of urban life—or, alternatively, the values of neighboring versus the values of buying and selling. Many people, then, brought with them into the resistance a critique of those whose independence from the local market and from local values entailed dependence on the Atlantic market and the wider world. It was not simply that, as British policies were making clear, such independence as could be gained by commerce meant increased dependence on markets, sources of credit, events, and powers far away. It was also that some Americans' freedom from local constraints spelled a consequent decline in their less powerful neighbors' control over their own lives. Nonimportation and nonconsumption pacts directly contradicted those who had begun to define liberty as their own independence from the obligations and entanglements of their local world.

Indeed, I do not think it is incidental that the patriot critique of Parliament's effort to derive revenue from the colonies expressed ideas for which colonists could find meaning closer to home. A basic premise applied to relations within the empire as it did to relations within local networks of exchange: it was wrong for one part of the community to try to gain at the expense of anther. By taxing colonial trade for revenue, England violated the purpose of economic exchange, the mutual advantage that transactions were supposed to secure. Parallels between empire and neighborhood may have provided a way that relatively ordinary Americans, unversed in the nuances of imperial relations or the niceties of constitutional thinking, understood such matters. Equally important, patriots' belief in mutuality, the invigoration of as-

[61] Morgan, "Puritan Ethic," pp. 96–97.

pects of plebeian culture, the licensing of ordinary men and women to oversee and ensure equity according to standards of a local community, and the suppression of aspects of genteel culture—these elements may well have constituted the cement in the cross-class coalition that precipitated resistance and revolution.[62] These characteristics of the nonconsumption, nonimportation movement were not incidental to many colonists' decision to join it. For many patriots the social changes inherent in the resistance represented more than a tactic for influencing Britain, more than a series of hardships to be endured as a means to another end.

If that is so, then there emerges another pattern, another rhythm characterizing the American Revolution as it unfolded over time. To Jameson, the Revolution represented a movement for political independence that had often unforeseen, often unintended social ramifications; the Revolution gained momentum through the 1770s and beyond. Viewed from the vantage point of the nonconsumption and nonimportation pacts, however, the Revolution can be seen to have suffered the loss of social dimensions as well. Patriots abandoned certain aspects of the resistance, foregoing aspirations for revising relations within neighborhoods as well as with the Atlantic market. To explain that shift we might look in part to the war, its duration, its difficulty, and the profound unsettling of economic life that it involved—all of which had effects on the original ideals of the movement. Without denying the force of Jameson's framework, we can add another—a move-

[62] Compare Breen, "'Baubles of Britain,'" pp. 73–104. Breen's article similarly argues that the nonimportation and nonconsumption movements were essential to the creation of patriot unity in the resistance era. For Breen, however, the key component to such unity beyond the local level was the anglicizing influence of the plethora of English imports enjoyed by eighteenth-century Americans throughout different communities. That consumer goods possessed a single, shared meaning, Breen argues, allowed Americans to establish a common political ground, rejecting Britain via its "baubles." As I hope is clear, my reading of nonimportation and nonconsumption emphasizes the significance of the social relationships in which imported goods played a role. Renouncing imported goods helped to produce unity less because those goods held meanings about which Americans agreed than because they figured in social practices and developments about which Americans were in conflict.

ment that had been social and political became a movement
more narrowly political and military. That transition in the
Revolution was not simple: it cost leaders of the patriot coalition some years and some effort to disentangle the movement
for Independence from popular participation, to suppress
plebeian cultural forms and insulate the movement from ideals such as fairness in prices and mutuality in exchange. Wartime struggles over those issues testify to the significance and
tenacity of the social commitments formed in the resistance
decade. Without doubt, "the transforming hand of revolution" touched many aspects of eighteenth-century society, but
in some respects patriots nonetheless discovered that their
reach had exceeded their grasp.

ALLAN KULIKOFF

Was the American Revolution a Bourgeois Revolution?

IN 1795 Mary Stevenson Hewson, who had arrived in Philadelphia from England a decade earlier, wrote her son, then
studying in England, about politics. Tutored by Benjamin
Franklin as a child when Franklin had stayed in Mary Hewson's mother's house, she learned political philosophy well.
"You did not expect politics from me I dare say," she wrote,
understanding the proper place of women, but she was "not
afraid of that—you or I shall ever endanger our liberty by
these sentiments." Her views, expressed in the letter, show
a strong sense of class prerogative. Decrying both "universal
liberty" and "perfect equality" as unattainable, she insisted
that "when people boast that in their nation all men are free
and equal they think only of their own class." Everywhere
"some men are set above the people, whether by hereditary
succession or election is of little importance while they are in
power." All rulers show the same "air of superiority," but in a
republic, like the United States, such airs "are more provoking than it would be from one whose station was always
above yours. Setting aside the permission of slavery," she concluded, "perhaps the government of this country is as good

The author is indebted to William Beik and Stanley L. Engerman for comments on an earlier version of this paper and to Alfred F. Young and especially Elizabeth Fox-Genovese for intensive discussions of issues
surrounding the concept of bourgeois Revolution.

as any, but I question whether the people are happier under it than under any other."[1]

This remarkable letter exposes the contradictions inherent in the American Revolution. Hewson challenged the ideology of popular sovereignty, an idea that legitimated the American republic—but longed for a more hierarchical government. Strongly embedded in Philadelphia Federalist society, she hardly showed solidarity with the Revolution made by her social inferiors a generation earlier.

Such examples of the contradictory results of the American Revolution as that found in Hewson's letter could be multiplied, and they defy easy explanation. Virginia planters manumitted thousands of slaves, influenced by the Revolution's promise of political and spiritual equality—but at the same time hundreds of ordinary planters signed racist proslavery petitions, seeking to protect ownership of their human property. The people-out-of-doors demanded their right as the people to determine public policy—but their rulers insisted that since free elections guaranteed popular sovereignty, all crowd actions be put down as against the people. The Revolution unleashed pent-up demands for economic equality *and* the right to pursue profit—and as a result wealth remained highly concentrated.[2]

---

[1] Mary Stevenson Hewson to Thomas Hewson, Feb. 18, 1795, Hewson Family Papers, microfilm, American Philosophical Society, Philadelphia. I am indebted to Susan Branson for this reference; her Ph.D. diss., "Politics and Gender: The Political Consciousness of Philadelphia Women in the 1790s," Northern Illinois University, 1992, greatly illuminates our knowledge of elite women's political interests.

[2] Peter J. Albert, "The Protean Institution: The Geography, Economy, and Ideology of Slavery in Post-Revolutionary Virginia," Ph.D. diss., University of Maryland, 1976, chaps. 4–7; Fredricka Teute Schmidt and Barbara Ripel Wilhelm, "Early Proslavery Petitions in Virginia," *William and Mary Quarterly*, 3d ser. 30 (1973):133–46; Gordon S. Wood, *The Creation of the American Republic, 1776–1787* (Chapel Hill, 1969), pp. 403–13; Allan Kulikoff, "The American Revolution, Capitalism, and the Formation of the Yeoman Classes," in Alfred F. Young, ed., *Beyond the American Revolution: Explorations in the History of American Radicalism* (DeKalb, Ill., 1993), pp. 80–119; Allan Kulikoff, "The Political Economy of Revolutionary War Service in Virginia," in John M. Murrin, ed., *War and Society in America from the Aztecs to the Civil War* (forthcoming).

These examples, and others like them, point to the need for a comprehensive theoretical framework to analyze the social dimensions of the American Revolution. Such a framework should encompass the contradictory goals of Revolutionaries, but it should also connect structural changes in the colonial economy to the coming of the Revolution and explain the process of change through the war, the creation of a new government, and the structural transformation that the Revolution encouraged. But common explanations of the Revolution do not even attempt to structure analysis around such questions. Instead, two generations of scholarship have enriched our knowledge of Revolutionary thought, the impact of ordinary people on the Revolution, and the formation of new governments, leaving us mired in details, unable to put the Revolution together as a coherent whole.

Perhaps our Revolution was a "bourgeois revolution," whose major impact was the spread of capitalism and the rise of a significant bourgeoisie and proletariat. The transition to capitalism, encompassing far more than the spread of markets, transformed social relations. White adult males, who had been independent proprietors owning the means of production (whether land or tools), lost their economic independence and began working as wage laborers (the proletariat) or became so deeply involved in commerce and credit that capitalists could demand what crops a farmer would plant, thereby denying him *control* of the means of production. At the same time a bourgeois or capitalist class formed that eventually came to own or at least control (through credit, banks, railroads) the means of production. Such control permitted the capitalists to expropriate part of the output of other classes and to employ the proletariat, which had only its labor power to sell.[3]

Such a framework, rarely pursued by American historians,

---

[3] This brief discussion greatly oversimplifies the transition to capitalism. For a discussion of the debate over rural capitalist transformation, see Allan Kulikoff, "The Transition to Capitalism in Rural America," *William and Mary Quarterly*, 3d ser. 46 (1989): 120–44, and idem, *The Agrarian Origins of American Capitalism* (Charlottesville, 1992), chaps. 1–2. Short definitions of *bourgeoisie* and *capitalism* are found in Tom Bottomore, ed., *A Dictionary of Marxist Thought* (Cambridge, Mass., 1983), pp. 54–55, 64–67.

plausibly resolves problems inherent in making a structural interpretation of a revolution. After looking briefly at the accomplishments and unresolved problems of social interpretations of the Revolution, we will explore it through the prism of bourgeois revolution. This essay, then, is not a synthesis but hypothetical history, a creative story consistent with our imperfect knowledge. Its purpose is not to close debate but to open it, to encourage historians to pursue other stories, perhaps contradictory to this one, but equally plausible.

Over sixty years ago J. Franklin Jameson argued that the American Revolution was a social movement that transformed "the relations of social classes to each other, the institution of slavery, the system of landholding, the course of business," all "in the direction of levelling democracy." Jameson painted vivid images of democratic revolution: the reduction of slavery, free settlement of the West, sale of loyalist estates to men of small means, abolition of primogeniture and entail, expansion of the franchise, disestablishment of established churches.[4]

Later historians have dismissed Jameson's portrait as exaggerated, pointing to errors in his presentation such as his failure to admit the viability of southern slavery. A revolution that failed to grant full citizenship to all adult white men, not to mention women and blacks, hardly deserves the label democratic, notwithstanding the achievements of the leaders of the Revolutionary generation. Critics, however, have obscured the changes that did occur, structural changes that sometimes proceeded in antidemocratic ways, toward the concentration of property and power, the development of capitalism, the destruction of the independence of farmers and craftsmen.[5]

The study of Revolutionary political ideology has produced immense benefits—an enhanced understanding of the reasons gentlemen and merchants, clergymen, and lawyers became alienated from England, vivid descriptions of

[4] J. Franklin Jameson, *The American Revolution Considered as a Social Movement* (1926; reprint ed., Princeton, 1967), pp. 9, 18.

[5] Lee Soltow, *The Distribution of Wealth and Income in the United States in 1798* (Pittsburgh, 1989); Sean Wilentz, *Chants Democratic: New York City and the Rise of the American Working Class, 1788–1850* (New York, 1984).

republican and liberal social visions of Revolutionary leaders, a fuller explanation of the relation between economic instability and the intellectual justifications of the Constitution. But intellectual historians privilege elite thought and rarely connect it to economic or social realities and therefore cannot see the dialectical relation between thought and action. Moreover they often ignore how contested that ideology was, how poorer women and men made their own Revolution.[6]

The flood of work on common people has illuminated popular ideology, class relations and conflict, uprisings of soldiers or farmers or artisans, plebeian culture, and popular literature. These historians have created entirely new Revolutions, populated by women, blacks, craftsmen, farmers, sailors, and Indians—Revolutions that often pursued contradictory goals. They have documented how the Revolution was, in Carl L. Becker's famous phrase, about "who shall rule at home" as well as "home rule."[7]

This impressive literature has raised new problems by its very richness. Failing to link the contradictory Revolutions of ordinary people, it creates confusion. More importantly, by privileging human agency—the ability of ordinary people to unite, make decisions, influence the course of events—these historians neglect or even deny the importance of structural constraints on behavior. Revolutionaries could make choices

---

[6] Bernard Bailyn, *The Ideological Origins of the American Revolution* (Cambridge, Mass., 1967), and Wood, *Creation of the American Republic*, remain the most brilliant examples. For a view that places the people-out-of-doors at the center of constitutional politics, see Alfred F. Young, "The Framers of the Constitution and the 'Genius of the People,'" *Radical History Review* 42 (1988):8–18.

[7] Alfred F. Young, "George Robert Twelves Hewes (1742–1840): A Boston Shoemaker and the Memory of the American Revolution," *William and Mary Quarterly*, 3d ser. 38 (1981):561–623, Gary B. Nash, *The Urban Crucible: Social Change, Political Consciousness, and the Origins of the American Revolution* (Cambridge, Mass., 1979), Kulikoff, *Agrarian Origins*, chap. 5; Linda K. Kerber, *Women of the Republic: Intellect and Ideology in Revolutionary America* (Chapel Hill, 1980), and Peter H. Wood, "'The Dream Deferred': Black Freedom Struggles on the Eve of White Independence," in Gary Y. Okihiro, ed., *In Resistance: Studies in African, Caribbean, and Afro-American History* (Amherst, Mass., 1986), pp. 166–87, and the essays in Young, ed., *Beyond the American Revolution*, constitute a small sample of a vast literature.

and influence events but only within those constraints. More-over the major consequences of the American Revolution, like the growth of capitalism, occurred despite the absence of de-liberate support by any class and the desire of many groups to evade such transformations.

BOURGEOIS REVOLUTIONS AND THE AMERICAN REVOLUTION

At first glance it hardly seems appropriate to label the Ameri-can Revolution a bourgeois revolution. The idea of bourgeois revolution evokes violent transformation, the struggle of well-organized and coherent classes against one another. A bour-geois revolution occurs, in this sense, after feudalism has de-cayed and a new capitalist class, driven by the need for the capitalists to expand, rises to challenge an entrenched feu-dal aristocracy.[8]

Despite the absence of both a feudal aristocracy and a well-developed bourgeoisie and proletariat, several historians have labeled the American Revolution a bourgeois revolution. Louis M. Hacker, for instance, contended in 1940 that Ameri-can capitalists were pitted against their English counterparts in a struggle for economic hegemony. The concept quickly fell into disrepute. Merchant capitalists, misidentified by Hacker as bourgeois, supported whatever side promised the greatest return. Men of capital, farmers, and artisans, the few and the many, supported both sides of the Revolution. Nor was the Revolution one in which a capitalist bourgeoisie van-quished some noncapitalist class, however defined. Northern capitalists and southern planters, Staughton Lynd insisted, united to support the Revolution but faced considerable op-position from the patriotic popular classes.[9] Conflicts between

---

[8] George C. Comninel, *Rethinking the French Revolution: Marxism and the Revisionist Challenge* (London, 1987), offers a Marxist critique of the idea of this version of bourgeois revolution in France.

[9] Louis M. Hacker, *The Triumph of American Capitalism: The Development of Forces in American History to the End of the Nineteenth Century* (New York, 1940), chaps. 12–14. Herbert Aptheker, *The American Revolution, 1763–1783* (New York, 1960), chap. 1, summarized and greatly modified this version of bourgeois revolution. For Staughton Lynd's ideas, see his *Class Conflict, Slav-*

capitalist and noncapitalist classes persisted for more than a century after the Revolution.

This vision of bourgeois revolution oversimplifies the history of political economy. The struggle to establish a capitalist political and economic order in Europe, England, and America took centuries. From English enclosure riots to Shays's Rebellion, from frontier squatters' demand for preemption of land to the Farmers' Alliance, rural folk demonstrated their hostility to capitalist social relations. Urban mechanics, sailors, and laborers protested equally vociferously when capitalists tried to undermine their traditional, collective, and often noncapitalist world, native-born and immigrant workers struggled together against early industrial capitalists, and slaveholders created an anticapitalist niche for themselves in an increasingly capitalist world economy. The Civil War, which pitted anticapitalist planters against early industrial capitalists, resulting in victory for free labor, more closely approximates this version of bourgeois revolution.[10]

Marxists, however, usually reject this concept of bourgeois revolution and turn from an evocation of conscious class conflict to a more subtle structural analysis. Christopher Hill, in a brilliant essay on the English Revolution of 1640 entitled "A Bourgeois Revolution?," argues that "the phrase in Marxist usage does *not* mean a Revolution made by or consciously willed by the bourgeoisie." That revolution, like all others, "was caused by the breakdown of the old society," the development of capitalist agriculture, for instance, within a still-feudal legal framework. He goes on to show how varied and contradictory the goals of revolutionaries were, how radicals attacked any attempt to impose capitalism. Notwithstanding the goals of most revolutionaries, the "*outcome*" of that revolution, Hill argues, "was the establishment of conditions far more favorable to the development of capitalism than those

---

ery, and the United States Constitution: Ten Essays (Indianapolis, 1967), chap. 1, esp. pp. 12–14.

[10] For the Civil War as a bourgeois revolution, see Barrington Moore, Jr., *Social Origins of Dictatorship and Democracy: Lord and Peasant in the Making of the Modern World* (Boston, 1966), chap. 3, and Lynd, *Class Conflict*, pp. 14–15.

which prevailed before 1640." Popular democracy was defeated, private property was enshrined in legal doctrine, the remaining peasants were dispossessed, and the English bourgeoisie ultimately was sustained in power.[11]

This Marxist concept of bourgeois revolution has great explanatory value when applied to the American Revolution. The Revolution came about, in part, because the tension between slowly developing capitalism and the desires of a large part of the populace to maintain noncapitalist relations of production could not be sustained when a political legitimacy no longer rested with the Crown and Parliament. Conflict with Great Britain ushered in forty years of intense—often radical—social conflict, with middling and poor men, and occasionally women, challenging the ruling classes in city and countryside.

Even if no social class consciously sought to impose or to oppose capitalist development, the Revolution did expedite movement toward a more bourgeois, capitalist society. The Revolution accelerated developments already under way in the North toward intensive economic growth and capitalism. Banking, public works, and the continental common market provided a favorable structure for capitalists, and the abolition of slavery in the North sustained the growth of an urban proletariat. Second, the ideology of possessive individualism, the idea that each person was a discrete individual rather than a member of a group, gained hegemonic power during the Revolutionary era. This hardly meant that America suddenly became "liberal," for different groups interpreted possessive individualism in conflicting ways. For instance, where employers used the language of free contracts to deny workers the traditional privilege of determining wages, journeymen turned similar language to a defense of these collective rights. And, third, the conflicts spawned in the Revolutionary strug-

[11] Christopher Hill, "A Bourgeois Revolution?" in J. G. A. Pocock, ed., *Three British Revolutions: 1641, 1688, 1776* (Princeton, 1980), pp. 109–39, quotations on pp. 110–11. A fully articulated argument about capitalism and the bourgeoisie within the Atlantic world, consistent with this analysis, can be found in Elizabeth Fox-Genovese and Eugene D. Genovese, *Fruits of Merchant Capital: Slavery and Bourgeois Property in the Rise and Expansion of Capitalism* (New York, 1983), esp. chaps. 7–8, 10–11.

gle shaped the character of social and economic conflict for generations: for a century women and men, the few and the many, producers and economic parasites, speculators and yeomen, capitalists and workers fought over the character of economic relations. The grounds of these struggles—the desirability of economic development, the protection of rights of journeymen to control their labor or farmers to graze livestock in unenclosed open fields—show the ways that capitalist relations of production structured social conflict.

This essay sketches out the structural tensions that underlay the coming of the Revolution and the spread of capitalist relations of production after the war. Then it will examine the diffusion of possessive individualism, analyzing Thomas Paine's *Common Sense,* the Declaration of Independence, and William Manning's *Key of Libberty.* Finally it will turn to the widespread class conflicts of the Revolutionary era, tracing the contours of conflict and the contradictory ways that blacks, white women, and white yeomen shaped individualism, sometimes twisting it against the best interests of capitalists.

THE REVOLUTION AND THE DIFFUSION OF CAPITALIST ECONOMIC RELATIONS

The American Revolution and the adoption of the Constitution were key events in the diffusion of capitalist economic relations throughout America. Building on pre-Revolutionary capitalist development around port towns, American capitalists and their allies used the opening provided by the Constitution to continue intensive economic development, industrialization, and the creation of a wage labor force.

Although English capitalists had financed colonial settlement and nearly all the colonists (especially southern staple producers) had participated in the market on occasion, colonial migrants often wished to escape capitalist relations of production increasingly common in England. The dynamic societies they created developed within the capitalist North Atlantic economy but remained outside of it. Northern farmers, who mostly owned the land they farmed, achieved communal self-sufficiency in food, avoided wage labor, and operated mostly outside a money economy. But they sent small surpluses to market, using the money they earned to buy consumer goods and sustain local exchange. Southern staple producers participated vigorously in markets, sustaining a large class of merchant capitalists, but the slave society they created was the very opposite of the system of the free labor, freely contracted, at the heart of capitalist economic relations.[12]

Late colonial economic development involved northern colonists more directly and intensively in international commodity markets than ever before. When warfare and poor crops reduced European grain supplies, Pennsylvania and Shenandoah Valley farmers seized opportunities to export grain to the Continent. As the wheat trade grew, a wealthy indigenous merchant class emerged. Integrated markets for commodities, moreover, began to appear in the colonies. Although towns like New York and Philadelphia were still tiny by later standards, they had grown sufficiently large to create demand for butter, cheese, vegetables, and fruit from the surrounding countryside, thereby encouraging a new form of market surplus farming.[13]

New forms of tenancy and labor relations arose from these structural economic changes. As the population grew and per capita land supplies diminished in settled areas, tenancy—and especially short-term leases—expanded in regions where it was already well known (like the Hudson River Valley) and in places tied to growing urban markets (like southeastern Pennsylvania). The beginnings of both extensive agricultural

[12] Kulikoff, "Transition to Capitalism"; Michael Merrill, "Cash Is Good to Eat: Self-Sufficiency and Exchange in the Rural Economy of the United States," *Radical History Review* 4 (1977):42–71; Lois Green Carr and Lorena S. Walsh, "Economic Diversification and Labor Organization in the Chesapeake, 1650–1820," in Stephen Innes, ed., *Work and Labor in Early America* (Chapel Hill, 1988), chap. 4; Allan Kulikoff, *Tobacco and Slaves: The Development of Southern Cultures in the Chesapeake, 1680–1800* (Chapel Hill, 1986), chaps. 3–4.

[13] The growing literature on colonial economic development is summarized in John J. McCusker and Russell R. Menard, *The Economy of British America, 1607–1789* (Chapel Hill, 1985), chaps. 9, 11, 13.

wage labor (as seen in the rise of cottagers in the Delaware Valley) and urban wage labor (which developed as urban slave imports and indentured servitude declined) could be seen by the 1760s and 1770s.[14]

A slow, imperceptible transformation of merchant capitalists—who had blended into the surrounding society, serving farmers and artisans—into a class of capitalists probably began during the late colonial era. In Philadelphia, for instance, Quakers saw the glaring contradiction between slavery and freedom and insisted in the 1770s that their members free their slaves. Such men, often merchants, then turned to wage labor, replacing traditional hierarchies with a cash nexus.[15]

One must not exaggerate these changes. Most colonial whites lived on their own farms or owned their own shops. Slaves and servants performed a substantial portion of manual labor in every colony. Colonial gentlemen hardly saw themselves as capitalists but demanded deference from their social inferiors. As tenancy increased, some landlords attempted to mask capitalist ground rent in traditional, almost feudal language.[16]

[14] Lucy Simler, "Tenancy in Colonial Pennsylvania: The Case of Chester County," *William and Mary Quarterly,* 3d ser. 43 (1986):542–69; Edward Countryman, *A People in Revolution: The American Revolution and Political Society in New York, 1760–1790* (Baltimore, 1981), pp. 13–25; Jean R. Soderlund, *Quakers and Slavery: A Divided Spirit* (Princeton, 1985); Gary B. Nash, "Slaves and Slaveowners in Colonial Philadelphia," *William and Mary Quarterly,* 3d ser. 30 (1973):223–56.

[15] The transformation of merchant capitalists into capitalists is a little-studied topic. Some dimensions of the problem can be seen in Fox-Genovese and Genovese, *Fruits of Merchant Capital,* esp. chaps. 1, 7. Soderlund, *Quakers and Slavery,* chaps. 4–6, and Thomas M. Doerflinger, *A Vigorous Spirit of Enterprise: Merchants and Economic Development in Revolutionary Philadelphia* (Chapel Hill, 1986), chaps 2, 7 8, illuminate the growth of a class of capitalists, without ever using this language.

[16] Rowland Berthoff and John M. Murrin, "Feudalism, Communalism and the Yeoman Freeholder: The American Revolution Considered as a Social Accident," in Stephen G. Kurtz and James H. Hutson, eds., *Essays on the American Revolution* (Chapel Hill, 1973), pp. 256–88; David Galenson, *White Servitude in Colonial America* (Cambridge, 1981), esp. chap. 7; Evarts B. Greene and Virginia D. Harrington, eds., *American Population before the Federal Census of 1790* (New York, 1932), pp. 104–5, 110–11, 119–20; Ira

Political and economic events of the Revolutionary era accelerated the thrust of this incipient capitalist development. The diffusion of commodity markets continued apace, encouraged by the new states and a federal Constitution that mandated a continental common market. Although such developments indicated the direction of change, the Revolution itself did not install capitalist economic relations. As we shall see, every step toward capitalism met with substantial resistance from such social classes as yeoman farmers and urban craftsmen.

The Revolution destroyed both the colonial political attachment to Great Britain and the legal constraints on development that Britain had imposed to provide a market for British manufactured goods. Massive state investments in internal improvements, so common in the early nineteenth century, were inconceivable as long as colonials attached themselves more to London than to neighboring colonies. However ineffective British laws restricting colonial industry may have been, the Revolutionary victory cleared legal hurdles to the settlement of land, home manufacturing, and industrialization. Moreover, warfare (both the Revolution and the later wars in Europe) cut off imports of textiles, especially encouraging home manufacture of cloth, a new putting-out industry, and eventually textile mills. Neither warfare nor the removal of legal constraints, of course, immediately triggered massive industrialization, but these events did make such developments easier once economic resources were in place.[17]

By eliminating all trade barriers and imposing federal mediation in economic disputes between states, the Constitution created a national common market. Such regulation did not

Berlin, *Slaves without Masters: The Free Negro in the Antebellum South* (New York, 1974), pp. 46–47; John M. Murrin, "The Myths of Colonial Democracy and Royal Decline in Eighteenth-Century America," *Cithara* 5 (1965):53–69; Kulikoff, *Tobacco and Slaves*, chap. 7.

[17] McCusker and Menard, *Economy of British America*, chaps. 13, 15; James A. Henretta, "The War for Independence and American Economic Development," in Ronald Hoffman et al., eds., *The Economy of Early America: The Revolutionary Period, 1763–1790* (Charlottesville, Va., 1988), pp. 45–87.

immediately lead to an explosion of interregional trade, however. Even on the eve of the Civil War, most farmers and artisans still traded with neighbors or sent their goods to other places within the region. Goods, however, *could* move freely. Once access to the Mississippi River was secured in 1803, frontier farmers in the Ohio Valley floated farm products to New Orleans, where they entered interregional or international trade. And as soon as the Erie and other canals opened in the 1820s and 1830s, a vigorous two-way trade of grain and manufactured goods developed between the West and East. The elimination of trade barriers and the commerce it encouraged expedited the formation of a more national class of merchants, making them into a more cohesive political group capable of influencing state and national economic policy. For example, New York cotton factors, rather than British merchants, dominated the growing southern cotton trade.[18]

Bankers, who played a key role in nineteenth-century economic development, owed their influence and even their existence to the Revolution and the Constitution. There were no organized private incorporated banks in pre-Revolutionary America. Despite British prohibitions, colonies often emitted paper money (sometimes using the value of land as collateral), frequently succeeding in creating a stable currency. The great inflation of the Revolutionary era soured merchants and their allies on state-printed paper money. As a result, three banks formed in port towns in the 1780s. Fearing a kind of legal Shaysism, the loss of the value of loans repaid in depreciated paper money, and the negative impact of differing state monetary policies on interstate commerce, delegates to the Constitutional Convention prohibited states from making paper emissions. Farmers, artisans, and merchants still needed far more money than the small supply of specie could provide, however. The federal government failed to print paper money, but until state emissions were retired, some paper money remained in circulation. Eventually the Bank of the United States and new state-chartered banks stepped into this

[18] Douglass C. North, *The Economic Growth of the United States, 1790–1860* (New York, 1966); Diane Lindstrom, *Economic Development in the Philadelphia Region, 1810–1850* (New York, 1978).

void, printing bank notes that could be used for currency and providing loans to capitalists bent on development. By 1798 there were 22 chartered banks in the United States, almost all in northern cities. Economic expansion and warfare in the years when Republicans ruled encouraged an explosion of bank formation: the number of chartered state banks grew from 29 in 1800 to 89 in 1811 and reached 208 in 1815 (with a total capital of $82,000,000).[19]

Bankers—who had often been merchants or merchant-farmers—became key figures in capitalist development. Banks were not good substitutes for state-funded land banks, however. As early as 1786, John Witherspoon attacked Philadelphia's Bank of North America, claiming "that banking companies give credit only so as to be serviceable to merchants, and those immediately connected to them, but do not extend it to husbandmen, or those who improve the soil, by taking mortgages for a considerable time." Studies of banking sustain Witherspoon's criticisms—merchants and retailers held four-fifths of the active accounts in the Bank of North America. Banks later helped finance early textile mills and frequently lent money for short periods to merchants and manufacturers, but less often granted mortgages or other loans to farmers. Bankers sometimes favored their own directors, further limiting their utility to ordinary farmers and mechanics. The only advantage most men received from banks was use of bank notes that circulated as currency.[20]

[19] Mary M. Schweitzer, "State-Issued Currency and the Ratification of the U.S. Constitution," *Journal of Economic History* 49 (1989):311–22; Curtis P. Nettels, *The Emergence of a National Economy, 1775–1815* (New York, 1962), pp. 75–88, 295–301; U.S. Bureau of the Census, *Historical Statistics of the United States: Colonial Times to 1970*, 2 vols. (Washington, D.C., 1975), 2:1018.

[20] Schweitzer, "Currency and the Constitution," p. 317; Doerflinger, *Vigorous Spirit of Enterprise,* pp. 296–310; Lance Edwin Davis and Peter Lester Payne, "From Benevolence to Business: The Story of Two Savings Banks," *Business History Review* 32 (1958):386–406; Harry R. Stevens, "Bank Enterprises in a Western Town," *Business History Review* 29 (1955):139–56; Alan L. Olmstead, "New York Mutual Savings Bank Portfolio Management and Trustee Objectives," *Journal of Economic History* 34 (1974):815–34; Olmstead, "Investment Constraints and New York City Mutual Savings Bank Financing of Antebellum Development," *Journal of Economic History* 32

In order to keep the country united in an era when cabals variously formed by Virginia Republicans, Aaron Burr, and New England Federalists threatened to tear the infant nation apart, entrepreneurs wished to foster more rapid communication and trade. Politicians disagreed on how to finance internal improvements but generally agreed on their necessity. During the early nineteenth century a combination of private initiative and state and federal action cut the time and cost of private communication and commerce. Between 1790 and 1820 mail was delivered over an ever-growing network of post roads, the cost of interurban travel declined by half, and the importance of domestic trade grew. The construction of canals during the 1820s and 1830s accelerated this process, binding the country ever-closer together. The development of this economic infrastructure provided markets for the credit and commodities produced by the growing class of financial and early industrial capitalists.[21]

The gradual transformation of commerce inevitably changed relations of production, impelling the decline of traditional systems of unfree and craft labor and the growth of wage labor. During the mid-eighteenth century most workers could be divided into five broad groups: farm operators and their families; farm hands; master craftsmen, journeymen, and apprentices; indentured servants; and slaves. A traditional hierarchy permeated the workplace: yeomen ran patriarchal households, making all economic decisions; farmhands and journeymen received a traditional, set wage; apprentices and journeymen expected to become master craftsmen once they had mastered the mystery of their trade; and servants and especially slaves understood (and often resisted) the absolute power of their masters. Relations between social classes

---

(1972):811–40; Andrew A. Beveridge, "Local Lending Practice: Borrowers in a Small Northeastern City, 1832–1915," *Journal of Economic History* 45 (1985):393–403; Naomi R. Lamoreaux, "Banks, Kinship and Economic Development: The New England Case," *Journal of Economic History* 46 (1986):647–68.

[21] See Allan R. Pred's impressive *Urban Growth and the Circulation of Information: The United States System of Cities, 1790–1840* (Cambridge, Mass., 1973).

depended upon the place of an individual in a social hierarchy, not upon a market nexus. Struggles occurred when subservient classes saw traditional rights—the appropriate journeyman's wage, the slave's Sunday holiday—denied by the master.[22] All of this began to dissolve under the impact of the Revolution.

Northern legislators and judges, responding to the implicit promise of the Declaration of Independence and pressure from below from slaves and concerned citizens, emancipated the region's slaves in the decades after the Revolution. Not only was chattel bondage inconsistent with the freedom the colonists had won from British "slavery," but it was "highly detrimental to morality, industry, and the arts." By the end of the Revolution the New England states (where slavery was least entrenched) had emancipated their salves, and Pennsylvania (where far more slaves lived) had passed a gradual emancipation bill, freeing newly born slaves when they reached adulthood. By 1800 just one of every fourteen blacks in New England and one of every ten in Pennsylvania was still enslaved. Emancipation proceeded more slowly in New York and New Jersey; gradual emancipation laws were passed between 1799 and 1804, but in 1820 nearly two-fifths of New Jersey's black people and a quarter of those in New York were still in bondage. Nearly all of these freedmen and freedwomen, facing discrimination and lacking the skills needed in the cities where most of them lived, worked for wages and formed a substantial part of a new urban proletariat.[23]

The emancipation of northern slaves was part of the process of the formation of an American proletariat in both city and countryside. This process proceeded most rapidly in the

[22] For contrasting surveys of colonial labor systems, see Marcus Rediker, "Good Hands, Stout Hearts, and Fast Feet: The History and Culture of Working People in Early America," *Labour / Le Travailleur* 10 (1982):123–44, and Richard S. Dunn, "Servants and Slaves: The Recruitment and Employment of Labor," in Jack P. Greene and J. R. Pole, eds., *Colonial British America: Essays in the New History of the Early Modern Era* (Baltimore, 1984), pp. 157–94.

[23] The standard work is Arthur Zilversmit, *The First Emancipation: The Abolition of Slavery in the North* (Chicago, 1967). The quotation, from the preamble to Pennsylvania's gradual emancipation law, is on p. 127.

growing cities of the new nation. Long before large factories opened, urban workers—both male and female—suffered a debasement of their skills, the atrophy of the system of apprenticeship, and the creation of sweatshops. Because they themselves worked on low profit margins, early urban manufacturers tried to organize the workplace rationally, dividing labor more minutely and paying market rather than traditional wages if they were lower. Despite persistent resistance from working men and women, they usually succeeded in imposing their will. Similar developments occurred in the rural hinterlands of the cities. Requiring seasonal labor for planting and harvest but few hired hands, commercial farmers enticed urban workers with high daily wages but released them when the harvest was complete. Agricultural laborers unable to find winter work subsisted in rural poorhouses, increasingly built in the generation after the Revolution.[24]

The degree to which any of these developments, from banking to canals, from manumissions to free labor, were linked to the Revolution is impossible to determine conclusively. Some—like the growth of wage labor—had already begun before the war; others—like canal construction—reached a peak a half-century after the Revolution had ended. But all were probably affected by the Revolution, either immediately or over the long-term. Before the Revolution, for instance, only radical groups like Quakers sought freedom for slaves, but the contagion of freedom the war provoked led to the end of northern slavery. Slave emancipation was an almost *immediate* effect of the Revolution. The end of northern slavery, in turn, accelerated the growth of urban free labor, a *long-term* economic process, because proletarians, some of them freed slaves from Philadelphia and the sur-

[24] Wilentz, *Chants Democratic*; Christine Stansell, *City of Women: Sex and Class in New York, 1789–1860* (New York, 1987); Paul G. E. Clemens and Lucy Simler, "Rural Labor and the Farm Household in Chester County, Pennsylvania, 1750–1820," in Innes, ed., *Work and Labor*, pp. 106–43; Winifred B. Rothenberg, "The Emergence of Free Labor Markets and the Transformation of the Rural Economy: Massachusetts, 1750–1855," *Journal of Economic History* 48 (1988):537–66; Carville Earle and Ronald Hoffman, "The Foundation of the Modern Economy: Agriculture and the Costs of Labor in the United States and England," *American Historical Review* 85 (1980):1055–85.

rounding communities, were needed to replace the now freed slaves. Similarly, the beginnings of American banking were triggered immediately by the Revolution, but the building of canals occurred as a result of independent economic policies, in part predicated upon bank loans.[25]

THE REVOLUTION AND THE IDEOLOGY OF POSSESSIVE INDIVIDUALISM

The Revolution not only provided an impetus for greater capitalist development but enshrined possessive individualism as a dominant national ideal shared by all classes. Possessive individualism is an approach to human relations that identifies each human being (or at least each citizen) as a separate person, attached to other individuals only by freely-made contracts, and rejects any attempt to group people on the basis of birth or ascribed status. Although such an ideology most often began as a justification for a full market society and the classical liberal ideas of free trade and unfettered development and labor relations that went with capitalism, it can logically support a range of policies, from tariffs to free trade, from an aristocracy of talents to a democratic polity whose goal is restraining capitalism. The term is almost the opposite of the kind of individualism (or "personalism") supposedly characteristic of the lone frontiersman who sought the autonomy possessive individualism granted to everyone. Such a mythic character lived outside of society, rejecting the free contracts, freely made, at the center of possessive individualism.[26]

[25] Gary B. Nash, "Forging Freedom: The Emancipation Experience in the Northern Seaport Cities, 1775–1820," in Ira Berlin and Ronald Hoffman, eds., *Slavery and Freedom in the Age of the American Revolution* (Charlottesville, Va., 1983), pp. 3–48; Nash, *Forging Freedom: The Formation of Philadelphia's Black Community, 1720–1840* (Cambridge, Mass., 1988); Sharon V. Salinger, *"To Serve Well and Faithfully": Labor and Indentured Servants in Pennsylvania, 1682–1800* (Cambridge, 1987), chap. 7, epilogue. See note 20, above, for banking.

[26] The classic work remains C. B. McPherson, *The Political Theory of Possessive Individualism: Hobbes to Locke* (London, 1962), but see also Joyce Oldham Appleby, *Economic Thought and Ideology in Seventeenth-Century England*

An ideology of possessive individualism developed within both the English ruling class and among radical groups during the seventeenth century as a justification for early capitalist development and a legitimization of the revolutions of 1640 and 1688. Such beliefs attained some importance in the colonies, especially among groups like middle-colony Quakers, but never gained political hegemony. Rather, they competed with contrasting political views like classical republicanism (sometimes democratic, more often merely anticommercial) and evangelicalism (individualistic and collectivist at the same time). Gentry classes, which achieved both economic superiority and political hegemony in the colonies by the mid-eighteenth century, justified their rule on the traditional grounds of status, family, and wealth, not on their achievements in a free marketplace.[27]

The ideology of possessive individualism, however, diffused rapidly during the American Revolution, enshrined in such popular tracts as Paine's *Common Sense* and Thomas Jefferson's Declaration of Independence. In order to make their Revolution, gentlemen and merchants had to attack British authority. The simplest way to accomplish that end was to deny the legitimacy of the Crown and Parliament because they were not sustained by the freely given consent of colonial citizens. Ordinary folk rapidly adapted these ideas of popular sovereignty as a political weapon and rejected all forms of communal or collective authority not sustained by popular demand.[28] The result, as we shall see, was not victory for a

---

(Princeton, 1978). I have borrowed the term *personalism* from Elizabeth Fox-Genovese.

[27] Barry Levy, *Quakers and the American Family: British Settlement in the Delaware Valley* (New York, 1988), chaps. 3–4, 7, argues that Pennsylvania Quakers were modern (read bourgeois) long before the Revolution. Debates over the relative importance of classical republicanism and liberalism are summarized in Lance Banning, "Jeffersonian Ideology Revisited: Liberal and Classical Ideas in the New American Republic," *William and Mary Quarterly*, 3d ser. 43 (1986):3–19, and Joyce Oldham Appleby, "Republicanism in Old and New Contexts," *William and Mary Quarterly*, 3d ser. 43 (1986):20–34.

[28] Wood, *Creation of the American Republic*, is the key work.

liberal republic but intense conflict over appropriate economic and political behavior by virtuous citizens.

Common Sense, the most widely circulated pamphlet in Revolutionary America, preached a gospel of possessive individualism in language so biblical, direct, and unadorned that even barely literate Americans could understand it. Its popularity was immediate: as many as 150,000 copies were sold in 1776 alone, enough to reach two-fifths of all the white households in the colonies. Readers included "common farmers and tradesmen," citizens persuaded by Paine that Independence was the only route for the colonies. Thousands of other Americans—women, poor whites, even slaves—too unlettered to read the pamphlet heard it read or overheard conversations about the message it contained.[29]

Paine justified his plea in *Common Sense* for the immediate independence of the colonies from England with a primer on eighteenth-century political theory, one tinged with possessive individualism. All monarchs, he insisted, lacked true legitimacy because they had not gained the assent of the people, as individuals, to their rule. Americans owed nothing, he added, to a British mother country but had a "natural right" to form a free government. Britain had merely disrupted American trade and involved her colonies in unwanted foreign wars. A new society, based upon individual rights, beaconed. After all, America had already "been the asylum for the persecuted lovers of civil and religious liberty from every *part* of Europe." Once free of the British king, Americans could devise a democratic republic, with annual elections, representatives responsible to the people, and—by implication—widespread citizenship.[30]

The Declaration of Independence, with its egalitarian preamble and its contract theory of government, circulated with great rapidity once it was signed. Read before the troops throughout the country and to crowds in every American city

[29] Thomas Paine, *Common Sense* (1776), ed. Isaac Kramnick (Harmondsworth, England, 1976), pp. 7–9; Eric Foner, *Tom Paine and Revolutionary America* (New York, 1976), chap. 3, quotations on p. 79.

[30] Paine, *Common Sense,* quotations on pp. 84, 98.

and village, it was read by thousands of others when it was reprinted in whig newspapers, its message passed to the smallest child through excitement, pomp, and celebration. The Declaration spoke to each person as an individual, unconstrained by status or tradition, connecting political rights and natural rights. Public reading of the Declaration linked each listener to British tyranny, to the momentous events about to happen, and to the formation of a new government of which each of them was a part. John Adlum, a youth living in York, Pennsylvania, captured the meaning of the Declaration for ordinary folk in a later reminiscence. James Smith, a signer, and two local dignitaries came to York on July 7, 1776, "to see how the good people of the town and its vicinity relished the said Declaration." After the document was read, Smith—who was also the colonel of the local militia regiment—spoke, "pointing out the advantages that it would be of to our country" and concluding by throwing "up his hat and [hurrahing] for liberty and independence. The militia on parade and others attending followed their example."[31]

Common folk—farmers, mechanics, laborers, soldiers— took seriously the political rights demanded by Tom Paine and by the Declaration of Independence. For example, townsmen in Lenox, Massachusetts, rejected the 1778 draft state constitution in part because it ignored individual rights. Since "all men were born equally free and independent" and had the rights of "enjoying and defending Life and Liberty and acquiring, possessing and protecting Property," the state should not exclude anyone from citizenship and the franchise, even the poor and the free Negroes, for that deprived them of their legitimate rights to have a voice in choosing their legislators. Such beliefs extended even to the slave societies of Maryland and Virginia, where numerous slave owners

[31] Debates over Thomas Jefferson's sources and early texts of the document are not relevant here. As written, the Declaration clearly espouses possessive individualism. See J. R. Pole, *The Pursuit of Equality in American History* (Berkeley, Calif., 1978), pp. 51–58. John H. Hazelton, *The Declaration of Independence: Its History* (1906; reprint ed., New York, 1970), chaps. 10–11, surveys the dissemination of the Declaration. For the York incident, see John C. Dann, ed., *The Revolution Remembered: Eyewitness Accounts of the War for Independence* (Chicago, 1977), pp. 115–16.

(some, but by no means all of them, Quakers) manumitted slaves in the 1780s and 1790s. Charles Copeland, of Richmond County, Virginia, manumitted his slaves "from natural reasons, that God created all men free; and that all Laws made to subjugate one part of the Human race to the absolute domination of another are totally repugnant to the clearest dictates of natural justice."[32]

RADICALISM, INDIVIDUALISM, AND THE PROMISE OF THE REVOLUTION

The Revolution, with its promise of popular rule, led to nearly forty years of radicalism and violence from the Stamp Act crisis until the election of Thomas Jefferson. Historians have only begun to uncover the magnitude of the intense struggles over who should rule at home. The unrest covered the country, North and South, from frontiers to old areas, from small towns to cities. Such struggles included urban crowd actions in the 1760s, ostensibly over British policy but also encompassing hatred of men of wealth; bread riots; land wars in New York and the Carolinas in the early 1770s over land security; warfare between loyalists and whigs in the back-country Carolinas; attempts, sometimes successful, to close courts to prevent collection of debts in the 1780s, culminating in Shays's Rebellion; attacks upon tax collectors and the hated whiskey excise tax in the 1790s throughout the American frontier, not merely the Whiskey rebels in western Pennsylvania and revolts against the 1798 direct tax in Pennsylvania and New York. Like the radicals of the English Revolution of 1640, participants in these actions sought a more democratic, less capitalist society than that espoused by merchants and lawyers.[33]

[32] Oscar Handlin and Mary Flug Handlin, eds., *The Popular Sources of Political Authority: Documents on the Massachusetts Constitution of 1780* (Cambridge, Mass., 1966), pp. 253–58; Albert, "Protean Institution," chap. 7, quotation on p. 272.

[33] Michael Smuksta, "Food Riots in America, 1710–1864," M.A. thesis, Northern Illinois University, 1974; Barbara Clark Smith, "Food Rioters and the American Revolution," *William and Mary Quarterly*, 3d ser. 51 (1994):3–38; Pauline Maier, "Popular Uprisings and Civil Authority in

The people-out-of-doors had often participated in crowd actions in town and countryside in pre-Revolutionary times, seeking a redress of grievances or a return to traditional rights. In contrast, rebels of the Revolutionary era challenged the ruling classes, demanding a democracy in which small propertyholders would determine public policy. They threatened the stability, even the existence, of the new states and nation by violence, or even worse, by controlling state legislatures. The rulers, especially Federalists, responded with horror, sometimes sending in troops. From our vantage point, victors and vanquished seem almost preordained. But the conclusion—one that reduced citizenship to elections and sustained policies that encouraged capitalist development—was apparent to neither small propertyholders nor their betters and was accomplished only with some bloodshed and suppression.

Revolutionary ideology, with its emphasis on individualism, had spread widely and stood at the heart of these conflicts, as the Fries Rebellion against the 1798 direct tax suggests. The tax, passed after the Whiskey Rebellion, when Federalists realized that excise taxes on whiskey were a poor way to raise revenue, assessed dwellings, land, and slaves. Republicans attacked it because "the farmer" had to "pay impost for every foot of land" while a capitalist paid "nothing for certificates

---

Eighteenth-Century America," *William and Mary Quarterly*, 3d ser. 27 (1970):3–35; Jesse Lemisch, "Jack Tar in the Streets: Merchant Seamen in the Politics of Revolutionary America," *William and Mary Quarterly*, 3d ser. 25 (1968):371–407; Dirk Hoerder, *Crowd Action in Revolutionary Massachusetts, 1765–1780* (New York, 1977); Richard Maxwell Brown, "Back Country Rebellions and the Homestead Ethic in America, 1740–1799," in Brown and Don E. Fehrenbacher, eds., *Tradition, Conflict, and Modernization: Perspectives on the American Revolution* (New York, 1977), pp. 73–99; Edward Countryman, "'Out of the Bounds of the Law': Northern Land Rioters in the Eighteenth Century," in Alfred F. Young, ed., *The American Revolution: Explorations in the History of American Radicalism* (DeKalb, Ill., 1976), pp. 39–69; Alan Taylor, "Agrarian Independence: Northern Land Rioters after the Revolution," in Young, ed., *Beyond the American Revolution*, pp. 221–45; David P. Szatmary, *Shays' Rebellion: The Making of an Agrarian Insurrection* (Amherst, Mass., 1980); Thomas P. Slaughter, *The Whiskey Rebellion: Frontier Epilogue to the American Revolution* (New York, 1986).

he purchased at a tenth part of their public value." Trying to defuse such criticism, Federalists insisted that "poorer classes of the community would be almost wholly exempt from the tax." When put into operation, the law was astonishingly progressive. Two-thirds of the revenue was to be raised from the tax on dwellings, and most of that was paid by gentlemen on their elegant homes. Frontiersmen paid an average of just twenty cents on their log cabins, levels so low as to suggest that assessors may have deliberately underestimated their wealth.[34]

However fair the tax may have been, middling German farmers in eastern Pennsylvania rebelled against it in many ways, from petitions and public meetings to tax resistance and intimidation of assessors. When troops led by John Fries freed several tax protesters from federal custody, he was captured, tried for treason, sentenced to hang, but reprieved by President John Adams. The protesters, Jeffersonian Republicans who supported the French Revolution (some wore "french cockades in their hats" to protest meetings), linked the law to the Stamp Act and called assessors and supporters of the act "Stamplers" and "Tory rascals," threatening to force one assessor "to go to the liberty pole and dance around it." At their meetings they made "a great noise; huzzaing for liberty, and democracy, damning the tories." They or their fathers had "fought for liberty" during the Revolution, and they "would fight for it again." The "house tax," along with the Alien and Sedition Acts, proved that "the government is laying one thing after another, and if we do not oppose it, they will . . . makes slaves of us." Listening to farmers like these Germans, Republicans ended the direct tax in 1802.[35]

[34] Lee Soltow, "America's First Progressive Tax," *National Tax Journal* 30 (1977):53–58 (see p. 54 for quotations from James Callender and from *Annals of Congress*); Soltow, *Inequality in the United States*; Peter Levine, "The Fries Rebellion: Social Violence and the Politics of the New Nation," *Pennsylvania Magazine of History and Biography* 60 (1973):242–43; Charles A. Beard, *Economic Origins of Jeffersonian Democracy* (New York, 1949), pp. 214–16.

[35] Levine, "Fries Rebellion," pp. 241–58, misses the ideological context of the rebellion documented in Thomas Carpenter, stenographer, *The Two Trials of John Fries on an Indictment of Treason; Together with a Brief Report of the*

Ideological debate, then, had major political and economic consequences, whether carried on in armed struggle or—more commonly—as part of less violent political and economic controversy. Who should enjoy the rights individualism promised? Individual rights, in bourgeois philosophical traditions from which Revolutionaries borrowed, was intricately linked to citizenship in civil societies. All men might be "created equal," but only full citizens enjoyed rights as discrete individuals; dependents only gained rights through their superiors.[36]

The language of individualism had become highly contested by the late eighteenth century. Different groups read differently the promise of the Revolution and the individualism it legitimated. Yeomen used individualism to support their collective aspirations (but not their wives') for a republic of small propertyholders. Patriotic women wished that the promises of individualism would be extended to them, but men, no matter their class, ridiculed that demand, forcing them to build individual identities in the bourgeois home. Black petitions for freedom or redress of grievances, couched in the language of equality, competed with white slaveholder demands for the protection of slave property. These visions of individualism clashed with the ideas of a free market, the division of labor, and the virtue of the pursuit of profit that capitalists slowly, but ultimately, embraced. Which version of individualism the government adopted would influence economic development and the prosperity of individuals. Once the state had suppressed violence, conflicting interpretations of individualism continued to structure class, gender, and racial struggles over development, the role of women, and racial equality for more than a century.[37]

Trials of Several Other Persons, for Treason and Insurrection (Philadelphia, 1800), esp. pp. 38, 40, 49, 58, 68, 75–77, 81, 105–6.

[36] Elizabeth Fox-Genovese, "Property and Patriarchy in Classical Bourgeois Theory," *Radical History Review* 4 (1977):36–59.

[37] This is an extremely complex subject. For my own thoughts, see "American Revolution and Yeoman Classes"; for women, see Kerber, *Women of the Republic*; for free blacks, see Nash, *Forging Freedom*, chap. 5.

An examination of the ideas of William Manning illuminates the collective uses to which individualism could be put. Manning, a middling yeoman farmer from Massachusetts, "never had the advantage of six months schooling" in his life. Yet this village sage wrote two tracts defending republicanism and liberty. Manning supported internal improvements like the Middlesex Canal and helped suppress Shays's Rebellion. He insisted that men as individuals were corrupt and showed little interest in defending the balanced government sought by classical republicans. Observing the freely organized combinations of men of substance, he urged farmers, mechanics, and laborers to organize politically to protect their rights. This idea of voluntarism, of freely contracted individual agreements, is a key ingredient of liberalism.

Yet Manning embedded individualism into a defense of the newly invented traditional rights of the freeholding yeomanry against the power of a monied aristocracy. Like the New York land rioters, the Carolina Regulators, and the Shaysites, he espoused a labor theory of value, writing that "labour is the soul parrant of all property—the land yealdeth nothing without it, & their is no food, clothing, shelter, vessel, or any nesecary of life but what costs Labour & is generally esteemed valuable according to the Labour it costs." But the few, through their combinations, their control of government, and their investment policies, threatened the very livelihood of yeomen. Far from seeking a liberal state permeated by wage labor, freely contracted, that protected the rights of capital, Manning sought protection for the property of small holders. "The soul end of Government," he insisted, "is the protection of Life, Liberty & property. The poor mans shilling aught to be as much the care of government as the rich mans pound." Therefore taxes "aught to be layed equilly according to the property each person purseses & the advantages he receives from it."[38] Men who agreed with Manning came to support cheap or free land, or—at a minimum—the rights of squat-

[38] Michael Merrill and Sean Wilentz, "*The Key of Libberty:* William Manning and Plebeian Democracy, 1747–1814," in Young, ed., *Beyond the American Revolution,* pp. 246–82; Samuel Eliot Morison, ed., "William Manning's *The Key of Libberty,*" *William and Mary Quarterly,* 3d ser. 13 (1956):202–54, quotations on pp. 217–18.

ters to buy the land they had settled at the minimum government price.

Federalists challenged such uses of individualism to support yeoman rights. Insisting upon individual initiative as the key to success, denying that any aristocracy prevented men from owning land, they decried any attempt by farmers to demand land or access to it as a right rather than a privilege to be earned by hard labor. Land should be developed so that farmers could fully participate in markets, and settlers should be kept off public land until it was surveyed.[39]

Blacks understood the implications of possessive individualism. Encouraged by colonial demands for freedom, slaves engaged in numerous small conspiracies between 1765 and 1776. Once Independence was declared, northern slaves began petitioning for freedom, insisting that the natural rights of individuals belonged to them. Massachusetts slaves, "detained in a state of Slavery in the Bowels of a free & Christian Country," petitioned the Massachusetts General Court in 1777 for immediate freedom for adults and emancipation of children at age twenty-one. They "apprehend that they have in common with all other men a Natural and Unaliable Right to that freedom which" God "hath Bestowed equalley on all menkind." Torn away from their homes by violence, living as good Christians, they had repeatedly petitioned for the freedom they deserved. Only when they were free would "the inconstancey of acting themselves the part which they condem and oppose in others" end. Notwithstanding poverty and proletarianization, free black men behaved like citizens, demanding schooling, forming churches and other voluntary societies, agitating for the end of the slave trade and of slavery, petitioning Congress, voting when allowed.[40]

Most whites in both North and South denied that black people should have full citizenship or even the partial free-

[39] Kulikoff, *Agrarian Origins,* chap. 3; Peter S. Onuf, "Liberty, Development, and Union: Visions of the West in the 1780s," *William and Mary Quarterly,* 3d ser. 43 (1986):179–213.

[40] Wood, "'Dream Deferred,'" pp. 166–87; Herbert Aptheker, ed., *A Documentary History of the Negro People in the United States,* vol. 1, *From Colonial Times through the Civil War* (New York, 1951), chaps. 1–2 (Massachusetts petition on pp. 9–10); Nash, *Forging Freedom.*

dom that emancipation brought. Philadelphia's elite whites, sympathetic to the plight of poor freed slaves, refused to help finance churches that blacks organized, preferring to keep them subservient. Hostility toward blacks in that city and elsewhere in the North increased after 1800, and most northerners wished blacks would not live among them.[41]

After a brief flurry of manumissions, southerners severely limited the rights of masters to free slaves. Virginians who signed proslavery petitions in 1784 and 1785 not only feared social chaos if many slaves achieved freedom but insisted that slaves were property, incapable of attaining the attributes of citizenship. Petitioners from Lunenberg County, for instance, linked Revolutionary individualism to slavery. "In order to fix a Tenure in our property on a Basis of Security not to be shaken in future," they wrote, we fought with England, creating "a Constitution . . . grounded on a full and clear Declaration of such rights as naturally pertain to Men born free." Among those individual rights of citizens was the right to hold property, including slaves. But the legislature threatened to consider general emancipation, which would "wreste from us . . . the most valuable indispensible part of our Property, our Slaves."[42]

White women, especially wives of propertied men, insisted that they be counted as individuals, for they had participated in the Revolution by boycotting tea, sewing homespun, and taking care of farms and businesses when husbands were away at war. They, too, read *Common Sense* and listened to readings of the Declaration of Independence. Abigail Adams was not alone in fearing the tyranny of giving "unlimited power" to husbands, urging them to "Remember the Ladies, and be more generous and favorable to them than your ancestors." Connecting citizenship to individual rights, she insisted that women "will not hold ourselves bound by any Laws

[41] Nash, *Forging Freedom*, esp. chap. 6. For the later story of discrimination against blacks in the North, see Leon F. Litwack, *North of Slavery: The Negro in the Free States, 1790–1860* (Chicago, 1961), esp. chaps. 3–5, and Leonard P. Curry, *The Free Black in Urban America, 1800–1850* (Chicago, 1981), esp. chaps. 2, 5–6.

[42] Albert, "Protean Institution," chap. 7; Schmidt and Wilhelm, eds., "Early Proslavery Petitions," pp. 133–46, quotations on pp. 140–41.

in which we have no voice, or Representation" but would rather "foment a Rebelion." Middling and wealthy white women in the Revolutionary era formed voluntary societies, began female academies, read Mary Wollstonecraft's *Vindication of the Rights of Woman,* and discussed politics among themselves and with husbands.[43]

Men, no matter their class, denied women access to individualism, for individualism was connected to citizenship, and women were supposed to be dependent upon men. Political leaders ridiculed, then suppressed, female attempts at public political participation; everywhere (with the temporary exception of New Jersey), men refused women the right to vote. John Adams's response to Abigail suggests fear both of sharing power with the dispossessed and of the end of proper subservience of dependents within family and republic. He pointed, only half in jest, to universal demands for rights: "We have been told that our Struggle has loosened the bonds of Government everywhere," he wrote. "That children and Apprentices were disobedient—that schools and colleges were grown turbulent—that Indians slighted their Guardians and Negroes grew more insolent to their Masters." But now women, "more numerous and powerfull than all the rest were grown discontented," equally threatening public order. Adams, for one, would not "repeal our Masculine systems," would not subject the country "to the despotism of the Peticoat."[44]

Middle-class women stood back from public political participation but manipulated the republican need for virtuous male citizens to their advantage. Accepting neither the implications of inferiority nor the strict separation of public and

[43] Abigail Adams to John Adams, Mar. 31, 1776, in L. H. Butterfield et al., eds., *The Book of Abigail and John: Selected Letters of the Adams Family, 1762–1784* (Cambridge, Mass., 1975), pp. 120–21; Branson, "Politics and Gender," chaps. 1–2; Kerber, *Women of the Republic,* esp. chaps. 2–3, 7–8; Mary Beth Norton, *Liberty's Daughters: The Revolutionary Experience of American Women, 1750–1800* (Boston, 1980), chaps. 6–9.

[44] John Adams to Abigail Adams, Apr. 14, 1776, in Butterfield et al., eds., *Book of Abigail and John,* pp. 122–23; Gregory Evans Dowd, "Declarations of Dependence: War and Inequality in Revolutionary New Jersey," *New Jersey History* 103 (1984):53–58.

private inherent in the ideology of republican motherhood, middling women tried to build autonomous lives in their own sphere of home and child nurture, demanding equality with husbands in the family and the right to control their own fertility. But they remained dissatisfied. Revolutionary mothers—and their daughters and granddaughters—remembered the promises of the Revolution when they formed voluntary associations to protect their sphere, lobbied to protect the property they brought into marriage, or even demanded the right to vote. The feminists at Seneca Falls deliberately copied the Declaration of Independence, with its message of universal citizenship, in their founding document.[45]

The debate between John and Abigail Adams illuminates the contradictions of possessive individualism in the Revolutionary era. A consistent respect for individuals would open the state to the unruly or dependent, but anything less seemed to forfeit the universal promise of rights Revolutionaries fought to attain. Far from unifying classes, consensus over individualism only served to deepen conflicts. Many-sided struggles for citizenship rights, supposedly guaranteed by the Revolution, continued for generations. Every group, without quite realizing it, tried to deny other groups full rights of individual citizenship, thereby precluding them from full humanity in societies defined by contract rather than by traditional hierarchical relations.

The American Revolution, then, can be dubbed a bourgeois revolution because its ideology meshed with bourgeois ideals, and the contingencies of war and state formation accelerated

---

[45] Linda K. Kerber brilliantly analyzes the literature on domesticity in "Separate Spheres, Female Worlds, Woman's Place: The Rhetoric of Women's History," *Journal of American History* 75 (1988):9–39; but see also Kerber, *Women of the Republic,* chap. 9; Ruth H. Bloch, "American Feminine Ideals in Transition: The Rise of the Moral Mother, 1775–1815," *Feminist Studies* 4 (1978):101–26; Nancy F. Cott, *The Bonds of Womanhood: "Woman's Sphere" in New England, 1780–1835* (New Haven, 1977). For the relation between individualism and early feminism, see Linda K. Kerber, "From the Declaration of Independence to the Declaration of Sentiments: The Legal Status of Women in the Early Republic, 1776–1848," *Human Rights* 6 (1977):115–24.

capitalist development. But the Revolution did not lead to a final or even partial victory for the bourgeoisie. It would take more than a century of conflict, a bloody Civil War, and innumerable class, racial, and gender struggles before individualism achieved undisputed ideological hegemony and corporate capitalists gained full political and economic power. Full individualism for all adults, embedded in capitalist relations of production, grew from these conflicts.

Northern development of a full market society, with growing classes of capitalists and proletarians, proceeded apace through the antebellum decades. But slavery, supported by cotton production, became even more fully embedded in the South. Contradictions between slavery and free labor, between individualism, in all its varieties, and the growing corporatism of proslavery writers and their supporters, ultimately led to the Civil War. The war helped complete the first American bourgeois revolution, begun nearly a century earlier. The Civil War settlement granted freed slaves voting rights, at least temporarily, but growing Southern capitalism (in the guise of sharecropping or urban wage labor) insured that blacks—and ultimately poorer whites—would become dependent upon markets controlled by northern capitalists and their southern allies. Equally severe contradictions between white, male individualism and the failure of the state to grant white women citizenship rights led to a century of struggle over women's property rights and, ultimately, female suffrage, and substantial tensions between black men, who were granted the franchise, and white women, who were not. The rights gained permitted married women to work and to participate in politics, but placed them at the mercy of the same free contractual society that had proletarianized so many men.[46]

[46] Moore, *Social Origins*, chap. 3; Barbara Jeanne Fields, "The Advent of Capitalist Agriculture: The New South in a Bourgeois World," in Thavolia Glymph, ed., *Essays on the Postbellum Southern Economy* (College Station, Tex., 1985), pp. 73–94; Ellen Carol DuBois, *Feminism and Suffrage: The Emergence of an Independent Women's Movement in America, 1848–1869* (Ithaca, N.Y., 1978); Elizabeth Fox-Genovese, "Women's Rights, Affirmative Action, and the Myth of Individualism," *George Washington Law Review* 54 (1986):338–74.

The ultimate victory of capitalism was predicated upon both the growing power of capitalists *and* the internal logic of individualism itself. Dependent groups, whether blacks or small propertyholders or women, could overcome hierarchical subservience to ruling-class white men, at least initially, only by reference to systematic individualism. Their spokesmen often tried to defend their collective rights using individualist rhetoric. But individualism is predicated upon free contracts made between individuals—on the "free labor, free men, free soil" early Republicans espoused. Free contracts, of course, protect only powerful individuals and are a poor means to protect collective rights, as such groups as nineteenth-century trade unionists and Populists discovered. Dissenters who insisted upon social rights, whether land reformers who urged the abolition of capitalist land markets or early utopian or Marxist socialists, found their programs labeled as alien because they rejected individualism.[47]

Where does the Revolution fit within these long, complex struggles over capitalism and bourgeois individualism? It was an essential first step, a sweeping away of remaining constraints on capitalist development, a crucial victory of the ideology of systematic individualism over the idea of collective rights. More than any other event it *created* the American bourgeoisie, helping to transform merchant capitalists into capitalists. That such radical change was not fully achieved by the Revolution is hardly surprising. The Revolution, then, was a bourgeois beginning.

[47] See esp. Fox-Genovese, "Property and Patriarchy," pp. 36–59, and idem, "Women's Rights," pp. 338–74.

JEAN B. LEE

Lessons in Humility

The Revolutionary Transformation of the Governing Elite of Charles County, Maryland

WHEN FRANCIS WARE ran for sheriff of Charles County, Maryland, in 1785, he was an attractive candidate. During peacetime since 1765, voters had regularly elected him to the legislature. He also had good military credentials. As a captain in the colonial militia, he served on the western frontier during the Seven Years' War. Early in the War for Independence, he was the second-highest officer in the Maryland Line of the Continental army, and he rose to colonel before ill health forced him to resign his commission in 1777. Even then, his efforts on behalf of the American cause did not cease because, for the remainder of the war, he served as the lieutenant of Charles County. In that capacity he procured men and arms for the military and coordinated local defense efforts.[1]

This essay is drawn from the author's *The Price of Nationhood: The American Revolution in Charles County* (New York, 1994). I am grateful to the publisher, W. W. Norton and Co., for permission to use portions of the book in this essay. I also wish to acknowledge, with deep appreciation, research support from the American Association of University Women, the Danforth Foundation, the Institute of Early American History and Culture, the National Endowment for the Humanities, the Society of the Cincinnati in the State of Virginia, the Thomas Jefferson Memorial Foundation, and the University of Wisconsin—Madison.

[1] Edward C. Papenfuse et al., eds., *A Biographical Dictionary of the Maryland Legislature, 1635–1789*, 2 vols. (Baltimore, 1979, 1985), 2:861; Charles

Ware handily won the sheriff's election. Before assuming office, he and several sureties had to post a customary performance bond of 200,000 pounds of marketable tobacco, an immense sum. It was their guarantee to the state of Maryland that Ware would faithfully discharge the duties of his office. Already ranked in the top tenth of local wealthholders, he could anticipate enriching his estate with the fees he would receive for performing those duties during his three-year term.[2]

Less than two years after his election, however, this man who stood near the pinnacle of his society was convicted in the General Court of owing more than £14,000 current money to the state of Maryland, on which interest was accruing at the

---

County Court Records, liber I3 (1759–60), fol. 257, Maryland State Archives, Annapolis; Mary K. Meyer, ed., "Genealogica Marylandia: Maryland Muster Rolls, 1757–1758," *Maryland Historical Magazine* 70 (1975):224–25; Rieman Steuart, *A History of the Maryland Line in the Revolutionary War, 1775–1783* (N.p., 1969), pp. 3, 143; William H. Browne et al., eds., *Archives of Maryland*, 72 vols. (Baltimore, 1883–1972), 16:304; *Laws of Maryland, Made and Passed at a Session of Assembly . . . June . . . One Thousand Seven Hundred and Seventy-Seven* (Annapolis, [1777]), chap. 17.

[2] Francis Ware received 548 votes, compared to 149 cast for the runner-up (Governor and Council, Commission Record, 1777–98, fol. 159, Md. St. Arch.). His performance bond is lost, but see that of sheriff Edward Boarman in the Charles County Court Records, liber Y3 (1778–80), fol. 24. That the amount pledged in the bonds was, indeed, an immense sum is demonstrated in statistics on productivity. Lorena S. Walsh has calculated a mean output of 749 pounds of marketable tobacco per laborer on the lower Western Shore of Maryland during the years 1782–89. Walsh, "Slave Life, Slave Society, and Tobacco Production in the Tidewater Chesapeake," in Ira Berlin and Philip D. Morgan, eds., *Cultivation and Culture: Labor and the Shaping of Slave Life in the Americas* (Charlottesville, Va., 1993), p. 175. Ware's standing among wealthholders is derived from an analysis of all surviving 1782 county assessment lists in Jean B. Lee, "The Social Order of a Revolutionary People: Charles County, Maryland, 1733–86," Ph.D. diss., University of Virginia, 1984, pp. 101–12, 366–73. Ware's property was assessed that year at £1,335 common money of Maryland, including 404 acres of land valued at £303 and 24 slaves valued at £905 (Charles County Tax Assessments, 1782, for the lower east hundred of Port Tobacco Parish, Maryland State Papers, Scharf Collection, box 96, Md. St. Arch.). On the profitability of the shrievalty, see Donnell M. Owings, *His Lordship's Patronage: Offices of Profit in Colonial Maryland* (Baltimore, 1953), pp. 70–71.

rate of 10 percent per year. Subsequently he suffered the humiliation of seeing the state seize and auction off part of his plantation as well as slaves, livestock, and even furniture. When trustees assumed control of the rest of his plantation, Ware was reduced to living as a tenant on the land that he so recently had owned. By 1800 the former legislator, colonel in the Maryland Line, and county sheriff was "reduced to extreme indigence."[3]

In ordinary times, Ware's insolvency might have resulted from personal mismanagement, overextension, or even corruption. But the 1780s and 1790s were not ordinary times in Charles County, and none of these factors was responsible. Rather, Ware was overwhelmed by the aftermath of the Revolution and a long, costly war. And he was not alone. He was part of his society's governing elite—by which I mean *local* officeholders. While not every member of that elite suffered as much as Ware, some did, and *all* lost wealth, power, or status during the 1780s. For these local leaders, the Revolution truly was a transforming experience, in ways that must have astonished them and their neighbors. My purpose is to describe that transformation.

In the colonial period, civil offices within the county were entirely appointive. The magistrates who tried suits and oversaw everything from poor relief to the condition of the roads, the sheriff who collected taxes and punished the convicted, the clerk who kept the public records, the constables who apprehended people accused of fornication, bastardy, and assault, the collector of proprietary quitrents, the deputy commissary who administered the probate of estates, and even the men who inspected planters' tobacco and declared what was marketable—these and others were appointed, not elected. The proprietary government filled the chief offices—justice, sher-

---

[3] Order to the coroner of Charles County, Apr. 1787, Loose Papers, 1779–88, General Court of the Western Shore, Md. St. Arch.; William Kilty to John Kilty, Sept. 10, 1789, Maryland State Papers, Red Books, 23:93, Md. St. Arch.; *Maryland Gazette* (Annapolis), Feb. 12, Aug. 13, 1789, Apr. 28, 1791, Dec. 26, 1793, Sept. 4, 1794; Gaius M. Brumbaugh, ed., *Maryland Records: Colonial, Revolutionary, County and Church*, 2 vols. (1915, 1928; reprint ed., Baltimore, 1967), 2:403.

iff, clerk, deputy commissary, and quitrent collector. In turn, the justices controlled most of the lesser offices.[4]

Without exception, the proprietary appointees were members of the local gentry, a group distinguished from "plain Country people" in several ways. Gentlemen were "people of considerable property," according to Nicholas Cresswell, a visiting Englishman. They had "fortunes," other white men a "competency." Whereas most inhabitants lived out their lives on plantations, received little or no formal education, and usually traveled no farther than church, a neighbor's plantation, or a nearby town, the gentry's world was, collectively, much broader. No local group was better educated or more widely traveled. In a society where one of every three white men signed his name with a mark, elite males appear to have been uniformly literate, and a few had access to the best formal education available in their day. Gentlemen also were acutely conscious of their status. They cherished their church pews, riding chairs, blooded horses, militia commissions, and honorific titles, whether official, ceremonial, or whimsical. One of the Smallwoods, who were among the wealthiest families in Charles County, was "commonly called King of the woods." When the Virginia Lees referred to Richard Lee, patriarch of the Maryland branch of the family and the senior member of the governor's council, they called him "Esquire Lee."[5]

[4] For proprietary offices, see Owings, *His Lordship's Patronage*, and *An Historical List of Public Officials of Maryland: Governors, Legislators, and Other Principal Officers of Government, 1632 to 1990*, in Browne et al., eds., *Archives of Maryland*, n.s. 1 (1990). For locally controlled offices during the late colonial period see the Charles County Court Records, libers I3 through X3 (1774–78). Anglican parish vestries, on which magistrates and other members of the gentry sat, appointed the tobacco inspectors. See, for example, the Journal of the Vestry of Trinity Parish, in "Abstracts of Early Protestant Episcopal Church Records of Charles County, Maryland" (N.d., typescript on deposit at the Martha Washington Chapter, Daughters of the American Revolution, Washington, D.C.), pp. 5, 7.

[5] The quotations, in order, are from Thomas Stone to Thomas Sim Lee, Dec. 20, 1781, Governor and Council, Pardon Papers, box 1 (1777–81), folder 82, Md. St. Arch.; Nicholas Cresswell, *The Journal of Nicholas Cresswell, 1774–1777* (New York, 1924), p. 26; Richard Lee, Jr., to [loyalist claims commissioners, ca. Mar. 26, 1784], American Loyalist Claims, ser. 2, A. O.

The social distance that the elite cultivated and enjoyed did not mean social isolation, however. Gentry hospitality was legendary. An illiterate planter named Benjamin Branson related what happened when he called upon his neighbor, Richard Lee, about 1766: "Squire Lee according to Custom asked me if I would drink a Dram or some Cyder. I in a merry Humour used freedom enough to say I had not eat my Breakfast. Mr Lee laugh'd and said I must wait 'till it was dress't. The Squire asked me if a cut of Bread and Cheese would do? I answered very well, which was ordered to be brought and Mrs Lee at the same time went out and presently returned with a Plate of Fresh Beef, hashed as good as ever I saw." The journal of Nicholas Cresswell, who visited the county on the eve of the Revolution, contains a litany of gentry attentiveness. He dined at plantations, danced nearly all night with "young ladys," watched "diverting plays" (which, he wrote, "seems very strange to me, but I believe it is common in this

---

13/40, fols. 100–101, Public Record Office; Charles County Court Records, liber Y3, fol. 596; Philip Ludwell Lee to [?] Lee, July 24, 1777, Lee Family Papers, 1638–1867, Virginia Historical Society, Richmond. The principal forms of wealth in the county were land and slaves. The Charles County Debt Book, 1774 (in Land Office Records, Md. St. Arch.) reveals that, of 585 male landowners counted that year, 37 held tracts of 1,000 or more acres, and less than 1 in 5 had 500 or more acres. The Charles County Sheriff's Account Book, 1769, Md. St. Arch., which covers only part of the county, lists 438 male taxpayers, only 4 of whom were assessed for 20 or more laborers. Tax lists from 1758, also incomplete, similarly yield a small proportion of very large planters. See table 3 in Jean B. Lee, "The Problem of Slave Community in the Eighteenth-Century Chesapeake," *William and Mary Quarterly,* 3d ser. 43 (1986):343. The statement on literacy is derived from analysis of the signatures and marks of 1,590 men, constituting nearly 90 percent of the county's free adult males, who took an oath of fidelity to the state in 1778. Charles County Court Records, liber X3, fols. 641–51. Education is treated in Lee, "Social Order of a Revolutionary People," pp. 232–68. For the gentry and church pews, riding chairs, and thoroughbred horses, see Browne et al., eds., *Archives of Maryland,* 31:297–98; Charles County Register of Wills, liber AD5 (1752–67), fols. 221, 242–43, liber AE6 (1767–77), fols. 133–34, Md. St. Arch.; *Maryland Gazette,* Mar. 22, 1764. Biographical information on gentry families is in Margaret B. Klapthor and Paul D. Brown, *The History of Charles County, Maryland* (La Plata, Md., 1958), and Papenfuse et al., eds., *Biographical Dictionary.*

Country"), got drunk ("Sick with my last night's debauch"), and went off to Annapolis in the company of several gentlemen.[6]

In other ways, too, the elite demonstrated noblesse oblige. Richard Lee "counsel[ed] his neighbours in their litigious contests, and he was always ready to give them his mature and best advice." Gentlemen watched over a local grammar school, secretly helped alleviate "honest poverty," paid for a rider who regularly carried mail to Annapolis, and provided a parish church with an organ, a rare musical instrument in the eighteenth-century Chesapeake. Such beneficence involved more than altruism, of course. It created "obligations," as Cresswell readily perceived. People of lower rank had more incentive to support the hierarchical social system of Charles and other Chesapeake counties if they benefited from it.[7]

Even among the elite, only a few were appointed to the most influential local offices, those of county court justice and sheriff. In the fifteen years after 1760, when the county's population was over 13,000 people, just twenty-six men sat on the court, and only one sheriff was not first a justice. All were Protestants (Catholics had been disfranchised in colonial Maryland since 1718), and nearly all were of English ancestry. These "principal Gentlemen" were planters and merchants, not lawyers. Theirs was country justice, and they insisted upon dispensing it with proper decorum. By the 1760s the court employed a man to beat a drum at quarterly sessions, which were held at the county seat in Port Tobacco. He was also to "wash the Court house the Saturday before the Court," sweep it daily during the session, and "Attend the Chief Justice at his Lodgins every morning by 9 O Clock and also at Dinner time." When a juryman "much in Liquor" fell asleep in the middle of a trial, he was fined, as was anyone found guilty of throwing balls against the courthouse.[8]

[6] Browne et al., eds., *Archives of Maryland,* 32:355; Cresswell, *Journal,* pp. 17–20, 23, 55.

[7] *Maryland Gazette,* Mar. 25, 1762, Feb. 15, 1787, Oct. 18, 1804; Browne et al., eds., *Archives of Maryland,* 34:740–44, 56:135; Cresswell, *Journal,* p. 26.

[8] Charles County Court Records, libers I3–X3; Thornton Anderson, "Eighteenth-Century Suffrage: The Case of Maryland," *Maryland Historical*

During the court sessions, twelve to fifteen "worshipfull justices" heard civil cases involving no more than £100 sterling, tried all criminal cases except those concerning whites accused of capital crimes, and handled many administrative matters affecting the general populace. Bound by common and statutory law, justices nevertheless exercised a good deal of discretion in apprenticing orphans, appointing constables and overseers of the roads, granting licenses for ordinaries, deciding whether slaves and adult white men were too old or disabled to be counted for tax purposes, and fining white women who bore bastard children. To the extent that public money was dispensed for welfare purposes in the county, the court dispensed it. The idea was to provide essential services like caring for and burying the indigent, but at minimal cost to taxpayers.[9]

Once the court spoke, individual justices often involved themselves in implementing its orders. No matter seemingly was too trivial to escape their notice. Hence justices served on commissions that the court appointed to mark and preserve landowners' boundaries. When a woman complained that a road leading from her plantation to a public tobacco inspection warehouse was "very hurtfull to her," two justices personally investigated, agreed that the road was too steep for rolling hogsheads to the warehouse, and recommended construction of an alternate route. When a visitor to the county

---

Magazine 76 (1981):143. Quoted material, in order, is from Owings, *His Lordship's Patronage,* p. 2; Charles County Court Records, liber P3 (1766–67), fol. 151, liber T3 (1770–72), fol. 593, liber I3, fol. 560. A census of 1755, the only late colonial census for the county, showed a population of 13,056 of whom 8,095 were whites. In 1782 the total population numbered 17,724. "An Account of the Number of Souls in the Province of Maryland, in the Year 1755," *Gentleman's Magazine* (London) 34 (1764):261; "Population in Maryland—1782," *The American Museum, or, Universal Magazine* 7 (1790):159.

[9]This paragraph is based on examination of all Charles County Court Records from 1759 to 1776, libers I3–X3. For the jurisdiction of the county courts, see "Maryland in 1773," *Maryland Historical Magazine* 2 (1907):362, and Morris L. Radoff, Gust Skordas, and Phebe R. Jacobsen, comps., *The County Courthouses and Records of Maryland: Part Two, The Records* (Annapolis, 1963), pp. 2–3.

notified the court that he had only enough money to "Pay his Passage and other Necessaries Sufficient to go home to his own Country or to get him Cured of his many Infirmities here," the court ordered one of its own members to obtain medical help. Another justice arranged board and care for a woman who petitioned that she was "in a most Deplorable Condition in as much as . . . She Cannot get any thing Towards a Lively Hood." Between court sessions, the magistrates attended to such matters and also helped keep the peace in their neighborhoods. A few even had private jails at their plantations, where persons accused of crimes could be held until the court next met.[10]

If the gentlemen justices behaved imperiously—as they sometimes were accused of doing—little could be done about it because they were proprietary appointees. Occasionally, very occasionally, someone complained to the House of Delegates, the popularly elected branch of the Maryland assembly. It usually summoned several justices. One would deign to appear, whereupon the house would examine the complaint and most likely conclude that the court had been inattentive, negligent, or, in one instance in 1751, had extended its "Power to the utmost Limits of the Law" by failing to hear "coolly, fully, and impartially, both Sides of the Question" before pronouncing judgment. After the justice ritually apologized for the court's shortcomings and "submitted to the Lenity and Determination" of the lower house, it ritually recommended "more Caution and Circumspection for the future." And that was the end of it.[11]

Much of this description of the county's governing elite—and of the social stratum to which they belonged—sounds typical of the Chesapeake gentry in the late colonial period. Even so, the Charles County elite seems strikingly different when compared with recent depictions of their counterparts elsewhere in the region. For nowhere, to my knowledge, is

---

[10] Charles County Court Records, liber I3, fol. 536, liber K3 (1760–62), fol. 405, liber M3 (1762–64), fol. 56; Browne et al., eds., *Archives of Maryland*, 32:360.

[11] Browne et al., eds., *Archives of Maryland*, 46:429–30, 446–47, 557–58 (quotations).

there any evidence that these men of "great influence" in their society were plagued with anxiety over indebtedness to British merchants. Nor was their style of living, either spiritual or material, significantly challenged by dissenting Protestants or anyone of lesser social rank. Whatever the extent of anxiety and social unrest elsewhere, the Charles County gentry appeared self-confident and unthreatened.[12]

The world of the gentlemen officeholders nevertheless was soon transformed by the American Revolution, and in three distinct phases: first, the period from the Stamp Act crisis of 1765 to announcement of the Coercive Acts in 1774; second, from the Coercive Acts to the end of the War for Independence; and third, the immediate postwar period. By 1790 the self-assured, successful governing elite of the colonial period was substantially, sometimes completely, humbled.

The transformation began slowly. Between 1765 and 1774 the magistrates never lost control amidst the gathering Revolution. Rather, both as officials and private persons, they were often in the forefront of extralegal activities through which local people protested British imperial policies and those of the proprietary regime. Hence the justices themselves shut the courthouse doors during the Stamp Act crisis and reopened them several months later. In response to the Townshend duties, members of the court signed the provincial nonimportation association. But when extralegal activities

[12] Recent works that treat, in a variety of contexts and Chesapeake locales, gentry anxieties and challenges to their dominance include Ronald Hoffman, *A Spirit of Dissension: Economics, Politics, and the Revolution in Maryland* (Baltimore, 1973), David C. Skaggs, *Roots of Maryland Democracy, 1753–1776* (Westport, Conn., 1973), Hoffman, "The 'Disaffected' in the Revolutionary South," in Alfred F. Young, ed., *The American Revolution: Explorations in the History of American Radicalism* (DeKalb, Ill., 1976), pp. 273–316, Rhys Isaac, *The Transformation of Virginia, 1740–1790* (Chapel Hill, 1982), T. H. Breen, *Tobacco Culture: The Mentality of the Great Tidewater Planters on the Eve of the Revolution* (Princeton, 1985), Allan Kulikoff, *Tobacco and Slaves: The Development of Southern Cultures in the Chesapeake, 1680–1800* (Chapel Hill, 1986), and Keith Mason, "Localism, Evangelicalism, and Loyalism: The Sources of Discontent in the Revolutionary Chesapeake," *Journal of Southern History* 56 (1990):23–54. The "great influence" remark is in Philip Richard Fendall to James Russell, Aug. 26, 1774, Russell Papers, bundle 3, Coutts and Co., London (microfilm), Virginia Colonial Records Project, Colonial Williamsburg Foundation Library, Williamsburg, Va.

spawned an incipient tax revolt in 1773, following collapse of
the proprietary tobacco inspection system, the court promptly
served notice that the undermining of county government
would not be tolerated. First the justices fined known tax
evaders. Then they fined and fired a constable who, by failing
to submit a list of the taxables in his district, had prevented
the collection of *any* public revenues there. Through these actions, the court set the limits of extralegal resistance in
Charles County.[13]

The second phase of the governing elite's transformation
was significantly more dramatic than the first. As colonial resistance intensified between 1774 and 1776, the court became
increasingly impotent and irrelevant. Although the justices
continued at first to hear criminal cases, frequent adjourn-
ments slowed debt litigation, the most common form of civil
suit. Then, as soon as the nonexportation provisions of the
Continental Association took effect in September 1775, debt
litigation virtually ceased. Within months country justice was
at a standstill. In March 1776 the court neglected to empanel
a grand jury, ceased criminal prosecutions, and conducted almost no business save for one telling exception—resolutions
of Maryland's Revolutionary Provincial Convention were entered in the official records. During the summer of Independence, as Marylanders mobilized men and resources for a
long war and turned to writing a state constitution, the
court—the locus of authority in colonial Charles County—
did not meet at all.[14]

If the court became moribund in the vortex of Revolution,

[13] Charles County Court Records, liber N3 (1764–66), Aug. 1765–Mar.
1766 sessions, liber U3 (1772–73), fols. 161, 171, 285; Horatio Sharpe to
Cecilius Calvert, Nov. 11, 1765, and nonimportation resolution of June 22,
1769, Browne et al., eds., *Archives of Maryland*, 14:239, 62:458–62, respectively; Jean H. Vivian, "The Poll Tax Controversy in Maryland, 1770–76:
A Case of Taxation *with* Representation," *Maryland Historical Magazine* 71
(1976):151–76. A detailed account of the coming of the Revolution in
Charles County may be found in Lee, *Price of Nationhood*, pp. 95–130.

[14] Alexander Hamilton to James Brown and Co., Aug. 20, 1775, in David
C. Skaggs and Richard K. MacMaster, eds., "The Letterbooks of Alexander
Hamilton, Piscataway Factor, Part 3, 1775–1776," *Maryland Historical Magazine* 62 (1967):151; William Fitzhugh to Russell, Jan. 6 [1775], Russell Papers, bundle 6; Charles County Court Records, liber X3, fols. 514, 517.

the justices did not. In fact, most of them helped guide the county from colonial status to Independence, and they did so by chairing popular meetings and serving on the local, extra-legal, committee of observation. Consequently the source of their authority changed. As justices, they were proprietary appointees; as committee members and chairmen of popular meetings, they were elected by the freemen. When those freemen decided who should rule at home—to invoke Carl L. Becker's famous phrase—they did not sweep aside the colonial governing elite. Of the thirteen men who presided over the court in 1774, at least eleven belonged to the committee of observation.[15]

Yet, by themselves, the justices qua committeemen could not possibly attend to the countless tasks generated in the Revolutionary crisis, including enforcing the Continental trade embargo, guarding against loyalism, collecting war materiel, and even controlling debt collections and litigation. Hence the freemen variously elected from thirty-two to ninety men to sit on the committee of observation, which from the summer of 1775 until early 1777 was the county's *only* functioning government. Remembering that just twenty-seven men served as magistrate or sheriff during the last *fifteen* years of proprietary rule, the committee signaled a major expansion of political leadership. Joining the magistrates on it were other members of the elite, including the county's last delegation to the proprietary assembly. Whether out of deference or preference, therefore, the freemen chose a gentry-led transition to the new political order.[16]

So did leaders in Annapolis when, under the Maryland constitution of 1776, local officeholding once again became appointive except for the sheriff. When the government commissioned a revived Charles County court in 1777, it was evident that the colonial governing elite had come through nearly three years of revolution and extralegal politics almost

---

[15]*Maryland Gazette*, June 16, Nov. 24, 1774, June 8, Oct. 19, 1775; see also Lee, *Price of Nationhood*, pp. 111–12, 115–16, 126–28; Carl L. Becker, *The History of Political Parties in the Province of New York, 1760–1776* (1909; reprint ed., Madison, Wis., 1960), p. 22.

[16]*Maryland Gazette*, Nov. 24, 1774, Oct. 19, 1775.

intact. Of thirteen justices who had presided in 1774, ten were returned to the court in 1777. Creating places for other gentlemen who had gained political prominence during those years, the governor also commissioned twelve new justices. Although appointed, the post-Independence court could legitimately claim public approval and support in a way that its colonial predecessor could not: in the years surrounding Independence, the freemen had elected nearly every justice, old and new, to the committee of observation.[17]

For the rest of the war, the state turned to the counties to ensure citizens' loyalty toward the American cause and to meet seemingly endless demands for men, money, and materiel. Without exception in Charles County, the state called upon the gentry to direct those efforts. To administer Maryland's oath of fidelity to all free white males, the state called upon the court. But to mobilize resources for fighting the war, the legislature created several new offices. As lieutenant of the county, Col. Francis Ware, with whom this essay began, coordinated the home guard and helped recruit soldiers for the army. Several commissaries, the most diligent and successful of whom was Daniel Jenifer, a senior member of the court, procured supplies for the military. And a new tax collector received payments in money and agricultural staples on behalf of the state.[18]

Wartime demands, unprecedented demands, required these officers to interact with local people on an unprecedented scale. The lieutenant personally persuaded planters' sons to join the army. The tax collector, for the first time in Maryland history, viewed and assessed all property belonging to every taxpayer. And the commissaries scoured the countryside for blankets, shoes, slabs of bacon, barrels of corn and flour, cavalry horses, and cattle on the hoof. In the process, the elite became mediators between often urgent requisitions from the state and the army, on the one hand, and people's

[17] Charles County Court Records, liber X3, fol. 563.

[18] Ibid., fols. 641–51; *Laws of Maryland, June 1777*, chap. 17; *Laws of Maryland, Made and Passed at a Session of Assembly . . . October . . . One Thousand Seven Hundred and Seventy-Seven* (Annapolis, [1777]), chaps. 4, 20; Papenfuse et al., eds., *Biographical Dictionary*, 2:484–85.

ability or willingness to respond, on the other. Although the commissaries and tax collector had coercive powers to extract resources from the public if necessary, they almost never used such powers. Instead, to repeat the words of one of the commissaries, they usually managed to "prevail on the people." And if prevailing did not always yield the county's full portion of men, supplies, and even taxes, the officers patiently explained the deficiencies to state leaders and expected them to understand. By the Battle of Yorktown, the officers had organized and managed the county's war effort with pragmatism and considerable success. And they had done so while being responsive to the public mood.[19]

Following the war, the governing elite—perhaps having learned too well how to be responsive to the populace—unknowingly embarked upon a collision course with the state of Maryland. For its part, the state had an important agenda, the same one that was on the minds of many Americans during the 1780s. That is, if republican government were to succeed, the state would have to be fiscally responsible, and it would have to maintain civil order. For their part, the county's officeholders seemingly ignored the state's agenda when postwar economic difficulties plagued the Chesapeake. In a manner reminiscent of the war years, a succession of sheriffs and tax collectors prevailed upon but did not coerce people to pay their county or state taxes, with the result that revenue collections were tens of thousands of pounds in arrears by 1786. In addition, when inhabitants resisted paying prewar debts to British creditors, several magistrates allegedly countenanced, perhaps even encouraged, the most serious riot in postwar Maryland. State officials did not ignore such happenings, and consequently they precipitated the third and final phase of the governing elite's Revolutionary-era transformation. It was a humiliating experience.

The riot occurred after county inhabitants had exhausted all legal means of postponing payment of prewar debts to British merchants. Protection of those debts in the Peace of

---

[19] The quotation is from Daniel Jenifer to Thomas Sim Lee, July 22, 1780, Browne et al., eds., *Archives of Maryland*, 45:21. Wartime mobilization of men and materiel is discussed in Lee, *Price of Nationhood*, pp. 154–84.

Paris allegedly was "a Stroke so unexpected that it has created a general amazement," since most people assumed that the war somehow canceled them. How much greater was their amazement, then, when British agents began pressing to collect interest as well. In the summer of 1784, however, the justices and jurors of the Charles County court refused to enforce such charges. Fumed one British agent, "The dread bodys has taken it into their heads, especially your County Gentry, to refuse to pay the Interest. It is said some of your Wiseacres of Majestrates has determined that point. How they may reconcile this conduct with their oaths to do justice according to the Laws of the Land, is, you may say, another affair." The justices in Charles and several other counties obliged debtors even more when an acute economic depression struck the Chesapeake in late 1785. Merely by adjourning court sessions during the following spring, they postponed the moment when debtors either had to settle their accounts or go to jail.[20]

On the day appointed for the Charles County court to reconvene in June 1786, all but two justices stayed away, thereby preventing a quorum. The two who appeared were Chief Justice Walter Hanson, who had been on the bench since the 1740s and had been active locally in the Revolution, and John Dent, a member of the court since the 1760s and a brigadier general of the militia during the war. Throughout

[20] Hamilton to James Brown and Co., Mar. 10 [1784], and to Robert Fergusson, July 17, 1784, in David C. Skaggs and Richard K. MacMaster, eds., "Post-Revolutionary Letters of Alexander Hamilton, Piscataway Merchant: Part 1, January–June 1784," *Maryland Historical Magazine* 63 (1968):30, and Skaggs and MacMaster, eds., "Post-Revolutionary Letters of Alexander Hamilton, Piscataway Factor: Part 2, July–October 1784," *Maryland Historical Magazine* 65 (1970):20. Although the peace treaty was silent about interest, the assembly had recognized it in 1782. *Laws of Maryland, Made and Passed at a Session of Assembly . . . April . . . One Thousand Seven Hundred and Eighty-Two* (Annapolis, [1782]), chap. 55. On economic depression and court closings, see Louis Maganzin, "Economic Depression in Maryland and Virginia, 1783–1787," Ph.D. diss., Georgetown University, 1967; Hamilton to James Brown and Co., May 24, 1786, Piscataway Letter Book, 1773–76, 1784–90, John Glassford and Co. Papers, Manuscript Division, Library of Congress; John Hoskins Stone to Walter Stone, Oct. 30, Dec. 27, 1786, Stone Family Papers, Maryland Historical Society, Baltimore.

the day, attorneys for British creditors tried to induce a necessary third justice to attend. When Samuel Hanson, Jr., nephew of the chief justice, finally took his seat as evening approached, the court, with unconcealed reluctance, began sentencing delinquent debtors to jail. Then suddenly the justices stopped and asked the attorneys whether they *really* meant to have people imprisoned. Thereupon Chief Justice Hanson reportedly depicted the jails rapidly filling "with Wretched and Unhappy Debtors" and announced that "he could not bear to send a Man to Gaol for debt" (although he had been doing just that for forty-five years). Unmoved, an attorney and war veteran named John Allen Thomas, who had filed more than one hundred British debt cases that term, persevered until the court resumed sentencing.[21]

That is when the riot broke out. Whether the chief justice's soliloquy was meant to signal "the Sense of the Court, and to rouse the People," as Thomas contended, is unclear. But unquestionably the justices saw the riot coming. It was impossible *not* to see a hundred men gathering just outside the courtroom window. Then, after the crowd rushed into the courthouse "in a most riotous and tumultuous Manner," the justices did not read the riot act. Instead, Chief Justice Hanson complimented the rioters on their sobriety, advised them "not to be so violent," and urged patience until Justice Dent could persuade a quivering attorney Thomas to save his life. How? By removing his name from every British suit he had filed, which would render them moot. Feeling very alone in

---

[21] Memorial of John Allen Thomas to Gov. William Smallwood, June 15, 1786, and Justices Walter Hanson, John Dent, and Samuel Hanson, Jr., to Smallwood [July 1786], Maryland State Papers, Executive Papers, box 59, Md. St. Arch. Information on Thomas and the justices is in Papenfuse et al., eds., *Biographical Dictionary,* 1:264, 409–10, 2:808–9, respectively. Surviving eyewitness accounts enable one to reconstruct the riot in unusual detail. See Jean B. Lee, "Maryland's 'Dangerous Insurrection' of 1786," *Maryland Historical Magazine* 85 (1990):329–44. The episode in Charles County was similar to outbursts of violence elsewhere in America during the 1780s. On crowd actions, compare Pauline Maier, "Popular Uprisings and Civil Authority in Eighteenth-Century America," *William and Mary Quarterly,* 3d ser. 27 (1970):3–35, and Thomas P. Slaughter, "Crowds in Eighteenth-Century America: Reflections and New Directions," *Pennsylvania Magazine of History and Biography* 115 (1991):3–34.

the packed courtroom, Thomas obliged. The rioters, their mission accomplished, quickly dispersed to the sounds of Hanson loudly proclaiming that filing so many lawsuits was "shameful."[22]

Thomas believed that Hanson and Dent, "so far from discountenancing such riotous Conduct, were actually behind the Curtain supporting it," and that Hanson particularly had incited the mob: "For this very humane tender hearted Old Gentleman who a few Minutes before could not bear to see a Man goe to Gaol for debt, could sit in Court perfectly unmoved, and forgetful of his Humanity & of his Oath, see a fellow Citizen assaulted and shamefully abused by a riotous and tumultuous Mob, without using one single Effort to prevent it." Several days after the riot, Thomas asked Gov. William Smallwood and the Maryland Council to investigate the justices' conduct. Furthermore, he framed what was at stake in unequivocal terms: "The Community at large" had been injured, and "if Proceedings of this kind pass unnoticed . . . all civil Liberty is at an End."[23]

Governor Smallwood, a native and resident of Charles County, reportedly was "much displeased" with the riot and "determined to have it searched to the bottom." Yet the executive in Revolutionary Maryland, as in other states, was notably limited. Smallwood and the Council therefore asked, but could not require, the two accused justices to come to Annapolis to explain themselves. Imperiously—as if they were sitting on the colonial court—Hanson and Dent declined and, instead, sent a written defense. While presenting themselves as paragons of rectitude and impartiality (and simultaneously attempting to discredit Thomas), they argued that "Uproar and Confusion" were so great during the riot, and the mob so large, that reading the riot act or calling out a posse would have been pointless. After all, they said, "nine tenths of the Multitude the[re] present were Engaged in [the riot]." Under

[22]Thomas memorial, June 15, 1786; deposition of Josias Hawkins, Aug. 1, 1786; deposition of Henry Massey Hanson, July 22, 1786; deposition of John Muschett, Aug. 8, 1786; Walter Hanson, Dent, and Samuel Hanson, Jr., to Smallwood, [July 1786], Executive Papers, box 59.

[23]Thomas memorial, June 15, 1786.

the state constitution, the only censure the governor and his advisers could invoke was removal from office, and that they declined to do. They merely pronounced the magistrates not guilty "of any Wilful violation of their Duty." The only person praised, and then rather faintly, was Thomas, for demonstrating "a becoming Zeal and Regard for Order and good Government."[24]

Yet if the justices were not excoriated, the riot was. Its immediate impact and potential dangers for country justice in Maryland simply could not be ignored. British debts may have been the ostensible cause, but suspicion was widespread that all debts and even the payment of taxes were in jeopardy. Furthermore, in the wake of the riot the county court system throughout Maryland nearly ground to a halt. Shades of 1765, when Maryland courts closed during the Stamp Act crisis, and of 1775, when they closed again as proprietary government disintegrated. Now, however, rioting was a threat not to British or proprietary rule but to the new republican state. Should this state prove impotent, what would replace it? "I am affraied," wrote one observer, that "by aiming at too much Liberty we shall lose it altogether."[25]

In strident tones, therefore, Smallwood issued a proclamation that denounced "riotous proceedings" as a threat to the welfare of the state, as "highly criminal" deeds that all magistrates, sheriffs, and citizens should "be vigilant and active in suppressing." He also ordered the incumbent Charles County

[24] Hamilton to James Brown and Co., July 10, 1786, Piscataway Letter Book, 1773–76, 1784–90, Glassford and Co. Papers, fols. 73–74; Smallwood to Walter Hanson and Dent, July 12, 1786, and to Thomas, July 12, 1786, Governor and Council, Letter Book, 1780–87, fols. 503–4, Md. St. Arch.; Walter Hanson to Smallwood, Aug. 3, 1786; and Walter Hanson, Dent, and Samuel Hanson, Jr., to Smallwood, [July 1786], Executive Papers, box 59. Council proceedings regarding the riot are in Browne et al., eds., *Archives of Maryland*, 71:122–23, 131. Information on Smallwood is in Papenfuse et al., eds., *Biographical Dictionary*, 2:741–42.

[25] Hamilton to James Brown and Co., July 10, 1786, Piscataway Letter Book, 1773–76, 1784–90, Glassford and Co. Papers, fol. 73; John Ridout to Sharpe, Aug. 9, 1786, Ridout Collection, Md. St. Arch. The worried observer was Alexander Hamilton, a Scottish tobacco factor who was at Port Tobacco during the riot. Hamilton to Fergusson, June 18, 1786, photocopy in Collection G333, Md. St. Arch.

sheriff, Francis Ware, to read the proclamation at the court-house and other public gathering places and to pepper the county with printed copies. So, too, twenty grand jurors of the Eastern Shore publicly denounced the riot in the *Maryland Gazette*. Promoting it to a "dangerous insurrection" perpetrated "by a set of infatuated men in Charles county," they warned that such disorder would have "dangerous and fatal consequences . . . if not timely discountenanced and suppressed." The wider community was issuing a loud message: no pretext for tumult existed in a political system with a written constitution and laws adequate to redress citizens' legitimate grievances. No matter how understandable or regrettable local people's problems, perceived threats to the welfare and survival of the young state government would not be tolerated.[26]

While that lesson about public order was being absorbed in Charles County, state officials were offering another—about fiscal responsibility. During the war, the legislature instituted ad valorem state taxes and in each county established a board of tax commissioners. They, in turn, appointed a collector. Benjamin Cawood, the Charles County collector from 1779 until the end of the war, operated much like the local procurers of military supplies. That is, he did not take up the full amount of taxes that were due. By 1780 his arrearages came to more than 300,000 pounds of tobacco. Revenue officers in other counties also had difficulty with collections, but by 1781 Cawood's arrearages were the largest in Maryland. While the war dragged on, the government at Annapolis did not press the issue. Afterward, it called Cawood to account. In 1784 state officials filed suit on his performance bond, the legal instrument in which he and his sureties pledged several hundred thousand pounds of currency for the faithful execution of his office. If taxpayers would not pay Cawood, the state would collect from him and his sureties.[27]

[26] *Maryland Gazette*, July 20, Sept. 21, 1786; Smallwood to Francis Ware, July 14, 1786, Governor and Council, Letter Book, 1780–87, fol. 504.

[27] Robert A. Becker, *Revolution, Reform, and the Politics of American Taxation, 1763–1783* (Baton Rouge, 1980), p. 231; Charles County Court Records, liber X3, fol. 621; *Laws of Maryland, Made and Passed at a Session of Assembly*

A measure of panic soon emanated from Charles County. When a surety named Robert Brent realized that state officials proposed to seize more than £3,000 of his property, the specter of poverty suddenly loomed before him. "Take Compassion on me," he begged Maryland's chief fiscal officer, "and the Rest of the Gentl[eme]n that are taken in with me . . . give us all the Indulgence that you Possoble can it being the only Chance to Save us poor Securitys and our famalys from Utter Ruining." Brent no doubt spoke the truth when he promised to "push" Cawood immediately and "use Every method [that] Lays in my power to gitt him to make a finish of his Arrears." Cawood, the collector, was more composed. By laboring "under a very heavy burthen" since 1780, he claimed, he had reduced his liability from 300,000 pounds of tobacco to 18,000. The state probably granted his request for more time to settle his accounts because the suit on his performance bond seems to have been dropped. His successors were not so fortunate.[28]

Charles Mankin began his three-year term in 1783 and, aided by high postwar tobacco prices, collected all taxes due for that year. Then, as economic depression settled over the Chesapeake, he, too, fell into arrears. An energetic, insistent man who was prone to use "very Improper Language," Mankin began seizing delinquents' property in lieu of taxes. But that proved a useless way to raise revenues because everyone

------

... *March* ... *One Thousand Seven Hundred and Eighty* (Annapolis, [1780]), chap. 30; Benjamin Cawood to Daniel of St. Thomas Jenifer, May 20, 1784, Red Books, 32:37. For the status of Cawood's accounts with the state, see balances due from county tax collectors for 1779–82 and an account of taxes collected in the counties for 1782 supplies, Nov. 16, 1782, Maryland State Papers, Pforzheimer Papers, box 1, Md. St. Arch. Compare Edward C. Papenfuse, "The Legislative Response to a Costly War: Fiscal Policy and Factional Politics in Maryland, 1777–1789," in Ronald Hoffman and Peter J. Albert, eds., *Sovereign States in an Age of Uncertainty* (Charlottesville, Va., 1982), pp. 134–56.

[28] Robert Brent to Daniel of St. Thomas Jenifer, Apr. 18, 1784, Executive Papers, box 46; Cawood to Daniel of St. Thomas Jenifer, May 20, 1784, Red Books, 32:37; Thomas Harwood's list of balances due for taxes on the Western Shore, Dec. 16, 1788, Vertical File, Md. Hist. Soc.

boycotted his distress sales. Although he managed to move Charles from dead last to midway among Maryland counties in terms of tax arrearages, he left office owing more than £10,000 in uncollected assessments. The state sued on his performance bond, won judgment against him, and in 1789 foreclosed on him and two sureties. When the men's property was auctioned off that year, Mankin lost everything—200 acres of land (aptly named "Mankin's Venture" and "Mankin's Folly"), six town lots in Port Tobacco, and all of his slaves, livestock, and furniture. The sureties lost another 400 acres and two slaves. Yet all of that property did not entirely cover the arrearages; Mankin still owed the state over £4,000 in back taxes.[29]

Well before anyone knew for sure that Mankin and his sureties were headed toward financial disaster, no one wanted to succeed him in office. The burdens of collecting were too heavy, the potential consequences of failure too high. Ultimately the county board of tax commissioners prevailed upon one of its own members to take the job, then explained to the governor that this unusual arrangement "wou'd not have happened if any other person cou'd have been got to undertake the Collection."[30]

The reluctant new collector was Hoskins Hanson, a magistrate. But that did not help him because, upon assuming office in 1786, he had the unrewarding task of dealing with taxpayers during the depths of the postwar depression. As of June 1787, Hanson had not forwarded to the state treasury a single shilling of tax money due from the previous year. Predictably by now, the state sued on his performance bond. One

[29] Petition of James Freeman to William Paca, undated, Southern Maryland Studies Center, Charles County Community College, La Plata, Md.; Charles Mankin to [Daniel of St. Thomas Jenifer?], July 27, 1784, and list of balances due from collectors for 1783–85, Executive Papers, boxes 50, 54; James Brice to Harwood, June 26, 1789, Governor and Council, Letter Book, 1787–93, fol. 57; William Kilty to John Kilty, Sept. 10, 1789, Red Books, 23:93; *Maryland Gazette*, July 30, Aug. 13, Oct. 29, 1789; account of taxes due from the Western Shore counties, Nov. 1, 1789, Pforzheimer Papers, box 1.

[30] Charles County tax commissioners to Smallwood, July 16, 1787, Executive Papers, box 62.

autumn day in 1789, well over 2,200 acres of land that had belonged to Hanson and his sureties went up on the auction block.[31]

Parallel to and, in Charles County, entwined with the tax collectors' travails were those of the sheriffs. Their ability to exact revenues for which they were legally responsible—including county tax levies, court fines, lawyers' fees, and marriage, peddlers', tavern, and liquor licenses—also was impeded during the 1780s. And that placed in jeopardy their performance bonds. Worse, three men successively elected sheriff—Benjamin Cawood (1779–82), Charles Mankin (1782–85), and Francis Ware (1785–88)—were in double jeopardy, Cawood and Mankin because they served as both sheriff and tax collector, and Ware because he had signed Mankin's collector's bond. Public offices that would have enhanced their wealth in better times instead impoverished them and some of their sureties during the 1780s.[32]

If one steps back and views the officers' difficulties as a whole, it is possible to see them caught in an ongoing Revolu-

---

[31] Charles County tax commissioners' certification of the account of Hoskins Hanson, Nov. 27, 1786, ibid., box 62, Harwood's list of Western Shore counties (including Charles) from which no tax money was received in 1786, June 30, 1787, ibid., box 64; Smallwood to tax commissioners in Charles and several other counties, July 6, 1787, Governor and Council, Letter Book, 1780–87, fol. 528; *Maryland Gazette*, Apr. 30, 1789. The disasters that befell tax collectors in Charles and other counties could not continue if the state hoped to retain any revenue officers. In late 1789 the assembly therefore halted the distress sales. Shortly thereafter it also designated an agent to arrange with collectors appointed since 1783 for payment of their arrearages and interest. The collectors could also reclaim title to property the state bought in 1789 and still retained if they paid the appraised value. Neither Hanson nor Mankin seems to have met the state's terms because property seized from them and their sureties was subsequently offered for sale. John Eager Howard to the sheriffs of Charles, Harford, and St. Mary's counties, Nov. 7, 1789, Howard to William Kilty, Nov. 8, 1789, John Kilty to William Kilty, Nov. 23, 1789, Governor and Council, Letter Book, 1787–93, fols. 77–78, 85; Council to the House of Delegates, Nov. 8, 1789, Executive Papers, box 67; *Maryland Gazette*, Nov. 19, 1789, Jan. 7, July 22, Sept. 30, 1790, Jan. 5, 1792.

[32] Governor and Council, Commission Record, 1777–98, fols. 91, 154, 159; *Maryland Gazette*, Oct. 29, 1789.

tion. From 1775 to 1783, the state government depended on the counties to support the war with everything from fresh recruits to donated silver, but how and the extent to which local quotas were filled was up to the people who organized the war effort at the local level. When state ad valorem taxation was first introduced, householders could pay in commodities sorely needed to feed the army. After the war, the state wanted taxes in currency, not wheat or pork. If the war forced one level of cooperation upon localities because American Independence hung in the balance, the 1780s forced a deeper level because republican government was at stake. For without regularly collected revenues—not just what local agents of the state managed to take up—neither current government expenses could be met nor the war debt retired. And without regularly collected revenues, the state could no more have viable government than if the courts fell victim to mobs.[33]

"When Taxes once become odious," mused someone at Annapolis in 1784, "I believe we shall find too little Energy in our republican Government to Enforce a Collection of them." The challenge to state officials during the 1780s was to find the energy to prove that prophecy wrong even during bad times, and no matter how much or little taxpayers, county collectors, and sheriffs cooperated. Although the assembly sometimes temporarily deferred tax collections, it did not revoke them. Collectors and sheriffs either had to remit everything people owed or suffer the consequences. Absent was any recognition from the state that the community should assume or at least share the burden in circumstances that were realistically beyond the control of local officials.[34]

The system through which the state called officeholders to account, the performance bond, had worked well during the colonial period, when relatively few demands were placed on

---

[33] Lee, *Price of Nationhood,* pp. 170–84; Papenfuse, "Legislative Response to a Costly War," pp. 134–42.

[34] John Beatty to Reading Beatty, Apr. 2, 1784, Joseph M. Beatty, Jr., ed., "Letters of the Four Beatty Brothers of the Continental Army, 1774–1794," *Pennsylvania Magazine of History and Biography* 44 (1920):240–41; *Laws of Maryland, March 1780,* chap. 30; *Maryland Gazette,* Feb. 1, 1787.

it. In the wake of a costly and disruptive war, in the crisis over collection of public revenues, the system broke down. In Charles County and elsewhere in Maryland during the 1780s, public offices involving collection of revenues became paths to personal financial ruin. No one could have been more surprised than Francis Ware, who had done as much as any man in the county to forward the Revolution. In 1787, just before the state moved against him, his property was assessed at nearly £2,300 current money. By the early 1790s he was too poor to qualify to vote, much less hold offices that so recently had been his for the asking. The old soldier's fortunes never improved. In 1800 county residents petitioned the legislature to authorize a local tax levy for his support, but the legislature rejected the stigma of public relief for a man who had served in the Maryland Line with "distinguished bravery and fidelity." Instead, the assembly, citing Ware's ill health and "misfortunes arising from those acts of benevolence which the duties of society often render indispensable," granted him half-pay for life at the rank of lieutenant colonel.[35]

Imagine the tensions created when local officers found themselves caught between the citizenry and a determined state government. Certainly Robert Brent was not the only surety who, abruptly confronted with the prospect of ruin, "pushed" the man whose performance bond he had signed. Nor could Thomas Stone have been the only attorney who let the sheriff know that "I must have what is due Me" in fees. And certainly the sheriffs and collectors pushed the citizenry in turn, as Joseph Nelson learned. At the November court in 1780 Nelson had pleaded no contest to a charge of pulling Virlinda Haislope "from her horse, Tearing her Cloaths, and making use of many threats to Accomplish his Designs." Assessed a £30 fine, he petitioned the court to remit it and, when Sheriff Cawood came by to collect, announced that he did not owe it. There the matter rested until Cawood got in trouble with the state. He then reappeared and demanded payment in specie that, because of postwar deflation, reportedly was

[35] Order to the coroner of Charles County, Apr. 1787, in Loose Papers, General Court of the Western Shore, 1779–88; *Maryland Gazette*, Sept. 4, 1794; *Votes and Proceedings of the House of Delegates of the State of Maryland, November Session, 1800* (Annapolis, [1801]), pp. 45, 61, 67.

worth six times the value of the original fine. One of the leaders of the courthouse riot was named Joseph Nelson.[36]

Although the sheriffs and collectors pressed citizens hard at times—as Cawood did in confronting Nelson, and Mankin in seizing delinquent taxpayers' possessions—the huge balances on their books when they left office suggest lack of success on that score. Householders who owed taxes, fees, and fines to the state or county were not without recourse. One was the communal cohesiveness Mankin encountered when he tried to sell delinquents' property but discovered that no one would even attend the sales. Then, too, some delinquents adopted a more individualistic approach—they simply ran away. From the vantage of local revenue officers, *they* were the ones who bore the brunt of concerted efforts by the state government to set things right during the 1780s.[37]

While their travails were the most sensational, at least one other class of public officers experienced analogous problems. These were tobacco inspectors, members of the elite, at whose warehouses British raiders had destroyed or stolen tobacco "during the tumults of the late war." Because they stored planters' tobacco until shipment, inspectors, too, had to post performance bonds and were personally liable for any losses. Compensating planters for hogsheads destroyed in a raid on his warehouse exhausted the wealth of one inspector and landed him in debtors' prison. The estates of deceased inspectors were equally liable, as two widows learned when they petitioned the assembly for relief. To their plea for a countywide levy to reimburse planters for property lost during raiding, the assembly turned a deaf ear. Not even acts of war absolved

[36] Brent to Daniel of St. Thomas Jenifer, Apr. 18, 1784, Executive Papers, box 46; Thomas Stone to Walter Stone, Jan. 15, 1786, Papers of the Stone Family of Maryland, fol. 163, Ms. Div., Libr. of Cong.; Joseph Nelson file, Governor and Council, Pardon Papers, box 5 (1790–91), folder 57; Muschett deposition, Aug. 8, 1786, Executive Papers, box 59. The only Joseph Nelson named in the 1782 tax records owned one hundred acres of land but no other assessed property. Charles County Tax Assessments, 1782, for Pomonkey Hundred, Scharf Collection.

[37] Mankin to [Daniel of St. Thomas Jenifer?], July 27, 1784, and Charles County tax commissioners' certification of the account of Hoskins Hanson, Nov. 27, 1786, Executive Papers, boxes 50, 62.

local officers from the obligations of their performance bonds.[38]

The magistrates certainly could empathize—because they, too, had continuing problems with the state. For not only did the state investigate their part in the Charles County riot, it also modified the size and composition of the county court and a separate, newly created orphans' court. In 1786—the year of acute depression, the riot, and no tax collections—the state reduced the number of magistrates, "not from any Doubt of their Sufficiency to discharge the Trust," the governor assured them, but for the sake of efficiency. The following year the justices of the orphans' court asked the governor to fill vacancies on that body with whomever he "Judge[d] most proper," all the while assuming he would choose from among the magistrates in order of seniority. When he did not, Walter Hanson, whose seniority made him chief justice of both local courts, was outraged and warned that the slight would "give great umbrage to the Gent who had by Custom a right to expect the appointment."[39]

By the time Hanson vented his anger in the autumn of 1787, at the very moment when a stronger national government was being launched, public officeholding and the conduct of public business were in disarray in Charles County. The combination of a county court under a cloud, former tax collectors, sheriffs, and tobacco inspectors in default and heading toward insolvency with their sureties in tow, and state intervention in the composition of the local courts—that combination alternately overwhelmed and infuriated an elite that previously had been quite content to exercise power and garner the status it accorded. Now, Hanson sighed, "I heartily

[38] *Maryland Gazette*, Sept. 20, Oct. 11, 1787, Mar. 27 (quotation), Sept. 18, Oct. 23, 1788, Sept. 19, 1793, Oct. 9, 1794.

[39] Smallwood to the justices of Charles, Prince George's, and Cecil counties, Mar. 10, 1786, justices of the Charles County orphans' court to Smallwood, Feb. 12, 1787, Walter Hanson to the justices of the orphans' court, Sept. 22, 1787, Executive Papers, boxes 56, 62. The legislature established separate county orphans' courts in 1777. *Laws of Maryland, Made and Passed at a Session of Assembly . . . February . . . One Thousand Seven Hundred and Seventy-Seven* (Annapolis, [1777]), chap. 8.

wish our County . . . could be at Peace and the Publick business Carried on in a regular and Consistant manner."[40]

The gentry reacted to the perils of officeholding, republican style, with a rash of resignations and refusals to serve. Whether citizens could obtain public services, even access to the courts, became problematic. Col. William Harrison declined appointment to the orphans' court. It could not always raise a quorum. After less than a year in office another man resigned as tobacco inspector with the explanation that "the business [is] So Very Fatiging & Perplexing, [I] think my Self not Equal to the Task." His successor did not last a year. Keeping an incumbent coroner became as difficult as finding a tax collector.[41]

As for the magistrates, they staged something of a strike because of the appointment of nonmagistrates to the orphans' court. The governor's action "has given great Offense" and allegedly was widely regarded as illegal, according to one magistrate. Justice Hoskins Hanson, passed over for an orphans' court appointment, thought himself extremely "ill used," and understandably so. For what disqualified him for a seat on the court was the tax collectorship that he had accepted only reluctantly, and that soon cost him nearly 1,000 acres of land because of his default on collections. So incensed was Hanson that he threatened not to serve in the magistracy, and his was not an idle remark. Soon most of the justices refused to perform their duties. Observed one of them in October of 1787, "At present it is very difficult & troublesome to get Business done from the remoteness [from the courthouse] of the few Magistrates who will do it." The spirit of noblesse

[40]Walter Hanson to the justices of the Charles County orphans' court, Sept. 22, 1787, Executive Papers, box 62.

[41]Col. William Harrison to Smallwood, Mar. 9, 1787, John N. Smoot to Smallwood, May 19, 1787 (quotation), Charles County tax commissioners to Smallwood, Apr. 19,1788, Daniel Jenifer to Howard, Feb. 16, 1789, ibid., boxes 62, 64, 68; State of Maryland to Francis Boucher Franklin, Jan. 2, 1787, Benjamin Fendall to Smallwood, Dec. 5, 1787, John Sanders to Smallwood, Apr. 7, 1788, ibid., box 57. In addition to their customary duties, county coroners were required to assume some that delinquent sheriffs and tax collectors no longer performed. Henry Barnes to Smallwood, June 20, 1788, Franklin to Howard, Apr. 19, 1789, ibid., boxes 66, 57.

oblige faltered when the magistrates thought themselves under attack.[42]

The county court sank into lassitude. Several justices either resigned or, because they lived "remote" from the courthouse, seldom appeared on the bench. Those in attendance in December 1787 reported, "Its with much difficulty the Court business can be Carried on in the manner it ought to be." In mid-1789 Justice Daniel Jenifer stated, "Tho it should seem from looking over the list of Magistreates, there are enough in this County, Yet . . . from a variety of Circumstances, it often happens that a sufficient number to conduct the business is not found on the Bench." Accomplishing out-of-court business was even more difficult, especially since fewer magistrates meant enlarged jurisdictions.[43]

The General Assembly solved the problem in 1790—not by honoring requests for more magistrates, but by creating five circuit courts, each comprised of a chief justice and two associate justices from each county in the judicial district. The old county courts were reduced to three men each—the chief circuit justice and the associate judges from that county—and any one of them could conduct judicial business. No longer did justices of the peace sit on the bench. Rather their duties became largely administrative—levying local taxes, overseeing tobacco inspection, and issuing licenses.[44]

In Charles County, reorganization of the court was the last act of a drama begun the day of the courthouse riot. When the curtain fell, the single most important locus of local power, gentry power, was drastically altered. The old court had survived the proprietary regime's demise, Independence, and the war. It succumbed—as did the revenue officers—to the

[42] Samuel Hanson (d. 1794) to Smallwood, Oct. 8, 1787 (quotation), George Dent et al. to Smallwood, Dec. 17, 1787, ibid., boxes 62, 66; *Maryland Gazette*, Apr. 30, 1789.

[43] Charles County justices to Smallwood, Dec. 8, 1787, Zephaniah Turner to Howard, May 6, 1789, Daniel Jenifer to Howard, Feb. 16, 1789, Executive Papers, boxes 62, 68.

[44] Charles County justices to Smallwood, Dec. 8, 1787, ibid., box 62; *Laws of Maryland, Made and Passed at a Session of Assembly . . . November . . . One Thousand Seven Hundred and Ninety* (Annapolis, [1791]), chap. 33.

disarray of the 1780s and the agenda of Maryland's post-Revolutionary government.

While the restructured court reinvigorated the administration of justice in the county, lassitude among other officials continued during the 1790s. The sheriff was late in submitting polling results for the presidential election of 1792. A man opened a store and sold liquor without a license (for which he was fined) because he could not locate a justice of the peace to issue a license. Roads became impassable, in one case because the overseer was in jail for debt. And in 1794 state officials waited in vain for the justices of the peace to recommend a slate of tobacco inspectors, then finally asserted, "As we have been at a loss to understand your intentions, we would recommend a stricter attention in future to . . . your duty in this particular."[45]

Although the breakdown of local government in Charles County may have been more severe than elsewhere in Maryland (the courthouse riot was the most serious civil disturbance of the postwar years), it was far from unique. Thus, the assembly several times postponed tax collections because collectors in many counties were in arrears and unable to fulfill their responsibilities. The state's prodding of local officials and seizure and sale of their property also occurred in many counties. And the 1790 law that reorganized the courts cited widespread problems of inefficiency and lack of uniformity in the administration of justice.[46] The exquisite difficulties, the wrenching transformations of local government and officeholding in postwar Charles County were part of a larger mosaic, a mosaic that infuses the term *Critical Period* with new meaning.

[45] Thomas Sim Lee to the sheriffs of Charles, St. Mary's, and Frederick counties, Governor and Council, Letter Book, 1787–93, fol. 167; Randolph B. Latimer to John Dent et al., Governor and Council, Letter Book, 1793–96, fol. 138; Governor and Council, Pardon Papers, box 5, folder 35, box 6, folders 19, 52, 90.

[46] Bountiful evidence supporting this statement is contained in state records and in notices in the *Maryland Gazette* both of sales of property seized from local officials and their sureties as well as an astonishing number of bankruptcy notices from them.

JEAN B. RUSSO

Chesapeake Artisans in the Aftermath of the Revolution

J. FRANKLIN JAMESON wrote of "the transforming hand of revolution." Joyce Oldham Appleby has stated that an American aged forty in the year 1800 "would have seen every fixed point in his or her world dramatically transformed" by the events of the Revolution and its aftermath. Within the Chesapeake, historians have pointed to the Revolution as a critical factor in the development of Baltimore as the preeminent urban center of the region; Gary Larson Browne has described the American Revolution as the "catalyst" for Baltimore's growth. Labor historians have similarly granted a crucial role to the Revolution in the development of a cohesive, self-conscious artisan class, whether in Baltimore, older cities like New York and Philadelphia, or towns like Lynn, Massachusetts.[1] But what of artisans who worked not in urban centers

[1] J. Franklin Jameson, *The American Revolution Considered as a Social Movement* (1926; reprint ed., Princeton, 1973), p.9; Joyce Oldham Appleby, "Commercial Farming and the 'Agrarian Myth' in the Early Republic," *Journal of American History* 68 (1982):838; Gary Lawson Browne, *Baltimore in the Nation, 1789–1861* (Chapel Hill, 1980), pp. 10–11; Edward C. Papenfuse, *In Pursuit of Profit: The Annapolis Merchants in the Era of the American Revolution, 1763–1805* (Baltimore, 1975), pp. 133, 158; Ronald Hoffman, *A Spirit of Dissension: Economics, Politics, and the Revolution in Maryland* (Baltimore, 1973), pp. 79–80; Charles G. Steffen, *The Mechanics of Baltimore: Workers and Politics in the Age of Revolution, 1763–1812* (Urbana, Ill., 1984); Sean Wilentz, *Chants Democratic: New York City and the Rise of the American Working Class, 1788–1850* (New York, 1984); Bruce Laurie, *Working People of Philadelphia, 1800–1850* (Philadelphia, 1980); and Paul G. Faler, *Mechanics and Manufacturers in the Early Industrial Revolution: Lynn, Massachusetts, 1780–1860* (Albany, N.Y., 1981). Richard Alan Ryerson, *The Revolution Is Now Begun: The Radical Committees of Philadelphia, 1765–1776* (Philadelphia, 1978), although

but in a rural economy—scattered across the landscape rather than clustered in towns, linked not to fellow craftsmen through shared work experiences but by birth and marriage to planters, who were themselves often cultivators of plantation lands, full participants in the civic life of the community, and dispersed throughout the social and economic structure rather than grouped at the bottom or among the middling sort? Did the Revolution transform their world or did the post-Revolutionary experience favor continuity over change? To examine these questions, this essay will focus on the lives of mechanics living in Talbot County, Maryland, in the years between 1760 and 1810, building upon the previous study of craftsmen in that county in the colonial period.

If Maryland represented a middle ground between slave and free societies, Talbot County represented a middle ground within Maryland and the Chesapeake. Talbot was and is an area of low-lying farmland, midway along the Eastern Shore of Maryland. Land in the county began to be taken up in the late 1650s as settlers moved up the western shore and across the Chesapeake Bay in search of suitable tobacco land. Talbot offered plantation sites along waterways to facilitate transport and a band of good soil running down the middle of the county but provided only poor land on the largest necks and average soil in the eastern, inland portion.[2] Thus, although tobacco was Talbot's staple crop through the early eighteenth century, scale of cultivation remained smaller and commitment to slave labor less extreme than was true for areas better endowed with good tobacco land. Planters in Talbot shifted from a predominantly servant to a predominantly slave labor force a decade or two later than did Anne Arundel planters,[3]

---

not a labor history, also examines the role of Revolutionary politics in defining mechanics as a separate, articulate interest group.

[2] Paul G. E. Clemens, *The Atlantic Economy and Colonial Maryland's Eastern Shore* (Ithaca, N.Y., 1980), pp. 46–47.

[3] Jean B. Russo, "Free Workers in a Plantation Economy: Talbot County, Maryland, 1690–1759," Ph.D. diss., The Johns Hopkins University, 1983, fig. 2.2, p. 86, and idem, "The Structure of the Anne Arundel County Economy," sec. 5, pp. 4–5, in Lorena S. Walsh, proj. dir., "Annapolis and Anne

for example, and the proportion of slaves among the county's population never exceeded 40 percent before the Revolution.[4] As overseas demand for wheat increased in the mid-eighteenth century, with Philadelphia millers expanding their supply network farther and farther down the Eastern Shore, Talbot planters acquired a second staple in wheat. By the 1750s and 1760s, a minimum of 55 percent of inventoried households raised wheat; at least 80 percent cultivated wheat and tobacco for export, as well as corn.[5] Talbot's economy by the Revolution thus represented a mix of tobacco and wheat as the export staples and a mix of slave and free labor as the work force. It was a diversified economy, as well, in that it always included a significant number of independent craft workers.

As a rural community, Talbot never replicated the range of craft skills available even in the minimally urbanized Chesapeake centers—that is, Williamsburg and Annapolis—let alone those of larger colonial cities (to say nothing of European urban areas), but certain basic crafts were represented from early settlement and others were added to or subtracted from the mix as the county developed.[6] Carpenters were among the earliest artisans and remained a major component of the craft workers until well into the nineteenth century. Blacksmiths constituted a smaller but equally vital group. Both supplied essential services that could not be supplanted by import substitution. Carpenters provided buildings and

---

Arundel County, Maryland: A Study of Urban Development in a Tobacco Economy, 1649–1776," NEH Grant RS-20199–81–1985, 1981.

[4] "The Population of Maryland, 1755," *Gentleman's Magazine* (London) 34 (1764), reproduced in Edward C. Papenfuse and Joseph M. Coale III, *The Hammond-Harwood House Atlas of Historical Maps of Maryland, 1608–1908* (Baltimore, 1982), p. 37; and Census of 1776, Talbot County, Maryland State Archives, Annapolis.

[5] Russo, "Free Workers," Appendix 5, p. 459.

[6] The following discussion is based upon Jean B. Russo, "Self-Sufficiency and Local Exchange: Free Craftsmen in the Rural Chesapeake Economy," in Lois Green Carr et al., eds., *Colonial Chesapeake Society* (Chapel Hill, 1988), pp. 389–432.

furniture; blacksmiths rarely made tools and utensils but did shoe horses and mend a wide range of metal objects, from plows and pots to watches and guns. Shoemakers represented a third major group of craftworkers, despite the abundance of shoes imported into the colony from England. With a ready supply of raw materials and a substantial demand for shoes, the market had room for both imports and local providers. Weavers and tailors occupied a similar niche in the economy. Cloth, again imported from overseas, dominated store accounts for decades, but buyers also existed for fabric woven from local wool and flax. Imported and homemade garments supplied part of the market for clothing, but skill, price, and time combined to protect a share for local tailors.[7]

While these five major craft groups persisted throughout the preindustrial period, the presence and duration of more minor crafts varied over time. Some appeared initially but vanished by the early eighteenth century, having found the rural rim of the Atlantic economy an inhospitable home. The county's one hatter and few glovers, butchers, and bakers comprised this group. Potential customers could supply their own food; ship captains and storekeepers offered ample stocks of gloves and hats. Others, most notably coopers, declined in numbers over the course of the eighteenth century. Planters' needs for hogsheads and barrels were great enough to encourage home production, while skill level and equipment costs did not erect a barrier against entry. Cooperage and, to a lesser degree, shoemaking were the two crafts most likely to be incorporated into the operations of individual plantations, with a consequent dampening effect on the number of free artisans. Still other mechanics first appeared in Talbot only in the mid-eighteenth century, as population growth and increasing levels of household wealth enlarged their pool of prospective customers. Carpentry became more specialized, with the addition of joiners, house carpenters, and eventually cabinetmakers. A few more saddlers plied their trade in the county, and a larger number of gold- and silversmiths found buyers for their wares.

[7] Ibid.

Table 1. Talbot County artisans, by craft, 1690–1810

Crafts group	1690–1759 No.	1690–1759 %	1760–85 No.	1760–85 %	1786–1810 No.	1786–1810 %
Woodworkers						
Carpenters	228	28	39	13	52	14
Coopers	59	7	6	2	3	1
Sawyers	53	7	12	4	8	2
Joiners	40	5	29	10	13	4
Wheelwrights	19	2	11	4	9	2
Coachmakers	0	0	5	2	8	2
Cabinetmakers	7	1	12	4	18	5
Millwrights	6	1	1	*	1	*
Turners	3	*	1	*	0	0
House carpenters	3	*	13	4	30	8
Chairmaker	1	*	0	0	0	0
	419	51	129	43	142	38
Clothworkers						
Tailors	74	9	37	12	37	10
Weavers	57	7	10	3	5	1
Hatters	1	*	5	2	13	4
Fuller	1	*	0	0	0	0
	133	16	52	17	55	15
Leatherworkers						
Shoemakers	72	9	27	9	46	15
Tanners	16	2	9	3	10	3
Saddlers	7	1	4	1	7	2
Glovers	4	*	0	0	0	0
Breeches maker	0	0	1	*	0	0
	99	12	41	13	63	20

This evolution of the craft network continued into the early national period[8] (see table 1). Carpentry, encompassing carpenters, joiners, and house carpenters, remained the dominant craft, with slightly more than one-quarter of the artisans in both the period from 1760 to 1785 and the twenty-five years from 1786 to 1810. The number of blacksmiths remained steady throughout, varying by only one or two men from 1740 to 1810 and constituting 7 percent of the total dur-

---

[8]The discussion of crafts prior to the Revolution is based upon Russo, "Free Workers," while evidence for craftsmen in the Revolutionary period and thereafter was gathered from Talbot County Land Records, Civil Court Judgments, Indentures, Wills, and Tax Assessments, all located at the Md. St. Arch.

Table 1.   Talbot County artisans, by craft, 1690–1810 (*cont.*)

Crafts group	1690–1759		1760–85		1786–1810	
	No.	%	No.	%	No.	%
Metalworkers						
Blacksmiths	53	7	28	9	26	7
Silversmiths	3	*	8	3	10	3
Brazier	1	*	0	0	0	0
Copper/tinsmiths	0	0	0	0	2	1
Watchmakers	0	0	1	*	6	2
	57	7	37	12	44	13
Shipbuilders						
Ship carpenters	42	5	26	9	29	8
Caulkers	4	*	0	0	0	0
Sailmakers	2	*	0	0	1	*
Blockmakers	2	*	0	0	0	0
Rigger	0	0	0	0	1	*
	50	5	26	9	31	8
Builders						
Bricklayers	25	3	9	3	7	2
Plasterers	13	2	2	1	7	2
Brickmakers	4	*	1	*	1	*
Glaziers	2	*	0	0	1	*
Mason	0	0	0	0	1	*
	44	5	12	4	17	4
Miscellaneous						
Barbers	4	*	1	*	3	1
Butchers	2	*	0	0	4	1
Bakers	2	*	1	*	2	1
Limners/music	0	0	0	0	4	1
Potter	0	0	0	0	1	*
	8	0	2	0	14	4
Total	810	96	299	98	366	102

SOURCE: Adapted from Jean B. Russo, "Free Workers in a Plantation Economy: Talbot County, Maryland, 1690–1759," Ph.D. diss., Johns Hopkins University, 1983, table 3.1, pp. 139–40; Talbot County and Provincial Records, Maryland State Archives, Annapolis.

*Figure less than .5.

ing those years. Tailors increased somewhat in number, to 37 in both intervals, and accounted for 12 and then 10 percent of all craftsmen. Shoemakers represented the last of the large groups of artisans to appear consistently in all periods. With 27 men in the Revolutionary years and 46 in the early national period, they accounted for 9 and then 15 percent of the total in the two spans. Four core crafts, then, continued to dominate, collectively encompassing nearly 60 percent of all artisans working in the county through the Revolutionary and early national periods.

Other trades continued the pattern of decline evident before 1760. There were few coopers and a dwindling number of sawyers. As with the making of barrels, sawing wood became the employment of slaves or the winter task of farmers and dependent sons. Few men specialized in the work by the end of the eighteenth century. A final trade declined in numbers as well, but for a different reason—not lack of demand but evolution in a more skilled direction. Only sixteen wheelwrights worked after 1760; other men who crafted vehicles for transportation now called themselves carriage- or coach- or chaisemakers and numbered a dozen. Twenty-eight men making carts and coaches represented triple the number working in the previous interval.

The appearance of coach- and carriagemakers points to the most striking change to occur in the occupational structure in the post-Revolutionary years—the emergence of a number of skills generally associated with a more cosmopolitan or urban clientele. Bakers and butchers, who had found the county inhospitable in the early 1700s, returned in the 1790s. The same pattern prevailed for barbers; the four early practitioners were followed a century later by three men. Two coppersmiths set up in business, the first specialists in a metal other than iron since brassworker John Jones died in 1702. One dancing master had offered his services to county residents briefly in the 1720s before leaving for a more receptive area; now the citizens of Talbot could patronize a limner, a musician, and a miniature painter. After decades with no hatter in the county, during the Revolutionary years there were five; in the post-Revolutionary period, thirteen hatters supplied Talbot residents with their wares. Members of the Bruff family had been silversmiths in Talbot since the late 1600s; Maj. Joseph Bruff carried on the trade at the courthouse in the third quarter of the century, and several of his kin continued after his death. But rather than being virtually the lone representatives of the luxury craft, they were only a few of the sixteen gold- and silversmiths and seven watchmakers at work in the county. No cabinetmakers set up shop in Talbot before 1740, but there were seven such men in the 1740s and 1750s. Twelve specialized in making furniture between 1760 and 1785, while eighteen men were at work in the last twenty-five years. One final group, ship carpenters, also experienced an increase in numbers after 1760. A slow but steady rise throughout the eighteenth century in the number of boatbuilders was sustained by the need for vessels during the Revolutionary War. The town of St. Michael's developed as a maritime center, although the stimulus to shipbuilding did not extend to the ship chandlery crafts; only one sailmaker and one rigger took up residence as specialists.

In sum, between 1760 and 1810, the core crafts of a rural area persisted as the predominant trades in Talbot County—carpentry, tailoring, shoemaking, and blacksmithing. A few others declined in prominence, most notably coopering, sawing, and weaving, while shipbuilding grew in importance. Several crafts that had failed to establish themselves early in the colonial period reappeared as the county became more urbanized; their representatives included bakers, butchers, barbers, and hatters. And a number of "urban" crafts appeared for the first time or in increased numbers—cabinetmakers, gold- and silversmiths, watchmakers, and painters. Two other firsts should be noted: the presence of Mrs. Peter Redhead, a milliner and the first woman to be designated by a skill rather than as widow, spinster, or wife, and the appearance of men like Lera Hall, a hatter, carpenters John and James Webster, and Moses Smith, a shoemaker—all free blacks and the first free black craftsmen in the county.

Developments in some crafts represent an evolutionary pattern that operated throughout the eighteenth century, affecting coopers, shoemakers, and sawyers most markedly. Low costs for equipment, steady demand within individual plantations, and readily acquired skills encouraged planters to incorporate these activities into the routines of their plantations. Opportunities for independent craftsmen declined accordingly, in absolute terms for coopers and sawyers and in relative terms for shoemakers. Although cordwainers or boot- and shoemakers, as they were variously known, remained a major occupational group, inventory and apprenticeship records make it clear that they shared their market with both planters and slaves, thus limiting potential growth.[9]

A number of the changes outlined here reflect the most significant development of the post-Revolutionary period, the appearance for the first time in the history of the county of a true urban area.[10] Towns had existed in Talbot in earlier years, of course. The legislature established Oxford in the town act of 1668 and designated it as the port of entry for the Eastern Shore in 1694, but the settlement had never established itself as an urban presence.[11] Factors representing British trading firms, particularly the Liverpool firms of Richard Gildart and Foster Cunliffe and Sons, set up stores there and a few artisans located in the town, but there was no urban infrastructure. The court met elsewhere, no church group congregated in Oxford, and craftsmen were few in number. Sales of Oxford lots rarely occurred; equally rare were county citizens who identified themselves as "of Oxford." Other towns—Yorke (the early county seat), Doncaster, Kings Town, and Dover—traced an even fainter pattern on the landscape. The county court had met since 1712 at a site near Pitts His Bridge, known until the 1780s only as "Talbot Court House." Over time, first one, then two, then as many as a half-dozen taverns located there, but Jeremiah Banning, an Oxford partisan, denigrated the settlement as late as the Revolution as consisting of only four houses and one store or tradesman's

[9] Russo, "Self-Sufficiency and Local Exchange," pp. 411, 418–19.

[10] Even here, the term *urban* is used in a relative sense. Easton's population in 1790 probably did not exceed 250 persons, while the other towns were much smaller—hardly more than villages or hamlets.

[11] John C. Reps, *Tidewater Towns: City Planning in Colonial Virginia and Maryland* (Williamsburg, Va., 1972), p. 109.

shop.[12] Banning exaggerated the insignificance of the community at the courthouse, but not by much.

Dramatic changes took place in the decade or so after the Revolution, however. As part of the reorganization of governmental agencies and functions that followed in the wake of Independence, the legislature in 1785 erected a town at the courthouse site. The enabling act appointed five commissioners to oversee surveying and selling lots in Talbot Town.[13] Three years later a second act designated the town, now renamed Easton, as the meeting place for the general court of the Eastern Shore.[14] The land office for the Eastern Shore subsequently made Easton its headquarters as well, and the town was considered the unofficial capital of the counties on the eastern side of the bay, with the expectation that the title would be officially bestowed in time. Lawyers followed the court, first one and then a second newspaper began publishing, merchants with Baltimore connections opened stores, one of the two branches of the Farmers' Bank (the other in Annapolis) began operation in the early 1800s, and craftsmen moved their shops into town. The Eastern Shore general court was terminated within six years and the town never became the official counterpart of Annapolis, but a critical mass was achieved during those early years that enabled Easton to survive after its initial raison d'etre vanished—something that had not been possible for most of the earlier Chesapeake towns.

Nor was Easton alone as a center of urban development. Renewed interest in Oxford lots is demonstrated by the increasing frequency of sale and resale. An enterprising factor took it upon himself to lay out and sell lots in a tract of land along the Miles River owned by the firm of Gildart and Gawith, an action of dubious legal merit, but one that did succeed as an example of townbuilding. The first sales occurred in December 1778 to capitalize on the stimulus to shipbuilding

[12] Jeremiah Banning, "Autobiography, 1733–93," no. 2433, fol. 6, Maryland Historical Society, Baltimore.

[13] William Kilty, ed., *The Laws of Maryland*, 7 vols. (Annapolis, 1799–1818), vol. 2, Nov. 1785, chap. 32.

[14] Ibid., Nov. 1788, chap. 16.

provided by the war effort;[15] by 1804 the town had grown large enough to warrant a successful petition to the legislature for incorporation as the town of St. Michael's.[16] Two very small but stable settlements grew up around crossroads on the Eastern Shore's main north-south route, towns with the Wild West names of Trappe and Hole in the Wall. Landowners began to subdivide larger holdings in the area of each settlement in the early 1780s, selling off their property generally in four-acre parcels—large lots by modern standards but very small landholdings for the time. Mean acreage for the colonial eighteenth century averaged from 350 to 375 acres; clearly purchasers of property at Trappe or Hole in the Wall or St. Michael's, with its half-acre lots, envisioned a different usage of their property than did the average landowner in Talbot.[17] Dennis Griffith's 1794 map of Maryland captures this new stage in the county's development; in addition to locating the towns already mentioned, Griffith also notes the settlements of Louis Town, Williamsburgh, Hook Town, and the still-breathing though nearly moribund Kings Town.[18]

Given the relatively small size of lots within these towns, it should not be surprising to find that many of the residents earned their livelihood from pursuits other than farming. A number were storekeepers, some operated taverns, a few were professional men, physicians, and—in Easton—attorneys, and many were artisans. Early purchasers of St. Michael's lots included wheelwright John Bruff and ship carpenters Jonathan and Perry Spencer and Thomas Lambdin. As James Dickinson began selling off lots from the tracts of Sandy Hill and Bozman's Addition (soon to be the town of Hole in the Wall), craftsmen like shoemaker Henry Delahay, carpenter William Walker, wheelwright Charles Gulley, joiner Noah Corner, and tailors John Heron and Samuel Mullikin each acquired a four-acre lot. Of the initial dozen and a half

[15] Talbot County Land Records, RS 21/80–150, for the earliest sales.

[16] Kilty, ed., *Laws of Maryland*, vol. 3, Nov. 1804, chap. 82.

[17] Mean landholding calculated from Talbot County Debt Books, Md. St. Arch.

[18] Dennis Griffith, Map of Maryland, 1794 [1795], Library of Congress.

purchasers of lots at Hole in the Wall, at least a dozen were artisans. The Mullikin family's division of their property into Trappe town lots proceeded more slowly. Merchant William Stevens supplied the major initiative for town clustering, but tailor James Mullikin and blacksmith Matthew Doyle were early residents.[19]

The most pronounced association between craftsmanship and town residence appeared in Easton. The earliest property owners in the vicinity of the courthouse had been tavernkeepers catering to the visitors who arrived on court days, but a few years before the legislature erected the town Henry Nicols, owner of one of the two tracts on which Easton was built, subdivided part of his land into a series of lots, all rented on long-term developmental leases. Merchant James Kennady, a newcomer from Delaware, took one lot, while a physician and three merchants leased four more. The remaining lots went to saddler William Meluy, cabinetmaker Caleb Hannah, and silversmith William Skinner.[20] As evidence of the potential for expansion that surrounded the rebirth of the town, only Skinner, of the eight buyers, belonged to an established Talbot family; the others had migrated from surrounding counties, undoubtedly anticipating the growth that would come with the branches of the state government.

Fragmentary tax records for 1786 include those for the towns of Oxford and Easton.[21] Owners of thirty-four houses paid taxes in that year, seventeen in Oxford, the older town, and sixteen in newly formed Easton, with one residence unknown. Fully 40 percent, at a minimum, of the properties belonged to craftsmen. Four resided in Oxford: two ship carpenters, James Cray and Nicholas Pamphilion; one blacksmith, Edward Bromwell; and one chaisemaker, Spedden Bromwell. Pamphilion and the Bromwells belonged to old Talbot families. Bromwells had owned a forge in Oxford since blacksmith Thomas Beswick left his land and tools to the widowed Rebecca Bromwell in 1718, while four other members of the family had been woodworkers. The first Pamphilion,

[19] Talbot County Land Records, liber RS21.

[20] Ibid., liber BS 23.

[21] Talbot County Tax Assessments, 1786.

Thomas, had been a ship carpenter in Oxford as early as 1714.

The ten artisans who lived in Easton, on the other hand, formed a more diverse group—not all as well established in the community, with a greater variety of trades, and producing wares more geared to an urban clientele. Silversmith Joseph Bruff and hatter John Bennett had lived at the courthouse site since before the Revolution, but both had died by 1786; their land was held by heirs. Bennett's estate was administered by James Seth, who had married Bennett's widow and was himself a hatter. John Dickinson IV, scion of a prominent Talbot family and distant kin of the Pennsylvania author of "Letters from a Farmer," also made hats for county residents. John Hopkins, whose extended family owned many acres adjoining Easton, worked as a carpenter and wheelwright, and Solomon Corner, Jr., was a joiner as were several of his kinsmen, although his brother Nicholas was an innkeeper in town. Tailor John Heron, cabinetmakers Tristam Needles and Thomas Wickersham, shoemakers Charles Pickering, Jr., and William Blake, and saddler Samuel Stevens completed the group. Wickersham, and perhaps Bennett, were newcomers to Talbot and Heron's roots in the county were shallow.

The association between urban places and the workshops of craftsmen continued as the towns developed. The surviving portion of the 1798 tax assessment covers only Easton property; the fifty lot owners included at least fifteen mechanics, while a minimum of eight more occupied rented housing. By 1804 nearly fifty craftsmen or their heirs owned property in or near Easton, eleven resided in St. Michael's, ten at Trappe, five at Hole in the Wall, and four in Oxford. The Oxford lot owners included two shoemakers, a blacksmith, and a cabinetmaker. Two shoemakers, two carpenters, and a blacksmith held land at Hole in the Wall, and Trappe land belonged to six carpenters, two weavers, a blacksmith, and a shoemaker. The growing maritime community of St. Michael's numbered four carpenters and four ship carpenters among its property owners, as well as a shoemaker, a rigger, and a silversmith. Traditional rural craftsmen, like shoemakers, blacksmiths, and carpenters, gathered in Easton too, but the town also claimed the rest of the silversmiths, the watchmakers, the coach- and carriagemakers, most of the tailors, the hatters, and most of the cabinetmakers. Ranks of urban craftsmen grow larger with the addition of renters to those owning property. Both leases and deeds turned over rapidly, but whenever the game of musical lots is stopped, mechanics made up a substantial portion of town dwellers.[22]

While the clustering of artisans in the nascent urban centers represented one postwar development, changes in the nature of apprenticeship represented a second contrast between the colonial and postwar experiences of Talbot's craft workers. Before the end of the eighteenth century, the institution of apprenticeship served a dual function. On the one hand, it provided shelter, food, and perhaps education within a surrogate family for (mainly) orphaned children lacking kin able to care for them; on the other hand, it supplied training in a useful skill that would enable children without an inheritance of real property to support themselves as independent adults. The judges of the orphans' court oversaw the placement of orphans with masters who would provide care and training and recorded the contracts governing such placement in the court records. Private indentures arranged craft training for children who were not orphans, but many contracts were not recorded and do not survive; other such apprenticeships may have been negotiated informally.

Between the years 1690 and 1760, the justices bound out nearly four hundred children for maintenance and training. For girls, who numbered 150 and accounted for 40 percent of the children, the court never specified training other than in the skills of housewifery, primarily sewing and spinning. Of the boys who were bound, the indentures of two-thirds provided for education in a skilled craft or trade, while one-

[22]Artisans did not desert the countryside, however. The 1804 list of property owners includes many scattered on rural sites throughout the county. For the most part, rural craftsmen continued almost exclusively to practice the basic crafts that had served the needs of county residents for over a century: carpentry, blacksmithing, coopering, weaving, and shoemaking.

Table 2. Indentures of Talbot County boys, 1690–1793

Training	1690–1759	1760–93
Craft skill	67%	37%
Noncraft	33%	
Farming & planting		49%
Maritime		1%
Professional		1%
None required		12%
Total	100%	100%
Craft skill		
Woodwork	42%	18%
Leatherwork	36%	48%
Tailor	7%	3%
Weaver	6%	18%
Blacksmith	4%	9%
Hatter	0%	3%
Bricklayer	4%	0%
Millwright	1%	0%
Total	100%	99%

SOURCE: Talbot County Court Records, 1690–1793, Maryland State Archives, Annapolis.

third received no training (see table 2). The latter group in the early years generally found themselves bound to members of the elite and likely worked along with indentured servants and slaves as field laborers. By the 1740s bastards accounted for most of those prepared only for agricultural work, and they typically went into the households of small planters.[23]

Changes occurred as well within the group bound to craftsmen. Overall, woodworking apprenticeships took 42 percent of the boys, leatherworking accounted for 36 percent, and tailoring and weaving for 13 percent. Most woodworking apprenticeships specified carpentry or cooperage, while shoemaking claimed most of the leatherworkers and accounted for the largest single group of boys. Of the remaining youths, six were placed with blacksmiths, five with bricklayers, and two with millwrights.

Over the course of the colonial period, a trend developed of assigning children to be trained in craft skills by planters

[23] Analysis drawn from Russo, "Free Workers," pp. 96–110.

rather than artisans. This movement was most pronounced for the crafts being incorporated into plantation households—cooperage and shoemaking primarily, carpentry, weaving, and tailoring to a lesser degree. Only practicing craftsmen undertook the training of smiths, bricklayers, and millwrights. Among the woodworkers, masters divided evenly between planters and artisans, but planters provided training only as carpenters, coopers, or sawyers; craftsmen trained wheelwrights, ship carpenters, and chairmakers. Before 1720 all children to be educated as tailors and weavers were bound to artisans, but after that date half received their training from planters. The trend toward plantation, rather than craft shop, training reveals itself most clearly with shoemaking apprentices. Before 1720 planters and artisans shared responsibility for preparation equally; after 1720 all but two of the twenty-five apprentices entered the households of planters for their training.

In the years between 1760 and 1793, when the apprenticeship law was revised, ninety boys came before the court to be placed in homes. The justices specified craft training for just slightly more than one-third of the children, reversing the percentages of the pre-1760 period. Fifty percent could expect no training other than in farming and planting. For 12 percent, the court did not require even that much education; the indentures mentioned no work-related training at all. Three of the ninety were black and two were bastards; all five belonged to the unskilled labor group. Among the children placed for craft training, fifteen were to learn shoemaking, six weaving, five carpentry, three blacksmithing, and one each were to become a cooper, hatter, tailor, and tanner. Masters who took apprentices as blacksmiths were themselves smiths or kinsmen of smiths. Richard Mansfield worked as a house carpenter; the other masters contracting to provide carpentry training were at the least related to carpenters who could have supplied training for the children their kinsmen bound. Thomas McKeel, who took an apprentice as a cooper, was himself a cooper, just as James Mattison and Samuel Swan were qualified by their own skills to train their apprentices as hatter and tailor respectively. Neither the tanner nor the masters taking in weavers, however, and only two of the fif-

133

teen accepting shoemaking apprentices were themselves craftsmen or kinsmen of artisans.[24] Traditional rural crafts thus continued to claim most of the children, and their masters continued to represent a mix of mechanics and planters.

With the enactment in 1793 of the "Act for the better regulation of apprentices," however, an effective cleavage occurred between the two functions of the colonial institution.[25] Responsibility for care and maintenance of orphaned or poor children was carried out independently of the need to train craftsmen and supply master mechanics with apprentice workers. The statute empowered the justices of the orphans' court to bind out as apprentices all poor, illegitimate, or orphaned children to some "manufacturer, mechanic, mariner, handicraftsman, or other person" to teach the children "some useful art or trade." The act authorized the trustees of the poor to make comparable arrangements for any child residing in the county's poorhouse. Finally, the legislation regularized the informal contracts made between masters and parents by permitting "any father [to] bind out his child as an apprentice, on reasonable terms," and requiring that a written indenture ratifying the agreement be drawn up and recorded with the registrar of the orphans' court, subject to a fine of £3 for failure to do so. With responsibility for arranging apprenticeships entrusted to three agents—justices, trustees, and fathers—and with the requirement that the indenture agreements be incorporated into the court records, both the formal and informal arrangements of the years before 1793 should be captured in the indentures volumes.[26]

Those volumes dramatically confirm the operation of a new order, but reveal its implementation to have taken a different course than might be expected merely from reading the statute. In the first two decades after enactment of the new law, indentures were recorded for 465 children, 429 of whom

---

[24] Talbot County Civil Court Judgments, 1760–93.

[25] Kilty, ed., *Laws of Maryland*, vol. 2, 1793, chap. 45.

[26] The following discussion of post-1793 apprenticeships is based upon contracts recorded in Talbot County Indentures, 1794–1804, 1804–12, and 1812–17.

were boys.[27] But of the latter number, only 57, or just 13 percent of the total, were placed with a master through the agency of either the justices or the trustees, and only 6 of those 57 children were placed with any of the groups enumerated by the law as suitable masters. The remaining 51 (89 percent) the justices and trustees bound with the requirement that they be taught farming, to be a waiter or servant, "to labor in the cultivation of the earth," or no skill at all. Arrangements for the other 372 boys were sanctioned either solely by parents or, in 308 cases, by the child himself, acting on his own or with the consent of a parent. The elaborate provisions outlined in the act for the maintenance of orphaned or poor children went largely unused, then, in Talbot. Rather, the system was taken over by children old enough to choose a guardian, which could be done at age fourteen, largely to provide themselves with training in a craft.

Table 3 outlines the training received by the children whose indentures were recorded between 1794 and 1813. Nineteen percent of the boys learned only agricultural or domestic skills or none at all, 5 percent of the apprentices entered professional or white collar fields, 3 percent went into maritime related work, and 1 percent into trades, while 71 percent agreed to indentures that would train them in a craft skill. Boys bound out to unskilled work averaged just under nine years of age, a figure that varied by little more than a year at most whether the children were orphaned, poor, or illegitimate, white or black. Young children, for whom maintenance was the most important consideration, were placed in farming households where their labor would be of some immediate use, thus partially offsetting the costs of their support. The average age of youths apprenticed to skilled trades and crafts, on the other hand, was fifteen years, with only sixteen children (just 5 percent) ten or younger. For older children, the

[27] Girls accounted for only 8 percent of the children bound out by any of the empowered parties. The proportion of girls included in the apprenticeship process had been declining over the course of the eighteenth century. By the end of the century, families were expressing a clear determination to keep orphaned female relatives from being placed in the homes of strangers. Only girls from households on the social and economic margins of society came before the court to be bound out.

Table 3.   Talbot County indentures, 1794–1813

Training	Total	%	White	Black
Boys				
None	10	2	3	7
Waiter/servant	3	1	0	3
Farming/planting	70	16	49	21
Professional	23	5	23	0
Maritime	14	3	14	0
Trades	3	1	3	0
Uncertain	1	*	1	0
Crafts	305	71	303	2
Total	429	99	396	33
Girls				
Housewifery	35	97		
Craft	1	3		
Total	36	100		

SOURCE: Talbot County Indentures, 1794–1813, Maryland State Archives, Annapolis.

*Figure less than .5.

training function of apprenticeship became the primary motivation for placement.

Indicative of that development, a final pronounced change occurred. The trend before enactment of the law had been away from apprenticeship to practicing craftsmen except in the most skilled trades. After passage of the 1793 act, *all* masters who signed indenture agreements to provide craft training were themselves men who earned their living from that skill. With the bond between master and apprentice forcefully reestablished within the art and mystery of the craft, who engaged apprentices during these two decades? Table 4 presents the distribution of apprentices for the period in question and confirms the changes that had been taking place in the craft structure of the county as well as the continuities that extended back through the colonial period. Shoemakers continued to account for the largest single group of apprentices, just as shoemaking had always been the largest craft represented regardless of who provided the training. Collectively, woodworkers indentured the largest number of children, as they always had. The skills of carpenters, house carpenters, and

Table 4.   Talbot County craft indentures, 1794–1813

Craft training	Total	%	Male	Female	White	Black
Woodworkers						
Carpenters	7	2	7	0	7	0
Carpenters & joiners	20	7	20	0	20	0
Sawyer	1	*	1	0	1	0
Wheelwrights	3	1	3	0	3	0
Coachmakers	14	5	14	0	14	0
Cabinetmakers	23	8	23	0	23	0
House carpenters	19	6	19	0	19	0
House carpenters & joiners	37	12	37	0	36	1
	124	41	124	0	123	1
Clothworkers						
Tailors	33	11	33	0	33	0
Weaver	1	*	0	1	1	0
Hatters	21	7	21	0	20	1
	55	18	54	1	54	1
Leatherworkers						
Shoemakers	57	19	57	0	57	0
Tanners	11	4	11	0	11	0
Saddlers	5	2	5	0	5	0
	73	25	73	0	73	0
Metalworkers						
Blacksmiths	18	6	18	0	18	0
Gold & silversmiths	3	1	3	0	3	0
Coppersmith	1	*	1	0	1	0
Clock & watchmakers	4	1	4	0	4	0
Pewterers	1	*	1	0	1	0
	27	8	27	0	27	0
Shipbuilders						
Ship carpenters	15	5	15	0	15	0
Riggers	2	1	2	0	2	0
	17	6	17	0	17	0
Builders						
Bricklayers & makers	2	1	2	0	2	0
Plasterers	5	2	5	0	5	0
Housepainter & glazier	1	*	1	0	1	0
Mason	1	*	1	0	1	0
	9	3	9	0	9	0
Total	305	101	304	1	303	2

SOURCE: Talbot County Indentures, 1794–1813, Maryland State Archives, Annapolis.
*Figure less than .5.

joiners overlapped, giving that enlarged craft a group of 83 apprentices in all. Tailors continued to be a major source of apprenticeship training, as did blacksmiths.

The weakened position of some traditional crafts clearly reveals itself in the indentures, however. Just one weaver took an apprentice, and she was Fanny Pasterfield, the sole girl of thirty-six to receive training other than in the traditional skills of housewifery. Only one sawyer took an apprentice, and that child was a one-year-old bastard; placement of such a young child from the fringes of society indicates the marginality by the second decade of the nineteenth century of sawing as a distinctive craft.

The indentures also point to crafts experiencing growth, as well as marking those in decline. Wheelwrights took only three apprentices, but carriage- and coachmakers acquired fourteen; the transportation trade was evolving in their direction, and most makers of wheeled vehicles began to adopt those designations. The market for finely crafted furniture encouraged cabinetmakers to take on twenty-three youths, while hatters—whose craft had vanished by the 1720s—returned to indenture twenty-one boys. The market for other luxury trades is attested to by the apprenticing of four clock- and watchmakers, one coppersmith and one pewterer, and three gold- and silversmiths. In all, the dozen trades of the previous two centuries doubled in these twenty years, training during that time nearly as many youths as had been educated in the preceding two hundred, not only in the traditional rural crafts but also in those catering to the growing urban population and others who aspired to a more cosmopolitan standard of living.

One final assessment of change and continuity compares the relative wealth of Talbot's mechanics for the post-Revolutionary period with the position of the county's craftsmen during the colonial period. Broadly speaking, before the Revolution, craftsmen as a group enjoyed a level of wealth slightly higher than that of colonists engaged solely in agriculture, but the comparison can be made only for the decedents in both groups whose estates went through probate.[28] For the

[28] Russo, "Free Workers," pp. 408–24.

Table 5.   Property ownership in Talbot County, 1783–1804

Percentage	1783	1786	1798	1804
Artisans*				
With personalty	10	18	11	13
With real property	13	18	13	18
Artisans				
Owning land	45	52	58	64
Owning slaves	43	n/a	36	32
All taxpayers				
Owning land	45	53	53	47
Owning slaves	42	n/a	47	39
Median wealth	n/a	£89	£29†	£24†
Artisans below median	n/a	67	60	50
Mean wealth				
Artisans	£118	£120	£215	£224
All taxpayers	£236	£257	£474	£448

SOURCE: Talbot County Tax Assessments, Maryland State Archives, Annapolis.

NOTE: Tax records for 1783 and 1786 give total wealth—personal and real property for each taxpayer; 1798 and 1804 assessments are divided into separate real and personal property lists. I have combined the means for each list to calculate an overall mean for those two years. All values are deflated.

*In total population.

†Real property is not included in determining the median value.

post-Revolutionary period, tax lists permit direct comparison within the living population (see table 5).

In 1783 craftsmen accounted for just over 10 percent of the 1,672 heads of household, paupers, and single men assessed in that year.[29] They represented only 5 percent of all pauper households but nearly 8 percent of those headed by men. Artisans may have comprised almost 15 percent of the category of single men, who paid only 15 shillings in taxes.[30] Of the largest group, property-owning taxpayers, mechanics made up 10 percent. Nearly half owned either land or slaves or both; 45 percent held real property and 43 percent possessed

[29] Talbot County Tax Assessments, 1783. Nonresidents accounted for 194 assessments, or 11.6 percent of the total.

[30] The singular lack of originality in naming makes it difficult to select the right man as the craftsman from among three or four with the same name.

slaves. Artisans matched the population at large in both respects; 45 percent of all households owned at least some acreage and 42 percent owned slaves. Both slaves and land contributed less to their wealth than was true for planters, however. Nearly 33 percent of the artisans owned small town or "suburban" lots of land, less than ten acres in size, while only 13 percent of all landowners held tracts that small. Only 15 percent of the slaveowning craftsmen possessed ten or more slaves, while 20 percent of all slave owners held ten or more.[31]

Overall, the distribution of wealth for craftsmen was less skewed than that of the total population; smaller percentages existed both of paupers and of the very wealthy. The numbers support the logical assumption that for those without the resources of either land or bound labor, possession of a skill enabled one to avoid destitution with more success than did lack of any skill. By the same token, skill alone was not sufficient to bring great wealth in an economy still largely tied to production of agricultural staples. The artisans in the top 10 percent of wealth ownership were men from well-established county families, heirs of both land and slaves, who probably derived much of their wealth and income from agricultural pursuits.

By 1786 mechanics accounted for 18 percent both of all taxpayers and of those owning real estate. Two-thirds, however, had estates valued at less than the median wealth,[32] and only one, cabinetmaker Tristam Bowdle with an estate of £649, appeared in the top decile of wealth holders. The mean value of all estates was £257; only eight craftsmen ranked higher on the list, and they represented just 8 percent—not 18—of those taxpayers. Carpenter John Cockey with £10, tailor James Roper with £28, or blacksmith Richard McMahan with £70 typified the craftsman of that year more accurately

[31] Slave ownership is an increasingly unreliable indicator of social and economic position in Talbot County, however, as Revolutionary ideology, religious conviction, and economic pressures all contributed to extensive manumission of slaves.

[32] All values are deflated to a base consisting of 1700–1709 prices, according to deflators created for the St. Mary's City Commission by P. M. G. Harris.

than did Tristam Bowdle. Mean value of wealth for mechanics in both 1783 and 1786 measured only half that of the total population. The apparent parity between craftsmen and other residents during the late colonial period had eroded by the end of the Revolution.[33]

No further comparison can be made for twelve years, until the records for 1798 permit a third opportunity to weigh the rewards of artisanal work against those of planting and farming. In that year, Talbot's artisans represented about 11 percent of those paying taxes on personal property and about 13 percent of land owners.[34] While 47 percent of all taxpayers owned slaves, only 36 percent of craftsmen possessed bound labor. As slaveowners, craftsmen averaged three fewer slaves per holding than the countywide average—5.7 slaves for artisans as opposed to 8.6 for all taxpayers. Only Perry Parrott, who by now styled himself a planter rather than a joiner, owned more than ten slaves, and he held only eleven. Thirty-six planters and farmers, on the other hand, owned more than ten slaves, with the largest owner, Edward Lloyd, having 309. Slightly higher percentages of craftsmen owned horses and cattle, animals that could be maintained on a small house lot, than did the total population, but the typical holding was much smaller—one or two horses, a few head of cattle. The horses were for riding or pulling a carriage and the cattle supplied the family with milk and meat; these were not herds of livestock raised for farmwork or for market.[35] Among owners of personal property, the county's artisans had a median value exactly half that of all taxpayers. Nearly two-thirds—a full 60 percent—of the mechanics had estates valued at less than the median for the county. Only four mechanics owned assets that placed them in the top 20 percent of wealth holders, and two

[33] Talbot County Tax Assessments, 1786.

[34] The difficulties of linking known craftsmen with specific individuals on the tax list make a precise calculation of the percentage impossible (ibid., 1798, District 2).

[35] The average holdings for craftsmen were 3.2 horses, 6.8 cows, 15.3 sheep, and 12.4 hogs; those for all taxpayers were 5.3 horses, 13.2 head of cattle, 21.9 sheep, and 16.4 hogs. The median number of horses owned by artisans was 2; of cattle, 3 head.

were men no longer active as craftsmen. Clearly, the decline in comparative position evident twelve years earlier had continued over the intervening period.

The final comparison can be made for 1804, the only year for which tax lists survive from the entire county. In that year, artisans accounted for approximately 13 percent of those assessed for personal property and for 18 percent of the owners or long-term lease holders of real property. As had been true for two decades, property holdings of craftsmen more likely consisted of half-acre town lots than of two or three hundred acres of arable land. Two-thirds of the artisans owning land in 1798 held less than fifteen acres (and most of those owned less than one acre); just under one-third worked two hundred or more acres, and no holding exceeded five hundred acres (nearly 10 percent of all owners held 500 acres or more). In 1804 almost the same percentage—60 rather than 67—owned less than 15 acres, while another 9 percent owned both town property and rural land. Craftsmen held an average of 98 acres, with a mean value of £101 and improvements assessed at a mean of £70, while noncraftsmen owned an average of 250 acres, with a mean value of £266 and improvements of £107. The only large artisan landowner was ship carpenter Perry Spencer, who held 1,685 acres. For non-artisans, 15 percent owned more than 400 acres and the largest estate—that of Edward Lloyd—totaled 11,484 acres.

Craftsmen paying personal property taxes in 1804 had a mean assessed value slightly greater than the mean in 1798. In 1798 the assets of artisans amounted to only half of those of the total population, but in 1804 their worth had risen to two-thirds of the wealth of all taxpayers. Median wealth for all had dropped slightly, but the relative position of mechanics had improved with regard to this measure also, for their median wealth equaled that of the population at large rather than falling below it, as had been the case a dozen years earlier. As a group their wealth had increased somewhat since 1798, with an even greater improvement in comparison to the population as a whole. Ship carpenter Perry Spencer ranked highest in personal wealth as in landholding, with assets valued at £386; no artisan placed among the 4 percent of all taxpayers with possessions totaling more than that amount.

In the broad period between 1783 and 1804, then, artisans held their own or slightly improved their position in comparison with noncraftsmen, but the improvement built upon a diminished base. The parity or above-average wealth that they had enjoyed before the Revolution had been lost by the end of the war. The change should not be attributed to the ravages of war, however, or to declining prospects in the postwar economy. Tax assessors used measurements of wealth weighted toward the predominantly agricultural economy— ownership of land, slaves, and livestock. As craftsmen became increasingly town-based in the postwar period, they necessarily owned less land, few slaves, and little livestock. Their town lots did not have the extensive outbuildings that were part of working plantations and farms. They often owned carriages and furnished their homes well, but such assets were minor components of the property enumerated by assessors. The result was a divergence in wealth between craftsmen as a whole and noncraft residents, and also between craftsmen who inherited or invested in rural property and those who did not. Artisans owning more than one hundred acres of land in 1804, for example, generally belonged to families resident in the county for over a hundred years and followed the more lucrative trades. They were ship carpenters, blacksmiths, tanners, and cabinetmakers rather than tailors or sawyers. Thus there were some continuities through this period as family connections, land ownership, and choice of trade continued profoundly to influence wealth, and some changes, as craftsmanship became increasingly associated with an urban work environment.

Within this context, however, continuity prevailed in the social and civic world. Craftsmen continued to participate in society in roles largely determined by their wealth, as had always been true. No artisan held office in the state legislature; the few wealthy enough to qualify were easily outranked by many wealthier planters and merchants. Nor, for the same reason, did any serve as justices of the peace or of the orphans' court. During the entire colonial period, less than a half-dozen artisans had filled these positions. But in the post-Revolutionary period, as before, mechanics did fill other civic offices. Hatter Edward Cox served a term as sheriff, house carpenter Levin Stevens and hatter John Martin Needles held the office of collector of the tax, cabinetmaker James Neall was one of the trustees of the poor, ship carpenter Perry Spencer held an appointment as one of the commissioners to establish new election districts, three artisans were among the commissioners appointed to erect the town of St. Michael's, and saddler William Meluy was one of five men authorized to sell shares in Talbot for the Union Bank of Maryland. Mechanics sat on grand and petit juries, appraised estates, stood surety for bonds, witnessed wills, and acted as executors and administrators for kin and for friends, as they had for over a hundred years.

Artisans had never formed a self-conscious, distinctive group within Talbot society during the colonial period, a situation that the Revolution did not change. When the town of Easton held a parade as part of its commemoration of George Washington's birthday in the year following his death, men who were not members of militia companies marched "two by two," not by crafts as was the custom in urban parades.[36] Again, while craftsmen did join the Methodist church, the new denomination already enjoyed widespread support on Maryland's Eastern Shore, and those artisans who belonged worshipped with planters and farmers in an occupationally diverse congregation. House carpenter William Alexander and tailors James Mullikin and James Chaplain acquired land near Trappe as trustees for a Methodist chapel, but they did so in conjunction with a kinsman of Chaplain's and five other men, all of whom were planters.[37] Trustees of Methodist property in Easton in 1790 included shoemaker John Blake and carpenters William Martin and James Vansandt but also innkeeper Alexander McCallum, physician Moses Allen, and merchant George Miller.[38] Similarly, to the extent that mem-

[36] Dickson J. Preston, *Talbot County: A History* (Centreville, Md., 1983), p. 150.

[37] Talbot County Land Records, RS 21/393, Apr. 1784.

[38] Ibid., BS 24/187, Sept. 1790.

bers of Easton's two Freemasons' Lodges can be identified, they were more likely to be drawn from the town's mercantile and professional groups than from craftsmen working there. Militia companies mixed men of all occupations; none was exclusively the domain of the county's artisans. Nor did volunteer fire companies provide the camaraderie and social cohesion that they afforded mechanics in large urban centers. Only Easton may have had a volunteer fire company, as the legislature in 1803 authorized purchase of a fire engine and construction of pumps.[39] But the managers of the lottery to raise the necessary funds consisted of two merchants, a newspaper editor, an attorney, and the court clerk. If a volunteer company was actually formed, it is unlikely that it functioned as a vehicle for artisanal self-consciousness. Nor, finally, did the Republican party serve as a means of expressing an "artisan republicanism." In the early 1800s Talbot was a Republican county, and leadership of the party rested firmly in the hands of the county's elite, beginning with its wealthiest resident, Edward Lloyd.[40] Artisan residents of Talbot participated actively in the affairs of the Republican party, but they shared control and membership in the party with planters, merchants, and professional men. Saddler William Meluy and ship carpenter Perry Spencer, for example, served on the committee to plan a jubilee celebrating acquisition of Louisiana, but they worked with merchant Thomas Coward, physician Samuel Dickinson, and planters Jacob Gibson, Samuel Stevens, Jr., John Turner, Jr., and James Nabb.[41]

Only one hint remains of a sense of community among any of the county's craft groups. The following announcement appeared in the *Maryland Herald and Eastern Shore Intelligencer* in August 1794:

[39] Kilty, ed., *Laws of Maryland*, vol. 3, 1803, chap. 28.

[40] See Whitman H. Ridgway, *Community Leadership in Maryland, 1790–1840: A Comparative Analysis of Power in Society* (Chapel Hill, 1979), for analysis of political parties and their leadership in Talbot. Ridgway concluded that in a traditional community such as Talbot, the oligarchy that ruled during the colonial period retained its control of local politics and officeholding throughout the first party system.

[41] *Republican Star,* May 8, 1804.

To all the ARCHITECTS and HOUSE CARPENTERS of the EASTERN SHORE OF MARYLAND

By the request of a number of Fellow-Mechanics, the Subscribers are authorized to give this public notice, that a meeting will be held at Easton, on Saturday the 30th day of August next, for the purpose of forming a society to adopt such rules and regulations as may be thought necessary for the better governing of that part of the Building Branch, and somewhat similar to those now existing in different parts of America.

> CORNELIUS WEST
> JAMES BENSON
> JAMES VANSANDT[42]

No evidence survives, however, to indicate that the meeting actually took place, how many people from what parts of the Eastern Shore might have attended, or what actions resulted from it.

James Vansandt advertised for apprentices in 1796 but had left Easton by 1801 to try his chances in the developing town of Washington, D.C.[43] West, who received the contract to construct a new courthouse in Easton in the early 1790s, needed a special act of the assembly in 1794 to help defray his costs. He appealed for a supplement to the original payment on the grounds that the price of materials, supplies, and labor had suddenly risen while construction was underway, leaving him with nothing for his own labor and expenses over three years once he had paid for materials and workmen.[44] West appears on the 1798 tax assessment as a pauper and not at all on the 1804 list.[45]

James Benson's career is the most difficult of the three to trace, for he belonged to the fourth generation of his family to live in the county. The James Benson who signed the ad-

[42] *Maryland Herald and Eastern Shore Intelligencer,* Aug. 26, 1794.

[43] Ibid., Apr. 5, 1796, and Talbot County Land Records, JL 29/120, June 1801. James Vansandt, "of the city of Washington," appointed shoemaker John Blake as his attorney in Talbot.

[44] Kilty, ed., *Laws of Maryland,* vol. 2, Nov. 1794, chap. 63.

[45] Talbot County Tax Assessments, 1798, District 2.

vertisement was assuredly the great-grandson of the physician, also named James Benson, who settled in Talbot in 1674. James's younger son Perry began his career as a carpenter and was one of the colonial artisans to serve in the lower house and as a justice of the peace.[46] Perry's only son James may also have been a carpenter for he contracted in the 1760s with the vestry of St. Michael's Parish to build an addition to the church and to supply the pews. James, too, served in the lower house, during the Revolutionary War, and was commissioned as a justice of the peace, although he did not qualify himself to take office.[47] His son James was probably the carpenter who joined with West and Vansandt in the call for an organization of carpenters, but whether he was the James Benson still in the county in 1804 it is impossible to say for that man may have been his cousin James, a shoemaker. Although James Benson was the most likely of the three signers to have persisted in Talbot, the subsequent careers of at least two of the three strongly suggest that nothing substantive came of their call for a meeting of all house carpenters and architects.

Continuity predominated in one other area as well. Neither the colonial period nor the post-Revolutionary years offer any evidence of organization of craftwork along the lines of protoindustrialization. During the colonial years, free artisans worked either as independent craftsmen, owning both their tools and workplaces, or occasionally as the individual employee of the noncraft owner of a specialized workplace.[48] While many divided their time between craft work and ag-

[46] Edward C. Papenfuse et al., eds., *A Biographical Dictionary of the Maryland Legislature, 1635–1789*, 2 vols. (Baltimore 1979–85), 1:131.

[47] Ibid., pp. 130–31.

[48] The two most prevalent fields in which such arrangements were likely to occur were blacksmithing and tanning. Both crafts utilized workplaces that represented a relatively substantial and immovable capital investment. If the work site became the property, through inheritance or purchase, of an owner not himself a trained artisan, economic prudence dictated that he rent the premises to a craftsman or hire one to work it for him. Christine Daniels, "The Town Smith and the Country Smith: Rural Craftsmen in Eighteenth-Century Maryland," unpublished paper, 1989, provides an illuminating analysis of this process.

ricultural routines, nothing in the surviving records suggests that their craftwork was organized by or carried out under the direction of an entrepreneur who supplied raw materials or marketed the finished product.[49] Shoemakers, for example, may have received credit in store accounts for finished shoes, but the debit side of their ledger records no charges for leather or other raw materials. The merchant simply accepted shoes, for which he could easily find customers, as payment for purchases of cloth, utensils, gloves, soap, sugar, rum, or any of the other myriad of goods that passed over his counter to all of his clientele.

The closest that any relationship came to protoindustrialization was the one that existed between Easton merchant Jesse Richardson and Easton silversmith James Bowdle in the early 1790s. Richardson's ledger debited Bowdle's account for the cost of gilt and plated buttons, while crediting it for "Federal buttons." Presumably Bowdle purchased plain buttons, embellished them with a design—perhaps an eagle—that made them "Federal buttons," and returned them to Richardson for credit against his account. Richardson was then free to sell the decorated buttons to his other customers.

---

[49]James A. Henretta argues for the existence of a *Kaufsystem* in late colonial Maryland using evidence presented in an essay by Lois Green Carr tracing economic development in Somerset County. In this instance, I believe that Henretta misinterprets Carr's findings. The evolution of regional specialization involving, among other elements, growth of crafts and home industries does not in itself demonstrate the presence of protoindustrialization. Chesapeake artisans were not obligated to sell their products at prices set by local merchants, with additional costs for commissions and excess profits. Rather they produced custom work for sale to, or exchange with, their neighbors at mutually agreed upon terms. They conformed, in fact, to the second of three rural manufacturing systems identified by Jacob M. Price, which he called the "independent rural artisan system," in which rural craftsmen owned both their tools and raw materials, and worked for a local market. See Henretta, "The War for Independence and American Economic Development," in Ronald Hoffman et al., eds., *The Economy of Early America: The Revolutionary Period, 1763–1790* (Charlottesville, Va., 1988), pp. 52, 82, and Jacob M. Price, "Reflections on the Economy of Revolutionary America," ibid., pp. 303–22. Carr's essay, "Diversification in the Colonial Chesapeake: Somerset County, Maryland, in Comparative Perspective," is included in Lois Green Carr et al., eds., *Colonial Chesapeake Society*, pp. 342–88.

Although there were several silversmiths at work in Easton during the early 1790s, Richardson had no similar arrangement with any of them; only Bowdle took plain buttons and returned decorated ones. Nothing in the account book suggests a relationship other than a mutually beneficial one between two independent businessmen, each of whom was free to look elsewhere, if he chose, for a partner.[50]

The one change in working relationships that does appear to have occurred after the Revolution was an increase in the scale of operations in the workplace. Colonial craftsmen worked alone for the most part, perhaps with the assistance of an occasional apprentice, a hired helper, or—more rarely—a slave. By the 1790s, however, a number of artisans began to take on several apprentices at one time. Cabinetmaker Joseph Neall apprenticed six boys between 1795 and his death in 1800; his younger brother James, also a cabinetmaker, assumed the indentures of three of the boys in 1800 and added ten more during the decade. Between 1802 and 1814 Neall never had fewer than 5 apprentices in his household (assuming that each served the full term of his indenture) and in 1804 and 1805 was assisted by eight youths; tailor Thomas Ball bound five apprentices, all in 1797; house carpenter and joiner Tristam Bowdle acquired eight youths between 1797 and 1807; hatter Thomas Harper, who had himself served a formal apprenticeship, indentured five boys between 1800 and 1804; and shoemaker George Sewall took on six apprentices between 1804 and 1813, to cite just a few examples.[51]

In addition to expansion through increased use of apprentices, a hierarchy of master and journeymen appears for the first time. By the early 1800s Talbot craftsmen had two newspapers in which to advertise their services, giving them a venue for attracting customers beyond personal acquaintance and word-of-mouth knowledge. Artisans appealed to customers by stressing their familiarity with current fashions, their ability to offer prices competitive with those in the Baltimore market, and the adequacy of their work force. When Robert

[50] Chancery Papers Exhibits, Jesse Richardson Ledger B, 1550, fol.63, Md. St. Arch.

[51] Talbot County Indentures, 1804–12 and 1812–17.

Spedden joined with his nephew Levin in the coachmaking trade, they advertised that they would "have a sufficiency of workmen" to execute all the orders that they received. William Patton, opening his shoe- and bootmaking business, announced that he had "supplied himself with workmen from Baltimore." James Ballentine informed readers that he was "now provided with assistance to enable him to transact business in the profession of house plastering." William Bromwell's selling point for his saddle- and harnessmaking shop stressed his supply of "competent workmen."[52] Levin Spedden had indentured just one apprentice prior to his advertisement. William Patton had taken on five apprentices in 1803, before he placed his advertisement, but they were all local boys, not "workmen from Baltimore."[53] Colonial craftsman rarely employed journeymen, but if the advertisers in the *Star* accurately described their establishments, the employment of journeymen was another new feature of post-Revolutionary craft operations.

The Revolution did not, then, cause the craftsmen working in Talbot to come together as a self-conscious interest group within society, but in what ways did the "hot sun of revolution" affect those county residents who earned their living primarily as artisans?[54] The most profound changes that occurred within the working environment of Talbot's craftsmen related to the development of a constellation of urban centers that became focal points for craftwork. The initial growth of long-lasting towns may have been stimulated by the Revolution, although it remains difficult to trace a direct link. Records of the state government do not suggest that Talbot was a major supply center during the war for any materiel other than tobacco, grains, and livestock. The goods collected in the county to provision troops generally left Talbot by water, probably utilizing existing shipping, although transport needs may have contributed somewhat to an increase in ship-

[52] *Republican Star,* Jan 4, Jan. 18, Aug. 16, and Dec. 27, 1803.

[53] Talbot County Indentures, 1794–1804.

[54] Jameson, *American Revolution as a Social Movement,* p. 32.

building. Chestertown and Head of Elk served as supply centers and, to a more limited degree, manufacturing centers on the Eastern Shore, but Baltimore—rather than the Eastern Shore communities—played the major role in equipping troops with clothing, ammunition, weapons, and other necessities, both through indigenous manufacturing and through the efforts of its merchant community.[55]

Talbot Court House at the end of the war differed little from the collection of court building and taverns that had characterized its existence for fifty years. But three years after the end of the war, the legislature, responding to a petition from "sundry inhabitants of Talbot county" stating that "the village at the court-house of the said county hath considerably increased in number of houses and inhabitants, [and] that the chief trade of the county is carried on there," for which reason they "prayed that the said village may be erected into a town," formally created a town around the courthouse.[56] With its designation as the site of the general court of the Eastern Shore, Easton began to grow in size and form a self-sustaining economy. The development of Easton thus flowed directly out of the War for Independence. The newly created state government, not provincial authorities, determined to designate an auxiliary administrative center for the Eastern Shore and thus supplied the stimulus for its growth.

Independence from imperial control of both political and economic life manifested itself in a variety of other ways—a more multifaceted involvement in local economies by American merchants, creation of local financial institutions, improvements in transportation and communication to stimulate commerce, and the growth of associations to remedy social ills and improve public welfare, among others. Domestic mercantile firms moved into the Eastern Shore as suppliers of merchandise for local shopkeepers. For Talbot,

[55] Journal of the Convention, Journals and Correspondence of the Council of Safety, and Journals and Correspondence of the State Council, in William H. Browne et al., eds., *Archives of Maryland*, 72 vols. (Baltimore, 1883–1972), vols. 11–12, 16, 21, 43, 45, 47–48; Browne, *Baltimore in the Nation*, pp. 10–11.

[56] Kilty, ed., *Laws of Maryland*, vol. 2, Nov. 1785, chap. 32.

this movement primarily took the form of links between Baltimore and Easton merchants, although the firm of Nicols, Chamberlaine, and Kerr was affiliated for a time with Wallace, Johnson, and Muir in Annapolis.[57] As noted earlier, Easton became the first town on the Eastern Shore to be served by banking facilities when the Farmers' Bank opened in 1805. Citizens' petitions asked the state legislature and county court for new and improved roads; for example, requesting enabling legislation for the creation of a road from Easton, "more likely to flourish if there was a convenient road from said town to navigable water . . . at the point of land called Cow Landing" (Easton Point), or appealing to the court for a "road through neighboring lands to places of public worship, mills, market towns, public ferries, and the Court House."[58] By the fall of 1803 two packets operated weekly between Easton Point and Baltimore for shipment of grain and other cargoes and transport of passengers.[59] The *Maryland Herald* and the *Republican Star* provided a forum not only for arguing the Federalist and Republican sides of political issues but also for local businesses to compete for customers and enlarge their markets. Civic improvements included the establishment in 1790 of a town market, formation of the Easton Academy in 1799, creation in 1807 of a board of agriculture, and incorporation of the Charitable Society of Easton in 1813.[60] Of the fourteen manufacturing companies chartered in the state between 1808 and 1816, one, the Manufacturing Company of the Eastern Shore, intended the manufacture of woolen, linen, and cotton cloth in Talbot.[61]

Within this more vigorous and independent economic climate, local mechanics found an expanded arena for enterprise. But it was an arena with strong continuities to the

[57] Papenfuse, *In Pursuit of Profit*, pp. 179, 180, 216–18.

[58] Kilty, ed., *Laws of Maryland*, vol. 2, Nov. 1787, chap. 24, and Talbot County Civil Court Judgments, June 1794.

[59] *Republican Star,* Sept. 13, 17, 1803.

[60] Kilty, ed., *Laws of Maryland*, vol. 2, Nov. 1790, chap. 14, Nov. 1799, chap. 56, vol. 4, Nov. 1807, chap. 169, and vol. 5, Dec. 1813, chap. 143.

[61] Ibid., vol. 4, Nov. 1811, chap. 118.

prewar period as well as changes reflecting postwar developments. The core traditional crafts continued to dominate in numbers of participants, pre-Revolutionary trends weakening the competitive position of independent coopers, sawyers, and weavers persisted into the early national period, and population growth, greater concentration of markets, and the continued spread of the consumer revolution supplied an increasing number of customers for growing numbers of craftsmen catering to buyers seeking amenities rather than necessities.

The most notable feature of the post-Revolutionary period—the creation of an urban-based artisan group—remains an ambiguous one. On the one hand, it can be interpreted as an indication of the maturation of craftsmanship within a still predominantly rural economy, characterized now by a more fully formed network of mechanics, working in specialized shops with the assistance of journeymen and apprentices, advertising their wares, and supplying a wider range of goods. On the other hand, did the separation of artisans from the land make their livelihood more precarious? For every Perry Spencer, who held the most property among artisans in 1804, there were several James Parrotts, Charles Gulleys, and Benjamin Wilmotts petitioning for relief under the insolvent debtors' act.[62] Tax assessment records suggest an overall decline in wealth, and therefore social position, for the county's craftsmen in the years after the Revolution, but that may be only an artifact created by the ability to examine for the first time the living population. More intensive analysis of inventories and extended prosopographical work are required before a reliable conclusion can be reached.

Nevertheless, the mechanic working in a shop on Washington Street in Easton on a bustling market day in the early 1800s carried on his craft in an environment very different from that experienced decades earlier by his father or grandfather at work on a plantation out in the countryside. "The transforming hand of revolution" had played little direct role

---

[62] Ibid., vol. 3, Nov. 1802, chap. 97, Nov. 1803, chap. 104, and Nov. 1804, chap. 110.

in shaping the changes that had occurred. But by bringing
political independence—freedom from imperial control and
restrictions and transfer of political power to bodies wishing
to encourage economic growth—the Revolution set the stage
upon which broader economic changes, predating the political revolution and subsumed for convenience sake under the
term Industrial Revolution, operated to transform the working environment. It would be decades more, however, before
the full implications of those changes would play themselves
out in the rural plantation economy. The independent status,
and social position derived from it, of Talbot's craftsmen
would not be eroded from within by capitalist takeover of raw
materials and markets but would be gradually worn away
over the nineteenth century as external manufacturers could
produce and sell more cheaply the shoes, clothing, metal
work, and other products crafted by local artisans.

MARCUS REDIKER

A Motley Crew
of Rebels

Sailors, Slaves, and the

Coming of the

American Revolution

IN OCTOBER 1765 a mob of sailors "armed with Cutlasses and
Clubs" visited the home of Charleston merchant Henry
Laurens; "*Liberty, Liberty, & Stamp'd Paper*" was their cry.
Eighty strong and warm with drink and rage, the crowd had
come for the stamped paper Laurens was rumored to have
stored in his home. They would, as Laurens later recalled,
"admit of no '*Parleys*' no '*Palabres*'"; they "not only menaced
very loudly but now & then handled me pretty uncouthly."
Finally convinced that Laurens did not have the paper, they
left and probably dispersed across the waterfront, straggling
into the smoky taverns and bare boardinghouses, onto the
damp wharves and creaky ships. Many of the sailors would
eventually leave the city, but their influence would remain.
Their direct action, in Charleston as in Boston and New York,
led to the founding of the Sons of Liberty, destined to be one
of the leading popular organizations in the Revolutionary
movement after 1765.[1]

The arguments presented here will be developed at greater length in Peter
Linebaugh and Marcus Rediker, *The Many-Headed Hydra: The Atlantic Working Class in the Seventeenth and Eighteenth Centuries* (forthcoming). I would like
to thank Ira Berlin, Wendy Goldman, Jesse Lemisch, Peter Linebaugh, and
Alfred F. Young for their criticism of earlier drafts.

[1] Extract of a letter from Henry Laurens to J. B., Esq., Oct. 26,1765, and
Laurens to James Grant, Jan. 31, 1766, George C. Rogers, Jr., et al., eds.,

A few months later, in January 1766, Charleston was again agitated with protest. A group of slaves, some of whom perhaps had joined with the seamen in the Stamp Act crowd, assembled and cried once more for "*Liberty.*" Their action, complained Laurens, caused "vast trouble throughout the province." Authorities mobilized armed patrols who stalked the city's streets for almost two weeks. One protest had led to another in which the demand for liberty took on a different, more radical meaning.[2]

Shortly after this event, Laurens noted that Charleston's harbor was "exceedingly crouded with Ships." The seafaring people who had brought the ships to port had grown "clamorous," which, Laurens observed, "has set the Protectors of Liberty"—soon to be the Sons of Liberty—"in motion and commotion again." South Carolina Governor William Bull looked back over the events of late 1765 and early 1766 described by Laurens and blamed Charleston's turmoil on "disorderly negroes, and more disorderly sailors." Laurens and Bull thus expressed precisely the central argument of this essay: sailors and slaves created much of the "motion and commotion" of the Revolutionary era in America, much

---

The Papers of Henry Laurens, 13 vols. to date (Columbia, S.C., 1968–), 5:39–40. Laurens estimated that roughly half the mob was made up of sailors from ports other than Charleston (people, he said, who "dread no body" and certainly not himself); the other half were townspeople, some of whom were disguised with "Soot, Sailors habits, Crape Masks, slouch hats, &ca." (ibid., p. 28).

[2] Laurens to John Lewis Gervais, Jan. 29, 1766, Rogers et al., eds., *Papers of Laurens,* 5:53–54. See also Arthur Meier Schlesinger, Sr., "Political Mobs and the American Revolution, 1765–1776," *Proceedings of the American Philosophical Society* 99 (1955):244; Carl Bridenbaugh, *Cities in Revolt: Urban Life in America, 1743–1776* (New York, 1955), pp. 313–14; Philip D. Morgan, "Black Life in Eighteenth-Century Charleston," *Perspectives in American History,* n.s. 1 (1984):233; Pauline Maier, "The Charleston Mob and the Evolution of Popular Politics in Revolutionary South Carolina, 1765–1784," *Perspectives in American History* 4 (1970):176; Peter H. Wood, "'Taking Care of Business' in Revolutionary South Carolina: Republicanism and the Slave Society," in Jeffrey J. Crow and Larry E. Tise, eds., *The Southern Experience in the American Revolution* (Chapel Hill, 1978), p. 277.

of the movement toward Independence between 1765 and 1776.[3]

This of course is not to say that sailors and slaves alone made the Revolution, but rather to emphasize that it took the combined power, energy, and volatility of a welter of revolts, some of them antagonistic and mutually incompatible, to destabilize imperial civil society and hence to make possible the world's first modern colonial war for liberation. Thanks to extensive research by a new generation of early American social historians, it is now clear that the American Revolution involved revolts by artisans, farmers, merchants, slaveowners, and evangelical Christians, all of whom sought, in one way or another, to make, remake, or perpetuate society in their own image. The revolutionary activities of sailors and slaves, in contrast, have not received the scholarly attention they deserve.[4]

This essay argues that free waged laborers (sailors) and unfree, unwaged laborers (slaves) fashioned their own revolts within the Revolution, using the political divisions and turmoil of the age to make their own "declarations of independence."[5] It also suggests that the revolts of these workers, free and unfree, were connected in important ways, and that, taken together, they were much more crucial to the genesis, process, and outcome of the Revolution than is generally understood. The activities of sailors and slaves during the 1760s and 1770s helped to propel America toward Independence and thus created from below a political field of force in which

[3] Laurens to Grant, Jan. 31, 1766, Rogers et al., eds., *Papers of Laurens*, 5:60. Laurens spoke here of "Masters" of ships, but as we shall see below, the seamen they employed caused much greater commotion in every colonial port, Charleston included. William Bull quoted in Maier, "Charleston Mob," p. 176.

[4] I wish to emphasize at the outset that the sailors discussed in this article were not simply "British" or "white"; they were in fact a multiracial group that included significant (and increasing) numbers of African-Americans.

[5] Benjamin Quarles, "The Revolutionary War as a Black Declaration of Independence," in Ira Berlin and Ronald Hoffman, eds., *Slavery and Freedom in the Age of the American Revolution* (1983; reprint ed., Urbana, Ill., 1986), pp. 283–304. See also the important book by Sylvia R. Frey, *Water from the Rock: Black Resistance in a Revolutionary Age* (Princeton, 1991).

everyone, including a nascent American ruling class, was forced to operate. The impact of their actions is thus written in the register of the social history of the Revolutionary era, but not only there, for their agency is also evident in the period's intellectual history, in the development of radical, liberal, and conservative strands of thought. Finally, the experience of sailors and slaves demonstrates how the American Revolution was part of broader cycles of rebellion in the eighteenth-century Atlantic world, in which deep continuities and connections informed a huge number and variety of popular struggles.[6]

It has been known since the 1968 publication of Jesse Lemisch's pathbreaking article "Jack Tar in the Streets" that seamen were prime movers in the American Revolution, helping to secure numerous patriot victories between 1765 and 1776. Seamen led a series of militant riots against impressment between 1741 and 1776, and indeed their agency was acknowledged by both Thomas Paine (in *Common Sense*) and Thomas Jefferson (in the Declaration of Independence), both of whom listed impressment as a major grievance and a spur to colonial liberation.[7]

What has been less fully appreciated is that merchant seamen entered the Revolutionary era with a tradition of militancy well in place. Over the course of the eighteenth century they had already learned to use portside riots, mutiny, piracy, work stoppage, and desertion to assert their own objectives as

[6] My effort to treat free and unfree workers as constituents of a larger working-class history follows the lead of the late Herbert G. Gutman. This theme has been reiterated by Graham Hodges in "Blacks and Whites at Work in Colonial New York and New Jersey: An Historiographic Approach" (Paper presented at the Conference on New York Labor History, New-York Historical Society, May 1988).

[7] Jesse Lemisch, "Jack Tar in the Streets: Merchant Seamen in the Politics of Revolutionary America," *William and Mary Quarterly*, 3d ser. 25 (1968): 371–407. My emphasis on the leading role of seamen in the struggle against impressment does not deny the importance of their allies, most notably merchants whose cargo might lie on the docks for a lack of seafaring labor, and other urban workers who were themselves at risk from the press gang.

opposed to those mandated from above by merchants, captains, and colonial and royal officials. They would learn new tactics in "the Age of Revolution," but so too would they contribute to the Revolutionary movement the vast amount they already knew.[8]

Part of what sailors knew was how to resist impressment, for this was a tradition that stretched back to thirteenth-century England. With the expansion of the Royal Navy and its requirement of vastly more maritime labor in the late seventeenth century and with the mobilization for each of the many wars of the eighteenth century, their struggles there took on a new intensity. When, after a quarter century's peace, England declared war against Spain in 1739, sailors and other workers began to battle press gangs on both sides of the Atlantic. Daniel Baugh writes that "in nearly every provincial port [of England] press gangs were steadily and effectively thwarted" during the 1740s. Fists and clubs flew in American ports as well, in Antigua, St. Kitts, Barbados, Jamaica, New England, and elsewhere.[9]

Seamen rioted in Boston in 1741, beating a Suffolk County sheriff and a justice of the peace for their assistance to the press gang of HMS *Portland*. They took to the streets again in

[8] Marcus Rediker, *Between the Devil and the Deep Blue Sea: Merchant Seamen, Pirates, and the Anglo-American Maritime World, 1700–1750* (Cambridge, 1987), chap. 5.

[9] Gary B. Nash, *The Urban Crucible: Social Change, Political Consciousness, and the Origins of the American Revolution* (Cambridge, Mass., 1979), pp. 221–22; John Lax and William Pencak, "The Knowles Riot and the Crisis of the 1740s in Massachusetts," *Perspectives in American History* 19 (1976): 166–67; Dora Mae Clark, "The Impressment of Seamen in the American Colonies," in *Essays in Colonial History Presented to Charles McLean Andrews by His Students* (New Haven, 1931), p. 217; Bridenbaugh, *Cities in Revolt*, p. 115; Richard Pares, "The Manning of the Royal Navy in the West Indies, 1702–1763," Royal Historical Society *Transactions* 20 (1937):48–49; Daniel Baugh, *British Naval Administration in the Age of Walpole* (Princeton, 1965), p. 162. The resistance within the British empire overlapped with and may have been connected to a burst of riots and strikes waged by Dutch seamen between 1737 and 1743. See Rudolf Dekker, "Labour Conflicts and Working-Class Culture in Early Modern Holland," *International Review of Social History* 35 (1990):407.

1742, when three hundred seamen armed with "axes, clubs, and cutlasses" attacked the commanding officer of the *Astrea* and destroyed a Royal Navy barge. They rose twice more in 1745, first roughing up another Suffolk County sheriff and the commander of HMS *Shirley*, then, seven months later, confronting Captain Forest and the crew of HMS *Wager* but losing two seamen to the flashing cutlasses of the press gang. Adm. Peter Warren warned in 1745 that the sailors of New England were emboldened by a revolutionary heritage: they have, he wrote, "the highest notions of the rights and liberties of Englishmen, and indeed are almost Levellers." Here he referred to one of the most radical and democratic groups of the English Revolution, who for a time held considerable power in Cromwell's New Model Army.[10]

Within the surge of militancy during the 1740s, seamen developed a tactic soon employed in numerous hot spots around the Atlantic. They began to burn the boats in which press gangs came ashore to snatch bodies, thereby cutting their contact with their ships and making the work of "recruitment" much harder, if not in many cases impossible. Comdr. Charles Knowles wrote in 1743 that naval vessels pressing in the Caribbean "have had their Boats haul'd up in the Streets and going to be Burned, & their Captains insulted by 50 Arm'd Men at a time, and obliged to take shelter in some Friends House." After Capt. Abel Smith of the *Pembroke Prize* had pressed some men near St. Kitts, a mob of seamen "came off in the road and seized the Kings boat, hawled her up . . . and threatened to burn her, if the Captain would not return the Prest Men, which he was obliged to do to save the Boat, & peoples Lives, to the great Dishonour of Kings Authority (especially in Foreign Parts)." These attacks on the property and power of the British state had considerable effect: by 1746 the captain of HMS *Shirley* "dared not set foot on shore for four

---

[10] Peter Warren to the duke of Newcastle, June 18, 1745, Julian Gwyn, ed., *The Royal Navy and North America: The Warren Papers, 1736–1752* (London, 1973), p. 126. On the transmission of the ideas and practices of the Levellers and other English revolutionaries around the Atlantic, see Peter Linebaugh, "All the Atlantic Mountains Shook," *Labour / Le Travailleur* 10 (1982):87–121.

months for fear of being prosecuted . . . or murdered by the mob for pressing."[11]

The most important early development within the cycle of protest against impressment took place in 1747, when, according to Thomas Hutchinson, there occurred "a tumult in the Town of Boston equal to any which had preceded it." The event began when "near 50" sailors deserted Commodore Knowles and HMS *Lark* for the higher wartime wages they would find in the ports of New England. In response, Knowles commenced a hot press and "swept the wharfs" of Boston, seeking to recapture deserters and seize new men to run his ship.[12]

A mob, initially consisting of three hundred seamen but later ballooning to "several thousand people," seized some officers of the *Lark* as hostages, beat a deputy sheriff and slapped him into the town's stocks, surrounded and attacked the provincial council chamber, and posted squads at all piers to keep naval officers from escaping back to their ship. The mob was led by laborers and seamen, black and white, of many ethnic and national backgrounds, all armed with "clubs, swords, and cutlasses." The "lower class," observed Hutchinson, "were beyond measure enraged."[13]

The mob did as their comrades had done in other Atlantic

[11] Charles Knowles to [?], Oct. 15, 1744, Admiralty Papers, 1 / 2007, fol. 135, Public Record Office; "The Memorial of Captain Charles Knowles" (1743), Adm. 1 / 2006, P.R.O.; Warren to Thomas Corbett, June 2, 1746, Gwyn, ed., *Warren Papers*, p. 262. The best treatment of the Knowles Riot is Lax and Pencak, "Knowles Riot," pp. 163–214, to which I am deeply indebted despite my disagreement with parts of their argument.

[12] Thomas Hutchinson, *The History of the Colony and Province of Massachusetts-Bay*, ed. Lawrence Shaw Mayo, 3 vols. (1936; reprint ed., New York, 1970), 2:330; William Shirley to the Lords of Trade, Dec. 1, 1747, and Shirley to the duke of Newcastle, Dec. 31, 1747, Charles Henry Lincoln, ed., *Correspondence of William Shirley, Governor of Massachusetts and Military Commander in America, 1731–1760*, 2 vols. (New York, 1912), 1:418, 421. Any deserter who got caught would suffer. Knowles himself had presided over hearings that awarded 90 to 180 lashes for flight. See Knowles to [?], Feb. 10, 1743, Adm. 1 / 2006, P.R.O.

[13] Of the eleven ringleaders arrested, five were seamen and four were laborers. See Lax and Pencak, "Knowles Riot," p. 186; Hutchinson, *History of Massachusetts-Bay*, 2:330.

ports, defiantly assaulting state property and power. They first considered burning a twenty-gun ship being built for the Crown in a local shipyard, then picked up what they thought was a naval barge and "carried it in Procession through the Town with an Intention to burn it." They "dragged it, with as much seeming ease through the streets as if it had been in the water." They eventually set it aflame on Boston Common.[14]

The sailors had originally assembled in the streets of Boston for "self-defense," but their protest had a positive dimension as well. As Knowles remarked: "The Act [of 1746] against pressing in the Sugar Islands, filled the Minds of the Common People ashore as well as Sailors in all the Northern Colonies (but more especially in New England) with not only a hatred for the King's Service but [also] a Spirit of Rebellion each *Claiming a Right* to the same Indulgence as the Sugar Colonies and declaring they will maintain themselves in it." Maintain themselves in it they did.[15]

Sailors thus defended their "liberty" and justified their resistance in terms of "right." This was the essential idea embodied in their activity, in their resistance to unjust authority. Samuel Adams, who was later described by a perceptive enemy as someone full of "serpentine cunning" who "understood Human Nature, in low life," very well, watched the maritime working class defend itself. He soon began to translate its "Spirit of Rebellion" into political discourse. According to John Lax and William Pencak, Adams used the Knowles Riot to formulate a new "ideology of resistance, in which the natural rights of man were used for the first time in the province to justify mob activity." Adams saw that the mob "embodied the fundamental rights of man against which government itself could be judged," and he justified violent direct action against oppression. But the self-activity of some common tars,

[14] Hutchinson, *History of Massachusetts-Bay*, 2:331; Shirley to the Lords of Trade, Dec. 1, 1747, Lincoln, ed., *Correspondence of William Shirley*, 1:415–16. It turned out that the barge did not belong to the Royal Navy but rather, it was claimed, to one of the protesters.

[15] Knowles, quoted in Lax and Pencak, "Knowles Riot," pp. 182, 186 (my emphasis); see also Lemisch, "Jack Tar in the Streets," p. 400.

long considered zealous abetters of liberty, came first. Their refusal of what they considered "slavery" produced a major breakthrough in libertarian thought that would lead ultimately to revolution.[16]

It will probably never be known precisely why Samuel Adams moved from "the rights of Englishmen" to the broader, more universal idiom of natural rights and the rights of man in 1747, but one likely reason may be found in the composition of the crowd that instructed him. For in truth Adams faced a dilemma; how could he watch a motley crew of Africans, Scotsmen, Dutchmen, Irishmen, Englishmen, and probably even others battle the press gang and then proceed to describe them as engaged simply in a struggle for "the rights of Englishmen"?[17] How could he square the apparently traditional Lockean ideas in his Harvard masters' thesis of 1743 with the activities of "Foreign Seamen, Servants, Negroes, and other Persons of mean and vile Condition" who led the riot of

[16] Douglass Adair and John A. Schutz, eds., *Peter Oliver's Origin & Progress of the American Rebellion: A Tory View* (San Marino, 1961), pp. 39, 41. See Lax and Pencak, "Knowles Riot," pp. 205, 214; Rediker, *Between the Devil and the Deep Blue Sea,* pp. 251–53. The interpretation offered here, stressing the ways in which the seamen's actions generated Revolutionary ideology, is exactly the opposite of that proposed by Bernard Bailyn, who sees the ideas of the Revolutionary movement as giving meaning to the seamen's "diffuse and indeliberate anti-authoritarianism." See Bailyn, with the assistance of Jane N. Garrett, *Pamphlets of the American Revolution: 1750–1776,* vol. 1, *1750–1765* (Cambridge, Mass., 1965), p. 583.

[17] Of the eleven men arrested as ringleaders of the riot, the names of only four, note Lax and Pencak, can be traced to New England through other records of this period ("The Knowles Riot," p. 199). Of those who apparently came from elsewhere, we may surmise that Edmund Sheay, Patrick Downey, Henry Fitzpatrick, and Thomas Fitzpatrick were Irish, and that Jacobus Dekenyrin was probably continental European, perhaps Dutch. See Patrick Hanks and Flavia Hodges, eds., *A Dictionary of Surnames* (Oxford, 1988), pp. 152, 185, 488. We know nothing about the "slaves" or "negroes" who took part in the riot, but an advertisement for a runaway less than a week before the riot suggests a possibility: "A Negro Man Servant, named *Nea,* about 30 Years of Age, speaks good English and French, a tall slender well set Fellow," who "had on a blew Jacket, and Breeches of same, speckled Shirt, and appears as a Sailor" (*Boston Gazette,* Nov. 24, 1747).

1747?[18] The very diversity of the rebellious subject may have forced his thought into the more revolutionary channel of "Natural right." It might also have made a difference to Adams that the riot was, in a most literal and widely understood way, a case of "the people" fighting for their "liberty," for throughout the eighteenth century the crew of a ship was known as "the people," who once ashore were on their "liberty."[19]

Liberty and natural right had apparently been years in the making, for the sailors in the streets of Boston saw their struggle as one that had a history. In an unusual public exchange with Massachusetts Governor William Shirley, the mob used "very indecent, rude expressions" to remind him of the murderous violence visited upon sailors by the press gang of HMS *Wager* in 1745. Indeed, almost everyone who commented on

[18] Adams's masters' thesis was an oral disquisition in which he argued the affirmative on the lawfulness of resisting "the Supreme Magistrate, if the Commonwealth cannot otherwise be preserved." There was apparently nothing of interest in his treatment of this "not uncommon" subject "at Harvard College commencements." John C. Miller writes: "Unfortunately no copy of his thesis has been found: evidently it was not remarkable enough to be preserved in hearers' notes or in the newspapers." See Miller, *Sam Adams: Pioneer in Propaganda* (Stanford, 1936), pp. 15–16.

[19] Quotation from *Independent Advertiser,* Jan. 4, 1748. Lax and Pencak say that the descriptions of the mob as consisting of foreign seamen, laborers, and African-Americans were "not truthful" ("Knowles Riot," p. 200). But they cannot account for the fact that everyone—Governor Shirley, the Boston Town Meeting, the Massachusetts House of Representatives, Thomas Hutchinson, William Douglass, and Samuel Adams—whether hostile or sympathetic to the mob—described its composition in similar ways. See Shirley to the Lords of Trade, Dec. 1, 1747, Lincoln, ed., *Correspondence of William Shirley,* 1:412; resolution of the Boston Town Meeting, Nov. 20, 1747, and resolution of the Massachusetts House of Representatives, Nov. 19, 1747, both in the *Boston Weekly Post-Boy,* Dec. 21, 1747; Hutchinson, *History of Massachusetts-Bay,* 2:332; William Douglass, *A Summary, Historical and Political, of the First Planting, Progressive Improvements, and Present State of the British Settlements in North America* (Boston, 1749), pp. 254–55; *Independent Advertiser,* Aug. 28, 1749; Amicus Patriae, *An Address to the Inhabitants of the Province of Massachusetts-Bay in New-England; More Especially, to the Inhabitants of New England; Occasioned by the Late Illegal and Unwarrantable Attack upon Their Liberties* (Boston, 1747), p. 4. (Lax and Pencak have convincingly identified Adams as the author of this pamphlet; see "Knowles Riot," pp. 205–6.) See also *Oxford English Dictionary,* s.v., "liberty" and "people."

the Knowles Riot considered the popular anger generated by the earlier clash to be a major cause. The deaths of two seamen were, as Samuel Adams put it, "still recent in our minds."[20]

The mob rattled the nerves of Governor Shirley further by asking him if he recalled the fate of Capt. John Porteous. Here they referred to the much-hated leader of Edinburgh's City Guard, convicted of murder after firing on a crowd that had assembled to witness the hanging of a popular smuggler. Porteous was subsequently given royal clemency, but was at last seized by a mob and "hanged upon a sign post." The "lower rank of the people" in Edinburgh saw the act "as the hand of God doing justice." These actions had taken place eleven years earlier, in 1736, but Governor Shirley remembered them well enough to beat a hasty retreat to Castle William, where he remained until the riots in Boston ran their course.[21]

The crowd remembered 1736 and 1745, but it also drew upon Boston's working-class traditions of festivity and self-organization. As chronicler William Douglass wrote in 1749, the press and the riot "happened a few days after the annual and most numerous and outrageous Muster of this Mob" on Pope's Day, November 5, when North and South End crowds, made up of sailors, servants, slaves, and workmen of all kinds, met in rowdy, brawling competition and celebration. Commodore Knowles himself made the connection between the riot and Pope's Day activities, saying confidently at one point that "the North End People were the Rebels."[22]

[20] Douglass, *A Summary*, pp. 253, 237–39; Shirley to the Lords of Trade, Dec. 1, 1747, Shirley to the duke of Newcastle, Dec. 31, 1747, Lincoln, ed., *Correspondence of William Shirley*, 1:415, 417, 422; Amicus, *An Address*, p. 3; Lax and Pencak, "Knowles Riot," p. 179.

[21] Shirley to Josiah Willard, Nov. 19, 1747, Lincoln, ed., *Correspondence of William Shirley*, 1:415; William Roughead, ed., *Trial of Captain Porteous* (Toronto, 1909), p. 103. It is worth noting that the mob leader who asked Shirley about Porteous was *not* Scottish; Shirley described him as a "local man."

[22] Douglass, *A Summary*, p. 239; Knowles, quoted in the deposition of Joseph Ballard, reproduced in John Noble, "Notes on the Libel Suit of Knowles v. Douglass in the Superior Court of Judicature, 1748 and 1749,"

The rioters thus drew upon the living past as they point ed the way toward the future. Their action in 1747 moved Samuel Adams and friends to found a weekly publication called the *Independent Advertiser,* which expressed a remarkable, even prophetic variety of radical ideas during its brief but vibrant life of less than two years. The paper reported on resistance to the press gang and on mutiny in other parts of the world. It supported the "natural right" to "self-defense" and vigorously defended the ideas and practices of equality, calling, for example, for popular inspection of the means by which a few people were acquiring excessive wealth. It went so far as to call for an "Agrarian Law or something like it," to support the poor working people of New England. It stood self-consciously on the side of popular power, concluding in one article that "the reason of a People's Slavery, is . . . *Ignorance of their own Power.*" Perhaps the single most important idea to be found in the *Independent Advertiser* appeared in January 1748: "All Men are by Nature on a Level; born with an equal Share of Freedom, and endow'd with Capacities nearly alike." The opening words of the Declaration of Independence of 1776 clearly echoed these thoughts, first expressed in the immediate aftermath of the riot of 1747 but destined to become weapons in the hands of abolitionists, workers, and women for centuries to come.[23]

It was not the only connection between 1747 and 1776. The actions of sailors probably also influenced what Bernard Bailyn has called "the most famous sermon preached in pre-Revolutionary America," what Charles W. Akers has called "the most important defense of the right to revolution made

---

Publications of the Colonial Society of Massachusetts 3(1895–97): 232. On Pope's Day, see Alfred F. Young, "English Plebeian Culture and Eighteenth-Century American Radicalism," in Margaret Jacob and James Jacob, eds., *The Origins of Anglo-American Radicalism* (London, 1984), p. 198.

[23] For "natural right" see *Independent Advertiser,* Feb. 8, 1748; mutiny: ibid., Mar. 6, 1749; resistance to the press gang: ibid., Apr. 18, 1748; "Agrarian Law": ibid., Jan. 25, 1748; "a People's Slavery": ibid., Mar. 14, 1748; "All Men": ibid., Jan. 11, 1748.

by an American before 1776," what Edmund S. Morgan has called "the boldest exposition of popular sovereignty before the Revolution"—Jonathan Mayhew's *A Discourse concerning Unlimited Submission and Non-Resistance to the Higher Powers,* delivered and published in Boston in early 1750.[24]

Mayhew, an eminent clergyman who was throughout his life extremely sensitive to the events that swirled around him, delivered his famous sermon at a time when the riot and its consequences were still the subject of discussion in Boston's newspapers. Moreover, he ministered at West Church, whose congregation was deeply involved in trade and maritime affairs, and who would have been deeply concerned by the riot, its causes, and its consequences. By 1748 Mayhew's preachings were considered heretical enough to get one listener, a young Paul Revere, a whipping by his father for his waywardness. By early 1749 Mayhew was tending toward what some saw as sedition, saying that it was not a sin to transgress an iniquitous law, presumably such as the one that licensed impressment.[25]

In writing the *Discourse concerning Unlimited Submission* in late 1749 and early 1750, Mayhew offered a partial but still radical defense of regicide and of the "Good Old Cause" of the English Revolution. He delivered his sermon on January 30, the anniversary of the execution of Charles I, which he considered not a day of mourning but rather a day for remembering that Britons will not be slaves. Like Adams before him he argued passionately for both civil disobedience and a right to resistance that utilized force; indeed, passive nonresistance, Mayhew claimed, was "slavery." It is difficult to imagine that Mayhew's own defense of "the right to revolution" could have been made without the action of the riot and the extensive discussion it prompted among Samuel Adams and

---

[24] Bailyn, *Pamphlets of the American Revolution,* p. 204; Charles W. Akers, *Called unto Liberty: A Life of Jonathan Mayhew, 1720–1766* (Cambridge, Mass., 1964), p. 84; Edmund S. Morgan, *Inventing the People: The Rise of Popular Sovereignty in England and America* (New York, 1988), p. 143.

[25] Akers, *Called unto Liberty,* pp. 53, 67, 84.

others who contributed to and read the *Independent Adver-tiser.*[26]

Boston in 1747 was in many ways only the beginning for the political struggles of seamen and for the articulation of a revolutionary ideology in America. Thereafter, Jack Tar took part in almost every port city riot in England and America for the remainder of the century. Whether in Newport, Boston, New York, Philadelphia, Charleston, London, Liverpool, Bristol, or the Caribbean, tars took to the streets in rowdy and rebellious protest on a variety of issues, seizing in practice what would later be defined as "rights" by philosophers and by legislators.[27] Here, as elsewhere, rights were not granted from on high; they had to be fought for, won, and defended.

Seamen and their various rebellions oscillated back and forth between England and the American colonies in the 1760s and 1770s, not least because the working classes of English and colonial cities experienced severe dislocation and distress with the end of the Seven Years' War in 1763. The years 1765–70 were especially tumultuous on both sides of the Atlantic. Seamen in particular had to contend with the demobilization of the Royal Navy, which always brought disastrous effects, not only on prospects for employment but on the material conditions (food, wages, discipline) of seafaring life.[28]

Such effects were visible in the Royal Navy by 1764, and sailors did what they could to resist them. The common men of the deep soon demonstrated "a spirit of Desertion," which

---

[26] Jonathan Mayhew, *A Discourse concerning Unlimited Submission* (Boston, 1750), reprinted in Bailyn, ed., *Pamphlets of the American Revolution*, pp. 213–47. See also Bailyn's comments on the sermon, pp. 213, 233, 242, and Akers, *Called unto Liberty*, p. 88.

[27] Rediker, *Between the Devil and the Deep Blue Sea*, pp. 249–53.

[28] On conditions after 1763, see Bridenbaugh, *Cities in Revolt*, p. 306; Edward Countryman, *A People in Revolution: The American Revolution and Political Society in New York, 1760–1790* (Baltimore, 1981), p. 56; Nash, *Urban Crucible*, chap. 12; Peter Linebaugh, *The London Hanged: Crime and Civil Society in the Eighteenth Century* (London, 1991), pp. 288–331; William Ander Smith, "Anglo-Colonial Society and the Mob, 1740–1775," Ph.D. diss., Claremont Graduate School and University Center, 1965, chap. 3.

the Admiralty hoped to break "by a sharpe look out and strict Justice on the Delinquents." For deserters John Evans, Nicholas Morris, and John Tuffin, "justice" took the form of 700 lashes on the back; for Bryant Diggers and William Morris it took the form of hanging. Rear Adm. Alexander Colvill claimed that these "were the most severe punishments I ever knew to have been inflicted." Ever-bloodier and deadlier punishments administered aboard naval ships imparted a new and desperate intensity to shoreside resistance against the press gang.[29]

As the struggle escalated during the mid-1760s sailors revived the ritualistic act of menacing and destroying the king's naval property. When a press gang from HMS *St. John* tried in June 1764 to capture a deserter named Thomas Moss from a Newport wharf, a mob of sailors and other maritime workers counterattacked, recaptured Moss, roughed up the lieutenant who led the press gang, and "threatened to haul [the king's] schooner on shore, and burn her." Later the crowd sent "a sloop and two or three boats full of men to the battery on Goat Island," from which they fired several cannonballs at the *St. John*.[30]

In July 1764 a New York mob attacked a press gang from the *Chaleur* and "drawed its boat before the City Hall and there burnt her." These sailors recovered the man who had been pressed, forced the naval captain to make public apology, and successfully resisted court efforts to convict someone of wrongdoing in the action.[31] Soon after, another mob of maritime workers, at Casco Bay in the province of Maine, seized a press boat, "dragged her into the middle of Town,"

[29] Lord Colvill to Philip Stephens, Sept. 9 and Nov. 30, 1764, Adm. 1 / 482, fols. 386, 417–19, P.R.O.; Neil R. Stout, "Manning the Royal Navy in North America, 1763–1775," *American Neptune* 23 (1963):175.

[30] Colvill to Mr. Stephens, July 26, 1764, John Russell Bartlett, ed., *Records of the Colony of Rhode Island and Providence Plantations in New England*, 10 vols. (Providence, 1856–65), 6:428–29; Thomas Hill, "Remarks on Board His Maj[esty]'s Schooner St. John in Newport Harbour Rhode Island," Adm. 1 / 482, fol. 372, P.R.O.

[31] Thomas Langhorne to Colvill, Aug. 11, 1764, Adm. 1 / 482, fol. 377, P.R.O. See also *Newport Mercury*, July 23, 1764.

and threatened to burn it unless a group of pressed men were freed.[32] In Newport in 1765 a mob made up of "the dregs of the people"—sailors, "boys and negroes"—seized the press tender of HMS *Maidstone,* carried it to a central location in town, and set it ablaze. When popular antagonism toward the customs service rose in the late 1760s, sailors began to attack *its* vessels. Thomas Hutchinson wrote that in Boston in 1768 "a boat, belonging to the custom-house, was dragged in triumph through the streets of the town, and burnt on the Common." Seamen and other workers threatened or torched other vessels belonging to the king in Wilmington, North Carolina, and in Nevis in 1765, in Newport in 1769 and 1772, and twice in New York in 1775.[33]

One of the central meanings of the boat-burning ritual may be found in the locations to which the vessels were drawn and destroyed, whether Boston Common in 1747 or outside New York City Hall in 1764. By carrying the vessels of naval and state power to a central site usually associated with popular power and civil authority, seamen not only warned local leaders not to cooperate with the king's representatives in the signing of press warrants, they also militantly—and symbolically—subordinated raw, coercive military power to more responsible instruments of government—civil authority. The ritual was in its essence antiabsolutist, designed to work, as Capt. Charles Knowles noted during the first wave of barge burning in the 1740s, "to the great Dishonour of Kings Au-

---

[32] Colvill to Stephens, Jan. 12, 1765, Adm. 1 / 482, fol. 432, P.R.O.

[33] Gov. Samuel Ward to Capt. Charles Antrobus, July 12, 1765, Bartlett, ed., *Records of the Colony of Rhode Island,* 6:447; Lords of Admiralty to Mr. Secretary Conway, Mar. 20, 1766, in Joseph Redington, ed., *Calendar of Home Office Papers of the Reign of George III, 1766–1768,* 4 vols. (London, 1879), 2:26; Hutchinson, *History of Massachusetts-Bay,* 3:138; Donna J. Spindel, "Law and Disorder: The North Carolina Stamp Act Crisis," *North Carolina Historical Review* 57 (1980):10–11; *Pennsylvania Journal,* Dec. 26, 1765; Adair and Schutz, eds., *Peter Oliver's Origin & Progress,* p. 69; Lemisch, "Jack Tar in the Streets," p. 392; David S. Lovejoy, *Rhode Island Politics and the American Revolution, 1760–1776* (Providence, 1958), p. 157; Paul A. Gilje, *The Road to Mobocracy: Popular Disorder in New York City, 1763–1834* (Chapel Hill, 1987), p. 63. On the intertwining of naval and customs authority see Stout, "Manning the Royal Navy," p. 174.

thority (especially in foreign Parts)." Sailors defied the king by twisting the longest and strongest arm of his power.[34]

In the late 1760s sailors and other parts of the maritime proletariat waged struggles that paralleled, linked, and overlapped with the "Wilkes and Liberty" movement in England and the patriot movement in America.[35] Indeed, Wilkes, who began to argue for the right to resist impressment in 1772, may have drawn the idea from the sailors of London who themselves fought a guerrilla war against press gangs in the early 1770s. Wilkes, who took up the position a full quarter century *after* the Knowles Riot, was slow to champion the seamen's cause.[36]

In 1768, amid the Wilkite agitation in London, came another momentous innovation in the seaman's cycle of struggle: it was nothing less than the invention of the strike, which originally referred to Jack Tar's decision to "strike" the sails of his vessels, thereby crippling the commerce of the empire's leading city and bringing the accumulation of capital to a halt. Seamen's strikes would subsequently appear on both sides of the Atlantic with increasing frequency, as would struggles over maritime wages. Wage actions in America took on an additional political meaning in the aftermath of the reorganization of British customs in 1764, when officials began to seize the nonmonetary wages of seamen, the "venture" they carried, freight-free, in the hold of each ship.[37]

[34] "The Memorial of Captain Charles Knowles" (1741), Adm. 1 / 2006, P.R.O.

[35] On John Wilkes and his popularity in England and America, see Pauline Maier, *From Resistance to Revolution: Colonial Radicals and the Development of American Opposition to Britain, 1765–1776* (New York, 1972), pp. 162–69; George Rudé, *Wilkes and Liberty: A Social Study of 1763 to 1774* (Oxford, 1962).

[36] Smith, "Anglo-Colonial Society and the Mob," p. 108. See also Nicholas Rogers, "Liberty Road: Opposition to Impressment in Britain during the War of American Independence," in Colin Howell and Richard Twomey, eds., *Jack Tar in History: Essays in the History of Maritime Life and Labour* (Fredericton, New Brunswick, 1991), pp. 53–75, which unfortunately privileges the liberal legal forms of resistance over the sailor's direct action.

[37] *Oxford English Dictionary*, s.v., "strike." For a partial listing of seamen's strike activity in England, see C. R. Dobson, *Masters and Journeymen: A Pre-*

Sailors and their families struck in Liverpool in 1775, when three thousand "men, boys, and women" assembled to protest a reduction in wages. When authorities fired upon the crowd, killing several, the strike exploded into open insurrection. Sailors "hoisted the red flag" and began to bombard the mercantile Exchange, leaving "scarce a whole pane of glass in the neighborhood." They also destroyed the property of several rich slave-trading merchants. One observer of the strife in Liverpool wrote, "I could not help thinking we had Boston here, and I fear this is only the beginning of our sorrows."[38]

Boston, the "Metropolis of Sedition," popped up in Liverpool on the eve of the Revolution. Did some of the same sailors take part in the political actions of these two great ports? Perhaps. And perhaps there were specific connections between one of the slogans uttered by seamen in the great river strike of 1768—"No Wilkes, No King!"—and the increasingly antiabsolutist radicalism of seamen in American ports. The extraordinary mobility of seamen ensured that both the experience and the ideas of opposition carried fast. If Pauline Maier is correct in saying that the American Sons of Liberty saw their own struggle as but "one episode in a worldwide struggle between liberty and despotism," is there any reason to think seamen, who had a much broader experience of both despotism and internationalism, would have seen matters differently?[39]

---

history of Industrial Relations, 1717–1800 (London, 1980), pp. 154–70. On the seamen's wage struggles in America in the 1760s and after, see Oliver Morton Dickerson, The Navigation Acts and the American Revolution (Philadelphia, 1951), pp. 218–19.

[38] R. Barrie Rose, "A Liverpool Sailors' Strike in the Eighteenth Century," Transactions of the Lancashire and Cheshire Antiquarian Society 68 (1958):85–92. Quotation about Boston from "Extract of a Letter from Liverpool, Sept. 1, 1775," Morning Chronicle and London Advertiser, Sept. 5, 1775, reprinted in Richard Brooke, Liverpool as It Was during the Last Quarter of the Eighteenth Century, 1775 to 1800 (Liverpool, 1853), p. 332. This is the only known case of a mob in England turning cannon on the authorities; the same had already happened in America ten years earlier in Newport, as discussed above.

[39] Maier, From Resistance to Revolution, p. 161; Linebaugh, London Hanged, chap. 9; Adair and Schutz, etc., Peter Oliver's Origin & Progress, p. 56.

The militancy of seamen in port, whether in London, Liverpool, or Boston, cannot be understood apart from their struggles at sea, where they continually battled the concentrated powers of captains and merchants, backed by the state. The seaman's militancy owed a great deal to his specific work experience on board the merchant ship, where daily cooperation in the running of the ship and collective struggles over food, pay, work, and discipline produced an oppositional outlook that seamen carried ashore. Seamen often brought to the ports a militant attitude toward arbitrary and excessive authority, and a willingness to sympathize with the grievances of others, to cooperate for the sake of self-defense. They were inclined to use direct action, violent if necessary, to accomplish collectively defined goals. In the 1760s their portside struggles began to take on an even broader significance because their workplace conflicts over work, exploitation, and impressment began to resonate with larger political discussions of "liberty" and "right."[40]

The 1730s and early 1740s were no less crucial in the history of African-Americans, for this was a period in which the winds of rebellion slashed through many of the slave societies of the New World. Their struggles included the First Maroon War in Jamaica (1730–40), slave rebellions in New Orleans (1730, 1732), St. John in the Danish Virgin Islands, and Dutch Guyana (1733), major plots in the Bahama Islands, St. Kitts, and New Jersey (1734), the great slave conspiracy in Antigua (1735–36), rebellions on St. Bartholomew, St. Martin's, Anguilla, and Guadeloupe (1736–38), the Stono Rebellion (1739), the "Great Negro Plot" in New York (1741), and a series of disturbances in Jamaica (early 1740s). This cycle of rebellion both expressed and enhanced what David Barry Gaspar has called a "Dangerous Spirit of Liberty."[41]

Although conspiracies and insurrections were rooted in local circumstances, they sometimes featured broader, even in-

---

[40] Lemisch, in "Jack Tar in the Streets," was the first to see "rioting as political expression" among seamen (pp. 378–79, 381–87, 390, 393–96).

[41] David Barry Gaspar, "A Dangerous Spirit of Liberty: Slave Rebellion in the West Indies during the 1730s," *Cimarrons* 1 (1981):79–91.

ternational, connections. The life of a slave named Will, who between 1733 and 1741 took part in the rebellion on St. John, then in the conspiracy on Antigua, and finally in the plot in New York, illustrates the movement and exchange of subversive experience among slaves. Another Antigua conspirator, banished from his own island, emerged as a leader of a plot on the Danish island of St. Croix in 1759. Samba, who led an unsuccessful revolt against a French slave-trading fort on the coast of Africa, then a mutiny aboard a slave ship, was finally broken on the wheel in New Orleans after plotting an insurrection in 1730. Gaspar has suggested that black sailors may have carried the news of Antigua's plot to other islands, just as their latter-day counterparts would do in the era of the Haitian Revolution, as shown by Julius S. Scott.[42]

A new wave of struggle against slavery was inaugurated in Jamaica in 1760 by Tacky's Rebellion, which was, according to sugar planter and historian Edward Long, "more formidable than any hitherto known in the West Indies." The revolt broke out in April among slaves in St. Mary's parish and spread quickly to involve thousands islandwide. Slaves shaved their heads to signify solidarity with the insurrection and their intention to join it.[43] The rebellion raged for several months, but by late summer the authorities had largely reestablished control, though sporadic guerrilla fighting would continue

[42] David Barry Gaspar, *Bondmen and Rebels: A Study of Master-Slave Relations in Antigua, with Implications for Colonial British America* (Baltimore, 1985), pp. 37, 210; Michael Craton, *Testing the Chains: Resistance to Slavery in the British West Indies* (Ithaca, N.Y., 1982), pp. 335–39; Peter H. Wood, *Black Majority: Negroes in Colonial South Carolina from 1670 through the Stono Rebellion* (New York, 1974); T. J. Davis, *A Rumor of Revolt: The "Great Negro Plot" in Colonial New York* (New York, 1985), p. 158; Herbert Aptheker, *American Negro Slave Revolts* (New York, 1943), pp. 181–82; "Account of the Negro Rebellion on St. Croix, Danish West Indies, 1759," *Journal of Negro History* 11 (1926):55. See also Gaspar's "A Dangerous Spirit of Liberty" and Julius S. Scott, "The Common Wind: Currents of Afro-American Communication in the Era of the Haitian Revolution," Ph.D. diss., Duke University, 1986.

[43] Edward Long, *The History of Jamaica, or, General Survey of the Antient and Modern State of That Island; Reflections on Its Situation, Settlements, Inhabitants, Climate, Products, Commerce, Laws, and Government,* 3 vols. (London, 1774), 2:462.

for another year. The canefields smoldered and damage to property was enormous. The carnage was among the greatest yet witnessed in the annals of Atlantic slave revolts: 60 whites killed, 300 to 400 slaves killed in military action or dead of suicide once their cause became hopeless, and another 100 slaves executed.[44]

Control was thus reestablished in Jamaica but apparently with small help from the merchant seamen who found themselves in Jamaica when the revolt broke out and who were quickly herded into the local militias to help put down the uprising. Overseer Thomas Thistlewood made it clear that some sailors spent their time wandering from one plantation to another to drink the grog and steal the silver spoons of terrified sugar planters. Indeed, Edward Long claimed that in the middle of the revolt a captured leader of the slave rebels told a Jewish militia guard: "As for the sailors, you see they do not oppose us, they care not who is in possession of the country, Black or White, it is the same to them." The rebel was convinced that after the island's revolution, the sailors will "bring us things from t'other side the sea, and be glad to take our goods in payment."[45]

Like the Knowles Riot of 1747, Tacky's Rebellion transformed revolutionary thought. In 1760, after Tacky's Rebellion had broken out but before it was suppressed, a man who called himself J. Philmore wrote a pamphlet entitled *Two Dialogues on the Man-Trade*. An internationalist who considered himself "more as a citizen in the world, than as a citizen of England," Philmore insisted that "all of the human race, are, by nature, upon an equality" and that one person simply could not be the property of another. He denied the "worldly superiority" of Christianity and thought the slave trade to be organized murder. Philmore had probably learned of Tacky's revolt by way of merchant seaman, for he made it his business

[44] On the shaved heads of the rebels see Douglas Hall, ed., *In Miserable Slavery: Thomas Thistlewood in Jamaica, 1750–1786* (London, 1989). For a good account of the revolt see Craton, *Testing the Chains*, pp. 125–39.

[45] Long, *History of Jamaica*, 2:460; Hall, ed., *In Miserable Slavery*, p. 98. Sailors in the Royal Navy, it should be noted, apparently did assist in putting down the rebellion in a couple of areas. See Craton, *Testing the Chains*, pp. 132–33, 136.

to frequent the docks. Much of the considerable amount he knew of the slave trade came, he claimed, "from the mouths of some sailors."[46]

Philmore supported the efforts of Tacky and his fellow rebels "to deliver themselves out of the miserable slavery they are in." His principle conclusion was clear, straightforward, and revolutionary: "So all the black men now in our plantations, who are by unjust force deprived of their liberty, and held in slavery, as they have none upon earth to appeal to, may lawfully repel that force with force, and to recover their liberty, destroy their oppressors; and not only so, but it is the duty of others, white as well as black, to assist those miserable creatures, if they can, in their attempts to deliver themselves out of slavery, and to rescue them out of the hands of their cruel tyrants."[47] He called for immediate emancipation. Like Samuel Adams a few years before him, Philmore justified the use of force against oppression.

Philmore's words must have caused a shudder among many, including the more activist Quakers who were opposed to slavery but committed to principles of nonviolence. Anthony Benezet, for example, used and reprinted several of Philmore's arguments but carefully deleted his defence of violence in the struggle for liberty. But Philmore's radical perspective nonetheless managed to enter the mainstream of antislavery thought in the form of "higher law" doctrine, through the argument that resistance to slavery was sanctioned by a moral law higher than the bourgeois law drafted by people who frequently had investments in slavery, the slave trade, or the empire as a whole. He had written that "no legis-

---

[46] J. Philmore, *Two Dialogues on the Man-Trade* (London, 1760), pp. 7–10, 14. For a brief discussion of Philmore, see David Brion Davis, *The Problem of Slavery in the Age of Revolution, 1770–1823* (Ithaca, N.Y., 1975), and the same author's "New Sidelights on Early Antislavery Radicalism," *William and Mary Quarterly*, 3d ser. 28 (1971):585–94. Evidence internal to the pamphlet suggests the moment at which it was written. Philmore wrote after many of his "countrymen had lost their lives," but before the revolt was suppressed. He explained that he was happy not that many had died but rather that so many slaves "had recovered their liberty" (p. 4).

[47] Philmore, *Two Dialogues*, pp. 51, 54. Philmore also defended the conspiracy in Antigua that had taken place in 1735–36 (p. 58).

lature on earth, which is the supreme power in every civil society, can alter the nature of things, or make that to be lawful, which is contrary to the law of God, the supreme legislator and governour of the world." It was, as David Brion Davis has pointed out, the original expression of what would eventually become perhaps the central idea in the continuing transatlantic struggle against slavery.[48]

Tacky's Revolt may well have helped to generate another breakthrough in antislavery thought on the western side of the Atlantic. When, in 1761, James Otis made his electrifying oration against the writs of assistance that allowed British authorities to attack the trade between New England and the French West Indies, he went beyond his formal subject to "assert the rights of the Negroes." He delivered his famous speech in February, in the wake of Tacky's Revolt, after a series of articles on the rising had appeared in Boston newspapers. When Otis published *The Rights of the British Colonies Asserted and Proved* (1764) he elaborated on this assertion, claiming that all men—"white or black"—"are by the law of nature freeborn." Thus did the language of natural right permanently enter the struggle against slavery in America, just as it had done, in the very same seaport, a few years earlier against impressment.[49]

---

[48] Anthony Benezet used and popularized the higher law argument in his *A Short Account of that Part of Africa Inhabited by the Negroes . . .* (Philadelphia, 1762), and again in *Some Historical Account of Guinea* (Philadelphia, 1771). It was eventually accepted by Granville Sharp and a great many others in the antislavery movement. See also Davis, *Problem of Slavery*, p. 332. Quotation is from Philmore, *Two Dialogues*, p. 45.

[49] James Otis, *The Rights of the British Colonies Asserted and Proved* (Boston, 1764), republished in Bailyn, ed., *Pamphlets of the American Revolution*, pp. 419–82. In this work Otis refers specifically to Jamaican slavery and to "the ferocity, cruelty, and brutal barbarity that has long marked the general character of the sugar islanders," by which he meant the sugar planters (p. 439). Such traits of character would have been on grisly display in the executions taking place in Jamaica in the months before Otis gave his speech, many of which were reported in Boston newspapers. See the *Boston News-Letter*, June 19, July 10, Sept. 18, Oct. 30, 1760; Feb. 2, 1761. It is worth noting, however, that the newspapers may not have added much to what Otis could have learned about the revolt from Boston's numerous sailors and merchants who traded to the Caribbean, whose case, after all,

One of the few substantive descriptions of Otis's speech of 1761 is the set of notes written by John Adams many years later. Otis was, that day, "a flame of fire," a prophet, "Isaiah and Ezekiel united." He gave a "dissertation on the rights of man in a state of nature," an antinomian account of man as "an independent sovereign, subject to no law, but the law written on his heart" or lodged in "his conscience." Adams claimed that no "Quaker in Philadelphia" ever "asserted the rights of negroes in stronger terms." Otis apparently called for immediate emancipation and advocated the use of force to accomplish it. Adams, for his part, "shuddered at the doctrine he taught; and I have all my lifetime shuddered, and still shudder, at the consequences that may be drawn from such premises."[50] The arguments for emancipation and the legitimate use of force suggest that Otis may have read Philmore's pamphlet or perhaps simply drew similar conclusions from Tacky's Revolt. In any case, after the revolt, Philmore's pamphlet, and Otis's oration, metropolitan and colonial antislavery thought would never be the same.

Tacky's Revolt initiated a new cycle of slave resistance that would shake every corner of the Anglo-Atlantic world and beyond. Major plots and revolts erupted in Bermuda (1761), Dutch Guyana (1762, 1763, 1772), Jamaica (1765, 1766, 1776), British Honduras (1765, 1768, 1773), Grenada (1765), Montserrat (1768), St. Vincent (1769–73), Tobago (1770, 1771, 1774), and St. Croix and St. Thomas (1770 and after). Veterans of Tacky's Revolt took part in a rising in British Honduras (where some five hundred rebels had been banished), as well as in three other revolts in Jamaica in 1765 and 1766.

---

he was arguing in his attack on the writs of assistance. For the background to Otis's address, see John J. Waters and John A. Schutz, "Patterns of Massachusetts Colonial Politics: The Writs of Assistance and the Rivalry between the Otis and Hutchinson Families," *William and Mary Quarterly,* 3d ser. 24 (1967):543–67.

[50] John Adams recalled: "Shall we say, that the rights of masters and servants clash, and can be decided only by force? I adore the idea of gradual abolitions! But who shall decide how fast or how slowly these abolitions shall be made?" All quotations are taken from Charles Francis Adams, ed., *The Works of John Adams,* 10 vols. (Boston, 1850–56), 10:247, 272, 314–16.

Magistrate John Fielding believed that some of the leaders of the insurrections of the 1760s had gained valuable subversive experience by passing through the black community of London.[51]

On the North American continent the reverberations of rebellion intensified after 1765, as demonstrated in important recent work by Peter H. Wood. He has argued that "black freedom struggles on the eve of white independence" multiplied as slaves seized the new opportunities offered by divisions between imperial and colonial ruling classes. Running away increased at a rate that alarmed slaveholders everywhere, and by the mid-1770s a rash of slave plots and revolts sent white fears soaring. Slaves organized themselves for risings in Perth Amboy, New Jersey, in 1772; in St. Andrews Parish, South Carolina, and in a joint African-Irish effort in Boston in 1774; in Ulster County, New York, Dorchester County, Maryland, Norfolk, Virginia, and the Tar River region of North Carolina in 1775. In the last of these, a slave named Merrick plotted with a white seafarer to make arms available and the intended revolt possible.[52]

Such conspiracy and exchange was facilitated by the strategic position that many urban slaves or free blacks occupied in the social division of labor. Northern ports, with their promise of anonymity and an impersonal wage in the maritime sector, served as a magnet to runaway slaves and free blacks throughout the colonial period and well into the nineteenth century.

[51] The importance of these events was not confined to their place of origin, for news of them was carried around the Atlantic by word of mouth and by newspaper. On the connections between Tacky's Revolt and the later risings in Jamaica and British Honduras, see Craton, *Testing the Chains*, pp. 138–40; O. Nigel Bolland, *The Formation of a Colonial Society: Belize, from Conquest to Crown Colony* (Baltimore, 1977), p. 73. On John Fielding, see Linebaugh, "All the Atlantic Mountains Shook," p. 117.

[52] See Wood, "'Taking Care of Business,'" p. 276, and "'The Dream Deferred': Black Freedom Struggles on the Eve of White Independence," in Gary Y. Okihiro, ed., *In Resistance: Studies in African, Caribbean, and Afro-American History* (Amherst, Mass., 1986), pp. 170, 172–75; Jeffrey J. Crow, "Slave Rebelliousness and Social Conflict in North Carolina, 1775 to 1802," *William and Mary Quarterly*, 3d ser., 37 (1980):85–86; Aptheker, *American Negro Slave Revolts*, pp. 87, 200–202; Benjamin Quarles, *The Negro in the American Revolution*, (Chapel Hill, 1961), p. 14.

Most found work as laborers and seamen. Slaves too were employed in the maritime sector, some with ship masters as owners, others hired out by the voyage. By the middle of the eighteenth century, slaves dominated Charleston's maritime and riverine traffic, in which some 20 percent of the city's adult male slaves labored. The freedom of Charleston's "Boat negroes" had long concerned the city's rulers, at no time more than when they involved themselves in subversive activities, as alleged against Thomas Jeremiah, a river pilot, in 1775. Jeremiah was arrested for stockpiling guns as he waited for the imperial war that would "help the poor Negroes." "Two or three White people," probably sailors, were also arrested, then released for lack of evidence, but nonetheless driven from the province. Jeffrey J. Crow has noted that black pilots were "a rebellious lot, particularly resistant to white control."[53]

The political effects of slave revolts and other forms of resistance were always complex, often fueling fear and repression on the one side and sometimes new arguments against slavery on the other. They helped to make chattel slavery a "nightmare" not only for the "colonial intelligentsia" but also for a huge portion of colonial society. But clearly slave resistance also helped to generate a great deal of the antislavery discourse during the first major surge of the movement between 1765 and 1776. According to Roger Bruns, Anthony Benezet,

[53] Gary B. Nash, *Forging Freedom: The Formation of Philadelphia's Black Community, 1720–1840* (Cambridge, Mass., 1988), p. 72; Quarles, *Negro in the American Revolution*, p. 84; Lemisch, "Jack Tar in the Streets," p. 375; Shane White, *Somewhat More Independent: The End of Slavery in New York City, 1770–1810* (Athens, Ga., 1991), p. 128. For the percentages of black workers in the maritime sector in the early nineteenth century, see Shane White, "'We Dwell in Safety and Pursue Our Honest Callings': Free Blacks in New York City, 1783–1810," *Journal of American History* 75 (1988):453–54; Ira Dye, "Early American Merchant Seafarers," *Proceedings of the American Philosophical Society* 120 (1976):358. On South Carolina, see Morgan, "Black Life in Eighteenth-Century Charleston," p. 200; Wood, "'Taking Care of Business,'" p. 276; Crow, "Slave Rebelliousness," p. 85; Henry Laurens to John Laurens, June 18, 1775, and June 23, 1775, Rogers et al., eds., *Papers of Laurens*, 10:184, 191. On the black seamen in the West Indies, see Gaspar, *Bondmen and Rebels*, pp. 109–11.

America's leading abolitionist, "wrote of slave uprisings all over the world and relayed them to his antislavery compatriots" through his correspondence, his pamphlets, and his books. Benezet took an international approach, carefully noting the incidence of slave resistance in the New World colonies of Great Britain, France, the Netherlands, and Portugal.[54]

Two of the Revolutionary era's most popular pamphleteers took notice of the militancy of slaves, and each was moved during the 1770s to include attacks on slavery in larger arguments for human liberty and freedom. John Allen, a Baptist minister who had witnessed the ferocious struggles of London's Spitalfields silk weavers through the 1760s, delivered (and then published) *An Oration on the Beauties of Liberty* after the burning of the revenue cutter *Gaspee* by sailors in 1773. In the fourth edition of his pamphlet, which according to John Adams was read to "large Circles of the Common People," Allen denounced slavery, not least for the "frequent revolts" of slaves, which "so often occasion streams of blood to be shed." Of this, he insisted, there were "recent proofs."[55]

Another man fair of pen and smitten with liberty, Thomas Paine, argued against slavery soon after his arrival in America in 1774. He repeated in diluted form Philmore's argument for self-liberation: "As the true owner has a right to reclaim his goods that were stolen, and sold; so the slave, who is proper owner of his freedom, has a right to reclaim it, however often sold." Paine signaled his awareness of the upswing

---

[54] F. Nwabueze Okoye, "Chattel Slavery as the Nightmare of the American Revolutionaries," *William and Mary Quarterly*, 3d ser. 37 (1980):12; Bruns's introduction to Anthony Benezet to Granville Sharp, Mar. 29, 1773, in Roger Bruns, ed., *Am I Not a Man and a Brother: The Antislavery Crusade of Revolutionary America, 1688–1788* (New York, 1977), p. 263. For Benezet's comments on the rising of slaves in Dutch Berbice in 1763, see Benezet to Joseph Phipps, May 28, 1763, ibid., pp. 98–99.

[55] John Adams, quoted in John M. Bumsted and Charles E. Clark, "New England's Tom Paine: John Allen and the Spirit of Liberty," *William and Mary Quarterly*, 3d ser. 21 (1964):570. Portions of Allen's pamphlet have been reprinted in Bruns, ed., *Am I Not a Man and a Brother*, pp. 257–62. On the struggles of Spitalfields weavers in the 1760s, see Linebaugh, *The London Hanged*, pp. 270–83.

in African-American resistance by referring to slaves as "dangerous, as they are now."[56]

Peter Wood concludes that between 1765 and 1776 North American slaves generated a "wave of struggle" that became "a major factor in the turmoil leading up to the Revolution": "It touched upon every major slave colony, and it was closely related to—even influential upon—the political unrest gripping many white subjects in these years." Allen and Paine in particular prove his point. Wood's treatment of this cycle of rebellion as "a significant chapter in the story of worker and artisan political unrest" invites us to link it to the Revolutionary struggles of other workers.[57]

It was within the crowd actions of the Revolutionary era, within those rowdy gatherings of thousands of men and women that created an unprecedented imperial crisis, that the trajectories of rebellion among sailors and slaves intersected. Thanks to the efforts of a recent generation of scholars who have insisted that common folk were important historical actors in their own right, it is now time to roll back some of the effects of history written during the Cold War and conclude once again, as Arthur Schlesinger, Sr., did forty years ago, that "Mob violence played a dominant role at every significant turning point of the events leading up to the War for Independence." Mobs were crucial to the protests against the Stamp Act, the Townshend Revenue Act, the increased power of the British customs service, the Quartering Act, the Tea Act, and Intolerable Acts, and therefore in the Revolutionary rupture itself.[58]

[56] Thomas Paine, "African Slavery in America" (1775), in Philip S. Foner, ed., *The Complete Writings of Thomas Paine* (New York, 1945), pp. 17, 19.

[57] Wood, "'Dream Deferred,'" pp. 168, 181. Wood argues that the cycle entered a new phase (to last until 1783) when Lord Dunmore made his famous proclamation (Nov. 15, 1775) that offered freedom to any slave who would fight in the king's army (p. 177).

[58] The highlights in the literature on mobs include Schlesinger, "Political Mobs," pp. 244–50; Gordon S. Wood, "A Note on Mobs in the American Revolution," *William and Mary Quarterly*, 3d ser. 23 (1966):635–42; Lemisch, "Jack Tar in the Streets"; idem, "Jack Tar vs. John Bull: The Role of New York's Merchant Seamen in Precipitating the Revolution," Ph.D. diss., Yale

Such crowd actions, which featured workers black and white, slave and free, were themselves episodes in the broader cycles of rebellion among waged and unwaged laborers in the eighteenth century. Sailors in particular were crucial to these crowds, and African-Americans, free and enslaved, also played a significant, if generally unappreciated, part. Boston's North Side and South Side mobs were, as far back as the 1740s, made up of mechanics, sailors, servants, and slaves. Indeed, perhaps the single most common description of mobs in Revolutionary America was "a Rabble of boys, sailors, and negroes."[59] Moreover, on almost every occasion when a crowd went beyond the planned objectives of the moderate leaders of the patriot movement, there were large numbers of sailors and often slaves in its midst.

And yet it is difficult to know precisely what role sailors and slaves played in colonial crowds, ironically enough because

---

University, 1962; Pauline Maier, "Popular Uprisings and Civil Authority in Eighteenth-Century America," *William and Mary Quarterly,* 3d ser. 27 (1970):3–35; idem, "Charleston Mob," pp. 173–96; idem, *From Resistance to Revolution;* Lee R. Boyer, "Lobster Backs, Liberty Boys, and Laborers in the Streets: New York's Golden Hill and Nassau Street Riots," *New-York Historical Society Quarterly* 57 (1973):280–308; Edward Countryman, "The Problem of the Early American Crowd," *Journal of American Studies* 7 (1977):77–90; idem, *A People in Revolution*; Dirk Hoerder, *Crowd Action in Revolutionary Massachusetts, 1765–1780* (New York, 1977), p. 17 (for agreement with Schlesinger); Nash, *Urban Crucible*; John K. Alexander, "The Fort Wilson Incident of 1779: A Case Study of the Revolutionary Crowd," *William and Mary Quarterly,* 3d ser. 31 (1974):589–612; Gilje, *Road to Mobocracy*; Young, "English Plebeian Culture," pp. 185–213; and several of the essays (some by the authors listed above) in Alfred F. Young, ed., *The American Revolution: Explorations in the History of American Radicalism* (DeKalb, Ill., 1976). A recent survey is Thomas P. Slaughter, "Crowds in Eighteenth-Century America: Reflections and New Directions," *Pennsylvania Magazine of History and Biography* 115 (1991):3–34.

[59] Several historians (Bridenbaugh, Foner, Gilje, Hoerder, Lemisch, and Nash) have called attention to the presence of African-Americans in Revolutionary crowds. Others have neglected the issue, perhaps in part because well-to-do citizens sometimes described mobs as consisting of "boys, sailors, and Negroes" in order to protect their own kind and to blame "disorder" on the poorer parts of urban society. Gilje writes, correctly in my view, that "youths, seamen, mechanics, laborers, and black slaves were the main participants" in early American crowds (*Road to Mobocracy,* p. 30).

their concerted actions were so effective. Early American mobs acted within relatively undeveloped civil societies that lacked police forces and, usually, standing armies; local militias could not easily be mobilized against them, because militiamen were often members of the crowds. Urban mobs thus created enormous disequilibrium because there were so few other institutions or corporate groups to counterbalance them and guarantee social stability. Local authorities were too close to the action at hand, imperial authorities too far away. Crowds were, therefore, extremely powerful in this context. They often succeeded in achieving their aims and usually managed to protect their own, which meant that individual members of the crowd were rarely arrested and prosecuted. Crowd activity itself was thus infrequently criminalized (even when it was condemned), a singular fact that makes it difficult for the historian to establish the precise social composition of early American crowds, as, for example, George Rudé has done for crowds in England and France in the eighteenth century. But this does not make the quest to understand the role of sailors and slaves impossible, for the very power of the crowd ensured that it would be the object of extensive commentary, if not the kind of direct legal analysis that would have come in the wake of repression.[60]

Interracial mobs, the potent if temporary unions of free, waged and unfree, unwaged laborers, helped to win numerous victories for the Revolutionary movement. The "Sons of Neptune" (sailors, themselves both black and white), other free blacks, and slaves were probably most united and most effective in their battles against impressment. The crucial Knowles Riot of 1747, which witnessed the birth of the Revolution's language of liberation, was led by "armed Seamen, Servants, Negroes, and others." Later, in 1765, "Sailors, boys, and Negroes to the number of above Five Hundred" rioted against impressment in Newport, Rhode Island, and in 1767

---

[60] Hoerder, *Crowd Action*, p. 14; George Rudé, *The Crowd in History* (New York, 1964). Maier stresses the weakness of colonial authorities, rather than the power of the crowd, in "Popular Uprisings and Civil Authority," pp. 19–20.

a mob of "Whites & Blacks all arm'd" attacked Capt. Jeremiah Morgan in a press riot in Norfolk. A mob of sailors, "sturdy boys & negroes" rose in the *Liberty* riot in Boston in 1768. Jesse Lemisch has noted that after 1763 "armed mobs of whites and Negroes repeatedly manhandled captains, officers, and crews, threatened their lives, and held them hostage for the men they pressed."[61]

Why African-Americans took to the streets to fight the press gang cannot be fully known, but that they did so at all is of interest, not least because getting aboard a naval ship was sometimes a way to freedom. Advertisements for runaway slaves demonstrated as much throughout the eighteenth century. Those who joined anti-impressment mobs probably sought to preserve bonds of family or some degree of freedom they had won for themselves. Perhaps they wanted to avoid the pestilence and punishment that ravaged many of the men impressed into the Royal Navy. Some may have simply preferred to stay with the devil they knew rather than risk a new one.

It may also be that African-Americans were attracted to the fight by the idiom through which seamen expressed their own opposition to impressment and service in the Royal Navy. On probably any dock, in any port, anywhere in America, there were sailors to be found who would—in the saltiest of language—denounce impressment as slavery plain and simple, governed by coercion, discipline, the lash, and a lack of rights. To take but one admittedly dramatic example: Michael Corbett and several of his brother tars fought against "being forced on board a man of war" in the port of Boston in 1769, claiming that "they preferred death to such a life as they deemed slavery." John Allen reiterated what many sea-

---

[61] Hutchinson, *History of Massachusetts-Bay,* 2:332; Bridenbaugh, *Cities in Revolt,* p. 309; Jeremiah Morgan to Francis Fauquier, Sept. 11, 1767, Adm. 1/2116, P.R.O.; Miller, *Sam Adams,* p. 142; Lemisch, "Jack Tar in the Streets," pp. 386, 391. For specific accounts of the riots, see *Newport Mercury,* July 16, 1764, and June 10, 1765; *New York Gazette, or Weekly Post-Boy,* July 12, 1764, and July 18, 1765; and *Weyman's New York Gazette,* July 18, 1765. See also Elaine Forman Crane, *A Dependent People: Newport, Rhode Island, in the Revolutionary Era* (New York, 1985), p. 113.

faring men had stated in practice and what Samuel Adams had written years before: that Americans "have a right, by the law of God, of nature, and nations, to reluct at, and even to resist any military or marine force." Allen then went on to insist on the moral equivalence between the impressment and enslavement. The press gang, he insisted, "ought ever to be held in the most hateful contempt, the same as you would *a banditti of slave-makers on the coast of Africa.*"[62]

The political critique of impressment as slavery dates back to the era of the English Revolution, when the Levellers and other radical groups denounced all forms of conscription. In their famous *Agreement of the People* (1647), the Levellers suggested that "the matter of impresting and constraining any of us to serve in the warres, is against our freedome; and therefore we do not allow it in our representatives." In a later pamphlet, *Foundations of Freedom* (1648), the Levellers outlined the antinomian basis of such resistance: "Every mans conscience being to be satisfied in the justnesse of that cause wherein he hazards his life." Peter Warren was thus correct in a quite crucial way when he claimed that the sailors of New England were "almost Levellers." As such, they and other seamen both expressed and expanded what Robin Blackburn has called "popular antislavery," which was both older and deeper than abolitionism proper.[63]

Workers white and black also participated in the popular upsurges against the Stamp Act, whose successful repeal was perhaps the key moment in the development of a Revolutionary movement in British North America. Peter Oliver observed that after the Stamp Act riots, "the *Hydra* was roused.

---

[62] During the fight, Michael Corbett harpooned a naval lieutenant in the throat, killing him, but was later acquitted in court by a verdict of justifiable homicide. See Oliver Morton Dickerson, comp., *Boston under Military Rule, 1768–1769, as Revealed in a Journal of the Times* (Boston, 1936), pp. 94–95, 110; John Allen, "Oration on the Beauties of Liberty," in Bruns, *Am I Not a Man*, pp. 258–59 (emphasis in original).

[63] Don M. Wolfe, *Leveller Manifestoes of the Puritan Revolution* (New York, 1944), pp. 227, 300. For other denunciations of impressment by the Levellers see pp. 125, 287, 320, 405. See also Robin Blackburn, *The Overthrow of Colonial Slavery, 1776–1848* (London, 1988), chap. 1.

Every factious Mouth vomited out curses against *Great Britain,* & the Press rung its charges against Slavery."[64]

The Stamp Act protests involved people of all classes, though sailors were singled out by many observers of the riots for their leadership and spirit. When commerce ground to a halt with the widespread refusal to use stamped paper, idle sailors, turned ashore and making no wages, became a volatile force in every port. Many an official must have agreed with the customs agent in New York who saw the power of "the Mob . . . daily increasing and gathering Strength, from the arrival of Seamen, and none going out, and who are the people that are most dangerous on these occasions, as their whole dependance for subsistence is upon Trade."[65]

Boston's mob took angry action against the property of stampman Andrew Oliver on August 14, 1765, then turned an even fiercer wrath against the house and refined belongings of Thomas Hutchinson twelve days later.[66] Then it was on to Newport, to which sailors likely carried the word and perhaps the experience of the tumults in Boston, and where loyalists Thomas Moffat and Martin Howard, Jr., suffered the same fate as Hutchinson on August 28.[67] In Newport, where the mercantile economy depended upon the labor of sailors and dockworkers black and white, the resistance to the Stamp

[64] Adair and Schutz, eds., *Peter Oliver's Origin & Progress,* p. 51; Edmund S. Morgan and Helen M. Morgan, *The Stamp Act Crisis: Prologue to Revolution* (Chapel Hill, 1953), pp. 208, 231–39.

[65] Nash, *Urban Crucible,* p. 366; Schlesinger, "Political Mobs," p. 244; Morgan and Morgan, *The Stamp Act Crisis,* p. 162.

[66] The likelihood that African-Americans took part in one or both of these crowds is suggested by the decision of popular leader Ebenezer Mackintosh to ban them from gatherings on Nov. 1 and 5, 1765. See Maier, *From Resistance to Revolution,* p. 70.

[67] Lovejoy notes that the attacks on Martin Howard, Jr., and Thomas Moffat began well before the publication of the Sept. 2 issue of the *Newport Mercury,* which carried the official news of the Boston tumults of Aug. 26. See his *Rhode Island Politics,* p. 105, and Sheila Skemp, "Newport's Stamp Act Rioters: Another Look," *Rhode Island History* 47 (1989):41–59.

Act was led by John Webber, probably a sailor and perhaps "a deserted convict."[68]

The actions taken by sailors, slaves, and others in Boston and Newport made the very threat of action all the more ominous in other colonies, as stamp distributors resigned before even receiving their commissions, and for good reason. The band of sailors known as the "Sons of Neptune" led three thousand rioters in an attack on New York's Fort George, the fortress of royal authority, which, like the multiracial conspirators of 1741, they tried to burn to the ground. In Wilmington, North Carolina, a "furious Mobb of Sailors &c." forced the stamp distributor to resign. Sailors also took part in mass actions against the Stamp Act in Antigua, St. Kitts, and Nevis, where they "behaved like young Lions."[69]

Seamen, with the occasional help of African-Americans, also played a major role in resisting the Townshend Revenue Act and the renewed power of the British customs service in the late 1760s and early 1770s. As Alfred F. Young has shown, seamen drew upon the custom of the sea to forge a new weapon in the arsenal of Revolutionary justice, the tarring and feathering that intimidated a great many British officials in the colonies. The clunk of the brush in the tar bucket echoed behind Thomas Gage's observation in 1769 that "the Officers of the Crown grow more timid, and more fearful of doing their Duty every Day."[70]

[68] Redington, ed., *Calendar of Home Office Papers*, 1:610; Morgan and Morgan, *Stamp Act Crisis*, p. 196. See also Louis P. Masur, "Slavery in Eighteenth-Century Rhode Island: Evidence from the Census of 1774," *Slavery and Abolition* 6 (1985):145; Crane, *A Dependent People*, pp. 63–64.

[69] Lloyd I. Rudolph notes that New York's mob featured "a large contingent of sailors and other waterfront characters." See his "The Eighteenth-Century Mob in America and Europe," *American Quarterly* 11 (1959):452; Spindel, "Law and Disorder," p. 8; *Pennsylvania Journal*, Nov. 21, Dec. 26, 1765. See also James Truslow Adams, *Revolutionary New England, 1691–1776* (Boston, 1923), p. 336; Lawrence Lee, "Days of Defiance: Resistance to the Stamp Act in Lower Cape Fear," *North Carolina Historical Review* 43 (1966):186–202.

[70] Young, "English Plebeian Culture," pp. 193–94; Thomas Gage, quoted in Schlesinger, "Political Mobs," p. 246. See also Steven Rosswurm, *Arms,*

One maritime action, the burning of the customs schooner *Gaspee* in Newport in 1772, proved to be another decisive moment in the development of the Revolutionary movement. "Lawless seamen" had long taken direct action against customs men, in Newport and elsewhere. After the *Gaspee* ran aground, three longboats crowded with sixty to seventy men boarded the ship, wounded the roundly despised Lt. William Dudingston, took him and his crew ashore, and set the vessel afire. These men were charged with what Lord Dartmouth described as "high treason, viz.: levying war against the King." The burning of the king's vessels had long signified as much.[71]

Most historians have held that merchants, John Brown in particular, were involved in the *Gaspee* affair, and perhaps too some artisans and farmers who had reasons of their own to dislike the customs service. But that sailors were involved, and centrally, there can be no doubt. Daniel Horsmanden, chief justice of the colony of New York and a member of the king's commission that investigated the *Gaspee* incident, was convinced that the act was "committed by a number of bold, daring, rash enterprising sailors." Horsmanden did not know if someone else had organized them or if these men of the sea had simply "banded themselves together."[72]

Seamen also led both the Golden Hill and Nassau Street riots in New York City and the King Street Riot, better remembered as the Boston Massacre. In both instances, sailors and other workers resented the ways in which British soldiers labored for less than customary wages along the waterfront; in New York they also resented the soldiers' efforts to destroy their fifty-eight-foot liberty pole, which, not surprisingly, resembled nothing so much as a ship's mast. Rioting and street

---

Country, and Class: The Philadelphia Militia and the "Lower Sort" during the American Revolution (New Brunswick, N.J., 1987), pp.32–33; Hoerder, *Crowd Action*, p. 241.

[71] Lemisch, "Jack Tar in the Streets," p. 398; Lovejoy, *Rhode Island Politics*, pp. 156, 159.

[72] Lovejoy, *Rhode Island Politics*, pp. 159, 164.

fighting ensued. Thomas Hutchinson and John Adams, among others, believed that the events in New York and Boston were related; perhaps they had common participants. Adams, who defended Captain Preston and his soldiers in trial, called the mob that assembled on King Street on "the Fatal Fifth of March" nothing but "a motley rabble of saucy boys, negroes and molattoes, Irish teagues, and out landish Jack Tarrs." Seamen also took part in the Tea Party, provoking Britain to a show of naked force in the Intolerable Acts, and an eventual confrontation that proved irreconcilable. During the Revolutionary War, sailors, free blacks, and slaves took part in mobs that harassed loyalists and diminished their political effectiveness.[73]

Occasionally the transit of radical ideas and practices—the oppositional ideas of "these most dangerous people"—can be traced from one port to another during the imperial crisis. Gov. William Bull of South Carolina, facing Stamp Act protests in Charleston, found that the "Minds of Men here were . . . universally poisoned with the Principles which were imbibed and propagated from Boston and Rhode Island." Soon, "after their example the People of this Town resolved to seize and destroy the Stamp Papers." Bull explained this development by noting that "at this time of Year, Vessels very frequently arrive" from Boston and Newport, where seamen and slaves had helped to protest the Stamp Act, just as they would do in Charleston. As it happened, "principles" as well as commodities were transported on those ships![74]

It is not surprising that "seamen, servants, boys, and negroes" should have made up such a large proportion of colonial crowds. They were, after all, a huge part of the urban population. According to the latest estimates, made by Gary B. Nash, Billy G. Smith, and Dirk Hoerder, seamen were the

[73] Boyer, "Lobster Backs, Liberty Boys, and Laborers in the Streets," pp. 289–308; Hiller B. Zobel, *The Boston Massacre* (New York, 1970); L. Kinvin Wroth and Hiller B. Zobel, eds., *Legal Papers of John Adams*, 3 vols. (Cambridge, Mass., 1965), 3:266; Hoerder, *Crowd Action*, chap. 13; Rosswurm, *Arms, Country, and Class*, pp. 46–48; Charles G. Steffen, *The Mechanics of Baltimore: Workers and Politics in the Age of Revolution, 1763–1812* (Urbana, Ill., 1984), p. 73.

[74] Bull quoted in Bridenbaugh, *Cities in Revolt*, pp. 313–14.

"largest single occupational group" in the colonial cities; moreover, free wage labor was increasing in all of the northern ports after 1763. Slaves, servants, apprentices, seamen, laborers, and poor craftsmen altogether made up some 50 to 60 percent of urban workingmen in the major colonial cities; slaves themselves made up roughly 15 percent of the group. It is, therefore, hardly surprising that urban crowds should have reflected this fundamental demographic fact.[75]

This bottom half of the urban class structure was connected by commonalities of culture as well. A subculture of apprentices, journeymen, servants, slaves, laborers, and sailors revolved around common work experiences and a common cultural life of revels, masques, fairs, May Day celebrations, street parties, taverns, and "disorderly houses." "Apprentices, servants, and even negroes" drank together in Hell Town in Philadelphia, just as "seamen and Negroes" caroused "at unseasonable hours" in Charleston. Black and white workers—slaves, free blacks, soldiers, sailors, and poor workingmen—congregated in 1741 at John Hughson's tavern in New York, where they planned a rebellion that would do in the "white people"—by which they meant the rich white people—of New York. Magistrate Daniel Horsmanden suggested that such taverns provided "opportunities for the most loose, debased, and abandoned wretches amongst us to cabal and confederate together and ripen themselves into these schools of mischief, for the execution of the most daring and detestable enterprizes. I fear there are yet many of these houses amongst us, and they are the bane and pest of the city. It was such that gave the opportunity of breeding this most horrid and execrable conspiracy." Grogshops, low tippling houses, and dancing cellars existed in every Atlantic port, much to the despair of colonial ruling classes who sought to criminalize and otherwise discourage contact between the free and unfree workers who used such settings to hatch conspiracies and

[75] Gary B. Nash, Billy G. Smith, and Dirk Hoerder, "Laboring Americans and the American Revolution," *Labor History* 24 (1983):418, 435. (Nash, Smith, and Hoerder note that class structure varied by city as they delineate common occupational patterns.) See also Nash, *Urban Crucible*, pp. 260, 320–21, and Sharon V. Salinger, *"To Serve Well and Faithfully": Labor and Indentured Servants in Pennsylvania, 1682–1800* (Cambridge, 1987), epilogue.

even to form a "maritime underground railroad" through which many escaped to freedom.[76] There was, therefore, a history of interracial cooperation that underlay the joint protests of sailors and slaves against impressment and other measures during the Revolutionary era.

Seamen and slaves thus expressed a militant mood summed up by Peter Timothy when he spoke of Charleston, South Carolina, in the summer of 1775: "In regard to War & Peace, I can only tell you that the Plebeians are still for War— but the noblesse [are] perfectly pacific." Their war was not always the conservative patriot's war, but it was war sure enough, and it pushed the Revolutionary vanguard to extreme positions and eventually to a declaration of independence. Contrary to those who have claimed that sailors, laborers, slaves, and other poor workingmen were in no position to participate in or "shape the revolutionary process,"[77] it is clear that these groups provided much of the spark, volatility, momentum, and sustained militancy for the attack on British policy after 1765.[78] In the process they provided an image of interracial cooperation that raises doubts whether racism was as monolithic in white society as is often assumed.[79]

[76] Eric Foner, *Tom Paine and Revolutionary America* (New York, 1976), pp. 48–50; Rosswurm, *Arms, Country, and Class,* p. 37; Salinger, *"To Serve Well and Faithfully,"* pp. 101–2; Morgan, "Black Life in Eighteenth-Century Charleston," pp. 206–7, 219; Davis, *Rumor of Revolt,* pp. 81, 194, 248 (Horsmanden quotation); Peter Linebaugh, "A Letter to Boston's 'Radical Americans' from a 'Loose and Disorderly' New Yorker, Autumn 1770," *Midnight Notes* 4 (1983); Gaspar, *Bondmen and Rebels,* pp. 138, 204; Rediker, *Between the Devil and the Deep Blue Sea,* chap. 1; N.A.T. Hall, "Maritime Maroons: *Grand Marronage* from the Danish West Indies," *William and Mary Quarterly,* 3d ser. 42 (1985):491–92. Crane notes a law passed in 1770 against "disorderly Houses kept by free Negroes and Mulattoes" in Newport (*A Dependent People,* p. 104).

[77] Hermann Wellenreuther, "Rejoinder" (to Nash, Smith, and Hoerder), *Labor History* 24 (1983):442.

[78] Peter Timothy, quoted in Maier, "Charleston Mob," p. 181; Countryman, *A People in Revolution,* pp. 37, 45.

[79] While arguing that some slaves did contribute directly to the patriot victory (hardly a controversial claim), I want to stress that I *am not* arguing that slaves shared the political ideals of a mainstream republicanism that was, in the opinion of Edmund S. Morgan, racist in its very essence (see

Indeed, the militant, interracial, working-class mob may have provided the most radical, and to loyalists and moderate patriots alike, the most frightening representation of liberty in the entire age of revolution. Paul Revere's famous but falsified pictorial account of the Boston Massacre quickly tried to make the "motley rabble" respectable by leaving black faces out of the crowd and putting into it entirely too many gentlemen.[80] The South Carolina Council of Safety complained of the attacks of sailors—"white and black armed men"—in December 1775.[81] It is not surprising, therefore, that well-to-do colonists often called the mob a "Hydra," a "many-headed monster," a "reptile," and a "many-headed power," using the same mythic terms that other parts of the Atlantic bourgeoisie had long used to describe and interpret its struggles against a diverse international working class.[82] Many-headedness was making its way toward democracy but not without fearful resistance from above.

The worries of the wealthy were understandable, for the politicized mob was one of the three most important "mass organizations" (along with the militia and the army) in the

---

Morgan, *American Slavery, American Freedom: The Ordeal of Colonial Virginia* [New York, 1975], chap. 16, pp. 385–87). Nor am I suggesting that racism did not exist among white workers, that sailors and slaves wanted the same things out of the Revolution, or that they supported it to the same degree. Many thousands of slaves, of course, deserted their masters for the British army.

[80] This is clearly and convincingly shown by Linebaugh in "A Letter to Boston's 'Radical Americans.'" The sailors of the schooner *Betsey* carried the news and the engraving of the massacre to London, where both were quickly republished and circulated more widely. See Clarence S. Brigham, *Paul Revere's Engravings* (Worcester, Mass., 1954), pp. 41–57.

[81] Quarles, *Negro in the American Revolution*, p. 125.

[82] William Godard, quoted in Steffen, *The Mechanics of Baltimore*, p. 73; Gouverneur Morris to Mr. Penn, May 20, 1774, Peter Force, ed., *American Archives*, 4th ser. 6 vols. (Washington, D.C., 1837–46), 1:343; Bull, quoted in Maier, "Charleston Mob," p. 185; "Poor Richard, 1747," in Leonard W. Labaree, ed., *The Papers of Benjamin Franklin*, 29 vols. to date (New Haven, 1959-), 3:106. Peter Oliver used the hydra and its poison to symbolize the "infectious growth of the revolution." See comments of Adair and Schutz in *Peter Oliver's Origin & Progress*, pp. xv, 35, 51–55, 88, 107.

Revolutionary movement, and it was certainly the hardest of the three to control.[83] Moreover, it was in most instances relatively democratic—almost anyone could join, and workingmen (but apparently not women) could rise to positions of momentary or long-term leadership. If relatively open, democratic crowds helped to make the Revolution, then their subsequent suppression by former revolutionaries was part of an American Thermidor, their condemnation by big landowners, merchants, and artisans part of a literal "enclosure movement" designed to move politics from "out-of-doors" to legislative chambers. When Samuel Adams, who helped to draw up Massachusetts's Riot Act of 1786, ceased to believe that the mob "embodied the fundamental rights of man against which government itself could be judged," he detached himself from an important source of democratic creativity and expression, the force that years ago had given him the best idea of his life.[84]

An excellent example of Thermidorian fears was a poem entitled *The Anarchiad,* written in 1786–87 by the Connecticut Wits (David Humphreys, Joel Barlow, John Trumbull, and Dr. Lemuel Hopkins) in specific response to Shays's Rebellion and in obvious memory of the popular insurgency and radical ideas that had fired the Revolutionary movement. The Wits expressed their hatred for mobs and popular action in no uncertain terms. They sneered at "democratic dreams," "the rights of man," and reducing all "To just one level." One of their darkest nightmares was what they called a "young DEMOCRACY from *hell.*"[85]

[83] This is not the place to enter into an extended discussion of the relationship between directed mobs and self-activating mobs. For a good discussion of the situation in Massachusetts, see Hoerder's conclusion to *Crowd Action,* pp. 368–77.

[84] Maier, "Charleston Mob," pp. 181, 186, 188, and idem, "Popular Uprisings and Civil Authority," pp. 33–35; Hoerder, *Crowd Action,* pp. 378–88. Gordon S. Wood notes that "once-fervent Whig leaders began to sound like the Tories of 1775" when confronted by the mobs, popular committees, and "People Out-of-Doors" in the 1780s. See his *Creation of the American Republic, 1776–1787* (Chapel Hill, 1969), pp. 319–28.

[85] David Humphreys, Joel Barlow, John Trumbull, and Lemuel Hopkins, *The Anarchiad: A New England Poem (1786–1787),* ed. Luther G. Riggs (1861; reprint ed., Gainesville, Fla., 1967), pp. 29, 56, 38, 69.

The Wits had not forgotten the role of sailors in the Revolution. In fact, in their imagined "state" of anarchy, the "mighty Jacktar guides the helm." He had been "Nurs'd on the waves, in blust'ring tempests bred, / His heart of marble, and his brain of lead." Having sailed "in the whirlwind" as a part of his work, this hardhearted, thick-headed man naturally "enjoys the storm" of revolution. The Wits alluded to the revolutionary acts of sailors when they referred to "seas of boiling tar."[86]

The rebellious actions of workers free and unfree thus illuminate the clashing, ambiguous nature of the American Revolution, particularly its libertarian origins, radical momentum, and conservative political conclusion. Direct actions undertaken by sailors and slaves to "deliver themselves" to freedom must be considered part of the ideological origins of both the American Revolution and the Revolutionary attack on slavery that ended in America with the Civil War. The intersection of the distinct trajectories of resistance of sailors and slaves during the 1760s and 1770s heightened the political instability and larger sense of crisis in America and pushed the colonies toward the Revolution. The political implications of both the separate and joint actions of sailors and slaves, in turn, hastened the sudden, reactionary retreat from the radical, universalistic language of 1776. The redefinition of the concept of race during the Revolutionary era may be yet another dimension of Thermidor.[87]

The ideas of Samuel Adams, J. Philmore, James Otis, John Allen, Thomas Paine, the Connecticut Wits, and others—whether radical or conservative, early or late in the Revolutionary era—reflected in one way or another popular "motion and commotion" and long-term cycles of struggle. Mass actions in Boston and St. Mary's Parish, Jamaica, generated powerful new ideas that would circulate around the Atlantic world for decades to come.

And if the mass actions of sailors and slaves affected the

[86] Ibid., pp. 14–15, 34.

[87] Barbara Jeanne Fields, "Slavery, Race, and Ideology in the United States of America," *New Left Review* 181 (1990):101.

intellectual history of the American Revolution, they also deeply influenced its organizational history. The militancy of workers black and white in Boston, Newport, New York, and Charleston led to the formation of the Sons of Liberty, the earliest intercolonial organization to coordinate anti-imperial resistance.[88] Richard B. Morris has written that New York's sailors "were organized as the Sons of Neptune, apparently antedating the Sons of Liberty, for whom they may well have provided the pattern of organization."[89] The commotions around the *Gaspee* incident in 1772 set in motion a new round of organization, for in the aftermath of this "bold enterprize" an even more crucial form of revolutionary organization, the committees of correspondence, began to be established throughout the colonies. To loyalist Daniel Leonard the committees were "the foulest, subtlest, and most venomous serpent ever issued from the egg of sedition."[90]

Direct action thus accelerated the process of political organization, but in an ambiguous if not contradictory way. For by 1766 a central goal of what Pauline Maier has called "ordered resistance" was to limit the initiative of the rowdier, more militant elements such as sailors and slaves. The more "respectable" parts of the movement wanted to defang the serpent. In New York, for example, the Sons of Liberty came into being as a reaction against the "threatened anarchy" of autonomous risings against the press and the Stamp Act in 1764 and 1765. Everywhere the Sons began to advertise themselves as the guarantors of good order, as the necessary counterpoint of the riots, violence, and lawlessness, the "motion and commotion" amidst which they themselves had been born. In so

[88] My emphasis on the mob as a progenitor of the Sons of Liberty is by no means to deny the importance of other sources such as the Loyal Nine and the Charleston Fire Company. See Maier, *From Resistance to Revolution*, pp. 85–86; Morgan and Morgan, *Stamp Act Crisis*, p. 257.

[89] Richard B. Morris, *Government and Labor in Early America* (New York, 1946), p. 189.

[90] Lovejoy, *Rhode Island Politics*, p. 159; Daniel Leonard, quoted in Esmond S. Wright, *Fabric of Freedom, 1763–1800*, rev. ed. (New York, 1978), pp. 77–78.

doing they showed that revolution and counterrevolution could advance together.[91]

And yet the revolutionary implications of the struggles of the 1760s and 1770s could not easily be contained, by the Sons of Liberty or by others, which supplies another argument for putting the radical ideas and practices of the Revolution in an Atlantic context. So doing provides a better basis for understanding later moments of resistance such as the rising incidence of mutiny after 1776 among British sailors, who doubtless told yarns of heroic battle against the press gangs and the king's authority in America. Soldiers black and white who served in the French army in America may have learned lessons of their own. Several of these veterans would later lead the modern world's second colonial war for liberation and its greatest slave revolt, in Haiti. Other veterans, from the eastern side of the Atlantic, may have led a series of revolts against feudal land tenure that accelerated the revolution in France. The news carried by Hessian soldiers back to their homeland would soon propel a new generation of settlers toward Revolutionary America. Several observers believed that news of the American Revolution helped to inspire slave rebels in Hanover Parish, Jamaica, in 1776, if indeed any inspiration was needed.[92]

Final words go to John Adams. Of the five workingmen killed in the Boston Massacre in 1770, he said, "The blood of the martyrs, right or wrong, proved to be the seed of the

[91] Maier, *From Resistance to Revolution*, pp. 76, 97–100; Gilje, *Road to Mobocracy*, p. 48.

[92] Arthur N. Gilbert, "The Nature of Mutiny in the British Navy in the Eighteenth Century," in Daniel Masterson, ed., *Naval History: The Sixth Symposium of the U.S. Naval Academy* (Wilmington, Del., 1987), pp. 111–21; Sidney Kaplan and Emma Nogrady Kaplan, *The Black Presence in the Era of the American Revolution*, rev. ed. (Amherst, Mass. 1989), pp. 68–69; Forrest McDonald, "The Relation of the French Peasant Veterans of the American Revolution to the Fall of Feudalism in France, 1789–1792," *Agricultural History* 25 (1951):151–61; Horst Dippel, *Germany and the American Revolution, 1770–1800: A Sociohistorical Investigation of Late Eighteenth-Century Political Thinking*, trans. Bernard A. Uhlendorf (Chapel Hill, 1977), pp. 228–36; Richard B. Sheridan, "The Jamaican Slave Insurrection Scare of 1776 and the American Revolution," *Journal of Negro History* 61 (1976):290–308.

congregation." Adams thus made clear the working-class origins of the Revolution and the new nation, for the blood of the martyrs, as everyone knew, was the blood of a journeyman, an apprentice, and three wage laborers: a ropewalker and two seamen, one of whom was a runaway slave of African and Native American ancestry who lived in the Bahama Islands. His name was Crispus Attucks. Of this martyr John Adams had said earlier, his "very looks would be enough to terrify any person," or at least any person like Adams himself. He might well have said the same about the "motley rabble" Attucks had led into battle, thereby speaking the fearful mind of the moderate leadership of the Revolutionary movement. And yet despite his efforts to distance himself from this motley crew, Adams knew that its motions and commotions had animated the Revolutionary movement. Adams came perhaps as close as he could to saying so in 1773, when he wrote a letter about liberty, addressed it to Thomas Hutchinson, and signed it "Crispus Attucks."[93]

[93] Schlesinger, "Political Mobs," p. 250; Wroth and Zobel, eds., *Legal Papers of John Adams*, 3:269; Adams, ed., *Works of John Adams*, 2:322. On Crispus Attucks, see Kaplan and Kaplan, *Black Presence*, pp. 6–8. I would like to thank Alfred F. Young for pointing out Adams's use of Attucks as a pen name.

BILLY G. SMITH

Runaway Slaves in the Mid-Atlantic Region during the Revolutionary Era

MOSES GRIMES LANDED in the York County, Pennsylvania, jail in early October 1764 on the suspicion of being a runaway slave. The jailer dismissed Grimes's claim to be free and instead advertised him in the newspaper as being "this Country born, about 5 feet 6 Inches high," wearing "a great Thickset Coat and Jacket, blue Breeches, with white Metal Buttons," and riding a "bay Horse." The notice advised Grimes's master to claim him and to pay the cost of interment within a month, otherwise Moses would be sold as a slave for the fees. Philip Graybill, probably a relative of the jailer, purchased Grimes a few months afterward. Nearly five years later, Moses apparently decided he would no longer be a slave, and he absconded at least four times in the next three years. During the evening of March 19, 1769, he fled, taking with him a considerable amount of clothing, which suggested his intention to be absent a long while. But Grimes was quickly apprehended and then sold to another York County resident. Moses left again just two months later. By this time he was "about 28 years of age" and had been waiting tables and taking care of horses at a tavern. By his master's reckoning, Grimes was also "very talkative, and given to lying" and would

I wish to thank Susan E. Klepp, Gary B. Nash, Julius S. Scott, Mechal Sobel, Jean R. Soderlund, Michael Zuckerman, and the members of the seminars sponsored by the Philadelphia Center for Early American History and the University of Delaware for their critical comments on various drafts of this essay.

likely try to "pass for a free man, and get somebody to forge a pass for him." One advantage Moses enjoyed was that he was "very yellow, and has passed for a Mulattoe."

Although recaptured, Moses was not deterred from his ambition to be free. He left, in company with a white apprentice, seeking, according to his owner, "to pass for a free Negroe." Caught and resold to a Philadelphia resident, Grimes ran again, prompting his master to offer a sixty-shilling reward— the equivalent of a month's pay for a day laborer—and to provide the following physical description of him: "Of a yellowish complexion, the fore part of his head shaved, and is rather bald, [and] he sometimes wears a wig." Grimes was active in Philadelphia's African-American community since he "is very religious, preaches to his colour, walks before burials, and marries." In addition, his master added, "he is very artful, pretends to be free, and will no doubt get a forged pass; he is very fond of liquor, and if spoke familiarly to pretends to simplicity and laughs." Grimes's master "supposed" that he had gone in 1772 either to North Carolina or to his previous residence in York County.

Grimes apparently served during the Revolutionary War. When Jane Wilson fled slavery in 1779, her master believed that she had run to her "husband in the regiment belonging to this state [Virginia] commanded by Col. Gibson, a Mulatto named Moses Grymes, who I am informed waits on Col. Brent." At this point Grimes disappears from the historical sources.[1]

Thousands of slaves fled bondage in the Mid-Atlantic re-

---

[1] Most vignettes in this essay are based on advertisements that appeared in the *Pennsylvania Gazette* (Philadelphia). The following issues contained notices for Moses Grimes: Oct. 18, 1764, Mar. 30 and July 13, 1769, May 17, 1770, and Nov. 25, 1772. Wilson was advertised in the *Pennsylvania Packet, or, the General Advertiser* (Philadelphia), Sept. 30, 1779. Hundreds of advertisements have been reproduced in Billy G. Smith and Richard Wojtowicz, eds., *Blacks Who Stole Themselves: Advertisements for Runaways in the Pennsylvania Gazette, 1728–1790* (Philadelphia, 1989), and in Richard Wojtowicz and Billy G. Smith, "Fugitives: Newspaper Advertisements for Runaway Slaves, Indentured Servants, and Apprentices," in Billy G. Smith, ed., *Life in Early Philadelphia: Documents from the Revolutionary and Early National Periods* (forthcoming).

gion during the eighteenth century. Some, like Moses Grimes, fled repeatedly, inadvertently enabling us to reconstruct a few aspects of their lives, at least as recorded in advertisements published by their masters. Others appear in the records only fleetingly, yet they still leave a powerful impression. Perhaps intending to pass as a "Cook of a Vessel," and thereby escape America altogether, Caesar ran away even though "he has both his legs cut off, and walks on his Knees." Although it limited her chances for a successful escape, Dorcas took both her infants when she fled to join her fugitive lover. Another Moses, after "endeavouring to prevail upon the Negroes in this neighbourhood to go with him and join the ministerial army," declared his personal independence in 1776, a few months after the Continental Congress affirmed the nation's separation from Great Britain. "It is hoped," his master raged, that "every lover of his country will endeavour to apprehend so daring a villain."[2]

These examples permit momentary glimpses into the world of fugitives and slaves during the Revolutionary era. Seven decades ago, J. Franklin Jameson wrote that a very "serious question, in any consideration of the [impact of the] American Revolution on the status of persons, is that of its influence on the institution of slavery." But Jameson addressed that issue by focusing solely on the actions of whites to the neglect of the endeavors of blacks. Of course scholars have subsequently vastly expanded our knowledge of the lives and cultures of slaves and of the myriad creative ways in which they resisted slavery and attempted to gain their freedom during the tumultous political events of the time.[3]

[2] *Pennsylvania Gazette:* Caesar, Sept. 20, 1789; Dorcas, Aug. 20, 1794; Moses, Sept. 25, 1776.

[3] J. Franklin Jameson, *The American Revolution Considered as a Social Movement* (1926; reprint ed., Princeton, 1967), p. 21. Only the most recent of the numerous excellent studies of slavery, abolition, and black life in the Mid-Atlantic during the eighteenth century can be cited here. These include Allan Kulikoff, *Tobacco and Slaves: The Development of Southern Cultures in the Chesapeake, 1680–1800* (Chapel Hill, 1986); Jean R. Soderlund, *Quakers and Slavery: A Divided Spirit* (Princeton, 1985); Gary B. Nash, *Forging Freedom: The Formation of Philadelphia's Black Community, 1720–1840* (Cambridge,

This essay analyzes escapees and slavery in Pennsylvania, Delaware, southern New Jersey, and northeastern Maryland during the eighteenth century, focusing in particular on the Revolutionary period. After briefly sketching a few aspects of slavery in that region, I will examine the characteristics of African-American fugitives and their escape patterns. Most runaways in the Mid-Atlantic, in contrast to fugitives in other areas, aimed permanently to liberate themselves, especially in the decades after 1760. Moreover, by absconding and resisting bondage, slaves not only established their personal freedom, but they also challenged the "peculiar institution" in the North and greatly hastened its demise during and after the Revolution.

The number of blacks enslaved in Pennsylvania, Delaware, and New Jersey increased from 7,066 in 1720 to 25,392 in 1780, then declined to 20,281 by the end of the century (see table 1). Most of that growth resulted from forced immigration as whites bought slaves from southern owners, the West Indies, and Africa. Slaves comprised about 5 percent of the inhabitants of the Mid-Atlantic during the eighteenth century, although this aggregate statistic conceals the importance of slave labor in particular locales. For example, enslaved blacks counted for 17 percent of the residents in certain New Jersey towns in 1790, for 25 percent of Philadelphia's citizens early in the century, and for 11 percent of the inhabitants of the three colonies in 1720.[4]

Mass., 1988); Gary B. Nash and Jean R. Soderlund, *Freedom by Degrees: Emancipation in Pennsylvania and Its Aftermath* (New York, 1991); and Shane White, *Somewhat More Independent: The End of Slavery in New York City, 1770–1810* (Athens, Ga., 1991).

[4] Statistics for New Jersey, 1720–80, are from the U.S. Bureau of the Census, *Historical Statistics of the United States: Colonial Times to 1970*, 2 vols. (Washington, D.C., 1975), 2:1168, reduced by estimates of the number of free blacks in Nash and Soderlund, *Freedom by Degrees*, p. 7. Delaware data, 1750–80, are from Patience Essah, "Slavery and Freedom in the First State: The History of Blacks in Delaware from the Colonial Period to 1865," Ph.D. diss., University of California, Los Angeles, 1985, pp. 21, 100–101. Delaware statistics, 1720–40, are estimated using the methodology developed by Essah. The slave populations of Pennsylvania and Philadelphia from 1720

Like whites, the vast majority of blacks lived in farm communities and engaged in the multitude of tasks associated with raising cereals and livestock. Black males spent much of their time in these pursuits, although a minority worked in such large-scale enterprises as mills, tanneries, and iron foundries, and many toiled as craftsmen during the slack winter months.[5] African-American women likewise labored in the fields and cared for animals, but they also performed domestic tasks associated at that time with their gender. However, both men and women crossed traditionally defined sexual boundaries in their employment. Simon, for instance, was one of many black males who "understands working on a farm, but more especially house and kitchen work, is an excellent cook, can wash, spin, sew, knit, &c."[6]

---

through 1780 are from Nash and Soderlund, *Freedom by Degrees*, pp. 5, 7, 15. All figures for 1790 and 1800 are from the U.S. Bureau of the Census, *A Century of Population Growth from the First Census of the United States to the Twelfth 1790–1900* (Washington, D.C., 1909), pp. 57, 133. Maidenhead, Lower-Freehold, and Middletown were a few New Jersey towns with a high proportion of slaves (U.S. Census Office, *Return of the Whole Number of Persons within the Several Districts of the United States* [Philadelphia, 1801], pp. 42–43). The best statistics for Philadelphia are calculated by Jean R. Soderlund, "Black Importation and Migration," *Proceedings of the American Philosophical Society* 133 (1989): 144–53.

[5] On the employment of slaves in the Mid-Atlantic, see Ira Berlin, "Time, Space, and the Evolution of Afro-American Society on British Mainland North America," *American Historical Review* 85 (1980): 46–47; Nash and Soderlund, *Freedom by Degrees*, pp. 3–40; Soderlund, *Quakers and Slavery*, pp. 69–73; Edgar J. McManus, *Black Bondage in the North* (Syracuse, N.Y., 1973), pp. 36–54; Jerome H. Woods, Jr., "The Negro in Early Pennsylvania: The Lancaster Experience, 1730–1790," in Elinor Miller and Eugene D. Genovese, eds., *Plantation, Town, and Country: Essays on the Local History of American Slave Society* (Urbana, Ill., 1974), pp. 447–48; Frances D. Pingeon, "Slavery in New Jersey on the Eve of the Revolution," in William C. Wright, ed., *New Jersey in the American Revolution*, rev. ed. (Trenton, N.J., 1974), pp. 51–52, 57; Arthur Cecil Bining, *Pennsylvania Iron Manufacture in the Eighteenth Century* (1938; reprint ed., Harrisburg, 1973), pp. 93–102; and Paul F. Paskoff, *Industrial Evolution: Organization, Structure, and Growth of the Pennsylvania Iron Industry, 1750–1860* (Baltimore, 1983), pp. 14–15.

[6] *Pennsylvania Gazette*, Jan. 26, 1785. See also Jean R. Soderlund, "Black Women in Colonial Pennsylvania," *Pennsylvania Magazine of History and Biography* 107 (1983): 49–68, and Debra Newman, "Black Women in the Era

Slavery assumed various forms in the Delaware Valley. In particular, the nature of bondage and the lives of slaves were different in the city from what they were in the country. Urban slaves generally worked in more diverse capacities than their rural counterparts. Domestic duties defined the work world of most black women in Philadelphia, and their owners sometimes hired them out to wash clothes, wait tables, and help out in taverns and inns. Males likewise labored around their masters' homes as cooks, coachmen, and personal attendants, but a great many worked as sailors, longshoremen, day laborers, and artisans. Even while they served valuable economic functions, slaves also frequently represented symbols of their owners' status.[7]

As in all slave societies, the needs of masters did much to shape the lives of bondpeople, setting the boundaries within which they lived and maneuvered and thereby influencing the nature of their culture and families. Owners held most slaves singly or in groups of two or three, meaning the majority of African-Americans in Pennsylvania and southern New Jersey worked side by side with their masters and often lived in their owners' home. Blacks in Delaware and northeastern Maryland more likely resided and labored in groups on large farms engaged in tobacco and wheat production. In more cramped urban quarters, slaves occupied back rooms and closets in their masters' houses and associated with whites in everyday affairs.[8]

---

of the American Revolution in Pennsylvania," *Journal of Negro History* 61 (1976): 276–89.

[7] Nash and Soderlund, *Freedom by Degrees*, pp. 20–22; Nash, "Slaves and Slaveowners in Colonial Philadelphia," *William and Mary Quarterly*, 3d ser. 10 (1973): 247–52; Soderlund, *Quakers and Slavery*, pp. 61–65; Berlin, "Time, Space, and Evolution," pp. 47–49; Allan Tully, "Patterns of Slaveholding in Colonial Pennsylvania," *Journal of Social History* 6 (1973): 286; McManus, *Black Bondage in the North*, pp. 41–42; Woods, "Negro in Early Pennsylvania," pp. 447–48. Numerous advertisements from the *Pennsylvania Gazette* offering slaves for sale, some of which indicated their occupations, further support this analysis of the jobs performed by urban bondpeople.

[8] Nash and Soderlund, *Freedom by Degrees*, pp. 14–40; White, *Somewhat More Independent*, pp. 3–21.

Table 1. Slave population in Philadelphia, Pennsylvania, New Jersey, and Delaware

					All three states	
Year	Philadelphia	Pennsylvania	New Jersey	Delaware	Number	% of all residents
1720	611	2,000	2,385	2,681*	7,066	10.7
1730	481	1,241	3,008	1,831*	6,080	6.2
1740	708	2,055	4,366	3,964*	10,385	6.6
1,750	798	2,822†	5,354	5,740	13,916	6.3
1760	978	4,309†	6,567	6,650	17,526	5.6
1770	1,375	5,561†	8,220†	7,050†	20,831	5.3
1780	450	6,855†	10,060†	8,477†	25,392	5.0
1790	301	3,760	11,423	8,887	24,070	3.6
1800	55	1,706	12,422	6,153	20,281	2.4

SOURCES: Statistics for New Jersey from 1720 through 1780 are from the U.S. Bureau of the Census, *Historical Statistics of the United States: Colonial Times to 1970,* 2 vols. (Washington, D.C., 1975), 2:1168, and reduced by estimates of the number of free blacks in Gary B. Nash and Jean R. Soderlund, *Freedom by Degrees: Emancipation in Pennsylvania and Its Aftermath* (New York, 1991), p. 7. The Delaware data for 1750 through 1780 are from Patience Essah, "Slavery and Freedom in the First State: The History of Blacks in Delaware from the Colonial Period to 1865," Ph.D. diss., University of California, Los Angeles, 1985, pp. 21, 100–101. The Delaware statistics for 1720 through 1740 are estimated using the methodology developed by Essah. The slave populations of both Pennsylvania and Philadelphia from 1720 through 1780 are from Nash and Soderlund, *Freedom by Degrees,* pp. 5, 7, 15. All figures for 1790 and 1800 are from the U.S. Bureau of the Census, *A Century of Population Growth from the First Census of the United States to the Twelfth, 1790–1900* (Washington, D.C., 1909), pp. 57, 133.

NOTE: Data for Philadelphia do not include slaves in its two suburbs, Southwark and the Northern Liberties.

*Data augmented by the estimated number of blacks not included in extant records.
†Data reduced by estimates of the number of free blacks.

Blacks consequently learned the rudiments of Anglo-American culture quickly. For many slaves, the acculturation process, as Ira Berlin has noted (though perhaps exaggerated), took "a matter of years, not generations." While slaves socialized with one another, especially in the urban setting, their physical isolation from each other in the countryside undermined their ability easily to forge a distinct African-

American culture. Still, even though blacks in the Delaware Valley, like their brothers and sisters in New England and New York, accepted many aspects of European culture, they struggled to maintain a separate identity and sense of community.[9]

Bondpeople in the middle colonies and states generally enjoyed less success than southern slaves in establishing and maintaining families. Philadelphia's African-Americans often led fragmented family lives, bearing relatively few children, living together infrequently, and forming short-term relationships at best. Birthrates among the city's slaves were low, in part because urban owners viewed slave children as an extra expense and an added burden, and Philadelphia masters actively discouraged their human property from reproducing. "Indeed," one newspaper contributor commented, "in this city, negroes just born, are considered as an incumbrance only, and if humanity did not forbid it, they would be instantly given away." The brisk market in slaves and the high mortality in the city also tore black families apart. Even though Philadelphia blacks struggled hard to establish viable families, circumstances beyond their control doomed most of their efforts.[10]

[9] Berlin, "Time, Space, and Evolution," p. 49. On the development of African-American cultures in northern areas, see Nash, *Forging Freedom,* chap. 3; White, *Somewhat More Independent,* pp. 92–95; and William Piersen, *Black Yankees: The Development of an Afro-American Subculture in Eighteenth-Century New England* (Amherst, Mass., 1988).

[10] "Another Letter to a Clergyman," *Pennsylvania Packet, or, the General Advertiser,* Jan. 1, 1780. These arguments and the evidence about the family lives of Philadelphia's slaves are developed more fully in Billy G. Smith, "Black Family Life in Philadelphia from Slavery to Freedom, 1750–1800," in Catherine E. Hutchins, ed., *Shaping a National Culture: The Philadelphia Experience, 1750–1800* (forthcoming). See also Soderlund, *Quakers and Slavery,* pp. 78–80, and, for similarities in New York City, see White, *Somewhat More Independent,* pp. 188–92. Yet information about the family lives and reproductive activities of black Philadelphians is fragmentary and remains open to other interpretations. Susan E. Klepp, for example, calculated considerably higher birthrates among the city's blacks before the Revolution, suggesting more success in the formation of black families (Klepp, "Seasoning and Society: Racial Differences in Mortality in Eighteenth-Century Philadelphia," *William and Mary Quarterly,* 3d ser. 51 [1994]: 473–506).

Slaves in the countryside were more capable of creating families and bearing children, in part because of greater acquiescence on the part of many masters who prized black children because of their potential productive value to their farms. In addition, as William Moraley, a New Jersey indentured servant noted, owners "make [slaves] some amends, by suffering them to marry, which makes them easier, and often prevents their running away." Yet both the physical distance between slaves and local unbalanced sex ratios curtailed family formation and reproduction, at least in comparison to slaves in the Chesapeake Bay region. The fact that most Mid-Atlantic bondpeople resided on small, scattered farms set limits on their ability to define their intimate interpersonal relations, and the gender differences among slaves who dotted the countryside exacerbated the problem by creating shortages of potential lovers and marriage partners.[11]

During the second half of the eighteenth century, the antislavery movement enjoyed notable successes that affected the lives of blacks. Influenced by both ideological and economic arguments against slavery, many Mid-Atlantic masters manumitted their slaves. More important, in 1780 Pennsylvania became the first state to end slavery by legislative act. But the institution of racial bondage was to be brought to a gradual rather than an abrupt conclusion: Children born to slaves after March 1 were freed after having served as bound ser-

---

[11] Susan E. Klepp and Billy G. Smith, eds., *The Infortunate: The Voyage and Adventures of William Moraley, An Indentured Servant* (University Park, Pa., 1992), p. 94. See Nash and Soderlund, *Freedom by Degrees*, pp. 38–40; Smith, "Black Family Life in Philadelphia"; Jean R. Soderlund and Gary B. Nash, "Slavery on the Periphery: Pennsylvania" (Paper presented at "Cultivation and Culture," a conference held at the University of Maryland, College Park, April 1989); Soderlund, *Quakers and Slavery*, pp. 78–85; Soderlund, "Black Importation and Migration," pp. 144–53; Berlin, "Time, Space, and Evolution," pp. 50–51; Merle G. Brouwer, "Marriage and Family Life among Blacks in Colonial Pennyslvania," *Pennsylvania Magazine of History and Biography* 99 (1975): 368–72. African customs also probably played a role in maintaining relatively low birth rates in both the country and city. See Russell R. Menard, "The Maryland Slave Population, 1658 to 1730: A Demographic Profile of Blacks in Four Counties," *William and Mary Quarterly*, 3d ser. 32 (1975): 41, and Eugene D. Genovese, *Roll, Jordan, Roll: The World the Slaves Made* (New York, 1976), pp. 498–99.

vants for twenty-one years if they were female or for twenty-eight years if they were male. The law failed to liberate any living slaves.[12]

Just as the law against slavery did not intend to bring bondage to a sudden halt, neither was it fashioned to "give any relief or shelter to any absconding or runaway negro." Masters retained the right to pursue and claim their human property, and the legal rewards and penalties for seizing fugitives or aiding their escape remained unchanged. Still, the gradual emancipation of slaves after 1780 encouraged the growth of a sizable free black community in Pennsylvania, especially in Philadelphia, and thus provided a haven where runaways might blend into a racially mixed population.[13]

During the final two decades of the century, Pennsylvania stood as an oasis in the midst of states which had not made the commitment to end slavery. By 1784 New England had joined the Keystone State in phasing out racial bondage, but proslavery forces in New York, New Jersey, Delaware, and Maryland continued strong resistance. New York took fifteen more years and New Jersey two more decades to legislate gradual emancipation.[14]

I used advertisements for runaway slaves that appeared in six of Philadelphia's newspapers to analyze African-American

[12] The antislavery movement is discussed in Arthur Zilversmit, *The First Emancipation: The Abolition of Slavery in the North* (Chicago, 1967), Soderlund, *Quakers and Slavery,* and Nash and Soderlund, *Freedom by Degrees.* Also see the recent debate in David Brion Davis, "Reflections on Abolitionism and Ideological Hegemony," *American Historical Review* 92 (1987): 797–812, and Thomas L. Haskell, "Convention and Hegemonic Interest in the Debate over Antislavery: A Reply to Davis and Ashworth," ibid., pp. 829–78. The legislation is in James T. Mitchell and Henry Flanders, comps., *The Statutes at Large of Pennsylvania from 1682 to 1801,* 18 vols. (Harrisburg, Pa., 1896–1911), 10:67–73.

[13] Mitchell and Flanders, comps., *Statutes at Large,* 10:71; Nash, *Forging Freedom,* chaps. 2 and 3; Ira Berlin, *Slaves without Masters: The Free Negro in the Antebellum South* (New York, 1974), pp. 37–38.

[14] Winthrop D. Jordan, *White over Black: American Attitudes toward the Negro, 1550–1812* (Chapel Hill, 1968), pp. 345–49; Zilversmit, *First Emancipation,* pp. 124, 155; Berlin, *Slaves without Masters,* pp. 20–29.

fugitives.[15] These notices chronicle the stories of 1,804 escapees and permit a systemic analysis of many of their characteristics.[16] For example, masters described the "typical" eighteenth-century runaway in that region as being a man in his mid-twenties, 5 feet 8 inches tall, born on the North American continent, and living in Pennsylvania, working as a craftsman, speaking some English, fleeing in solitude during the summer months, seeking to "pass for a free man," and being worth a reward of 50 shillings for his capture. Of course, this composite depiction disguises as much as it reveals. As always, human experience varied tremendously, and runaways cannot be accurately captured by a single description or one set

[15] Because of the large number of newspapers published in Philadelphia, and because some issues are no longer extant, it was impossible to count all the fugitives advertised in every city newspaper. Since Benjamin Franklin's *Pennsylvania Gazette* was the most widely circulated and longest lasting newspaper, I used its advertisements to anchor my study of runaways, and I combed each of its issues between its founding in 1728 and 1796. I also counted the fugitives advertised in all published issues of the *American Weekly Mercury* (1719–46) and the *Pennsylvania Chronicle* (1767–74). I tabulated all advertised runaways in the *Pennsylvania Ledger* (1775–83) and in the *Pennsylvania Packet* (1771–90) for six of their years of publication, and in the *Aurora* (1792–96) for two of its years of publication. Gary B. Nash generously shared data on advertisements for slaves escaped from urban Philadelphia and Chester County, Pennsylvania, included in another dozen city newspapers between 1771 and 1796. I deleted duplicate advertisements among all the newspapers from the tally of advertised fugitives. To estimate the total number of advertised runaway slaves in all of the city's newspapers, I calculated the advertised escapees in the "missing" or unsurveyed issues of a specific newspaper from the ratio of the number of known advertised fugitives in that same newspaper compared to the advertised runaways in the *Pennsylvania Gazette* during the appropriate time period.

[16] The strengths and weaknesses of these advertisements as historical records are discussed in Smith and Wojtowicz, eds., *Blacks Who Stole Themselves*, pp. 4–5. It is important to note that the advertisements by no means indicate *all* of the escape attempts by blacks living in the middle colonies and states since fugitives often went unadvertised. As Peter H. Wood notes, advertised runaways probably represent "little more than the top of an ill-defined iceberg" (*Black Majority: Negroes in Colonial South Carolina from 1670 through the Stono Rebellion* [New York, 1974], p. 240). See also Betty Wood, *Slavery in Colonial Georgia, 1730–1775* (Athens, Ga., 1984), pp. 170–72, and Philip D. Morgan, "Colonial South Carolina Runaways: Their Significance for Slave Culture," *Slavery and Abolition* 6 (1985): 57–58.

of statistics. The following pages thus explore these characteristics of escapees in some detail.

The vast majority of the advertised runaways escaped from
the colonies and states in the Delaware Valley area: 49 percent
ran from Pennsylvania (including 18 percent from Philadelphia), 9 percent from Delaware, 16 percent from New Jersey,
and 16 percent from northeast Maryland. An additional 10
percent fled from Virginia, New York, and New England.

Running away was primarily a male activity. Although they
comprised half of the slave population, women accounted for
only one of every ten fugitives.[17] That the burden of child
care fell disproportionately to them undoubtedly limited their
escape opportunities since few willingly abandoned their off-
spring. In only one recorded incident did a woman leave her
child behind (although some men apparently abandoned
their families). Moreover, because women were more intimately involved with their children and likely valued family
ties more strongly than did men, women commonly may have
taken unexcused vacations to visit their relations. Expecting
their voluntary return, their masters probably hesitated to
pay for an advertisement and to offer a reward, which partially accounts for the low number of advertised female fugitives. Hagar Jones, for example, obtained "a pass for 8 days,
in order to visit a child of her's in the city of Philadelphia," but
when she failed to reappear, her owner waited several months
before placing a notice in the newspaper. The involvement of
slave women primarily in domestic work limited their geo-

[17] The proportion of advertised women runaways in the Mid-Atlantic remained constant throughout the eighteenth century. Women accounted for
about one of every ten escapees in Virginia as well, although women absconded in higher proportions in the lower South. Data on fugitives in Virginia and South Carolina are analyzed by Lathan Algerna Windley, "A
Profile of Runaway Slaves in Virginia and South Carolina from 1730
through 1787," Ph.D. diss., University of Iowa, 1974, pp. 63–146. See also
Wood, Black Majority, pp. 239–68, Wood, Slavery in Colonial Georgia, pp. 169–
87, Daniel E. Meaders, "South Carolina Fugitives as Viewed through Local
Colonial Newspapers with Emphasis on Runaway Notices, 1732–1801,"
Journal of Negro History 60 (1975): 288–319, and Daniel C. Littlefield, Rice
and Slaves: Ethnicity and the Slave Trade in Colonial South Carolina (Baton
Rouge, 1981), pp. 115–73.

graphic mobility, their knowledge about the surrounding countryside, and their chances to flee. Women also calculated that they would encounter substantially greater obstacles earning a living and passing as a free person than would black males. Finally, the vulnerability of black women escapees to sexual exploitation discouraged many from taking flight.[18]

Vigorous young slaves between the ages of twenty and forty comprised about three-quarters of the escapees. Children obviously encountered great difficulty making their way as fugitives. And most older slaves may have decided to remain enslaved because of family connections, the partial security available to aged bondpeople, and the physical tribulations of life on the run. In addition, many slaves may not have lived long lives, and masters probably advertised older, less valuable fugitives less aggressively.[19]

The physical appearance of runaways offers clues about their experiences, treatment, and background. The bodies of many African-Americans reflected the travails of their life. Ishmael and Toby, for example, limped because their feet had been frostbitten, and many others sustained injuries while working with farm implements or livestock. Whites commonly suffered similar afflictions, but slaves endured much physical abuse largely unknown to Anglo-American workers. Because Friday resisted his capture in Africa, he had "a Scar on his left cheek . . . and some large ones on his Arms." Tony

[18] *Pennsylvania Gazette*, Feb. 20, 1772. On women fugitives, see Deborah Gray White, *Ar'n't I a Woman? Female Slaves in the Plantation South* (New York, 1985), Linda Brent, *Incidents in the Life of a Slave Girl*, ed. Maria Child (San Diego, 1973), pp. 91, 93, 148, 162, and Billy G. Smith, "Black Women Who Stole Themselves in Eighteenth-Century America" (Paper presented at the Berkshire Conference for Women's History, Poughkeepsie, N.Y., June 1993).

[19] The age distribution of advertised fugitives in the Mid-Atlantic was constant throughout the century, and it resembled that of Virginia runaways; escapees in South Carolina were somewhat younger. See Windley, "Profile of Runaway Slaves," pp. 63–146. According to Edgar J. McManus, runaways in New York were similarly youthful (*A History of Negro Slavery in New York* [Syracuse, N.Y., 1966], p. 106). We know little about life expectancy among Mid-Atlantic slaves, although Klepp found higher mortality rates for blacks than for whites in Philadelphia, in "Seasoning and Society."

was "scarr'd on his Shoulders by Correction," while the backs of Dick, Will, and Ben were "much scarified," "full of scars, by severe whipping," and "much whipped." With no sense of the cruel irony of his own words, William Payne wrote that his fourteen-year-old slave Hagar had "a Scar under one of her Breasts, supposed to be got by Whipping and an Iron collar about her Neck," and that "she is supposed to be harboured in some Negroe Quarter, as her Father and Mother encourage her in these elopments, under a pretence that she is ill used at home."[20]

Approximately 2 percent of all fugitives had been disfigured by beatings. The proportion decreased over time, from 8 percent between 1728 and 1750, to 1 percent during the century's third quarter, and to a handful after 1775. The trend may indicate an actual decline in the use of corporal punishment against slaves, influenced perhaps by the general reform movement to limit physical correction, at least among lawbreakers. It also might suggest that flogging became less acceptable publicly as antislavery sentiment increased. Thus, when Will, "his back . . . cruelly scarred with severe whipping," absconded in 1783, his master took pains to assure newspaper readers that the marks had been inflicted "for running away before I got him."[21]

The advertisements raise questions about the supposedly "benign" system of slavery in the Delaware Valley region, at least in terms of physical abuse. Because slaves formed a small minority of the population, and whites feared race revolts less intensely in the Mid-Atlantic area, historians have sometimes assumed that discipline was less brutal than on large farms and plantations in the South. But while 2 percent of escapees advertised in the Delaware Valley bore whip scars, masters identified only 3 percent of fugitives with similar marks in Virginia and just 1 percent in South Carolina and Georgia. Beatings thus may have been as common in the Mid-Atlantic as in the South. A handful of northern masters branded their

[20] *Pennsylvania Gazette:* Ishmael, Apr. 21, 1790; Toby, May 31, 1764; Friday, Sept. 2, 1762; Tony, Apr. 14, 1745; Dick, Aug. 17, 1760; Will, Oct. 20, 1773; Ben, July 20, 1774; Hagar, Nov. 6, 1766.

[21] Ibid., May 14, 1783.

bondpeople, and they once again blamed the practice primarily on whites in the West Indies, the southern colonies, and traders in Africa. Fugitives in the South more often bore these permanent physical marks of ownership than did escapees in the Delaware Valley: 1 percent of the latter were branded, compared to 2 percent in Virginia, 3 percent in South Carolina, and 6 percent in Georgia.[22]

A few owners in the Mid-Atlantic shackled their bondpeople, especially those who ran away repeatedly; 2 percent of fugitives endured such confinement. Jack wore "an Iron Collar round his Neck, with a short Prong, a little crooked at the Point, which might be pretty easily hid or covered," while another Jack "had on a pair of handcuffs." Owners took even more precautions with other slaves: Dick "has a collar round his neck, and a chain to his leg"; a collar with "an Ox Chain fastened to it" hampered Cyprus; an "Iron Collar, and a Pair of Iron Fetters double rivetted" bound Shadwell; Cato "had irons on his legs, and about his neck"; and Bill "had a case hardened horse lock on one of his legs." Nearly all manacled slaves had fled previously, and, while these instruments undoubtedly stopped some people from absconding, they apparently did little to impede many from eloping again. From past experience, masters knew that most would readily free themselves of the mechanisms. Cato "probably has cut [his irons] off, as he has done several times before on the like occasion." Dick thoughtfully carried along a hammer and chisel to free himself, while Cuff Dix, a hammerman in a forge, possessed the necessary skills and access to tools with which to accomplish the task. Pero many have had his collar removed "by some ill-disposed neighbour."[23]

Africans often marked themselves as part of their cultural tradition. "Customary to Guinea Negroes," Hannah bore "scars on her cheeks" and Tom "hath some scars in his face."

[22] Comparative data are from Windley, "Profile on Runaway Slaves," pp. 63–146, and Wood, *Slavery in Colonial Georgia*, p. 183. For the conditions of slavery in New York, see White, *Somewhat More Independent*, chap. 4.

[23] *Pennsylvania Gazette:* Jack, Sept. 13, 1764; Jack, Oct. 25, 1770; Dick, May 10, 1770; Cyprus, Oct. 22, 1761; Shadwell, July 8, 1762, and Sept. 26, 1765; Cato, May 5, 1748; Bill, Aug. 30, 1750; Cato, May 5, 1748; Dick, May 10, 1770; Dix, May 24, 1775; Pero, Apr. 28, 1773.

One young woman, "supposed to be a Whedaw Negroe," was "mark'd round the Neck with three Rows like beads." Like a few other escaped males, Henry had "on each Side a Hole through his Nose, and one through each Ear," while Jacob and Christmas possessed "sharp filed Teeth." Some slaves appeared particularly formidable to whites: Jemmy had "a Scar in each Temple, a Hole in each Ear, and scars cut on each Arm," and Joe wore "the crown of his head shaved, with a ridge of wool left all round, and a foretop, which he turns back; a brass or iron ring in his left ear; a scar near his right eye, and another on his breast."[24] The advertisements designated that 2 percent of runaways carried such bodily signs, but the custom did not cut deeply into slave culture in the Mid-Atlantic. While almost half (49 percent) of the African natives bore such symbols, none of the runaways identified as being born in North America or the West Indies adopted that fashion.

The decision to flee obviously was an extraordinarily important one that held, literally, grave implications. If unsuccessful, runaways faced punishments ranging from being whipped, shackled, or sold to being maimed, branded, or killed during or after recapture. Even fugitives who succeeded in passing as free persons traded stability, friends, and family for a future filled with uncertainty. Although slaves treasured the possibility of freedom, they still must have realized that the problematic nature of a successful escape, the difficulties of maintaining one's liberty, the painful separation from family and friends still enmeshed in bondage, and the creation of a meaningful life in an alien, racist society would all be extremely arduous. Given these circumstances, only a minority of bondpeople chose to elope.

Owners offered various explanations for the flight of their slaves. Some, astigmatized by their benign view of bondage, were blind to the reasons why their slaves would abscond. The advertisements described the personalities of 13 percent of

[24] Ibid.: Hannah, Feb. 21, 1776; Tom, Sept. 22, 1748; "Whedaw Negroe," June 27, 1734; Henry, Oct. 27, 1763; Jacob, June 26, 1766; Christmas, June 15, 1757; Jemmy, July 5, 1759; Joe, Sept. 1, 1773.

fugitives, and masters categorized one-quarter of that group as being "shy," "complaisant," or of "meek countenance," surely not people who would resist bondage. Clearly perplexed, Toby's owner wrote "that this slave should runaway, and attempt getting his liberty, is very alarming, as he has always been too kindly used, if any thing, by his master, and in whom his master has put great confidence, and depended on him to overlook the rest of his slaves, and he had no kind of provocation to go off." John Holt could not fathom the ingratitude of Charles, a mulatto whom John had purchased out of jail: "When he became my servant, I intended to have shipped him to the West Indies, and sold him there; and kept him in Prison till I should get an Opportunity; but on his earnest Request, solemn Promises of his good Behaviour, and seeming Penitence, I took him into my Family upon Trial, where for some Time he behaved well, and was very serviceable to me. Deceived by his seeming Reformation, I placed some Confidence in him, which he has villainously abused."[25]

Masters occasionally specified that the catalyst of their slave's escape resulted from an immediate crisis event rather than long-simmering resentment of injustice. Sam was caught stealing a few items which, his owner believed, "was the cause of his flight, and may probably induce him to go a great distance, to avoid punishment." George, Cato, and Dick "were discovered carrying on illicit traffic with infamous whites in the neighbourhood, and ran off for fear of punishment." Bondpeople also escaped when separated from their friends and loved ones through sale or the dispersal of the estate at their owners' deaths. The case of eighteen-year-old Hannah is illustrative. In August 1765 Michael Hulings, who lived near Philadelphia's wharves, offered Hannah for sale, advertising her as having been "bred" in his own family. A tavernkeeper a few miles from the city purchased her in October. Two months later Hannah eloped, returning, her new master believed, either to her family in Philadelphia or to her brother and sister in Wilmington where Hulings had hired them out. Slaves occasionally fled as a reaction to inhumane treatment, although masters rarely provided details about the abuse

---

[25] Ibid.: Toby, Mar. 25, 1755; Charles, Apr. 29, 1762.

which they may have inflicted on their bondpeople before they escaped.[26]

A few blacks took flight when disappointed in their expectation of gaining freedom legitimately. John Richardson was "well known about Chester [County], by a trial he had for his freedom, but being disappointed of his expectations, he was sent home, and continued" for a brief time before absconding. Bob ran when his owner died, claiming "that his late master promised he should be set free." Having herself fled the slave revolt in Saint Domingue, Mrs. Chambre settled with her two slaves, Magdalen and Zaire, in Philadelphia. After "five calendar months and three weeks"—one week shy of the six months required by law to make her slaves free—Chambre moved to Burlington, New Jersey. Magdalen and Zaire immediately returned to Philadelphia and sued (unsuccessfully) for their freedom, asserting that their owners' residence in the state actually exceeded the necessary "six lunar months, in computation of time."[27]

Like conservatives who blame social unrest on outside agitators, masters often accused other whites or free blacks of stealing or convincing their slaves to abscond. Dr. John Finney was unsure whether Betty had been "Stolen, stray'd, or Run-away," but he thought that she had "been taken from hence by an Oyster-Shallop, Benjamin Taylor Master, bound for Philadelphia, and may be sold on some Part of the River." Like Betty, Sambo and Jemmy were new arrivals in America who barely spoke English and were, by their masters' reckoning, liable to abduction. Sambo's owner believed that "he is either stolen or decoyed away," while Jemmy's master was "suspicious that the said fellow is (by some ill disposed person or other) stolen and carried into the back woods." More than

[26] Ibid.: Sam, Mar. 7, 1771; George, Cato, and Dick, Aug. 18, 1734; Hannah, Aug. 29 and Dec. 12, 1765. On the illegal "trafficking" in stolen goods between whites and blacks in eighteenth-century Virginia, see Mechal Sobel, *The World They Made Together: Black and White Values in Eighteenth-Century Virginia* (Princeton, 1987), pp. 50–51.

[27] *Pennsylvania Gazette:* Richardson, Sept. 5, 1771; Bob, July 28, 1784. The case of Magdalen and Zaire is in Helen T. Catterall, ed., *Judicial Cases concerning American Slavery and the Negro,* 5 vols. (1926; reprint ed., New York, 1968), 4:17.

a few whites railed against "designing People" who would "countenance the escape" of their property. By their actions, runaways intensified the tension between slaveholders and abolitionists and increased the level of public awareness and debate about the institution of slavery.[28]

Crisis events seem not to have sparked the flight of most runaways even though a few, like Jess, "took a very precipitate resolution to decamp, insomuch that he did not stay to put on his hat or shoes."[29] But the seasonal pattern of escape attempts suggests that many slaves planned their departure well in advance. Rather than spontaneously responding to specific episodes—a series of actions that would have produced a random schedule of leave taking—fugitives usually selected the times to flee that would maximize their chances for success. Charting the escape attempts throughout the year produces a modified sine wave pattern as most runaways chose to elope during warmer temperatures (see figure 1). The average of 4 percent of fugitives who left each month during the winter grew to 8 percent monthly during the spring and peaked at 12 percent each month from June through September before declining during the late autumn. Seasonal changes in the intensity of agricultural labor account for part of this pattern of escape attempts. But that slave artisans absconded in an identical pattern suggests that most fugitives calculated the timing of their escape.[30]

Examples of advanced planning abound as slaves stole clothing, food, blankets, and cash, obtained forged passes, inquired about directions, equipped canoes and small boats, and plotted their escape with other bondpeople, indentured servants, and free whites. Like at least 22 percent of all fugi-

---

[28] *Pennsylvania Gazette:* Betty, Sept. 18, 1740; Sambo, July 11, 1765; Jemmy, Dec. 6, 1753. One owner expressed her anger at people she suspected of helping her slaves escape in an advertisement in the July 28, 1748, issue of the newspaper.

[29] Ibid., July 30, 1777.

[30] These statistics are derived from the 1,804 fugitives advertised in Philadelphia's newspapers. Slaves in South Carolina absconded in a more random fashion, indicating less planning on their part (Windley, "Profile of Runaway Slaves," pp. 63–146).

Figure 1
Seasonality of Escape Attempts

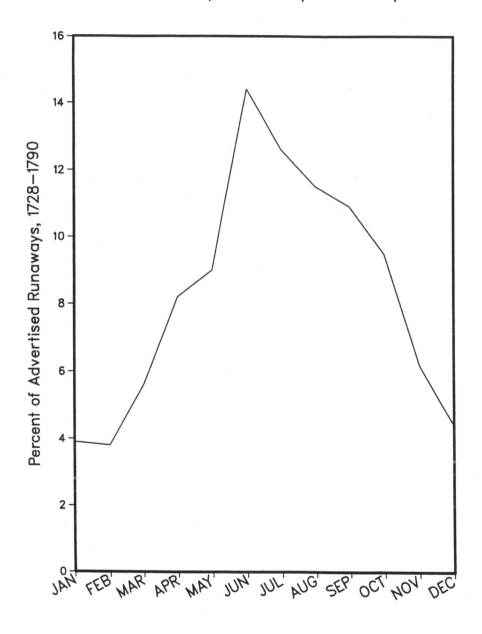

Percent of Advertised Runaways, 1728–1790

tives, Will took extra apparel, some of which he sold. Dan saved the money he earned from playing the fiddle to help finance his departure. Charles carried away a "Variety of Clothes" when he eloped, including "two or three Coats or Suits . . . and several other Waistcoats, Breeches, and Pairs of Stockings; a blue Great Coat, and a Fiddle." Charles apparently spent considerable time amassing capital for his escape, having, according to his master, "embezzled Money sent by him to pay for Goods, borrowed Money, and taken up Goods in my Name unknown to me, and also on his own Account, pretending to be a Freeman. By this villainous Proceeding I suppose he has collected a considerable Sum of Money."[31]

The objectives that masters attributed to escapees are suggestive about the motives and goals of fugitives. Although undoubtedly sometimes mistaken, owners indicated that they knew the probable intent of 286 runaways: approximately 10 percent sought to reunite with family and friends, an equal proportion headed for specific geographic locations, while the vast majority (79 percent) attempted, through a variety of strategies, to gain their freedom (see table 2). Besides these purposes ascribed to them by whites, some African-Americans searched for new masters while others felt that the need to take a "vacation" from the pressures of life in bondage exceeded the risks of punishment.

Some slaves fled to their spouses. When Sam absconded, his master noted that he "has a wife [in Philadelphia], a Negroe . . . who it is thought secrets him," and Dick jumped ship to go "to Dover, as he has a Wife there." Stephen Carpenter advertised for an escaped "Negroe Woman, about 45 Years of Age," who he supposed was in the Quaker City where "she has a Husband, a Baker by Trade." Sue, another forty-five-year-old black woman, took refuge in Baltimore "where she remained for some time, by the name of Free Poll." She may have met her spouse at that point before being apprehended, for when she escaped again, during the Revolutionary War, her master warned that "she is now about Philadelphia, waiting for the return of her husband, as she

---

[31] *Pennsylvania Gazette:* Will, Dec. 12, 1787; Dan, June 30, 1779; Charles, Apr. 29, 1762.

Table 2. Escape objectives of runaway slaves

Objective	1728–50 % (N = 27)	1751–75 % (N = 138)	1776–90 % (N = 121)	1728–90 % (N = 286)
Freedom				
Pass as free	0	30	37	30
Leave on ship	22	17	12	15
Join military	0	3	11	6
To Philadelphia	30	12	21	17
Pass as Indian	0	3	0	1
To Indians	0	3	0	1
To backcountry or N. Carolina	30	10	0	8
To swamps	0	1	0	0
Total	81	78	80	79
Family and friends				
To family or previous home	0	11	5	7
To free blacks	0	4	2	3
Total	0	15	7	10
Geographic area				
New England	0	0	1	0
N.Y. and N.J.	7	2	11	6
West Indies	4	1	1	1
England	4	1	0	1
Southern colonies (not Carolinas)	4	3	0	2
Total	18	6	12	10

SOURCE: Advertisements for 1,324 runaway slaves printed in the *Pennsylvania Gazette* (Philadelphia).

NOTES: Masters did not specify the objectives of 1,038 escapees. Percentages do not add up to 100 because of rounding.

calls him; a free Mulattoe, named Mark Stubbs, who sailed from Baltimore in a ship called the Enterprize." Because Congamouchu "talked much of his wives" in Africa, his master believed that he "will endeavour to get off by water" in order to return to them.[32]

A handful of runaways visited more than one wife, in the

[32] Ibid.: Sam, July 5, 1753; Dick, June 5, 1765; Carpenter's slave, Feb. 7, 1763; Sue, May 16, 1781; Congamouchu, June 22, 1769.

polygynous tradition associated with West Africa. Charles first eloped in 1782 and stayed away for nearly three years, "in which time he married two wives . . . by one of which he had three children." After his second escape, Charles's master expressed his moral outrage: "I do apprehend he will reside chiefly . . . with his *plurality of wives* (notwithstanding it is against the laws of Moses and the United States)." Peter, "a smooth tongued artful fellow, a noted liar, a great villain, and fond of liquor," posed a continual problem for his owner. He had "been a run away almost ever since he was 20 years of age; he has lived in New-Jersey . . . has been [on] a voyage or two to sea; has lived in Philadelphia, in Bucks county and almost every part of Chester county." He apparently enjoyed an active love life in each of these places, for in addition to his "Indian wife," he had "children by four black women, to all of whom he says he is lawfully married." His master was perplexed about which of his wives Peter "will apply to conceal him."[33]

Escapees sought out their parents as well. Declaring her intention "to see her mother this winter," twenty-year-old Nancy ran away from her owner in the Northern Liberties. Sambo, a seventeen-year-old slave in Chester County, presumably headed for the Pennsylvania capital, "as his mother lives in the city." And determined to visit his father and mother in Maryland, Jack escaped twice within six months from his Philadelphia master.[34]

Still, the proportion of advertised runaways who, according to their masters, strove to reunite with their kin was substantially lower in the Delaware Valley than in the Chesapeake or the Lower South. Owners who advertised in Philadelphia newspapers specified that 7 percent of fugitives struggled to return to relatives or to their previous home, and that an additional 3 percent fled to "free blacks," presumably friends. By comparison, advertisements in newspapers in other areas indicated that 33 percent of runaways in Virginia and 69 percent in South Carolina probably spent their time "visiting"

---

[33] Ibid.: Charles, Sept. 21, 1785; Peter, Apr. 13, 1796.

[34] Ibid.: Nancy, Dec. 4, 1793; Sambo, Oct. 15, 1794; Jack, Oct. 21, 1772.

their families and acquaintances.[35] The difference between the goals of Mid-Atlantic fugitives and of those in the South is best explained by the greater obstacles northern slaves encountered in establishing families and friends. Before 1750, when the African-American population of the Delaware Valley was small, scattered, and primarily imported, slaves experienced particular difficulty initiating and maintaining intimate personal relations with others of their race. As a result, not a single owner who advertised in Philadelphia's newspapers before midcentury believed that his or her slave had left to visit kin.

Of course, a considerable number of runaways throughout early America went unadvertised because their masters anticipated that they would return voluntarily after having seen their kinfolk or simply having enjoyed their freedom for a few days. Owners thus waited for more than a month before placing notices for 40 percent of the fugitives described in Georgia newspapers, while probate inventories and planter correspondence in South Carolina frequently mentioned "missing" slaves who had never been advertised.[36] Similar phenomena are evident in the Delaware Valley. The advertisement for Frank, for example, did not appear for nearly five months after he absconded. And five weeks after Jack departed, his master commented that "said fellow would have been advertised before, but he had a trick of absenting him-

---

[35] The figures for Virginia and South Carolina are calculated using only advertisements in which masters indicated the fugitive's supposed destination (Gerald W. Mullin, *Flight and Rebellion: Slave Resistance in Eighteenth-Century Virginia* [New York, 1972], p. 108; Morgan, "Colonial South Carolina Runaways," pp. 67–68). A similar pattern among Chesapeake slaves is evident in Allan Kulikoff, "The Origins of Afro-American Society in Tidewater Maryland and Virginia, 1700 to 1790," *William and Mary Quarterly*, 3d ser. 25 (1978): 253–54.

[36] Wood, *Slavery in Colonial Georgia*, p. 171; Morgan, "Colonial South Carolina Runaways," pp. 57–58. Philip D. Morgan and Michael Nicholls discovered a similar phenomenon in their joint study of runaways in eighteenth-century Virginia ("Slave Runaways in Eighteenth-Century Virginia" [Paper presented at the Eighty-third Annual Meeting of the Organization of American Historians, Washington, D.C., 1990]).

self for two or three weeks at a time and then returning home; it was thought he might do the same now."[37]

Some African-Americans fled as a way to change their masters. The right to locate another owner was informally accepted by many blacks and whites in Pennsylvania and New Jersey. Silvia Dubois, a New Jersey slave, reminisced that "when the slave thought the master too severe, and the slave and the master did not get along harmoniously, the slave had a right to hunt a new master." Thus, Syron "had a pass, without a limited time, to look for a master"; Sambo went away "under Pretence to get a Master"; and Jack "says he has liberty from me to look for another master." James McHenry provided the following pass to his slave: "The bearer has permission to look out for a master. . . . His price is two hundred Dollars." Eleanor Moore advertised that Rose "has been dissatisfied with her place for some time past, [but] if she returns, she shall have the liberty to choose a master."[38]

Some escapees decided it was prudent to work for whites under conditions of semifreedom, thereby gaining some protection from their previous owner. After fleeing from Maryland to Philadelphia, Penn indentured himself as a servant to John Meredith. When Jack left bondage in Chester County, "he was met by a certain . . . James Rigbee, who took him into Maryland, and kept him in his employ for near 9 months, but finding he could no longer keep him . . . he delivered him up to his master."[39] The common complaints of owners against other whites who employed escaped slaves and the descriptions of the experiences of bondpeople who had fled previously indicate that fugitives might find people who would

---

[37] *Pennsylvania Gazette:* Frank, Nov. 22, 1764; Jack, May 23, 1781.

[38] C. W. Larison, *Silvia Dubois, a Biografy of the Slav Who Whipt Her Mistres and Gand Her Fredom,* ed. and trans. Jared C. Lobdell (New York, 1988), p. 54. *Pennsylvania Gazette:* Syron, Dec. 7, 1769; Sambo, Dec. 19, 1765; Jack, Jan. 11, 1770; Rose, Dec. 3, 1794. The pass for James McHenry's slaves is in the Papers of the Pennsylvania Abolition Society, box 3A, ser. 4, Historical Society of Pennsylvania, Philadelphia.

[39] *Pennsylvania Gazette:* Penn, Aug. 31, 1774; Jack, Sept. 5, 1771.

harbor them either because of their antislavery sentiment or their need for cheap labor.

No matter what other objectives whites may have attributed to escapees, liberty was the ultimate goal of most runaways. As Jim's owner succinctly expressed it: "I believe he has nothing in view but freedom."[40] Masters presumed that four of every five fugitives were attempting to escape bondage entirely. Once again, the aims of runaways in the Delaware Valley contrasted with the objectives of escaped slaves in other regions, since owners assumed that only two of every five runaways in Virginia and one of five in South Carolina endeavored permanently to establish their freedom.[41]

The number of fugitives varied over the course of the eighteenth century, primarily in response to changing opportunities for successful escape. From approximately 7 annually before 1750, escapees advertised in Philadelphia's newspapers increased to 43 each year during the century's third quarter, exploded to 102 annually during and immediately after the Revolution, and then declined to 53 each year after 1785 (see figure 2). This variation in escape attempts is also apparent when the number of advertised fugitives is compared against the region's slave population.[42]

Fugitives adapted their strategies to changing conditions over time (see table 2). Runaways enjoyed limited options before midcentury: They could attempt to hide or to get a berth as a sailor aboard an oceangoing vessel, flee to the frontier (commonly defined as the Pennsylvania backcountry or North Carolina), or seek anonymity in the nearest city, Philadelphia. The greater number of runaways during the century's third quarter resulted from increased slave importation

[40] Ibid., Aug. 2, 1786.

[41] Mullin, *Flight and Rebellion*, p. 108; Morgan, "Colonial South Carolina Runaways," pp. 67–68.

[42] For every ten thousand slaves who lived in Pennsylvania, New Jersey, and Delaware (see table 1), the following number of fugitives are estimated (by the method specified in note 15, above) to have been advertised in Philadelphia newspapers: 8.0 from 1719 through 1746, 15.7 from 1747 through 1761, 30.3 from 1762 through 1775, 41.3 from 1776 through 1784, and 23.0 from 1785 through 1796.

Figure 2
Estimated Number of
Advertised Fugitives
and Slave Population

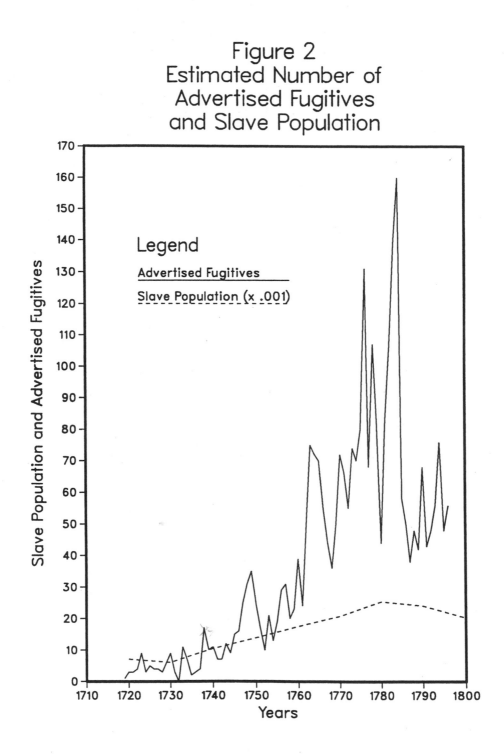

during the Seven Years' War and the expanding options available to escapees. As Delaware Valley residents purchased more bondpeople to fill their labor needs during the war, the slave population and, consequently, the number of fugitives, increased. Moreover, the growing number of free blacks in the region and the war itself provided more opportunities for runaways. For the first time, masters asserted that fugitives might attempt to "pass as free" in a society in which not all African-Americans were enslaved. While both ships and the Pennsylvania capital remained popular destinations, escape to the French army offered an additional alternative.

The American Revolution, the antislavery movement, and the continued growth of the free black population further widened the latitude of fugitives during the century's final decades. More owners than ever believed that their slaves would pretend to be free people, and especially that they would find camouflage in the growing urban population of African-Americans who lived without masters. Whites also feared, quite correctly, that bondpeople would join the enemy or take advantage of the turmoil of the war to escape. When Lord Dunmore invited blacks to flee to his forces in 1775 and Sir Henry Clinton extended the invitation more broadly four years later, thousands of slaves responded. The British occupation of Philadelphia in 1777 and 1778 was a godsend for escape-minded slaves, many of whom seized the providential opportunity. That the Black Guides and Pioneers, a company of African-Americans, belonged to the occupation forces strengthened the resolve of many slaves to take a stand for their personal liberty. Seizing the new opportunities and motivated increasingly by the radical rhetoric that raised expectations for freedom, slaves fled at very high rates during the Revolutionary War.[43]

Caesar, Tone, Moses, James, and Cuff Dix all absconded early in the conflict, hoping to make it to territory controlled by Virginia's last royal governor. Since "Negroes in general think that Lord Dunmore is contending for their liberty," ac-

[43] See Benjamin Quarles, *The Negro in the American Revolution* (Chapel Hill, 1961), and idem, *Black Mosaic: Essays in Afro-American History and Historiography* (Amherst, Mass., 1988). Nash discusses the actions taken by Philadelphia blacks during the Revolution in *Forging Freedom*, pp. 46–65.

cording to Dix's master, "it is not improbable that said Negroe is on his march to join his Lordship's own black regiment, but it is hoped he will be prevented by some honest Whig from effecting it." In September 1777 Dick "joined the British then at the Head of the Elk" in Maryland as they marched toward Philadelphia, while Peter fled the day before the army arrived in the Quaker City. Women took advantage of the new circumstances as well: Peg "went into Philadelphia, whilst the British troops were there," where she may have encountered Phyllis and Poll, who earlier had left their masters. Scores of African-Americans boarded the ships when the British evacuated the city, and others continued to flee after the occupation. Constables apprehended four men in January 1780 "on suspicion of their designing to go to the enemy," while Simon "was seen . . . in company with some straggling troops belonging to the French army" in 1782.[44]

Slaves continued to abscond in significant numbers after the Revolution. The number of runaways peaked during the early 1780s, primarily because Pennsylvania's 1780 gradual emancipation law inadvertently encouraged slaves to take leave of their masters. When the statute failed to free any living blacks, dozens of disappointed slaves took to their heels. Many believed they could meld successfully into the rapidly growing community of free blacks centered in the City of Brotherly Love. As the news about emancipation circulated through the slave community, some mistakenly thought that they would gain legal freedom if only they could reach Pennsylvania. As one Virginia master commented in his advertisement, "The slaves in this state generally supposing they may obtain their freedom by going into Pennsylvania makes it highly probable that he is in some part of that state." Fleeing Baltimore, Dick and Ned "were heard to say they intended [to go] a little beyond Philadelphia, where they would be free." Whites in nearby areas feared and exaggerated Pennsylvania's actions. James Hutchings of Baltimore thought that

[44]*Pennsylvania Gazette:* Caesar and Tone, Aug. 13, 1777; Moses, Sept. 25, 1776; James, Oct. 30, 1776; Dix, July 17, 1776; Dick, Feb. 6, 1782; Peter, June 2, 1779; Peg, July 7, 1779; four men, Jan. 19, 1780; Simon, Sept. 18, 1782. Advertisements for Phyllis and Poll appear in the *Pennsylvania Ledger,* May 6, 1778.

his escaped slaves "have taken asylum, in the Pennsylvania State, under the cover of a law, fraught with great mischiefs and inconvenience to her sister States."[45]

Many bondpeople also were aware that they might find refuge among whites with antislavery feelings. When Ned initially escaped from Lancaster County, he encountered "two gentlemen in bucks county, who gave six dollars to a lawyer to help them to set him free." Ned absconded again several months later, heading, his master believed, once again to Bucks County to locate the men who "were such good friends to him." Charles tried to use the abolitionist movement to his own advantage by pretending "to have been set free by the people called Quakers."[46] As slavery began to wilt in Pennsylvania during the century's final years, bondpeople continued to abscond in large numbers. Just as no American soldier wanted to be the last one to die in Vietnam, so no African-American wanted to be the last slave to be held in captivity in the Keystone state.

In political terms, running away always was a forceful but highly personal act of rebellion. During and after the Revolution, those individual deeds, though not coordinated by any group, assumed considerably greater importance as a direct challenge to the peculiar institution in the Mid-Atlantic. Runaways struck at the economic heart of slavery and thereby hastened its demise during the century's final decades. Whites who supported emancipation in the Delaware Valley frequently were motivated by idealistic arguments, but it was slavery's declining profitability in parts of that region that enabled abolition to succeed. Runaways exacerbated the economic problems of their masters. Many slaveowners must

[45] For a similar argument about slave escapees after 1780, see Soderlund and Nash, "Slavery on the Periphery: Pennsylvania." The best estimates of the growth of the free black population in urban Philadelphia are as follows: 57 in 1767, 114 in 1775, 241 in 1780, 1,849 in 1790, and 6,028 in 1800 (Soderlund, "Black Importation and Migration"). The Virginian's advertisement is in the *Pennsylvania Packet*, Oct. 22, 1789. *Maryland Journal and Baltimore Advertiser* (Baltimore): Dick and Ned, Feb. 25, 1785; Hutching's slave, Sept. 6, 1785.

[46] *Pennsylvania Gazette:* Ned, Apr. 9, 1788; Charles, May 25, 1785.

have perceived that the problem of physically holding onto their labor force, especially young males, the most valuable slaves, was growing more acute. In addition, blacks usually escaped during the summer and fall, the times when their labor was most valuable to their agricultural masters.

In the complicated interaction between slaves and masters, African-Americans often manipulated whites by using escape and other forms of resistance as weapons to coerce their owners into making concessions. Some slaves used flight to force their masters to negotiate for their freedom. After Harry, Azor, and Joseph absconded during the 1790s, their owners agreed to emancipate them in return for their pledge of a few more years of faithful service. Although Magdalen and Zaire (discussed earlier) did not gain their freedom by escape, they used this leverage to bargain successfully with their mistress to change their status from perpetual slaves to bound servants.[47]

As slavery became more vulnerable, losing much of its legal and moral foundation in the Mid-Atlantic during the post-Revolutionary decades, many bondpeople issued an additional challenge: they simply refused to do their masters' bidding. Their names and the charges against them tumble off Philadelphia's prison dockets. Fortune, Lawrencine, and Tobias were all jailed several times for "refusing to obey" their masters or "to promise better behaviour." Sally had a "very turbulent ungovernable Temper" and rejected her owner's commands. Caesar "obstinately" refused and Frank "positively" refused to behave themselves. Charles fled five times in three months, but Amy held the record by absconding eight times in a single week. By these actions, hundreds of slaves tried to force their masters' hands. Choisi succeeded. After serving a month in the workhouse for declining "to obey

---

[47] The cases of Harry and Azor are in the Papers of the Pennsylvania Abolition Society, box 4B, ser. 4. Joseph's case is from "Small Minutes as Related by Different Blacks & Not Entered in the Minute Book," Acting Committee, Loose Minutes, Apr. 13, 1796, ibid. Magdalen and Zaire appear in the following entries of the Vagrancy Dockets, Philadelphia City Archives: July 14, 1794, Feb. 9 and Oct. 12, 1796. In the last two entries, the status of the two women changed from slaves to bound servants. The various ways slaves negotiated for their freedom are discussed in Nash and Soderlund, *Freedom by Degrees*, chap. 5.

the Lawfull commands of his Master," he refused "to return to his Masters Service" and drew another month's sentence. Following several more confrontations, Choisi's master finally agreed to free him if he would serve for three more years. The problem owners faced was widespread: between 1793 and 1797, they confined nearly 700 blacks to Philadelphia's workhouse at a time when the city contained fewer than 200 and the state only about 2,000 slaves.[48]

This type of resistance by African-Americans hastened the demise of slavery in the North. In Pennsylvania, for example, slavery died a much quicker death than was mandated by the gradual emancipation legislation, as masters, responding to pressure from their bondpeople, often agreed to manumit their human property in return for a pledge of several more years of service as an indentured servant. Northern slaves thus played an active role in their own emancipation.[49]

Blacks who absconded and disobeyed their masters not only risked their lives to gain personal advantage, but they also undermined the system of racial bondage by making it too costly and troublesome to their owners. In addition, they established an enduring legacy of solidarity and rebellion that linked their struggles with that of nineteenth-century black abolitionists and resistant slaves who were inspired by their actions. Finally, by joining with other blacks to construct viable communities in northern cities, they provided way stations, destinations, and hope for succeeding generations of slaves who would steal themselves and follow the North Star to freedom.

[48] Vagrancy Dockets, Philadelphia City Archives: Fortune, Dec. 12, 1797, and Mar. 6, 1798; Lawrencine, Jan. 1 and Feb. 22, 1797; Tobias, Aug. 4 and Sept. 7, 1796; Sally, Aug. 13, 1795; Caesar, Mar. 10, 1796; Frank, Apr. 9, 1796; Charles, Feb. 5, 1793; Amy, Feb. 9, 1793; Choisi, Nov. 1 and 9, Dec. 28, 1796, and Feb. 20, 1797. For the estimated number of slaves in Philadelphia and Pennsylvania in 1780 and 1800, see table 1.

[49] The demise of slavery and various ways that slaves obtained their freedom are discussed in Nash and Soderlund, *Freedom by Degrees,* pp. 4–7 and chap. 5.

ALAN TAYLOR

"To Man
Their Rights"

The Frontier

Revolution

IN NOVEMBER 1787 Col. Timothy Pickering lamented his inability to maintain Pennsylvania's legal authority over the rebellious Yankee settlers of Luzerne County in the upper Susquehanna Valley. Pickering blamed the local settler insurgency on "the natural instability of the common people" compounded by frontier isolation from established authority and well stirred by populist demagogues. And he detected a national pattern. "The discontents in the county of Luzerne are not the result merely of disaffection to the government of Pennsylvania. The peculiar circumstances of the United States have encouraged bad men in several of them to throw off their allegiance to excite the common people to rebellion & to attempt the erecting of New States." Pickering regarded the "bad men" as class traitors: rogue gentlemen "of talents, but of desperate fortunes," who, for want of restraining virtue, recklessly pursued their self-interest by encouraging popular turmoil. Pickering worried that "no one can say what would be the final issue of the contest, in the present weak state of the federal union and general discontent and spirit of revolt so prevalent among the people of these states."[1]

Pickering's alarm about the extent of backcountry unrest

[1] Col. Timothy Pickering to George Clymer, Nov. 1, 1787, Julian P. Boyd and Robert J. Taylor, eds., *The Susquehannah Company Papers*, 11 vols. (Wilkes-Barre, Pa., and Ithaca, N.Y., 1930–71), 9:255–59.

during the 1780s was widely shared and well founded. In Maine, aggrieved settlers and frustrated local politicians combined to agitate for separation from Massachusetts. They found inspiration in Vermont, where the settlers had seceded from New York and used force to keep their independence. Hundreds of Massachusetts and New Hampshire farmers resisted the collection of taxes and debts during Ely's Rebellion of 1782 and Shays's Rebellion of 1786–87. The tenant farmers living along the New York–New England border frequently rioted against their landlords and in favor of secure freehold land. In Western New York unscrupulous land speculators sought to preempt the region by leasing it for 999 years from a few compliant Iroquois sachems; these speculators meant to evade a New York state law that forbade private purchases of land from the Indians in western New York. To uphold their brazen deal, the leaseholders encouraged the settlers in western New York to secede and organize their own state. Western Pennsylvania was also rife with squatters, secessionist schemes, and tax resistance. Meanwhile squatters in the Ohio country defied federal troops and made plans to organize their own state. George Washington dubbed them "a parcel of banditti, who will bid defiance to all authority." In Kentucky hundreds of settlers seeking free lands hoped to escape Virginia's jurisdiction and its landlords by supporting separatist proposals hatched by some competing land speculators. In Tennessee, dissident settlers and speculators cooperated to secede from North Carolina and to form the state of Franklin. Surveying the whole frontier, a Connecticut newspaper aptly concluded in 1787, "We see *banditties* rising up against law and good order in all quarters of our country." Washington worried that "the Western Settlers . . . stand, as it were, on a pivet—the touch of a feather would almost incline them any way."[2]

[2] Ronald F. Banks, *Maine Becomes a State: The Movement to Separate Maine from Massachusetts, 1785–1820* (Portland, Maine, 1973), pp. 3–25; Robert E. Moody, "Samuel Ely: Forerunner of Daniel Shays," *New England Quarterly* 5 (1932):105–34; David P. Szatmary, *Shays' Rebellion: The Making of an Agrarian Insurrection* (Amherst, Mass., 1980); Oscar Handlin, "The Eastern Frontier of New York," *New York History* 18 (1937): 50–75; Thomas P. Slaughter, *The*

As Pickering noted, most of the frontier separatist movements of the 1780s were alliances between two distinct but compatible groups: penurious settlers seeking free or cheap homesteads *and* aggressive land speculators who lacked the proper connections to realize their ambitions through the existing state governments. The two groups allied to defy the legal and political establishments and the old-money land speculators who had invested in more reputable land titles. In sum, the scramble for wilderness lands newly wrested from the Indians generated a series of triangular contests from Maine to Tennessee involving settlers and two competing sets of speculators—well-established gentlemen and aspiring, opportunistic new men. Ultimately, the contending speculator camps struggled for the power to collect payments from the settlers; but in the short run, the competition created opportunities for the first settlers in a given district to demand free or cheap homesteads in return for their support. In general, the first settlers found it in their interest to enlist with the opportunists who needed armed force to circumvent the established legislatures and courts that favored the land titles of more reputable men of entrenched wealth and status.

But we should be careful not to equate settlers and opportunists, not to regard the latter as exemplifying the behavior and aspirations of the former. In fact, the settlers had their own agenda and readily deserted or sought new allies as circumstances shifted. Nor should we regard the settlers as simply the pawns of the opportunists. The upstart speculators responded to opportunities created by settlers of more modest means and aspirations. Indeed, settler resistance could exist without speculator allies, as was the case in Maine. This

---

Whiskey Rebellion: Frontier Epilogue to the American Revolution (New York, 1986), pp. 29–60, 86 (second Washington quotation); Andrew R. L. Cayton, *The Frontier Republic: Ideology and Politics in the Ohio Country, 1780–1825* (Kent, Ohio, 1986), pp. 2–11 (first Washington quotation, p. 7); Patricia Watlington, *The Partisan Spirit: Kentucky Politics, 1779–1792* (New York, 1972), pp. 46–78; Thomas Perkins Abernethy, *Western Lands and the American Revolution* (New York, 1959), pp. 288–310; extract from the *Connecticut Courant,* Sept. 10, 1787, in Boyd and Taylor, eds., *Susquehannah Company Papers,* 9:188.

essay will examine the triangular contests for the frontier with special attention to the related conflicts in Vermont and in northern Pennsylvania's Susquehanna Valley.[3]

DISAFFECTION AND OPPORTUNISM

In eighteenth-century America, men acquired fortunes and political power by obtaining titles to lands on the fast-settling frontier. No other path to wealth and power was more promising on a continent of fertile soil and fecund people. Access to extensive lands conquered from the Indians encouraged colonists to marry relatively young (four to five years younger than in Europe) and to bear additional children. Consequently, even apart from immigration, the population grew at a rate of about 3 percent annually, a doubling by natural increase every twenty-five years. Because almost every family sought a farm, each new generation doubled the demand for land, putting increased pressure on the beleaguered Indians. Given the demographic facts of North American life, those men who acquired titles to large tracts of unsettled land could reap rich profits by retailing farms as the tide of settlement reached their domains. In a detailed memorandum meant to shape his extensive land speculations, Gen. Henry Knox noted, "The price of any commodity whatever may be raised

---

[3] Historians of the early American frontier disagree in how they describe the relationship of settlers and land speculators. Frederick Jackson Turner and his intellectual heirs, the Progressive historians, depict an adversarial relationship; revisionists, such as Charles S. Grant and Bernard Bailyn, insist that settlers and large-scale speculators were inclined to cooperate in a shared pursuit of the profits from rising land values. Both cases can be sustained because at different times in separate places each scenario was true. I mean to argue that neither the bipolar nor the unitary concept of the settler-speculator relationship works well for the American Revolutionary generation. See Ray Allen Billington, "The Origins of the Land Speculator as a Frontier Type," *Agricultural History* 19 (1945):204–12; Charles S. Grant, *Democracy in the Connecticut Frontier Town of Kent* (New York, 1961), pp. 1–65; Bernard Bailyn, *The Peopling of British North America: An Introduction* (New York, 1986), pp. 65–86. The latter conflates settlers and speculators. For a work that treats resisting settlers simply as pawns of petty speculators, see Sung Bok Kim, *Landlord and Tenant in Colonial New York: Manorial Society, 1664–1775* (Chapel Hill, 1978), pp. 281–345.

in two ways, either by diminishing the quantity for sale, or by increasing the demand. But the extension of settlements and the increase of wealth and population operate at once in both these ways upon American lands: not only diminishing the quantity for sale, but increasing the means and the eligibility of making further purchases and settlements." Titles were licenses to collect payments from whoever wanted to use the land; they were valuable only to the degree that their owners could induce actual settlers to buy them. A settler found it in his interest to buy a title when the landlord could resort to a court of law and prevail in a lawsuit for trespass or ejectment. So, in the last analysis, the power of the courts to enforce their will gave titles their value. And the courts favored the titles created by governors and legislatures and awarded to their political favorites rather than titles asserted by squatters or by those who bought deeds from the Indians without official license.[4]

Ordinarily, colonial settlers accepted that they had to pay a landlord to obtain a piece of the forest. But when landlords behaved in a blatantly predatory manner, they aroused the ordinarily dormant but always potent fear that the rich were hoarding the wilderness in order to "enslave" the common people. At such moments, settlers imagined themselves as verging on the degradation of European peasants, for they knew that without secure property they were ripe for exploitation by the powerful. The settlers of Orange County, North Carolina, anticipated a dreadful life of "wooden shoes and uncombed hair" for want of secure homesteads. William Prendergast, a leader in the New York tenant rebellion of 1766, said that "it was hard they were not allowed to have *any property.*" He knew that people without property could not long keep their liberty. When alarmed by impending domina-

---

[4] Jim Potter, "Demographic Development and Family Structure," in Jack P. Greene and J. R. Pole, eds., *Colonial British America: Essays in the New History of the Early Modern Era* (Baltimore, 1984), pp. 136, 149; Henry Knox, "Facts and Calculations Respecting the Population and Territory of the United States of America," Henry Knox Papers, vol. 53, 138, Massachusetts Historical Society, Boston. For a fuller discussion of titles see Alan Taylor, "'A Kind of Warr': The Contest for Land on the Northeastern Frontier, 1750–1820," *William and Mary Quarterly,* 3d ser. 46 (1989): 3–26.

tion, rural Americans suddenly could imagine the better society of equal rights and justice that Hermon Husband of the North Carolina Regulators called a "new government of liberty" or a "New Jerusalem." Both alarmed and inspired, settlers strove to secure the property that endowed liberty. They denounced their landlords as parasites, rallied around the cheapest alternative titles they could obtain, and organized militias to defend themselves from eviction and to oust anyone who assisted the landlord.[5]

Growing settler unrest encouraged the emergence of a new brand of land speculator—less reputable and less well connected men ready to proffer quasi-legal and cut-rate land titles. The opportunists capitalized on the growing number of settlers who felt cheated and who wanted cheap lands. The opportunists concocted alternative titles either by extending the bounds of bordering colonies and states or by plying cooperative Indian sachems with alcohol and trade goods. Then the opportunists retailed their titles to farm-sized lots at reduced rates in order to fill their lands with supportive settlers prepared forcefully to repel the law officers of the established courts in the existing states. Opportunists appealed to the poorest settlers, those least able to pay the higher prices demanded by the holders of the more reputable titles created by colonial and state governments. In a pamphlet written to support the Indian-deed claim of Col. John Henry Lydius to about one million acres in what is now Vermont, Dr. Thomas

---

[5] Richard Maxwell Brown, "Back Country Rebellions and the Homestead Ethic in America, 1740–1799," in Richard Maxwell Brown and Don E. Fehrenbacher, eds., *Tradition, Conflict, and Modernization: Perspectives on the American Revolution* (New York, 1977), p. 79; Prendergast quotation in Edward Countryman, *A People in Revolution: The American Revolution and Political Society in New York, 1760–1790* (Baltimore, 1981), p. 50; Orange County settlers' quotation in A. Roger Ekirch, *"Poor Carolina": Politics and Society in Colonial North Carolina, 1729–1776* (Chapel Hill, 1981), p. 190; idem, "'A New Government of Liberty': Hermon Husband's Vision of Backcountry North Carolina, 1755," *William and Mary Quarterly*, 3d ser. 34 (1977):632–46; Ruth H. Bloch, *Visionary Republic: Millennial Themes in American Thought, 1756–1800* (New York, 1985), pp. 72–73, 183–84; Taylor, "'A Kind of Warr,'" pp. 3–26; Kim, *Landlord and Tenant*, pp. 281–415; Countryman, *A People in Revolution*, pp. 36–71; Thomas L. Purvis, "Origins and Patterns of Agrarian Unrest in New Jersey," *William and Mary Quarterly*, 3d ser. 39 (1982): 613–21.

Young insisted that such cheap titles furnished "many poor families with the means of a very comfortable living, who must otherwise groan with poverty." In an "Invitation to the Poor Tenants of New York," Thomas Rowley of Rutland County, Vermont, promoted the suspect titles based on New Hampshire grants; by recruiting settlers among New York's tenants, Rowley hoped simultaneously to undermine the economic base of that colony's landlord class and strengthen the numbers committed to resisting their claims to Vermont. He urged,

> Come all you laboring hands that toil below,
> Among the rocks and bands, that plow and so;
> Upon your hired lands, let out by cruel hands,
> 'Twill make you large amends to Rutland go.
> Your patroons forsake, whose greatest care
> Is slaves of you to make, while you live there;
> Come, quit their barren lands, and leave them in their hands,
> 'Twill ease of[f] you your bands to Rutland go.

The opportunists gambled that once they had placed a body of well-armed settlers on the land, the governments would have to bow to the fait accompli, and the gentry would have to welcome the victors to their club. By undercutting the titles manufactured by governors and their councils and upheld by the courts, the opportunists threatened the entire basis of political authority in eighteenth-century America, the dispensation of land grants to construct networks of interest binding influential men together in support of the established institutions of governance.[6]

During the 1760s and early 1770s innovative landgrabs proliferated along the entire frontier arc. Small-scale speculators from New England exploited suspect titles created by New Hampshire's unscrupulous governor, Benning Wentworth, to lay claim to northeastern New York (present-day Vermont). To defy New York's posses and surveyors, the

---

[6] Dr. Thomas Young, *Some Reflections on the Dispute between New-York, New-Hampshire, and Col. John Henry Lydius of Albany* (New Haven, 1764), pp. 14–15; Thomas Rowley quotation in John C. Williams, *The History and Map of Danby, Vermont* (Rutland, 1869), p. 240.

claimants recruited well-armed settlers by offering free grants to the first comers and prices as low as two cents per acre to subsequent arrivals. "They are crowding up to this Country as if all New England was set on fire," one Vermont resident observed in 1771. To retain their bargains, the settlers in western Vermont organized a de facto government of local committees and a militia known as the Green Mountain Boys. Meanwhile aspiring land speculators from Connecticut meant to seize northern Pennsylvania; they organized the Susquehannah Company in 1753, negotiated a treaty of purchase with some intoxicated Iroquois Indians, and began to sell titles for nominal amounts to settlers who came from Pennsylvania, New Jersey, and New York, as well as from New England. Farther south, Judge Richard Henderson of North Carolina and his partners financed transappalachian exploration by Daniel Boone, organized the Transylvania Company, and in March 1775 negotiated a purchase of twenty million acres—nearly all of present Kentucky and much of northern Tennessee—from a group of Cherokee Indians for trade goods worth £10,000, the equivalent of two to three cents an acre. Henderson won over most of the region's new settlers by offering them lands at the low price of twenty shillings per hundred acres; he meant to wrest the region away from Virginia and establish a distinct colony. Another cartel based in North Carolina and known as the Watauga Association pursued a similar strategy to secure eastern Tennessee for £2,000 and to bring the local settlers into their scheme.[7]

VERMONT

The frontier opportunists became even more daring and formidable after the outbreak of the Revolutionary War in 1775.

[7] Chilton Williamson, Sr., *Vermont in Quandary, 1763–1825* (Montpelier, 1949), pp. 12–18; Charles A. Jellison, *Ethan Allen: Frontier Rebel* (Syracuse, N.Y., 1969), pp. 18–38; Matt Bushnell Jones, *Vermont in the Making, 1750–1777* (Cambridge, Mass., 1939), pp. 20–66, 225–26; Florence May Woodward, *The Town Proprietors in Vermont: The New England Proprietorship in Decline* (New York, 1936), pp. 45–55; John Munro to Gov. William Tryon, Nov. 6, 1771, in Edmund Bailey O'Callaghan, ed., *The Documentary History of the State of New York*, 4 vols. (Albany, 1850–51), 4:453; Boyd and Taylor, eds., *Susquehannah Company Papers*, 1:lxiv–lxxxvii; Malcolm J. Rohrbough, *The*

Exploiting the Revolutionary upheaval, opportunists from Maine to Tennessee went into the state-making business. The elimination of royal authority over the wilderness added to the uncertainty over who could create legitimate land titles. And the colonists' Declaration of Independence from Great Britain set a precedent for aggrieved frontiersmen and canny opportunists to cite in their efforts to break away from the regimes of the eastern seaboard. The would-be leaders of projected frontier states built popular support by promising the first settlers better terms (often free land) than those offered by the land speculators of the established states. Once the new leaders had secured their new state, they meant amply to reward themselves from the offices of government and from the remaining stock of unsettled lands within their jurisdiction. In effect, through state-making, the opportunists meant to seize the most important path to wealth and power on the North American continent—the authority to build an "interest" by making, selling, and enforcing land titles. For ambitious men with few scruples, Revolutionary state-making promised meteoric social mobility.[8]

Vermont was the prototype for the opportunistic state-making associated with the Revolution. In January 1777 a convention of delegates from seventeen townships established the republic of Vermont, independent of both New York and New Hampshire. Six months later another convention adopted a populist constitution for the republic. The new government was dominated by a group of opportunists known as the Arlington Junto because most resided in that town during the war: Ethan Allen, his brother Ira, and their friends Thomas Chittenden and Matthew Lyon. The popular and pliable Chittenden presided over the new republic's council of state; the shrewd and secretive Ira Allen filled most of the other major posts—treasurer, secretary of state, and surveyor general; Lyon served as Ira Allen's chief deputy and

---

Trans-Appalachian Frontier: People, Societies, and Institutions, 1775–1850 (New York, 1978), pp. 21–25; Abernethy, *Western Lands and the American Revolution*, pp. 123–34.

[8] Peter S. Onuf, *The Origins of the Federal Republic: Jurisdictional Controversies in the United States, 1775–1787* (Philadelphia, 1983), p. 131.

as clerk of the Vermont assembly; Ethan Allen rarely held formal office but influenced the government through his three allies.[9]

The Arlington Junto exercised their control over Vermont's land to build an "interest," or faction, that would keep them in office so that they could ultimately enrich themselves from the residue of the republic's unsettled forest. In the short run, they had to dispense land generously to cultivate men who would help them weather the threats of British invasion, internal disaffection, and New York's continuing efforts to suppress the Vermont republic. In the long run, the Arlington Junto meant to secure their own wealth and social preeminence by speculating in New Hampshire land grant titles to over 75,000 acres of Vermont's very best land, principally in the then unsettled Onion River Valley (now the Winooski River Valley) around present-day Burlington. Over the course of their dozen-year stewardship of Vermont, they accumulated thousands of additional acres farther north. If Vermont survived and prospered, the Junto would reap fortunes from their extensive, albeit legally dubious, land claims.[10]

The Junto's first task was to curry support among the settlers and thereby obtain the militia needed to repel the British and to intimidate New York's authorities and their local supporters. To that end, Vermont abrogated the claims of New York's landlords and endorsed the New Hampshire grants that most settlers relied upon for title. Settlers without any titles could obtain cheap grants to "public lands" from the Vermont assembly. This policy promised settlers that they need make no additional payments for purchase or for quitrents to New Yorkers so long as Vermont remained independent. Consequently, the interest of most settlers as freeholders depended on the survival of the Junto's republic. Moreover, the Junto sustained popularity by minimizing taxes, financing

[9] Ibid., pp. 127–45; Aleine Austin, *Matthew Lyon: "New Man" of the Democratic Revolution, 1749–1822* (University Park, Pa., 1981), pp. 20–22; Countryman, *A People in Revolution*, p. 156; Jellison, *Ethan Allen*, pp. 178–93; Jones, *Vermont in the Making*, pp. 347–93.

[10] Jellison, *Ethan Allen*, pp. 178–93; Williamson, *Vermont in Quandary*, pp. 26–27, 75–76.

their regime virtually without taxes through 1780 by confiscating and auctioning the lands of alleged loyalists. The Junto's broad definition of "loyalist" extended to anyone who supported New York's jurisdiction or land titles. Junto members often profited from their positions by purchasing the best properties at bargain prices. The regime also minimized the costs of defense (postponing the introduction of significant taxes) by entering secret negotiations with the British authorities in Canada. The Vermont leaders purchased a de facto state of neutrality during the war's later years by promising (perhaps disingenuously) to persuade their constituents to rejoin the British empire. A reputation for cheap land and for low taxes made Vermont a haven for hard-pressed New England yeomen who flocked to the region during the war, swelling the ranks of the militia that the Junto needed to stay in power. By serving the ambitions of rogue gentlemen, common yeomen eased their own access to freehold prosperity, leaving the landlords and rulers of New York to fume in futility. The Junto sustained their republic because it offered the common yeomanry better access to cheap, fee-simple homesteads than did New York's authorities and landlords.[11]

The Junto's second task was to use their land titles to counteract New York's influence in Congress and to buy the goodwill of leading men in other state governments. The land committee of the Vermont assembly allocated generous grants of wild land in fifty new townships at token prices to useful and powerful outsiders: members of Congress, Continental army generals, and the leaders of state governments. The grantees included John Paul Jones, John Adams, Oliver Wolcott, generals John Sullivan and Horatio Gates, and President John Witherspoon of Princeton. The grantees' interest in their new townships merged with the interest of the Arling-

[11] Jellison, *Ethan Allen*, pp. 196–200, 247–49; Austin, *Matthew Lyon*, pp. 22–24; Michael A. Bellesiles, "The Establishment of Legal Structures on the Frontier: The Case of Revolutionary Vermont," *Journal of American History* 73 (1987): 899–900; Michael A. Bellesiles, *Revolutionary Outlaws: Ethan Allen and the Struggle for Independence on the Early American Frontier* (Charlottesville, Va., 1993); Williamson, *Vermont in Quandary*, pp. 67–74; Onuf, *Origins of the Federal Republic*, pp. 135–38; Woodward, *Town Proprietors in Vermont*, pp. 111–13.

ton Junto because the township grants would prove valuable only if the republic preserved its independence from New York. Into the bargain, members of the Junto sought further enrichment by naming themselves and their allies partners in many of the grants. Thomas Chittenden, for example, held interests in at least forty-two new townships.[12]

By securing the support of both resident yeomen and many nonresident gentlemen, the Arlington Junto weathered the war and remained in control of their republic until Ethan Allen's death in 1789. New York could never secure a congressional commitment to suppress the Junto, in part because of Vermont's growing "interest" in Congress and in part because of fears that coercion would drive the rogue republic into the British embrace. In 1791 the Junto's successors negotiated peace with New York. In return for an indemnity of $30,000, New York surrendered its claims and permitted Vermont to enter the Union. Following the Junto's example, the new state government used land grants to reward the New York politicians—including Alexander Hamilton, John Jay, and William Duer—who had consummated the deal over the bitter opposition of their state's governor, George Clinton. The Arlington Junto had retained power long enough to secure Vermont's statehood and to consolidate their private claims to substantial landholdings.[13]

The success of the Arlington Junto attests to the new avenues to wealth and authority opened by the Revolution and exploited by men of great ambition but of only middling property and without patronage from the established elite. Short on the social graces, family ties, and literary education necessary for acceptance among the nation's gentility (who in-

[12] Jellison, *Ethan Allen*, pp. 208–35; Austin, *Matthew Lyon*, pp. 25–29; Woodward, *Town Proprietors in Vermont*, pp. 114–16, 129–31; Williamson, *Vermont in Quandary*, p. 76.

[13] Alfred F. Young, *The Democratic Republicans of New York: The Origins, 1763–1797* (Chapel Hill, 1967), p. 57; Williamson, *Vermont in Quandary*, pp. 165–82; E. Wilder Spaulding, *His Excellency, George Clinton, Critic of the Constitution* (New York, 1938), pp. 142–45; Edward Porter Alexander, *A Revolutionary Conservative: James Duane of New York* (New York, 1938), pp. 202–3; Austin, *Matthew Lyon*, pp. 61–62.

cluded New York's landlords), the members of the Junto had made a virtue of necessity, obtaining Vermont leadership and estates by cultivating popular suspicion of prominent and wealthy outsiders. Before squandering his fortune on unwise investment in foreign commerce and political intrigue, Ira Allen had become one of the richest men in Vermont. The other members of the Junto were more fortunate. Matthew Lyon had come to America an Irish immigrant and an indentured servant, but he obtained in Fairhaven, Vermont, a four-hundred-acre tract unusually rich in iron, lumber, and water-power. During the 1780s and early 1790s he established a profitable complex with a sawmill, gristmill, paper mill, iron-works, tavern, store, newspaper, and farm. He also became a United States congressman who won notoriety as an extreme Jeffersonian. Ethan Allen secured a fourteen-hundred-acre farm of choice riverside land in Burlington and another 12,000 acres of fast-appreciating forest land in new townships. It was less than the great estates of the New York grandees he had contended with—men like James Duane and Philip Schuyler—but it was far more than he had begun with as the son of a Connecticut yeoman. Thomas Chittenden also achieved new wealth and power from his leadership in Vermont's revolution. In 1789 the Rev. Nathan Perkins, the Congregationalist pastor of orderly West Hartford, Connecticut, expressed distaste after he visited Governor Chittenden and toured his frontier estate. Perkins found anomolous and disquieting the new wealth of a man of humble origins and crude manners. "A low poor house,—a plain family—low, vulgar man, clownish, excessively parsimonious,—made me welcome,—hard fare, a very great farm,—1000 acres,—hundred acres of wheat on the Onion River—200 acres of extraordinary interval land. A shrewd, cunning man—skilled in human nature and in agriculture—understands extremely well the mysteries of Vermont, apparently and professedly serious." Men of established standing were uneasy that the Revolution had enriched clusters of new men without the cultured, genteel tone and without the established patrons previously expected as prerequisites for admission to the eighteenth-century American elite. It profoundly alarmed the genteel that upstarts could grow rich and influential by abetting popular unrest.[14]

EXTENDING VERMONT

The Arlington Junto's success and the new nation's postwar turmoil combined to encourage other ambitious opportunists to make other Vermonts. During the 1780s and early 1790s in Maine, western New York, northern and western Pennsylvania, Ohio, Kentucky, and Tennessee, aggrieved settlers and canny opportunists spoke of adopting the "Vermont plan" or of establishing "a Second Vermont," to the profound alarm of entrenched gentlemen. As late as 1801 a Susquehanna opportunist "referr'd to the success of Govr. Chittendon and the Allens in forming the State of Vermont and gave his opinion that the same thing might be effected here with greater ease."[15]

The recent Revolution and the weakness of the new state

[14]Gordon S. Wood, "Interests and Disinterestedness in the Making of the Constitution," in Richard Beeman et al., eds., *Beyond Confederation: Origins of the Constitution and American National Identity* (Chapel Hill, 1987), pp. 69–109; Rev. Nathan Perkins, *A Narrative of a Tour through the State of Vermont from April 27 to June 12, 1789* (Woodstock, Vt., 1920), p. 17; Austin, *Matthew Lyon,* pp. 26, 30–33; John Page, "The Economic Structure of Society in Revolutionary Bennington," *Vermont History* 49 (1981):76–79; Williamson, *Vermont in Quandary,* pp. 26–27; Jellison, *Ethan Allen,* pp. 322–24; Alexander, *A Revolutionary Conservative,* pp. 70–73, 84–85.

[15]For endorsements of Vermont see [Samuel Ely], *The Appeal of the Two Counties of Lincoln and Hancock from the Forlorn Hope, or Mount of Distress* (Portsmouth, N.H., 1796), pp. 20, 23; Maj. William Judd to Zebulon Butler, Feb. 1, 1782, "Extract of a Letter from Wayne County," July 21, 1801, Boyd and Taylor, eds., *Susquehannah Company Papers,* 7:97–98, 11:139. For fears of Vermont, see David Cobb to William Bingham, Sept. 7, 1797, Frederick S. Allis, Jr., ed., *William Bingham's Maine Lands,* 2 vols. (Boston, 1954), 2:859; George Washington to James Madison, Mar. 31, 1787, John C. Fitzpatrick, ed., *The Writings of George Washington,* 39 vols. (Washington, D.C., 1931–44), 29:192; and Peter S. Onuf, "Settlers, Settlements, and New States," in Jack P. Greene, ed., *The American Revolution: Its Character and Limits* (New York, 1987), p. 181. For backcountry disaffection during the 1780s and 1790s see Onuf, *Origins of the Federal Republic,* pp. 149–72; Slaughter, *Whiskey Rebellion,* pp. 28–44; Watlington, *Partisan Spirit,* pp. 36–78; and Abernethy, *Western Lands,* pp. 288–310.

governments and their confederation created a sense of uncertainty and possibility during the 1780s and early 1790s.
People questioned every form of allegiance to authority.
Widespread discontent among the yeomanry with the taxes
and debts collected by their betters inspired in most states a
spate of riots that escalated into overt rebellions in parts of
New England and Pennsylvania. While established gentlemen
dreaded the disorders as harbingers of violent, leveling anarchy, opportunists dispassionately calculated how they could
profit from the turmoil. One of those opportunists was Dr.
Timothy Hosmer, a Connecticut land speculator determined
to profit by wresting the upper Susquehanna country away
from Pennsylvania. In early February 1787, while the New
England Regulators commanded by Daniel Shays waged an
insurgency against the state troops of Massachusetts, Hosmer
wrote to the Susquehanna settlers,

> Will it not be Advantageous to the Susquehannah Settlement, let
> the event Go which way it will. If Government succeeds those
> opposers must look for some other Place to make their Residence
> and I have no doubt but numbers of them will flee to your
> Goodly Country: If they Fail (the Government Troops) we Shall
> be Flung into a State of Anarchy, from which a new form of Gov-
> ernment must Grow, from the Feebleness of the present Foederal
> Government, . . . a Monarchical (government) of some kind will
> it is most probable Grow out of it. If so, we have all the reason to
> draw this Conclusion That the holders of the Lands will have it
> secured to them after the Revolution for undoubtedly there will
> be an anihilation of State lines under a one Headed Government.
> That we shall not have to Quarell with a State but have a Tryal
> before Majesty which I had rather Submit to Tho' it were a Nero
> or Caligula Than to the Land Jobing Jockying State of Pennsyl-
> vania.

It seemed that bold and resourceful men could take advantage of the Revolutionary flux to pursue interest in defiance
of any government, republican or monarchical.[16]

[16] Timothy Hosmer to John Paul Schott, Feb. 2, 1787, in Boyd and Taylor, eds., *Susquehannah Company Papers*, 9:21–22; see the similar sentiments
in Judd to Butler, Jan. 11, 1787, ibid., 9:5–6. Circulating widely among
the receptive settlers of the upper Susquehanna, Hosmer's words quickly

The leaders of the Susquehannah Company were opportunists bent on obtaining the northern third of Pennsylvania despite a December 1782 ruling by a special federal tribunal at Trenton in favor of that state's claim to the long-contested region. Most of the old guard among the company shareholders accepted the Trenton decision and gave up the contest. But in 1784 the Susquehanna Valley's Yankee settlers, led by Col. John Franklin, independently organized a militia that drove out the soldiers and tenants sent by Pennsylvania to occupy the region. The settlers' success inspired a few daring, ambitious, and unscrupulous investors to revive the moribund Susquehannah Company during the summer of 1785. But for the settlers' initiative, there would have been no opportunity for upstart speculators to advance their counterclaim to the Susquehanna country.[17]

The new leaders of the Susquehannah Company were remarkably akin to the Arlington Junto. Both sets of opportunists were aggressive, entrepreneurial, and daring men of middling property, and most members of both groups came from the Connecticut–New York borderland, a region known for land speculation and controversy. Dr. Joseph Hamilton, Col. John McKinstry, Capt. Solomon Strong, Zerah Beach, Dr. Caleb Benton, and Maj. William Judd of the Susquehannah Company all embodied the stereotype of the crafty, calculating, self-righteous Yankee speculator so disliked and distrusted by their New York neighbors. Some of the new leaders had inherited small interests in the pre-Revolutionary Susquehannah Company, but none had been prominent in company affairs until the reorganization of 1785. Their initial bond came from shared membership in freemasonry, which in late eighteenth-century Connecticut was synonymous with political and religious free-thinking. Joseph Hamilton, the company's preeminent new leader, inherited his penchant for aggressive and contentious land speculation from his father,

---

became an article of faith among the inhabitants. See Joseph Sprague to Pickering, Feb. 20, 1787, ibid., 9:64.

[17] Introduction, ibid., 5:xxi–lii; Oscar Jewell Harvey, *A History of Wilkes-Barre, Luzerne County, Pennsylvania* (Wilkes-Barre, Pa., 1927), 3:1476–78.

David Hamilton, one of the first settlers and proprietors of
Sharon in northwestern Connecticut, near the New York border. Father Hamilton had invested in the New Hampshire
Grants and in the Susquehannah Company, banking in both
cases on settler resistance to make good his suspect titles. The
youngest of three sons, Joseph Hamilton moved across the
border to Hudson, Columbia County, New York, and became
a doctor and innkeeper—careers often associated in Revolutionary America with religious and political unorthodoxy. He
also became a leading freemason. John McKinstry was another Hudson freemason and innkeeper who joined Hamilton in the new company's leadership. Solomon Strong was
a Connecticut-born sawmill owner in nearby Claverack, New
York, until obliged to flee from a counterfeiting indictment to
the Susquehanna country. Zerah Beach was a storekeeper and
Caleb Benton was a doctor; both were residents of Amenia,
Dutchess County, New York, near the Connecticut line, and
both were sons of Yankee fathers. William Judd of Plainville,
Connecticut, was a man of more established connections—a
Yale graduate (1763), successful lawyer, and Continental army
officer. But he was prone to bursts of relentless, reckless ardor,
as in September 1775 when he led a provocative and fool-
hardy raid against Pennsylvania, only to land in a Philadelphia jail. And he was an avid freemason who became master
of Connecticut's grand lodge in 1792. Alienated from Connecticut's religious and political establishment, he became a
leading Jeffersonian.[18]

The one new leader who did not fit the opportunist mold
was the one who was an actual Susquehanna settler, John

[18] Harvey, *History of Wilkes-Barre*, 3:824–25n, 1498n, 1569n; Dorothy A.
Lipson, *Freemasonry in Federalist Connecticut, 1789–1835* (Princeton, 1977),
pp. 69–71, 88; George Clinton to Benjamin Franklin, Dec. 13, 1786, in
Boyd and Taylor, eds., *Susquehannah Company Papers*, 8:423; James H.
Smith, ed., *History of Dutchess County, New York* (Syracuse, N.Y., 1882), p. 339;
Stephen B. Miller, *Historical Sketches of Hudson* (Hudson, N.Y., 1862), p. 77.
Connecticut's freemasons opposed that state's congressional religious estab-
lishment and most became leading Jeffersonians at odds with the state's
governing Federalists. On medicine's association with unorthodoxy see
Pauline Maier, *The Old Revolutionaries: Political Lives in the Age of Samuel Adams*
(New York, 1980), pp. 131–34.

Franklin. He shared little with the nonresident leaders besides birth in northwestern Connecticut to the son of a petty investor in the Susquehannah Company. Principled, pious, and fearless, Franklin devoted his life to the settlers' cause and rarely availed himself of his opportunities, as the company's clerk and treasurer, to become rich through land speculation. He was content with a modest farm and sawmill and with his fellow settlers' esteem. He used the nonresident leaders to obtain needed funds for the settler resistance, as they used him to advance their ambitions. Dr. Hamilton understood that Franklin was the key figure in the Susquehanna resistance. On behalf of the nonresident speculators, Hamilton assured Franklin that "we have got the money chest in possession, we are very sensible of, but then you have the key, no righteous wheel will move until you move and that in such manners as to make the world know you are in earnest." [19]

By attaching themselves to the settlers' resistance led by Colonel Franklin, the company's new directors hoped to intimidate Pennsylvania's rulers into a quick compromise. If that failed, the Susquehannah Company's upstart leaders planned to follow Vermont's precedent and declare their claim an independent state. Franklin explained, "We must sweep in settlers to make ourselves strong; then if a writ of ejectment under Pennsylvania is served, we will rise and beat off the sheriff; and if Pennsylvania sends out a party against us, we will embody and drive them out; and then we will openly proclaim a new state, comprehending the Susquehannah Purchase." Several of the Susquehannah Company's new leaders—Benton, Hamilton, and McKinstry—also speculated in an equally brazen sister scheme by the "New York Lessees" to rob New York, their home state, of its western lands by obtaining Indian leases for 999 years and by declaring that region a new state. Apparently the opportunists hoped to

[19] Louise Welles Murray, *A History of Old Tioga Point and Early Athens* (Athens, Pa., 1907), p. 492; James Edward Brady, "Wyoming: A Study of John Franklin and the Connecticut Settlement into Pennsylvania," Ph.D. diss., Syracuse University, 1973, pp. 11, 308–12; Harvey, *History of Wilkes-Barre* 3:1227–30n; David Craft, *History of Bradford County, Pennsylvania* (Philadelphia, 1878), pp. 102, 107; Dr. Joseph Hamilton to Col. John Franklin, Sept. 10, 1787, in Boyd and Taylor, eds., *Susquehannah Company Papers*, 9:187.

merge their two overlapping companies and their two projected states, one extracted from New York and the other
from Pennsylvania.[20]

In search of the necessary expertise in Revolutionary state-
making, the company leaders turned to Ethan Allen. Aware
that interest was Allen's god, Joseph Hamilton recruited him
by offering a gratuity of twelve full shares in the company in
August 1785. The son of an original Susquehannah Company
proprietor, Allen was flattered by the company's offer and delighted by the new stage on which to strut in pursuit of more
adventure, acclaim, and property. Speaking from experience,
he advised the Susquehannah settlers, "Crowd your settlements, add to your numbers and strength; procure fire-arms,
and ammunition, be united among yourselves. . . . Liberty &
Property; or slavery and poverty; are now before us." In April
1786 Allen toured the upper Susquehanna to boost settler
morale. He seems to have taught the settlers the violent pro-
fanity that was his chief stock-in-trade. In the wake of Allen's
visit, a shocked Pennsylvania supporter named Obadiah Gore
reported, "Men Up the river are breathing out Threatnings.
. . . [They] make use of the most Blasphemous Expressions
that I ever heard being Uttered from any person." Thereafter
old age, a new marriage, and his Vermont affairs diverted Allen's attention from the Susquehanna. Nonetheless, until his
death in 1789, rumors persisted among the settlers that Allen
would soon return with one thousand armed Green Mountain Boys.[21]

[20] John Franklin quotation in John J. AcModer deposition, Dec. 22, 1788,
Boyd and Taylor, eds., *Susquehannah Company Papers,* 9:524–25; Samuel
Gordon to Obadiah Gore, Oct. 15, 1787, ibid., 9:240–41; Orsamus Turner,
*History of the Pioneer Settlement of Phelps and Gorham's Purchase, and Morris' Re-
serve* (1851; reprint ed., Geneseo, N.Y., 1976), pp. 106–10. New York's Gov.
George Clinton reacted quickly before the Lessees could establish more
than a few dozen settlers on the land; at Clinton's orders, Herkimer County's sheriff dispossessed the Lessees' settlers, burned their cabins, and arrested their leaders. The pretensions of the New York Lessees collapsed.

[21] Jellison, *Ethan Allen,* pp. 316–19; Ethan Allen's receipt, Aug. 19, 1785,
in Boyd and Taylor, eds., *Susquehannah Company Papers,* 8:256; Ethan Allen
to Butler et al., Oct. 27, 1785, ibid., 8:270–71; William Montgomery to
Pennsylvania's Council, May 17, 1786, ibid., 8:329; "An Address from the
Inhabitants of Wyoming," Sept. 12, 1786, ibid., 9:394–401; William Hooker

The violent contest between the competing speculators of opposing states created an opportunity for poor men to obtain free homesteads. In July 1785 the new leaders promised a half-share in the company to "every Able bodied and effective Man" who settled in the valley and agreed to "submit himself to the Orders of this Company." A half-share entitled every new settler to a homestead of at least one hundred, and as many as two hundred, acres that he could retain only if the company defeated Pennsylvania. By 1786 about half of the upper valley's five hundred adult male settlers were newcomers—"Half-Share Men"—and the other half were pre-1783 "Old Settlers." By all accounts, the Half-Share Men were refugees from poverty. In August 1786 Timothy Pickering toured the Susquehanna country and described the newcomers as "men destitute of property, who could be tempted by the gratuitous offer of lands, on the single condition that they should enter upon them armed, 'to man their rights,' in the cant phrase of those people." Another Pennsylvania official, Thomas Cooper, later characterized the resistance as a coalition of "the unprincipled speculators in half share rights, and the poor, industrious, but obstinate and deluded people who confide in these men."[22]

The company leaders put great stock in the power of interest to sustain settler resistance. Hamilton advised, "Men thus Planted and desperate The angels from Heaven, unless Divinely Commissioned, could not disposses. . . . my Friends go on, go on, but for God sake preserve rule and good order among yourselves, but let no man be among you but who feels himself Interested, let him be pleased with his situation if possible. This is the only true Policy." John McKinstry insisted

---

Smith to Charles Biddle, Aug. 10, 1786, ibid., 8:380; Gore to Pickering, Nov. 12, 1787, ibid., 9:267; Harvey, *History of Wilkes-Barre*, 3:1498–1500.

[22] Pickering quotation in Octavius Pickering and Charles W. Upham, *The Life of Timothy Pickering*, 2 vols. (Salem, Mass., 1829), 2:259, 266; Susquehannah Company Minutes, July 13, 1785, in Boyd and Taylor, eds., *Susquehannah Company Papers*, 8:247–50; Thomas Cooper to Tench Coxe, July 13, 1801, ibid., 11:118. For other accounts of settler poverty on the upper Susquehanna see Craft, *Bradford County*, pp. 87–90, 438; and Johann David Schoepf, *Travels in the Confederation [1783–1784]*, trans. and ed., Alfred J. Morrison, 2 vols. (Philadelphia, 1911), 1:170–74, 186.

"that the Pennsylvanians would never fight like those who are particularly concerned." By giving away a small part of their vast claim to armed settlers, the company leaders meant to obtain the forces needed to wrest the rest of the region away from Pennsylvania; the leaders expected subsequently to profit by retailing farms to later settlers.[23]

Most of the Half-Share Men came from the Yankee borderland bisected by the boundary line between eastern New York and western New England. The Yankee borderlanders were experienced in organized extralegal violence meant to protect their small homesteads from the taxes, rents, and purchase payments sought by New York's landlords and Massachusetts' magistrates. In the 1750s and in 1766 those on the New York side of the line had organized a violent resistance against the rents charged by that colony's landlords. Defeated, many Yankee tenants subsequently migrated north to participate as Green Mountain Boys in Vermont's rebellion against some of the same landlords. During the Revolution and the 1780s, the Yankees on the Massachusetts side of the line resisted the collection of taxes and debts by massing in armed force to close down the courts. When one state's authorities triumphed over resistance, the most disgruntled yeomen sought refuge on the other side of the border. New York tenants sought succor in Massachusetts and Connecticut during the 1750s and 1760s, and the defeated Regulators of Massachusetts found havens in Vermont and New York in 1787. The region was also notorious for harboring counterfeiters who evaded arrest by shifting back and forth across the legal borders. By the mid-1780s, Vermont could no longer satisfy the hunger for cheap land among borderlanders frustrated by the defeats of the tenant uprisings and of the New England Regulation. The disaffected began to spill over into the Susquehanna country, bearing with them a readiness "to man their rights" with armed force.[24]

[23] Col. John McKinstry, quoted in Thomas Wigton deposition, Sept. 8, 1787, in Boyd and Taylor, eds., *Susquehannah Company Papers*, 9:183; Hamilton to John Franklin, Mar. 24, 1786, ibid., 8:311–12.

[24] Staughton Lynd, *Anti-Federalism in Dutchess County, New York: A Study of Democracy and Class Conflict in the Revolutionary Era* (Chicago, 1962), pp.

The Susquehannah Company's new leaders were well placed to recruit the borderland's disaffected yeomen. Most of the new leaders were transplanted Connecticut Yankees dwelling in eastern New York's Columbia or Dutchess counties, the cockpits of violent antirentism. Moreover, many of those new leaders were doctors or innkeepers, men especially well positioned to know the area and to communicate with its inhabitants. Joseph Hamilton's tavern lay by an important ferry across the Hudson River, a strategic location for recruiting and directing Yankee emigrants. With tempting offers and populist rhetoric, the speculators tapped the borderland's growing surplus of defiant families. In November 1787, in the immediate wake of the defeat of Shays's Rebellion, one emigrant to the Susquehanna reported, "In order to incourage Settlers to come into their country & settle, I see a writing . . . signifying that Each settler should have a certain Quantity of Land gratis, &c., &c. Subtill arguments are made use of to persuade the people to repair to a New Country to avoid the heavy Taxes their new Masters lay on them."[25]

In addition to wooing actual settlers with free homesteads, the Susquehannah Company also tried to buy support among America's leading men. Once again the Arlington Junto provided the model. In 1794–95 the company authorized 234 new townships, each five miles square, and embarked on an aggressive program of surveying and promotion. Shares in the new townships were sold cheap, or given away, to influential men like Theodore Sedgwick, a United States senator from Massachusetts. Settler resistance made this program of creating new land titles possible, as the Half-Share Men

37–54; David J. Goodall, "New Light on the Border: New England Squatter Settlements in New York during the American Revolution," Ph.D. diss., State University of New York at Albany, 1984; Handlin, "The Eastern Frontier of New York"; Countryman, *A People in Revolution*, pp. 5–71; Robert J. Taylor, *Western Massachusetts in the Revolution* (Providence, 1954).

[25] Zerah Beach to Butler, Sept. 21, 1785, in Boyd and Taylor, eds., *Susquehannah Company Papers*, 8:262; Hamilton to John Franklin, Mar. 24, 1786, ibid., 8:310; Gordon to Nathan Dennison, Nov. 24, 1787, ibid., 9:305.

chased away the surveyors for Pennsylvania's landlords and protected those working for the Susquehannah Company.

In the Susquehanna scheme, settler strength and speculator interest supported one another. On the one hand, a formidable settler commitment to an upstart title attracted the attention of outside investors on the alert for a promising speculation. On the other, the accumulation of speculator interest in a landgrab bolstered settler confidence in ultimate victory, for they knew the importance of wealth and influence in a political struggle. To boost morale, Colonel Franklin and other local leaders actively circulated among their neighbors the letters of support received from influential gentlemen living in other states. In September 1796 Clement Paine, a Susquehanna settler leader exulted, "The title of our land is growing in repute; many persons of respectability and influence, particularly in Connecticut, Massachusetts, New York, Rhode Island, and Vermont, have purchased and made themselves interested in the business."[26]

But Paine spoke too soon, for few outsiders of significant standing bought Susquehannah titles, and almost all who did quickly lost interest. Although successful in the first half of their program—to establish a settler constituency—the company failed in the second—to develop a substantial interest among the nation's leaders. In large part this was because of the countercampaign waged by Tench Coxe, a Pennsylvania land speculator and the state's land office secretary, for the hearts and minds of America's elite. In 1801 he vigorously denounced the Susquehannah Company in a pamphlet freely distributed to the "Governors, Senators, and Representatives, Judges, Members of the State legislatures, Lawyers, Landed men, &c, the Attorney general of the United States, and every other public Man from . . . Washington to Massachusetts." Coxe effectively warned them that they would reap nothing but trouble and expense by assisting the Susquehannah re-

---

[26] Susquehannah Company Minutes, Feb. 20, 1795, ibid., 10:214–16; Dr. Caleb Benton to John Jenkins, Oct. 26, 1795, ibid., 10:329; Clement Paine to Seth Paine, Sept. 20, 1796, ibid., 10:381. For the circulation of letters see Pickering to Samuel Hodgdon, Mar. 16, 1788, ibid., 9:338.

bels. Moreover, the American elite had begun to reach a new consensus that it was dangerous and unseemly to carry their competition for wealth and power to extremes that empowered men of little property. After the reformation of the federal government with the ratification of a new Constitution in 1788, gentlemen had reunited in support of established legal institutions; they became loath to undermine another state's jurisdiction and land titles. Consequently, after 1788 the Susquehannah Company failed to attract as much support among America's political leaders as Vermont had enjoyed during the preceding decade. The company's inability to match the wealth and prowess of their Pennsylvania competitors discouraged the resisting settlers. To highlight their advantage, the Pennsylvania speculators formed an association and published a broadside meant to intimidate the settlers: "The Associators are highly respectable in number and character. The property they have at stake is immense. Their Committee is active and industrious. Council of eminence in the law have been applied to, for the support of prosecutions against offenders." An effective argument, it cracked the settler confidence; within five years most of the settlers came to terms and agreed to buy Pennsylvania titles.[27]

CONCLUSION

All of the coalitions of opportunists and settlers formed during the 1780s fell short in their schemes to create additional Vermonts. When Kentucky and Tennessee won separate statehood and admission to the Union in 1792 and 1796, it was with the consent of their mother states, Virginia and North Carolina. That consent came after the new regimes promised to preserve the status quo in land titles. Maine did not win separate statehood until 1820, and again only after it had become clear that the new leaders would not tamper with

[27] Coxe to Cooper, June 26, 1801, ibid., 11:88; Broadside of the Pennsylvania Landholders' Association, Apr. 14, 1801, ibid., 11:53; Jacob E. Cooke, *Tench Coxe and the Early Republic* (Chapel Hill, 1978), p. 366 n. 51.

the land titles already created by Massachusetts and already sold to regular land speculators. Secessionist schemes in western New York and northwestern Pennsylvania also crumbled.[28]

The post-Revolutionary alliances of settlers and opportunists ultimately failed because they frightened the established gentlemen into creating a federal government capable of stifling frontier disaffection. Peter S. Onuf has demonstrated that jurisdictional conflicts between the states during the 1780s built a new consensus among America's gentlemen in favor of vesting sovereignty in a central government that could guarantee the territorial integrity of every member state. Those jurisdictional conflicts originated in the efforts by settlers and upstart speculators to create and uphold alternative land titles. After the ratification of the federal Constitution in 1788, state-making ceased to be a viable option for opportunists. Frontier dissidents, like the Susquehannah Yankees, who looked to federal courts or Congress for succor against state authorities, invariably had their hopes blasted. Pro-Spanish and secessionist intrigues persisted in Kentucky and Tennessee, but ultimately they came to nothing. During the 1790s frontier dissidents who violently defied federal authority, like the Whiskey Rebels of western Pennsylvania, were vigorously suppressed. As a result, the disaffected within states had to seek compromises from their state legislatures. For example, during the first decade of the nineteenth century, Pennsylvania mollified the Yankee settlers within the fifteen oldest and most populated Susquehanna townships by selling them titles for an average of thirty-two cents per acre. But most of the Half-Share Men lived in newer settlements excluded from the compromise legislation; they had to pay more—two to three dollars per acre—to Pennsylvania's land speculators or give up and move on. Their abettors, the Sus-

---

[28] Paul W. Gates, *Landlords and Tenants on the Prairie Frontier: Studies in American Land Policy* (Ithaca, N.Y., 1973), pp. 13–47; Rohrbough, *Trans-Appalachian Frontier*, pp. 56–63; Alan Taylor, *Liberty Men and Great Proprietors: The Revolutionary Settlement on the Maine Frontier, 1760–1820* (Chapel Hill, 1990).

quehannah Company, gained nothing from the long and expensive struggle.[29]

Moreover the new federal government assumed control of the vast domain of wilderness land lying west of Pennsylvania and north of the Ohio River. There the federal government enforced the Northwest Ordinances of 1785 and 1787, a program of land sales and territorial government specifically designed to preclude further trouble from combines of squatters and opportunists. By mandating a relatively high minimum price for land (one dollar per acre) and by insisting upon government surveys in advance of sale and settlement, the Northwest Ordinance of 1785 encouraged compact, orderly settlement by commercial farmers who could be relied upon to support the federal government as the source of their titles. The Northwest Ordinance of 1787 mandated hierarchical territorial governments dominated by a governor, a secretary, and three territorial judges all appointed by the distant national government. The ordinance delayed statehood until a territory's population topped 60,000 in the expectation that the previous period, if supervised by gentlemen landlords and governors, would teach the inhabitants, in the words of Arthur St. Clair, Ohio's first territorial governor, "habits of Obedience and Respect."[30]

With the Northwest Ordinances, Congress acted to restore the primacy of true gentlemen in retailing, settling, and governing frontier lands. The restrictive policy appealed to prestigious gentlemen like George Washington who were appalled at the competition from upstart speculators of limited means but aggressive ambition. In 1784 he had complained, "Men in these times talk with as much facility of fifty, a hundred, and even 500,000 Acres as a Gentleman formerly would do

---

[29] Onuf, *Origins of the Federal Republic;* Introduction, in Boyd and Taylor, eds., *Susquehannah Company Papers,* 11:xxix–xxx; Rosewell Welles and Alexander Scott to Gov. Thomas McKeen, Mar. 4, 1808, ibid., 11:524.

[30] Peter S. Onuf, "Liberty, Development, and Union: Visions of the West in the 1780s," *William and Mary Quarterly,* 3d ser. 43 (1986):179–213; Onuf, "Settlers, Settlements, and New States," pp. 171–96; Cayton, *Frontier Republic,* pp. 12–50, St. Clair quotation p. 35; Malcolm J. Rohrbough, *The Land Office Business: The Settlement and Administration of American Public Lands, 1789–1837* (New York, 1968), pp. 4–23.

of 1000 acres. In defiance of the proclamation of Congress, they roam over the Country on the Indian side of the Ohio, mark out Lands, Survey, and even settle them." In 1787 Congress agreed to make a special sale at reduced rates of 1,500,000 acres to the Ohio Company, a cartel of great men, principally Continental army officers from New England and their friends in Congress. The company members impressed Congress as "men of very considerable property and respectable characters." Their spokesman, Manasseh Cutler, promised that they would "begin *right*" by carefully screening prospective settlers so that there would be "no *wrong* habits to combat, and no inveterate systems to overturn . . . no rubbish to remove." Impressed with that promise, Washington's administration drew upon leading members of the Ohio Company to command Ohio's territorial government.[31]

For the moment, the federal government stifled the symbiosis of squatter and petty speculator in the Ohio territory. But it would revive in a new form after 1800 through the vehicle of state politics, when Jeffersonian "friends of the people" cast out the Federalist "fathers of the people" throughout the West. The Jeffersonian leaders of Ohio, who ousted St. Clair and his Ohio Company allies from office in 1802, were small-scale speculators who knew how to win votes among the common people insulted by Federalist paternalism. The new Ethan Allens and John Franklins of the West were men like Nathaniel Massie and Thomas Worthington of Ohio who, as surveyor-speculators and Jeffersonian politicians, had found that they could profitably work within and dominate the new system of federal land sales and state governments. But the common settler got little more than the catharsis that came from electoral crusades against the haughty Federalist "aristocrats." The common settlers had lost their leverage for want of any further demand for their services as militias on behalf of upstart titles.[32]

[31] Onuf, "Liberty, Development, and Union," pp. 184–93, Washington quotation p. 192; Onuf, "Settlers, Settlements, and New States," pp. 171–96, Cutler quotation p. 185; Cayton, *Frontier Republic*, p. 17.

[32] Rohrbough, *Land Office Business*, pp. 44–48; Cayton, *Frontier Republic*, pp. 51–94.

GREGORY H. NOBLES

"Yet the Old Republicans Still Persevere"

Samuel Adams,

John Hancock,

and the Crisis of Popular

Leadership

in Revolutionary

Massachusetts, 1775–1790

BY 1776, MOST American radicals knew where their movement
was going; they only worried about how they would get there,
and who would lead them. In March of that year, just a few
months before the Continental Congress declared American
independence from Britain, Mercy Otis Warren wrote to
John Adams to offer her opinions on "the form of government which ought to be preferred by a people, about to shake
the fetters of monarchic and aristocratic tyranny." Like Adams, Warren declared herself an "admirer of republican government" because it was "a form productive of many excellent
qualities, and heroic virtues in human nature which often lie
dormant for want of opportunities of exertion." Yet like many
other self-professed republicans, she worried that "American
virtue has not yet reached that sublime pitch" necessary for

successful self-government: republican ideals had to be imple-
mented by real people, and Warren feared that the flaws of
human nature would render many people unable (or unwilling) to act with selfless virtue. Therefore she looked to republican leaders like Adams to set the tone and standards for the
rest of society. On the eve of Independence she could only
hope "that America has more than *one politician,* who has the
abilities to make the character of the people, to extinguish
vices and follies he finds, and to create the virtues he sees
wanting."[1]

Her hope soon gave way to disdain and despair. In a letter
to Adams three years later, she noted "a spirit of party" and
moral decline among the political leaders in her own state of
Massachusetts: "The votaries of pleasure, men of *pretended*
taste and refinement, make no inconsiderable figure, while
many others worship only at the shrine of *Plutus.*" Many of
the men who had led Massachusetts into the Revolution were
now threatening to lead it to ruin. In closing, she offered only
one note of encouragement: "Yet the old republicans (a solitary few) still persevere, their hands untainted by bribes—
though poverty stares them in the face—and their hearts un-
shaken by fear, amidst the dissipation and folly, the levity, luxury, and wickedness of the times."[2]

Clearly, something had gone wrong in Massachusetts. In so
short a time, the bright prospects for political and moral advance that had at least seemed possible in 1776 now seemed
to have dimmed. For Mercy Otis Warren and the "solitary
few" who still adhered to the Old Republican standards, the
Revolutionary era had already become a source of disappoint-
ment. The people and their leaders had had their republican
virtue put to the test, and most of them had failed.

The Old Republicans' sense of loss was not merely a case of
self-serving sour grapes. Something *had* gone wrong in Massachusetts. At the outset of the Revolutionary War, no other
former British colony seemed as well prepared as Massachu-

[1] Mercy Otis Warren to John Adams, March 1776, Letter Book of Mercy
Otis Warren (1770–1800), Mercy Otis Warren Papers, pp. 162–64, Massachusetts Historical Society, Boston.

[2] Warren to Adams, July 29, 1779, ibid., pp. 176–77.

setts to stand as a strong, independent state. Massachusetts had been the center of radical activity in the colonies since the 1760s, with a group of remarkably articulate and active whig ideologues. These popular leaders had forged an effective alliance with the common people, first in the Boston area and then throughout the countryside. In 1774–75 the radical movement mobilized widespread opposition and, eventually, armed resistance to British rule. By early 1776, the British army and most of its loyalist sympathizers evacuated Massachusetts, leaving the patriots firmly in control. Throughout the war, Massachusetts never faced any serious threat of British invasion or military occupation as did most of the other former colonies. Moreover, it never suffered the fierce internal fighting between armed patriot and loyalist factions that turned the Revolution in New York, New Jersey, and especially the southern states into a vicious, "uncivil war."[3] Massachusetts remained comparatively staunch and secure, one of the most united of the states to endure the Revolutionary struggle.

Yet the Revolution revealed serious social and political divisions that eventually shattered the surface appearance of unity. The internal conflict in Massachusetts did not reflect the dominant divisions of the Revolutionary era—the struggles between Britain and America and between loyalists and patriots—although those divisions certainly contributed to the sense of crisis. Rather it was a conflict that stemmed from divisions among people—common folk and leaders alike—who considered themselves essentially on the same side, allies in the cause of republicanism. It was a conflict over the nature of republicanism itself, a question of how the standards of republican government would be defined and by whom. In

[3] For examples of internal conflict in other Revolutionary states, see John Shy, "Armed Loyalism: The Case of the Lower Hudson Valley," and "The Military Conflict Considered as a Revolutionary War," in idem, *A People Numerous and Armed: Reflections on the Military Struggle for American Independence* (New York, 1976), pp. 181–224; Joseph S. Tiedemann, "Patriots by Default: Queens County, New York, and the British Army, 1776–1783," *William and Mary Quarterly,* 3d ser. 43 (1986):35–63; and Ronald Hoffman, Thad W. Tate, and Peter J. Albert, eds., *An Uncivil War: The Southern Backcountry during the American Revolution* (Charlottesville, Va., 1985).

Massachusetts that question remained unanswered throughout the war and well into the first years of peace.

The purpose of this essay is not to offer a detailed discussion of Massachusetts politics during the Revolutionary era:
other historians have done that.[4] Rather, the goal is to explore
the standards of political leadership in a popular movement
like the American Revolution by examining the changing
fates of Samuel Adams and John Hancock. In Massachusetts,
they were the two men most strongly identified with the Revolutionary movement *as a movement,* as a mass mobilization of
the common people. True, other men—John Adams, Elbridge Gerry, Joseph Hawley, James Otis, and James Warren,
to name a few—played critical roles as popular leaders in
Revolutionary Massachusetts. But Samuel Adams and John
Hancock were the critical conduits between the classes, two
men who seemed most able to operate at any level, whether
in the streets and crowded meetinghouses with the common
people or in parlors and private chambers with the political
elite. From the 1760s through the 1780s, they spoke both to
and for the common people, and they always stood in the
middle of the movement. But they also stood far apart on the
spectrum of style and status—Adams the older, impecunious,
high-principled professional politician, the "last of the Puritans"; Hancock the younger, free-spending, popularity-
seeking political neophyte. Thus they offer two especially
valuable political portraits, two sharply contrasting images

[4]Useful works on political developments in Massachusetts during the
Revolutionary era include Charles W. Akers, *The Divine Politician: Samuel
Cooper and the American Revolution in Boston* (Boston, 1982); John L. Brooke,
*The Heart of the Commonwealth: Society and Political Culture in Worcester County,
Massachusetts, 1713–1861* (Cambridge, 1989); Richard D. Brown, *Revolu-
tionary Politics in Massachusetts: The Boston Committee of Correspondence and the
Towns, 1772–1774* (Cambridge, Mass., 1970); Van Beck Hall, *Politics without
Parties: Massachusetts 1780–1791* (Pittsburgh, 1972); Stephen E. Patterson,
Political Parties in Revolutionary Massachusetts (Madison, Wis., 1973); William
Pencak, *War, Politics, and Revolution in Provincial Massachusetts* (Boston, 1981);
Ronald M. Peters, Jr., *The Massachusetts Constitution of 1780: A Social Compact*
(Amherst, Mass., 1978); David P. Szatmary, *Shays' Rebellion: The Making of an
American Insurrection* (Amherst, Mass., 1980); and John Tyler, *Smugglers and
Patriots: Boston Merchants and the Advent of the American Revolution* (Boston,
1986).

that help define the standards of popular leadership in the Revolutionary era.

The standards of popular leadership are important, because they reveal a great deal about the standards of the people. Even when historians consider the American Revolution as a social movement (as J. Franklin Jameson put it in the 1920s) or study it "from the bottom up" (as Jesse Lemisch argued in the 1960s), they still have to look at its leaders.[5] Popular leaders provide an important human focus, a means of personifying the goals of the movement. They are not socially isolated ideologues or wily propagandists who create a mass movement through the force of intellectual, moral, or emotional appeals. To a great extent, quite the reverse is true: popular movements create their own leaders. They propel certain people into positions of prominence, endowing them with the status of spokesperson or sometimes even symbol.

The burden of being a symbol is a heavy one, and few people bear it well, and certainly not for long. Some of the most prominent popular leaders of the 1760s and early 1770s—and here Samuel Adams is a notable example—fell from favor with the people by the 1780s, no longer commanding the influence or esteem they once did. In turn, Adams and some of his allies also began to express doubt that the common folk had the wisdom and virtue necessary to govern themselves in a proper republican manner. On the other hand, Hancock seemed only to gain power and prominence during the course of the Revolution. Although many of his social and political peers, especially Old Republicans like Mercy Otis Warren, questioned his intelligence and integrity, Hancock proved to be a great favorite of the common people. Especially in the period of political crisis in the 1780s, he was the one individual who most effectively embodied political legitimacy and helped hold the commonwealth together. In general, gauging the rise and fall of popular leaders like Samuel Adams and John Hancock may be one of the best barome-

[5] J. Franklin Jameson, *The American Revolution Considered as a Social Movement* (Princeton, 1926); Jesse Lemisch, "The American Revolution Seen from the Bottom Up," in Barton J. Bernstein, ed., *Towards a New Past: Dissenting Essays in American History* (New York, 1968).

ters of political change in reconsidering the American Revolution as a social movement.

In the early stages of the Revolutionary movement, Samuel Adams and John Hancock were commonly portrayed as a matched pair of provocateurs, a political odd couple considered inseparable by friends and foes alike. George Robert Twelves Hewes, Alfred F. Young's remarkable Revolutionary man in the street, claimed to have dumped tea into Boston harbor alongside Adams and Hancock (the latter recognizable, in part, because of his ruffles sticking out under his Indian disguise).[6] In fact, Adams and Hancock were not actually onboard ship with the other participants in the Boston Tea Party, but whether Hewes was accurate or not is almost beside the point; in the memory of a common man like Hewes, Adams and Hancock *must* have been among the patriots on deck. A less sympathetic Bostonian, Chief Justice Peter Oliver, wrote that Hancock was "as closely attached to the hindermost Part of Mr. Adams as the Rattles are affixed to the Tail of a Rattle Snake."[7] Hancock himself emphasized the connection between the two when he commissioned John Singleton Copley to paint their portraits, which hung side by side in the Hancock mansion on Beacon Hill.[8]

The British wanted to hang the two men themselves. By 1775 Adams and Hancock lived constantly with the threat of arrest, and on the night of April 18, when the British troops marched on Lexington and Concord to capture patriot arms and ammunition, Gen. Thomas Gage also had hopes of capturing the two most troublesome radicals. Adams and Hancock escaped, but Gage did not give up his desire to get them;

[6] Alfred F. Young, "George Robert Twelves Hewes (1742–1840): A Boston Shoemaker and the Memory of the American Revolution," *William and Mary Quarterly*, 3d ser. 38 (1981):561–623, esp. pp. 590–92, 600. Herbert S. Allan, *John Hancock: Patriot in Purple* (New York, 1948), pp. 140–41, also recounts Hewes's story but discounts its accuracy.

[7] Quoted in John Langdon Sibley and Clifford K. Shipton, *Biographical Sketches of Those Who Attended Harvard College*, 17 vols. (Boston, 1873–1975), 13:423.

[8] Ibid., p. 425.

in June 1775, when he offered amnesty to Massachusetts radicals, he explicitly excluded Adams and Hancock, "whose offenses are of too flagitious a nature to admit of any other consideration than of condign punishment."[9] By that point, both Adams and Hancock were on their way out of Massachusetts and headed for Philadelphia, where they would serve in the Second Continental Congress.

Just after they arrived in Philadelphia, Adams received a letter from James Warren, warning that "All Bodies have their Foibles. Jealousy, however groundless, may predominate in yours."[10] Warren's prediction was soon borne out in Adams's relationship with Hancock. Their political paths began to diverge, and their personal contrasts turned increasingly to conflict. Hancock became a highly visible member of the Congress, serving as president in 1775 and 1776. He eventually broke ranks with his radical Massachusetts colleagues, however, and drifted into an alliance with more conservative members from New York and the southern states; at best, he was slow to embrace Independence.[11] Still, although Adams may have been a prime mover for American Independence, Hancock had the prime spot on the Declaration of Independence. (His famous signature, of course, is written with a flourish above the others, while Adams's is the third down in the far right column.)

Adams worked not so much in Hancock's shadow as in the background, using his consummate skills as a "parliamentary whip" to build coalitions and control committees.[12] On several notable occasions he succeeded in defeating Hancock's plans and deflating his ego. In 1775, when Hancock put himself forward for the generalship of the Continental army, Samuel Adams and his cousin John voted to give the post to a south-

[9] Allan, *John Hancock*, pp. 193–94.

[10] James Warren to Samuel Adams, June 21, 1775, Photostat Collection, Mass. Hist. Soc.

[11] Allan, *John Hancock*, pp. 229–31; William M. Fowler, Jr., *The Baron of Beacon Hill: A Biography of John Hancock* (Boston, 1980), p. 207.

[12] The term *parliamentary whip* comes from Jack N. Rakove, *The Beginnings of National Politics: An Interpretive History of the Continental Congress* (New York, 1979), p. 103.

erner, George Washington. Two years later, when Hancock resigned from his position as president of the Congress, Samuel Adams led his New England colleagues in refusing to offer Hancock a vote of thanks for his services. In arguing that no single representative should be accorded special honor, Adams stuck to a sound republican principle, but he also struck a sound blow to Hancock's pride.[13]

Adams's victories over Hancock in Congress may have been satisfying in the short run, but they did not prevent Hancock's subsequent political success. When Hancock left Congress and returned to Massachusetts, he enjoyed an illustrious political career as long as he lived, serving as the first governor elected under the new constitution in 1780 and winning reelection every time he ran. In 1788 his support for the federal Constitution was deemed critical to the success of the federalist faction in the Massachusetts ratifying convention. Some federalists even hinted that he would be a possible candidate for the nation's first president or, certainly, vice-president. In short, Hancock's political star was on the rise throughout the Revolutionary era, and no one in Massachusetts could match his prominence or popularity.[14]

By contrast, Samuel Adams's political career reached its peak before the Revolution and began to decline in the 1780s. Indeed, most of the Adams biographies pay scant, if any, attention to his career after 1775, even though he held public office throughout the Revolutionary era.[15] He served in the Continental Congress from 1774 to 1781, and he regularly held a seat in the state senate from 1782 to 1789. Although

[13] William V. Wells, *The Life and Public Services of Samuel Adams*, 3 vols. (Boston, 1888), 2:308–9, 503–4; John C. Miller, *Sam Adams: Pioneer in Propaganda* (Stanford, 1936), pp. 333–37; Allan, *John Hancock*, pp. 195–96; Fowler, *Baron of Beacon Hill*, pp. 191–92, 207–8.

[14] See especially Allan, *John Hancock*, and Fowler, *Baron of Beacon Hill*.

[15] See, for instance, Miller, *Sam Adams*, which devotes only two chapters out of fourteen to Adams's political career after 1774. Other biographical works—notably, Cass Canfield, *Samuel Adams's Revolution, 1765–1776* (New York, 1976), and Stewart Beach, *Samuel Adams: The Fateful Years, 1764–1776* (New York, 1965)—do not even consider Adams's later years. Only Wells's nineteenth-century biography offers a detailed treatment of Adams's career *during* the Revolution (*Samuel Adams*, vols. 2 and 3).

he repeatedly sought the governor's chair, he always lost to Hancock. It was Hancock, in fact, who put Adams in line to become governor by supporting him for lieutenant-governor in 1789; then, when Hancock died in 1793, Adams stepped into the position. But Adams's two terms as governor were undistinguished, and he retired from public life in 1797 an unhappy and unpopular man. Despite his long record of public service, he still remains more noteworthy as a political organizer than as an elected official.

More to the point, Adams stands out not so much for his political accomplishments as for his political character. He was the very model of the republican revolutionary—a staunch, stable, self-disciplined, self-sacrificing, puritanical patriot. Yet as Pauline Maier has shown, he has not always been well treated by historians, especially some of Jameson's contemporaries.[16] Ralph Volney Harlow, who published a study of Adams in 1923, just two years before Jameson delivered his lectures on the Revolution, not only attacked Adams as a dishonest propagandist but asserted that he "was not entirely normal, and he was probably a neurotic." According to Harlow's crude psychobiography, Adams was a failure in life who had a severe inferiority complex and "turned to politics because in that kind of activity he found relief from his troublesome mental problems."[17] John C. Miller, whose 1936 book on Adams is still the standard biography, took a more balanced view but nonetheless described him as a "Pioneer in Propaganda."[18] In general, historians writing in the period between the World Wars and in the early years of the Cold War took a dim view of Adams, often portraying him as a de-

[16] Pauline Maier, "Coming to Terms with Samuel Adams," *American Historical Review* 81 (1976):12–37; see also idem, *The Old Revolutionaries: Political Lives in the Age of Samuel Adams* (New York, 1980), chap. 1.

[17] Ralph Volney Harlow, *Samuel Adams, Promoter of the American Revolution: A Study in Psychology and Politics* (New York, 1923), pp. 38–39, 64–65. Even more recent analyses of Adams's character have slipped into the language of psychological disorder. William Pencak, for instance, has written of Adams's "exaggerated, even paranoid" political stance in the wake of the Revolution. See Pencak, "Samuel Adams and Shays's Rebellion," *New England Quarterly* (1989):65.

[18] Miller, *Sam Adams.*

vious, almost demented man who manipulated and sometimes misled the docile masses.

By comparison, Maier and other historians have offered a more positive portrait of Adams as a principled political leader who set a high personal standard of republican virtue. They emphasize his roots in New England Puritanism, his Calvinist commitment to the common cause. William Appleman Williams credits Adams with being a true radical, "a man who went to the root of the human condition and tried to evolve a program that would sustain and extend that humanity." Like his Puritan forbears, he believed in a "corporate Christian commonwealth . . . [and] he committed himself to that ideal with the vigor and *elan* of all great revolutionaries." Similarly, Jack N. Rakove has described Adams as "a recognizable revolutionary 'type' . . . [whose] ascetic devotion to the mundane tasks of political organization set him apart even from his closest colleagues . . . whose public mask and private personality became so tightly fused that even he no longer knew where one ended and the other began." In short, Adams was, to use Bruce Mazlish's term, a "revolutionary ascetic" in the tradition of Cromwell and in anticipation of Robespierre.[19]

If Samuel Adams was the American Revolution's Robespierre, John Hancock was its Danton. Compared to Adams, Hancock seems a surprisingly flawed figure to rise as a leader in a republican revolution. Scarcely anyone has given him much credit for intellect or originality. One caustic loyalist critic writing in 1776 dismissed Hancock as "a man whose brains were shallow and pockets deep."[20] In her history of the American Revolution, Mercy Otis Warren barely restrained

[19] Maier, "Coming to Terms with Samuel Adams," esp. pp. 30–37; William Appleman Williams, "Samuel Adams: Calvinist, Mercantilist, Revolutionary," *Studies on the Left* 1 (1960):57; Rakove, *Beginnings of National Politics*, pp. 6, 298; and Bruce Mazlish, *The Revolutionary Ascetic: Evolution of a Political Type* (New York, 1976). I am grateful to my colleague John Garver for bringing Mazlish's book to my attention. I must point out, though, that while I find many of Mazlish's observations to be quite perceptive and useful, I do not find his emphasis on psychological categories an ultimately satisfying form of historical or biographical explanation.

[20] Quoted in Wells, *Samuel Adams*, 2:431.

her disdain for Hancock, describing him as "a young gentleman of fortune, of more external accomplishments than real abilities . . . [whose] fickleness could not injure, so long as he was under the influence of men of superior judgment."[21] Even Hancock's more sympathetic modern biographers make few claims for his mental abilities. Herbert S. Allan notes that Hancock was "intellectually inferior to many of the statesmen he presided over" in the Continental Congress, and William M. Fowler, Jr., admits that he was not in the same intellectual league with Thomas Jefferson or John Adams: "He wrote nothing of an extraordinary nature and seems never to have been much interested in any of the great issues of the time beyond those of mundane politics."[22] In general, most explanations for Hancock's rise to political prominence in the patriot movement usually point not to his head but to his pocketbook.

By most accounts, Hancock was the wealthiest man in Boston in the decade before the Revolution. He was not, however, the most financially astute. He inherited the family fortune in 1764, at the age of twenty-seven, and proceeded to squander much of his wealth on parties, fancy clothes, luxury goods, and other forms of personal display. Although he continued to run the family mercantile house built up by his father and uncle, he was not a successful businessman; in fact, even after allowing for the difficulties of doing business in an era of increasing governmental interference, one of Hancock's biographers has still judged him "a failure as a merchant."[23]

Hancock's financial troubles in the 1760s may well have turned him against the Crown initially, but it was Samuel Adams who nurtured his animosity and helped him change careers from merchant to professional politician. Adams and his fellow political leaders in the Caucus Club gave Hancock their stamp of approval when he was elected one of Boston's four representatives to the General Court in 1766. Adams is reputed to have said that by choosing Hancock, the people of

[21] Mercy Otis Warren, *History of the Rise, Progress, and Termination of the American Revolution,* 3 vols. (Boston, 1805), 1:212.

[22] Allan, *John Hancock,* p. 191; Fowler, *Baron of Beacon Hill,* p. 280.

[23] Allan, *John Hancock,* p. 144.

Boston "have made that young man's fortune their own." A decade later, a Boston loyalist characterized Hancock as an "Orator and Milch Cow of the Faction but whether Public Spirit or Vanity has been his Governing principle is uncertain." What is certain, however, is that Adams and his colleagues knew how to make good use of Hancock's money, good looks, and smooth style, and in the early years of his political career, Hancock served as a useful front man for the whig faction.[24]

Yet Hancock's wealthy background also made him suspect in the eyes of his allies. In an era that called for self-denial and republican simplicity, Hancock seldom surrendered his self-indulgent love of display. His trip to join the Continental Congress in Philadelphia in 1775 was a case in point. As the Massachusetts and Connecticut delegations approached New York, thousands of militiamen and citizens thronged the roads leading to the city to greet the members of Congress. Hancock's carriage was in the lead, and a crowd sought to unharness his horses and pull the vehicle themselves. Hancock protested and finally prevailed upon them not to do so, but the next day he confessed to his wife that "I was much obliged to them for their good wishes and opinions—in short, no person could possibly be more noticed than myself."[25] Two years later, on his return trip to Boston, Hancock traveled with an entourage of light horsemen, a perquisite no other member of the Massachusetts delegation enjoyed. In this case, the procession apparently created more resentment than respect, because Hancock and his horsemen did not pay their tavern bills along the way but told the tavernkeepers to charge the government. John Adams, who took the same route with Samuel Adams the following week, wrote that the tavernkeepers were annoyed, but the loyalists were delighted: "They scoff at them for being imposed upon by their king, as they call him. Vanity is always mean; vanity is never rich enough to be generous."[26] Back in Boston, however, Hancock did lit-

[24] Ibid., pp. 95–96; Fowler, *Baron of Beacon Hill*, pp. 64–65; "Tory Account of Boston Whigs, Apr. 18, 1775," Photostat Coll., Mass. Hist. Soc.

[25] Allan, *John Hancock*, p. 186.

[26] Ibid., pp. 264–65; Wells, *Samuel Adams*, 2:504–5.

tle to counter such criticisms. According to one newspaper account, "John Hancock of Boston appears in public with all the state and pageantry of an Oriental prince. He rides in an elegant chariot. . . . He is attended by four servants dressed in superb livery, mounted on fine horses . . . and escorted by fifty horsemen with drawn sabres."[27]

The martial appearance of Hancock's procession is revealing, for it points to a part of his life he could never satisfy as easily as his love of luxury—his desire for military prominence. Hancock's military career, such as it was, began in 1772, when Gov. Thomas Hutchinson made him captain of the Company of Cadets, the governor's honor guard. The position was more a political plum than a military post, and Hutchinson gave it to Hancock in the hope of exploiting what appeared to be a rift between Hancock and the whig leadership of Boston. But Hancock made the most of his command, paying for fancy new uniforms out of his own pocket and parading his men before the Boston populace.[28] When Hancock went to Congress in 1775, he had bigger dreams of military power. He considered himself at least a viable candidate for general-in-chief of the American army, and he was crestfallen when John Adams and Samuel Adams engineered the selection of George Washington instead. Swallowing his pride, Hancock offered his services to Washington but was politely denied a place on the general's staff. Hancock later took out his frustrations on Samuel Adams, seeking to implicate him in the "Conway Cabal," the abortive attempt to have Washington relieved of his command. But Adams survived the rumors, and Hancock gained neither favor with Washington nor a position in the army.[29]

Hancock's main military role in the Revolution was as senior major general of the Massachusetts militia, but even in

[27] Allan, *John Hancock,* p. 275; for a similar reference to Hancock as an "Eastern Prince," see James Warren to John Adams, June 7, 1778, in *Warren-Adams Letters,* 2 vols. (Boston, 1917–25), 2:19–21.

[28] Allan, *John Hancock,* pp. 125–27; Fowler, *Baron of Beacon Hill,* pp. 139–40.

[29] Allan, *John Hancock,* pp. 195–97; Wells, *Samuel Adams,* 2:500–504; Miller, *Sam Adams,* pp. 333–35, 344–50.

this capacity he received much more criticism than credit. In 1778, when combined American and French forces made ready to attack the British stronghold at Newport, Hancock had an excellent opportunity to be part of the military command. Unfortunately, storms and unfavorable winds scattered the French fleet and made the allied attack impossible, and the Franco-American force had to retreat. Hancock, however, returned to Boston even before the general retreat, and for that his enemies ridiculed him as a military dilettante. James Warren sneered that Hancock's participation in the operation was all for show, that he "staid Just long enough to gain among the Multitude the popular eclat, and then left it so soon as to make the more discerning laugh." Upon returning to Boston, Warren wrote, "Genl Hancock has made most magnificent entertainments for the Count [d'Estaing] . . . with much military parade. On this occasion the General had an [opportunity] of Exhibiting a Specimen of his Military Talents."[30]

In short, John Hancock was hardly a paragon of character or a profile in courage. He was a young man who inherited a family fortune but quickly proved he had little talent in the family business, who rose to high political office but had little talent for dealing with complex political ideas, who held a relatively safe position in the militia but had little talent for actually leading men in battle. Even his friends considered him superficial, and his enemies ridiculed him as shallow and cowardly. That such a man could be a candidate for high office would seem almost unthinkable.

It certainly seemed unthinkable to many of Hancock's contemporaries, especially the Old Republicans of Massachusetts.

[30] James Warren to John Adams, Oct. 7, 1778, *Warren-Adams Letters*, 2:52; James Warren to Samuel Adams, Sept. 30, 1778, Photostat Coll., Mass. Hist. Soc. For a critical assessment of Hancock's role in the Rhode Island campaign, see Fowler, *Baron of Beacon Hill*, pp. 232–34. For a somewhat more sympathetic treatment, see Lorenzo Sears, *John Hancock: The Picturesque Patriot* (1912; reprint ed., Boston, 1972), pp. 250–60. Even Sears admits, however, that "Hancock was not a military genius. That he ever aspired to anything beyond the captaincy of his Cadet Company must be taken as one of the instances of mistaking one's calling, and of the love of the pomp and circumstance of war apart from its inconveniences and hardships, suffering, and peril" (p. 257).

Samuel Adams was generally circumspect in his criticism of Hancock, but he clearly had Hancock in mind when he expressed concern about the kinds of leaders the new republican government would produce. In 1777, while he was serving in Congress, Adams wrote James Warren to express his hope that the people of Massachusetts would take great care in choosing a governor. The governor, "whether a wise Man or a Fool, . . . [would] in great Measure form the Morals and Manners of the People." Adams said he hated to suggest that the people could be misguided or deluded enough to choose a fool, "but alas! Is there not such a possibility?" He went on to "assure my self of better things" and to affirm his faith in the wisdom of the people."[31] Three years later, after the ratification of the Massachusetts constitution, he was not so sure. "Human nature," he wrote, "is too much debased to relish the republican principles in which the new government of the Commonwealth of Massachusetts is now founded." Not only were people "prone enough to political idolatry," but the experience of living so long as subjects under a system of government "calculated to make servile men rather than free citizens" had left "the minds of many of our countrymen . . . inured to a cringing obsequiousness." Again Adams pointed to the role of political leaders in shaping the morals of the people, and he warned against the moral defects of some potential governors: "Should vanity and foppery ever be the ruling taste among the great, the body of the people would be in danger of catching the distemper. . . . I pray God we may never be addicted to levity and the folly of parade."[32] Adams did not mention Hancock by name, but he scarcely had to. The references to "vanity," "foppery," "the folly of parade," and especially "idolatry" all pointed directly to the picture of Hancock in the eyes of his critics.

James Warren and Mercy Otis Warren, two of Adams's

[31] Samuel Adams to James Warren, Oct. 29, 1777, *Warren-Adams Letters*, 1:375–77.

[32] Samuel Adams to Elbridge Gerry, Nov. 27, 1780, Harry Alonzo Cushing, ed., *The Writings of Samuel Adams*, 4 vols. (New York, 1904–8), 41:228–29.

strongest political allies, exercised much less restraint in their vilification of Hancock. They repeatedly ridiculed him as the "idol of straw," the "man of straw," the "great image." James Warren insisted that Hancock was little more than a tool for tepid Revolutionaries, "men who were so hid in Holes & Corners a few years ago that it was difficult to find them, & when found dared not tell you which side they belong'd to." This party had once "worship'd Hutchinson [and] they all now worship another who if he has not H's abilities certainly equals him in ambition & Exceeds him in vanity."[33]

Moreover, unlike Adams, the Warrens did not fall back on guarded optimism about the wisdom of the people. Rather they suspected that the people were easily seduced by Hancock's extravagance. Writing to Adams in 1778, James Warren warned that "an old Roman Republican would make an awkward figure here in these days of refinement & might exclaim O Tempora O Mores till his heart ached without any effect." "How long the Manners of this People will be uncorrupted & fit to Enjoy that Liberty you have so long Contended for I know not. . . . They will soon be fit to receive some ambitious Master."[34] Mercy Otis Warren complained bitterly that "we have seen a man without abilities idolized by the multitude and fame on the wing to crown the head of imbecillity; we have seen a people trifling with the priviledge of *election,* and throwing away the glorious opportunity of establishing liberty and independence on the everlasting basis of virtue, we have heard them trumpet the praises of their idol of straw, and sing of sacrifices he never had the courage to make."[35] The indictment of John Hancock thus became an indictment of the people. The people had had their chance at choosing men to lead them in a new Revolutionary society, and they had foolishly thrown their votes away on a facile "im-

[33] James Warren to Samuel Adams, Aug. 18, 1778, Photostat Coll., Mass. Hist. Soc.

[34] James Warren to Samuel Adams, June 28, 1778, and Oct. 25, 1778, ibid.

[35] Mercy Otis Warren to Elbridge Gerry, June 6, 1783, Letter Book of Warren, p. 470.

age." To self-styled "old Roman Republicans" like the Warrens, the political popularity of an "idol of straw" like John Hancock was a sure sign of the failure of republicanism.

To come to terms with republicanism, we must come to terms with John Hancock. We cannot deny his political popularity, so we must try to explain it. It would be easy, perhaps, to dismiss him, as many of his contemporary critics and not a few modern historians have done, as a shallow charlatan, a professional politician pandering to a gullible public. We could accept the assessment of one of Hancock's recent biographers that popular acclaim was "the ruling passion of his life," and that, at best, "he was motivated inherently by . . . enlightened self-interest."[36] But to do so leaves us with a view of Hancock as little more than a one-dimensional "man of straw," far too simple a portrait of a man who remained at the center of Revolutionary politics for almost thirty years. Moreover, such a view of Hancock leaves us with a distorted and certainly discouraging view of the political implications of the American Revolution as a social movement. Unless we are willing to accept the jaundiced judgment of contemporary critics that Hancock's popularity was little more than proof of the people's folly and gullibility, we must appreciate the changing nature of popular politics in Revolutionary Massachusetts. In short, the only way to make sense of Hancock's remarkable career is to consider it within the political culture of a revolutionary people.

The vast historical literature on Revolutionary Massachusetts has made one point abundantly clear: The common people were by no means docile or exceedingly deferential, nor were they easily duped by elite leaders. From the first public protests of the Stamp Act crisis in 1765 to the outbreak of armed hostilities in 1775, the common people of Massachusetts, both in the port towns and in the countryside, had become a potent political force, disciplining and eventually

---

[36] Allan, *John Hancock,* p. 232. For a similar evaluation, see Patterson, *Political Parties in Revolutionary Massachusetts.* According to Patterson, Hancock and his political allies "appealed to no set of principles nor to any particular interest" but "were probably motivated by no other principle than to make Hancock governor" (pp. 195, 216).

deposing obnoxious officials.[37] Suspicion of men in high positions was not confined to pro-British officials alone but was
also directed at leaders of the emerging republican society.
Popular concern about the political power of prominent leaders infused the debates over the attempts to frame a state constitution in 1778 and 1780. In 1779 a convention of towns in
western Massachusetts declared that "we are of opinion that
it is the Duty of Virtuous Leaders to Preserve the Liberty of
the People over whom they Preside, and whenever from a
desire to Agrandize Themselves they Endeaver to Persuade
the People to submit to Arbitrary Infringements of their
Rights, they not only forfeit their Title to the Respect which
is Due to a Virtuous Member of Society, But Deserve to be
Treated with the Severity due a Traitor." [38] This statement captures an important element of the political transformation
taking place in Revolutionary Massachusetts. The point is not
that common people rejected elite leadership out of hand; the
revolution "from the bottom up" never brought about that
sweeping a social inversion. The people did, however, make
clear their commitment to regulate their leaders, to make
them know and uphold the responsibilities of "Virtuous
Leaders" to "the People over whom they Preside." Above all,
they made it clear that leaders could no longer take their positions for granted, could no longer expect to govern sure of
the gratitude of a deferential people. People now looked at
their leaders with a wary eye.

Yet they still looked upon John Hancock with favor.
Throughout the critical period of making a revolution and a
constitution, despite the frequent attacks on elite leadership
and an undemocratic political system, Hancock remained politically unscathed, at least in the eyes of the vast majority of
voters. One of the most eloquent expressions of this popularity came not from voters, in fact, but from two nonvoters in

[37] The best analysis of the role of common people in Revolutionary politics is Dirk Hoerder, *Crowd Action in Revolutionary Massachusetts, 1765–1780*
(New York, 1977). See also the works listed above in note 4.

[38] Committees of a Number of Towns in the Western Part of the County
of Hampshire to the Selectmen or Committee of Safety in Northampton,
Mar. 30, 1779, Joseph Hawley Papers, Mass. Hist. Soc.

the Massachusetts militia, Capt. Samuel Talbot and Lt. Lemuel Gay, both of Stoughton. They wrote to Hancock in November 1780, shortly after his election to the governorship, to protest what they saw as the inherent injustice in the commonwealth's new political system. Above all, they complained about the property qualifications for suffrage, especially because they, like many of their fellow soldiers, had been "by ye Constitution disfranchised, for want of property, lost by many in their struggle for freedom." The restrictions on their rights in the civil sphere made it virtually hypocritical for them to carry out their duties in the military: "We can no longer with truth encourage our fellow soldiers, who are so poor as to be thus deprived of their fundamental Rights, that they are fighting for their own freedom; and how can an Officer possess'd of ye generous feelings of humanity detach any of them into a service in which they are not interested." To make their point more compelling, they argued that even the militia was more democratic than the state: in the militia, at least, common soldiers were able to elect their commissioned officers. But because they did not have the power to choose their leaders in civil government, they "decline[d] acting under such a form of government (except in private life) that appears repugnant to ye principles of freedom." Accordingly, they resigned their commissions. They took care, however, to make a distinction between Hancock as governor and the flawed system that elected him. Praising Hancock for his "Capacity, Integrity, & Patriotism," they conceded that they were "fully sensible of ye Wisdom of ye People in placing your Excellency at the Head of ye Commonwealth."[39] In this regard, the two men reflected the sentiments of thousands of other citizens of Massachusetts.

There is, of course, no way to "prove" what were the popular perceptions of John Hancock; the eighteenth century had no public opinion polls or periodic approval ratings or any of the other elaborate means of gauging political sentiment that are available to students of twentieth-century politics. Even election results are imprecise indicators of the voters' values.

[39] Capt. Samuel Talbot and Lt. Lemuel Gay to John Hancock, Nov. 16, 1780, Hancock Family Papers, Mass. Hist. Soc.

Yet more than any other prominent leader, Hancock seems to have been able to rise above the political divisions emerging in Revolutionary Massachusetts. To understand this apparently charmed political life, it is necessary to look past the image and explore the social reality behind the role he played on the public stage of popular politics.

One element that stands out above all is Hancock's largesse, his frequent habit of dispensing communal and personal favors. Throughout the Revolutionary era, Hancock repeatedly dug deep into his own pockets to provide for the people: he gave money to churches, firewood to the poor, and a fire engine to the city of Boston. He was also a major source of jobs and loans, and even a critic like John Adams observed that "not less than a thousand families were, every day in the year, dependent on Mr. Hancock for their daily bread."[40] On one level such acts of public and private benevolence might seem little more than evidence of noblesse oblige, political paternalism, even eighteenth-century ward-heeling. Stephen E. Patterson has suggested, for instance, that in the winter of 1777–78, Hancock's donation of 150 cords of firewood to the Boston poor and his willingness to accept payment for debt in paper currency rather than hard money represented an attempt to curry favor with voters in anticipation of an upcoming gubernatorial election.[41] No doubt it was. But within the context of the Revolutionary era, and especially within the context of Massachusetts politics, Hancock's largesse also bespoke the emergence of a new relationship between the elite politician and the common people. Hancock was not just reaching down to give them charity; he was reaching *out* to gain their loyalty. In doing so he was moving from the traditional politics of deference to the politics of interdependence—that is, from the assumption of inherent status to the acceptance of mutual recognition.

Political relationships are often best symbolized by personal gestures. Consider again, for instance, the glimpse we have of the encounter between Hancock and George Robert Twelves

---

[40] Allan, *John Hancock,* pp. 98–99; Fowler, *Baron of Beacon Hill,* p. 63; Sibley and Shipton, *Biographical Sketches,* 13:419.

[41] Patterson, *Political Parties in Revolutionary Massachusetts,* pp. 186–87.

Hewes, the subject of Young's study. When Hewes first met Hancock, in 1762 or 1763, Hancock invited the young shoemaker to join him in greeting the New Year. Though Hewes was terrified to be in the presence of such a prosperous man, Hancock put him at ease, shared a toast with him, and sent him on his way with a gift of money. A few years later, to celebrate the repeal of the Stamp Act, Hancock extended a similar favor to all the common people of Boston. While he "gave a grand and elegant Entertainment to the genteel Part of the Town," he also "treated the populace with a pipe of Madeira Wine" set out in front of his house.[42]

This act of "treating" the common people with drink invites several interpretations, but we can perhaps best understand it by looking beyond Massachusetts to the broader political context of the American colonies, especially to the South. As Rhys Isaac has shown, such gestures of generosity can be "read" in a dramaturgical sense as a form of role-playing, in which the various actors both understood and accepted the meaning of the parts they played. In Virginia, for instance, "treating" at the militia muster and at the polling place was not simply a way for members of the gentry to buy support with a barrel of rum. Rather, it signified a recognition of "the expectation of a mutual exchange of services" between men of high and low social status.[43] It did not break down class boundaries—indeed, it helped reinforce them—but it did define bonds of mutuality that stretched across those boundaries and made men political allies, if not equals. By the same token, Hancock's providing a pipe of Madeira did not erase the distinction between the "genteel part" inside his house and the "populace" on the lawn. It did, however, demonstrate that he recognized the stake, not to mention the role, that the common people had had in the Stamp Act controversy.

The critical question, of course, is what the common people recognized in Hancock. To be sure, Hancock acted in a different political culture from that of the Tidewater gentry, and

[42] Fowler, *Baron of Beacon Hill*, p. 65.

[43] Rhys Isaac, *The Transformation of Virginia, 1740–1790* (Chapel Hill, 1982), pp. 111–13.

we cannot too readily assume that the common people of Massachusetts found the same meaning in a rich man's treat as would the yeomen of Virginia. Still, compared to a prominent political figure like Thomas Hutchinson, the arrogant elitist who disdained the poor and blamed them for their own poverty, Hancock must have seemed a refreshingly different sort of leader, a member of the elite who was willing at least to acknowledge those below him on the social ladder.[44] Perhaps the common people could look past Hancock's apparent vanity and self-indulgent display to see a man who used his personal wealth for the public good. In that regard, his providing for a shared celebration at the end of the Stamp Act crisis was an important gesture, for it expressed a sense of common cause that would become increasingly important in the decade to come. As Young has explained, the Revolutionary era was a time in which a common man like Hewes "won recognition as a citizen; his betters sought his support and seemingly deferred to him."[45] Hancock clearly accepted this process of mutual recognition, even role reversal, better than did his opponents in pre-Revolutionary Massachusetts, especially Thomas Hutchinson. Moreover, he accepted it better than did some of his fellow leaders in the Revolutionary movement, perhaps especially Samuel Adams.

For Hancock and Adams, the real measure of this new political understanding came at the end of the Revolution, with the outbreak of the Massachusetts Regulation, or Shays's Rebellion, the agrarian insurrection that swept the western counties of Massachusetts in 1786–87. Although the war was won, and the Revolution was apparently a success, the Regulation raised serious questions about the Revolutionary settlement in Massachusetts and, indeed, threw the whole meaning of the Revolution into doubt.

There was no doubt, however, about Samuel Adams's re-

---

[44] For a brief yet valuable comparison of Hutchinson and Hancock as different sorts of "Great Men" in Massachusetts politics, see Ronald P. Formisano, *The Transformation of Political Culture: Massachusetts Parties, 1790s–1840s* (New York, 1983), pp. 31–32.

[45] Young, "George Herbert Twelves Hewes," pp. 561–62, 570, 590–92.

sponse to the Regulation: he insisted that it be suppressed and its leaders hanged. Such staunch opposition to popular mobilization might seem odd, even hypocritical, coming from Adams, a man who had once promoted protest against an established government and had himself been targeted for hanging. Moreover, Adams knew from his own experience as a radical organizer that there was little the authorities could do to stop a growing mass movement. Writing to Elbridge Gerry in 1774, Adams explained that "when the passions of a multitude become headstrong, they generally will have their course; a direct opposition only tends to increase them." There was no point in expecting to pacify people with a "lecture of morality."[46] But by the 1780s morality was precisely the issue for Adams. Just as he attacked the rich for their luxuriousness, so he condemned the poor for their rebelliousness. The extralegal means he and his radical allies had used to oppose an oppressive British government were no longer necessary or legitimate; popular elections now took the place of popular protest. More to the point, the creation of a republican government also created a collective obligation to republican principles, strict standards of virtue to which the people must adhere, or at least aspire. If they could not uphold those standards, the fault was their own, a failure of their collective character, a weakness of their will. Accordingly, republican principles now justified repressive penalties: "In monarchies, the crime of treason and rebellion may admit of being pardoned or lightly punished; but the man who dares to rebel against the laws of a republic ought to suffer death."[47]

Fortunately for the accused Regulator leaders, Samuel Adams did not have the authority to act on his principles. In April 1787 state elections brought sweeping changes in Massachusetts politics—among them, the return of John Hancock to the governor's chair. Hancock had resigned this office in 1785, thus avoiding direct responsibility for the crisis in the commonwealth. Coming just as the insurrection was dying

[46] Samuel Adams to Elbridge Gerry, Mar. 25, 1774, Cushing, ed., *Writings of Samuel Adams*, 3:83.

[47] Wells, *Samuel Adams*, 3:246.

out, Hancock's reelection reflected a widespread sentiment for reconciliation and reform.

From the western counties, where several Regulator leaders were held in jail, came repeated appeals for pardon. Ebenezer Mattoon, a justice of the peace in Amherst and a loyal supporter of the government during the insurrection, was one of many writers who sought to intercede on behalf of Henry McCulloch, a young man from nearby Pelham who was reputed to have been one of Daniel Shays's lieutenants. Mattoon acknowledged that the government had every right to execute McCulloch, but to do so would be unfortunate and politically unwise. Arguing that the "tempers of the people" were now growing moderate, Mattoon suggested that clemency for McCulloch would "conciliate the town of Pelham to the government, and be attended with very happy consequences." The choice was clear: "If he is spared the town of Pelham is attached to government, if he is executed . . . the affections of the town is lost."[48] Mattoon understood that although the farmers in the west had surrendered their arms, they had not yet surrendered their "affections" to the government.

Hancock apparently understood that too, and at the last minute before the scheduled execution, he pardoned McCulloch and another condemned man. By doing so, was he just taking the easy path of political pragmatism? Perhaps. But he was also taking an important step toward defining the emerging relationship between a leader and the people in a republican society. Hancock's response reflects not so much adherence to a set of fixed political principles as acceptance of an unfolding political process. In the case at hand, by stop-

[48] Ebenezer Mattoon to Thomas Cutler, May 6, 1787, vol. 189, pp. 300–301, Massachusetts Archives, Boston. For a fuller discussion of the political significance of Henry McCulloch's fate, see Gregory H. Nobles, "The Politics of Patriarchy in Shays's Rebellion: The Case of Henry McCulloch," in Peter Benes, ed., *Families and Children*, The Dublin Seminar for New England Folklife: Tenth Annual Proceedings, 1985 (Boston, 1987), pp. 37–47; and Nobles, "Shays's Neighbors: The Context of Rebellion in Pelham, Massachusetts," in Robert A. Gross, ed., *In Debt to Shays: The Bicentennial of an Agrarian Rebellion* (Charlottesville, Va., 1993), pp. 185–203.

ping the execution at the last minute, he was both asserting and surrendering some of his power as an elected leader. More to the point, by offering pardon to an individual rebel, he was offering political recognition to the people as a whole, reaching out to acknowledge them in an act of reconciliation, even negotiation.

The notion of negotiation provides a useful perspective on our understanding of Hancock's leadership in the context of a revolution—especially a revolution "considered as a social movement." As E. P. Thompson has suggested, the relationship between a patrician leader and the common people was "more active and reciprocal . . . than the one normally brought to mind under the formula 'paternalism and deference.'"[49] That was especially true in an era of radical change like the American Revolution. Framing a constitution or establishing a government or even suppressing an insurrection did not bring that process of change to an end. Even though the people were in the process of making the transition from a revolutionary crowd to a republican electorate, they were not completely pacified. They still assumed the autonomy and the authority to take extraordinary, sometimes extralegal, action; they retained the right to subject their leaders to popular control, correction, or, as the Shaysites put it, regulation.

To suggest that John Hancock engaged in this important, albeit implicit, process of negotiation is not to suggest that he was an exceptionally wise or virtuous leader. While he may have been a better man than some of his more caustic contemporary critics would have us believe, he still does not have to stand as the epitome of the popular leader or the best embodiment of the people. In fact, the notion of negotiation makes that unnecessary. It emphasizes the distinct, separate identities of the people and their leaders. It allows us to see that, for all his flaws, foppery, and follies, a man like Hancock could still be a valuable ally of the common people. They did not have to be duped by his display or fooled by his facade to choose him as their leader. They had only to recognize his

[49] E. P. Thompson, "Patrician Society, Plebeian Culture," *Journal of Social History* 7 (1974):396.

usefulness to their movement. In a word, common people could be pragmatic, too.

In 1789, in the wake of the Regulation, John Hancock and Samuel Adams reached a reconciliation of their own. They stood together as governor and lieutenant-governor, respectively, and took the oath of office, as Clifford K. Shipton notes, "wearing practically identical suits of domestic manufacture."[50] Their appearance together suggested that Hancock had come to adopt something of Adams's modest style, and Adams had come to accept Hancock's elevated status. For four years, until Hancock's death in 1793, they were once again political allies, sharing the responsibility of administering the affairs of Massachusetts.

Soon after Samuel Adams's death, in fact, the two came even closer together. They emerged as twin symbols of what Ronald P. Formisano has called the "Revolutionary Center" of early nineteenth-century politics. Massachusetts Federalists and Republicans wanted to wrap themselves in the memory of the "Sacred War," and Adams and Hancock seemed best to embody the spirit of liberty that post-Revolutionary politicians—the Republicans, at least—sought to make their own.[51] With the tension and antagonism between the two plastered over by popular memory of their involvement in a virtuous struggle, the old rivals both became Old Republicans at last.

The tendency to fit Old Republicans into a new political framework did not end in the early nineteenth century. Rather, it was only beginning. From the Jacksonian era to the New Deal to the present day, each generation has had to come to terms with the Revolutionary generation, to find some way to make radical leaders comprehensible in the context of current politics. Recently, for instance, Samuel Adams has been described as "perhaps the most 'modern' of Revolutionary leaders in the sense that he lived, quite simply, for politics alone."[52] By the same token, John Hancock's latest biogra-

---

[50] Sibley and Shipton, *Biographical Sketches*, 13:443.

[51] Formisano, *Transformation of Political Culture*, pp. 57–62.

[52] Rakove, *Beginnings of National Politics*, p. 225.

pher has concluded that Hancock "deserves to be enshrined as America's first modern politician," a "flexible and adaptable" man who "could cope with changes in his political environment."[53] Such attempts to make Adams and Hancock into models of modernity may offer a useful reminder about the roots of political behavior, but they also run the risk of reducing eighteenth-century revolutionaries to predictable prototypes of the twentieth-century professional politician.

More to the point, even in the context of the Revolution itself, we cannot leave Adams and Hancock as ideal types. To be sure, each of them might suggest strikingly different standards of political virtue. Adams, perhaps in his own eyes and certainly in those of his political allies, seemed a pillar of republican principle compared to the facile "man of straw." Hancock's supporters could counter that their man was not a rigid ideologue but a pragmatic democrat whose popularity stemmed from his willingness to accommodate the common people. Yet neither image is altogether accurate, nor can either fully reflect the roles Adams and Hancock played in Revolutionary Massachusetts.

Ultimately the important point about both Adams and Hancock is that they were not political symbols, but political activists, popular leaders in a broad-based revolutionary movement. As leaders, they could help define the movement, but they could not direct it. Every true revolutionary movement—our American Revolution, all revolutions since, and all revolutions still to come—is fundamentally a popular revolution, a social movement that requires a radical rethinking of the relationship between the people and their leaders. The principles of political leadership that propel a social movement do not only come down from the top. They also come up from below, from the people who make the movement. The task, then, is not only to see popular leaders as they saw themselves (and each other) but also to understand how they

[53] Fowler, *Baron of Beacon Hill,* p. 280. For a different view, that "Hancock was far closer to Hutchinson and other eighteenth-century notables than he was to nineteenth-century politicians," see Formisano, *Transformation of Political Culture,* pp. 31–32.

may have been seen by those who chose them to lead. Defining that relationship was one of the critical problems for the people who made the American Revolution, and it is no less a problem for those who write about the Revolution today.

ROBERT A. GROSS

White Hats
and Hemlocks
Daniel Shays and
the Legacy of the
Revolution

AMERICANS, IT HAS been said repeatedly since Alexis de
Tocqueville visited these shores in the early 1830s, are notoriously indifferent to history, preferring to anticipate the future
rather than dwell on the past. But ours is, in fact, a selective
memory through which a few perdurable myths work across
the generations to fashion a comforting national identity. Appropriately, in a country that likes to think itself new, the
guardians of tradition—writers, educators, clergymen, politicians—celebrate acts of "creation and innovation." Our national myths pay tribute to great explorers and inventors, to
legendary founders of states and makers of constitutions. Defeated rebels and lost causes need not apply.

Back in 1940, when Progressive history was at its height,
the scholar Arthur E. Morgan lamented the widespread neglect of Daniel Shays. "What does the average American know
about Shays' Rebellion?" Morgan asked. "Only that just after
the American Revolution a number of 'malcontents' in western Massachusetts made some kind of disturbance, apparently because of high taxes, and the rebellion was put down.
This was about all one could learn from the average American
school textbook of the past century." A half-century later,
Shays has receded even further from collective memory.
When asked to list individuals connected with "American his-

tory from its beginning through the end of the Civil War," college students spontaneously recall the heroes of the Revolution—George Washington, Benjamin Franklin, and Thomas Jefferson—and even such lesser lights as Paul Revere and Betsy Ross. Nobody volunteers the name of Daniel Shays. He is equally absent from the list of "What Literate Americans Know," the compendium of items supposedly essential to "cultural literacy" prepared by the best-selling author E. D. Hirsch, Jr. Despite national commemorations of the Revolution and the Constitution in the space of little more than a decade (1975–88), Shays and the movement he sometimes led never penetrated popular consciousness. Shays's Rebellion has yet to receive its Bicentennial "minute."[1]

If the "little rebellion" that rocked western Massachusetts in 1786–87 and reverberated through the capitals of the new republic has left little imprint on the general public, it has mattered deeply to more than a few Americans over the past two centuries. The concern is not merely scholarly; in the nineteenth and early twentieth centuries, before popular and professional history had gone separate ways, the name of Daniel Shays evoked powerful passions among custodians and critics of the American political tradition. And with good reason. As the single moment at the dawn of Independence when the new republic threatened to dissolve into civil war, the agrarian uprising with which Shays is forever linked inescapably challenges celebrations of America's rise from colony to nation.

Ever since 1776 our identity as a nation has been defined, quite literally, by the myth of the Revolution as a spontaneous rising of the people, free and united, against British oppression. Originating in whig propaganda, this idealization of the

[1] Arthur E. Morgan, "An Early American Social Revolt," *Survey Graphic: Magazine of Social Interpretation* 29 (1940):618; Michael Frisch, "American History and the Structures of Collective Memory: A Modest Exercise in Empirical Iconography," *Journal of American History* 75 (1989):1130–55; E. D. Hirsch, Jr., *Cultural Literacy: What Every American Needs to Know*, expanded ed. (New York, 1988), pp. 152–215. Interestingly, every one of the individuals most commonly named by college students in Michael Frisch's survey appears on Hirsch's list of "What Literate Americans Know." Americans are consistent in whom they choose to remember and forget.

American cause was elaborated, during and after the war, into a full-dress historical interpretation. And with the ratification of the Constitution, the "spirit of 1776," which inspired the Declaration of Independence, was joined to the "miracle at Philadelphia" that produced the Constitution. In the hands of nationalist wiiteis, every step on the road to Independence—the Stamp Act protests, the Boston Tea Party, the clash between minutemen and regulars at Concord's Old North Bridge on April 19, 1775—led to the establishment of the national government in 1787–88. In this triumphal drama, the Revolution fulfilled the destiny of America as the citadel of liberty and self-government—Abraham Lincoln's "last best hope on earth."[2]

Shays's Rebellion disrupts this celebration. The popular uprising exposed the rifts among the victorious patriots, revealing social tensions and ideological divisions dating back to the beginnings of protest against British imperial policies. Beneath the facade of consensus lies an unseemly record of economic rivalries, personal ambitions, mutual enmities, social stereotypes, political paranoia, and deep-seated doubts about the capacity of Americans for self-rule. The entire episode, though concentrated in the New England countryside, dramatized the profound alienation of common folk everywhere from the new governments they had brought into being. It crystallized, in turn, the reservations and the anxieties felt by many in the whig elite about the virtue of the people they presumed to lead. In the supercharged rhetoric of the day, onetime comrades-in-arms confronted each other as enemies—as they would briefly in battle at Springfield Armory and Petersham field. The danger of violence soon passed, but in the aftermath came the successful movement by Continental leaders to form a new national government, endowed with the energy and power to curb "anarchy" and "licentiousness" in the states. That movement was hardly due to Shays's Rebel-

[2] Michael G. Kammen, *A Season of Youth: The American Revolution and the Historical Imagination* (New York, 1978); Arthur H. Shaffer, *The Politics of History: Writing the History of the American Revolution, 1783–1815* (Chicago, 1975), pp. 102–41; Lester H. Cohen, "Creating a Usable Future: The Revolutionary Historians and the National Past," in Jack P. Greene, ed., *The American Revolution: Its Character and Limits* (New York, 1987), pp. 309–30.

lion alone. Still, it left an unsettling legacy for future generations. For if the formation and ratification of the Constitution were driven in part by fear of "the people"—the very ordinary folk who had fought the War for Independence—how do we commemorate our origins as a democratic nation?

In the critical period of the 1780s, few Americans had the occasion or the detachment to reflect on the ambiguities of the Revolution. They certainly did not in the troubled Commonwealth of Massachusetts. There the rural protests against the program of hard money and heavy taxes adopted by the state government in order to pay the Revolutionary War debt provoked a cascade of charges and countercharges that continues to resound today. On one side, spokesmen for the countryside portrayed their crusade as a new fight for independence, this time against a patriot elite more oppressive than the Crown officials it had displaced. On the other side, the Friends of Government proclaimed their mission to rescue the republic from self-seeking demagogues at the helm of a temporarily deluded people. In this polarized debate, numerous voices of moderation and dissent were submerged; it was easy to lose sight of the farmers who shared the grievances of the rebels but declined to close courts or to take up arms and of the tradesmen who denounced mob violence but sought to conciliate the disaffected. But on one point, all participants in the Massachusetts crisis agreed: they affirmed loyalty to the Revolution and to the republican ideal.

Later generations have taken one party or the other at its word. Over the course of the two centuries since the end of the "horrid and unnatural rebellion," as it was officially dubbed by the Massachusetts General Court, diverse Americans have identified themselves for or against Daniel Shays. Nineteenth-century writers invoked the rural uprising to warn against Jacksonian demagogues, southern secessionists, and Populist reformers. In the twentieth century activists and writers on the left embraced Shays as the embodiment of their cause—the champion of ordinary people against privileged elites. A recent journalistic account of American veterans from Valley Forge to Vietnam even extols Shays as the exemplary hero for our time: "To this day," remark Richard Severo and Lewis Milford, "the United States has not produced anyone quite like him; no doomed rebel who touches our hearts so, at least those few of us who know who Daniel Shays was. We like to lionize and idealize the dreamers who fight city hall in our novels and films. But few of us dare to be like them, and none of us has been like Shays. No other former soldier has gone to such lengths to correct a Government abuse." A foe of commercial capitalism, a model for Vietnam veterans, Shays can also aid mythmakers on the right; in that role, he becomes the angry taxpayer in revolt against Big Government. In this vein, it is surely appropriate that a direct descendent of Daniel Shays now sits in Congress, a Republican representative—albeit a liberal one—from Connecticut.[3]

Shays's Rebellion has thus provided a screen onto which historically minded Americans in every generation have projected their own political ambitions, ideological agendas, and social anxieties. Bound up with the Revolution and Constitution, the uprising is etched into our collective memory, however dimly recalled today, and has become a piece of popular culture. As symbol and event, it plays a mythic part in our historiography, too. In popular and academic accounts, Shays's Rebellion has carried the emotional and intellectual burden of changing attitudes toward the Revolution and the fulfillment of its promise in American life.

The first history was contemporaneous with the event, appearing not long after the defeat of the insurrection; it spawned two centuries of writing in its wake. This body of scholarship, launched by the Revolutionary generation itself and then sustained by diverse intellectuals—gentlemen-amateurs, aspiring journalists, political pundits, professional historians—across a shifting landscape of thought, offers a striking register of American cultural history. As Warren Susman has noted, how we interpret the past is itself an artifact of culture, through which we can read the preoccupations and

---

[3] Richard Severo and Lewis Milford, *The Wages of War: When America's Soldiers Came Home—From Valley Forge to Vietnam* (New York, 1989), p. 12. On the several strategies by which historians and others package the past to serve the needs of the present, see David Lowenthal, "The Timeless Past: Some Anglo-American Historical Preconceptions," *Journal of American History* 75 (1989):1263–80.

values of our predecessors.[4] At the same time, through close analysis of historical writings, we can trace the dialectical process by which a dominant interpretation becomes oversimplified through repetition and generates its own revision and repudiation. In Shays's Rebellion, the subject of historical argument for two hundred years, we have an extraordinary case in point. This essay charts that long debate; it is, at once, an inquiry into popular memory and an exploration of historiography—or better, a study of the interplay between the two. By uncovering the various layers of meaning that have been successively attached to the event, it undertakes an archaeology of the Revolution in what was once confidently called "the American mind." Alternatively, in the spirit of J. Franklin Jameson, we might call this enterprise a small inquiry into "the American Revolution Considered as a Cultural Movement."

Ironically, the earliest historian of the insurgency, writing in the immediate aftermath of the explosion, just months after the rebels had been routed, offered the most dispassionate, seemingly impartial account to appear in the century or more after the event. As clerk of the state House of Representatives throughout the 1780s, George Richards Minot had witnessed and recorded at first hand the unfolding of the entire crisis from the perspective of the legislature. His official role was to keep the journal of the assembly; unofficially, he summarized the proceedings for the *Massachusetts Magazine*. Neutral in public, the young Harvard graduate and lawyer, a man in his twenties and a scion of Boston's mercantile class, was privately outraged by the insurgency and by the vacillations of the legislature in quelling it. Decapitating Shays, he confided to his diary, was a sure way to cut short the rebellion. But such personal opinions were not the main spur to *The History of the Insurrections, in Massachusetts, in the Year Seventeen Hundred and Eighty Six, and the Rebellion Consequent Thereon,* published in 1788. Minot, an ambitious man of letters, composed the work to answer English and European critics who were chortling from across the ocean that the disorders in

---

[4] Warren Susman, *Culture as History: The Transformation of American Society in the Twentieth Century* (New York, 1984).

Massachusetts proved the folly of popular government. Determined to vindicate the commonwealth and the cause of republicanism, the stern advocate of law and order soft-pedaled his views and produced an impersonal, authoritative narrative of popular protest and government response, notable for its seeming impartiality and balance. In Minot's telling, the insurrection was but a passing irritation, not a fatal condition, and it was readily put to rest by a "lenient" but effective government.[5]

Minot's exposition of the insurgency was a very sophisticated work, well beyond the crude polemics of the day. For Minot, Shays's Rebellion represented, fundamentally, a test of *governance*. Such a perspective came naturally even to a minor member of the elite, who looked out on the spreading disorder in the countryside through the eyes of the legislators in Boston, whose every decision he silently wrote down. For the first time in its history, the Commonwealth of Massachusetts, operating under the newly ratified constitution of 1780, was confronted by an uprising of the people, whose voluntary consent to laws made by elected representatives formed the very basis of republican government. Riots and rebellions, Minot observed, were familiar in the regimes of Europe, but unprecedented in "the annals of Massachusetts, either under the royal or republican government." How had such disturbances come about? And how had the rulers of the republic met the challenge of upholding authority while conciliating the people? Centering on these questions, Minot put the best face possible on the decisions of government, in a calm, reasoned, but unmistakably partisan justification for virtually each and every move.[6]

The first problem before Minot was to account for the widespread unrest. Extremists among the Friends of Government had dismissed the complaints of farmers out of hand, but not

---

[5] George Richards Minot, *The History of the Insurrections in Massachusetts. In the Year Seventeen Hundred and Eighty Six. And the Rebellion Consequent Thereon* (1788), 2d ed. (Boston, 1810); Robert A. Feer, "George Richards Minot's *History of the Insurrections:* History, Propaganda, and Autobiography," *New England Quarterly* 35 (1962):203–28.

[6] Minot, *History*, pp. 169–71.

Minot; he readily conceded the existence of acute economic distress throughout the countryside. Yes, taxes and debts were heavy and money scarce. But those ills were not the fault of government. Public expenditures and hence taxes had swollen for a simple reason—revenues were required to pay off the massive public debt that Massachusetts had contracted to fight the war. They constituted the price of Independence, which no honorable citizenry could refuse. The enormous load of private debts under which the inhabitants staggered was equally due to the Revolution. Courts had been closed in the west for most of the conflict, and hence many obligations went uncollected, earning interest all the while. With the return of peace, the bills came due. Adding to these woes, many people, starved for consumer goods during the war, had rushed to buy imported luxuries on credit when trade with Britain was restored. Unfortunately, demands for payment arrived just as the economy was plunging into depression. Minot catalogued the numerous sufferings of the state: the destruction of the fisheries, the decay of farming, the loss of markets for mercantile trade, the outflow of specie to pay for British goods. No wonder there was so little money in circulation. But what could the government do? Surely not endorse that nostrum of the backcountry, paper money, which would only add more instability and injustice to economic life. In the face of these difficulties, Minot concluded, the people of Massachusetts could justly lament their fate, but the fault lay in themselves or in forces beyond the government's control.[7]

This careful, conscientious consideration of popular complaints was essentially a restatement of the legislature's official *Address to the People* in the fall of 1786, an elaborate defense of its financial measures. So, too, was Minot's unwillingness to concede any of the political "grievances" of the backcountry, to which he gave passing attention. Neither lawyers nor the county courts, eminent for their "antiquity and past utility," merited attacks by the public; they were merely the impersonal instruments of creditors in a grave economic crisis. But if the policies and practices of government were as well founded as he said, Minot had to confront an intellectual di-

[7] Ibid., pp. 5–22.

293

lemma. Why had the government failed to persuade the disaffected with the obvious merits of its case?[8]

Once again Minot reverted to the powerful impact of the Revolution, not on the purses, but on the minds of the people. The patrician lawyer knew that he was living through tumultuous times that had shaken popular habits of deference to the roots. No longer did common folk submit contentedly to a government "established by their forefathers, and receiving their implicit obedience from the force of habit." The Revolution had been a momentous school of political education. "In a society where that great prerogative of human nature, self government, has been literally exercised," ordinary individuals had gained confidence in their own judgments of public affairs. And so, having sacrificed enormously to enjoy a new era of freedom, they resented any "abridgments of their liberties," however necessary. "They could not realize [that is, accept] that they had shed their blood in the field, to be worn out with burdensome taxes at home," Minot wrote, with uncommon sympathy for the hardships of the lower orders, "or that they had contended, to secure to their creditors, a right to drag them into courts and prisons." In the grip of such grievances, citizens did not simply grumble about taxes and pay; newly politicized, they took direct action to assert their rights.[9]

In this understanding of the sources of popular unrest, Minot managed, uniquely among the literary defenders of the government, to sidestep controversy over who was to blame for the rebellion. Having attributed the insurrection to the disruptive forces of the Revolution, to a clash between rising expectations and disappointing realities, he was free to dissect the divisions of the state in the neutral voice of a modern political scientist. The insurgents, Minot observed, were a diverse lot, encompassing discordant elements. Many were moderates, willing to put pressure on government through county conventions in order to effect limited reforms; they were "entangled" with radicals who demanded the "annihila-

[8] Ibid., p. 37; Massachusetts General Court, *An Address from the General Court to the People of the Commonwealth of Massachusetts* (Boston, 1786).

[9] Minot, *History*, pp. 16, 22–26.

tion of both publick and private debts, and who aimed to revise and extinguish the constitution." The insurgents
included men on both sides of the Revolution: violent loyalists, still bitter at their defeat, allied with "flaming, but disappointed patriots." And while "the great body of the
disaffected" sincerely demanded greater popular control over
government, a few among them were extreme conservatives
in disguise, exploiting the movement in order to provoke reaction against "the democratick principles of the constitution." As Minot gauged it, a third of the population belonged
to this coalition of "the discontented." An equal fraction were
neutrals, unwilling to risk a stand. But the final third, consisting of "the men of property," proved the "more powerful
body." These Friends of Government backed the state for a
variety of reasons, about which Minot was refreshingly can-
did. Some, public bondholders and private creditors, acted
from "motives of safety," others clung to government out of
traditional reverence for authority, but the dynamic agent
among them was a core of enlightened patriots, committed to
the principles of the Revolution. These selfless souls "saw the
use which might be made of the commotions of the people by
designing men, for the purpose of enslaving them," and they
"too sensibly recollected the blood and treasure, which had
been expended in obtaining the constitution, to renounce it
for temporary evils." [10]

While Minot succeeded in transcending the passions of the
moment to produce an astute social analysis of the contending
parties, he had never lost sight of his central purpose. His
narrative of the movement of events—from the first court
closings in the late summer of 1786 through the special session of the General Court during the fall and the escalating
confrontation in the countryside down to the blast of cannon
at Springfield Armory, the rout of the insurgents at Petersham, and the punishment and pardoning of the rebels in the
legislature—is an extended vindication of government actions throughout the crisis. At every step of the way, aggressive, recalcitrant foes provoked a lenient, reluctant
government to take ever-stronger measures to uphold au-

[10] Ibid., pp. 103–6.

thority. In the emergency fall session of the legislature called to resolve the crisis, members offered significant relief to the countryside—a suspension of tax collections and a temporary Tender Law for the payment of debts—and resisted calls for repression. It was the startling news that the protesters were forming militia companies that galvanized the house into suspending the guarantees of habeas corpus. Likewise, the administration of James Bowdoin did everything possible to avoid bloodshed until absolutely necessary; it even sent a secret emissary to Shays, promising a pardon if he gave up the cause. Only continued defiance by the insurgents prompted the final resort to arms. Even in victory, government was magnanimous. Gen. Benjamin Lincoln readily pardoned insurgents in the countryside who surrendered their weapons and took oaths of allegiance. In Boston, the house declined to enact harsh punishments for the rebels until it became clear that some diehards in the backcountry were continuing the fight. Though a few insurgents were eventually tried and convicted of treason, they escaped the gallows through last-minute reprieves. Throughout the crisis, the government's acts of repression were marked by respect for the constitution and the forms of law, in sharp contrast to the deceitful, lawless insurgents. In the end, Minot suggested, the Commonwealth of Massachusetts had provided a signal lesson to governments everywhere, under the severe test of popular challenge: "Thus was a dangerous internal war finally suppressed, by the spirited use of constitutional powers, without the shedding of blood by the hand of the civil magistrate; a circumstance, which it is the duty of every citizen to ascribe to its real cause, the lenity of government, and not to their weakness; a circumstance too, that must attach every man to a constitution, which, from a happy principle of mediocrity, governs its subjects without oppression, and reclaims them without severity." Through the wisdom of the magistrates, Massachusetts had solved a problem that had beset governments for ages—it had invented a republican remedy for popular rebellion.[11]

As the first extended account of Shays's Rebellion to reach readers on both sides of the Atlantic, *The History of the Insurrec-*

[11] Ibid., pp. 59–62, 86–89, 98–101, 138–41, 160–71, 192.

tions in Massachusetts instantly commanded the field. With his dispassionate, seemingly objective approach, Minot easily conveyed an air of impersonal authority; his was, truly, the *official* story. But the book succeeded beyond measure. Minot did not simply frame discussion in print of Shays's Rebellion; he monopolized it. In similar controversial episodes of the early republic like the Whiskey Rebellion, the competing parties took up the pen in a bitter war of books almost as soon as they had laid down arms. Not in Massachusetts; in the wake of defeat, the Shaysites retreated into silence. Rural outsiders to cosmopolitan culture, they never had a representative in the eighteenth-century Republic of Letters. But Minot's domination of the discourse lasted well beyond the age of Shays. His *History* stood unchallenged as the only book-length work of nonfiction about the insurrection for more than a century and a half. Not until Marion L. Starkey issued *A Little Rebellion* in 1955 was there a single rival, and it would take another twenty-five years before a second, David P. Szatmary's *Shays' Rebellion,* appeared.[12]

Embraced as the standard authority on its subject, Minot launched the school of interpretation that will be dubbed "White Hats" from the insignia—scraps of white paper—that the Friends of Government wore in order to identify themselves and to symbolize their devotion to words on paper, such as constitutions and contracts. That version of events went virtually uncontested in our histories from the first narratives of the new nation to appear after Independence, through the

---

[12] Thomas P. Slaughter, "The Friends of Liberty, the Friends of Order, and the Whiskey Rebellion: A Historiographical Essay," in Steven R. Boyd, ed., *The Whiskey Rebellion: Past and Present Perspectives* (Westport, Conn., 1985), pp. 9–30; Marion L. Starkey, *A Little Rebellion* (New York, 1955); David P. Szatmary, *Shays' Rebellion: The Making of an Agrarian Insurrection* (Amherst, Mass., 1980). Curiously, two major dissertations on Shays's Rebellion between 1900 and 1958 never saw print, and a third was published nearly three decades after it was completed. Remaining in the archives were Joseph Parker Warren, "Shays' Rebellion," Ph.D. diss., Harvard University, 1900, and Bernard Donovan, "The Massachusetts Insurrection of 1786," Ph.D. diss., Boston College, 1938. Robert A. Feer, "Shays' Rebellion," Ph.D. diss., Harvard University, 1958, was recently published in the series Harvard Dissertations in American History and Political Science (New York, 1988).

burgeoning of antiquarian studies of Massachusetts in the second half of the nineteenth century, down to the beginnings of professional scholarship in this century. For the most part, writing on Shays's Rebellion was an occasional thing, a few pages in the saga of the Confederation and Constitution, a section in local histories of western Massachusetts. Like a glacier, the Massachusetts crisis moved imperturbably through the shifting seas of historical interpretation. It was always stolidly there, a necessary point of negotiation in the passage from colony to nation. With Minot as their guide, historians cut a safe path through the subject—the policies of Massachusetts during the 1780s were necessary and sound, the officials honorable patriots all, the rebellion unjustified. Not a one among them shared the faith of Thomas Jefferson, who remarked unflappably, on hearing of the insurgency in 1786, that "a little rebellion now and then is a good thing, and as necessary in the political world as storms in the physical. . . . It is a medicine necessary for the sound health of government." In the conservative project of nationalist historians, Americans had forfeited the right to revolution, once they established a republic of their own. Devoted to the consolidation of the Union, self-appointed custodians of the past repeatedly hauled out the riots and disorders of Shays's Rebellion to teach lessons of loyalty and submission to law. By the Civil War, the protests in Massachusetts had become a minatory case in the *History of American Conspiracies,* included along with the uprising of Pontiac and the riots of the Paxton Boys in a formidable *Record of Treason, Insurrection, Rebellion, &c., in the United States of America, from 1760 to 1820.*[13]

[13] Michael Kraus, *A History of American History* (New York, 1937), pp. 140–41, 147, 155–58, 188–89, 246; Thomas Jefferson, quoted in Starkey, *Little Rebellion,* p. 111; Orville Victor, *History of American Conspiracies: A Record of Treason, Insurrection, Rebellion, &c., in the United States of America, from 1760 to 1820* (New York, 1863). The repudiation of the theoretical right to revolution began as early as the 1790s in South Carolina, according to Michael Zuckerman, as anxious slaveholders hastily erected barriers against the ideological currents of the French Revolution. The ideal of the universal rights of mankind had overturned white rule on nearby Saint Domingue, in a bloody conquest of power by the blacks. In the wake of that event, elite South Carolinians, having already muted their onetime Revolutionary faith

The heirs of Minot were, in fact, more fervent than the master in denunciation of Shays's Rebellion. With his solicitude for America's reputation abroad, Minot had striven mightily to rescue the republican experiment from the taint of the insurgency. In his telling, the people of Massachusetts continued faithful sons of liberty even as they defied the law; the government, in turn, remained responsive to citizens even as it suppressed rebellion. Despite the upheaval, the system worked. In this effort to depict a secure republican consensus, Minot was led to ignore the doubts, the disdain, even the ridicule of common folk that were freely expressed by his peers at the height of the crisis. His literary successors were less circumspect. In the era of the early republic, it was still important to defend the national character; consequently, in Mercy Otis Warren's *History of the Rise, Progress, and Termination of the American Revolution* (1805) and Alden Bradford's *History of Massachusetts* (1825), the insurgents were treated as misguided but honest souls. They were ignorant of the reasons for public policies and so prey to rumors and lies. Under the influence of Revolutionary ideals, they held "improper notions of government" and resisted restraint. And they were desperate "to relieve themselves from debts which they couldn't pay." Still, popular discontent would never have exploded into violence had it not been skillfully "wrought up" by a few "artful and unprincipled men." Left to themselves or, even better, guided by patient, enlightened leaders, the common people respected the law.[14]

---

in the face of political challenge within, gave the coup de grace to those ideals. According to my reading of the historiography of Shays's Rebellion, it would take New Englanders another generation to reach the same reactionary end point. Michael Zuckerman, "Thermidor in America: The Aftermath of Independence in the South," *Prospects* 8 (1983): 360–65.

[14] Mercy Otis Warren, *History of the Rise, Progress, and Termination of the American Revolution*, 3 vols. (Boston, 1805), 3:346–56; Alden Bradford, *History of Massachusetts from July, 1775, When General Washington Took Command of the American Army, at Cambridge, to the Year 1789 (Inclusive), When the Federal Government Was Established under the Present Constitution* (Boston, 1825), pp. 248–59; Shaffer, *Politics of History*, pp. 126–29; Lester H. Cohen, "Explaining the Revolution: Ideology and Ethics in Mercy Otis Warren's His-

This mild paternalism turned into dark distrust of democracy from midcentury on. Prompted by revulsion from the partisan battles and egalitarian politics of the Jacksonian age and disturbed still more by the class divisions of an emerging industrial society, the conservative gentlemen who watched over the nation's past found in Shays's Rebellion a bleak confirmation of their worst fears. The most extreme expression of this perspective, an angry, scornful broadside against "the lawless outbreaks of popular force," appeared, curiously enough, in a local history of western Massachusetts by a native son, Josiah Gilbert Holland, in 1855. Today the insurgency serves as a badge of local identity for many in the Connecticut Valley; in Holland's time it was no source of local pride. Ithamar Conkey, a native of Pelham who had come down from the hills to settle in neighboring Amherst, where he became a notable lawyer and judge, tactfully avoided all mention of Shays and the troubles of 1786–87 when he delivered the official address at the centennial of his home town in 1843. Holland was more blunt. The aspiring son of a luckless machinist and inventor, Holland had spent his childhood shuttling about the Connecticut Valley; too poor to attend college, he had briefly tried a career in medicine before finding his calling in journalism. As literary editor for Samuel Bowles's *Springfield Republican,* he identified profoundly with the larger world of cosmopolitan culture. It was thus natural for Holland to view the backcountry rebellion from his vantage point in the commercial hub of Springfield, where the insurgents had once stormed the courts, encountered forcible opposition, and marched into cannon fire on Armory Hill. Resolved to rehabilitate western Massachusetts from its past opposition to the advancing American nation, Holland refought the battles of the 1780s with as much fury and invective as anybody had shown at the time. Indeed, the several chapters he devoted to the rebellion constituted a latter-day *Anarchiad,* the nasty mock-epic of the insurgency published in the newspa-

---

torical Theory," *William and Mary Quarterly,* 3d ser. 37 (1980):200–218. See also Richard Hildreth, *The History of the United States of America, from the Discovery of the Continent to the Organization of Government under the Federal Constitution,* 3 vols. (New York, 1849), 3:472–77.

pers of 1786–87 by the Hartford Wits, the onetime literary celebrities of the Valley. For his baleful view of the rebels as rogues and cheats, seduced into rebellion by artful knaves, Holland was doubtless indebted to the spiteful satire of its Federalist authors—David Humphreys, Joel Barlow, John Trumbull, and Lemuel Hopkins.[15]

It is tempting to dismiss out of hand Holland's cascade of insults, his reduction of Shays's Rebellion to a morality play. But his writing had lasting impact on the White Hat school. For one thing, Holland redefined the economic stakes of the struggle. To Minot and others, the insurrection was an understandable, though unjustified, response to *real* economic distress produced by the combined burden of public charges and private debts. Holland shrugged off the toll of taxes in a few paragraphs and simplified the whole affair into an immoral bid by desperate debtors to flee their bills. It was true, he conceded, that the war had imposed severe costs, leaving "a people never rich . . . extremely poor." But many of those people had only themselves to blame. In the excitement of war, they had relaxed old habits of steady labor and thrift and contracted an insidious "love of luxury and indolence." Hungry for the easy life, they went on a buying spree when trade with Britain was restored. But the unhappy day of reckoning soon arrived. Caught with overdue bills while money was scarce, rural spendthrifts squirmed to avoid payment or their day in court. It is no "subject of marvel," Holland observed, "that when a proportion of the people felt themselves helplessly within the power of their creditors, they should grow restive, and seek in untried channels the relief which common means failed to command." Any measure that promised relief was welcome—paper money, tender laws, or stopping the

---

[15] Ithamar Conkey, *A Centennial Address, Delivered at Pelham, Massachusetts, January 16, 1843* (Amherst, Mass., 1843); Josiah Gilbert Holland, *History of Western Massachusetts. The Counties of Hampden, Hampshire, Franklin, and Berkshire. Embracing an Outline, or General History, of the Section, an Account of Its Scientific Aspects and Leading Interests, and Separate Histories of Its One Hundred Towns,* 2 vols. (Springfield, Mass., 1855); Richard B. Sewall, *The Life of Emily Dickinson,* 2 vols. (New York, 1974), 2:595–96; David Humphreys, Joel Barlow, John Trumbull, and Lemuel Hopkins, *The Anarchiad,* in Vernon Louis Parrington, ed., *The Connecticut Wits* (New York, 1926).

courts. "More than any other cause—more than taxation or deterioration of money," concluded Holland, "the wide existence of private indebtedness, and the legal efforts made for the collection of claims, operated to bring about the uneasiness and its shameful and disastrous results."[16]

If the rank-and-file insurgents were outright deadbeats, skipping out on their debts, their leaders, in Holland's view, were even worse. They came in three types: "adventurers, demagogues, and desperadoes." Men without principle or character, they jumped at the opportunity "to take advantage of popular discontent, to win notoriety to themselves, and advance their own interests." Absent any respectable claim to leadership, their only chance lay in popular rebellion. Such an "adventurer" was Daniel Shays, whom Holland castigated as a scheming social climber lacking "those higher sensibilities which mark a high nature and a noble man." Giving new life

[16] Holland, *History of Western Massachusetts*, pp. 230–34. Forrest and Ellen Shapiro McDonald have recently argued that the reigning view of Shays's Rebellion as the struggle of a "band of embattled farmers, oppressed by and deeply indebted to an avaricious and heartless merchant class," was invented in 1879 by Edward Bellamy and popularized among "leftist and reform circles" at the turn of the century. Such an interpretation, they maintain, is a projection of the ideological concerns of the twentieth-century left onto the embattled yeomen of the Revolutionary era. Besides offering evidence to discredit the significance of private debts as the cause of the insurrection, the McDonalds claim that the earliest historians of the farmers' uprising were unanimous in the belief that public abuses—taxes and courts—not private debts, had created the unrest. By my reading of the historiography, this judgment is completely wrong. Every historian of Shays's Rebellion in the early republic emphasized the *interplay* of taxes and debts in spawning the crisis. And as Holland's *History of Western Massachusetts* indicates, it was an antebellum conservative, not a Gilded Age Populist, who oversimplified the story into a debtors' revolt. Whatever distortions people on the left have committed, they are surely no worse than the McDonalds' Reaganite conception of the insurgency as a modern taxpayers' revolt: "Now that most Americans, or at least most of them outside the Washington, D.C., metroplitan area, have come once again to realize that the greatest danger to their liberties arises from excessively large and expensive government," they write, "perhaps the time has arrived for scrapping an interpretation that reflects the rhetoric of populism and for returning to one that reflects the realities of the 'late Disturbances in Massachusetts'" (McDonald and McDonald, *Requiem: Variations on Eighteenth-Century Themes* [Lawrence, Kans., 1988], pp. 72–76).

to old anecdotes that had been circulated in 1786–87, Holland, himself a poor boy from the hills aiming to make good, claimed that Shays had cheated his way into a captain's rank. No gentleman by birth or character, he thereupon exposed his lack of honor by selling his Lafayette sword. The only talents Shays possessed were the low arts of the politician: "He was plausible, ambitious, of good address and appearance, and possessed undoubted courage." A ready "tool" of the "seditious spirit" when it bid fair to place him at the head of "multitudes," Shays was anxious to desert the cause when it appeared doomed to fail. "He was bound to the insurrectionary movement by no tie of principle, no active conviction of right, no controlling motive of love for the public good." [17]

Dishonesty and selfishness were, to Holland, the keys to Shays's Rebellion. Out of private vices—the shirking of debts, the scheming for power—had come public wrongs that disordered a commonwealth. Nothing Holland said was new. His blaming the debtors for their own woes, his mordant view of the common people as ripe for the plucking, his disgust at the self-serving schemes of Shays and company—all resonated opinions held by many commentators in 1786–87, which Holland retailed as fact. He cited not a shred of evidence to prove that the insurgents were the deserving victims of their own consumer binge. But the significance of his work derived not from its reconstruction of reality but from its articulation of the ideology that had governed contemporary perceptions of the insurgency among the upper ranks of society. Alarmed at political and social mobility during the Revolution, many gentlemen attributed the unrest in the countryside to amoral politicians who stirred riots to advance themselves. If only common people had stayed in their proper place! Endorsing this hierarchical perspective, Holland scuttled Minot's republican earnestness and developed a damning indictment of unruly crowds and democratic disorder.

Holland's formula held for the next half-century. It was, in fact, perfectly suited to the needs of conservatives in the Gilded Age, when a new agrarian revolt, based in the cotton fields of the South and the wheat belt of the Midwest, chal-

[17] Holland, *History of Western Massachusetts*, pp. 292–95.

lenged the power of eastern merchants and financiers. Responding to the same structural dilemmas in farming that had prompted Shays's Rebellion—falling prices, scarce currency, burdensome debts—Greenbackers and Populists revived the familiar call for cheap money and greater public control over the economy. Inevitably, the rural uprising reawakened interest in Shays's Rebellion, especially since it coincided, fortuitously, with the centennials of the Massachusetts insurrection and of the United States Constitution. A spate of publications—local and national histories, reprints of original documents—poured forth during the high tide of the era of Populism and Progressivism; altogether, almost half of the thirty or so local studies of the Massachusetts insurgency that appeared in print from 1788 through the mid-1970s were published in the three decades between 1885 and 1915.[18] A few of these writings explicitly sympathized with the agrarian protests. Others reflected the growing filiopietism of old-stock New Englanders, retreating into the rural past as an escape from the threatening hordes of immigrants and workers in a class-divided, urban-industrial landscape. None of this work altered the historical viewpoint of White Hats a bit. If anything, the pro-government writers only heightened the national visibility of Shays's Rebellion as a symbol of popular excess. In his influential *The Critical Period of American History, 1783–1789* (1888), which originally appeared in serial form in the *Atlantic Monthly* and became "probably the most widely read book ever published on the formation of the U.S. Constitution," John Fiske popularized the familiar indictment of the insurgents for a vast audience beyond New England. For Fiske, the insurrection was the culmination of national malaise during the bleak postwar era of the Confederation. Though he admitted the crushing burden of taxes and debts, Fiske was as contemptuous of the insurgents as Holland. Naive victims of "the paper money craze," with little respect for private property, the protesters lacked any comprehension of the national plight. They were narrowly concerned only to save themselves from the law. Fiske, son of an old, prosperous

[18] John D. Haskell, Jr., *Massachusetts: A Bibliography of Its History* (Boston, 1976). See index under "Shays's Rebellion."

Yankee family in Hartford, carried on the New England tradition of the "wealthy amateur" historian, composing his books as a literary avocation to supplement his librarian's salary from Harvard College. But his version of events proved no different from that of the emerging leaders of the historical profession. In his volume for Harpers's American Nation series, *Confederation and Constitution* (1905), Andrew Cunningham McLaughlin put the imprimatur of the new-style academic, with his university-based Ph.D., on the well-worn prejudices of earlier amateurs. A safe, hard-money man, he was as sure as anyone that the insurgents were simply "improvident debtors" in flight from their legal obligations. The cry for cheap paper perfectly expressed their low character; with inflated ambitions and exaggerated language, the rebels carried everything to extremes. "The vicious, the restless, the ignorant, the foolish . . . were coming together to test the strength of Massachusetts." Alarmed at the crisis, "thoughtful men" appraised the dangers to the republic and set about establishing a strong, national government, with the power to insure "domestic Tranquility." [19]

With McLaughlin, White Hat history achieved a dreary apotheosis. There was nothing left to say; in the embattled pages of the nationalists at the turn of the century, the long, unrelenting campaign against the insurgency ended in parody of the past. Sensitive to the vicissitudes of his time, Minot had located the rebels in a changing, Revolutionary world that had altered not just the economy but politics and society too. But from Holland on, the story had shrunk into a symbolic encounter between selfishness and patriotism. To the defenders of government, there were no real issues, no authentic grievances, no Revolutionary ideals gone astray. The rebellion had a simple cause: the self-seeking of the wretched

[19] Michael Kraus, *The Writing of American History* (Norman, Okla., 1953), pp. 120–26; Kraus, *History of American History;* Michael G. Kammen, *A Machine That Would Go of Itself: The Constitution in American Culture* (New York, 1986), p. 24; John Fiske, *The Critical Period of American History, 1783–1789* (Boston, 1888), pp. 177–86; Richard Hofstadter, *The Progressive Historians: Turner, Beard, Parrington* (New York, 1968), pp. 24, 26; Andrew Cunningham McLaughlin, *The Confederation and the Constitution, 1783–1789* (New York, 1905), pp. 154–67.

debtors and their scheming leaders. This view of the matter reflected an economic interpretation of history, applied in a partial, elitist form. For the nationalists exempted the magistrates of Massachusetts from any comparable scrutiny. When the legislature funded depreciated state securities at par and paid them in coin, enriching speculators handsomely in a single stroke, it aroused no suspicion; the honorable members were just upholding public credit. When the body repudiated "rag money," it was conforming to the natural laws of economics. There was nothing personal in the actions of James Bowdoin, Samuel Adams, Henry Knox, and company. Wise servants of the public good, they perceived the impersonal dictates of objective circumstances and did their duty. By this logic, Shays's Rebellion was abstracted from history entirely and transformed into a timeless battle between propertyholding virtue and penniless vice.

This class-conscious caricature of historical reality was bound to generate opposition in a gathering Age of Reform. At the very moment McLaughlin wrote, challenges were appearing in the academic world, among local historians, and in the popular press. In 1900 Edward Bellamy's fictional account of the insurgency in Berkshire County, *The Duke of Stockbridge: A Romance of Shays' Rebellion,* originally serialized in a western Massachusetts newspaper two decades before, was issued posthumously as a book. Attracting readers from the immense following Bellamy had won for his best-selling utopian novel, *Looking Backward,* the work restored the conflict to human terms in an insightful rendering of the rebels' abortive struggle within an aristocratic social order. Not long after, Joseph Parker Warren, having completed his Harvard University dissertation on Shays's Rebellion, was assuring readers of the *American Historical Review* that, contrary to conservative myth, the insurgency was *not* a movement "to overthrow the state government, and to establish some purely democratic or even communistic system in its place." And in 1903, at a gathering of the historical society of Clinton, Massachusetts, a small town on the fringe of Shaysite country in Worcester County, a local judge with a desire for historical "impartiality" opened an inquiry into the farmers' grievances and ruled in their favor. None of these efforts had a radical intent. But to treat the complaints and the actions of the insurgents seriously, as matters for detailed, empirical research, was to put aside the special pleading and smug moralism of the White Hats and to prompt a reconsideration of all parties to the affair. And when joined to the revolt against a business-dominated society that was launched by Progressive intellectuals in the 1920s, these small forays into the late eighteenth century gave rise to the second school of Shaysite historiography, designated "Hemlocks" for the evergreen emblems the rebels wore in their hats.[20]

The rehabilitation of the insurgents owed most to the assiduous scholarship of Jonathan Smith, the lawyer and judge in Clinton, whose work was issued as a pamphlet by the town historical society in 1905 and gained currency two decades later through James Truslow Adams's influential work *New England in the Republic, 1776–1850*. Raised on a farm in Peterborough, New Hampshire, the son of a hard-working, substantial deacon, Smith (1842–1930) knew at first hand the constant, strenuous labors required to wrest a living from the New England backcountry. He had experienced both the trials of combat as a young soldier in the Union army and the hardships of a postwar economy that eroded the security of rural families. By dint of long struggle, he had managed to graduate from Dartmouth College at age twenty-nine, then gone on to thrive in the law. But he never forgot his origins. Perhaps for that reason, Smith was skeptical of all the histories of Shays's Rebellion, "strongly colored with the opinions of those actively engaged in its suppression, and also of the conservative classes, who had no sympathy with the movement." Though devoted to sound money himself, though as certain as any Friend of Government in 1786 that rebellion "cannot

---

[20] Joseph Parker Warren, "The Confederation and the Shays Rebellion," *American Historical Review* 11 (1905): 42; Edward Bellamy, *The Duke of Stockbridge: A Romance of Shays' Rebellion*, ed. Joseph Schiffman (1900; reprint ed., Cambridge, Mass., 1962); Jonathan Smith, *Some Features of Shays' Rebellion. The Annual Address before the Clinton (Mass.) Historical Society, by Jonathan Smith, President of the Society, September 14, 1903* (Clinton, Mass., 1905), reprinted as "The Depression of 1785 and Daniel Shays' Rebellion," *William and Mary Quarterly*, 3d ser. 5 (1948):77–94; Hofstadter, *Progressive Historians*, pp. 23–43, 181–89.

be justified on either legal or moral grounds," the fair-minded lawyer presumed that "as in every other popular agitation, there were two sides," which ought to be examined in "a more judicial spirit than was possible a century ago." From that open-minded inquiry, he concluded, the insurgents stood forth "in a truer and better light."[21]

Judge Smith's intellectual strategy involved little more than a lawyer's painstaking investigation into the facts of a case. Taking on the insurgents as his client, Smith delved into the historical merit of their grievances. How heavy were debts and taxes? How many cases went to court? How burdensome were the costs of litigation? How exploitative were the officers of the law? Focusing his inquiries on Worcester County, especially the several communities in the northeast part that were centered around the old shire town of Lancaster (from which Clinton had been set off), and following the example of several nineteenth-century antiquarians, Smith explored the official records of towns, county, and state. His results confirmed the justice of farmers' complaints. By his reckoning, the public debt of Massachusetts in 1786 amounted to $43 per person, ten times the level of his own day. Taxes, in turn, approached close to $200 for every head of family, "more good money than the farmer saw during the entire twelve months." Add to that the massive private indebtedness, which in the prevailing hard times gave rise to four thousand lawsuits in Worcester County in just the years 1784 and 1785—one for every head of family, already groaning under the tax collector's demands. Those "unfortunates," who were unable to satisfy their creditors' claims, were crowded into the Worcester jails where, in 1785, 92 out of 103 souls languished for lack of money, amidst scenes that Smith likened to the miseries depicted in Dickens's *Little Dorrit*.

In the judge's opinion, however, not every complaint had validity. According to a list of official charges for two civil cases in 1786, court costs were not exorbitant but actually "much

<hr />

[21] Charles Knowles Bolton, "Jonathan Smith," *Proceedings of the Massachusetts Historical Society* 68 (1944–47):466–69; Smith, "Depression of 1785," pp. 77–78, 93.

less than they are now." Nor did lawyers deserve the oppro-
brium they had received. Far from being ill-educated petti-
foggers who stirred up needless lawsuits to enrich themselves,
as was commonly said, the men admitted to the Massachusetts
bar during the first decade of Independence (1776–86) were,
for the most part, respectable college graduates. In Smith's
view, a Harvard man was, by definition, no "shyster." Lawyers
were no more at fault for doing well in a credit crisis than
were doctors for seeing and charging numerous patients during a plague. To Judge Smith, the legal system neither caused
nor exacerbated the troubles in the 1780s. A neutral instrument of society, it simply registered the unhappy consequences of an economy in distress.[22]

Having established that the cries of pain from the countryside deserved sympathy, Smith proceeded to challenge the
standing stereotype of the protesters. "The malcontents were
not the rabble," he wrote. Instead, they comprised the producing classes—farmers, mechanics, laborers—who found
their leadership among men in the upper orders. Smith discovered that three-quarters of twenty-one "prominent actors"
indicted for treason in Worcester County in April 1787 were
listed as "gentlemen"; the remainder were "yeomen." Even
more, the top commanders of Shays's army had all fought in
the Revolution, many with three to five years' service to their
credit. "It would not be wide of the truth to call it a movement
organized and sustained by revolutionary soldiers." And what
had prompted such patriots to rise up against the state? It
was, Smith suggested, a feeling of betrayal by the very government they had sacrificed so much to create. Paid for their
army service in paper certificates that had rapidly depreciated
after the war, these former Continentals had been forced by
sheer necessity to sell the unredeemed notes to speculators
for a song. But the worst of it was that they were now being
taxed unbearably, perhaps even losing their farms, to pay in-

[22] Smith, "Depression of 1785," pp. 80–84; Grindall Reynolds, "Concord
during the Shays Rebellion," in *A Collection of Historical and Other Papers*
(Concord, Mass., 1895), pp. 195–244; Samuel A. Green, "Groton during
Shays's Rebellion," *Groton Historical Series: A Collection of Papers Relating to the
History of the Town of Groton, Massachusetts* 1 (1887).

terest in cash on claims that rightly belonged to themselves. Then again, the bulk of the countryside shared their economic plight. With such an abundance of misery, Smith was convinced that "a majority of the people" in the rural communities of central and western Massachusetts were "in secret or open sympathy" with the rebellion.[23]

The final step in Smith's reasoning solved the puzzle of the insurgency. If the rebels were respectable patriots, suffering genuine economic distress, they could not be dismissed as extreme radicals, out to overturn the social order. A reading of rural protests—petitions to the legislature, town instructions to representatives, resolves of county conventions—confirmed Smith's hunch. All the citizens had ever wanted from the government was relief from the crushing burden of private debt. But a distant, uncaring administration ignored their pleas. It foolishly treated their restrained demonstrations as acts of treason, ordered the arrests of the ringleaders, and drove them into reluctant revolt. "Until by the acts of the state officials the malcontents were thrown on the defensive," Smith concluded, "the movement was simply an effort on the part of the farmers and mechanics to preserve what little property they had and save themselves from the debtors' prison." Shays's Rebellion had been entirely unnecessary. A wise government could have put a quick stop to the affair by suspending the collection of debts. Given the insensitivity and miscalculations by the Bowdoin administration, the "rebellion—if rebellion it may be called"—amounted to a misdemeanor, under "extenuating" circumstances. The real crime, the judge implied, was the stupid misjudgment by the state.[24]

This closely reasoned defense of the insurgents was both less and more challenging to the White Hats than it initially appeared. Familiar with the practices of the county courts, Smith pioneered in the use of their records as a way of gauging the gravity of the economic crisis. The evidence he compiled on litigation and imprisonment for debt marked a significant addition to the slender body of fact about the pre-

[23] Smith, "Depression of 1785," pp. 88–89.

[24] Ibid., pp. 84–93.

vailing circumstances in the mid-1780s. The few novel details he adduced, together with some scraps in other works of local history, would be cited over and over again by Hemlock historians in succeeding decades. In the innocent days before "the new social history," nobody bothered to follow up on Smith's lead and reconstruct either society or the courts. The crucial point to defenders of the rebellion was that Smith had set forth the objective conditions that exculpated, if they did not justify, the insurgents' resort to arms. This line of argument, however, was no answer to the best, most sophisticated cases for the government. Minot had openly conceded the widespread existence of economic privation; Smith was merely repeating what everybody already knew—though with hard, substantial facts to back him up. Indeed, Smith and the historians who followed in his wake had absorbed a central tenet of the pro-government case: cold, impersonal necessities served to justify political acts. In the process, they skirted around the problem of understanding who among the rural population had enlisted in Shays's army and who had remained, for whatever reasons, passive sympathizers or perhaps neutral spectators of the affair.

On the other hand, Smith's essay skillfully turned the tables on the White Hats. If the insurgents were true sons of the Revolution, seeking temporary protection against unjust loss of their farms, and if the resort to arms came only after government moved aggressively to punish the rebels, then the central problem was how the Bowdoin administration could have failed so utterly to understand the people it ruled. Judge Smith had nothing to offer on this matter. But the question hung in the air, waiting to be seized. It would be the lever by which the Hemlock historians of the 1920s and 1930s pried open the chambers of government and exposed the seamy scandals inside.

The key to this new perspective was, of course, the intellectual revolution wrought by Charles A. Beard, Carl L. Becker, Arthur M. Schlesinger, Sr., and a generation of Progressive historians during the opening decades of the twentieth century. In that vibrant Age of Reform, iconoclastic intellectuals in numerous fields repudiated the arid formalism and the complacent certitudes of their elders. The conventional paradigm of American thought, the abstract, moralistic framework that governed the conservative approach to the past, was dismantled with gusto by a formidable wrecking crew. In the view of the rising generation, the received wisdom mystified the temporary arrangements of an unequal society by elevating them into timeless natural laws; it thereby cut the mass of Americans off from the controlling realities of their lives. But once the scaffolding was pulled down, the dirty secret was revealed—the basic institutions of American life served the selfish interests of the rich and powerful. In democratic outrage at this discovery, the Progressives enlisted Clio on the side of the people.

With a muckraking approach to knowledge, the new generation waged an unrelenting assault on the American past, particularly the world of the Founding Fathers. Wielding the "economic interpretation of history" with surgical brilliance, Charles Beard cut through the heroic myth of the Constitution and its framers. Far from saving a trembling nation from the verge of anarchy, as John Fiske had claimed, the Federalists had carried out a conservative counterrevolution in their own financial interest. Through the specific devices of the Constitution, the tough-minded speculators in government securities who sat at the Philadelphia Convention were coldly calculating to line their own pockets at public expense. Beard's argument focused closely on the delegates at Philadelphia, linking their hidden, personal interests to the decisions behind the scenes; consequently, he made only passing mention of Shays's Rebellion as one of the "popular movements in the states." Neither did his fellow historians, Becker and Schlesinger, who reconnoitered the early years of the Revolutionary movement in the leading ports to similar effect. As Becker and Schlesinger saw it, the commercial elite was as self-interested at the start of the Revolution as at the end. Stirring up opposition to Britain to protect their profits from imperial regulations and taxes, the merchants unwittingly unleashed a radical challenge from the lower orders against their own power. The story of the Revolution thus became, in Becker's formulation, not only a struggle for "home rule" but a fight over "who should rule at home." That description could have applied just as aptly to the situation of Massachusetts in 1786.[25]

Curiously, hardly anyone made that connection in the heyday of Progressive reform; then, all at once in the 1920s, everybody did. The key text in precipitating the new awareness of Shays's Rebellion was the work of a nonacademic writer, James Truslow Adams, who had gained a considerable following among general readers with a successful trilogy on New England. A Wall Street broker turned historian, with a gift for synthesizing the ideas and research of others in lively prose, Adams wrote in the Progressive vein but in a mood chastened by the defeat of reform, within and beyond the United States, after World War I. As he surveyed the contemporary scene, Adams noticed a distinctive "post-war psychology" that invariably emerged among the diverse classes "after every great conflict." In the wake of World War I, that "psychology" had meant a hasty retreat by the privileged classes into narrow, money-minded conservatism and a bitter explosion of conflict with the masses, as in the 1919 steel strike and the Palmer raids. For Adams, essentially the same process of reaction and struggle pushed post-Revolutionary Massachusetts into Shays's Rebellion.[26]

[25] Hofstadter, *Progressive Historians*, pp. 181–89; Charles A. Beard, *An Economic Interpretation of the Constitution of the United States* (1913; reprint ed., New York, 1965), p. 40; Arthur M. Schlesinger, Sr., *The Colonial Merchants and the American Revolution, 1763–1776* (New York, 1918); Carl L. Becker, *The History of Political Parties in the Province of New York, 1760–1776* (1909; reprint ed., Madison, Wis., 1960), p. 22. Beard did note that the disorders in Massachusetts deepened the "despair" among the representatives of "personalty" at the failure of republican government to advance their interests. And in analyzing the distribution of votes for and against the Constitution in Massachusetts, he remarked upon the strong Antifederalist sentiment in Worcester County, "the centre of the Shays rebellion in behalf of debtors." Such comments could easily have furnished the basis for a larger interpretation of the insurgency and its relation to the Constitution. As will be seen below, it would take another decade before Beard would offer this argument. Beard, *Economic Interpretation*, pp. 58–61, 262–63.

[26] Kraus, *History of American History*, pp. 523–29; James Truslow Adams, *The Founding of New England* (Boston, 1921); idem, *Revolutionary New England, 1691–1776* (Boston, 1923); idem, *New England in the Republic, 1776–1850* (Boston, 1926), p. 159; Allan Nevins, *James Truslow Adams: Historian of the American Dream* (Urbana, Ill., 1968), pp. 32–40. The Marxist writer A. M.

Adams's account of the insurrection was elaborated in two chapters ("Growing Unrest" and "Rebellion") of *New England in the Republic, 1776–1850,* the third and closing volume in his saga of the region, for which he had already won the Pulitzer Prize. For the book as a whole, Adams took as his central theme "the continued struggle of the common man to realize the doctrines of the Revolution in the life of the community." In this narrative of the drive for democracy, Shays's Rebellion proved a depressing stumbling block; it resulted in the execution of the grim resolve of the patriot elite to put a halt to the Revolution and the expansion of popular power.

With his sentiments squarely behind the people, Adams laid out the familiar grievances of common folk—taxes and debts, scarcity of money, lack of political power—and affirmed the respectability, patriotism, and orderly methods of the insurgents. Nothing in this argument was new; though he had read the printed sources himself, Adams closely followed the logic and evidence of Judge Smith down to his predecessor's distaste for paper money and rejection of popular complaints about lawyers. But Adams decisively altered the historiography of Shays's Rebellion by his hostile assault on the Massachusetts elite. Where nineteenth-century writers had identified with the forces of law and order, Adams viewed the actions of merchants and magistrates with a cynicism bred by his years of dealing with financial speculators on Wall Street and by disillusion at the political outcome of World War I. In his first volume on *The Founding of New England,* Adams had pioneered in the repudiation of Puritanism popular among intellectuals in the 1920s. Now he extended the indictment to the heirs of "the petty aristocracy of clergy, lawyers, and merchants" who had founded the Massachusetts Bay Colony on a "rigid suppression" of dissent. Descending from mean-spirited men, "singularly impervious to ideas," the hypocritical patriot elite had aroused the lower orders to resist

---

Simons did connect Shays's Rebellion and the move for the Constitution in an aggressive campaign by capitalist creditors to consolidate their power as a ruling class. But Simons's ideas were apparently not picked up by others until the 1930s. See A. M. Simons, *Social Forces in American History* (1911; reprint ed., New York, 1925), pp. 88–99.

British rule by promising an expansion of popular power, only to forget such calculated propaganda as soon as Independence was achieved. "It was all very well, when the common people were to be goaded into action in the war, for the 'well-born' . . . to talk about all men being created equal," Adams remarked, "but once the war was won, the old doctrines of the peculiar rights of the 'well-born' to govern and the peculiar sanctity of their property came once more to the fore." Coldly indifferent to the economic plight of the countryside, the "reactionaries" had nothing but insults and repression for the protests. The young Fisher Ames, who had sat out the war composing poetry and studying law, derided the insurgents as "bankrupts and sots." Even Samuel Adams, "the arch-conspirator and manipulator of the Boston mobs," invoked the sanctity of legal institutions. Given such rigid opposition, given the "stupidity and vacillation" of the legislature in the face of the crisis, given the desperation of the backcountry, Adams asked, "What was left for the discontented but violent action?" For Adams and the historians who followed, Shays's Rebellion was no longer a test of governance. It had turned into a basic matter of *social justice*.[27]

The assault on the Massachusetts magistrates furnished the final ingredient for the making of Hemlock history. It was now the motives and the decisions of the elite, rather than the insurgents, that became the constant object of attack in interpretations that steadily widened the significance of Shays's Rebellion for American history. The year after Adams's contribution, two classics of Progressive historiography—Charles and Mary Beard's *The Rise of American Civilization* and Vernon Louis Parrington's *Main Currents in American Thought*—located the Massachusetts insurrection within the new popular paradigm: the rag-tag band of poor debtor-farmers who marched with Shays waged a valiant battle for democracy against commercial, creditor interests, launching a long tradition of struggle linking them to the Jacksonians, the Populists, and the rising cotton and cornbelt rebellion of the 1920s. In an easy extension of the argument

---

[27] Adams, *New England in the Republic*, pp. 141–44, 148–49, 154; Nevins, *James Truslow Adams*, pp. 19–20.

of *An Economic Interpretation of the Constitution,* the Beards portrayed the commercial elite of Massachusetts and the other states as an active, dynamic force, aggressively pursuing its own economic interests against any and all challengers and, in the process, triggering the Revolution and Constitution. Within the commonwealth, a "conservative party of merchants, shippers, and money lenders" imposed a propertyholders' constitution under which the privileged enjoyed lucrative profits; through this rigged political system, the canny conservatives bestowed a great windfall upon speculators in the public debt while taxing farmers and laborers to excess. Such action soon provoked "a populist movement" that stimulated, in turn, the forces of reaction. Having emancipated themselves in the Revolution from British restraints over trade, the assertive capitalists of the new republic were determined to keep control over economic affairs and to check any initiatives from below. To this end, hoping to alarm propertyholders everywhere, such extreme nationalists as Henry Knox purposely exaggerated the aims of the insurgents, deceptively portraying the Shaysites as levelers who intended to confiscate and redistribute wealth. As Parrington emphasized, "It was Shays's Rebellion, that militant outbreak of populism . . . which crystallized the anti-democratic sentiment, and aroused the commercial group to decisive action. . . . It provided the object lesson in democratic anarchy which the 'friends of law and order' greatly needed." Moving quickly to exploit the moment, the conservative forces hastened on to the Philadelphia Convention and the triumph of "counter-revolution."[28]

Perhaps inevitably, such concerted action by conservative nationalists took on the semblance of conspiracy. During the 1930s and 1940s, under the impact of the Great Depression and the New Deal, as liberals battled the "economic royalists" of Wall Street, as militant farmers in the prairies stopped courts to prevent foreclosures, and as organizers for the left

[28]Charles A. Beard and Mary R. Beard, *The Rise of American Civilization,* 2 vols. (1927; reprint ed., New York, 1930), 1:297–309, 544, 665, 685, 759, 772, 798; 2:711; Vernon Louis Parrington, *Main Currents in American Thought: An Interpretation of American Literature from the Beginnings to 1920,* vol. 1, *The Colonial Mind, 1620–1800* (New York, 1927), pp. 271–82.

heralded a rising revolution by working people, intellectuals were quick to credit the most extreme scenarios of 1786–87. In 1932, fast upon the notorious suppression of the murals he had painted on commission for the new Rockefeller Center, the Communist artist Diego Rivera set about producing a vast panorama of class struggle, "A Pageant of America," on the walls of the "ramshackle" New Workers' School at West Fourteenth Street in New York City. One huge fresco featured Shays's Rebellion. In the foreground of the mural, a heroic Daniel Shays, seated on horseback, leads his army of black and white farmers, armed with pitchforks and muskets, into the mouths of government cannon. In the distance stand the figures of reaction, the "big bourgeoisie" of George Washington and his aristocratic European friends, planted on a landscape of exploitation, symbolized by a courthouse, slave mart, Masonic temple, and church. In this reading of events, which the Mexican Rivera fashioned out of the research done for him by faculty and students at the Workers' School, a "new ruling class" was consolidating a "bourgeois revolution," crushing the hopes of the common people in a successful conspiracy that would shortly impose a safe, national government through the Constitution. Rivera's mural portrayed the central theme in studies of Shays's Rebellion for the next two decades by Marxists and non-Marxists alike. Against innocent, oppressed workers—farmers and laborers—a coalition of monied men plotted to impose undemocratic rule.[29]

Interestingly, this view was endorsed not only by left-wing intellectuals but also by rural citizens in Daniel Shays's old home of Pelham. By the 1890s Shays and his followers were no longer ignored in the history of the town; C. O. Parmenter gave them a prominent place in his 1898 *History of Pelham,* stressing the hardships of the post-Revolutionary era without

[29] Diego Rivera, *Portrait of America,* explanatory text by Bertram D. Wolfe (New York, 1934), pp. 30–31, 97–105; Bertram D. Wolfe, *Diego Rivera: His Life and Times* (New York, 1939), pp. 372–74; Robert A. East, "The Massachusetts Conservatives in the Critical Period," in Richard B. Morris, ed., *The Era of the American Revolution: Studies Inscribed to Evarts Boutell Greene* (New York, 1939), pp. 349–91; Millard Hansen, "The Significance of Shays' Rebellion," *South Atlantic Quarterly* 39 (1940):305–17; Morgan, "Early American Social Revolt," pp. 618–19.

justifying the resort to arms. Over the succeeding decades, the townspeople increasingly identified with Shays. That deepening kinship was due in good measure to the fact that the forces of eastern Massachusetts were once again invading the west, this time to dam up the Swift River Valley and inundate its tiny towns, for the sake of supplying water to the thirsty inhabitants of Boston. Among the towns scheduled for elimination was little Prescott, once a hamlet of Pelham, where Daniel Shays had kept his homestead in 1786. In the face of this intrusion, which culminated in the erection of Quabbin Reservoir during the Great Depression, the five hundred or so inhabitants of rural Pelham renewed their pride in the Rebellion. Joining with Shays enthusiasts to commemorate the 150th anniversary of the insurrection in 1936, they laid a plaque on a huge boulder in front of the Pelham meetinghouse, with a bold inscription: "To Commemorate Daniel Shays of Pelham, Captain in the American Revolution, Leader in the Shays Rebellion, against Unjust Laws." No longer a rebel even in his neighbors' eyes, Shays was now a folk hero in a populist pantheon.[30]

The quest for a more impartial history of Shays's Rebellion thus ended in a new mythology of the left. Historiography had become hagiography. In the orthodoxy that gained sway during the 1930s and 1940s, the insurgents were simply overburdened farmers and laborers, the sturdy patriots of 1776, driven by desperation to renew the struggle against oppres-

---

[30] C. O. Parmenter, *History of Pelham, Mass., from 1738 to 1898, Including the Early History of Prescott* (Amherst, Mass., 1898); *Springfield Sunday Union and Republican*, Sept. 23, 1928, Sept. 20, 1936; *Daily Hampshire Gazette*, Sept. 21, 1936; the newspaper clippings are included in the Shays's Rebellion Collection, Pelham Historical Society, Pelham, Mass. I am grateful to Robert Keyes of Pelham for giving me access to these materials. The populist view of Shays's Rebellion was also diffused in the volume on Massachusetts prepared by the Federal Writers' Project of the WPA. Treating the insurgency as a touchstone of the Revolution, the *Guide* carefully identified both minor and major sites of confrontation in 1786–87. See *The WPA Guide to Massachusetts: The Federal Writers' Project Guide to 1930s Massachusetts with a New Introduction by Jane Holtz Kay* (New York, 1983), pp. xxvii, 5, 43–44, 256, 302, 312, 360, 437, 479, 482, 525, 549, 552, 602. Originally published as *Massachusetts: A Guide to Its Places and People* (Boston, 1937).

sion. Arrayed against them was the phalanx of power, the un-
holy alliance of merchants, magistrates, professionals, and
speculators that was plundering the people and betraying the
Revolution. The contest between the two parties set virtue
against vice—innocent farmers against avaricious men of
trade—in a continuing confrontation throughout American
history. But this interpretation, however subtly argued, was as
partial as the pro-government view it displaced. It essentially
repeated the same charges, rehearsed the same self-
justifications that the Shaysites themselves had presented at
the time. The verdict of history was on their side.

Yet the new orthodoxy was the mirror image of the old.
Drawing on many of the same sources—newspapers, petitions, official documents, letters of prominent politicians—
nineteenth-century writers had employed, Hemlock historians merely inverted the perspective of their predecessors.
They may have seen themselves as men of convictions, without illusions, striding forth to rectify error and reveal truth.
But in the course of their readings, they had unconsciously
absorbed the assumptions of the past so as to reproduce a
familiar structure of interpretation. Theirs was the conspiracy
theory of the White Hats turned upside down. In both perspectives, a little body of selfish, ambitious men—in the one
case, demagogues from below, in the other, merchants and
magistrates from above—plotted to seize power and exploit
the people for personal gain. The conspirators resembled one
another in their social location; they were, invariably, *outsiders*
to the communities they assailed. To established gentlemen,
Shays was a social upstart, emerging from the depths to bid
for power; to the backcountry, eastern merchants represented
an intrusive, alien world. The plotters were alike, too, in their
single-minded pursuit of coherent ends. Their economics and
politics were of a piece. The bulwark of economic privilege,
the ruling class of Massachusetts was, to Hemlock historians,
equally the champion of elitist government; in turn, White
Hats portrayed the insurgents as egalitarians in society and
populists in the state. Happily, the worst designs of the respec-
tive invaders fell short of victory, owing to resistance from
selfless defenders of the common good. Though they argued

competing cases, White Hats and Hemlocks were locked into the same worldview, which replicated the prevailing paradigm of politics in the Revolutionary age.

Assimilating the language and assumptions, the very structure of thought, of the eighteenth-century people they studied, writers of both schools unwittingly perpetuated a conspiratorial view of history and society that had once been the hallmark of Enlightenment. When Progressive intellectuals burrowed beneath the surface of events, in search for the secret schemes of designing men, they were reaffirming the best insights of the eighteenth century. As Gordon S. Wood has shown, in the age of Samuel Adams and Daniel Shays the mysterious movements of history—the rise and fall of kings, the advance and decay of civilizations—were no longer attributed to the hidden hand of God or the grip of fate. Instead, the course of events reflected human agency; society was the product of the intentions of men. Such purposes were, invariably, conscious and rational—deliberate calculations, based on known interests and ideals, in service of planned ends. In its own time, this new perspective emancipated thought, enabling men and women to cut through venerable traditions and superstitions and to assert their own reason and will. But in a still hierarchical world, where the self-seeking maneuvers of individuals and groups for political gain were condemned as "faction," it also spawned the growth of conspiracy theories on all sides to public disputes. As a state senator and principal advisor to Governor Bowdoin in 1786–87, Samuel Adams blamed the popular insurgency on "designing men . . . imposing upon credulous though well-meaning persons" to produce "discord and animosity." That, of course, was exactly what loyalist writers had said about Adams only a decade before. The self-serving view of the eighteenth-century Court, this perspective provoked a parallel response from rural spokesmen for the Country. Bound by rationalist, consensual assumptions, nobody in Shays's Rebellion could presume the innocent intentions of opponents or admit the legitimacy of conflicts of interest. Bequeathed across the centuries, this framework of analysis prompted historians' obsession with the schemes and plots of the little cabals—the conniving bondholders, the loyalist doctors, the tight band of soldiers and speculators in the Ohio Company, the reactionary provocateurs—that have been accused of fomenting the crisis of Shays's Rebellion.[31]

Joint heirs to an eighteenth-century frame of mind, White Hats and Hemlocks were, in their different ways, loyal sons of the American Revolution. To the defenders of government, James Bowdoin and Samuel Adams aimed only to preserve the fruits of Independence—liberty and republicanism—against a hostile world. The advocates of the insurgents were no less fervent in their embrace of the Revolution, but they relocated the true spirit of 1776 in the brave spirits of the backcountry. In the bitterness of debate, each side questioned the loyalty of the other. Progressive historians, to be sure, were eager to expose the lukewarm patriotism of the merchant class, but they skipped right over the halfhearted enthusiasm among many in the backcountry. Nobody bothered to explore the diverse meanings of the Revolution to all parties in the dispute, to set the conflicts of the era in the long perspective of Massachusetts history, or, more radically, to probe the many ties, personal, political, and cultural, that still bound insurgents, neutrals, and Friends of Government alike to a more traditional, pre-Revolutionary world.

While they shared common premises of thought, White Hats and Hemlocks arrived at mutually exclusive views. The conspirators of one school were the Revolutionary heroes of the other, and vice versa. But not always. In what is surely the most lurid scenario of Shays's Rebellion ever written, Forrest McDonald combined the paranoia of the White Hats with the economic interpretation of the Progressives and carried both

[31] Gordon S. Wood, "Conspiracy and the Paranoid Style: Causality and Deceit in the Eighteenth Century," *William and Mary Quarterly*, 3d ser. 39 (1982):401–41; William Pencak, "Samuel Adams and Shays's Rebellion," *New England Quarterly* 62 (1989):66; Douglass Adair and John A. Schutz, eds., *Peter Oliver's Origin & Progress of the American Rebellion: A Tory View* (San Marino, 1961); James H. Hutson, "Country, Court, and Constitution: Antifederalism and the Historians," *William and Mary Quarterly*, 3d ser. 38 (1981):356–68; Forrest McDonald, *E Pluribus Unum: The Formation of the American Republic, 1776–1790* (Boston, 1965), pp. 145–54; Sidney Kaplan, "Veteran Officers and Politics in Massachusetts, 1783–1787," *William and Mary Quarterly*, 3d ser. 9 (1952):29–57; East, "Massachusetts Conservatives," pp. 375–84.

to enthusiastic excess. In *E Pluribus Unum* (1965), an account of the making of national government out of a loose confederation of sovereign states, McDonald surveyed Massachusetts politics in the mid-1780s and found plotters lurking everywhere, on all sides of the dispute, in an eighteenth century Hobbesian war of all against all. As McDonald set the forces in motion, both government and insurgents fulfilled the worst fears of their enemies. The little coterie in control of Massachusetts, McDonald argued, consisted of new, inexperienced men, arrivistes in trade and state, who had rushed into the vacuum of power caused by the departure of the loyalists only to encounter economic and political challenges beyond their ken. "Changed world commercial conditions" demanded creative solutions, such as the opening up of the China trade by Salem merchants. No easier were the dilemmas of governance over a republic that had never commanded much loyalty from distant farmers in the west. But in the face of these difficulties, what did the "mediocrities" and "submediocrities" in Boston do? First, they proved their incompetence in trade by overimporting British goods on credit in 1783–84; then, with the prospect of bankruptcy before them, they demonstrated their stupidity in politics by turning to the state to bail them out. Having bought up public securities on the cheap and gotten them funded at par, these "bungling Bostonians" pressed for rapid repayment of interest and principal in coin. Their strategy was simple: "Save themselves by bleeding their neighbors." Should that gambit succeed, "the new rich would be secure in their fortunes, and the taxpayers of Massachusetts would be impoverished."

Naturally, the farmers of the west, with little cash and less patience, resented the claims on their purses. Having resisted the authority of the state from 1776 to 1780, they wanted only to be left alone in their parochial affairs. However, in McDonald's judgment, the common people were insular and ill-informed, a gullible mass easily stirred into rebellion by "malcontents" with self-seeking aims. "Ne'er-do-wells" abounded in every New England town, he explained, providing raw material and leadership for rebellion. Some hung around the taverns, eager for excitement, in exchange for liquor or pay. A few were angry Revolutionary veterans, grown poor in their country's service; they "had the plausibility that makes for leadership in troubled times." Such agitators would have gotten nowhere, but for a handful of "well-heeled Tories," who had been waiting and praying for "the moment of counterrevolution to come." "Somehow (nobody knows how) some of these men (nobody knows how many, or for sure, exactly which) got together and began to think of turning local turbulence to much grander account." With the money supplied by these unreconciled loyalists, McDonald suggested, militant farmers began drilling in the western hills. Popular protests soon brought tax relief from the legislature in Boston, but to no avail. Self-seeking tax collectors hid the news of reform in order to profit from inside information. Nor did the government's promise of pardon win over the insurgents. The leaders of the rebellion suppressed the offer so as to keep the movement alive. As a result, the mass of Shays's army marched into Gen. William Shepard's cannon out of "a great and general fear" of government reprisals that was altogether unfounded. "Almost all were afraid of something, even if they knew not what. Ignorance had taken them this far, and fear would take them further." On the other side, James Bowdoin's administration was no better informed. Thanks to the deliberate propaganda of the crafty Henry Knox, who seized upon the disorders to promote the cause of extreme nationalism, the elite in Boston and elsewhere in the republic believed that Shays and his men meant to overturn government and redistribute property in common. Hence, they provoked the debacle at Springfield Armory, a confrontation that need never have happened, was quickly over, but produced, in its wake, the Constitution of the United States. Out of such connivings and contingencies a nation was born.[32]

The elaborate fantasies of McDonald brought the conspiracy theories of White Hats and Hemlocks to a bizarre culmi-

[32] McDonald, *E Pluribus Unum*, pp. 127–32, 145–54. McDonald, in collaboration with Ellen Shapiro McDonald, repeats the same interpretation, often in the very same words, in his essay "On the Late Disturbances in Massachusetts," published in *Requiem* in 1988 (pp. 59–83). This piece contains little new evidence, but adds a polemical thrust against the liberal and left-wing historians who have distorted Shays's Rebellion to serve their own ideological purposes.

nation. Crediting the wildest charges on all sides—polemics in the press, loose testimony before state commissions—and presuming, without evidence, the motives and influence of the principal parties, McDonald took the worst imaginings of the time as fact. In his presentation, a tiny clique in Boston was plundering the people for its own gain—exactly as the Shaysites charged. At the same time, the insurgents *were* ignorant plowjoggers, deceived and manipulated into rebellion by "artful, designing men"—exactly as the Friends of Government claimed. In McDonald, the "paranoid style" of eighteenth-century partisanship became a cynical, twentieth-century exposé of chicanery and subversion at the nation's start. But now the political progressivism of Charles Beard and his generation was gone. McDonald's muckraking seemingly had no point, except to show the accidental origins of the Constitution. Perhaps for that reason, it existed in a historiographic world apart—the latter-day flowering of an exotic atavism from the past.[33]

Yet McDonald was less idiosyncratic than he first appears. His lonely obsession with secret schemers and hidden manipulators notwithstanding, he stood at the end of a generation-long effort to rewrite the history of the Revolution and Shays's Rebellion. As we have seen, by 1940 writers on the left had driven defenders of the Massachusetts magistrates from the field. In place of an enduring battle between virtuous patriots and immoral rebels—the gospel according to White Hats—the Progressive scholars had erected a new orthodoxy of a fundamental conflict between privileged capitalists and the mass of working people. That contest was hardly unique to the 1780s; indeed, time and again it recurred in American life with essential elements intact, so that each additional episode in the struggle produced only a sense of déjà vu. Always one

[33] James H. Hutson, "The Origins of 'The Paranoid Style in American Politics': Public Jealousy from the Age of Walpole to the Age of Jackson," in David D. Hall, John M. Murrin, and Thad W. Tate, eds., *Saints and Revolutionaries: Essays on Early American History* (New York, 1984), pp. 332–72. For a similar critique of McDonald's "crude version of economic determinism," which mimicked the flaws in Charles Beard's analysis even as he attempted to refute it, see Lee Benson, *Turner and Beard: American Historical Writing Reconsidered* (New York, 1960), pp. 139–40, 167–74.

found a deep-seated conflict of material interests between the few and the many; invariably, out of that split crystallized a vast ideological divide. The outcome might vary, here a victory for democracy, there a setback, but the story was inevitably the same. In the end, Progressive history came to seem as timeless, as *ahistorical,* as the work it superseded. As a result, beginning tentatively in the 1940s and accelerating in the 1950s, a rising group of young scholars subjected the new version of Shays's Rebellion to radical scrutiny and, with the aim of rehistoricizing events, cut away its central props. Through a close inspection of Massachusetts politics and society during the immediate years of Revolution and Independence (1775–87), the new generation introduced a fresh sense of accident and contingency to events that White Hats and Hemlocks had foreclosed. In the process, however, they opened the way for McDonald's inventions, which reduced the grand drama of 1786–87 to the scale of opéra bouffe.

We have come conveniently to denote the new generation of scholars "consensus historians," whose every effort, at a time of ideological contest with communism, was devoted to denying the presence of social conflict in the American past. Not so, however, for revisionists of Shays's Rebellion. A consensus history of a popular uprising is, after all, something of an oxymoron. If any moment before the Civil War exposed the fault lines in American society, it was surely Shays's Rebellion. Appropriately, the new generation never questioned the *reality* of the division between government and insurgents in the Massachusetts crisis, nor did they doubt the *validity* of popular grievances. Readily accepting the intellectual legacy of Jonathan Smith, these scholars portrayed a familiar scenario of heavy taxes, crushing debts, and scarce money in a depressed countryside. They were also quick to agree that the rural dissidents originally wanted relief, not revolution, and that they moved into rebellion only after government failed to meet popular needs. The once-controversial claims of Hemlock history had become the accepted basis upon which all future scholars would build. But the revisionists challenged existing understandings of how and why the crisis had come about, how it was interpreted by the opposing parties, and how it fit into the larger movement of the Revolutionary era and of American history as a whole. Their reaction against the conventional wisdom of the day set the terms for a new debate over the meaning of Shays's Rebellion that would last into the 1980s and provide the immediate backdrop for the bicentennial commemoration of the event.

Consensus history took shape gradually, by fits and starts, in a series of related inquiries that coalesced into a new orthodoxy about Shays's Rebellion by the mid-1950s. Nobody issued any manifestos to repudiate the old school or to herald the arrival of the new. But the turning point of scholarship can be located precisely, in a quietly subversive set of essays by Oscar and Mary Flug Handlin just before and after World War II. Without declaring their radical purpose, the Handlins challenged the prevailing notion that Revolutionary Massachusetts had been divided into two contending parties: a small, conservative elite of merchants and magistrates, on one side, and the militant mass of working people, on the other. Such an interpretation, they conceded, might fit the decade of resistance to British imperial policies between 1765 and 1775. This view had, of course, long since been established by Arthur M. Schlesinger, Sr., the Progressive historian who had been Oscar Handlin's mentor at Harvard; the student was not yet ready to question the master. Instead, the Handlins shifted attention to the period after 1776, where the way was clear for revisionism. Pre-Revolutionary parties, they contended, did not persist into the period after Independence; with the removal of the loyalists from politics, the whig coalition fractured into diverse rivalries among individuals and groups amidst the unsettlements of revolution and war. No common interest joined artisans in the towns and farmers in the countryside. On such wartime matters as price controls and in the postwar debate over the U.S. Constitution, the two groups took opposing stands. In fact, rural communities were divided among themselves in the long fight over the Massachusetts constitution. Most importantly, the Handlins shattered the assumption that merchants constituted a unified, powerful bloc throughout these turbulent years. Far from it. The upheaval of Revolution had swept through the counting-houses and the wharves of Boston. With the removal of the loyalists the merchant community lost the great body of its members, but their places were quickly taken by traders from the outports and by nouveau riche from the lower ranks, reaping the wartime rewards of privateering. So many new men, with such diverse origins, could hardly combine for common ends, much less be labeled a class.

> Certainly, in this transitory period [the Handlins wrote] when all the problems of government were new, such oversimplification falsifies a complex and involved process. . . . The merchants needed time to acquire and consolidate control, and even to become conscious of their own identity and interests in the unclear, rapidly changing, and confused condition of the state's economy. The young, the strangers, the newly risen needed time to discover they were a class, to sever old ties and establish new ones, to maintain their interests and discover how to protect them.

In short, no stable basis for class politics survived the war. Ironically, the constant fluctuations of the Revolutionary era disrupted the very continuity of society upon which Progressive historians had founded their case for radical conflict between socioeconomic groups.[34]

Having unsettled the basic social categories of Hemlock history, the Handlins went on to undermine a second prop of the Progressive analysis, the notion that contending groups could rationally calculate and promote their interests in the continuing contest over public policy. That may have been so in the late colonial era, but in the fluid circumstances of the Revolution, Massachusetts lawmakers were obliged constantly to make decisions on unfamiliar matters with no precedents to guide them. At the outset of the war necessity dictated the case; there seemed no alternative to paper money. But soon economic life became unpredictable—currency depreciated, prices skyrocketed, shortages of basic goods were rife. In this setting, patriots divided up according to economic interests, but nobody could foretell the consequences of the choices

[34] Oscar Handlin and Mary Flug Handlin, "Radicals and Conservatives in Massachusetts after Independence," *New England Quarterly* 17 (1944):343–55 (quotation p. 354).

they made. The link between intentions and results, so essential to the Progressive account of class struggle, was cut.[35]

This reappraisal of politics and society during the war carried important implications for the study of Shays's Rebellion. No longer could historians portray the merchants of Massachusetts as an entrenched elite, pursuing well-calculated ends. Instead, as the Handlins demonstrated in *Commonwealth* (1947), the commercial forces who dominated decisions on money and taxes in the mid-1780s formed a newly emergent group, certainly devoted to their own purses but divided among themselves and insecure in their control over the state. Perhaps it was owing to these circumstances, rather than to any inherent features of the social order, that the merchants proved so short-sighted in their management of the commonwealth. Having provoked a confrontation with debtor-farmers in 1786–87, the victors soon recognized the wisdom of appeasing their opponents. Political conciliation took the place of economic conflict. Contrary to the Progressives' view, Shays's Rebellion was merely a brief disturbance in a new, post-Revolutionary order, *not* the expression of enduring social divisions.[36]

The Massachusetts crisis was thus once again a test of *governance,* as it had been for George R. Minot back in 1788. In these terms, revisionist historians could readily admit that the Massachusetts leaders had flunked the challenge before them. Repeatedly, the state government was described as "inefficient" and "insensitive," torn between refusing reform and placating the people. Robert J. Taylor blamed the insurrection on the maladroit policies of the Bowdoin administration: "Self-deluded and confused," it compiled "a singularly poor record for positive action upon the people's grievances." Richard B. Morris agreed in a depiction of "Insurrection in Massachusetts" that was colored by his experiences of the Great Depression and New Deal. As in the 1930s, so in the

[35] Oscar Handlin and Mary Flug Handlin, "Revolutionary Economic Policy in Massachusetts," *William and Mary Quarterly,* 3d ser. 4 (1947):3–26.

[36] Oscar Handlin and Mary Flug Handlin, *Commonwealth: A Study of the Role of Government in the American Economy: Massachusetts, 1774–1861* (New York, 1947), pp. 33–51.

1780s, a conservative government, operating in a political system that favored propertyholders, was confronted by a profound economic depression, stirring widespread popular discontent. How did that government react? It proved as myopic as the lamented administration of Herbert Hoover; Bowdoin and company treated the Shaysites exactly as the Republican president and his commanding officer, Gen. Douglas MacArthur, did the rag-tag Bonus Army in 1932—and with the same catastrophic results. "Had a serious attempt been made to deal with these grievances," Morris judged, "there would have been no rebellion." Fortunately, the vindictive Bowdoinites were swiftly replaced by a conciliatory, reform-minded governor and legislature. Morris omitted the explicit parallel between the administration of John Hancock and that of Franklin D. Roosevelt, but the implication was hard to miss:

> The lesson seems patent to a generation now staggering from crisis to crisis. We must continue to achieve the ends of democracy under the rule of law. The attempts of minorities, whether bearing the banners of Fascism or of Communism, to achieve their objectives by force or to subordinate our national interest to those of a foreign power cannot be tolerated today any more than in Washington's time. Nevertheless, if we wish minority groups to accept majority rule we must give them reason to feel that they are a part of the whole, that under democracy they will not be reduced to a status of second-class citizens, that no groups may enjoy special privileges.

For Morris, a New Deal liberal writing at the dawn of the Cold War, Shays's Rebellion offered a parable for the times.[37]

---

[37] Robert J. Taylor, *Western Massachusetts in the Revolution* (Providence, 1954), pp. 132, 136; Richard B. Morris, "Insurrection in Massachusetts," in Daniel Aaron, ed., *America in Crisis: Fourteen Crucial Episodes in American History* (New York, 1952), pp. 46, 48–49. In an essay published in 1940, Arthur Morgan explicitly likened John Hancock, the victor in the gubernatorial election of 1787, to Franklin D. Roosevelt. One of the richest men in New England, Hancock promptly turned against his class upon resuming office in 1787 and backed popular demands for economic reform ("Early American Social Revolt," pp. 618–19).

By portraying the Massachusetts government as insensitive and inefficient, rather than oppressive and corrupt, the revisionists removed the Massachusetts insurrection from its place in the inexorable movement of social forces and restored the event, in all its contingency, to a specific time and place. In principle, the change of focus meant a fresh appreciation of *human agency* in the crisis. But in practice, the new history of Shays's Rebellion was nearly as impersonal as the old. There were no conspirators, no self-seeking classes in the revisionists' scenario. Then again, few individuals or groups commanded close inspection in these accounts. Having jettisoned class analysis, the consensus historians ceased to explore the motivations of the ruling elite. Government proved inefficient, not malign, its failings due to miscalculations, not original intent. The Bowdoin administration earned considerable blame from the historians but escaped real responsibility for its acts. Somehow the system had failed, but only by accident owing to the temporary occupants of office.[38]

The more consensus historians pursued the insurrection, the less significant it seemed. When Marion Starkey took up the subject in 1955, the crisis became "a little rebellion" and no more. The whole affair, she suggested, came down to mutual misperceptions and misunderstandings on both sides. Although they were moved by a "burning sense of grievance," backcountry farmers were victims of their own rural isolation and ignorance. Remote from Boston, "ill-informed" about politics, barely served by the press, they were easy prey to "hearsay" and rumor. No wonder they so misjudged the sources of their ills. Then again, Starkey thought, the Massachusetts elite was equally "obtuse," misinterpreting the rural protests and converting "commotions" into "rebellion." What Progressives had considered a violent outburst of class conflict amounted to a simple breakdown of communications.[39]

[38] See, for example, Alden T. Vaughan, "The 'Horrid and Unnatural Rebellion' of Daniel Shays," *American Heritage* 17 (1966):50–53, 77–81.

[39] Starkey, *Little Rebellion*, pp. xx, 16–17.

How, then, had the insurgents come to perceive public policies as oppression? Consensus historians returned to the formulations of Minot, who had stressed the ideological impact of the Revolution upon common people. The movement for self-government had exercised "a profound educative force," in the words of Robert Taylor. Once content to defer to the lofty River Gods of the Connecticut Valley, western Massachusetts farmers acquired heightened political consciousness in the Revolution, rejected traditional rule by elites, and demanded a government close to the people under a constitution written and ratified by their representatives. Indeed, as Robert A. Feer maintained in his widely read but long unpublished Harvard dissertation on Shays's Rebellion, this transformation of popular attitudes was the key to the insurrection. As a colony, Massachusetts had weathered equivalent economic depressions and specie shortages without provoking rural rebellion. Moreover, Feer argued in a fresh analysis of the crisis, the economic situation was "serious" in the mid-1780s but not dire. Suits for debt and auctions of property for overdue taxes had actually peaked in the mid-1780s, before the insurrection, while the number of hapless souls imprisoned for debt had been "greatly exaggerated." Why, then, an uprising in 1786–87? The solution resided in the forces unleashed by the Revolution. "Rebellion came, not simply because there was a specie shortage, high taxes, and a burdensome private debt," Feer maintained, "but because these conditions existed *at the same moment that men and women expected and believed themselves entitled to the good life.*" The Declaration of Independence had guaranteed every man the pursuit of happiness, and in postwar Massachusetts citizens insisted upon that natural right. In petition after petition demanding relief from state taxes, Feer observed, rural people cited their sacrifices for liberty and Independence. Had all their labors been in vain? With considerable subtlety, Feer revived and reaffirmed the essential insight of Minot: tragically, the Revolution had stimulated popular visions of "the good life," but in the financial burden it left behind, it blocked the attainment of those hopes. True sons of the Revolution, the insurgents were living and dreaming beyond their means, calling for liberty, but declining to pay its costs.[40]

If the Shaysites were only impatient Jonathans, demanding prompt payment of the promises of 1776, then surely the insurrection signaled no great divide among Americans. On one side, the insurgents took up arms only as a last resort; on the other, said Feer, government remained respectful of the law and constitution. The bloodletting was limited and soon over. "The Rebellion . . . provides impressive evidence of basic social stability," Feer concluded. "The same characteristics which enabled Massachusetts to make the transition from royal to republican government without upsetting the social structure of the community permitted her to fight a rebellion without wanton destruction."[41]

A popular rebellion that revealed social unity: such was the paradox posed by the consensus historians. But the ironies of the uprising multiplied still more when Louis Hartz took up the subject during the little surge of writing on the rebellion in the mid-1950s. If the contending parties in Massachusetts had been sure of one thing, it was that they disagreed fundamentally with their adversaries. According to Hartz, they were self-deceived. The influential political scientist seized upon the Massachusetts crisis as the test case for his interpretation of "the liberal tradition" in American politics. Daniel Shays, in his view, represented "the outermost limit of American radicalism" in the Revolutionary era; if even he could be fitted into the national consensus, then Hartz's argument for liberal exceptionalism was home free. No problem. Set against the socialist Babeufs of the French Revolution, burning with class resentment, Shays appeared a lukewarm "petit-bourgeois," interested only in preserving his land. Eager to advance themselves, the insurgents were "small capitalists in the American backwoods," Lockean liberals all, as fully the products of a free, middle-class society as their opponents in Boston. That was, in fact, the source of their strength. "When the Massachusetts radicals frightened the nation," Hartz pronounced, "they did so in the mood of unhappy kindred spir-

[40] Feer, "Shays' Rebellion," chaps. 1–2, esp. pp. 64–67, 69, 73–74.

[41] Ibid., pp. 201, 227, 524.

its, not in the mood of wholesale antagonists. They were inside, rather than outside, the liberal process of American politics." [42]

Downgraded to a petty, needless quarrel among a people united on liberal principles, what remained of Shays's Rebellion? For Starkey, as for Forrest McDonald, the Massachusetts insurrection was significant only for its unanticipated effect—hastening the movement for national government under the Constitution. But even that claim was challenged by Robert Feer, in a brief essay that downplayed the importance of the subject to which he had devoted his graduate career. Had Shays's Rebellion, he asked, been indispensable to the writing or adoption of the Constitution? Not at all. The leading Federalists—Washington, Alexander Hamilton, John Jay, James Madison—were convinced of the imperative to strengthen the national government long before the Massachusetts crisis; plans for the Philadelphia Convention were well underway before the first courts were closed in the commonwealth; the Founding Fathers only occasionally had the insurrection on their minds when they drew up the new frame of government, and the few who did worry out loud about the event were as likely to oppose the Constitution as not; even in Massachusetts, few people were terrified by the insurgency into supporting ratification. Shays's Rebellion, Feer concluded, had been a great bugbear of politics, frightening only to feeble spirits. "In all likelihood, the Constitutional Convention would have met when it did, the same document would have been drawn up, and it would have been ratified even if Shays's Rebellion had not taken place." [43]

By the time consensus historians were done, the Massachusetts insurgency had become an event of little significance, a minor incident that had gotten out of hand owing to the incompetence of politicians and later manufactured into a major crisis by credulous, overdramatic writers. Put in its proper place, Shays's Rebellion was a passing matter for local stu-

[42] Louis Hartz, *The Liberal Tradition in America: An Interpretation of American Political Thought since the Revolution* (New York, 1955), pp. 70–78.

[43] Robert A. Feer, "Shays's Rebellion and the Constitution: A Study in Causation," *New England Quarterly* 42 (1969):388–410.

dents of Massachusetts; it hardly deserved notice by serious historians of the nation. No one said so directly, but just about everyone got the message. For two decades, Shays's Rebellion fell out of mainstream historiography. To be sure, old-line Progressives such as Merrill Jensen and his students continued to insist upon the centrality of socioeconomic conflict between "mercantile-creditors" and agrarian debtors at the nation's start, as evidenced in the Massachusetts insurrection. Farther to the left, in an account of the *Early Years of the Republic* (1976) that reiterated the themes of the 1930s, Herbert Aptheker gave extended attention to the popular uprising that threatened the consolidation of the "bourgeois-democratic" Revolution under the patriot elite: "This rebellion was clearly one of class versus class—of poor versus rich and specifically of the debtors against the creditors." But for the most part the consensus school prevailed. Through the 1960s and early 1970s, even such critical historians as Gordon Wood agreed upon the essential irrelevancy of Shays's Rebellion to the constitutional and ideological struggles of the new republic.[44]

The dismissal of the insurgency as a sideshow in the Revo-

[44] Merrill Jensen, *The New Nation: A History of the United States during the Confederation, 1781–1789* (New York, 1950), pp. 307–12; Jackson Turner Main, *The Anti-Federalists: Critics of the Constitution, 1781–1788* (Chapel Hill, 1961), pp. 59–63; Herbert Aptheker, *Early Years of the Republic: From the End of the Revolution to the First Administration of Washington (1783–1793)* (New York, 1976), pp. 35–38, 142–47; Gordon S. Wood, *The Creation of the American Republic, 1776–1787* (Chapel Hill, 1969), pp. 412–13. Wood writes: "Shays's Rebellion was irrelevant to the major constitutional difficulty experienced in the Confederation period—the problem of legal tyranny, the usurpation of private rights under constitutional cover." By these terms, one might argue just the opposite. Shays's Rebellion posed the problem of how a supposedly representative government under a popularly written and ratified Constitution could so alienate a vast body of constituents as to push them into armed rebellion. Moreover, as Wood observes, in the aftermath of the insurgency the defeated rebels and their sympathizers turned to the ballot box and gained the power to effect their ends through the legislature in an assertion of the same "popular despotism" that was alarming elites throughout the states. See J. R. Pole, *Political Representation in England and the Origins of the American Republic* (Berkeley, Calif., 1966), pp. 226–44.

lution could not last. With the rise of a New Left and the revival of radical history from the mid-1960s on, writers one again heralded the dissenting voices in the American past. Shays's Rebellion came back in fashion. This time, however, scholars did more than champion the farmers' cause, though they certainly sympathized with popular grievances. Hemlock history was not yet dead. In its revitalized form, it embraced fresh disciples of the Progressives and young radicals on the New Left, allied in a concentrated assault upon the onetime mavericks of consensus who had become the reigning establishment. As in earlier debates with the past, the revolt of the young claimed to stake out new ground, but in key respects the rising generation followed in the direction of the elders they meant to reject.

The first object was to place socioeconomic conflict back at the center of American politics. Merrill Jensen had never abandoned that approach to the Revolutionary era, and at the University of Wisconsin he trained a generation of students in his own version of the Progressive paradigm. Employing the latest techniques of quantitative history, these scholars analyzed the records of the states, notably, roll call votes in the legislatures, and tallied them against social profiles of assemblymen and the communities they represented. The result was a remarkable map of the political landscape that refuted the case for consensus. Back in 1944 Oscar Handlin had launched the break with Progressive history by challenging the idea of continuous "radical" and "conservative" parties in Massachusetts, rooted in social divisions, throughout the long era of resistance, revolution, and Independence (1765–95). Set against the hard data of Jensen's students, the image of fluid politics in a changing state was credible no more. Contrary to Handlin, the splits in Massachusetts politics after Independence were of long standing, and they revealed a *systematic* division between competing blocs of communities dating back to the late colonial era. The dominant party included the most "commercial-cosmopolitan" places—eastern ports, river towns, farming districts near urban centers—all intimately involved in trade and the wider world, all notable for considerable economic inequality and social diversity within. Its "localist" adversary stood at the opposite end of the spectrum. The least-developed towns were small agrarian outposts, distant from markets, isolated from newspapers, lawyers, and cosmopolitan culture, but egalitarian and homogeneous within. Between these two poles were a good many towns whose leanings were less predictable but more often than not were won over to the "commercial-cosmopolitan" side—especially when their representatives were justices of the peace tied in to the patronage network of the state. This alignment of forces endured over a great many issues, including mobilization against Britain, the adoption of a state constitution, the treatment of loyalists, and the postwar policies on money and taxes. The pertinacity of Massachusetts voters was stunning. Leaders in politics and trade might come and go through the changing times, but the fundamental divisions of the state remained the same. Socioeconomic differences drove politics, as the Progressives had always said.[45]

The great appeal of the new scholarship is that it enriched the social analysis of Revolutionary politics. The standard categories of the Progressives had always seemed thin—merchants versus farmers, creditors versus debtors, east versus west. Without muting these distinctions, the work of Van Beck Hall, Jackson Turner Main, and Stephen E. Patterson added considerable depth. In the arena of politics people did not merely defend or assert material interests born of wealth and occupation, though they certainly did that. They also expressed the worldviews—the inherited cultures and the explicit beliefs—that stemmed from geography and class. Pursuing this insight, Jensen's students portrayed a sharp ideological divide within the republican "consensus." Lo-

[45] Van Beck Hall, *Politics without Parties: Massachusetts, 1780–1791* (Pittsburgh, 1972); Jackson Turner Main, *Political Parties before the Constitution* (Chapel Hill, 1973); Stephen E. Patterson, *Political Parties in Revolutionary Massachusetts* (Madison, Wis., 1973). Jensen disdained the category "Progressive history" on the ground that it lumped together historians of disparate political views and then distracted scholars from close reading of texts. I share his discomfort with labels but think he does fit into a well-established school of thought (Merrill Jensen, *The American Revolution within America* [New York, 1974], pp. 221–24).

calists, not surprisingly, insisted upon government close to home; suspicious of "high-flyers" in the capital, hostile to social difference without and within, these communities struggled to preserve familiar agrarian ways. Their rivals in the commercial entrepôts were, by contrast, the self-styled sophisticates of the eighteenth century, comfortable with gentility, tolerant of difference, acutely conscious of status and rank; for them, government belonged in the hands of the "better sort," entrusted by their inferiors to manage affairs for the common good. Such contrasting mentalities ran through the fights of the 1780s over money, taxes, courts, and constitutions. They formed perceptions of issues, sustained alliances, and shaped the very language of politics. Behind the patterns of politics lay the contours of culture.

It was out of this broad concern with culture that the latest, full-scale assessment of Shays's Rebellion by a historian on the left has emerged. In *Shays' Rebellion* (1980), the first monograph since Starkey, David Szatmary reinterpreted the insurrection from a perspective that fused politics with the "new social history," as practiced on both sides of the Atlantic. Following the pioneering models of such English scholars as E. P. Thompson and Eric Hobsbawm, he sought to place the contending parties in the Massachusetts crisis in the context of their social-cultural worlds. For Szatmary, Friends of Government and insurgents were products of competing ways of life. In the seats of power were the aggressive representatives of an advancing, "acquisitive, individualistic" world of commerce. Arrayed against them stood the besieged hosts of "a largely subsistence, family-based, community-oriented culture of independent farmers." The violent clash between the two forces, Szatmary argued, registered "the tumultuous effects of the transition from traditional society to merchant capitalism."[46]

Coercive capitalism, on one side; cooperative communalism, on the other: Szatmary's analysis recalled the terms of the 1930s but with a crucial difference. He went beyond the familiar distinction between merchants and farmers to ex-

---

[46] Szatmary, *Shays' Rebellion*, pp. xiv, 37.

337

plore the dynamics of their competing systems. His work drew heavily on recent studies of rural *mentalité* in early New England, entangling *Shays' Rebellion* in a developing controversy over the character of preindustrial agriculture. The economy of the backcountry, Szatmary maintained, was geared to the needs and the preferences of households and communities. Farmers neither specialized in cash crops for market nor engaged in trade for profit. They raised a variety of produce and livestock for annual subsistence, with a small surplus for exchange; when they did swap with neighbors or buy from storekeepers, money seldom changed hands, accounts were irregularly settled, and interest never accumulated on unpaid bills. Such practices were not simply adaptations to necessity, such as the scarcity of labor, capital, or cash; rather, in Szatmary's view, they affirmed the deliberate choices of backcountry people for a neighborly, noncompetitive way of life. Sustaining the independence of landowners in an interdependent community, the household economy offered an alternative to capitalism in the countryside.[47]

Now enter the advancing agent of the marketplace, the country storekeepers. Driven to expand sales, merchants moved into the backcountry with imported manufactures and fancy items and gradually enmeshed farmers in commercial exchange. The techniques were simple—offering easy credits, accepting farm goods in payment, encouraging surplus production. Soon the yeomanry was "increasingly being dragged into the marketplace" and obliged to deal with an antithetical culture. Merchants traded for personal gain, not reciprocal advantage, according to Szatmary; they prized money and profit as ends in themselves. When necessary, they put their own survival over all else. Thus it was that in 1784–86 an international credit crunch, emanating from

[47] Ibid., pp. 1–18; Michael Merrill, "Cash Is Good to Eat: Self-Sufficiency and Exchange in the Rural Economy of the United States," *Radical History Review* 4 (1977):42–71; James A. Henretta, "Families and Farms: *Mentalité* in Pre-Industrial America," *William and Mary Quarterly*, 3d ser. 35 (1978):3–32. For a recent review of the debate, see Allan Kulikoff, "The Transition to Capitalism in Rural America," *William and Mary Quarterly*, 3d ser. 46 (1989):120–44.

London, set off the crisis that culminated in Shays's Rebellion. Alarmed at excessive imports by American merchants, British wholesalers suddenly demanded payment of outstanding bills, triggering a chain reaction of debt collections throughout New England, with coastal merchants suing rural storekeepers, who, in turn, called on their country customers to settle accounts—but now *in cash,* not farm goods. With little coin in circulation and "oppressive" taxes upon them, rural people had no means to pay. The result was the wave of suits for debt, imprisonments, and foreclosures that swirled through the countryside, touching, by Szatmary's count, two-thirds of the men who joined the insurgents and arousing widespread fears that the independent yeomanry would soon descend into tenancy. That dread of "lordships," rooted in the communal culture of the yeomanry, was the springboard for the insurrection.[48]

Indeed, the culture of the countryside shaped the very organization of resistance. In the first sustained analysis of the rank-and-file insurgents, drawn from the lists of men receiving pardons from the state, Szatmary found that theirs was an inclusive movement, embracing farmers, artisans, and laborers, long accustomed to helping one another out. Close ties of kinship bound them together; fathers and sons, brothers and cousins marched to close the courts. Initially, according to Szatmary, they wanted limited reform—a suspension of debt suits—within the traditional system. But in the face of an unresponsive, repressive government, the insurgents moved to radical, then revolutionary goals. By the attack on the Springfield Armory, the Shaysites had burst the bounds of republican consensus.[49]

The turn to cultural analysis not only illuminated the mental world of the two parties, it also explained why their violent conflict was "almost inevitable." Szatmary endorsed the notion of consensus historians that the Massachusetts crisis arose from failures of communication. But the misperceptions, he noted, were *systemic,* not accidental; they reflected the opposing systems of thought and action in which the adversaries

[48] Szatmary, *Shays' Rebellion,* pp. 10–36, 66–67 (quotation p. 17).

[49] Ibid., pp. 60–63, 91–98.

were enmeshed. Merchants and farmers were strangers to one another, locked into mutual incomprehension by competing interests and contrary cultures. Committed to the absolute sanctity of contracts, as enforced through the remorseless machinery of the courts, the merchants and magistrates could not tolerate the farmers' demands for economic relief. Nor could they admit the legitimacy of the protests. "From their market perspective," Szatmary wrote, "the commercial and professional elite equated reformist objectives, militarily pursued, with radical attacks upon ordered society." Misreading the rural mood, the men in power detected a conspiracy to overturn the state and then, by resorting to repression, produced the very movement they feared. The dynamics of "the two worlds of New England" spawned a self-fulfilling prophecy.[50]

Szatmary's emphasis upon systems in conflict was a welcome alternative to earlier approaches. On the one hand, he could explain the clash between merchants and farmers on *impersonal* grounds; no conspiracies were required. On the other hand, he could allow for misunderstandings on both sides without trivializing the insurgency as an accident that need not have happened. He was the first scholar to place the debt crisis of the mid-1780s in a detailed, international context; he widened the panorama of the insurrection as well, noting that the disorders in western Massachusetts were part of a larger pattern of rural unrest in the new republic. Standing above the fray, with a detached perspective on both sides, Szatmary promised the first full account of Shays's Rebellion that had neither heroes nor villains. But that was not to be. For all the language of social analysis, all the talk of competing cultures, Szatmary was no less a Hemlock than his predecessors. He continued to treat the insurgents as brave veterans of the Revolution while stressing the antipopular sentiments of the patriot governing class; overlooked were the apathy and loyalism of many common folk before 1776 and their early war-weariness thereafter. Even more, Szatmary biased the story against the merchants. Where backcountry people joined in voluntary cooperation, the lords of trade invariably

[50] Ibid., pp. 37, 70–76.

turned to harsh coercion. Farmers *opted* for self-sufficiency; they were *dragged* into the market. The insurgency was a neighborly protest movement, something of a military husking bee. By contrast, the state army, financed by rich merchants, was manned by unwilling volunteers, the sons and servants of the elite, dispatched to do their masters' bidding. Szatmary skipped over equivalent evidence of hierarchy and community pressure on the rebels' side. By such invidious comparisons, the contrast between cultures fell into special pleading. The insurgents, it appeared, enjoyed not only a better case but a morally superior way of life.[51]

Even more, Szatmary opened up the social history of Shays's Rebellion only to constrict understanding of town and country alike. His categories of "traditional society" and modern merchant capitalism reified both. He exaggerated the isolation of backcountry people from markets and underplayed their ample desires for consumer goods. His yeomen were so economically self-sufficient that it is difficult to comprehend why they proved vulnerable to debt collections in 1784–86. Furthermore, neither the rural communities nor the towns were as united in the crisis as Szatmary indicated. Accepting the polarized rhetoric of the day, he overlooked the many people in the countryside who harbored grievances against Boston but declined to close courts or take up arms, and the considerable numbers in trading centers who condemned the riots but disdained the vindictive measures of government as well. Even in the legislature, a good number of representatives proved willing to forgo the logic of competitive capitalism and grant short-term relief from taxes and debts. Indeed, in the interest of avoiding confrontations with debtors, the commercial elites in other states accepted temporizing measures. Why did the merchants and magistrates of Massachusetts lack such wisdom? An emphasis upon competing

[51] In his view of the Regulation as part of a larger story of agrarian rebellion, Szatmary was following the lead of Barbara Karsky, whose essay anticipated his analysis in important ways. See Karsky, "Agrarian Radicalism in the Late Revolutionary Period (1780–1795)," in Erich Angermann, Marie-Luise Frings, and Hermann Wellenreuther, eds., *New Wine in Old Skins: A Comparative View of Socio-Political Structures and Values Affecting the American Revolution* (Stuttgart, 1976), pp. 87–114.

cultures cannot resolve these problems of political choice. Without personalizing politics, we still need to know how and why diverse individuals and groups, in a variety of social and economic settings, reached their positions when debate turned to action and men got ready for battle in late January 1787—or perhaps took no stand at all.

With Szatmary, then, the social history of Shays's Rebellion ended in a recapitulation of conventional wisdom on the left. Nearly two hundred years after the event, the categories of Hemlocks and White Hats carried the day. Consensus historians still repeated George Minot's sophisticated justification for government. Progressives and their successors continued to insist upon the oppressions of government and the legitimacy of the farmers' revolt. Each generation's interpretation bore a heavy burden from the past. Torn between a close-up on individual leaders and a panorama of impersonal conflict, stuck with an incomplete picture of economy and society in the Revolutionary era, historians groped for an understanding of the Massachusetts crisis and its larger significance for New England and the nation as a whole.

On the eve of the bicentennial of Shays's Rebellion, the central problem for historians remained the same ideological dilemma that had confronted George Minot and his contemporaries—how to reconcile the uprising with the myth of the Revolution? Consensus historians admitted Shaysites and Friends of Government equally into the whig pantheon; scholars on the left continued to insist that the authentic meaning of the Revolution—the promise of democracy and equality—resided with the rebels. But after two hundred years such commitments had become mere badges of identity, with little persuasive power. They were also at odds with emerging directions in the scholarship. At long last, historians have begun to acknowledge the complexity of the Massachusetts crisis and to explore its origins in a changing society and culture. No longer do the citizens of Massachusetts divide into two starkly polarized camps; seen in their local communities, where the contest of loyalties was waged, the participants adopt a variety of stances, depending not only on their economic situations but also on their religious outlook, political inclinations, wartime experiences, relations with neighbors, and connections with the wider world. In this framework, no group in 1786–87 wears the true colors of the Revolution. The self-consciously republican magistrates in Boston were divided in sentiment, committed to the ideal of an activist citizenry, yet expecting deference from common folk. Contradictions abounded in the countryside as well. In some places, men with huge debts, perched on the edge of bankruptcy, enlisted in the government army; in others, local creditors, faithful to their neighbors, joined the insurgency. Nowhere was this a simple fight between veterans who had fought the war and lost the peace and civilians who had stayed at home and profited in speculation and trade. Even in the hill town of Pelham, where Daniel Shays had his home, the ranks of the Regulators were filled with boys in their teens, who had been too young to enlist in the Continental forces.

Indeed, many inhabitants of the backcountry had been latecomers to the Revolutionary struggle, joining the patriot movement only in 1774–75 when the royal government threatened the independence of their towns. Once that immediate danger dissolved they proved to be "summer soldiers and sunshine patriots," grumbling about the costs of war even as some benefited from cheap money and expanding trade. On all sides there were adventurers and confidence men, eager to remake themselves in the contest for power. It was an age of fluid loyalties and unstable identities. Having abandoned allegiance to one sovereign, many people were prepared to calculate their commitment to another. In a dispersed, rural society, where people enacted their lives in local settings but freely moved about from place to place in search of opportunity, political attachments were flexible, easily made and just as easily dropped. Ethan Allen's Vermont, carved out of New Hampshire and New York in the turbulence of the Revolution, provided a model for restless settlers on the frontiers of every state. It is thus quite plausible that a delegation of Shaysites did secretly negotiate with the British governor-general in Canada, in hopes of obtaining their goals. And why not? Feeling betrayed by one set of rulers, they may have sought support from another with no more compunction than did the Continental Congress in forging its alliance with France.[52]

In the late twentieth century, an era of rising nationalisms and crumbling empires, we are suddenly witnesses to a dramatic upheaval of the geopolitical landscape and in the hearts and minds of the world's peoples, a historic moment not unlike the Revolutionary era of Daniel Shays. That experience may perhaps enable us to stand back from the "commotions" of Massachusetts and the new republic two centuries ago and sympathize with all parties to that dispute. If there are many ways to imagine political community, then surely the inhabitants of the new commonwealth were entitled to contest the terms of their post-Revolutionary order. To demand that they remain true to the spirit of 1776, as historians have repeatedly done, is to impose the teleology of American mission upon the past.

That was precisely what the earliest historians of the Revolution intended. Writing in the 1780s and 1790s, patriot intellectuals were appalled by the avarice, expediency, and corruption of the contemporary scene, including, of course, Shays's Rebellion. Against their hopes for a virtuous republic, they weighed the "licentiousness" of the rising generation; from that contrast developed the intellectual strategy that shaped their representation of the Revolution. Determined to teach morality by example, they invented a movement for Independence that never was—unified from the start, devoted to republican principle throughout, intent on preserving a simple, frugal existence of well-ordered liberty. No matter that many colonists were faint at heart, that they craved compromise with England up to the very end, that thousands became loyalists and many others neutrals in the war, that new men of wealth climbed to power in the crisis, that popular mobs revenged private as well as public wrongs, in short, that all the vices of which the historians complained were amply displayed in the two decades from 1765 to 1788. Such evidence was suppressed in the interests of the morality

[52] See the essays in Robert A. Gross, ed., *In Debt to Shays: The Bicentennial of an Agrarian Rebellion* (Charlottesville, Va., 1993), and Daniel Shelton, "'Elementary Feelings': Pelham, Massachusetts in Rebellion," senior honors thesis, Amherst College, 1986.

tale. The resulting fabrication was coherent, compelling, and enduring. Within its terms, the reputation of Shays's Rebellion would be debated for two centuries. The irony is that the political struggle in Massachusetts—to patriot historians, one of the disturbing signs of the times—contributed to the very myth of the Revolution in which it would long be encased. Born in fluid, ambiguous circumstances, the uprising became in defeat a fixture of the American heritage, forced to play its part in competing versions of the national saga. If that role has finally come to an end, its longevity will nonetheless always serve as a marker in our cultural history. In Shays's Rebellion we come to realize the truth of John Adams's familiar judgment on the entire era: the real American Revolution lay in the hearts and minds of the people.[53]

[53] Cohen, "Creating a Usable Future," pp. 309–27.

ALFRED F. YOUNG

American Historians
Confront
"The Transforming
Hand
of Revolution"

In AUGUST 1926 Charles A. Beard published an enthusiastic review of John Franklin Jameson's book *The American Revolution Considered as a Social Movement.* Jameson sent him a warm letter of appreciation and clarification, and Beard responded with even more lavish praise.[1] The exchange is a convenient point from which to launch an inquiry into the achievement of Jameson in the context of the scholarship of his day, the remarkable durability of his little book of four lectures, and

I wish to thank Ronald Hoffman, Jesse Lemisch, and Gary B. Nash for their astute critical comments on the manuscript; Staughton Lynd, Jackson Turner Main, Morey D. Rothberg, and Peter H. Wood who read sections of it, correcting my errors and adding to my knowledge; Paul Buhle, Edward Countryman, Stephen Foster, Mary Furner, John Kaminski, Pauline Maier, Peter Novick, Ellen Schrecker, and James M. Smith who answered my queries; and James A. Henretta who criticized an early version. Peter J. Albert edited the manuscript with consummate skill and infinite patience. I alone am responsible for the interpretations advanced.

[1] J. Franklin Jameson to Charles A. Beard, Aug. 10, 1926, and Beard to Jameson, Aug. 14, 1926, in Elizabeth Donnan and Leo F. Stock, eds., *An Historian's World: Selections from the Correspondence of John Franklin Jameson* (Philadelphia, 1956), pp. 319–20. Jameson's book was published by Princeton University Press.

the way American historians have dealt with the Jameson thesis and the larger, still unresolved issue of what Jameson called "the transforming hand of revolution." Beard has since been battered and some would say buried, but his ghost still haunts historical studies, and were he to appear he might be tempted to borrow the comment John Adams made about Thomas Jefferson from his deathbed, on July 4, 1826, when he was told that Jefferson who also lay dying was still alive: "J. Franklin Jameson still survives."

In 1950, when a historian published the results of a poll of 103 scholars (drawn from "an approximate cross section of the profession") as to the ten "best" works in American history published between 1920 and 1935, Jameson's book came in fourteenth with 26 votes. At the head of the list were Vernon Louis Parrington's *Main Currents in American Thought* (84 votes), Frederick Jackson Turner's collection of essays on the frontier (83), followed by Charles and Mary R. Beard's *Rise of American Civilization* (58), Carl L. Becker's *Declaration of Independence* (51), and Arthur M. Schlesinger, Sr.'s, *New Viewpoints in American History* (32). Jameson clearly held a place on the hit parade of Progressive historians. Counterprogressive "consensus" history was only a cloud on the historical horizon.[2]

Four years later Frederick B. Tolles, in a full-dress revaluation of Jameson's book in the *American Historical Review,* summarized the serious challenges to Jameson's hypotheses but concluded that "basically the 'Jameson thesis' is still sound, and what is more important, still vital and suggestive, capable of further life, still greater usefulness." The tide, however, was already turning. Edmund S. Morgan, in what became the most influential short work of synthesis on the American Revolution, *The Birth of the Republic* (1956), recognized Jameson's "influential essays" as a book that "helped focus attention on the internal conflicts that accompany such changes" as the American Revolution. But he was convinced there was "no

---

[2]John W. Caughey, "Historians' Choice: Results of a Poll on Recently Published American History and Biography," *Mississippi Valley Historical Review* 39 (1952):293, 299.

radical rebuilding of social institutions at this time," the Revolution bringing only "a host of incalculable, accidental, and incidental changes in society." A decade later Jack P. Greene pronounced the Progressive interpretation of the Revolution associated with Beard, Becker, Schlesinger, Sr., and presumably Jameson, "shattered and deeply discredited."[3]

Scholars continued to pay deference to Jameson, however, even as they substituted alternative syntheses of the Revolution. Gordon S. Wood called Jameson "the starting point for appreciating the social changes of the Revolution." James A. Henretta thought the book "remains a good summary of the social changes of the revolutionary era." In 1987 Richard B. Morris, one of the few senior historians who kept the door open to the Jameson thesis in the 1960s, summed up his own reflections on social change in the era by entitling a chapter in his last book "A Cautiously Transforming Egalitarianism." Greene in the late 1980s paid Jameson the ultimate homage by devoting a conference to defining the "limits" of change in the Revolutionary era.[4]

Jameson's thesis was diffused and widely accepted (1920s-50s), then rejected (1950-60s), and finally revived in very different guise (1960s-90s). "In the last quarter century," Linda K. Kerber wrote in 1990, "responding in part to the pressing questions of our own time, a new generation of historians have offered their own rich interpretations of the experience of the revolutionary generation." This new research "has tended to restore *rebellion* to histories of the American Revolution" by dealing with "the ways in which marginal people—

---

[3] Frederick B. Tolles, "The American Revolution Considered as a Social Movement: A Re-Evaluation," *American Historical Review* 60 (1954):1–12; Edmund S. Morgan, *The Birth of the Republic, 1763–1789* (Chicago, 1956), pp. 96, 98; Jack P. Greene, *The Reappraisal of the American Revolution in Recent Historical Literature* (Washington, D.C., 1967); Greene, ed., *The Reinterpretation of the American Revolution, 1763–1789* (New York, 1968), introduction.

[4] Bernard Bailyn et al., *The Great Republic: A History of the American People* (New York, 1977); James A. Henretta et al., *America's History* (Chicago, 1987), p. 207; Richard B. Morris, *The Forging of the Union, 1781–1789* (New York, 1987), chap. 7; Jack P. Greene, ed., *The American Revolution: Its Character and Limits* (New York, 1987), pp. 1–13.

blacks, women, the impoverished—shaped the revolution and were in turn affected by it." To this list others would add farmers, middling artisans, and American Indians. Historians, she writes, have also developed "broader conceptualizations of political ideology." What unites this diverse scholarship is an appreciation of "the radicalism—both social and intellectual—of the American Revolution."[5]

As a consequence, the issue of "the transforming hand of revolution"—Jameson's provocative concept—after a long exile has been restored to a central place in the historiography of the era. An examination of how historians have dealt with a single historian may be of value if it takes us to the heart of this larger issue his scholarship raised, the extent to which the American Revolution was a transforming event. It also sheds light on how a historian, in Edmund Morgan's words, "may reflect, however remotely, the needs of his time."[6]

In this essay I propose first, to summarize the Jameson thesis; second, to locate and analyze Jameson's achievement and limitations in the context of the scholarship of his own time; and third, to analyze the way successive schools of historical interpretation have considered the thesis. In the course of this discussion I will take up the alternative ways in which historians have dealt with the larger question of transformation in the American Revolution, which alone justifies such a long voyage through twentieth-century historiography.

I. THE JAMESON THESIS: THE TEXT

The Jameson thesis is disarming in its simplicity, as is the form of the book: four short lectures, no more than thirty thousand words, the equivalent today of a hefty journal article, without notes, without a bibliographic essay, and with only a hint

[5] Linda K. Kerber, "The Revolutionary Generation: Ideology, Politics, and Culture in the Early Republic," in Eric Foner, ed., *The New American History* (Philadelphia, 1992), pp. 25–49, citations at pp. 26, 44.

[6] Edmund S. Morgan, *The Challenge of the American Revolution* (New York, 1976), p. x.

within the text as to the evidence he was drawing on. Delivered as lectures at Princeton in 1925, published the next year by Princeton University Press, it was something that only Jameson at age sixty-six, "the wise and honored elder statesman of the historical profession," as John Higham has called him, could get away with.[7]

The American Revolution, Jameson argued, was "a political revolution" that had "social consequences." This was the gist of the thesis. It was "vain to think of the Revolution as solely a series of political or military events." The Revolution began one way and ended another. At no point did Jameson claim there was either "a social revolution," "a revolution within," or an "internal revolution"—these were the phrases of later scholars. He argued by metaphors heavy with physical analogies. The Revolution was "a stream." "But who can say to the waves of revolution: Thus far shall we go and no farther. . . . The stream of revolution, once started, could not be confined within narrow banks, but spread abroad upon the land. Many economic desires, many social aspirations were set free by the political struggle, many aspects of colonial society profoundly altered by the forces thus let loose." This was perhaps his fullest statement of his overall thesis.[8]

He expressed his underlying assumption in another analogy: "The various fibres of a nation's life are knit together in great complexity. It is impossible to sever some without loosening others, and setting them free to combine anew in widely different forms." He also offered the physical analogy of heat. "Whatever . . . was outgrown or exotic seemed to be thrown into the melting-pot, to be recast into a form better suited to the work which the new nation had before it. The hot sun of revolution withered whatever was not deeply rooted in the soil."[9]

Mystical as these analogies seem at first glance, they represented Jameson's quest for a vocabulary to express an analysis

[7] J. Franklin Jameson, *The American Revolution Considered as a Social Movement* (1926; reprint ed., Boston, 1956); John Higham, *History: The Development of Historical Studies in the United States* (Englewood Cliffs, N.J., 1965).

[8] Jameson, *American Revolution as a Social Movement*, pp. 8, 26, 9.

[9] Ibid., pp. 9, 32.

of a process of revolution that did not exist outside the framework of Marxism. He posited generic stages in revolution, and while the physical analogy of the stream overrunning its banks seemed to deny agency, he left no doubt that different groups of people moved revolutions from one stage to another. "Therefore the social consequences of a revolution are not necessarily shaped by the conscious or unconscious desires of those who started it, but more likely by the desires of those who came into control of it at later stages of its development. . . . Certain it is that, in some of our states at least, it [the American Revolution] fell ultimately into quite other hands than those that set it in motion." He then asked "who were in favor of the Revolution, and who were against it?" offering a short analysis that took into account class, occupation, race, nationality, and age. "The strength of the revolutionary party," he concluded, "lay most largely in the plain people, as distinguished from the aristocracy. It lay not in the mob or rabble" of the cities "but in the peasantry, substantial and energetic though poor, in the small farmers and frontiersmen."[10]

After devoting most of his first lecture, "The Revolution and the Status of Persons," to sketching these broad outlines of his thesis, Jameson devoted a few pages to the political changes that brought social change, in particular the suffrage that he believed was "much extended" and led to the elevation of voters "in their social status" and a decline of deference. He then devoted the remainder of his attention to slavery as an issue, focusing on the growth of antislavery sentiment among whites that led after the war to emancipation in the northern states, individual acts of manumission in the South, and the checking of slave importation. His emphasis was on the "leaven" of the Revolution leading to "very substantial progress."[11]

Jameson's second lecture was on "The Revolution and the Land," which he summed up as "the freeing of the soil from all connection with the feudal land-law, the breaking up of large estates, [and] the universal extension, in the North at

[10] Ibid., pp. 12, 18.

[11] Ibid., pp. 18–19, 25–26.

least, of that system of small or moderate farms, cultivated by the owner's own hands." In his judgment "we may properly give a place of great prominence to the land" because "political democracy came to the United States as a result of economic democracy."[12]

Jameson devoted his third lecture, "Industry and Commerce," using "industry" in the broad sense of productive economic activity, to the ways in which the stimulus of war and the liberating effects of Independence benefited agriculture, manufactures, and maritime trade. He considered the war not as a disruption; for most Americans "industrial life went on during these seven years . . . without cessation in its development." Farmers, "their minds . . . widened by the war," supported "much-needed" agricultural improvement societies. The prewar anti-importation movement and the war itself "called into existence or stimulated" a variety of manufactures and spurred household or domestic production as well. Maritime commerce was stimulated by privateering that overshadowed both the navy and commercial ventures. Independence provided a "release from fetters" that led to the opening of "new channels of trade." The only drawback to this litany of progress was the "weakness" of the Confederation government, which is why the architects of stronger federal government "found their best helpers among the commercial classes." The American Revolution, Jameson concluded, "brought ultimate benefit to the agriculture, the manufactures, and the commerce" of the nation.[13]

In his fourth and final lecture, a grab bag called "Thought and Feeling," Jameson attempted to suggest "the imponderable effects" of the Revolution "in the field of public opinion and popular emotion." Sketching the growth of humanitarian reform, nationalist feeling, and education, he devoted most of his attention to religion—the organization of denominations on a national basis and the disestablishment of church from state that made "religious freedom and equality . . . America's chief contribution to the world's civilization." Jameson closed the lecture and the book by mentioning the de-

[12] Ibid., pp. 49, 27, 29.

[13] Ibid., pp. 49, 51, 59, 69, 71, 73.

nominations of the future whose growth he suggested might be correlated with "the idea of the natural equality of all men." He offered it as an illustration of the underlying holistic assumption of the lectures: "The thesis that all the varied activities of men in the same country and period have intimate relations with each other, and that one cannot obtain a satisfactory view of any one of them by considering it apart from the others."[14]

II. THE JAMESON THESIS: THE CONTEXT

This was the thesis, deceptively simple in the lectures, simplified still further by any summary. On what scholarship was it based? Jameson provided no notes and made almost no internal references to scholars. He revealed some of his primary sources—European travelers' accounts, the letters of leaders, an occasional memoir or diary. But he gave no sign of having gone through any major bodies of sources; he offered examples but made no effort to pile proof on proof; his evidence was, in the best sense, impressionistic. And his erudition was clear. To understand what it was based on one must attempt an archaeology of the layers of his hitherto unpublished writing of the 1890s that the recent edition of his papers makes possible.[15]

What was it about Jameson's little book that inspired such admiration among so many scholars over so many decades? The exchange between Beard and Jameson helps to situate Jameson in the context of the scholarship of their time. Beard welcomed the book because it was "by one of the first scholars in America . . . a master of the older generation." It marked "the definitive close of the Bancroftian or romantic era" in scholarship that Beard had tried to deflate. The review, with the barbed caption "A Challenge to Windbags," was written

[14] Ibid., pp. 74, 90, 100.

[15] Morey D. Rothberg and Jacqueline Goggin, eds., *John Franklin Jameson and the Development of Humanistic Scholarship in the United States*, vol. 1, *Selected Essays* (Athens, Ga., 1993). Also see Morey Rothberg, "John Franklin Jameson and the Creation of *The American Revolution Considered as a Social Movement*," in this volume.

from outside the academy, appearing in the *New Republic*, the founding magazine of Progressive politics. Beard identified himself as among those who "have long been watching eagerly the flight of birds at the annual meetings of the American Historical Association hoping for new signs." He read each chapter as supporting his own economic interpretation. "The Status of Persons" was "a euphemistic title employed to cover the class arrangements of American society"; the "substance" of the business was economic; "the line-up of forces was essentially economic." In chapter 2—on the land system—Beard seized on Jameson's argument that "political democracy came to the United States as a result of economic democracy"; "the abundance of cheap land was the prime factor." Chapter 3 he saw as supporting a thesis of *An Economic Interpretation of the Constitution*. "The grooms of the sacred cow will not thank him for his page on privateering" nor for seeing that "the pathway to the creation of a firmer union led through considerations of commercial regulations." Only chapter 4—on humanitarian reform, ideas, and religion—Beard thought "shows how much hard preliminary work must be done before culture can be geared with economics and war." "A truly notable book" he concluded, "carefully organized, cut with a diamond point to a finish, studded with novel illustrative materials, gleaming with new illumination, serenely engaging in style, and sparingly garnished with genial humor."[16]

Jameson wrote to Beard to thank him—with one exception it was "the only serious review" he had seen—but he discreetly distanced himself from Beard. He was appreciative but clearly wanted to take up the insinuation that he was "a late convert to the economic interpretation of history." First of all, he wrote, "I will tell you confidentially that the four lectures only convey the substance of six that I gave to a small audience at Columbia University in 1895." His Princeton sponsors knew this; that was not the point. What struck Jameson as he set about revising his lectures of 1895 and surveyed

[16] Charles A. Beard, "A Challenge to Windbags," *New Republic*, Aug. 11, 1926, p. 344.

the books, dissertations, and articles published in the previous thirty years was "how little had been done to illuminate that period from the social and economic point of view—how little needed to be changed in my statements." Strictly speaking, this was not true, but he wanted Beard to know he had formulated his thesis long before the landmark monographs of Charles Henry Lincoln (1901), Becker (1909), Beard (1913), and Schlesinger (1918) had appeared. Secondly, Jameson resisted Beard's effort to pigeonhole him in a passage that has been echoed by countless scholars over the years. "There is some tendency to classify historical scholars particularly rigidly as of new and old schools, as if one must be distinctly of one school or the other and as if there had been a sharp transition, whereas I should think there has been a gradual one, and the new history does not seem so altogether new to me as many represent." [17]

In his reply Beard was mildly apologetic. "I quite understand how you feel about being driven into any particular corner, such as an economic interpretation, and it is far from my desire to drive anyone there." But he doubled his appreciation. "I wish that some rich man or wise college president (if such there be) had in 1895, when you first drafted these lectures, emancipated you from all routine work, freed your powers, and given you unlimited mechanical service and permitted you to devote your talent to the theme of the book. . . . If that had been done we should now have at least one great historical work in America lifted above 'was uns alle bandigt das Gemeine.'" He ended by agreeing "that there is a lot of embattled nonsense in the chatter about old schools and new." [18]

[17] Jameson to Beard, Aug. 10, 1926, in Donnan and Stock, eds., *Correspondence of Jameson*, pp. 319–20; Charles Henry Lincoln, *The Revolutionary Movement in Pennsylvania, 1760–1776* (Philadelphia, 1901); Robert Gough, "Charles H. Lincoln, Carl Becker, and the Origins of the Dual-Revolution Thesis," *William and Mary Quarterly*, 3d ser. 38 (1981):97–109.

[18] Beard to Jameson, Aug. 14, 1926, John Franklin Jameson Papers, box 59, Manuscript Division, Library of Congress. See Donnan and Stock, eds., *Correspondence of Jameson*, p. 320, for an excerpt. The only prior exchange between the two was in 1914 over a review Beard thought was marked by

Beard's reaction was based on who Jameson was and on the gulf between them. Beard, the iconoclast, had become the consummate gadfly. As author of *An Economic Interpretation of the Constitution* (1913), he had incurred the wrath of conservatives, including the trustees of Columbia University, who misread the book as have so many scholars since, as indicting the pocketbook motives of the Founding Fathers and questioning their sincerity and patriotism. In 1917 he had resigned from Columbia to protest the firing of two political opponents of the war from the faculty. In 1926, a gentleman farmer on his Connecticut dairy farm, he and his wife Mary Ritter Beard were in the final stages of their monumental two-volume *Rise of American Civilization* (1927), with its breathtaking, Olympian economic interpretation of the sweep of American history. A public intellectual, he published his review in the organ of the "new liberalism" to which he was a regular contributor.[19]

By contrast, Jameson (1859–1937) was, in 1926, at the peak of the American historical establishment he had helped bring into being. Recipient of the first Ph.D. in history from Johns Hopkins University in 1882, Jameson was a founder of the American Historical Association (AHA), its president in 1907, and managing editor of the *American Historical Review* from 1895 to 1901 and 1905 to 1928. After teaching for twenty-three years at Hopkins, Brown, and the University of Chicago, in 1905 Jameson became the second director of the Carnegie Institution's Bureau (later Department) of Historical Research in Washington. He would serve there for twenty-three years until 1928 (continuing as managing editor of the *American Historical Review*) and then would serve as chief of the manuscripts division at the Library of Congress until his death in 1937. Over his lifetime there was not a major

---

"personal animus" (Beard to Jameson, Oct. 8, 1914, Jameson to Beard, Oct. 10, 1914, Jameson Papers, box 279). Unpublished documents kindly provided by Morey Rothberg.

[19] Richard Hofstadter, *The Progressive Historians: Turner, Beard, Parrington*, (New York, 1968), chap. 6; for Beard's writings, see Howard K. Beale, ed., *Charles Beard: An Appraisal* (Lexington, Ky., 1954), pp. 265–86.

institutional historical project in American history—the *Dictionary of American Biography*, the National Historical Publications Commission, the National Archives—that did not bear his mark. He was Mr. History, a tall, dignified, somewhat austere man with a neatly trimmed beard who wore a winged collar.[20]

Professionalizing American history came at a price. As Peter Novick has demonstrated, Jameson "drove out the amateurs" with a vengeance. He not only "turned the profession over to academics"—as opposed to the patricians, antiquarians, and social scientists who had dominated it—but to two or three dozen professors in half a dozen elite universities in the Northeast who in 1907 could not even abide the founding of the Mississippi Valley Historical Association (now the Organization of American Historians).[21] Jameson managed the *American Historical Review* in an autocratic style and dominated the AHA to such an extent that he became a principal target of an insurgency in 1913–15 opposed to "an oligarchy" and "an Eastern establishment" and favoring a more democratic governance and ownership of the *Review* by the association. Jameson later fobbed off the rebellion as an "interesting tempest in a teapot," but at the time he devoted enormous energy to quelling it. Beginning in 1917, each summer for twenty years Jameson convened a private "convivium historicum" at a New England resort to set policy for the profession. He

---

[20] Higham, *History*, pp. 20–25. For a brief biography, see Richard Schrader, "J. Franklin Jameson," in Clyde N. Wilson, ed., *Twentieth-Century American Historians* (Detroit, 1983), pp. 236–40; for brief articles by fourteen contributors, see Ruth Anna Fisher and William Lloyd Fox, eds., *J. Franklin Jameson: A Tribute* (Washington, D.C., 1965); for a chronological bibliography of Jameson's writings by Donald Mugridge, see Fisher and Fox, eds., *Jameson Tribute*, pp. 103–37, expanded in Rothberg and Goggin, eds., *Selected Essays*, pp. 355–57; Morey D. Rothberg, "'To Set a Standard of Workmanship and Compel Men to Conform to It': John Franklin Jameson as Editor of the *American Historical Review*," *American Historical Review* 89 (1984):957–75.

[21] Peter Novick, *That Noble Dream: The "Objectivity Question" and the American Historical Profession* (Cambridge, 1988), pp. 183–85; Mary Furner, *Advocacy and Objectivity: A Crisis in the Professionalization of American Social Science, 1865–1905* (Lexington, Ky., 1975).

learned how to reform in order to conserve, a tactic a later AHA establishment would repeat in 1969 to quell a far more serious rebellion.[22]

Politically, Jameson was at first a mugwump, then a conservative Progressive in tune with Teddy Roosevelt and Woodrow Wilson, whom he especially admired. He was a Brahmin by adoption. His social values, captured by Morey D. Rothberg with exquisite skill, were those of a New England, Anglo-Saxon elitist; he was anxious in the 1880s about the hordes of working-class immigrants from southern and eastern Europe and fearful in the 1890s of the Populists as spokesmen for the "unintelligent farmers" (as he was of the Shaysites in the 1780s for their "plebeian" and "lawless insurrection").[23] He had a touch of genteel anti-Semitism and of noblesse oblige to Negroes. He published an article by W. E. B. DuBois in the *American Historical Review* in 1907 (the only article by a black to appear in that journal until John Hope Franklin's presidential address in the 1970s). But Jameson, the grandson of an abolitionist, was self-righteous when DuBois requested that he capitalize *Negro*.[24]

In his politics his brand of Progressivism was very different from Beard's, contrary to the facile critics of the 1950s who lumped historians of that era in a single Progressive political stereotype (even while scholars were rapidly revising it). If young Charles Beard taught workers' education courses in London, was a founder of the labor college Ruskin Hall, and campaigned in New York City for the Jewish socialist Morris

[22] Ray Allen Billington, "Tempest in Clio's Teapot: The American Historical Association's Rebellion of 1915," *American Historical Review* 78 (1973):348–69; Billington, *Frederick Jackson Turner: Historian, Scholar, Teacher* (New York, 1973), pp. 338–43; for the "convivium historicum," see Jameson to "Dear Colleague," Aug. 10, 1934, Jameson Papers. "This annual gathering of professors of history (taking place for the 18th time, I think) will be held. . . . This notice and invitation is sent to all 'full professors' of history in New England and adjacent parts."

[23] Rothberg and Goggin, eds., *Selected Essays*, pp. 29, 56–57, 227–28.

[24] Jameson to W. E. B. DuBois, July 22, 1910, Donnan and Stock, eds., *Correspondence of Jameson*, p. 133. But see August Meier and Elliott Rudwick, "J. Franklin Jameson, Carter G. Woodson, and the Foundations of Black Historiography," *American Historical Review* 89 (1974):1005–15.

Hillquit on the Lower East Side, young Jameson in Baltimore recoiled from the urban masses at political rallies and from a Jewish candidate he found loud and vulgar. If Beard brought down the wrath of Columbia's wealthy trustees for his iconoclasm, Jameson was appointed a department chairman at Chicago at a time when such appointments had to be acceptable to John D. Rockefeller and then became the head of a department in Andrew Carnegie's Institution and a fund-raiser par excellence among wealthy philanthropists. Jameson defended academic freedom at Brown.[25] But in World War I, while Beard supported both the war and the right to dissent from it, Jameson unabashedly fine-tuned the *American Historical Review* to patriotism. With other Progressives he enlisted in George Creel's Committee on Public Information where he was responsible for authenticating *The German Bolshevik Conspiracy,* "a pseudohistorical certification of manifestly forged documents."[26] Thus if Beard was in a wing of Progressivism "which shaded off into reformist socialism,"[27] Jameson was in the centralizing, professionalizing wing, reforming in order to conserve from threats of radicalism.

Yet Jameson was complex. He had an intellectual passion for social history that linked him to Beard and the "New History" of James Harvey Robinson. The terms *social* and *economic* were then used loosely; well into the twentieth century universities offered courses in the "social and economic history" of the United States or Medieval Europe. In graduate school Jameson was smitten with the European and English scholars who suggested the potential of the field, especially by Henry Thomas Buckle and Hippolyte Taine. In one of his first lectures as an instructor at Hopkins in 1885 he expressed his critique of conventional history in classical imagery: "Our political histories have for the most part been Iliads; they are filled with the deeds of chieftains . . . while the rest of the well-greaved Achaians stand in their ranks unnoticed and unsung." Later he would use the same passionate rhetoric of

[25] Morey D. Rothberg, "Striking a Blow for Academic Freedom in the 1890s . . . ," *Brown Alumni Monthly* 87 (May 1987):18–22, 29.

[26] Novick, *That Noble Dream,* pp. 64, 519, 521, quotation p. 124.

[27] Ibid., p. 96; Hofstadter, *Progressive Historians,* chap. 5.

others who discovered this gap: "No view is truthful that leaves out of account ideals which animated these toiling millions." There was no "paucity" of sources; he counseled a young scholar to do the history of "the less articulate classes" for colonial America.[28]

At Hopkins he took from Herbert Baxter Adams's seminars the canons of the new scientific history—mastery of the documents, analysis, presentation in scientific monographs or journal articles, and the eventual assembling of these "bricks" into works of synthesis. But he was impatient with Adams's "germ theory" of the evolution of American institutions from Germany and Anglo-Saxon England. He had arrived at a frontier interpretation of American history at about the same time as Frederick Jackson Turner. In fact, Jameson's unpublished lectures of 1885 and 1891 anticipated Turner's "Significance of the Frontier" paper of 1893, and his own 1895 lecture at Barnard, "The West in the American Revolution," was as rhapsodic about the influence of the frontier as anything Turner ever wrote. The timing suggests that Jameson, who left Hopkins in the fall of 1888, and Turner, who received his degree there in 1890, had developed their ideas concurrently. Jameson consistently was an admirer of Turner's "fruitful" mind and brought him into the inner circle of the AHA.[29]

Jameson's view of the American Revolution also owed much to the imperial school of historians taking shape in the 1890s in a mood of Anglo-American rapprochement that was consummated in World War I. Like them, he was steeped in En-

[28] J. Franklin Jameson, "An Introduction to the Study of the Constitutional and Political History of the States," in Rothberg and Goggin, eds., *Selected Essays*, pp. 18, 24; Jameson to Caroline Hazard, Oct. 8, 1926, Donnan and Stock, eds., *Correspondence of Jameson*, p. 320.

[29] J. Franklin Jameson, "Lectures on the Constitutional and Political History of the South" (1891), and Jameson, "The American Revolution as a Social Movement: Lectures on Slavery and the West" (1895), in Rothberg and Goggin, eds., *Selected Essays*, pp. 62–165, 203–30; for the origins of the frontier thesis, see Lee Benson, *Turner and Beard: American Historical Writing Reconsidered* (New York, 1960), parts 1 and 2; Billington, *Frederick Jackson Turner*, chap. 5.

glish and European history and cool to George Bancroft's patriot-charged narrative. The imperial scholars—George Louis Beer, Herbert L. Osgood, and later Charles M. Andrews and Lawrence Henry Gipson—were trying to look dispassionately at the Revolution from the vantage point of Britain and the loyalists. A major part of Jameson's first lecture in 1895 (given again in 1920 but abandoned in 1925) was devoted to rehabilitating the loyalists. In centering his attention on internal American developments, however, he clearly parted company with the imperial school.[30]

With the recent publication of Jameson's early lectures of 1885, 1890, and 1891, and the only two 1895 lectures at Barnard that have survived, it is possible to see how Jameson's prior scholarship fed into *The American Revolution as a Social Movement,* the name he originally gave to his 1895 lectures. The states provided the framework as he developed the constitutional and political history of the colonial and Revolutionary eras (1885), the history of political parties (1890), and a constitutional and political history of the South (1891). He began with constitutions and laws, but by 1891 he was dealing with the subjects that would become central in 1895—entail and primogeniture, the separation of church and state, the suffrage, land policy. He was also discovering intense political conflict. Massachusetts, he concluded, experienced "a social as well as a political revolution, new strata everywhere came to the surface." In Virginia he focused on the "radical reformers," looking through the lens of Jefferson's memoirs, at the disestablishment of the church and reforms of the land system. His studies of the South were suffused with a sense of class but strangely devoid of the presence of slavery. In his research, judging by internal evidence, he worked outward from politics into the society, not through any systematic investigation but through such sources as the diary of Devereux Jarrett or David Ramsay's contemporary history.[31]

[30] Morey Rothberg, introduction to Rothberg and Goggin, eds., *Selected Essays,* pp. xxvii–xlvii.

[31] Jameson, "American Revolution as a Social movement," ibid., pp. 203–30.

In 1895 his six lectures, built on this array of incompletely shaped essays on state polity and parties, moved squarely into social and economic history. For the next decade he seems to have done no new research on these topics. At Chicago (1901–5), where he taught graduate courses on the constitutions of the states and on political parties, he very likely embellished his earlier lectures, finding new examples. After 1905, in his new position at the Carnegie, he did no sustained research on the themes he began in the 1890s. But he now had a scholarly institution in which to fulfill his passion for social history.[32]

In 1907 he devoted his presidential address to the AHA to a plea to study religion for its potential to reach "the lives of out of the way communities or of inarticulate classes not represented in literature." "Millions have felt an interest in religion where thousands have felt an interest in literature or philosophy, in music or art."[33] In 1912 he made an ardent plea to the Carnegie trustees for the utility of social history. "What information regarding the past," he asked, "will be demanded by a socialized, probably in some sense socialistic America," using the term in the loose way contemporaries applied it to reform that expanded the role of government. The "drum and trumpet" historian "has his place." But "social and economic history will surely assume a greater place than political history. Where hitherto men have interrogated the past concerning the doings of generals and politicians, they will be more prone to interrogate it concerning"—and here he reeled of a list of topics that "the new history" was addressing—"the holdings of public and private land, the course of prices, the migration of settlers and of crop areas, the rise of trade unions, the development of new religions, the status of the negro, the advance of education or of missions, or of the spirit of toleration."[34]

At the Carnegie a major thrust of the projects he initiated and supervised was social: a guide to archives for religious

[32] Jameson letters, 1901–5, Donnan and Stock, eds., *Correspondence of Jameson*, pp. 78–89, and letters, 1915–24, ibid., pp. 176–302.

[33] Jameson, "The American Acta Sanctorum," in Rothberg and Goggin, eds., *Selected Essays*, pp. 166–82.

[34] Jameson, "The Future Uses of History," ibid., pp. 314–15.

history, multivolume documentary collections on the slave trade and the laws on slavery, a collection of sources on privateering and piracy (which he himself edited), Charles O. Paullin's *Atlas of the Historical Geography of the United States*, which mapped, besides political boundaries, the distribution of populations, land patterns, and a host of social factors.[35]

Thus in the long interim between 1895 and 1925, while he did not pursue the social history of the Revolution per se, his intellectual activities contributed to the 1925 lectures. As managing editor of the *American Historical Review* he stayed on top of the scholarship of the Revolution, assigning book reviews, reviewing all submissions, and editing documents. In 1925, in response to a query from Britain, he could evaluate in detail the work of a dozen major colonialists.[36] And if he had not himself turned the manuscripts, through the Carnegie projects he had a perspective on a range of social themes.

Why did it take Jameson thirty years to revise and publish his 1895 lectures? The subject is worth pursuing for what it reveals about the way historians are shaped by their life experiences and capacities, the canons of the profession, and the politics of their time.[37] Rothberg offers the insightful suggestion that trapped between his conservative political values and his passion for social history, Jameson "suppressed" the lectures, instead promoting the study of social history by others.[38] He may have been trapped in three other ways. In the late 1890s the book probably fell victim to his own intense careerism, one of the bitter fruits of the new academic profes-

[35] Rothberg, introduction to Rothberg and Goggin, eds., *Selected Essays*, p. xxxv; Rothberg, "The Brahmin as Bureaucrat: J. Franklin Jameson at the Carnegie Institution of Washington, 1905–1928," *Public Historian* 8 (1986):47–60; John Tracy Ellis, "American Religious History," and John K. Wright, "The Atlas of the Historical Geography of the United States," in Fisher and Fox, eds., *Jameson Tribute*, pp. 9–23, 66–79.

[36] Jameson to J. Holland Rose, Sept. 19, 1925, Donnan and Stock, eds., *Correspondence of Jameson*, p. 311.

[37] Ray Allen Billington, "Why Some Scholars Rarely Write History: A Case Study of Frederick Jackson Turner," *Mississippi Valley Historical Review* 50 (1963):3–27.

[38] Rothberg, "Jameson and the Creation of *The American Revolution Considered as a Social Movement.*"

sionalism. Jameson's early academic career was less than brilliant. He was an "associate," then an instructor at Hopkins for six years after receiving his degree in 1882 and published little. Brown, where he landed his first job, was a small Baptist school. He was in pursuit of a job at Barnard when he gave the lectures there in 1895. Barnard made him an offer but Jameson took umbrage at the salary and turned it down. Immediately after, he was appointed the first managing editor of the new *American Historical Review,* then a part-time job that he held while at Brown. Still in the job market, in 1901 he was appointed head of the University of Chicago's department of history. He helped plan the Department of Historical Research at the Carnegie Institution with himself in mind and was disappointed when someone else was appointed as the first director. *The American Revolution as a Social Movement* in its original form was too bold and too inchoate a book to have helped his career between 1895 and 1905.[39]

He may also have been trapped, secondly, by the conventions of publication of the new scientific history: presentation for an audience of specialists either as an annotated monograph or article. The interpretive analytical essay, a form Turner pioneered in 1893 in "The Significance of the Frontier," was not yet established.[40] In 1895 Jameson seems not to have been prepared to commit himself to the kind of sustained research in primary sources necessary to document so innovative a thesis. He had never published a monograph; his doctoral thesis on the origin of municipal institutions in New York City, in the early Hopkins mode when dissertations were less formidable than they later became, was no more than an extended essay.[41] At Brown he gave lectures to supplement his income, organized a collection of essays by others, and prepared a potboiler, the *Dictionary of United States History.*

[39] Jameson letters, 1888–1901, Donnan and Stock, eds., *Correspondence of Jameson,* pp. 44–77.

[40] Hofstadter, *Progressive Historians,* chap. 1.

[41] Donnan and Stock, eds., *Correspondence of Jameson,* p. 25 n. 50, claim the subject of the thesis was the common lands of Easthampton; I am indebted to Morey Rothberg for correcting this (Rothberg conversation with author, February 1993).

His only published book, *The History of Historical Writing in America* (1891), was a collection of deftly turned lectures on major historians.[42] But in none of these efforts had he brought a large, diverse mass of primary materials under control. Nor was he prepared to issue a rousing call to arms for the study of his subject as had Turner. Had he risked publication in the late 1890s, he would have been out on a limb. The landmark monographs of the Progressive interpretation of the Revolution did not appear until the first two decades of the twentieth century.[43]

Jameson was also caught, thirdly, in a trap of his own making, namely his perception of himself as a historian. "I know I am not good in many branches of historical work," he confided in 1903 at age forty-four to his best friend after two years at the University of Chicago. "I could never be an excellent historian, I am not a first-rate teacher, I am not making a success of my present position. My own talent, if I know myself, lies in the direction of Heuristik," a term he used to mean suggesting lines of inquiry for other scholars to pursue. Not until 1905 did he achieve the job he had created to suit his talents—director of the Carnegie's new research department.[44]

After fifteen years at the Carnegie, Jameson defined himself as "an historical powder monkey." "That is what I am for," he eagerly replied to a request for bibliographic help from the ailing Woodrow Wilson in 1922, "to help real historians . . .

---

[42] J. Franklin Jameson, *The History of Historical Writing in America* (New York, 1891); Jameson had also written *Willem Usselinx, Founder of the Dutch and Swedish West India Companies* (New York, 1887), and edited two volumes in the series Original Narratives of American History, 19 vols. (New York, 1906–7), for which he was the general editor.

[43] Lincoln, *Revolutionary Movement in Pennsylvania* (1901); Carl L. Becker, *The History of Political Parties in the Province of New York, 1760–1776* (Madison, Wis., 1909); H. J. Eckenrode, *The Revolution in Virginia* (Boston, 1916); Charles A. Beard, *An Economic Interpretation of the Constitution of the United States* (New York, 1913); Beard, *Economic Origins of Jeffersonian Democracy* (New York, 1915); Arthur M. Schlesinger, Sr., *The Colonial Merchants and the American Revolution* (New York, 1918).

[44] Jameson to Francis A. Christie, Mar. 6, 1903, Donnan and Stock, eds., *Correspondence of Jameson*, pp. 85–86.

to pass forward ammunition to historical gunners, or gun-men." The self-demeaning answer was poignant—as if exer-cising scholarly judgment as editor of a journal and initiating massive publications and archival projects were not function-ing as a "real historian." He had internalized the self-abasing hierarchy of values of the profession that assigned the highest status to publication of a book. "You know I have never writ-ten a book," he said ruefully to Allan Nevins some years later. He probably accepted Princeton's offer to do the 1925 lec-tures (which required publication) because it was as close as he would get to producing what the profession would accept as a book. And he turned to the American Revolution as a social movement because it was the only large subject that he had more or less laid out.[45]

Undoubtedly, if Jameson was not more conservative in 1895 than he was in 1895, he was more calculating. He was a consummate strategist who had learned how to anticipate and deflect criticism. He had watched the storm over Beard's eco-nomic interpretation of the Constitution; he was aware that Turner's lyricism about the frontier played better in Madison than in the Ivy League. Scarred in quelling the rebellion in the AHA, after 1920 he was in trouble at the Carnegie. The traditional skepticism among the natural scientists there to-ward history as a science was out in the open under a new director, a paleontologist, and would lead the trustees to let Jameson go and close the Department of Historical Research in 1927. In 1925 Jameson may have felt he was under scru-tiny. All of this, taken together, may account for the unmistak-able caution in the lectures.[46]

He talked and wrote as if he was protecting his flanks from hidden adversaries. *The American Revolution as a Social Move-ment* of 1895 became *The American Revolution Considered as a Social Movement* in 1925. He reduced his thesis to a heuristic, that is, a suggestion to pursue a hypothesis. The revised title

[45] Jameson to Woodrow Wilson, May 12, 1922, ibid., p. 270; Allan Nev-ins, "The Sage and the Young Man," in Fisher and Fox, eds., *Jameson Trib-ute*, p. 43.

[46] Jameson letters, 1925–28, Donnan and Stock, eds., *Correspondence of Jameson*, pp. 303–31.

simply asked the reader to "consider" the American Revolution as a social movement. Of course, he never claimed it was a "social revolution" or an "internal revolution," a phrase Merrill Jensen turned in 1940. To Jameson it was a political revolution that "had important social consequences," softened still further to "some social consequences." He would be content, he said in a teasing retreat, "if some who hear him are convinced that here is a field of history deserving further and deeper study."[47] The choice of the word *social* undoubtedly was also deliberate. The distinction between social and economic may have been vague, but Jameson knew how explosive Beard's analysis of the Founding Fathers had been, even after he tried to soften the blow by making the title *An Economic Interpretation of the Constitution,* implying it was one among other possible interpretations. Jameson's avoidance of documentation may also have been conscious; he thereby skirted the burden of the monograph for proof, turning to a genre, a short collection of reflective essays, that overcame the procrustean demands of "scientific" history.

Jameson may have been accurate in claiming to Beard that "everything that is a matter of doctrine was already in the text read in 1895."[48] Yet in condensing his 1895 lectures, as the two surviving drafts reveal, he pulled back from his sweeping claims. Slavery as an issue to which he devoted an entire lecture in 1895 he reduced to several pages. The argument was the same, stressing the positive gains of the Revolution, but the subject had lost its importance by eliminating the intense debate and was reduced to a minor episode in American history, as Jameson, Turner, and others in flight from the liberal commitments of abolitionism, the Civil War, and Reconstruction believed it should be. Jameson also eliminated his lyrical chapter on the West, retaining some of its argument here and there in his discussion of land and democracy; he saluted the frontiersman but abandoned the original Turneresque tone. Most important of all, when Jameson told Beard that nothing had been written on the subject in the thirty years gone by,

[47] Jameson, *American Revolution as a Social Movement,* pp. 10–11.

[48] Jameson to Beard, Aug. 10, 1926, Donnan and Stock, eds., *Correspondence of Jameson,* p. 319.

he was reading political history out of his interpretation: It was as if the work of Becker, Schlesinger, and Beard that had introduced the internal political dimension had no bearing on the Revolution as a social movement. By shunting aside politics (which had been uppermost in his history in the early 1890s), Jameson eliminated conflict from his analysis.

Yet two major political events of the intervening years impinged on Jameson, sharpening his analysis. World War I was on his mind, enabling him at several points to draw an important distinction between the influence of the war and the influence of the Revolution on late eighteenth-century America. So was the Russian Revolution, which he called "the greatest of all revolutions, the one destined evidently to be the most momentous in its consequences." He was emboldened in his interpretation of the "natural history" of revolution by the phases through which it had passed.[49] Thus, if in 1925 he adopted a strategy that in many ways retreated from 1895, he also tightened his argument by focusing on a single unifying theme, demonstrating at age sixty-six a grasp of the Revolution as a whole that had eluded him at age thirty-six.

III. JAMESON'S ACHIEVEMENT

What was Jameson's achievement in the context of the scholarship of his own time? It was both more and less than Beard recognized. Had Jameson published the lectures in 1895 soon after he had delivered them, conceivably his book might have had an effect on studies of the American Revolution comparable to Frederick Jackson Turner's "The Significance of the Frontier," delivered 1893. But then again, judging by the two lectures of 1895 that have survived, they would not have been as good a book as the lectures he released in 1925—focused, finely honed, and suggestive, rather than diffuse, sweeping, and strident. Coming as it did in the mid-1920s, the book was a coda to the meteoric works of Becker, Schlesinger, and Beard while it might have been a prologue. Yet Jameson accomplished something the other Progressive historians did not.

---

[49] Jameson, *American Revolution as a Social Movement*, p. 11.

First, he shifted the focus of scholarly attention from the origins of the Revolution to the results. All "schools" focused on the origins. Andrews, to Jameson the "chief authority on the colonial period," focused exclusively on the imperial relationship. Gipson, his successor, would take thirteen volumes to get to 1776.[50] Schlesinger took the colonial merchants only through the making of the Revolution, while Becker presented the struggle for "who should rule at home" in New York only from 1765 to 1776. Turner, while not concerned with the Revolution per se, called attention to the importance of land, sectional conflict, and western state-making in the post-Revolutionary era. Among the Progressives, Beard alone focused frontally on the results, treating the contest over the Constitution and the Hamiltonian-Jeffersonian conflicts as the capstone of the Revolution.

Second, Jameson dared to analyze the American Revolution in the generic category of revolutions. "Is there such a thing as a natural history of revolutions" through various "stages?" he asked. He drew on three revolutions for his answer. "The English Revolution" of the 1640s (his phrase) at first was "the affair of moderate statesmen, like Pym and Hampden"; then it "fell into the hands of men like Cromwell"; and finally, in the Commonwealth, "men of far more advanced views . . . radicals had come into control of the movement." As for the French Revolution, "everyone knows how its history is marked by distinct successive periods." And he had no fear in 1925 of adding to his roster the Russian Revolution, which had passed from one stage to another, transforming Russian society by 1925 "to an extent which no one would in 1913 have dreamed to be possible."[51] Jameson never explored the "radicals" of the American Revolution and disassociated himself from the Jacobins of the French Revolution (but felt no need to make clear he was not a communist). Yet he clearly attempted to rescue the American Revolution

---

[50] Jameson to Rose, Sept. 19, 1925, Donnan and Stock, eds., *Correspondence of Jameson*, p. 311; Lawrence Henry Gipson, *The British Empire before the American Revolution*, 14 vols. (New York, 1936–79).

[51] Jameson, *American Revolution as a Social Movement*, p. 11.

from conservative filiopietists who by the 1890s, as Michael G. Kammen points out, had reduced it to a War for Independence and a unique American experience.

Thirdly, without denigrating the leaders of the Revolution, Jameson shifted attention from elites to the "plain people." True, he defined them solely as small propertyholding farmers, distancing himself from "the mob and rabble" of the cities, and he had nothing to say about slaves, women, or the propertyless laboring classes. But Beard and Schlesinger studied elites, and Schlesinger and Becker focused on merchants and middling leaders who mobilized mobs. Jameson was closer to Turner and scholars of the South who dealt with a sectional clash of frontier and Tidewater aristocracy. And if he was more comfortable framing his history around abstract issues, he made it possible for others to study the people themselves—to go from antislavery to the slaves, from religious liberty to the Baptists, from the expanding economy to the rising middling men.

Finally, Jameson tried to grasp the American Revolution in a holistic way. That "all the varied activities of men in the same country and period have intimate relations with each other, and that one cannot obtain a satisfactory view of any one of them by considering it apart from the others" was not a self-evident truth to historians.[52] In flight from Becker's factional and class conflict and Beard's economic-interest conflict, Jameson played down political activity but did not jettison it. Schlesinger would take social history in the direction of history with the politics left out; not Jameson, whose thesis rested on the impact of the political on the social. By distinguishing his thesis from the more political, conflict-driven theses of the other Progressives, he won more of a hearing for the American Revolution considered as a social movement.

If there was a certain pose in Jameson's tentativeness, there was also a certain wisdom. He was asking scholars to "interrogate the past" with questions they had not asked in fields of study that did not exist. His book was an invitation to an inquiry, a door-opener in the study of American history.

[52] Ibid., p. 100.

IV. THE PROGRESSIVE HISTORIANS

To enter the domain of historiography one has to pass through the thorny thicket in which scholars are sorted out by "schools." The dangers in such exercises have been persistently deplored by scholars of almost all persuasions. Jameson's lament to Beard in 1926 of the tendency to classify historians rigidly is recurrent. Four decades later Merrill Jensen was convinced "that the moment we start pasting labels on historians and groups of historians mental rigor mortis sets in." By 1974 Jensen thought it would be in order to abandon "such labels as 'Progressive,' 'consensus,' 'new conservative,' 'neo-whig,' 'New Left' and the like." Writing at the same time, Bernard Bailyn was critical of the "uncontrollable inner dynamic" of bibliographic essays on the Revolution in which "trends or schools are detected and criticized before they are fully developed" and "general interpretations are pounced upon before the ink has dried." Moreover the entire process, as Richard Morris complained, frequently leads to distortion, to setting up straw men to knock down.[53]

Yet for all the pitfalls of bad historiography—pigeonholing, dismissive labeling, distortion—it remains true, as Edmund Morgan, another foe of lumping, remarked in 1976, that "historical understanding of the Revolution has proceeded in a series of reactions, one generation emphasizing problems and espousing views that the previous generation seemed to neglect or reject." Morgan's contention that "the successive reactions have carried us to new levels of perception" smacks of the whig history he has deplored. "The so-called consensus historians," Morgan argued, "could scarcely have reached their own understanding of the Revolution without attention to the Progressives who emphasized the internal conflicts of

---

[53] Merrill Jensen, "The American People and the American Revolution," *Journal of American History* 57 (1970):10; Jensen, *The American Revolution within America* (New York, 1974), pp. 221–24; Bernard Bailyn, "Lines of Force in Recent Writings about the American Revolution" (Paper presented at the Fourteenth International Congress of Historical Sciences, San Francisco, 1975), pp. 3–4; Richard B. Morris, *The American Revolution Reconsidered* (New York, 1967), p. 177.

the Revolution. Similarly New Left historians, while returning to the themes of conflict have also built on the work of those with whom they disagree." Yet it is reassuring to be reminded that "since the time needed to produce a historian is a good deal less than a lifespan, a lively dialogue has been possible among generations of scholars."[54] It is only unfortunate that more scholars have not accepted Morgan's invitation to a dialogue and that leading historians were often more interested in closing doors than in opening new ones.

For a quarter of a century after his book appeared in 1926, the Jameson thesis stayed alive largely on the strength of the Progressive paradigms for American history as a whole advanced by Beard, Turner, and Parrington and on the strength of the Progressive synthesis of the Revolution. He was the arch in the bridge between the interpretations of the origins of the Revolution introduced by Becker and Schlesinger and its consequences, offered by Beard. While Jameson may have "thrilled younger scholars," as John Higham writes, "by publishing an almost radical economic and social interpretation of the American Revolution," there was no Jameson school. He had no graduate students to pursue or test his insights, and as the powerful dean of the historical profession, he had few detractors. Indeed, judging by the number of copies of his book sold over twenty-five years—a scant 1,356—one wonders how many historians read Jameson; then again, there were not many historians and, in those quaint days before paperbacks, teachers put required reading on library reserve shelves. But over the 1930s and early 1940s scholars tested a number of his themes. And by the end of the interwar period a number of works synthesized the results of the Revolution, carrying his argument in different directions.[55]

The first generation of Progressive historians, Jameson's contemporaries, publicized his thesis but contributed little to exploring his hypotheses. Jameson's argument passed rapidly into both the stream of scholarship and the popular percep-

[54] Morgan, *Challenge of the American Revolution*, pp. 174–75.

[55] Higham, *History*, p. 185; W. Stull Holt, "Who Reads the Best Histories?" *Mississippi Valley Historical Review* 40 (1954):617.

tion of the American Revolution through Charles and Mary Beard's magisterial *Rise of American Civilization* (1927). Over time it sold at least 130,000 copies and shaped the outlook of several generations of left and liberal intellectuals; in the late 1930s the *New Republic* ran a series of articles on "The Books That Changed the World" in which Beard was ranked with Thorstein Veblen and John Dewey. The Beards, in six well-turned pages in which they uncharacteristically mentioned Jameson and his work by name, summed up "a far-reaching transformation in the land system" and the "shocks" felt by the clergy as well as the landed gentry. "In nearly every branch of enlightened activity, in every sphere of liberal thought," the Beards wrote, "the American Revolution marked the opening of a new humane epoch." "If a balance sheet is struck," they concluded, "then it is seen that the American Revolution was more than a war on England. It was in truth an economic, social, and intellectual transformation of prime significance."[56]

For the other leading Progressive historians, Turner and Parrington, Jameson's book came too late to be absorbed into their scholarship. But they did not need him; they sustained Jameson. Frederick Jackson Turner (1861–1932) published little in the two decades before his death, but his collected essays on the frontier (1921) and his essays on sectionalism (1932) gave a long afterglow to the argument he had first advanced in 1893. His glorification of the traits of the frontiersmen and western influences on democracy sustained Jameson's rather Turnerian interpretation of the Revolution.[57] Vernon Louis Parrington (1871–1929) in *Main Currents in American Thought,* published in 1927 but written some years before, had already reached the conclusion that the Revolution brought the triumph of "the republican" ideal over mon-

[56] Charles A. Beard and Mary R. Beard, *The Rise of American Civilization,* 2 vols. (1927; reprint ed., New York, 1930), 1:291; Hofstadter, *Progressive Historians,* pp. 291–96.

[57] Frederick Jackson Turner, "The Old West," in Turner, *The Frontier in American History* (New York, 1920), pp. 67–125; Turner, *The Significance of Sections in American History* (New York, 1932).

archy and aristocracy, and "out of this primary revolution came other revolutions, social and economic, made possible by the new republican freedom."[58]

Arthur M. Schlesinger, Sr., and Carl L. Becker, who began their scholarship with pathbreaking monographs on the origins of the Revolution, evaded the Jameson question of transformation for the rest of their careers. Schlesinger admired Jameson: he introduced the 1956 paperback edition of the book as "an epoch-marking if not epic-making event," linking it to the publication in 1927 of the Beards' *Rise* and the first volume in his own History of American Life series in social history. But after his book on the merchants in 1918 and a few essays, Schlesinger did not return to the Revolution for more than thirty years. Then he elaborated the Progressive interpretation at its weakest point, the theme of propaganda. The first generation of Progressive historians, suspicious of ideas as rationalizations of interests and devoid of empathy with urban laboring classes, never rose above the conception of the people as "the mob," manipulated by the propaganda of whig leaders. Schlesinger was responsible for the metaphor likening the mob to "Frankenstein's monster," created by their betters but "impossible to control," an image that seemed to foreclose scholarship on the subject. Thus there was a logic to his devoting one of his last books to the newspaper war against Britain from 1764 to 1776, based on his old assumption that propaganda aroused the masses. In his History of American Life volumes Schlesinger took American history to the extreme of a depoliticized social history. "I thought it was a mistake to write social history with politics omitted," Becker wrote to him; "I never understood why politics is not social."[59]

[58] Vernon Louis Parrington, *Main Currents in American Thought: An Interpretation of American Literature from the Beginnings to 1920* (1927), 3 vols. in 1 (New York, 1930), 1:190–93; Hofstadter, *Progressive Historians*, chaps. 10–11.

[59] Arthur M. Schlesinger, Sr., introduction to Jameson, *American Revolution as a Social Movement*, pp. vii-xii; "The American Revolution," in Schlesinger, *New Viewpoints in American History* (New York, 1922), p. 172; Schlesinger, *Prelude to Independence: The Newspaper War on Britain, 1764–1776*

Becker, for his part, took the Revolution in the direction of an intellectual history that left out both the politics and social history. After his 1909 work on New York, Becker suggested gingerly that his dual revolution thesis applied to other colonies. He dramatized his thesis brilliantly in "The Spirit of '76," an imaginative essay in the guise of a fictitious memoir of a conservative New York whig confronting a radical whig to his left and a loyalist aristocrat on his right. His forays into intellectual history produced a masterful analysis of the Declaration of Independence and another on the "climate of opinion" of eighteenth-century intellectual life, but almost all of his work ended the Revolution in 1776. Then from the mid-1930s on he devoted himself to well-honed essays defending the liberal democratic tradition confronted with totalitarianism and to espousing historical relativism. Self-defined as a historian of European intellectual history, he trained students who worked in European, rather than American history.[60]

Gradually in the 1930s and early 1940s, the mills of academic history ground out doctoral monographs taking up Jameson "heuristics." Not surprisingly, this afterglow of Progressive scholarship was bright at Columbia University, where Beard and the "New History" had flourished and where

---

(New York, 1958); Carl L. Becker to Arthur M. Schlesinger, Sr., Feb. 14, 1933, cited in Novick, *That Noble Dream*, pp. 178–79; Higham, *History*, pp. 194–95.

[60] Carl L. Becker, *The Eve of the Revolution* (New Haven, 1918); Becker, *The Declaration of Independence: A Study in the History of Political Ideas* (New York, 1922); Becker, *The Spirit of '76 and Other Essays* (Washington, D.C., 1927), pp. 9–58; Becker, *The Heavenly City of the Eighteenth-Century Philosophers* (New Haven, 1932); Milton M. Klein, "The Dilemma of Carl Becker," in Alden T. Vaughan and George A. Billias, eds., *Perspectives on Early American History: Essays in Honor of Richard B. Morris* (New York, 1973), pp. 120–66; Burleigh T. Wilkins, *Carl Becker: A Biographical Study in American Intellectual History* (Cambridge, Mass., 1961), p. 121, summarizes Louis M. Hacker's criticism, "namely, that Becker was in effect a timid academician who always stopped on the *eve* of revolutions instead of following their entire course" (Hacker, "Historians of Revolution," *New Republic*, Jan. 8, 1936, pp. 260–61).

Schlesinger had done his thesis and Becker had studied. Evarts B. Greene, who had shifted from institutional to social history, directed a number of theses in the Revolutionary era, and Columbia appointed Allan Nevins, a warm admirer of Jameson whose solid 1924 book on the political history of the American states in the Revolutionary era anticipated Jameson but lacked his flair.[61] In addition, Columbia gave doctorates to a handful of Marxist students drawn to early American history in the 1930s.

One focus of Columbia dissertations was land policy in the Hudson Valley. Irving Mark established the long history of agrarian conflict between tenant and landlord that continued during the Revolution, and Harry B. Yoshpe found the distribution of confiscated land from loyalist landlords far less democratic than Jameson hypothesized. Postwar social and economic change was another theme. Sidney I. Pomerantz's book on New York City from 1783 to 1803 was a case study of the "leaven" of the Revolution in humanitarianism, social policy, religion, and culture. Jameson's third chapter on industry and commerce was fleshed out by Robert A. East's depiction of postwar business corporations, banks, and large-scale speculation. Others added dimensions missing in Jameson: the transformation of eighteenth-century deism from a gentlemen's cult to a popular movement, the emergence of a body of opinion about women, and the development of indentured servitude.[62]

With scholarship such as this available by the late 1930s and early 1940s scholars began producing syntheses of the trans-

---

[61] Allan Nevins, *The American States during and after the American Revolution, 1775–1789* (New York, 1924). Nevins reviewed Jameson's book very favorably in the *American Historical Review* (32 [1926–27]:167–68), in a section entitled "Minor Notices," another sign of Jameson's self-deprecation.

[62] Irving Mark, *Agrarian Conflict in Colonial New York, 1711–1775* (New York, 1940); Harry B. Yoshpe, *The Disposition of Loyalist Estates in the Southern District of the State of New York* (New York, 1939); Sidney I. Pomerantz, *New York, an American City, 1783–1803: A Study of Urban Life* (New York, 1938); Robert A. East, *Business Enterprise in the American Revolutionary Era* (New York, 1938); Herbert Morais, *Deism in Eighteenth-Century America* (New York, 1934); Mary S. Benson, *Women in Eighteenth-Century America: A Study of Opinion and Social Usage* (New York, 1935). For scholarship at other universities, see Tolles, "American Revolution as a Social Movement."

formations of the Revolution more empirically based and more tough-minded than Jameson's. Among them were Greene, "a scholar and gentleman of the older generation," as Richard Morris called him, and Curtis P. Nettels and Merle Curti, both second-generation Progressives. Evarts P. Greene's volume in the History of American Life series took synthesis in the direction Schlesinger promoted—social history with very little politics. Politics, while there, was lost in a catalog of information on social, economic, and intellectual subjects without any integrating themes stronger than growth, progress, and the development of an American nationality. Greene, who spoke of Jameson's volume as no more than "a suggestive brief survey," gave himself a broad canvas. He took nine chapters to survey prewar colonial society and culture to provide a base for measuring change, devoted two to the war, and then five to the postwar years. He fleshed out Jameson's themes but lost the thread. On the other hand, in summarizing social change he was more balanced than Jameson: "The young republic made some progress towards realizing the Revolutionary ideal of equality. . . . Yet the conservative classes were still strong. The antislavery efforts of Southern liberals failed save in the prohibition of Negro importations by the border states. Property qualifications [to vote] though somewhat reduced, were still general, and Jefferson's efforts to equalize educational opportunities came to nil."[63]

By contrast Curtis P. Nettels, in *The Roots of American Civilization* (1938), a textbook that was more than a text, offered the first socioeconomic, conflict-oriented analysis of the colonial era as well as the origins and results of the Revolution. In the chapter "The Revolution Within"—the first use of this telling phrase—Nettels acknowledged Jameson's book as "the best general discussion of themes of this chapter." But unlike

[63] Richard B. Morris, "History over Time," *William and Mary Quarterly,* 3d ser. 41 (1984):455–63; Evarts B. Greene, *The Revolutionary Generation, 1763–1790* (New York, 1943), pp. 328–29, and chaps. 11–16; see also Morris, ed., *The Era of the American Revolution: Studies Inscribed to Evarts Boutell Greene* (New York, 1939), a collection of essays, some of which showed "class overtones in the Revolution," by Morris, Morais, Pomerantz, East, Michael Kraus, and others.

Jameson, Nettels depicted a sharp conflict between a "democratic or popular party" and "a conservative party," linking struggles over forming the new state governments, the currency question, and the distribution of land. More class-oriented than Jameson, Nettels recognized that "most of the gains of democracy were made at the expense of British interests and Loyalists rather than at the expense of the conservatives who supported the revolutionary cause. The latter held their own."[64]

Merle Curti, in *The Growth of American Thought* (1943), a book marking the coming-of-age of American intellectual history, presented a new synthesis of the "thought and feeling" of the Revolutionary era Jameson had not grasped. Curti was the epitome of the second generation of Progressive historians; a student of both Turner and Schlesinger, he thanked Beard for his "searching criticisms" of his manuscript. But unlike his mentors, Curti elevated the history of ideas, reaching down especially to ideas of the "plain people" that had eluded even Parrington. Using a rich array of ephemeral original sources, he called attention to such neglected grass-roots spokesmen of the Revolutionary era as Ethan Allen and William Manning. His analytical framework took a sense of conflict from Beard rather than Jameson. There was "a revolutionary shift in emphasis" and an "expanding enlightenment" followed by a "conservative reaction." The Revolution in Curti's judgment "did not democratize American intellectual life," but "it did much to democratize American thought."[65]

These three early syntheses summed up one era of inconclusive scholarship but could not anticipate another. They

[64] Curtis P. Nettels, *The Roots of American Civilization: A History of American Colonial Life* (New York, 1938), chap. 24, quotation p. 386; Nettels, *The Money Supply of the American Colonies before 1720* (Madison, Wis., 1934), his doctoral thesis; for Nettels's acerbic commentary on Harvard historians in 1937 and his radical politics, see Novick, *That Noble Dream*, pp. 181–82, 244–45.

[65] Merle Curti, *The Growth of American Thought* (New York, 1943), chaps. 6–8, quotations at pp. 153, 129; for Curti's radical politics, see Novick, *That Noble Dream*.

were harbingers of the postwar era in which the University of Wisconsin overtook Columbia as the center of the second generation of Progressive historians and as the creator of a third. Nettels taught at the University of Wisconsin from 1933 to 1944, Curti from 1942 to 1968 in a department whose leading Americanists were all Progressives.[66]

At Wisconsin Merrill Jensen (1905–80) was regarded as "the leading, currently active spokesman for the Becker-Beard school," as E. James Ferguson, a student long close to him wrote in 1975. "Jensen does not repudiate this categorization, but he is rather amused by it; he does not regard himself as a member of any school. . . . Jensen over a long period has merely stuck, as he would say, to recording the facts, aware of but undistracted by shifting fashions of interpretation." To Ferguson he was "essentially pragmatic, disdainful of ideology" yet "vaguely populist, combining a sympathy for the common man with a realistic sense of human motives and a hardheaded recognition of how the loaves and fishes are divided." Born and bred in rural South Dakota where he taught a one-room grade school, Jensen received his B.A. and M.A. at the University of Washington and his Ph.D. in 1934 from Wisconsin where Nettels was his teacher.[67]

For forty years Jensen made the issue of internal transformation and the divisions within the Revolutionary generation the focus of his scholarship. He had his students read Jameson, but he and they drew their problematics from Becker and Beard, not Jameson. "Even the historians who have seen the Revolution as a social movement," he wrote in criticism of Jameson, "have not tied that movement to the political history

[66] Curtis P. Nettels, "History Out of Wisconsin," *Wisconsin Magazine of History* 39 (1955–56):113–24. In this brag sheet of scholars who had studied, received their Ph.D.s, or taught at Wisconsin and had made their mark on the profession, for early American history Nettels listed Turner, Becker (a student of Turner), Orin G. Libby, Nettels, Jensen, Curti, and Robert E. Brown. For postwar Progressivism, see Paul Buhle, ed., *History and the New Left: Madison, Wisconsin, 1950–1970* (Philadelphia, 1990).

[67] E. James Ferguson, "Merrill Jensen: A Personal Comment," in James Kirby Martin, ed., *The Human Dimensions of Nation Making: Essays on Colonial and Revolutionary America* (Madison, Wis., 1976), pp. 5–6.

of the times."[68] In the first phase of his scholarship Jensen dealt with the Confederation era, first the shaping of the Articles of Confederation adopted in 1781, then the fruits of the Revolution in the period from 1781 to 1789. His consistent goal was to rescue the period from historians who looked at it through Federalist eyes from the hindsight of the victors' Constitution of 1787.

In 1940 Jensen introduced the phrase "the internal revolution" and stayed with the concept, if not the term, which he rephrased in 1974 as *The American Revolution within America*. Jameson's milder social interpretation was confused with this sweeping concept; Jameson was caught in the heavy cross fire leveled against Jensen by his critics. In *The Articles of Confederation* Jensen argued that the political revolution of 1776 was "predominantly an internal revolution carried on by the masses of the people against the local aristocracy" achieved by victories of "radicals" over "conservatives." In effect, he added an element of class conflict to Becker's thesis and extended it colony by colony. The "radical ascendancy was of brief duration, but while it lasted an attempt was made to write democratic ideals and theories of government into the laws and constitutions of the American states. Fulfillment was not complete . . . and once independence was won, the conservatives soon united in undoing, so far as they could, such political and economic democracy as had resulted from the war." The major part of the book was devoted to the writing and ratification of the Articles of Confederation. The Revolution, ran Jensen's thesis, was "essentially, though relatively, a democratic movement," and the Articles of Confederation "were the constitutional expression of this movement." Thus radicalism for Jensen, unlike Jameson, was not a spillover from the political revolution into other fields, but a democratizing political movement that made the Revolution of 1776 possible.[69]

---

[68] Merrill Jensen, *The Articles of Confederation: An Interpretation of the Social-Constitutional History of the American Revolution, 1774–1781* (Madison, Wis., 1940), p. 5; the book sold 2,000 copies by 1959, and 38,000 by its eighth printing in 1981 (Michael Stevens, "Merrill Jensen," in Wilson, ed., *Twentieth-Century American Historians*, p. 237).

[69] Jensen, *Articles of Confederation*, chap. 1, quotations pp. 5, 14–15.

In his second book, Jensen took up Beard's battle to deflate John Fiske's filiopietist interpretation of the era as *The Critical Period* (1888), a time of stagnation and disaster from which the Federalist saviors rescued the country. Ostensibly he paid homage to Jameson by devoting two chapters to "the spirit of the new nation" and "the betterment of humanities" and five chapters to the expanding economy—all fuller and richer than Jameson. But he framed these within a political narrative in which interest groups of all sorts fought over the fruits of the Revolution. The subtext was that the achievements of the era did not justify the political consolidation of 1787. It was not a time of social or economic instability; Shays's agrarian rebellion was a tempest in a teapot used by nationalists. Thus if Jensen could not explain why it was indeed a "critical period" for hard pressed farmers and desperate urban mechanics, he gave the fullest, most balanced picture of the era.[70]

Fortified with a sense of how the Revolution turned out, in the next phase of his scholarship Jensen turned back to how it began. In 1955 he published a massive collection of documents on the colonial era in which he balanced sources for the internal history of the colonies with sources for the imperial relationship. With some 225 documents that included not only the standard acts, petitions, and resolutions, but also correspondence drawn from unpublished manuscripts, newspaper accounts, and statistical tables, all accompanied by introductions and concise bibliographic essays, the book was a scholar's guide to the history of the Revolution. Jensen published a detailed history of the coming of the Revolution in 1968; it is the fullest one-volume narrative of the period, embracing both the imperial and internal politics of the Revolution. His aim was "not a search for causes or principles" but "a political history" that emphasized "the deeds of men rather than their motives." Because this book was "necessarily a history of thirteen separate colonies" many of which "were divided into 'factions' or 'parties,'" the history that emerged was "one of extraordinary intricacy,'" which probably dismayed

---

[70] Jensen, *The New Nation: A History of the United States during the Confederation, 1781–1789* (New York, 1950).

critics who had stereotyped the Progressive interpretation as simplistic.[71]

In his last book in 1974, based on four lectures, Jensen returned to the theme of transformation over the entire era from 1765 through 1787. And in retirement he rounded out his long exploration of divisions within the Revolutionary generation by turning to the debates capping the era, directing two large-scale documentary projects, one on the first federal elections and the second on the history of the debates on the ratification of the Constitution. The latter, still in progress, piling up the debates over the Constitution state by state and day by day, in the public forum in newspapers and pamphlets as well as in official conventions, opened new vistas to popular political thought that scholars have only begun to explore.[72]

Over the years Jensen modified his original interpretation in response to his critics. In 1959, in the third printing of *The Articles of Confederation,* he confessed that had he called his chapter "Discontent within the Colonies, 1763–1774," he might have avoided the acrimony over the term "internal revolution." But while he stuck to his central assumption, namely, that colonial political society was undemocratic, he shaded his argument: "The war for independence was accompanied by a degree of democratization, and in part was the result of demands for political and social change both before and after 1776." Insisting that "it matters little whether one calls the political and social process 'internal revolution' or 'political and social change,' change there was."[73] He concluded, secondly, that the "new men" he had identified as

[71] Jensen, ed., *American Colonial Documents to 1776,* English Historical Documents, vol. 9 (London, 1955); Jensen, *The Founding of a Nation: A History of the American Revolution, 1763–1776* (New York, 1968), p. xiii.

[72] Jensen, *The American Revolution within America* (New York, 1974); Jensen et al., eds., *The Documentary History of the First Federal Elections, 1788–1790,* 4 vols. (Madison, Wis., 1976–89); Jensen et al., eds., *The Documentary History of the Ratification of the Constitution,* 10 vols. to date (Madison, Wis., 1976–).

[73] Jensen, *The Articles of Confederation: An Interpretation of the Social-Constitutional History of the American Revolution,* 3d printing (Madison, Wis., 1959), p. xix.

"radicals" might better be called "popular leaders," because "few if any men such as Samuel Adams, Patrick Henry, and Christopher Gadsden had any interest in or program for 'internal' reform." It was a clarifying distinction, since widely adopted. Third, he eased away from the old Progressive stereotype of the manipulated mob. "The mob was a political power to be reckoned with," he wrote in 1974, and "mass meetings accustomed ordinary people to take part in politics as they never had before." While thus open to "popular participation," he continued to stress the effective but often opportunistic leadership of the popular leaders, as had Becker.[74] Fourth, he clarified the timing of radicalism. Before 1774–75, the movement for revolution was not, he granted, a democratic movement "except by inadvertence"; from 1776 on, democratic thought flowered as Americans confronted the restructuring of their governments. Fifth, he gave greater recognition to social radicalism, to what he called the "elusive undercurrents" or the "levelling spirit"—the "idea of an equal distribution of property"—and the erosion of deference to men of property, currents that helped make the Revolution "in part a 'people's' revolution."[75]

Jensen was sometimes his own best critic. He regretted that he had not paid more attention to political ideas that shaped democratic action.[76] Other criticisms eluded him. He was indifferent to theory. Jensen equated "historical materialism" with "economic determinism" and read Beard as favoring not economic determinism but "the economic interpretation of politics."[77] In the 1960s he was impatient with historical methods drawn from the social sciences; he dismissed the quantitative analysis of the distribution of wealth pursued by

[74] Ibid., p. xxi; Jensen, *American Revolution within America*, pp. 26–27 and chap. 2.

[75] Jensen, "American People and American Revolution."

[76] Jensen, ed., *Tracts of the American Revolution, 1763–1776* (Indianapolis, 1967), pp. xiii-lxix.

[77] Jensen, "Historians and the Nature of the American Revolution," in Ray Allen Billington, ed., *The Reinterpretation of Early American History* (San Marino, Calif., 1966), p. 122.

his student Jackson Turner Main as "sociology."[78] And while he welcomed the new practitioners of "history from the bottom up" who studied mechanics and seamen, the Midwestern farm boy joked about them as "asphalt flowers" for their seeming eastern, urban bias.[79] Confronted from the 1960s on with obituaries burying the Progressive interpretation as in "erosion" and then as "shattered and deeply discredited," he was not in a mood to face its weaknesses or suffer graduate students who questioned fundamental Progressive assumptions.[80]

Challenging the Progressive paradigm in Madison was difficult; the "three parts of the god-head here at Wisconsin— the Father, the Son, and the Holy Ghost," Warren Susman wrote in 1950, were Turner, Beard, and Parrington.[81] The department's graduate system encouraged a master-disciple relationship. Jensen's doctoral students, some fifty in all, worked within the Progressive paradigm, yet they often modified or amplified Progressive themes, strengthening them. Among his early students, E. James Ferguson made a major revision in Beard's argument about the way funding and assumption worked, sustaining the relevance of the issue. He also established a full-blown nationalist agenda as early as 1783, which gave a firmer base to an economic interpretation of the Federalists of 1787 than Beard's immediate pocketbook

[78] Jackson Turner Main, "Main Travelled Roads," *William and Mary Quarterly*, 3d ser. 41 (1984):444–54.

[79] Comment on papers by Jesse Lemisch and Alfred F. Young presented at Conference on Early American History, Newberry Library, Chicago, 1974, typescript in author's possession. William B. Hesseltine, a Wisconsin Progressive, similarly dismissed Richard Hofstadter's *Age of Reform* (New York, 1955) as "asphalt-oriented"; see Novick, *That Noble Dream*, p. 340.

[80] Jack P. Greene, "The Flight from Determinism: A Review of Recent Literature on the Coming of the American Revolution," *South Atlantic Quarterly* 61 (1962):235–59; for Greene's essays in 1967 and 1968, see Greene, *Reappraisal of the American Revolution*, and Greene, ed., *Reinterpretation of the American Revolution*.

[81] Warren Susman to Paul W. Gates, Jan. 14, 1950, cited in Novick, *That Noble Dream*, pp. 346–47; for a list of Merrill Jensen's doctoral students and their theses, see Martin, ed., *Human Dimensions of Nation Making*, pp. 365–67.

thesis. Jackson Turner Main and Van Beck Hall developed hypotheses about party divisions in the states in the 1780s around more complex dichotomies than Beard's. Among Jensen's later students, Joseph A. Ernst and Marc Egnal pushed the study of the economic origins of the Revolution into the field of political economy. Ronald Hoffman's sophisticated study of the Revolution in Maryland added new dimensions to the struggle within elites as well as between elites and poor farmers during the war. Hoffman portrayed a gentry frightened by the threat of social revolution ready to sacrifice part of their wealth to preserve their power, a theme Jensen incorporated in his last book.[82]

Jackson Turner Main, grandson of Frederick Jackson Turner and Jensen's most productive and innovative early student, was alone in making social as well as political transformation in the Revolutionary era the central focus of his scholarship. In *The Social Structure of Revolutionary America* (1965), a pioneering work in the new social history, Main attempted to measure social change nationally, making use of massive numbers of probate records and tax lists. "He told me," Main wrote of Jensen, "my book on the social structure was sociology, which damned it, and as far as I know he didn't read it." Comparing colonial society in the 1750s and 1760s with society in the late 1780s, Main examined the economic class structure, North and South, social mobility, social classes and their cultural patterns, as well as contemporary opinions about class. He concluded with candor that "the effects of the Revolution seemed on the whole to have been less than I ex-

---

[82] E. James Ferguson, *The Power of the Purse: A History of American Public Finance, 1776–1790* (Chapel Hill, 1961); Ferguson, "Political Economy, Public Liberty, and the Formation of the Constitution," *William and Mary Quarterly*, 3d ser. 40 (1983); Van Beck Hall, *Politics without Parties: Massachusetts, 1780–1791* (Pittsburgh, 1972); Joseph A. Ernst, *Money and Politics in America, 1755–1775: A Study in the Currency Act of 1764 and the Political Economy of Revolution* (Chapel Hill, 1973); Marc Egnal, *A Mighty Empire: The Origins of the American Revolution* (Ithaca, N.Y., 1988); Ernst and Egnal, "An Economic Interpretation of the American Revolution," *William and Mary Quarterly*, 3d ser. 29 (1972); Ronald Hoffman, *A Spirit of Dissension: Economics, Politics, and the Revolution of Maryland* (Baltimore, 1973); for changes in elites, see James Kirby Martin, *Men in Rebellion: Higher Government Leaders and the Coming of the American Revolution* (New Brunswick, N.J., 1973).

pected"; change had to be traced over a longer period of time, and he later deprecated the book as "at once pioneering and obsolescent." When he returned to the question a few years later, he felt that subsequent research had still not resolved the issue. Yet looking at the overall picture, Main, with the strongest base of evidence yet assembled, affirmed Jameson. "The Revolution contributed to the decline of deference, delayed the trend towards an economic and social aristocracy, and momentarily reversed the growing concentration of wealth. Whether intended or not, and whether permanent or not, these changes registered a clear gain for social democracy." [83]

In his analysis of political change, Main was more confident of a pattern of democratization. In a second large-scale quantitative project comparing the socioeconomic composition of the state senates before and after the war and in an article on the assemblies, Main amassed impressive evidence for the democratization of the state legislatures. Turning to an analysis of voting patterns in the legislatures in the 1780s, Main found evidence of distinct blocs which, when correlated with his socioeconomic findings on the members, suggested a division between what he dubbed "cosmopolitan" and "localist" parties. In the late 1780s Main saw this alignment coming into play in the conflict over ratifying the proposed federal Constitution. [84]

The Wisconsin school thus sustained a sophisticated, complex political side of the Becker-Beard interpretation but, save for Main and Hoffman, more or less passed by the Jameson themes about society and "thought and feeling." Jensen found the Counterprogressive interpretation that assigned causation to a set of ideas such as the belief in a conspiracy as "a form of intellectual determinism which I do not find any

[83] Jackson Turner Main, *The Social Structure of Revolutionary America* (Princeton, 1965); Main to Young, Aug. 5, 1993; Main, "Main Travelled Roads," p. 451; Main, *The Sovereign States, 1775–1783* (New York, 1973), p. 348.

[84] Main, *The Upper House in Revolutionary America, 1763–1788* (Madison, Wis., 1967); Main, "The American Revolution and the Democratization of the Legislatures," *William and Mary Quarterly*, 3d ser. 23 (1966):391–407; Main, *Political Parties before the Constitution* (Chapel Hill, 1973).

more satisfactory than economic determinism." He was any-thing but simplistic. "Complexity, conflict and change," Thomas P. Slaughter observed, are the hallmarks of Jensen's narrative work, as he "piles fact upon fact, nuance upon nu-ance, variation upon variation," so much so that the "evidence can bewilder."[85] If there is a place for the analysis of politics and conflict in the Revolutionary era, there is a resiliency to Jensen's tough-minded analysis. As the smoke of the barrage cleared—a barrage to which we will next turn—he remains one of the few scholars with an imposing command of large bodies of original sources who worked out a vision of the Rev-olutionary era that linked its transformations to its origins.

V. THE COUNTERPROGRESSIVES—PART 1

"If one had to choose a single term to characterize the domi-nant tendency in postwar American historical writing," writes Peter Novick in his commanding survey of the "objectivity question" and the historical profession in the United States, "'counterprogressive' would seem the best choice, for no project was more central to historians from the late 1940s on-ward than the revision and refutation of the alleged deficien-cies of the progressive historians who had preceded them." He adds, "As is usual in such revisionist projects, the new school constructed something of a straw man to battle against"; the revisionists "exaggerated" the dominance of Turner, Beard, and Parrington, and often "vulgarized" their theses "so as to present a broader target." Richard B. Morris said the same thing at the time about the treatment of Jame-son, who "said many sensible things, but it is now fashionable to exaggerate his thesis in order to decapitate a straw man."[86]

[85] Merrill Jensen, "Commentary on Bernard Bailyn's Paper at the AHA Meeting, Philadelphia, 1963," typescript in author's possession; Thomas P. Slaughter, "In Retrospect: Merrill Jensen and the Revolution of 1787," *Reviews in American History* 15 (1987):691–701.

[86] Novick, *That Noble Dream,* p. 332; see the influential contemporary analysis by John Higham, "The Cult of the American Consensus: Homoge-nizing Our History," *Commentary* 27 (1959):93–100, and Higham, "Beyond Consensus: The Historian as Moral Critic," *American Historical Review* 67 (1962):609–25, reprinted in Higham, *Writing American History: Essays on Modern Scholarship* (Bloomington, Ind., 1970), chap. 8; Higham, *History,*

Postwar historians were adamant that their own scholarship, unlike that of their Progressive forebears, was not "disfigured by presentism," as Novick puts it. As Edmund S. Morgan reviewed his long, fruitful career, he insisted that "the whole school of consensus history, if there is a school, is sort of accidental." It was "simply the result of historians looking closely at episodes that had not been looked at so closely before and saying 'Hey, I don't see this happening.'"[87] A decade before, however, while reflecting on the shifts in the direction of his own scholarly interests since World War II, Morgan pointed out that "the influence of the present upon [the historian] is so strong, albeit so subtle, that he may not be aware of it." When "different historians have found different things in the same records," he observed, "the differences may come simply from keener perception or from taking a closer look, but they are also affected, consciously or unconsciously, by the time and place in which the historian lives and by the people who live there with him. . . . An historian's understanding of the Revolution may thus reflect, however remotely, the needs of his time, which may differ from the needs of earlier times and differ also from year to year within his own lifespan."[88]

How a historian of the Revolution "may . . . reflect, however remotely, the needs of his time" is a subject most scholars have been reluctant to address in their contemporaries. Historians have no hesitation in pointing out how George Bancroft's democratic, patriotic version of the Revolution "reflected" his Jacksonian convictions or Charles Beard his Progressivism. But they are not comfortable with books like Michael G. Kammen's, which explore the Revolution in "the American historical imagination" or "the transformation of tradition in American culture" that imply a current cultural and political context in which historians function. Yet a much

---

chaps. 5–6; Morris, *American Revolution Reconsidered*, p. 77. I recall Higham as coining the term *consensus history.*

[87] Novick, *That Noble Dream*, p. 321; David T. Courtwright, "Fifty Years of American History: An Interview with Edmund S. Morgan," *William and Mary Quarterly*, 3d ser. 44 (1987):336–69, quotation pp. 360–61.

[88] Morgan, *Challenge of the American Revolution*, p. x.

adopted research handbook advises students to read historians "by a sort of triangulation: here I stand; there to the left or right, stands Macaulay [or whoever]; and beyond are the events that he reports" and warns that doing this "is not the same as dismissing an author having 'doped out' that he is a Whig, a Catholic." This kind of relativism is obviously a two-edged sword; no historian wants to see his or her scholarship reduced to a reflection of the time. Only recently have a minority of scholars been willing to grant that their questions are inspired by the "needs" of their own time or to claim their history is the better for their own life experiences or convictions.[89]

Reading Peter Novick's deeply researched, even-handed study of the published writings and revealing private correspondence of historians early in the Cold War, it is remarkable not how remotely but how directly leaders of the profession responded to and indeed shaped "the needs of [their] time." "In the late forties and early fifties," which, as Novick writes, were "the height of the cold war," "a sense of urgent crisis, and impending Armageddon, was widespread" among scholars. The crusade against communism abroad with its correlate, an inquisition into political heresy at home, settled a dark pall on emerging postwar academic communities.[90]

Conyers Read's presidential address to the AHA in 1949, "The Social Responsibilities of the Historian," was a call to arms. "Total war, whether it be hot or cold, enlists everyone and calls upon everyone to assume his part. The historian is no freer from this obligation than the physicist." In 1950, Samuel Eliot Morison (a rear admiral by virtue of his multivolume history of United States naval operations in World War II) issued a jeremiad in his AHA presidential address: the historian "owes respect to tradition and folk memory . . . historians, deal gently with your people's traditions." The

---

[89] Michael G. Kammen, *A Season of Youth: The American Revolution and the Historical Imagination* (New York, 1978); Kammen, *Mystic Chords of Memory: The Transformation of Tradition in American Culture* (New York, 1991); Jacques Barzun and Henry F. Graff, *The Modern Researcher* (1957), rev. ed. (New York, 1970), pp. 183–84.

[90] Novick, *That Noble Dream*, chap. 10, quotation p. 314.

years 1920 to 1940, he continued, were "two woeful decades" in which "historians were robbing the people of their heroes . . . insulting their folk memory of great figures they admired." He issued a call for "a sanely conservative history of the United States." Daniel Boorstin, expiating his brief sin as a Communist in the 1930s, explained to the House Committee on Un-American Activities in 1953 that his form of opposition to communism "has been an attempt to discover and explain to my students, in my teaching and in my writing, the unique virtues of American democracy."[91]

Other scholars conformed. On the left, disassociation from Marxism was obligatory. Merle Curti, in his presidential address to the Mississippi Valley Historical Association, included a passage disavowing Marxism, "to be on the safe side." In these "dark and wintry times," Curti wrote to Thomas C. Cochran, "I can't swim with the current and being a notoriously poor swimmer I can't swim against it." While Cochran remained convinced "of the essential soundness of most of historical materialism," he too was "disinclined to try to swim against the overwhelming current" and concluded "I guess what I've done is to build an ivory tower called the Social Science approach to history." Younger scholars without tenure were more vulnerable. Lee Benson, who wrote from an "implicit Marxist standpoint," fearful of making it explicit, said "during the 1950s, and for some time thereafter, I—for one—was intellectually terrified."[92]

[91] Ibid., pp. 318 (Read), 315–16 (Morison), 328 (Boorstin). For an analysis written in the 1960s, see Jesse Lemisch, *On the Active Service in War and Peace: Politics and Ideology in the American Historical Profession* (Toronto, 1975).

[92] Novick, *That Noble Dream*, pp. 330 (Curti), 325 (Cochran), 332 (Benson). For heresy-hunting in the academic world, ibid., chap. 11, and Ellen Schrecker, *No Ivory Tower: McCarthyism and the Universities* (New York, 1986). For diverse historians affected, see the references in Schrecker's index to Daniel Boorstin, John W. Caughey, Natalie Zemon Davis, Sigmund Diamond, Moses Finley, Philip S. Foner, Sidney V. James, Richard Schlatter, Vera Shlakman, and Dirk Struik, an incomplete list. For the experience of three left historians with inquisitorial committees see the interviews with Natalie Zemon Davis, William Appleman Williams, and Herbert G. Gutman in Henry Abelove et al., eds., *Visions of History* (New York, 1983), pp. 97–122, 125–46, 187–216; Sigmund Diamond, *Official Stories, Little Secrets: On*

Graduate students were especially vulnerable. At Columbia in 1947 I chose to do an M.A. thesis on "New York City in the Hysteria of the Alien and Sedition Laws, 1798–1800," because I wanted to see if I could learn how the country responded to what Jefferson called "the reign of witches." I suppose this made me politically suspect. I can remember standing in front of a newspaper kiosk before the Columbia subway entrance on Broadway and catching out of the corner of my eye my thesis director staring at me to see which newspaper or magazine I would choose. I left Columbia (overcrowded with four hundred history graduate students) for Northwestern where Lawrence "Bill" Towner and I (with an assist from George McGovern) cranked out leaflets against the Mundt-Nixon Bill, a new threat in the growing witch hunt, on a departmental mimeograph machine with the blessings of our advisor, Ray Allen Billington.

For a number of reasons Charles Beard (1874–1948) and to a lesser extent Carl Becker (1873–1945) were the prime targets of a generalized attack on Progressive history. Their philosophy of history and their politics were under fire long before the 1950s, when their scholarship on the Revolution came under review. In the interwar years Beard and Becker were the leading advocates of historical relativism. "The attack on moral relativism," Novick points out, "was part of an effort to rearm the West spiritually for the battle with totalitarianism," first against fascism in the late 1930s and during World War II and then against communism in the late 1940s. As early as 1938 Howard Mumford Jones lamented Beard's "unfortunate influence . . . from the point of view of keeping alive a necessary patriotic glow in the juvenile breast." J. H. Hexter, Novick writes, "saw an intimate connection between Becker's relativism and Nazi historical practice." Later, Robert E. Brown, chief prosecuting attorney of Beard and Becker, recycled the old charge that Becker's moral relativism and liberalism led him to skate "on the thin ice of communism," a

---

the Trail of the Intelligence Agency–University Complex, 1944–55 (New York, 1991).

red-baiting accusation J. Franklin Jameson in the 1930s found beneath contempt.[93]

Secondly, by the onset of World War II, Beard's "isolationist" politics had made him a pariah among internationalist-minded liberals and antifascist leftists. Beard's economic analysis of the internal domestic forces that shaped foreign policy led him to oppose Roosevelt's interventionist foreign policies. He devoted his last book in 1948 to proving Roosevelt's complicity in bringing on America's entry into the war.[94]

Thirdly, during the Cold War onslaught against Marxism, Beard's economic interpretation was equated with economic determinism, which was equated with Marxism and, in the absence of influential Marxist intellectuals in the United States, Beard became a surrogate for Marxism. Merely to raise the subject of the economic interests of the patriots of 1776 or of the Framers of 1787 was to question their "sincerity" or their "motives." In 1913 in Marion, Ohio (home of Warren G. Harding), the *Ohio Star* ran a banner headline in response to Beard's book on the Constitution: "Scavengers, Hyena Like, Desecrate the Graves of the Dead Patriots We Revere."[95] A half-century later, Barry Goldwater, the conservative Republican candidate for president, wrote columns in the same vein. With celebration the touchstone of loyalty, Beard, a relentless explorer of interests that lay behind official cant, was a dangerous model.

By the early 1950s a number of books popular among intellectuals were setting the new parameters of historical inquiry. David M. Potter told us we were *A People of Plenty* and the economist John Kenneth Galbraith wrote that we were *An Affluent Society*, which led the historian Jack P. Greene to conclude that "the absence of serious internal economic problems

[93] Novick, *That Noble Dream,* pp. 283 (Jones and Hexter); Robert E. Brown, *Carl Becker and the American Revolution* (East Lansing, Mich., 1970), chap. 7; Jameson to Mrs. Grattan Doyle, Dec. 9, 1935, in Donnan and Stock, eds., *Correspondence of Jameson,* pp. 358–59.

[94] Hofstadter, *Progressive Historians,* chap. 9.

[95] Cited in Ellen Nore, *Charles A. Beard: An Intellectual Biography* (Carbondale, Ill, 1983), p. 63.

and the general levelling of society [since the war] has enabled [historians] to avoid that central preoccupation with economic questions that led many scholars of the progressive school to wrench Revolutionary events out of context by superimposing some of the a priori assumptions and tenets of economic determinism." The sociologist Daniel Bell intoned *The End of Ideology* and the theologian Reinhold Niebuhr warned against "utopian visions of historical possibilities" and "Jeffersonian illusions about human nature," which may be why Cecelia M. Kenyon was so little challenged when she dismissed Thomas Paine as the "Peter Pan of the Age of Reason" who could not see the "dark side of human nature." "The outburst of McCarthyism"—of guilt by accusation and guilt by association— Richard Hofstadter points out, "instead of provoking a radical response, aroused in some intellectuals more distaste than they had ever thought they would feel for popular passions and anti-establishment demagogy. The populism of the right inspired a new skepticism about the older populism of the left." Such distaste for what Hofstadter called *The Paranoid Style in American Politics* turned most scholars away from examining the urban mobs, agrarian riots, slave insurrections, evangelical Great Awakenings, millennialist outbursts, and other forms of "enthusiasm" or "fanaticism" that in the eighteenth century were sources of radicalism.[96]

By the mid-1950s the major interpretive works in American history were slamming the door to the questions the Progressive historians had opened up about the Revolution. If Hofstadter was right in 1948 that liberal and conservative antagonists shared a consensus of values through American history, then there was more reason to explore agreements rather than disagreements in the founding generation. If Daniel Boorstin was right in *The Genius of American Politics* (1953), his offering of loyalty, that "the most obvious peculiar-

[96] Greene, "Flight from Determinism," p. 258; Cecelia M. Kenyon, "Where Paine Went Wrong," *American Political Science Review* 45 (1951):1086–99; Hofstadter, *Progressive Historians*, p. 438; Hofstadter, "The Paranoid Style in American Politics," *Harpers Magazine,* November 1964, reprinted in Hofstadter, *The Paranoid Style in American Politics and Other Essays* (New York, 1967).

ity of our American Revolution is that in the modern European sense of the word, it was hardly a revolution at all," then there was "wisdom in the naiveté" of the Daughters of the American Revolution. If Louis Hartz was right in *The Liberal Tradition in America* (1955) that America was "born free" because it had no feudal past, then Jameson's destruction of "feudal relics" in the land system was no more than "a mopping up operation."[97] If Robert E. Brown was right in 1955 that colonial Massachusetts was an equalitarian "middle class" society and a political democracy, then there was no need for change and Becker's and Jensen's dual revolution went out the window. And if Brown was right in 1956 and Forrest McDonald right in 1958 in their demolition jobs on Beard's interpretation of the Constitution, then the entire Progressive temple was in a state of collapse and by implication Jameson's piece of the arch had fallen in.[98]

The climate of opinion among leading early American historians changed with a speed that suggests that "the needs of [their] time" may have predisposed their response. The angry, one-sided polemics by Brown and McDonald against Beard were not surprising. McDonald's sympathetic biographer speaks of him as "unabashedly conservative" (and in 1964 chairman of the Goldwater for President committee in Rhode Island). He was a business historian who had written one book about the utilities industry of Wisconsin that was financed by the industry and would go on to write a biography that rehabilitated the utilities magnate Samuel Insull.

[97] Hofstadter, *The American Political Tradition and the Men Who Made It* (New York, 1948), pp. 15, 18; for his second thoughts twenty years later, see Hofstadter, *Progressive Historians*, chap. 12; Daniel Boorstin, *The Genius of American Politics* (Chicago, 1953), chap. 3, pp. 68–69; Louis Hartz, *The Liberal Tradition in America: An Interpretation of American Political Thought since the Revolution* (New York, 1955).

[98] Robert E. Brown, *Middle-Class Democracy and the Revolution in Massachusetts, 1691–1780* (Ithaca, N.Y., 1955); Robert E. Brown and B. Katherine Brown, *Virginia, 1705–1786: Democracy or Aristocracy?* (East Lansing, Mich., 1964); Robert E. Brown, *Charles Beard and the Constitution: A Critical Analysis of "An Economic Interpretation of the Constitution"* (Princeton, 1956); Forrest McDonald, *We the People: The Economic Origins of the Constitution* (Chicago, 1958).

What was surprising was the speed with which these prosecuting-attorney historians were canonized by liberal scholars who valorized balance and a judicious temperament. "Negative writing is always unpleasant," Morgan remarked, which perhaps is why he left it to others. What was also surprising was the way established scholars denied a hearing to the sophisticated analysis of critics of Beard like Lee Benson and Richard Hofstadter, who pointed out the "dualism" and "ambiguity" in Beard's interpretation.[99]

Jameson at first escaped such shabby treatment. Frederick B. Tolles's even-handed appraisal of the state of the Jameson thesis in 1954 was critical yet sympathetic. Tolles, a Quaker who had written a biography of George Logan, the Quaker resister to the Quasi War with France in 1798, pointed to the serious shortcomings in Jameson's hypotheses. On the status of persons, he had simplified what happened to the old aristocracy and the loyalists and overlooked such dependent classes as women and indentured servants. The Revolution "made less difference in the status of persons than Jameson believed." On the bedrock subject of land, the changes in entail, primogeniture, and quitrents were largely symbolic and the distribution of confiscated loyalist estates led to "considerably less diffusion and democratization of landownership . . . than Jameson supposed." The economic changes in commerce and industry were both more and less than Jameson perceived. In his chapter on "Thought and Feeling," Jameson in general "overlooked or underestimated the dynamic forces already present in the society of colonial America." Yet Tolles could forgive Jameson "a few oversights" and "overstatements." He pronounced the thesis "still sound, and what is

[99] For McDonald's value judgments of modern revolutions, see his *E Pluribus Unum: The Formation of the American Republic, 1776–1790* (Boston, 1965), pp. 235–56; for his politics and other scholarship, see Justus Doenecke, "Forrest McDonald," in Wilson, ed., *Twentieth-Century American Historians,* pp. 258–59; for Brown's political judgments, see his *Carl Becker,* pp. 265–67, and his *Reinterpretation of the Formation of the American Constitution* (Boston, 1963), pp. 56–63; see also, Courtwright, "Interview with Morgan," p. 367; Benson, *Turner and Beard,* pp. 95–150; Richard Hofstadter, "Beard and the Constitution: The History of an Idea," *American Quarterly* 2 (1950):195–213.

more important, still vital and suggestive, capable of still further life, still greater usefulness."[100]

Morgan's *The Birth of the Republic, 1763–1789,* in 1956 measured the shifting tide. A volume in the Chicago History of American Civilization series commissioned by Daniel Boorstin, it "drew together and consolidated all of the emerging scholarship opposed to Charles Beard," as three of his students put it in introducing his festschrift. This well-honed, lucid synthesis was nothing if not Counterprogressive, explicitly critical of Becker, Beard, Jameson, and Jensen; in tone it was remarkably defensive, assuming that the "motives" of the patriots were under attack. At every point Morgan seized on the most extreme version of the Progressive interpretation to deflate it. Regarding Becker: "To magnify the internal conflict in the same proportion as the revolt against England is to distort it beyond recognition." Regarding Jameson: there was "no radical rebuilding of social institutions"—a claim Jameson had never made—but only "a host of incalculable, accidental and incidental changes in society, many of which tended towards a redistribution of wealth." Regarding Beard: if the Framers of the Constitution had "self-interest" or "selfish interest," it was "undeniable" that their personal economic interests were involved, but the delegates to the Constitutional Convention also had a "selfish interest in bringing about a public good." Indeed, this was the thrust of Morgan's entire interpretation; in each crisis "self-interest led to the enunciation of principles which went far beyond the point at issue."[101]

Morgan may have been slaying more than the Beard-

[100] Tolles, "American Revolution as a Social Movement," pp. 1–12; Tolles, *George Logan of Philadelphia* (New York, 1953).

[101] David D. Hall, John M. Murrin, and Thad W. Tate, eds., *Saints and Revolutionaries: Essays on Early American History* (New York, 1984), p. xi; Morgan, *Birth of the Republic,* pp. 100 (Becker), 96, 98 (Jameson), 94–95, 190 (Beard); Morgan, "The American Revolution: Revisions in Need of Revising," *William and Mary Quarterly,* 3d ser. 14 (1957):3–15, reprinted with a preface in Morgan, *Challenge of the American Revolution,* pp. 43–44, and with an author's postscript in *In Search of Early America: The William and Mary Quarterly, 1943–1993* (Williamsburg, Va., 1993), pp. 44–53.

Becker-Jameson hydra. He had grown up in Cambridge where his father was a professor of law at Harvard and where he earned his B.A. in 1937. He spent 1938 at the London School of Economics where his mentors included Harold Laski, England's leading socialist intellectual, and R. H. Tawney, celebrated for *Religion and the Rise of Capitalism,* and where "most of the people I knew were, I guess, what would be called 'fellow travellers,' that is sympathetic to the Communist party and the Marxists." He was "disillusioned" by the politics of the left and regarded Marxist analysis as "simplistic." For a time a conscientious objector, he spent the war as a skilled tool and die maker. Back to Harvard for graduate school, he admired most Samuel Eliot Morison, who had long been engaged, as Robert Skotheim puts it, in rehabilitating the Puritans, as "a courageous, humane, brave, and significant people," and Perry Miller, who admired "the majesty and coherence of Puritan thinking" and was convinced that "the mind of man is the basic factor in human history." Both were bent on rescuing intellectual history from the degrading embrace of social history and the Puritans from economic determinist stereotypes fostered by Parrington and James Truslow Adams.[102] Morgan thus turned away from the path that led Tawney and Max Weber to explore Protestantism in its relation to capitalism and away from the path that led another admired Harvard teacher and friend, F. O. Matthiessen, a Christian socialist, to leftist activism and a social interpretation of the great writers of the American Renaissance, a seminal work in American Studies.[103] Morgan joined another crusade; Miller and Morison "made it necessary to take Puri-

[102] Courtwright, "Interview with Morgan," pp. 336–69; for the historiographic context, see Robert Allen Skotheim, *American Intellectual Histories and Their Historians* (Princeton, 1966), chap. 5, quotations pp. 174 (Morison) and 187 (Miller).

[103] Edmund S. Morgan, "The American Revolution as an Intellectual Movement, " in Arthur M. Schlesinger, Jr., and Morton White, eds., *Paths of American Thought* (Boston, 1963), pp. 11–33; F. O. Matthiessen, *American Renaissance: Art and Expression in the Age of Emerson and Whitman* (London and New York, 1941); Paul Sweezy and Leo Huberman, eds., *F. O. Matthiessen, 1902–50: A Collective Portrait* (New York, 1950).

tanism seriously," to "address what they said and wrote and read and taught," as he put it in 1966. He approached the American Revolution in the same spirit—to pursue "the American Revolution as an intellectual movement," the title of an essay that laid down the gauntlet to Jameson. The "distinguishing feature of the new historians"—among whom he numbered himself—in revising the Progressives, he wrote recently, "was not really their assumption of consensus among Americans but their insistence on taking seriously what the colonial leaders said they were fighting about."[104]

Morgan's first foray into the American Revolution in 1953—"my first real book after my dissertation" on the Puritan family—was a richly textured study in collaboration with Helen M. Morgan, his wife, of the two years of the Stamp Act crisis, 1765–66. One of the most influential books on the Revolution, the thrust was Counterprogressive. The Morgans rejected the prevailing interpretation that the colonists in responding to British taxation drew a distinction between internal and external taxation. They also rejected the Progressive contention that it was the economics and not the principle of taxation that was at stake and that the patriots, as Becker wrote, "step by step, from 1764 to 1776 . . . modified their theory to suit their needs." The Morgans found that the colonists objected on principle to all forms of parliamentary taxation and not simply to internal taxes. Second, in vivid accounts of the resistance led by the Sons of Liberty, they concluded that "the episodes of violence . . . were planned and prepared by men who were recognized at the time as belonging to the 'better and wiser part'" who never lost direction of events. Frankenstein had not created a monster, as Schlesinger had argued; the mob had little agency. Third, to "show the other side of the picture and thus achieve a kind of balance," they offered sympathetic chapter-length portraits of

[104] The quotations are from Edmund S. Morgan, "The Historians of Early New England," in Billington, ed., *Reinterpretation of Early American History*, p. 51, and Morgan, "The Second American Revolution," review of Gordon S. Wood, *The Radicalism of the American Revolution*, *New York Review of Books*, June 25, 1992, p. 23; for analysis of Morgan, see Marian J. Morton, *The Terrors of Ideological Politics: Liberal Historians in a Conservative Mood* (Cleveland, 1972), chap. 5, and Higham, *History*, p. 224.

five leading loyalist officials, "sufferers from that resistance," among them Thomas Hutchinson. The book was thus a peculiar blend, rescuing whig thought from the economic interpretation of the Progressives while embracing the imperial school's sympathies with suffering loyalist gentlemen and a distaste among conservatives and liberals for the mob.[105]

These conclusions in 1953, based on the opening crisis of 1765–66, cast a long shadow over Morgan's interpretation of the entire Revolutionary era in *The Birth of the Republic*. The Revolution "was a history of the Americans' search for principles." The first was "the principle that taxation was the exclusive right of their own elected representatives," held consistently through the entire era. The colonists' attachment was "sincere" and "genuine" and there was "no incongruity in their coupling of principle and self-interest"; they held to the principle of liberty "as a way of safeguarding the property which they regarded as the only security for life and liberty." The second principle they discovered was "equal rights," asserted in the Declaration. In the years that followed, while there was no "rebuilding of society," it was "possible to see the ideal [of equality] beginning to take shape and operating, if only fitfully, against the grosser social inequalities of the day." The third principle was national union, achieved in the Constitution of 1787, "the final fulfillment" of the struggle to make property secure and to link representation with taxation and equal rights.[106]

After a decade and more devoted to exploring the Puritans, when Morgan turned once again to the Revolution in 1967, he linked it to Puritanism. The Revolution in all of its phases, he argued, "was affected by, not to say guided, by a set of values inherited from the age of Puritanism." The Puritan ethic stressing frugality and frowning on extravagance, encouraging productive manufactures and discouraging speculation, informed the prewar movements for nonimportation

---

[105] Edmund S. Morgan and Helen M. Morgan, *The Stamp Act Crisis: Prologue to Revolution* (1953), 2d rev. ed. (New York, 1962); Edmund S. Morgan, "Colonial Ideas of Parliamentary Power," *William and Mary Quarterly*, 3d ser. 5 (1948):311–41; Becker, *Declaration of Independence*, chap. 3.

[106] Morgan, *Birth of the Republic*, pp. 51–52, 88–89, 96, 100, 132, 156–57.

and nonconsumption, the divisions during the war over corruption, and the movement to encourage American manufacturing and independence during the 1780s and 1790s.[107]

In the early 1970s as Morgan turned from New England to Virginia to explore the origins of the labor system, he was struck by the fact that "the rise of liberty and equality in this country was accompanied by the rise of slavery." The "central paradox in American history," he said in his presidential address to the Organization of American Historians in 1972, was "that two such contradictory developments were taking place simultaneously . . . from the seventeenth century to the nineteenth." The book that resulted from this exploration, *American Slavery, American Freedom: The Ordeal of Colonial Virginia* (1975), the three editors of Morgan's festschrift claimed, was "perhaps a more profound and desperate story of social conflict than anything the Progressives had ever written about colonial America." They wondered if perhaps the book was "a response to the war in Vietnam, a war replete with senseless massacres and exploitation." The Progressives, it was true, had never come to grips with slavery, but as Peter H. Wood pointed out, "the action and the anguish" in Morgan's Virginia "continue to belong largely to Europeans," not African-Americans.[108]

Surprisingly, this discovery of "the central paradox" led to no changes in Morgan's consensus interpretation of the Revolution. Quite the contrary, he thought that "the development

---

[107] Morgan, "The Puritan Ethic and the American Revolution," *William and Mary Quarterly*, 3d. ser. 24 (1967): 3–43, reprinted in *In Search of Early America*, pp. 78–108. Morgan's books on the Puritans were *The Puritan Dilemma: The Story of John Winthrop* (Boston, 1958), *The Gentle Puritan: A Life of Ezra Stiles, 1727–1795* (New Haven, 1962), *Visible Saints: The History of a Puritan Idea* (New York, 1963), *Puritan Political Ideas, 1558–1794* (Indianapolis, 1965), and *Roger Williams: The Church and the State* (New York, 1967).

[108] Morgan, "Slavery and Freedom: The American Paradox," *Journal of American History* 59 (1972):5–29; Morgan, *American Slavery, American Freedom: The Ordeal of Colonial Virginia* (New York, 1975); Hall, Murrin, and Tate, eds., *Saints and Revolutionaries*, p. xii; for Morgan's reaction, see Courtwright, "Interview with Morgan," pp. 358–59; Peter H. Wood, "'I Did the Best I Could for My Day': The Study of Early Black History during the Second Reconstruction, 1960 to 1976," *William and Mary Quarterly*, 3d ser. 35 (1978):185–225.

of slavery is perhaps the key to the consensus that prevailed in colonial America, for slavery meant the substitution of a helpless, closely guarded lower class for a dangerous, armed lower class that would fight if exploited too ruthlessly." This prevented the recurrence in 1776 of the class conflict of Bacon's Rebellion in 1676. So too did the "extraordinary social mobility" in the colonies and the war against Britain that "tended to suppress or encompass social conflict." "With a majority of laborers in chains and with the most discontented freemen venting their discontent in loyalism, the struggle over who shall rule at home was unlikely to bear many of the marks of class conflict." The social system contained the conflict.[109]

He left the argument of *The Birth of the Republic* intact in a second edition in 1977. In discussing the results of the Revolution, he added a page on slavery, acknowledging that "the blessings of liberty had grown side-by-side with the burdens of slavery, and the two were locked in an embrace not easily broken." But he let stand his earlier optimistic summary; he could still see the ideal of equality beginning to take effect, "if only fitfully, against the grosser social inequalities of the day." Slavery, an issue that David Brion Davis, Winthrop D. Jordan, and a host of scholars had moved to a central place in the history of the Revolution, remained peripheral in Morgan's narrative, and African-Americans as actors were not a presence.[110] In his third edition in 1992 Morgan saw no reason to change this sunny appraisal. He now added one sentence—a response to the "needs of his time"?—granting that the ideal of equality did not operate effectively against the inequality of women. "Although the Revolution called upon women to undertake jobs formerly reserved to men, and though they emerged from it with an enlarged view of their role in society,

[109] Morgan, "Conflict and Consensus," in Stephen G. Kurtz and James H. Hutson, eds., *Essays on the American Revolution* (Chapel Hill, 1973), pp. 289–309.

[110] Morgan, *The Birth of the Republic*, 2d ed. (Chicago, 1977); David Brion Davis, *The Problem of Slavery in Western Culture* (Ithaca, N.Y., 1966); Davis, *The Problem of Slavery in the Age of Revolution, 1770–1823* (Ithaca, N.Y., 1975); Winthrop D. Jordan, *White over Black: American Attitudes toward the Negro, 1550–1812* (Chapel Hill, 1968).

they did not achieve any fundamental change in the inferior status English and colonial law had allotted them." But these racial and gender paradoxes were not allowed to intrude on his original evaluation of the Revolution as a successful search for the principles of liberty and equality. It was a Revolution without losers save for suffering loyalist émigrés, or at least it was a world where the principle of equality would eventually trickle down to the unequals.[111]

Perhaps this is what Daniel Boorstin may have had in mind in his editor's foreword to the third edition in 1992 when he praised Morgan for avoiding "fashionable atomizing fads [which] obscure the wisdom and heroism" of the Founders, the "fads," presumably, of black history, women's history, or artisan or agrarian or Indian history. Boorstin also pointed to "recent events abroad in what was once the Soviet Union [which] have dramatized the weakness of dogmatic empires and a priori ideology as the cement for a changing society." In his bibliographic essay in 1992 Morgan still defined the historians' debate over the Revolution in terms of Beard and his critics, a debate long faded and redefined. Morgan concludes his most recent book with an analysis of the decline of deference, which he attributes to the experience of the war. In 1992 he acknowledged the way in which "the needs of his time" may have impinged on his scholarship, using the very words of a liberal critic of *Birth of the Republic* thirty-five years before. "Working in what an older critic called 'the flush times of mid-twentieth century capitalism,'" he wrote, the historians of the post-war generation "were perhaps less sensitive than their predecessors to internal conflicts among the Revolutionary Americans." But those conflicts, it would seem, remain "pretty small potatoes." An admirer of men of consistent principles, Morgan thus remained consistent in his interpretation.[112]

[111] Morgan, *Birth of the Republic*, 3d ed. (Chicago, 1992), pp. 95–96.

[112] Ibid., pp. ix (Boorstin), 191–92 (Morgan); Courtwright, "Interview with Morgan" ("small potatoes"); Morgan, *Inventing the People: The Rise of Popular Sovereignty in England and America* (New York, 1988); for his 1992 comment see Morgan, "The Second American Revolution," p. 23; for the original review see Max Savelle, *William and Mary Quarterly*, 3d ser. 14 (1957):608–18.

"No Morgan school exists," his students insist, "no point of view sustained by generations of disciples," although their work reflects "his confidence in intellectual history and his long standing interest in the Puritans." He concurs. Among over fifty doctoral students, more have written about the Puritan "saints" than the "revolutionaries," and among the latter several have mapped territory uncharted by Morgan. Especially in recent decades many have responded creatively to the "needs of their times."[113] But with notable exceptions they have not challenged the interpretation he has presented with an unmatched cogency and consistency for over forty years.

VI. AGAINST THE GRAIN

When an old paradigm is under assault and a new one vying to replace it, books often appear that do not fit the ascendant trend and seem to be a voice from the past. Sometimes they are the work of an older generation; often they are the voice of a graduate student not caught up in prevailing fashions. Such voices against the grain are often not appreciated when they appear and are not recognized until years later.

In the 1950s it took a while for the Cold War to freeze scientific inquiry in the ice of consensus history. If the prospect of a nuclear Armageddon made coexistence unlikely among the superpowers, a strange kind of coexistence flourished in the uniquely American, publisher-driven books in the "Problems of Interpretations" anthologies, the first of which was known as "the Amherst series," which presented students with arrays of conflicting historical views. Students were asked to evaluate spokesmen for the various schools: Andrews or Gipson for the imperial school, Louis M. Hacker for economic determinist Marxism, Jameson and Tolles for the Revolution as a social movement, Morgan for the Revolution as an intellectual movement, and, after the 1960s, Bailyn for the ideological interpretation and Jesse Lemisch for history "from the bottom up." The pattern was similar in the Bobbs-Merrill series in the 1960s that reprinted single articles at a cheap price, very

---

[113] Hall, Murrin, and Tate, eds., *Saints and Revolutionaries*, p. xiii; for a list of Morgan's students and their theses, ibid., pp. 373–79.

popular in an age before xeroxing. For the Revolutionary period, students (and their teachers) could read articles by Jensen, Ferguson, Main, their critics Bailyn, Brown, Greene, Kenyon, McDonald, Morgan, Tolles, and Wood, as well as by William Appleman Williams, Staughton Lynd, and Lemisch of the New Left and scholars who fit no categories. These publications are a reminder of the healthy skepticism of many historians to all determinisms, and an eclectic willingness to borrow a little from this interpretation and a little from that.[114]

Scholarly works appeared during these years that were not incorporated into Counterprogressive paradigms. Books by Elisha P. Douglass, Benjamin Quarles, Curtis P. Nettels, Robert R. Palmer, and the scholarly career of Richard B. Morris provide examples of scholarship that actually enhanced older interpretations, including Jameson's.

Douglass is an example of a doctoral student trying to pursue an old hypothesis that had not died. He introduced his book on the struggle for political democracy state by state, initially a thesis at Yale directed by Leonard W. Labaree, as an effort to deal with an aspect of the social movement Jameson had neglected, "the struggle of certain less privileged groups within the ranks of the revolutionary party to obtain equal political rights." He was exploring Becker's internal struggle past 1776. While Douglass stressed the conservatism of the outcome and halted at constitutions rather than political practice, he portrayed conflicts over the structure of government that were intense, widespread, and often class-oriented. More sympathetic to the democrats than the conservative whigs, Douglass offered a yardstick by which to measure achievement of the democratic ideal. Thomas Jefferson, for example, emerged as more moderate than radical when contrasted to grass-roots democrats.[115]

---

[114] Earl Latham, ed., *The Declaration of Independence and the Constitution* (Boston, 1956), and John C. Wahlke, ed., *The Causes of the American Revolution* (Boston, 1962), both volumes in the much-used "Amherst series"; George A. Billias, ed., *The American Revolution: How Revolutionary Was It?* (New York, 1965); *Index to the Bobbs-Merrill Reprint Series in American History* (Indianapolis, 1973).

[115] Elisha P. Douglass, *Rebels and Democrats: The Struggle for Equal Political Rights and Majority Rule during the American Revolution* (Chapel Hill, 1955).

Benjamin Quarles's *The Negro in the American Revolution* (1961) was simply a book ahead of its time by a pioneer African-American scholar. In the 1950s and early 1960s the scholarly debate on slavery spun around the axis of what slavery did to African-Americans with Kenneth M. Stampp's northern abolitionist view challenging Ulrich B. Phillips's benevolent racism, and after 1959 around Stanley M. Elkins's interpretation of the slave system as a concentration camp that infantilized blacks. Quarles's carefully researched study focused on what blacks did in the war from 1775 to 1783, fighting as bearers of arms in the American militia or army, or serving as spies and laborers, or taking flight from slavery to fight "in the king's service" and after the war evacuating to Nova Scotia with the British. Such a book built around the agency of blacks in resistance to slavery fit not at all into any framework of the Revolution or of slavery and lay fallow.[116]

Curtis P. Nettels's *The Emergence of a National Economy, 1775–1815* (1962) was a voice from the past—the magnum opus of a second-generation Progressive published twenty-five years after his initial scholarship. A thorough, almost encyclopedic inventory of the economic changes wrought in the Revolutionary era, it seemingly pursued no themes. But it provided ample evidence for the changes in the land system Jameson had suggested in his second chapter and for the burgeoning of commerce and manufacturing, the theme of Jameson's third chapter. It was an economic history of the Revolution, not an economic interpretation, and coming as it did when intellectual and ideological interpretations were in vogue, it was probably used more as a work of reference than interpretation.[117]

Robert R. Palmer's ambitious work of synthesis in the late 1950s, a magisterial two-volume comparative study of the late

[116] Benjamin Quarles, *The Negro in the American Revolution* (Chapel Hill, 1961). Quarles received his Ph.D. at Wisconsin in 1940; see August Meier and Elliott Rudwick, *Black History and the Historical Profession, 1915–1980* (Urbana, Ill., 1986), for the historiography of slavery and, for Quarles, pp. 115–16; see also David Brion Davis, "Slavery and the Post–World War II Historians," *Daedalus*, Spring 1974, 1–16.

[117] Curtis P. Nettels, *The Emergence of a National Economy, 1775–1815* (New York, 1962).

eighteenth-century revolutions in Europe and the United States, sustained the ailing Jameson thesis in unexpected ways. A scholar of the French Revolution and a student of Carl Becker, Palmer offered the first comparative history of revolutions since Crane Brinton's and one of the last to include the American Revolution. Very much aware that he was writing at a moment when "those who discount the revolutionary character of the American Revolution seem to be gaining ground," Palmer asserted that "my own view is that there was a real revolution in America and that it was a painful conflict in which many were injured."[118]

To gauge the extent of social change, Palmer offered two "quantitative and objective measures: how many refugees were there from the American Revolution, and how much property did they lose in comparison to the [émigrés from the] French Revolution." Estimates of the number of loyalist refugees ranged from 60,000 to 100,000. Taking the lower figure, Palmer calculated that this represented 24 émigrés per thousand population compared to 5 per thousand in the French Revolution. Then, taking conservative figures for both countries to measure the confiscation of property, Palmer concluded that "revolutionary France, ten times as large as Revolutionary America, confiscated only twelve times as much property from its emigres." Looking at the political impact of loyalist migration, Palmer wrote that "it must always be remembered than an important nucleus of conservatism was permanently lost in the United States." French émigrés by contrast returned to France.[119]

In examining the political dimensions of change, Palmer emphasized the way Americans institutionalized the concept of "the people as constituent power" in creating state constitutions. The Revolution "was revolutionary because it showed how certain abstract doctrines, such as the rights of man and the sovereignty of the people, could be 'reduced to practice' as [John] Adams put it." Palmer found the Revolution as a

[118] Robert R. Palmer, *The Age of the Democratic Revolution: A Political History of Europe and America, 1760–1800*, 2 vols. (Princeton, 1959–64), 1:187–88.

[119] Ibid., pp. 188–90

whole "really a revolution" but cloaked in "ambivalence." "It was conservative, it was also revolutionary and vice versa. It was conservative because colonial Americans had long been radical by general standards of Western Civilization. . . . It was conservative because the colonies had never known oppression, excepting always for slavery—because as human institutions go, America had always been free." If these conclusions fell in with the thrust of consensus scholarship, the rest did not. The Revolution "was revolutionary because the colonists took the risk of rebellion, because they could not avoid a conflict among themselves, and because they checkmated those Americans who as the country developed most admired the aristocratic society of England and Europe. . . . Elites for better or for worse would henceforth be on the defensive against popular values."[120]

Richard B. Morris was a scholar who moved away from the Progressive interpretation of the Revolution without closing the door to Jameson and the issue of transformation. He received his degree in legal history from Columbia in 1929 and taught at the City University of New York until he received the call from Columbia in the 1940s. He was an outsider; a Yale professor described him to Jesse Lemisch, a Yale undergraduate on his way to Columbia graduate school, as "a most energetic little man (of your same religious background)." In 1946 Morris published *Government and Labor in Early America*, a massive study of the white colonial laboring classes, free and indentured, based on ten years of research in 20,000 court cases from Maine to Florida. Its importance was not apparent at the time either to scholars of the Revolution or of labor history. In a long chapter Morris richly documented "concerted action among workers" including "political action by working-class groups" before, during, and after the Revolution. Morris located the urban classes the Progressive historians were unable to recognize, identifying the first American labor movement and filling in the missing "plain people" in the Revolution whom Jameson could only see as "peasant proprietors." His unmatched two-volume collection of docu-

---

[120] Ibid., p. 235

ments of the Revolution, coedited with Henry Steele Commager, emphasized the experiences of the common people during the war and included a chapter on the Progressive theme, "The Struggle for Democracy at Home."[121]

"As I read more deeply into the American Revolutionary period," Morris reminisced, "I came to feel that the fashionable Populist-Progressive interpretation represented an oversimplification of the facts, and I parted company with much of the interpretation as regards the Confederation period." But in the mid-1960s, despite his sharp differences with Merrill Jensen, he held to the formulation that there were "The Two Revolutions," one against Great Britain, the other internal, which was "marked by liberative currents, class currents, and egalitarian urges. . . . Clearly there is something more to the Spirit of '76 than 'redcoats go home.'"[122]

Earlier he had abandoned a massive study of early American slavery—not yet a fashionable field—shifting his energies to elites, editing the papers of John Jay and producing a full-dress study of the diplomacy of the Revolution. But he did not abandon his earlier concerns. His own scholarship on the Confederation, he felt, focused "on the people rather than the leaders." "This is where my interpretation of the period departs from both the Populist-Progressive school and the consensus historians." In 1976, in his presidential address to the AHA, citing the scholarship of the New Left and new social history of the decade gone by, he spoke with verve of "a people's revolution" that began "an era of innovation unprecedented in that day and age." He laid stress, as did Palmer, on the "new men" who rose in the era of the Revolution. While he felt that "the case for significant social change during the Revolution still needs to be made," he was confident

[121] Leonard W. Labaree to Jesse Lemisch, summer 1957, cited in Lemisch, "Radicals, Marxists, and Gentlemen: A Memoir of Twenty Years Ago," *Radical Historians' Newsletter* 59 (November 1989); Richard B. Morris, *Government and Labor in Early America* (New York, 1946); Morris and Henry Steele Commager, eds., *The Spirit of 'Seventy-Six: The Story of the American Revolution as Told by Participants* (New York, 1958), chap. 10; Morris, *American Revolution Reconsidered*, chap. 2, pp. 76, 84; Morris, "History over Time," p. 461.

[122] Morris, "History over Time," p. 462.

that "indubitably reform in . . . diverse categories helped create a more egalitarian and pluralistic society."[123]

A decade later in his last book he encapsulated these changes in the chapter "A Cautiously Transforming Egalitarianism," half of which he devoted to "persons forgotten," namely "poor whites," "black people," "native Americans," and "women." "After more than half a century of interpreting the past," Morris offered a "confession." "Honest historians must be prepared to concede that new situations, additional documentation and further reflection may modify our earlier views." His openness to new trends was testimony to the persisting pull of a social interpretation of the Revolution, if not of Jameson.[124]

Reviewing recent reactions among scholars to the works of Douglass, Quarles, Nettels, Palmer, and Morris, it is striking how historians now testify to their durability. Douglass's book in Gordon Wood's judgment is "important in emphasizing the radical and populist impulses in the states." Quarles's study is to Peter Wood "the judicious and pathbreaking study," and the editors of a volume of essays on slavery in the Revolution dedicated the book to him and three other pioneer African-American scholars. The standard survey of the literature on the economy takes it for granted that Nettels's thorough study of the impact of the war raises questions that merit further exploration. A scholar of the new history of colonial labor speaks of Morris's 1946 book as "a neglected classic . . . at the zenith of labor history." An informal survey in the 1990s of a score of historians of the Revolution for their opinions of Palmer's book finds a near-consensus on his "amazing ability" to transcend the historiography of his time and enthusiasm for his interpretation. Such belated recogni-

---

[123] Morris, *The Peacemakers: The Great Powers and American Independence* (New York, 1965); Morris et al., eds., *John Jay . . . Unpublished Papers . . .* , 2 vols. (New York, 1975–80); Morris, "'We the People of the United States': The Bicentennial of a People's Revolution," *American Historical Review* 82 (1977): 1–19; for Morris's career, see Peter Coclanis, "Richard B. Morris," in Wilson, ed., *Twentieth-Century American Historians*, pp. 307–14; for a bibliography, see Vaughan and Billias, eds., *Essays in Honor of Richard B. Morris*, pp. 376–85.

[124] Morris, *Forging of the Union*, chap. 7.

tion should give heart to scholars who go against the grain; it is also a warning to judge each piece of nonconforming scholarship on its merits.[125]

VII. THE COUNTERPROGRESSIVES—PART 2

"This book," Bernard Bailyn wrote in 1974 in introducing his biography of Thomas Hutchinson, the leading loyalist of the American Revolution, "which depicts the fortunes of a conservative in a time of radical upheaval and deals with the problems of public disorder and ideological commitment, was not written as a tract for the times. . . . But it would be foolish to deny that I have been influenced in writing it by the events of the late 1960's, when the original drafts were written. . . . My understanding has been sharpened by the course of American politics in the 1960's and early 1970's."[126]

If the first wave of Counterprogressive interpretations of the Revolution was shaped in the 1950s in the Manichean atmosphere of cold war and the need to lay the ghost of Charles Beard, the second wave associated with the ideological interpretation of Bernard Bailyn and Gordon Wood was more complex. It unfolded in the early 1960s in an atmosphere where revisionist scholarship was more secure and the nation, guided by the best and the brightest in Washington, seemed headed towards Arthur M. Schlesinger, Jr.'s, *Vital Center* and a renewal of the reform impulse. Then as the civil rights movement became Black Power, and the movement against the Vietnam War and the youth counterculture turned re-

---

[125] On Douglass: Bailyn et al., *The Great Republic*, p. 319; on Quarles: Peter H. Wood, "'I Did the Best I Could'"; on Nettels: John J. McCusker and Russell R. Menard, *The Economy of British North America, 1607–1789* (Chapel Hill, 1985), pp. 360–61; on Morris: Marcus Rediker, "Good Hands, Stout Hearts, and Fast Feet: The History and Culture of Working People in Early America," in Geoff Eley and William Hunt, eds., *Reviving the English Revolution: Reflections and Elaborations on the Work of Christopher Hill* (London, 1988), pp. 242–43; on Palmer: William Pencak, "A Second Look: R. R. Palmer's *The Age of the Democratic Revolution:* The View from America after Thirty Years," *Pennsylvania History* 60 (1993):73–92.

[126] Bernard Bailyn, *The Ordeal of Thomas Hutchinson* (Cambridge, Mass., 1974), pp. vii-viii.

form into rebellion, the ideological interpretation seemed to veer off into opposition to "radical upheaval" and "public disorder."

If Edmund Morgan rejected Jameson's thesis of "the transforming hand of revolution" outright, Bernard Bailyn and Gordon Wood cast a new interpretive mold in which "the transforming radicalism of the revolution" (Bailyn's phrase) flowing from the dominant ideology became a central theme. It was this latter theme that Bailyn seemed to abandon but which Wood pursued.

The weight Bailyn attached to ideas in his ideological interpretation of the Revolution surprised his graduate students who, as Wood wrote in a festschrift in 1991, thought of him in the 1950s and early 1960s as a historian of colonial America for whom "society itself" was "the central subject of study and analysis." His research had illuminated the merchant class of colonial New England, the social context of early American education, and the relation of politics to social structure in Virginia. In the study of politics his students thought of him as committed to a "hard-boiled Namierism," skeptical of the causal role of ideas. Bailyn dedicated his edited volume on the pamphlets of the Revolution to his Harvard mentor and colleague Oscar Handlin, a historian who had led social history into new terrain.[127]

Bailyn's ideological interpretation of the Revolution was unmistakably Counterprogressive. Earlier he had distanced himself from some of the shapers of consensus scholarship. He characterized Daniel Boorstin's study of colonial America as an "apologia for his disillusioned conservatism." He regarded Robert Brown's claim that colonial Massachusetts was

---

[127] Gordon S. Wood, "The Creative Imagination of Bernard Bailyn," in James A. Henretta, Michael G. Kammen, and Stanley N. Katz, eds., *The Transformation of Early American History: Society, Authority, and Ideology* (New York, 1991), pp. 16–50; on the "vital" place of the Hutchinson biography in Bailyn's interpretation of the Revolution, see Jack N. Rakove, "'How Else Could It End?' Bernard Bailyn and the Problem of Authority in Early America," ibid., pp. 60–62; Bailyn, *The New England Merchants in the Seventeenth Century* (Cambridge, Mass., 1955); Bailyn, "Politics and Social Structure in Virginia," in James M. Smith, ed., *Seventeenth-Century America* (Chapel Hill, 1959), pp. 90–115; Bailyn, *Education in the Formation of American Society: Needs and Opportunities for Study* (Chapel Hill, 1960).

a middle-class democracy as "very confusing" for its failure to distinguish between the legal existence of a relatively wide franchise and its exercise and "anachronistic" in its use of the concept of democracy. But Bailyn had accepted the Hartzian premise of the Counterprogressive critique. "Reforms that made America seem to the enlightened world like the veritable heavenly city of the eighteenth-century philosophers had been matters of fact before they were matters of theory and revolutionary doctrine," he wrote. In the Revolution the leaders "undertook to complete, formalize, systematize, and symbolize what previously had been only partially realized, confused, and disputed matters of fact."[128]

The *Ideological Origins of the American Revolution* (1967), originally published in 1965 as the extended introduction to the first of four projected volumes of pamphlets of the Revolution, was the outgrowth of his study of over four hundred pamphlets, some seventy-two of which he selected to edit for the John Harvard Library. The Progressive historians from Schlesinger on had read the pamphlets as propaganda. Philip Davidson called his book *Propaganda and the American Revolution;* John C. Miller subtitled his biography of Samuel Adams *Pioneer in Propaganda.* "The more I read," Bailyn wrote, "the less useful, it seemed to me, was the whole idea of propaganda in its modern meaning when applied to the writings of the American Revolution." Reading the pamphlets from the "interior" view, he was convinced "that the fear of a comprehensive conspiracy against liberty throughout the English-speaking world ... lay at the heart of the Revolutionary movement." His study of the pamphlets, he wrote, "confirmed my rather old-fashioned view that the American Revolution was above all else an ideological, constitutional, political struggle and not primarily a controversy between social groups undertaken to force changes in the organization of the

---

[128] Bailyn, review of Daniel Boorstin, *The Americans: The Colonial Experience, New Republic,* Dec. 15, 1958, p. 18, cited in Novick, *That Noble Dream,* p. 334; Bailyn, "The American Revolution," in John Garraty, *Interpreting American History: Conversations with Historians,* 2 vols. (New York, 1970), 1:85–86; Bailyn, "Political Experience and Enlightenment Ideas in Eighteenth-Century America," *American Historical Review* 67 (1962):339–51.

society or the economy"—a formulation in which the words *primarily* and *undertaken* made for a needlessly overstated antithesis.[129]

But if his reading of the pamphlets confirmed Bailyn's "old-fashioned" view of the origins of the Revolution, it suggested a newfangled view of the consequences or arguably a new version of J. Franklin Jameson's interpretation. The book in its original form in 1965 as the introduction to *Pamphlets of the American Revolution* was called "The Transforming Radicalism of the American Revolution,"[130] and, if Bailyn retreated to a less threatening title, he did not abandon his bold formulation. Chapter 6, "The Contagion of Liberty," explored the impact of political ideas on antislavery thought, the disestablishment of religion, and the decline of deference, a terrain Jameson had opened, and on radical democratic thought, a subject Jameson had avoided.

To Jameson the Revolution had been inadvertently radical, a stream overflowing its banks; to Bailyn it was inherently radical, the consequence of the "logic of revolutionary thought" and of the "intellectual dynamism" of ideas. Bailyn posited two major intellectual transformations. The first was "a new world of political thought," which "crystallized in effect three generations of political experience" of the eighteenth century. "The radicalism the Americans conveyed to the world in 1776 was a transformed as well as a transforming force." Then, beginning in 1775–76, the movement of thought "swept past boundaries that few had set out to cross, into regions few had wished to enter." In an array of rich metaphors, in which agency was lost, this process was sometimes mechanical ("a spillover"), sometimes a disease ("the contagion of liberty"), sometimes a firestorm ("defiance of constituted authority leaped like a spark from one flammable area

---

[129] Bailyn, with the assistance of Jane N. Garrett, ed., *Pamphlets of the American Revolution, 1750–1776,* vol. 1, *1750–1765* (Cambridge, Mass., 1965), pp. vii-xii; Philip Davidson, *Propaganda and the American Revolution, 1763–1783* (Chapel Hill, 1941); John C. Miller, *Sam Adams: Pioneer in Propaganda* (Stanford, Calif., 1936); Schlesinger, *Prelude to Independence;* Bailyn, *The Ideological Origins of the American Revolution* (Cambridge, Mass., 1967), p. vi.

[130] Bailyn, ed., *Pamphlets of the American Revolution,* p. xv.

to another, growing in heat as it went"), and sometimes altogether mysterious (conditions were "touched by the magic of revolutionary thought"). Thus while "in no obvious sense was the American Revolution undertaken as a social revolution"—*undertaken* offering another misleading caricature of Progressive claims—"the order of society" was "transformed as a result of the Revolution" or at least a basis for transformation was laid in "changes in the realm of belief and attitude." [131] In defending his interpretation, Bailyn later insisted that "it does not minimize the social and political changes that the Revolution created; it does not deny—indeed it alone explains—the upsurge of reformist zeal that is so central a part of the Revolution." [132]

Bailyn did not explore the "spillover" of the radicalism of Revolutionary thought. He edited only the first volume of pamphlets, which went to 1765, leaving in limbo the pamphlets of the mid-1770s that would have demonstrated the "contagion of liberty" in full epidemic. And the thrust of his own scholarship in these years lay entirely in amplifying the proof of the ideological origins of the Revolution, whether he was dealing with whig leaders, Thomas Hutchinson, the chief American loyalist, Protestant ministers, or the intellectual world of an ordinary Son of Liberty, Harbottle Dorr, a Boston shopkeeper. [133]

In the late 1960s and early 1970s, Bailyn's argument and tone shifted. Earlier he portrayed the radical patriots as principled, rational, and ideological, even when driven by a paranoid conception of conspiracy. [134] He and his students, especially Pauline Maier, building on the pioneering work of George Rudé, rescued the mob from the accusations of contemporary loyalists and historians of all schools that the rioters "were mindless instruments, passive tools of unscrupulous

[131] Bailyn, *Ideological Origins*, pp. 161–62, 230, 236, 271, 302, 305.

[132] Bailyn, "The Central Themes of the American Revolution," in Kurtz and Hutson, eds., *Essays on the American Revolution*, p. 15.

[133] The essays are assembled in Bailyn, *Faces of Revolution: Personalities and Themes in the Struggle for American Independence* (New York, 1990).

[134] Bailyn, "A Note on Conspiracy," in Bailyn, ed., *Pamphlets of the American Revolution*, 1:86–89.

demagogues like [Ebenezer] McIntosh," the shoemaker prominent in the Boston Stamp Act demonstrations. "Far from being empty vessels," Bailyn argued, the rioters "shared actively the attitudes and fears of the intellectual leaders of the Revolutionary movement."[135] Now Bailyn seemed to identify himself with Thomas Hutchinson, as had Edmund Morgan in *The Stamp Act Crisis,* and to distance himself from the radicals. In his biography of Hutchinson, his radical whig opponents became "demagogues" and "malcontents" who included "wild men, alarmists, the political paranoids, the professional agitators." They were "paranoics" driven by "passion and personal discontent" to make a "scapegoat" of Hutchinson. He thus reduced to a crude psychological determinism a group he had previously portrayed as rational. And the mob now appeared as "brutal," "savage," "more and more savage," and in effect mindless.[136] The historian reaches the "ultimate stage of maturity," Bailyn wrote, "where partisanship is left behind, and the historian can find an equal humanity in all the participants, the winners and the losers."[137] Between 1964 and 1974 Bailyn's winners, the patriots, top and bottom, lost some of their humanity.

This shift in Bailyn's value judgments of radicals was striking in his commentary on Thomas Paine. In 1965 in the comparative context of the pamphlets, Bailyn considered *Common Sense* "that brilliant pamphlet," agreeing explicitly with Harold Laski that Paine "with the exception of Marx [was] 'the most influential pamphleteer of all time.'" In the late 1960s *Common Sense* was still "a brilliant rhetorical production" and "a brilliant pamphlet by any measure." But by 1973 Paine was "savage," "enraged," "an ignoramus," "a bankrupt corset maker," whose writing was "slapdash," "crude," and "slightly

[135] Ibid., p. 583; Pauline Maier, "Popular Uprisings and Civil Authority in Eighteenth-Century America," *William and Mary Quarterly,* 3d ser. 27 (1970):3–35, reprinted in *In Search of Early America,* pp. 138–61, with author's postscript, pp. 161–62; Maier, *From Resistance to Revolution: Colonial Radicals and the Development of American Opposition to Britain, 1765–1776* (New York, 1972).

[136] Bailyn, *Ordeal of Thomas Hutchinson,* pp. 15, 72–73, 125, 133–34, 139, 182.

[137] Ibid., pp. viii–xii; Bailyn, "Central Themes," p. 15.

insane," and by 1975 Bailyn dismissed his writings as "marginal."[138]

In his attitude to other historians by the 1970s Bailyn demonstrated what Gordon Wood calls an "aversion" and a "particular antipathy" to a social interpretation of the Revolution that "confused and troubled even some of his former students." "He has been apparently unwilling to entertain any sort of social interpretation of the Revolution," Wood wrote. "Since his discovery of ideology, Bailyn has repeatedly denied that the Revolution had social origins and social impulses and has gone out of his way to refute those historians who have tried to find any."[139]

A contextualist analysis of Bailyn's own writings—the only method open to outsiders—suggests he was obsessed with the emergence of a wide range of historians who had not fallen in with either an intellectual or ideological reading of the Revolution. He lumped together as "neo-Progressives" second and third generation Progressives, the first wave of the New Left and the new social history, and even other consensus scholars and heretics among his students. In a paper delivered to a conference of scholars of the Revolution in 1971, one had to guess who were his contemporary targets from the arrows of "nots" he shot from his quiver. "The outbreak of the revolution was not the result of social discontent, or of economic disturbances, or of rising misery [Gary Nash? Kenneth Lockridge? James Henretta?], or of those mysterious social strains that seem to beguile the imaginations of historians straining to find peculiar predispositions to upheaval [Jack Greene? Gordon Wood?]. Nor was there a transformation of mob behavior or of the lives of the 'inarticulate' [Jesse Lemisch? Staughton Lynd?] in the pre-revolutionary years that accounts for the disruption of Anglo-American politics."[140]

[138] Bailyn, *Ideological Origins*, pp. 285–86; Garraty, *Conversations with Historians*, pp. 87–88; Bailyn, "Common Sense," in *Fundamental Testaments of the American Revolution*, Library of Congress Symposia on the American Revolution (Washington, D.C., 1973); Bailyn, "Lines of Force," p. 10.

[139] Wood, "Creative Imagination," p. 35.

[140] Bailyn, "Central Themes," pp. 12–13. The identification of the scholars is made explicit in Bailyn, "Lines of Force."

Earlier he thought "there can be some benefits from what the New Left historians are attempting to do"; the study of the mob "should yield some useful social data."[141] In 1975 in a paper before an international congress of historians he pilloried scholars pursuing the study of "the mob," "the helpless and inarticulate," seamen, and slaves as being for the most part "hopelessly presentist" or driven by "extreme and polemical presentism." He felt compelled to reassure European scholars still steeped in the comparative study of revolutions that in the American Revolution "there was no massive challenge from below," as in the English Civil War, and "no peasant uprising, no millennarian or anarchistic or jacobin communistic rebellion." Bailyn attempted to withdraw the American Revolution altogether from the generic category of revolutions.[142]

What accounts for Bailyn's differences with his critics hardening into "aversion" and his judgment of the radical whigs changing from principle to paranoia? What "events of the late 1960s" might have impinged on a professor at Harvard University writing about rioters who had destroyed Thomas Hutchinson's manuscript history of Massachusetts in 1765 while demolishing his house? One can only speculate: students storming University Hall in Harvard Yard bent on uncovering the dean's files; students at Columbia University occupying buildings and destroying a scholar's manuscript; the AHA undergoing what Robert R. Palmer, its president, called "the most turbulent business meeting in the whole history of the association . . . something like a revolution and probably also a counterrevolution"—one could go on with a litany of parallel national political events. Kenneth Lynn, a Harvard professor of American Civilization, believes Bailyn "learned a great deal from his experience in the Harvard Bust. He learned what it felt like to be an establishment insider who knows that the social order he is fighting for has made grave mistakes, but whose first duty is to preserve its integrity from the onslaughts of anarchy." Arguably an obses-

---

[141] Garraty, *Conversations with Historians*, pp. 86–87.

[142] Bailyn, "Lines of Force," pp. 8–20, 24–34. This essay was not published or reprinted in Bailyn, *Faces of Revolution*.

sion with presentism in other scholars has its own presentist roots.[143]

Bailyn never published his angry polemic of 1975 and in 1981, after a semblance of equilibrium was restored to American society, Harvard, and the historical profession, in an expansive mood in his presidential address to the AHA Bailyn said, "We are all Marxists in the sense of assuming that history is profoundly shaped by underlying economic or 'materialist' configurations and by people's responses to them." This together with his massive "Peopling of British North America" project led Gordon Wood to conclude that "he has returned to social history with a vengeance and has reminded us that he is still the social historian he always was." In 1992 with the radicalism of the American Revolution on the agenda of historians, Bailyn in the preface to the second edition of *Ideological Origins* reminded readers that "in fact I called the book when it was first published *The Transforming Radicalism of the American Revolution*." He expanded the volume to include a chapter on the Constitution of 1787 as "the final and climactic expression of the ideology of the American Revolution" but left in limbo "the contagion of liberty." It was thus a theme he had asserted but not developed.[144]

If Bailyn did not pursue "the transforming radicalism of the American Revolution," Gordon Wood did. Of all Bailyn's

---

[143] Kenneth Lynn, "The Regressive Historians," *American Scholar* 47 (1978), reprinted in Lynn, *The Airline to Seattle: Studies in Literary and Historical Writing about America* (Chicago, 1983), pp. 190–93; for events of the 1960s, see Todd Gitlin, *The Sixties: Years of Hope, Days of Rage* (New York, 1987); for events at Harvard, see Lawrence E. Eichel et al., *The Harvard Strike* (New York, 1970); for scholarship and politics at Harvard, see John Trumpbour, ed., *How Harvard Rules* (Boston, 1989), 379–97; for the activities of radical historians, see Jonathan M. Wiener, "Radical Historians and the Crisis in American History, 1959–1980," *Journal of American History* 76 (1989):399–434, and Novick, *That Noble Dream*, chap. 13; Robert R. Palmer, "The American Historical Association in 1970," *American Historical Review* 76 (1971):1–2.

[144] Bailyn, "The Challenge of Modern Historiography," *American Historical Review* 87 (1982):1–24, quotation at p. 6; Wood, "Creative Imagination," p. 44; Bailyn, *Ideological Origins of the American Revolution*, 2d ed. (Cambridge, Mass., 1992), p. v, postscript, pp. 321–79.

students—"a peculiarly headstrong set of students who argued continually with him and with each other," as Pauline Maier put it—Wood did the most to challenge and at the same time expand his mentor's interpretation. While Wood's book *The Creation of the American Republic, 1776–1787* (1969) took a place alongside *Ideological Origins* in the canon of the ideological interpretation, Wood was persistently in tension with Bailyn. In an influential article in 1966, he argued that the very success of the Bailyn thesis pointed to the need for a new socioeconomic interpretation of the Revolution. Wood rejected the scholarship of the Progressive historians because it "explicitly rejected the causal importance of ideas"; for Bailyn "ideas counted for a great deal."

Indeed, Wood wrote, for Bailyn "the ideas of the Revolutionaries take on . . . a dynamic self-intensifying character that transcended the intentions and desires of the historical participants." He "has ended by demonstrating the autonomy of ideas as phenomena where the ideas operate as it were over the heads of the participants, taking them in directions no one could have foreseen." Whig thought showed "fear and frenzy," "enthusiastic extravagance," and a "paranoic obsession." "The very nature of the Americans' rhetoric," Wood argued, "reveals as nothing else apparently can the American Revolution as a true revolution with its sources lying deep in the social structure. For this kind of frenzied rhetoric could only spring from the most severe sorts of social strain." The sources of the strain therefore required investigation. "It may be," Wood concluded, "that the Progressive historians in their preoccupation with internal social problems were more right than we have recently been willing to grant."[145]

In his own book that followed, Wood did not fulfill the promise of this hypothesis; but if he did not take on the challenge to portray the "reality" that underlay "the rhetoric," as

[145] Gordon S. Wood, "Rhetoric and Reality in the American Revolution," *William and Mary Quarterly*, 3d ser. 23 (1966):3–32, reprinted in *In Search of Early America*, pp. 54–77. For a list of Bailyn's students and their theses, see Henretta, Kammen, and Katz, eds., *Transformation of Early American History*, pp. 261–66; for Maier's comment, see her introduction to the 1991 edition of *From Resistance to Revolution*, p. viii; Maier to author, Sept. 20, 1991.

did several other scholars of politics, his analysis of the rhetoric restored conflict in the realm of ideas to the period from 1776 to 1787. Accepting Bailyn's ideological construct of the origins of the Revolution, he argued that after 1776 the Revolution "broadened into a struggle among Americans themselves for the fruits of independence, [and] became in truth a multifaceted affair with layers below layers." Some deepgoing, underlying social conflict was implicit in this rhetorical conflict. "How to keep them down" was a "central question" to whigs after Independence, and while Wood never defined "them," through his dense forest of quotations from contemporary sources one caught occasional sight of an agrarian rebel, an urban mechanic, or more likely a self-interested "new man" of the middling sort pushing into politics.[146]

This vision of 1776–87 as a period of intense ideological conflict, however undefined the interests, raised serious questions about Bailyn's interpretation of 1765–76. "The dominant fact of the earlier years," wrote Bailyn, "had been the intensification of the ideological passions first ignited by the Stamp Act crisis and their final bursting into open insurrection." Thereafter the ideas "were turned to positive uses in the framing of the first state constitutions [and] in the transforming of regressive social institutions." But "passions cooled as ordinary life reasserted itself and cultural, sectional, and social difference . . . became important." As Wood argued, "Bailyn's notion that ideas are ascendant and important at particular ideologically exciting times in the past—until social conditions reassert themselves—suggests a kind of seesawing up-and-down fluctuation between ideology and social behavior that . . . does violence to the full reality of human action."[147]

As Wood reached 1787, his analysis of the rhetoric implied

[146] Wood, *The Creation of the American Republic, 1776–1787* (Chapel Hill, 1969), p. 83; for Wood's subsequent analysis, see "The Democratization of Mind in the American Revolution," in *Leadership in the American Revolution*, Library of Congress Symposia on the American Revolution (Washington, D.C., 1974), pp. 63–88, and see the works by Wood discussed in section XII of this essay, "Toward a New Synthesis?" below.

[147] Wood, "Creative Imagination," p. 37.

a Progressive-like reality. The crux of the movement for the Constitution of 1787 was an effort by the elite to control the "vices of the political system," which Wood, like James Madison, located in the volatile, popular politics of the state legislatures, responsive to "the people out of doors." The Constitution thus was "in some sense an aristocratic document designed to curb the democratic excesses of the Revolution." This rattled Beard's ghost. At the conclusion of his magnum opus, Wood asked other scholars to "assess the immense consequences of the social forces released by the Revolution," an invitation that beckoned Jameson from the grave.[148]

The Bailyn-Wood thesis wedded to J. G. A. Pocock's "civic humanism" was rapidly absorbed into a "Republican synthesis" that, as Wood writes, was not at all Bailyn's intention and "is an object lesson in the unanticipated consequences of purposive action."[149] Joyce Oldham Appleby likened the discovery of republicanism "to the response of chemists to a new element. Once having been identified, it can be found everywhere." It was also challenged convincingly by Appleby's own analysis of liberalism as an ideology competing with republicanism, a "second language" that was equally revolutionary but more "modern" than republicanism and had special resonance among the "upwardly mobile" seeking their own "self-interest."[150]

By 1982 Robert Shalhope, who in 1972 considered the republican synthesis pervasive, found that the research of the ten years gone by "makes clear that it is no longer possible to see a single, monolithic political ideology characterizing

---

[148] Wood, *Creation of the American Republic,* pp. 626–27.

[149] Wood, "Creative Imagination," pp. 28–29, and Bailyn, *Ideological Origins,* 2d ed., pp. v-viii.

[150] Joyce Oldham Appleby, "Republicanism and Ideology," *American Quarterly,* 3d ser. 37 (1985):461–73, reprinted in Appleby, *Liberalism and Republicanism in the Historical Imagination* (Cambridge, Mass., 1992), quotation p. 277; see also idem, "Liberalism and the American Revolution," and idem, "The Social Origins of American Revolutionary Ideology," in idem, *Liberalism and Republicanism,* pp. 140–60, 161–87.

American thought on the eve of the Revolution."[151] And in 1992 Daniel T. Rodgers's review of "the career of a concept" summed up what was missing: "It squeezed out massive domains of culture—religion, law, political economy, ideas of patriarchy, family and gender, ideas of race and slavery, class and nationalism, nature and reason—that everyone knew to be profoundly tangled in the revolutionary impulse." John Shy summed up twenty years of skepticism of a wide range of scholars when he said in an interview, "What is troubling me at this moment about the state of American historical writing and thinking about the revolutionary period is the assumption that there is a single unitary culture that holds something that can be accurately described as an ideology. . . . And frankly I just don't believe it. I am ready to be *convinced,* I think, but I *have* not been convinced."[152]

Almost all of this challenge dealt with the argument on terrain Bailyn and Wood had staked out in the realm of ideas or at the point of origins. "The transforming radicalism of the American Revolution" went untested at the point of consequences and in social and economic terrain until the emergence of historians of "the New Left" and "the new social history."

VIII. THE NEW LEFT

Among historians there were two New Lefts: the first around *Studies on the Left* (1959–67), a journal founded by graduate students in history at the University of Wisconsin associated with William Appleman Williams and the "radicalism of dis-

[151] Robert Shalhope, "Toward a Republican Synthesis: The Emergence of an Understanding of Republicanism in American Historiography," *William and Mary Quarterly,* 3d ser. 29 (1972):49–80; Shalhope, "Republicanism and Early American Historiography," *William and Mary Quarterly,* 3d ser. 39 (1982):334–56, quotation p. 346.

[152] Daniel T. Rodgers, "Republicanism: The Career of a Concept," *Journal of American History* 79 (1992):11–38, quotation p. 17; for a critique in the Progressive tradition, see Colin Gordon, "Crafting a Usable Past," *William and Mary Quarterly,* 3d ser. 46 (1989):679–95; for John Shy, see Loretta Valtz Mannucci, "Four Conversations on Future Directions in Revolutionary War Historiography," *Storia Nordamericana* 2 (1985):118–19.

closure"; the second, beginning later in the 1960s, associated with Staughton Lynd and Jesse Lemisch and "history from the bottom up," which found expression in the *Radical History Review* (1973–). The two groups shared a distaste for the politics and historiography of the Old Left but were in tension with each other. Eventually, as Peter Novick has pointed out, "the new, left-oriented historians who became visible within the profession during the 1960s came to be capitalized, reified and often tacitly homogenized as 'New Left historians.' This was a largely empty and misleading designation, lumping together individuals of the most diverse orientation, and often, innocently or maliciously, associating them with the most extreme wing of the student movement." Yet distortions aside, there were New Left historians of the Revolution who laid out contrasting radical visions of the transformations of the era that challenged Progressives as well as Counterprogressives.[153]

New Left historians found few models in an Old Left American historiography dating to the 1930s either for doing history or interpreting the Revolution. The Old Left scholarship on the Revolution was in different ways a tail on the Progressive kite. In the late 1930s, on the one hand, was Louis M. Hacker's *Triumph of American Capitalism,* a highly schematic economic determinist Marxism with no sense of agency, which saw the Revolution as the triumph of mercantile capitalism leading inevitably to the victory of industrial capitalism. Hacker was an economist at Columbia whose interpretation circulated in the 1950s (long after he recanted his youthful exuberance), probably because it fit the caricature of Marxism

---

[153] Novick, *That Noble Dream,* chap. 13, quotation pp. 417–18; Wiener, "Radical Historians," pp. 399–444. For the first New Left, see *Studies on the Left* (1959–67). For the second New Left, see Barton J. Bernstein, ed., *Towards a New Past: Dissenting Essays in American History* (New York, 1968); *Radical America* (1967–); Paul Buhle, "History, United States," and "New Left," and Elliot Shore, "Radical Professional and Academic Journals," in Mary Jo Buhle, Paul Buhle, and Dan Georgakas, eds., *Encyclopedia of the American Left* (New York, 1990). For a contemporary critique, see Irwin Unger, "The 'New Left' and American History: Some Recent Trends in United States Historiography," *American Historical Review* 72 (1967):1237–63, and Unger, ed., *Beyond Liberalism: The New Left Views American History* (Waltham, Mass., 1971).

as economic determinism. At the other pole was a book by Jack Hardy, *The First American Revolution,* brought out by International Publishers, which read the Sons of Liberty radicals as if they were a vanguard party leading the masses to revolution. Becker's dual revolution and Jameson's social movement were understated in Hacker and overstated in Hardy. The most important Marxist monograph of the era, Herbert Aptheker's pathbreaking study of slave revolts (1943), had far reaching implications for the study of both the Revolution and slave resistance that were not integrated into an analysis either by Marxists or any other historians. The Old Left of the popular front era took American democratic traditions seriously but fell into a kind of whig history celebrating liberal heroes like Thomas Jefferson and radicals like Samuel Adams and Thomas Paine as forerunners of their own radical tradition.[154]

William Appleman Williams was the most important scholar of elites in the New Left and one of the few to devote major attention to the founding era. His influential synthesis, *Contours of American History,* suggested a new periodization for American history, defined around the stages of capitalism. The first third of this book was devoted to "The Age of Mercantilism, 1740–1828," the second to "The Age of Laissez Nous Faire, 1819–1896" and the last third to "The Age of

[154] Paul Buhle, *Marxism in the United States* (London and New York, 1987), chaps. 5–7; Buhle, "American Marxist Historiography, 1900–1940," *Radical America* 4 (1970):5–36; Louis M. Hacker, *The Triumph of American Capitalism: The Development of Forces in American History to the End of the Nineteenth Century* (New York, 1940); Hacker, "The American Revolution: Economic Aspects," *Marxist Quarterly* 1 (1937):46–67, widely reprinted in the 1950s; Jack Hardy, *The First American Revolution* (New York, 1937); Elizabeth Lawson, ed., *Samuel Adams: Selections from His Writings* (New York, 1946); Herbert Aptheker, *American Negro Slave Revolts* (New York, 1943); idem, *Essays in the History of the American Negro* (New York, 1945): Herbert Morais, *The Struggle for American Freedom: The First Two Hundred Years* (New York, 1944); Philip S. Foner, ed., *The Complete Writings of Thomas Paine,* 2 vols. (New York, 1945); for postwar Marxist scholarship, see Aptheker, *The American Revolution, 1763–1783* (New York, 1960); Foner, *Labor and the American Revolution* (Westport, Conn., 1976); see also Harvey Kaye, "Capitalism and Democracy in America: Leo Huberman's *We the People,*" in Kaye, *The Education of Desire: Marxists and the Writing of History* (New York, 1992), chap. 6.

Corporate Capitalism, 1882–."[155] The last concept won more converts than the first. A graduate student at Wisconsin, then a member of the Department of History (1957–68) at its Progressive ebbtide, Williams drew from the Progressive scholarship of Curtis Nettels and Merrill Jensen. But Williams was more left than his Progressive colleagues. Active in the early civil rights movement, he was hounded by the House Committee on Un-American Activities and was probably the only historian to have the honor of having the manuscript of his current book, *Contours*, subpoenaed by that committee. Williams was also more theoretical. An admirer of Beard as a "Tory radical," he attempted to dissolve the theoretical impasse in the debate over Beard by shifting attention from the pocketbook interests of individuals to the political economy and world outlook of their class. "Reality is not economics vs ideals or of politics vs either," he argued. "Reality instead involves how a political act is also an economic act, of how an idea of freedom involves a commitment to a particular economic system."[156]

Williams saw the leaders of the Revolution as a coalition of interest groups among the "gentry," who in breaking from the British Empire wanted to establish their own mercantilist empire. Expansion had a central place in American policy from the outset. The leaders were bent on building "a rising empire" or an "empire of liberty" (phrases common to men like Franklin and Jefferson), dedicated both to "expansion across space" on the continent and commercial markets overseas. Very much aware of the radicalism of the era, Williams

---

[155] William Appleman Williams, *Contours of American History* (1961; reprint ed., New York, 1988); Michael Wallace, interview with William Appleman Williams (1980), in Abelove et al., eds., *Visions of History*, pp. 125–46; Williams, "My Life in Madison," in Buhle, ed., *History and the New Left;* Herbert G. Gutman and Warren Susman, "Memories of Madison in the Fifties," *Radical History Review,* no. 36 (1986):101–9.

[156] Williams, "Confessions of an Intransigent Revisionist," *Socialist Review* 17 (September-October, 1973):94, reprinted in Henry Berger, ed., *A William Appleman Williams Reader* (Chicago, 1992), pp. 336–44; Williams, "Charles Austin Beard: The Intellectual as Tory Radical," in Harvey Goldberg, ed., *American Radicals: Some Problems and Personalities* (New York, 1957), reprinted in Berger, ed.; *Williams Reader,* pp. 105–15.

saw James Madison's effort to "extend the sphere" of the republic in 1787 as the gentry's solution to "the long pattern of discontent and unrest among the middle and lower classes." But he reinterpreted radicals of the Revolution; he saw Samuel Adams, for example, as "a true Calvinist and thoroughgoing mercantilist" who was "dedicated to the ideal and reality of a corporate Christian commonwealth" and thus was "a revolutionary without being a radical." To Williams the true radicals in American history were those who dissented from empire as a way of life.[157]

Williams, who directed some forty doctoral dissertations, won recognition, writes Novick, as "the single most important figure in the reconceptualization of the history of American foreign policy." His insight into the political economy of the Revolution was picked up by scholars anxious to break out of a narrow economic determinism, but his emphasis on the centrality of expansion probably was little appreciated by historians of the Revolutionary era who usually compartmentalized foreign from domestic policy.[158]

Lynd and Lemisch were characteristic of the other trend of New Left historiography: an emphasis on the agency of the common people, an avowed identification of the historian with movements for radical change in contemporary society,

[157] Williams, *Contours*, chaps. 3–5; Williams, "The Age of Mercantilism: An Interpretation of American Political Economy, 1763–1828," *William and Mary Quarterly*, 3d ser. 15 (1958):419–37; Susman to Gates, Jan. 8, 1961, cited in Peter Novick, "American Leftist Historians" (Paper presented at the Ninety-third Annual Meeting of the American Historical Association, San Francisco, December 1978); Williams, "Samuel Adams: Calvinist, Mercantilist, Revolutionary," *Studies on the Left* 1 (1960), reprinted in Williams, *History as a Way of Learning* (New York, 1973).

[158] Novick, *That Noble Dream*, p. 446. For examples see Egnal, *Mighty Empire;* Ernst, *Money and Politics in America;* John Nelson, *Liberty and Property: Political Economy and Policymaking in the New Nation, 1789–1812* (Baltimore, 1987); for an echo of the expansionist theme, see Drew R. McCoy, *The Elusive Republic: Political Economy in Jeffersonian America* (Chapel Hill, 1980); for Williams's general influence, see "Excerpts from a Conference to Honor William Appleman Williams," *Radical History Review,* no. 50 (1991):39–70, especially pp. 47–48 (Martin Sklar), and Bradford Perkins, *"The Tragedy of American Diplomacy:* Twenty-Five Years After," *Reviews in American History* 12 (1984).

and a sense of moral passion in the presentation of history. Each focused on the Revolutionary era exploring groups that were blanks in the books of almost all historians, Lynd on tenant farmers and urban mechanics, Lemisch on the merchant seamen.

Both began their scholarship as graduate students in the "bottom of the fifties and the bad times before the sixties became *The Sixties*," as Lemisch has put it in a memoir, which is less a puzzle than it seems. Both grew up in Old Left families in New York. Lynd's parents were the critical sociologists Helen and Robert Lynd of *Middletown* and *Middletown in Transition* fame. Lemisch's mother was a rank-and-file Communist "totally unschooled in Marxism," Lemisch writes, "who bred in me a street level variety which may have been better than the real thing." As undergraduates, Lynd at Harvard (1946–51) and Lemisch at Yale (1953–57) were members of the student left. At Columbia, Richard Morris, sui generis for his interest in colonial labor history, directed Lynd's doctoral thesis and Lemisch's master's work before Lemisch returned to Yale to do his thesis under Edmund Morgan. While becoming a historian, Lynd was contributing articles to *Studies on the Left*, the *New Republic*, *Commentary*, and *Liberation*, where he interpreted Henry David Thoreau as "an admirable radical," a forerunner of his own Quaker commitments; Lemisch wrote for the *Nation*.[159]

Not until both were well into their scholarship did the mass political movements emerge in which they took part. Each acknowledged the interrelatedness of their experience as historians and activists. From the mid-1960s "the civil rights and anti-war movements," Jonathan M. Wiener writes, "gave participants an experience of making history from below. . . . The

---

[159] Jesse Lemisch, "Looking for Jack Tar in the Scholarly Darkness, or, The Political Context of History from the Bottom up at the End of the '50s" (Paper Presented at the "Jack Tar in History" conference, Halifax, Nova Scotia, October 1990); Staughton Lynd, "Father and Son: Intellectual Work outside the University," *Social Policy*, Spring 1993, pp. 4–11; Lynd, "Henry Thoreau: The Admirable Radical," *Liberation*, February 1963, pp. 21–26; Lemisch, "Who Won the Civil War, Anyway?" *Nation*, Apr. 9, 1961; for the context, see Maurice Isserman, *If I had a Hammer . . . The Death of the Old Left and the Birth of the New Left* (New York, 1987).

revival of political opposition among the most oppressed (blacks) and the most incorporated (students) required analysis; it suggested a different sense of how history was made, not simply by elites, from the top down, but in the interaction of social groups holding power in different forms." Lynd's shift of attention to the issue of slavery and to the abolitionists paralleled his activity as director of the Mississippi Freedom Schools in 1964 and as a teacher at Spelman, a black college. His exploration of the intellectual roots of American radicalism paralleled his role in the movement against the war in Vietnam and his citizens' peace mission to Hanoi in 1965. Lemisch, who had been arrested for civil disobedience in 1963 and 1965, writes that he came "to a deeper understanding of the phenomenon of 'riot'" in August 1968 in Chicago as he made his way across the chaos and tear gas of Michigan Avenue after the police broke up a demonstration at the Democratic party convention. The movements, as Wiener put it, "rapidly *became* a source of intellectual energy for those developing critical perspectives on consensus history." [160] So did the powerful examples of the recovery of plebeian history by the English revisionist Marxist scholars—of George Rudé on the crowd, Eric Hobsbawm on "primitive rebels," Christopher Hill on Puritan radicals, and especially E. P. Thompson, who sought to rescue the "agency" of the common people from "the enormous condescension of posterity." [161]

Staughton Lynd epitomized left historians trying to break out of the Progressive paradigm. Looking back in 1967, he wrote, "My own initial attitude toward the Progressive histori-

---

[160] Wiener, "Radical Historians," pp. 412–13, emphasis added; Lynd and Thomas Hayden, *The Other Side* (New York, 1966); Lemisch, "Looking for Jack Tar."

[161] George Rudé, *The Crowd in History* (New York, 1964); Eric Hobsbawm, *Primitive Rebels: Studies in Archaic Forms of Social Movements in the 19th and 20th Centuries* (New York, 1965); Christopher Hill, *The World Turned Upside Down: Radical Ideas during the English Revolution* (New York, 1972); E. P. Thompson, *The Making of the English Working Class* (1963; reprint ed., New York, 1966); see the interviews with Thompson (1976, 1978) in Abelove et al., eds. *Visions of History*, pp. 3–46; Harvey Kaye, *The British Marxist Historians: An Introductory Analysis* (Oxford, 1984); for George Rudé see Kaye, *The Education of Desire*, chap. 2.

ography of Turner, Beard, Becker, and Parrington, was un-
critical. I did not expect to be driven beyond Beard, to lay
greater stress than he did upon city artisans, upon slavery,
upon the role of ideas. These themes were imposed, one at a
time, by the subject matter itself." "Beyond Beard" was the
title he gave to his essay in synthesis, "After Carl Becker," the
title he and I gave to the introduction to a brace of articles on
the mechanics of New York City, his dealing with 1775 to
1787, mine from 1788 to 1801.[162]

Lynd used a single locale, Dutchess County, as a microcosm
to test Becker and Beard and implicitly Jameson, pioneering
a case study approach long before it became commonplace.
Dutchess County on the east bank of the Hudson River, with
its vast estates of landlord aristocrats and tenants and a small
middling class of farmers and entrepreneurs, while atypical,
was a rich laboratory. What he found was a complex picture
in which "the same economic groups, to a striking extent the
same leaders, confronted each other in the tenants' rising of
1766, the struggle during the Revolution over the confiscation and sale of loyalist lands, and in the battle over ratification of the Constitution." Tenants fought for the confiscation
and then the sale of the land they farmed, winning a struggle
in which the middling gentry foes of the landlords (the Anti-
federalists to be) supported them. Thus, Lynd added agency
to Jameson's lifeless discussion of the redistribution of land
and complexity to Beard's simplified analysis of the alignments in New York on the Constitution.[163]

[162] Lynd, *Class Conflict, Slavery, and the United States Constitution: Ten Essays*
(Indianapolis, 1967), pp. 8–9; Lynd and Alfred F. Young, "After Carl
Becker: The Mechanics and New York City Politics, 1774–1801," the introduction to Lynd, "The Mechanics and New York City Politics, 1774–1788,"
and Young, "The Mechanics and the Jeffersonians, 1789–1801," *Labor History* 5 (1964):215–76. Lynd and I presented these papers at a session of the
Organization of American Historians in 1962; I later worked with him as
general editor of the American Heritage Series, for which he edited *Non-
Violence in America: A Documentary History* (Indianapolis, 1966); in 1967–68 I
served with Christopher Lasch as cochair of the Ad Hoc Committee to Defend Academic Freedom in Illinois, formed to defend Lynd in the Chicago cases.

[163] Lynd, "Who Should Rule at Home? Dutchess County, New York, in
the American Revolution," *William and Mary Quarterly*, 3d ser. 18

In New York City, Lynd found the faceless "rabble" of Becker and Jameson to be composed of politically conscious mechanics, who after 1775 developed a radical democratic program and after the war formed "a mechanic interest" in alliance with merchants behind the Constitution of 1787 in support of their own manufacturing and commercial needs. He thus explained a group Beard could not account for. Interested in the interplay of elites with subordinate classes, he saw the New York gentry in 1787 as "a governing class on the defensive," who turned to national power to curtail the state power they had lost to the new middling men, an alternative to Beard that substituted a viable analysis of class for narrow economic interest.[164]

Lynd went "beyond Beard" most sharply in the importance he attached to slavery in the making of the Constitution and Jeffersonian democracy. Beard's dichotomy between "personalty" (liquid capital) and "realty" (land), he argued, had submerged a more fundamental distinction between slaveholding southern planters and northern yeoman. "The slave, though he spoke few lines, should be moved front and center" because "to whatever extent the Constitution betrayed the promise of the Declaration of Independence, it did so most of all for the Negro." Lynd grappled with the puzzle of the old Confederation Congress in New York passing an ordinance banning slavery in the Northwest with the consent of the South shortly after the delegates at the Philadelphia Constitutional Convention ninety miles away broke the impasse between North and South by adopting the three-fifths compromise over representation in the House. This, he argued, as have other scholars since, was the result of an accom-

---

(1961):330–59; Lynd, *Anti-Federalism in Dutchess County, New York: A Study of Democracy and Class Conflict in the Revolutionary Era* (Chicago, 1962), winner of the Loyola University Press's William P. Lyons Masters Essay Contest for 1960.

[164] Lynd, "Capitalism, Democracy, and the United States Constitution: The Case of New York," *Science and Society* 27 (1963):385–414, reprinted as "A Governing Class on the Defensive: The Case of New York," in Lynd, *Class Conflict*, chap. 5, pp. 109–32.

modation over slavery, the fundamental compromise of 1787.[165]

Lynd's search for the eighteenth-century intellectual origins of the radical tradition that found fulfillment in the higher law radicalism of Thoreau and Martin Luther King, Jr., took him beyond Becker and beyond Bailyn. In a book-length "exploratory sketch," he located in the English dissenting radicals of the 1760s and 1770s, especially James Burgh and John Cartright, a cluster of beliefs not addressed in the prevailing view of the Commonwealthmen. "Dissenting radicalism raised awkward questions about the absolute right of private property," which found echoes in Jefferson's doctrine that "the earth belongs to the living." And the dissenting belief in "active freedom of conscience" grafted on to Quaker sensibilities led to the justification of individual resistance to unjust laws.[166]

Reflecting on "the elements" that a future analysis of the Revolution based on findings such as his own might include, Lynd offered a tentative New Left synthesis. The American Revolution "was waged by a coalition of diverse social groups." "Internal conflict," he believed, was "a secondary aspect of the revolution of 1776 which in fact was primarily a war of national independence." This was Becker with the proportions changed. Secondly, "the popular elements in this coalition . . . often clashed with their upper-class leaders," and this fear among the elites of domestic insurrection "was a principle motive for the formation of the United States Con-

---

[165] Lynd, "Beyond Beard," in Bernstein, ed., *Towards a New Past*, pp. 46–64, quotation p. 58; Lynd, "The Compromise of 1787," *Political Science Quarterly* 81 (1966):225–50, "On Turner, Beard, and Slavery," *Journal of Negro History* 48 (1963):235–50, and "The Abolitionist Critique of the United States Constitution," in Martin Duberman, ed., *The Anti-Slavery Vanguard: New Essays on the Abolitionists* (Princeton, 1965), pp. 209–39, all three reprinted in Lynd, *Class Conflict*, chaps. 6–8, pp. 135–213; for recent scholarship see Paul Finkelman, "Slavery and the Constitutional Convention: Making a Covenant with Death," in Richard R. Beeman, Stephen Botein, and Edward C. Carter II, eds., *Beyond Confederation: Origins of the Constitution and American National Identity* (Chapel Hill, 1987), pp. 188–225, and Gary B. Nash, *Race and Revolution* (Madison, Wis., 1990), p. 204.

[166] Lynd, *Intellectual Origins of American Radicalism* (1968; reprint ed., Cambridge, Mass., 1982).

stitution." So much for consensus history. Thirdly, "the upper class leaders ... were themselves divided into two basic groups, Northern capitalists and Southern plantation owners, and the Constitution represented not a victory of one over the other but a compromise between them." This was Beard fundamentally revised. There was "a second revolution which determined what kind of society the independent nation would become ... a bourgeois revolution comparable to the French Revolution, but it was directed not against England but against slavery and took place not in 1776 but in 1861." Here was the Beard of *Rise of American Civilization* cast in a different conceptual framework. Thus to Lynd the American Revolution was both less and more of a transforming event than portrayed by either the Progressives or their critics.[167]

These insights were the product of a meteoric decade as a historian and activist. The target of national right-wing political attacks, the victim of a bruising academic freedom fight at two Chicago colleges in 1967–68, denied tenure at Yale in 1968, his appointment by history departments in a host of Illinois and Indiana institutions blocked by administrators, Lynd was blacklisted.[168] In 1969, at a tumultuous annual meeting of the AHA attended by some two thousand, he led an unsuccessful effort to condemn the war in Vietnam; then, as an opposition candidate for the presidency, he won 396 votes to 1,004 for Robert Palmer, a rebellion that led the AHA to a more far-reaching reform than under Jameson in 1913.[169] Lynd, without much choice and never convinced that

[167] Lynd, *Class Conflict*, pp. 13–14, and Lynd, "Beyond Beard," in Bernstein, *Towards a New Past*, pp. 50–54.

[168] On Lynd at Yale, see Lynd, "Academic Freedom: Your Story and Mine," *Columbia University Forum* 10 (Fall 1967):23–28; Edmund S. Morgan and C. Vann Woodward, "Academic Freedom: Whose Story?" *Columbia University Forum* 11 (Spring 1968):42–43, with a reply by Lynd, pp. 50–51.

[169] Wiener, "Radical Historians," p. 422; Novick *That Noble Dream*, chap. 13; Lemisch, "Radicals, Marxists, and Gentlemen," pp. 2, 7–9. The AHA subsequently established three divisions, Research, Teaching, and Professional; in 1970 it established the Ad Hoc Committee on the Rights of Historians, in response to a resolution I introduced in the annual meeting. I served on this committee, chaired by Sheldon Hackney, and on the subcommittee responsible for the investigation of individual violations of academic

a radical activist historian should commit himself to a lifetime in academia, left early American history. He went to law school and began a second creative career as a labor lawyer and activist applying his New Left insights to twentieth-century labor history and American law.[170]

Jesse Lemisch was the godfather of "history from the bottom up," a phrase used by Turner in 1923 and Caroline F. Ware in 1940 that did not come into common parlance until the movements of the 1960s gave it resonance.[171] It was in currency in the circles of the Students for a Democratic Society in which Lemisch moved. The subtitle of Lemisch's thesis, "Jack Tar vs. John Bull: The Role of New York's Merchant Seamen in Precipitating the Revolution," announced his bold theme. The heart of it was a reexamination of the Stamp Act crisis, not as an event in the search for principle, the theme of his mentor, Edmund Morgan, but as an event in the emergence of a popular movement. The seamen were the true "radicals" who pushed "liberal" leaders into action.[172]

---

freedom, in the course of which I read the documents in the Lynd and Lemisch cases and some forty others. For the abridged report and the "Statement of Professional Standards" adopted by the AHA, see *AHA Newsletter* 12 (December 1974):9–13.

[170] Interview with Lynd (1977), in Abelove et al., eds., *Visions of History*, pp. 149–65; Lynd, "Intellectuals, the University, and the Movement," with a response by Lemisch, "Who Will Write a Left History of Art While We Are Putting Our Balls on the Line?" (1968), reprinted in *Journal of American History* 76 (1989):479–86; Lynd and Alice Lynd, eds., *Rank and File: Personal Histories by Working Class Organizers* (1973), 3d ed. (New York, 1988); Lynd, *The Fight against Shutdowns: Youngstown's Steel Mill Closings* (San Pedro, Calif., 1982); Lynd, "The Genesis of the Idea of a Community Right to Industrial Property in Youngstown and Pittsburgh, 1977–1987," *Journal of American History* 74 (1987–88):926–58.

[171] Turner to Carl Blegen, Mar. 16, 1923, cited in Novick, *That Noble Dream*, p. 442; I recall encountering the term in Caroline F. Ware, ed., *The Cultural Approach to History* (New York, 1940); Lemisch, "Towards a Democratic History," Students for a Democratic Society Radical Education Project Occasional Paper (1967).

[172] Jesse Lemisch, "Jack Tar vs. John Bull: The Role of New York's Merchant Seamen in Precipitating the Revolution," Ph.D. diss., Yale University, 1962; Lemisch, "New York's Petitions and Resolves of December 1765: Liberals vs. Radicals," *New-York Historical Society Quarterly* 49 (1965):313–26.

His since-famous "Jack Tar" article of 1968 broadened the scope of the argument in time and place. Challenging the stereotype of "jolly Jack Tar" and Samuel Eliot Morison's image of the seaman as "a clean young farm boy on the make," Lemisch suggested there were many sailors like Ishmael in Herman Melville's *Moby-Dick* "who left the land in flight and fear, outcasts, men with little hope of success ashore . . . dissenters from the American mood." He revealed a long history of struggle against colonial impressment often in spectacular riots that made more credible the large-scale participation of seamen in crowd actions in Atlantic seaports after 1765. In effect he uncovered a new cause of the Revolution, illuminating a forgotten clause of the Declaration of Independence. Lemisch felt he had tested the contention of the loyalist Peter Oliver that the "Mobility of all Countries [were], perfect Machines, wound up by any Hand who might first take the Winch." He found that "the seaman had a mind of his own and genuine reasons to act, and that he did act—purposefully." He also felt that Bailyn's claim that the "demonstrations by transient sailors and dock workers" were "ideologically inert" was not proved. Granting that "it might be extravagant to call the seamen's conduct and sense of injustice" ideological, yet, he argued, "there are many worlds and much human history in the vast area between ideology and inertness."[173]

Lemisch's essay "The American Revolution Seen from the Bottom Up," appearing about the same time, was akin to Turner's ardent appeal to scholars in 1893 to do the history of an unexplored subject and to Jameson's "heuristic." What might the history of the Revolution look like if scholars approached it from a different vantage point? Lemisch conceded that, insofar as the elite were concerned, the

[173] Lemisch, "Jack Tar in the Streets: Merchant Seamen in the Politics of Revolutionary America," *William and Mary Quarterly*, 3d ser. 25 (1968):371–407. I published this essay as "The Radicalism of the Inarticulate: Merchant Seamen and the Politics of Revolutionary America," in Young, ed., *Dissent: Explorations in the History of American Radicalism* (DeKalb, Ill., 1968). I reviewed Lemisch's scholarship in Young, "History from the Bottom Up: Twenty Years After," at the "Jack Tar in History" conference, Halifax, Nova Scotia, October 1990.

Revolution may well have been as conservative as Daniel Boorstin claimed but pounded on the assumptions that there was a consensus behind the elite or that the actions of the lower classes could be explained by "manipulation, propaganda, and the mindlessness of the people." The "inarticulate" "had adequate reason to act on their own, [and] had the capacity to act on their own." The history of "the powerless, the inarticulate, the poor," he concluded, "has not yet begun to be written."[174]

He next made "a struggle to get inside Jack Tar's head," attempting "an experimental history" in which he treated the British prisons as a laboratory to study the behavior of ordinary men without the presence of elites or outside political leaders. Sailors set up self-government, established a code of ethics, and voiced their patriotism in songs and celebrations. All but a few rejected the opportunity to go free by becoming turncoats. Putting "inarticulate" in quotation marks to correct a misreading of his earlier essay, he relied on little used memoirs of seamen to construct a collective portrait of articulateness.[175]

Lemisch's contribution to the debate over transformation in the Revolution was to establish a consciousness among ordinary people. To trace consciousness over time, he attempted a full scale biography of Andrew Sherburne, a seamen and prisoner of war, a work still in progress. The youthful son of a New Hampshire carpenter, Sherburne was lured to sea on a privateering vessel, taken prisoner of war, returned from Britain broken in health, eked out a living on the Maine frontier, and became a preacher in the Baptist church where he found community akin to what he had experienced as a prisoner. He went to Ohio to farm worthless land, received a veteran's pension, lost it in red tape, and went to Washington to fight for it. He ended his life in poverty, writ-

---

[174] Lemisch, "The American Revolution Seen from the Bottom Up," in Bernstein, ed., *Towards a New Past*, pp. 3–43.

[175] Lemisch, "Listening to the 'Inarticulate': William Widger's Dream and the Loyalties of American Revolutionary Seamen in British Prisons," *Journal of Social History* 3 (1969):1–29.

ing his autobiography and selling it door to door for two dollars—a painful reminder of the broken promises to the losers of the Revolution.[176]

To advance history from the bottom up, Lemisch moved in several directions. He wrote critical analyses of other historians; he offered an influential critique of the government's historical publications programs for failing to support the editing of papers other than those of "great white men." In response to those who dismissed the New Left as presentist, he offered in 1969 a scathing indictment of the present-mindedness of the historical establishment since World War II that the *American Historical Review* and the *Journal of American History* refused to print and that was published in Canada in 1975.[177] And finally he engaged in a series of exchanges with his critics on the Marxist Left, responding to charges that he romanticized the masses, failed to acknowledge the hegemony of ruling classes, and treated the bottom in isolation from the top.[178]

In 1966 the history department at the University of Chicago did not renew Lemisch's appointment. Daniel Boorstin found Lemisch's "sea stories" interesting but deplored his emphasis on class. In 1968 the chairman, William H. McNeill, informed him, "Your convictions interfered with your schol-

[176] Lemisch, "The American Revolution and the American Dream: A Short Life of the Reverend Andrew Sherburne, a Pensioner of the Navy of the Revolution" (Paper presented at a conference in honor of Edmund S. Morgan, New Haven, 1979).

[177] Lemisch, "Bailyn Besieged in His Bunker," *Radical History Review* 3 (1976):72–83; Lemisch, "Radical Plot in Boston (1770): A Study in the Use of Evidence," *Harvard Law Review* 84 (1970):485–504, a critique of Hiller Zobel, *The Boston Massacre;* Lemisch, "The American Revolution Bicentennial and the Papers of Great White Men," *AHA Newsletter* 9 (November 1971):7–21; Lemisch, "The Papers of a Few Great Black Men and Few Great White Women," *Maryland Historian* 7 (1975):60–66; Lemisch, "Present-Mindedness Revisited: Anti-Radicalism as a Goal of American Historical Writing since World War II," published as *On Active Service in War and Peace.*

[178] Aileen Kraditor, review of Bernstein, ed., *Towards a New Past, American Historical Review* 74 (1968):528–29; response by Lemisch and rejoinder by Kraditor, *American Historical Review* 75 (1969):1766–69; Joan Scott and Donald Scott, "Toward History," with a rejoinder by Lemisch, "New Left Elitism," *Radical America* 1 (1967):35–53.

arship." Lemisch continued in academia but, as he recently put it, "Great Institutions began to shun me."[179]

At the time the three pathbreakers of the New Left had a greater impact on young historians of modern rather than early American history. At first the *William and Mary Quarterly* was open. Under Lawrence W. Towner it published articles by Williams (1961) and Lynd (1962), and under Thad W. Tate published Lemisch (1968). It published a critique of "Jack Tar" that questioned only whether seamen were typical as well as Lemisch's response. But the gatekeeping journal in the field reviewed only one of Lynd's three books and ignored Williams's book as out of scope. In 1971 the Institute of Early American History and Culture invited neither Lemisch nor Lynd to a conference of representative scholars on the bicentennial of the Revolution. "Why didn't they invite Jesse and Staughton?" I remember Edmund Morgan asking me at lunch. Nor was there a welcome mat in Williamsburg for the British New Left historians whose seminal works also went unreviewed. The Council of the Institute long reserved a slot for someone in British history, but in 1977 when as chair of the nominating committee I brought in the name of Christopher Hill, they voted it down. The Institute's 1989 volume listing 2,001 recommended books carries some eighty-five titles in British history, but not one by Hill, Thompson, Rudé, or Hobsbawm. Recently Lynd has appeared as a reviewer in the *Quarterly,* and the journal's readers voted Lemisch's "Jack Tar" one of the most influential articles in the past fifty years.[180]

Lynd demonstrated that it was possible, by substituting class for economic interest and exploring subordinate classes, to

---

[179] Lemisch, author's postscript to "Jack Tar in the Streets," reprinted in *In Search of Early America*, pp. 136–37.

[180] Ibid.; James H. Hutson, "An Investigation of the Inarticulate: Philadelphia's White Oaks," *William and Mary Quarterly*, 3d ser. 28 (1971):3–25; Lemisch with John K. Alexander, "The White Oaks, Jack Tar, and the Concept of the 'Inarticulate,'" *William and Mary Quarterly*, 3d ser. 29 (1972):109–34; Lynd, *Intellectual Origins;* Lynd, review of Herbert Aptheker, *Anti-Racism in U.S. History, William and Mary Quarterly*, 3d ser. 50 (1993):631–34; David L. Ammerman and Philip D. Morgan, comps., *Books about Early America: 2001 Titles* (Williamsburg, Va., 1989), pp. 12–14.

arrive at a more sophisticated version of the dual revolution than had Becker, Beard, or Jensen. In pushing slavery to the center of the Revolutionary stage, he would be joined in time by a host of scholars. Lemisch's "Jack Tar" essay was a tour de force. Scholars have told me that after reading it as undergraduates, they decided to become historians. It created a subject that scholars did not know existed, demonstrating in a tone that was genuinely exploratory that there were sources to do history from the bottom up. Edmund Morgan likes to tell the story that it was the last time he would tell a graduate student there were no sources for a subject.

Lemisch was a founder of the early American crowd as a field of study. Rudé created the field for England and Europe. Bailyn, Wood, and Maier broke the stereotype of the mindless, manipulated mob but, before there was sufficient evidence, they substituted for it a single type of crowd sharing the mind of the whig pamphleteers.[181] Lemisch opened the door to what later research has shown to be a wide range of crowds. Lynd and Lemisch showed it was possible to find agency and consciousness below, if not ideology. And both challenged the complacent celebration of the Revolution, allowing scholars who followed to come to grips with its dark side, whether of slaves abandoned by the Founding Fathers or the Ishmaels and Andrew Sherburnes of America.

IX. THE NEW SOCIAL HISTORY

The "new" social history of the 1960s and 1970s laid a basis for reopening the question of transformation in the American Revolution by launching a systematic analysis of colonial society. The new social history paralleled the development of New Left history, sharing the same interest in "history from the bottom up" yet diverged from it in intellectual sources, focus, and methodology.

[181] Thomas P. Slaughter, "Crowds in Eighteenth-Century America: Reflections and New Directions," *Pennsylvania Magazine of History and Biography* 115 (1991):3–34; for a reassertion of the communitarian interpretation, see Paul A. Gilje, *The Road to Mobocracy: Popular Disorder in New York City, 1763–1834* (Chapel Hill, 1987).

In the "old" social history epitomized by the volumes in the History of American Life series edited by Schlesinger and Dixon Ryan Fox, successive unlinked chapters described society, education, recreation, literature, and so on, with what Beard called an "impressionistic eclecticism." "It represented the New History [of the early twentieth century] at its worst," Peter Novick writes, "shapeless and sprawling; 'liberal' in its avoidance of the issues of power (social history as 'history with the politics left out'); 'progressive' in its emphasis on rapid social change with no attention to long-range structural dynamics."[182]

At its best, in focused monographs, the old social history actually was more solid. Scholars who were steeped in their sources organized their subject empirically. Usually they fit no paradigm, indeed that may have been their source of strength. Examples are Carl Bridenbaugh's two volumes on the colonial cities, Morgan's studies of the family in New England and Virginia, studies of colonial women by Julia Cherry Spruill or Elizabeth Anthony Dexter, of the laboring classes by Morris and Towner, or of the Negro in colonial society and in the Revolution by Lorenzo Johnston Greene and Benjamin Quarles. Such works survive and are still mined by scholars.[183]

The "new social history," James Henretta wrote when its trends had become clearer, "does not resemble a coherent subdiscipline but rather a congeries of groups." One group drew especially on the French *Annales* school with its emphasis on achieving "total" history, on the trends of long duration that provided an underlying structure to eventful history, and

---

[182] Novick, *That Noble Dream*, pp. 178–80; Higham, *History*, pp. 194–95.

[183] Carl Bridenbaugh, *Cities in the Wilderness: The First Century of Urban Life in America, 1625–1742* (New York, 1938); Bridenbaugh, *Cities in Revolt: Urban Life in America, 1743–1776* (New York, 1955); Edmund S. Morgan, *The Puritan Family* (Boston, 1944); Morgan, *Virginians at Home* (Williamsburg, Va., 1952); Julia Cherry Spruill, *Women's Life and Work in the Southern Colonies* (Chapel Hill, 1938); Elizabeth Anthony Dexter, *Career Women of America, 1776–1840* (Francistown, N.H., 1950); Morris, *Government and Labor;* Lawrence W. Towner, "A Good Master Well Served: A Social History of Servitude in Massachusetts, 1620–1750," Ph.D. diss., Northwestern University, 1955; Lorenzo Johnston Greene, *The Negro in Colonial New England, 1620–1776* (New York, 1942); Quarles, *Negro in the American Revolution.*

its use of methods of quantification to achieve rigorous statistical analysis. A second group, which included the New Left, drew intellectually from the liberated revisionist Marxism of England; it was untraditional in focusing on agency and consciousness but traditional in its methods.[184]

Politically both groups were moved by the unprecedented popular movements of the late 1960s and early 1970s to recover the common people left out of conventional history. By 1975 Jack Greene, the perennial chronicler of historical trends who, the decade before, thought he was attending the wake of the social interpretation of the Revolution, wrote enthusiastically about the way the new history "reorders our priorities about the past." "It has become clear that the experience of women, children, servants, slaves and other neglected groups are quite as integral to a comprehensive understanding of the past as that of lawyers, lords, and ministers of state."[185]

The two histories had a common foe—so-called elitist history that ignored the vast majority and was excessively political, constitutional, and ideological; they parted company in focus. The New Left was concerned with movements and redefining the political to include the crowd, "primitive rebels," and cultural resistance. For colonial American history the new social historians by contrast were interested in the uneventful *longue durée* that captured trends in demography, family patterns, social structure, social mobility, social stratification, and literacy.[186] Both were interested in consciousness, but the new social historians were apt to deduce consciousness from behavior and their methods usually were quantitative. Dealing with what they could count, perhaps unconsciously, they per-

[184] James A. Henretta, "Social History as Lived and Written," *American Historical Review* 84 (1979):1293–1322, quotations pp. 1295–96.

[185] Jack P. Greene, "The 'New' History: From Top to Bottom," *New York Times*, Jan. 18, 1975.

[186] Daniel Scott Smith, "A Perspective on Demographic Methods and Effects in Social History," *William and Mary Quarterly*, 3d ser. 39 (1982):442–69; for surveys of this scholarship, see Jack P. Greene and J. R. Pole, eds., *Colonial British America: Essays in the New History of the Early Modern Era* (Baltimore, 1984).

petuated the notion that the common people were inarticulate and the historian had to speak for them after Lemisch, for example, had pulled back from the concept.

The contribution of the first wave of new social historians was to open up two large subjects, the contours of the small community—typically the New England town—and class stratification in the large seaboard cities. Initially few scholars of the small towns were interested in the Revolution, much less the Jameson thesis; indeed, the town studies usually stopped before the Revolution. Jackson Turner Main's social history discussed earlier was doubly exceptional in studying the social structure of the country as a whole both after as well as before the Revolution.[187]

The foray into the social structure of the major cities was opened up by James Henretta's analysis of tax records in Boston showing the growing class stratification in the colonial era (followed a few years later by Allan Kulikoff's analysis of the continuation of these trends after the war).[188] But Gary Nash led the first full-scale inquiry taking on the three largest communities, New York, Philadelphia, and Boston, with statistical analysis of a massive array of estate inventories, tax lists, and poor relief records that enabled him to measure social change over the century before the Revolution. The picture that emerged was of a growing concentration of wealth, "the crumbling of economic security for the lower middle class," and below that, widespread, chronic poverty. Unlike most other social historians, Nash went on to explore the "linkages" between this "restructuring of society" and the transformation of urban politics before and during the Revolutionary crisis, providing a dimension hitherto missing to explain urban radicalism. Unlike others in the new social history, Nash also gave major attention to race, measuring, for example,

[187] Richard R. Beeman, "The New Social History and the Search for 'Community' in Colonial America," *American Quarterly* 29 (1977):442–43; an exception was Robert A. Gross, *The Minute Men and Their World* (New York, 1976).

[188] James A. Henretta, "Economic Development and Social Structure in Colonial Boston," *William and Mary Quarterly*, 3d ser. 22 (1965):75–92; Allan Kulikoff, "The Progress of Inequality in Revolutionary Boston," *William and Mary Quarterly*, 3d ser. 28 (1971):375–412.

changing patterns of slaveholding in colonial Philadelphia. And in the first work of its kind, *Red, White, and Black*, he explored the interactions of Indians, Europeans, and African-Americans in colonial America.[189]

Whether or not they were disciples of the methods of the new social history, historians continued to find the social themes of the Revolution compelling. Several essays in the volume sponsored by the Institute of Early American History, which were sandwiched between the Counterprogressive essays of Bernard Bailyn and Edmund Morgan, obdurately explored Jamesonian hypotheses. John Shy, a military historian, convinced that "no question has aroused more interest and drawn more scholarly energy than the one posed by Jameson: did the Revolution change American society?" examined the social effects of seven years of war. Focusing on the triangularity of the struggle in which "two armed forces contended less with each other than for the support and control of the civilian population," he saw a "great middle group of Americans" who were "almost certainly a majority of the population . . . people who were dubious, afraid, uncertain, indecisive." "A great many of these people were changed by the war," and "the revolutionary war, considered as a political education for the masses, helps to fill the explanatory gap" contributing to "the rapid erosion of deferential political behavior."[190]

---

[189] Gary B. Nash and James T. Lemon, "The Distribution of Wealth in Eighteenth-Century America: A Century of Change in Chester County, Pennsylvania, 1693–1802," *Journal of Social History* 2 (1968):1–24; Nash, ed., *Class and Society in Early America* (Englewood Cliffs, N.J., 1970); Nash, *Red, White, and Black: The Peoples of Early America* (Englewood Cliffs, N.J., 1974); Nash, "Urban Wealth and Poverty in Pre-Revolutionary America," *Journal of Interdisciplinary History* 4 (1976):545–84; G. B. Warden, "Inequality and Instability in Eighteenth-Century Boston: A Reappraisal," *Journal of Interdisciplinary History* 4 (1976):585–620; Jacob M. Price, "Quantifying Colonial America: A Comment on Nash and Warden," *Journal of Interdisciplinary History* 4 (1976):701–9; Nash, "Up from the Bottom in Franklin's Philadelphia," *Past and Present*, no. 77 (1977):57–83.

[190] John Shy, "The American Revolution: The Military Conflict Considered as a Revolutionary War," in Kurtz and Hutson, eds., *Essays on the American Revolution*, pp. 121–56, quotations, pp. 122, 126, 147, 154; Shy, *A People Numerous and Armed: Reflections on the Military Struggle for American Independence* (New York, 1976).

William G. McLoughlin, dealing with the growth of religious liberty, thought that the Revolution "provided so many changes in so short a period that Jameson may have rightly described it as social revolution, at least in the area of religion." Unlike Jameson or his critics, McLoughlin located the agency of change in the Dissenters, especially the Baptists of New England, whose long war against the standing order he would unfold in a small library of books.[191]

Rowland Berthoff and John M. Murrin, with characteristic iconoclasm, rejected as conjectural the new hypotheses about the social origins of the Revolution to return to an old question central to Jameson, the effects of the Revolution on the land system. Skeptical of historians who reduced the abolition of entail and primogeniture to an issue of only symbolic importance, Murrin and Berthoff argued that "most colonies in the eighteenth century experienced what European specialists would recognize as a 'feudal revival.'" Challenging Louis Hartz's rarely questioned assumption that America had no feudal past, they contended that "feudal projects [that] collapsed in the seventeenth century, not because America was too progressive to endure them but because it was too primitive to sustain them," took on new life in the eighteenth century. "Between 1730 and 1745," old claims were revived and consolidated from Carolina to New York "not to restore feudal relationships but for the income they might produce" from tenancy. Outside New England this feudal revival "was as diverse as it was profitable, provoking more social violence after 1745 than perhaps any other problem." "We can only guess what sort of society the feudal revival might have produced had it gone unchecked for another half century. . . . But because the Revolution happened when it did the feudal revival was truly destroyed." But if Jameson thus underesti-

---

[191] William G. McLoughlin, "The Role of Religion in the Revolution: Liberty of Conscience and Cultural Cohesion in the New Nation," in Kurtz and Hutson, eds. *Essays on the American Revolution*, pp. 197–255; see also idem, *Isaac Backus and the American Pietistic Tradition* (Boston, 1967); idem, *New England Dissent, 1630–1833: The Baptists and the Separation of Church and State*, 2 vols. (Cambridge, Mass., 1971); idem, *Revivals, Awakenings, and Reform: An Essay on Religion and Social Change in America, 1607–1977* (Chicago, 1978); and idem, ed., *The Diary of Isaac Backus*, 3 vols. (Providence, 1980).

mated the dimensions of this issue, he overestimated the democratizing effect of the sale of confiscated loyalist land. "The long-term tendency," Murrin and Berthoff concluded, was "towards greater inequality with marked class distinctions."[192]

The consequence of all these exploratory forays into colonial society was to reopen analysis of the transformation question, not at the point of consequences, Jameson's focus, but at the point of origins. This systematic analysis of late colonial society provided insight into the social origins of the Revolution as well as a base line for measuring change after the Revolution.

In the early 1970s the social-science oriented historians who generalized about these trends—Jack P. Greene, Kenneth A. Lockridge, James A. Henretta—usually framed them in modernization theory. Greene became interested in "the preconditions of Revolution." Historians interested in "the causal pattern of revolution," he claimed in 1973, sidestepping Bernard Bailyn, "now give as much attention to social strain as to political and ideological conflict; to social dysfunction, frustration, anomie, and their indices as to weaknesses and tensions within the political system." He postulated two hypotheses, first, "that colonial society underwent a dramatic erosion of internal social cohesion over the period from 1690 to 1760, and second, that the social structure was becoming more and more rigid and social strain correspondingly more intense." But Greene was dubious about a "direct causal relationship" between such social strains and the Revolution, arguing that the "broader social revolution" of "modernization" was "in many respects far more crucial to an understanding of the first two centuries of American life and far more worthy of scholarly attention than the American Revolution" because it "would have been completed with or without the American Revolution."[193]

[192] Rowland Berthoff and John M. Murrin, "Feudalism, Communalism, and the Yeoman Freeholder: The American Revolution Considered as a Social Accident," in Kurtz and Hutson, eds., *Essays on the American Revolution*, pp. 256–88, quotations pp. 264, 267, 272, 281.

[193] Jack P. Greene, "The Social Origins of the American Revolution: An Evaluation and an Interpretation," *Political Science Quarterly* 88 (1973):1–2, 22.

Kenneth Lockridge, like Nash and unlike Greene, tried to find links between long-range social change and the Revolution. He was the author of an influential demographic study of Dedham, Massachusetts, in transition in its first hundred years from a communal utopia to a "modern" town, and of a pioneering study of the growth of literacy in New England. Revisiting the Dedham of the late eighteenth century, he found that New England was becoming "seriously overcrowded" and "more and more an old world society." He summed up the major trends of the half century before the Revolution as "increasing population density, pressure on land supply, migration, concentration of wealth, social differentiation and commercial dependency." He then asked, "How might men have reacted to these changes? How might their various reactions have entered into the debates of those who sought to give political definition to the new nation?" He concluded there was a "sharpened concern over the concentration of wealth and the decline of social equality" that provided the "reality" for the "rhetoric" examined by Gordon Wood in the intense conflict of 1776 to 1787 between "democracy" and "aristocracy." [194]

James Henretta's extended "interdisciplinary" essay in 1973 was in many ways a summa of the point at which the new social history had arrived in the early 1970s. The Revolution took place in the context of an evolution of long-range social trends. There was a "crisis of American colonial society." "For nearly a generation a succession of religious struggles, economic disturbances, and armed conflicts had shaken the foundations of social stability, creating a tense social environment conducive to an aggressive, even violent reaction to new and unexpected pressures" from the imperial relationship. Unlike most scholars of social change, he allowed for agency. "By destroying the established system of government and au-

---

[194] Kenneth A. Lockridge, *A New England Town, the First Hundred Years: Dedham, Massachusetts, 1636–1736* (New York, 1970); Lockridge, *Literacy in Colonial New England: An Enquiry into the Social Context of Literacy in the Early Modern West* (New York, 1974); Lockridge, "Social Change and the Meaning of the American Revolution" *Journal of Social History* 6 (1973): 403–49, quotations pp. 414, 405, 417; Lockridge, "Land, Population, and the Evolution of New England Society, 1630–1790," *Past and Present*, no. 39 (1968):62–80.

445

thority, the quest for home rule had made it possible for previously powerless groups to raise the question of who should rule at home."[195]

But as Henretta measured the "parameters of change" after the Revolution, he found only a "modicum of social mobility" and an uneven democratization of the political process. "Except for the disruptions produced by the war itself and by Loyalist emigration . . . most of the changes that took place during these years represented the culmination of previous trends." The "acceleration of the historical process had followed *linear* lines of development." In effect this repudiated Jameson. Turning to blacks and women, Henretta struck a harsh judgment. While "some previously disadvantaged groups, like the militant farmers of the interior and urban artisans, had also been sufficiently prepared by past events that they were able to seize the historical moment and realize some of their goals through purposeful political and social action . . . other deprived groups were not." The abolition of slavery "did not touch the overwhelming majority of the black population," and the new ideology of republicanism was little applied to women. "The liberation of blacks and of women was intimately connected," Henretta argued with a jolting boldness, "because both occupied the same type of structural position within the American social order. Both were members of a caste, one racial, and the other sexual . . . [both] were the legal chattels of the white male section of the population. . . . They joined those who were white and male, but also poor and propertyless as members of the hidden and oppressed *majority*."[196]

For Henretta, therefore, the American, in comparison to other revolutions, was not a "total" revolution but "rather a movement for home rule led, managed, and ultimately controlled by those groups who occupied privileged positions in the society." By 1815 the end of two centuries of social evolution was "urban middle class capitalism" in the North and "a rural landed aristocracy" in the South. Those who expressed

[195] James A. Henretta, *The Evolution of American Society, 1700–1815: An Interdisciplinary Analysis* (Lexington, Mass., 1973), p. 158.

[196] Ibid., pp. 169, 173.

optimism about the performance of these societies "were as a rule neither red, nor black, nor poor, nor female."[197] The first wave of new social history thus beckoned scholars to focus on the groups still missing the transforming benefits of either the Revolution or the new social history.

X. *EXPLORATIONS:* NEW LEFT, NEW SOCIAL, NEW PROGRESSIVE

The American Revolution: Explorations in the History of American Radicalism (1976) became in time something of a benchmark, a point at which to measure the challenge to reigning interpretations. Edmund Morgan considered it "the most important book on the Revolution yet produced by historians of the New Left." "It would be impossible to do justice to the range of interpretive insights offered in this book," he wrote. "It gives a new lease on historiographical life to the contest over who should rule at home." The collection made its way in the field fairly rapidly, suggesting that it filled a need for those groping for an alternative vision of the Revolution. Richard Morris cited six essays in his presidential address to the AHA in 1976 as evidence of the ways in which "ordinary people gave a distinct cast" to the era, making it "a people's revolution." In 1982 Robert Shalhope, reviewing the state of the "republican synthesis" he had found pervasive in 1972, analyzed the essays as embodying the central themes of the "fragmentation" of the ideological school. It was "no longer possible to see a single, monolithic political ideology characterizing American thought on the eve of the Revolution."[198]

"New Left" hardly conveyed the range of politics and historiographic traditions of the eleven essayists and myself as editor. I thought of it as a mix of new social, new Progressive,

[197] Ibid, p. 225; see also Richard D. Brown, *Modernization: The Transformation of American Life, 1600–1865* (New York, 1976).

[198] Edmund S. Morgan, "The American Revolution: Who Were 'the People'?" *New York Review of Books,* Aug. 5, 1976; Morris, " 'We the People' "; Shalhope, "Republicanism and Early American Historiography"; Kammen, *A Season of Youth,* p. 40; Alfred F. Young, ed., *The American Revolution: Explorations in the History of American Radicalism* (1976), 7th printing (DeKalb, Ill., 1993).

New Left, new feminist and other histories that fit no categorization. I was looking for scholars who, like myself, were trying to open old themes in new ways. I had begun my
exploration of the Revolution in the grim 1950s with a study
of the Democratic Republicans of New York from 1763 to
1797 that early had convinced me of the role of the Revolution in democratizing American political culture. I assumed
politics was defined in a world of parties, associations, and
elections as conveyed by newspapers, pamphlets, and broad-
sides, which may have owed something to my experience in
the Old Left. When I set out to explore mechanics more intensively, I was impressed by the power of the scholarship of
Lynd and Lemisch, who became fellow-explorers. And by the
late 1960s and early 1970s I was inspired by Rudé and
Thompson who showed that it was possible to recover the
"crowd" and the belief systems of artisans and by the success
of my friend Herbert G. Gutman in recovering the workplace
and community culture of American preindustrial classes. I
was going down various unmarked paths to get at the laboring classes in Boston—the ritual of Pope's Day, popular
culture conveyed by graphic arts, the life history of a shoemaker.[199]

[199] Young, *The Democratic Republicans of New York: The Origins, 1763–1797*
(Chapel Hill, 1967). I had edited *Dissent: Explorations in the History of American Radicalism;* the opening essays in that book were by Lynd and Lemisch,
who were both invited to take part in the 1976 volume. I had also served
with Leonard W. Levy as one of the two general editors of the American
Heritage Series (45 vols. [Indianapolis, 1965–75]), whose contributors to
the early history ranged across the spectrum (Morgan, Perry Miller and
Alan Heimert, Jensen, Kenyon, Lynd), and which included the first volumes of modern sources on slavery (Willie Lee Rose), women's history
(Gerda Lerner), and the black experience (August Meier, Elliott Rudwick,
and John Bracey); for my scholarship: "Pope's Day, Tar and Feathers, and
Coronet George Joyce, Jun.: From Ritual to Rebellion in Boston" (Paper
presented at the Anglo-American Scholars Conference, New Brunswick,
N.J., 1973); Young, "English Plebeian Culture and Eighteenth-Century
American Radicalism," in Margaret Jacob and James Jacob, eds., *The Origins
of Anglo-American Radicalism* (London, 1984), pp. 185–213; Young, "George
Robert Twelves Hewes (1742–1840): A Boston Shoemaker and the Memory
of the American Revolution," *William and Mary Quarterly,* 3d ser. 38 (1981),
reprinted in *In Search of Early America,* pp. 234–88.

I chose historians who were involved in major research touching on the theme of radicalism in the Revolution and who, as it happens, were at unusually productive points in their careers. Some had recently published books (Ira Berlin, Ronald Hoffman, Joseph Ernst, Francis Jennings), others were close to completing books (Gary Nash, Dirk Hoerder, Eric Foner, Edward Countryman, Rhys Isaac) which have since won recognition as major works of synthesis. Joan Hoff Wilson's essay would win the distinction of the Berkshire Prize in women's history.

I did not know the politics of most of the scholars I invited until they handed in autobiographical prefaces for their essays. I was partial to "outsiders" who might bring a fresh perspective—which meant to non-Americans (Isaac and Hoerder), to Americans long abroad (Countryman and Marvin L. Michael Kay), or to scholars drawn to the Revolution to cope with a long-range analytical issue (Berlin, Jennings, Wilson). Two were students of Merrill Jensen (Hoffman, Ernst); a number were practitioners of the new social history, like Nash, engaged in quantifying an analysis of urban social structures, or Wilson, drawing on demography and family reconstitution to analyze the status of women, or Isaac, reading "body language" to decode evangelical and gentry ways of life in Virginia.

The essays registered a perceptible shift of attention in the phase of the Revolution under study. Six of the eleven focused on the time of origins to 1776, but one took Thomas Paine, the quintessential radical of the era, through the Revolution, one dealt with the war and the resistance of the "the disaffected" to the gentry, and three dealt with results of the Revolution for women, free blacks, and American Indians— groups then on the edge of the historiography of the Revolution. Although no one was inspired by Jameson, the essays and the expanded scholarship in the authors' books had major implications for the study of the internal transformations in the Revolution in at least four ways.

They revealed, first, the agency of the common people in shaping events. The crowd, both urban and rural, took on new life. In the major cities the growing class stratification and the long tradition of popular movements against elites revealed by Gary Nash provided a context for crowd action during the political crisis with Britain. Crowds in the most "mobbish" town, Boston, as mapped by Dirk Hoerder fit no single pattern; some were self-led, some whig-led; some were consensual; others struggled for their own identity. In the countryside Edward Countryman showed a long history of popular struggles over land for New Jersey, the Hudson Valley, and what became Vermont, while Marvin L. Michael Kay portrayed the Regulators of backcountry North Carolina as engaged in a class conflict against their local elites rather than in a sectional conflict.[200]

Class conflict, in general, was neither scanty nor sporadic, nor was it muted by the war. Wherever there was a prior history of intense class antagonism in the countryside, and patriot leadership was from the elite, there was a wartime pattern of loyalism or "disaffection" among the "lower" orders. Ronald Hoffman traced this with acuity for Maryland, Delaware, and the southern interior. Wartime inflation and profiteering could also produce intense conflicts in the cities over price control, dividing artisans.[201]

Second, the essays suggested the kinds of ideologies scholars were likely to encounter—in political economy, evangelical religion, and democratic thought—if free from the assumption of a uniform consensual ideology. There was a

[200] Gary B. Nash, "Social Change and the Growth of Prerevolutionary Urban Radicalism," in Young, ed., *The American Revolution*, pp. 3–36; Nash, *The Urban Crucible: Social Change, Political Consciousness, and the Origins of the American Revolution* (Cambridge, Mass., 1979); Dirk Hoerder, "Boston Leaders and Boston Crowds," in Young, ed., *The American Revolution*, pp. 233–72; Hoerder, *Crowd Action in Revolutionary Massachusetts, 1765–1780* (New York, 1977); Edward Countryman, "Out of the Bounds of Law: Northern Land Rioters in the Eighteenth Century," in Young, ed., *The American Revolution*, pp. 37–70; Countryman, *A People in Revolution: The American Revolution and Political Society in New York, 1760–1790* (Baltimore, 1981); Marvin L. Michael Kay, "The North Carolina Regulation, 1766–1776: A Class Conflict," in Young, ed., *The American Revolution*, pp. 71–124.

[201] Ronald Hoffman, "The 'Disaffected' in the Revolutionary South," in Young, ed., *The American Revolution*, pp. 273–318; Hoffman, *A Spirit of Dissension*.

political economy implicit in the whig ideology of elites revealed by Ernst and the possibility of a distinct political economy among farmers. There were also clear signs of the "moral
economy" Thompson had identified in eighteenth-century
English crowds in Countryman's land rioters. Evangelical religion in Virginia as explored by Isaac armed Baptists and
Methodists to challenge not only the Anglican religious establishment but the entire value system of the planter elite.
Paine's success in Foner's analysis revealed the immense popularity of a strain of English thought—democratic and egalitarian—lying beneath the Commonwealthman ideology as
well as a commitment to the tenets of capitalism. All these
were strands of a popular ideology. They did not permit, I
thought, a claim for a distinct ideology among those below,
but neither did they permit scholars to continue on the bland
assumption of a consensus behind a single patriot ideology
descended from a single English tradition.[202]

Third, in dealing with consequences of the Revolution, the
authors pushed the subject into dark terrain not in keeping
in 1976 with the celebratory fife-and-drum tones of the Bicentennial. The Revolution was not fought to free the slaves,
but Berlin portrayed a revolution in black life. African-
Americans, who achieved freedom by their own efforts or by
acts of individual manumission in the South or of state governments in the North, forged the first free black communities. Jennings saw American Indians who fought against the
Americans on the side of the British, their traditional protectors, as engaged in effect in a series of peasant wars fought
against the barons who resisted the king; after the disaster of
the American victory they continued to resist the new United
States. Through the eyes of women, Wilson perceived only

[202]Joseph A. Ernst, "Ideology and an Economic Interpretation of the
Revolution," in Young, ed., *The American Revolution*, pp. 159–86; Ernst,
Money and Politics in America; Rhys Isaac, "Preachers and Patriots: Popular
Culture and the Revolution in Virginia," in Young, ed., *The American Revolu-
tion*, pp. 125–56; Isaac, *The Transformation of Virginia, 1740–1790* (Chapel
Hill, 1982); Eric Foner, "Tom Paine's Republic: Radical Ideology and Social
Change," in Young, ed., *The American Revolution*, pp. 187–232; Foner, *Tom
Paine and Revolutionary America* (New York, 1976).

the illusion of change; their legal status, economic position, and social condition, she argued, were probably worse after than before the Revolution.[203]

Fourth, this cluster of scholarship suggested to me a new way of measuring the success of radical movements—by their capacity to influence those in power. There was a process by which the pressures of internal radicalism and the sheer need of elites to mobilize popular support during a long war forced the creation of a new type of sophisticated conservatism. The Revolution led to upheavals that gentry struggled to control, whether it was crowds in Boston before the war, or during the war price control rioters in Philadelphia, poor Maryland farmers disaffected from the effort to conscript them, or evangelical farmers in Virginia in search of religious liberty. Authors showed would-be ruling classes learning, as had New York's aristocratic patriot Robert R. Livingston, "to yield to the torrent if they hoped to direct its course." They accommodated artisans and farmers but bent relatively little to outsiders to the political system: African-Americans, American Indians, or women (or so it seemed to me in 1976).[204]

The essays stimulated criticism from many points on the historical spectrum. Edmund Morgan thought they "succeeded in demonstrating a large amount of class antagonism"

[203] Ira Berlin, "The Revolution in Black Life," in Young, ed., *The American Revolution*, pp. 349–82; Berlin, *Slaves without Masters: The Free Negro in the Antebellum South* (New York, 1974); idem, "Time, Space, and the Evolution of Afro-American Society in British Mainland North America," *American Historical Review* 85 (1980):44–78; Francis Jennings, "The Indians' Revolution," in Young, ed., *The American Revolution*, pp. 319–48; Jennings, *The Invasion of America* (Chapel Hill, 1975); Joan Hoff Wilson, "The Illusion of Change: Women and the American Revolution," in Young, ed., *The American Revolution*, pp. 338–446.

[204] Robert R. Livingston to William Duer, June 12, 1777, cited in Young, *Democratic Republicans*, p. 15; Young, afterword in Young, ed., *The American Revolution*, pp. 449–62; Young, "Conservatives, the Constitution, and the 'Spirit of Accommodation,'" in Robert A. Goldwin and William A. Schambra, eds., *How Democratic Is the Constitution?* (Washington, D.C., 1980), pp. 117–47, and, in a revised version, "The Framers of the Constitution and the 'Genius of the People,'" in *Radical History Review*, no. 42 (1988):7–47, with commentary by Barbara Clark Smith, Linda K. Kerber, Michael Merrill, Peter Dimock, William Forbath, and James A. Henretta.

but that "the content of this popular ideology remains elusive and seems to consist more in attitude than in general ideas which can be differentiated from those of the Whig ideology." Jesse Lemisch, on the other hand, did not think several scholars drew out enough consciousness; he criticized Hoerder for deducing the consciousness of crowds from behavior and Wilson for relying on quantitative data to measure changes in consciousness among women, a criticism implicit in later books about women in the Revolution by Linda Kerber and Mary Beth Norton. An historian of the Wisconsin school thought the essayists (as well as Lynd, Lemisch, and Young) who searched for popular ideology were wrong to accept the premise of the importance of ideology while an intellectual historian considered the collection "Beard-dominated" in its orientation around interests and its skepticism about the importance of ideas. Such disparate reactions I thought reflected the mix in the book and the fact that scholars were working out pieces of the puzzle in search of a new overview.[205]

The collection as a whole pointed to new possibilities for the study of transformation in the Revolution. If the emphasis on the agency of the common people was valid, then forces came into being that might transform the society. Paine could no longer be put down as the "Peter Pan of the Age of Reason" or as a "bizarre" figure of "marginal" influence, nor could evangelical enthusiasts and radical crowds be dismissed as paranoid foes of intellectualism. Rural rebellion, while sporadic, seemed to be a recurring constant before and after the Revolution. And in light of Revolutionary ideals, the real "losers" were redefined as African-Americans, Native Americans, and American women, people who could no longer be shunted aside as "minorities" or as passive victims. If, as Morgan generously wrote, the book gave "a new lease on historiographical life to the contest over who should rule at home," Becker's political formulation, it also took out leases on ground that historians were only beginning to enter. It

[205] Morgan, "The American Revolution: Who Were 'the People?'"; Jesse Lemisch, review of Young, ed., *The American Revolution, American Historical Review* 82 (1977):737–39; Gordon, "Crafting a Usable Past," pp. 691–95; Rodgers, "Republicanism: The Career of a Concept," pp. 24–27.

helped to shift the axis of inquiry among scholars who were redefining the questions in the transformation debate.

XI. THE TRANSFORMATION OF EARLY AMERICAN HISTORY

In 1949 when I started to prepare for my Ph.D. exam at Northwestern University I began a loose-leaf notebook, devoting a page to each important scholar in early American history I assumed I was responsible for: Henry Adams, Andrews, Bancroft, Becker, Beer, Beard, through Gipson, Jameson, Perry Miller, Morison, Parkman, Parrington, down to Turner, Thomas Jefferson Wertenbaker, and Louis B. Wright. I had a few pages on subjects ("mercantilism as cause") and a page for "Negro history" (Ulrich B. Phillips, Herbert Aptheker, and John Hope Franklin), with many more titles from a course I had taken with Melville Herskovits in Anthropology ("African Retentions in the New World") because no one in history taught "Negro history." I had no page for Indians; presumably Francis Parkman sufficed. Early in the 1950s, as a young instructor at Wesleyan, I remember traveling up to Boston to join my former classmate, Bill Towner, at a conference of the Colonial Society of Massachusetts at Parkman's restored mansion on Beacon Hill. I was not only in the presence of Perry Miller and Samuel Eliot Morison, who were on my list, but over sherry I could chat with what seemed like all the rising young men in colonial history. I remember Miller telling good-naturedly how vexed he was with some moviemaker he was advising who could not grasp that the Puritans did not usually wear black clothing. What passion went into breaking stereotypes at Harvard when it came to the Puritans. After the lobster Newburg, we all climbed to the attic to tour Parkman's restored study where a metal grid frame that the partially blind historian used to guide his handwriting lay on his desk.

Today a graduate student might still compose a list of the "greats" (a much shorter list), but he or she is more likely to consult the Institute of Early American History and Culture's guidebook, *Books about Early America,* subtitled *2001 Titles,* focus on several subjects in more than fifty categories, and plead for a concentration on a few themes. Today all the capable young men and women in early American history could not fit into a large auditorium in Williamsburg, let alone Parkman's second floor living room, and most would not be inclined to make a pilgrimage to the shrine of a blatantly racist historian who saw Indians, blacks, Catholics, and the lesser breeds thronging America through the vision of a very WASP Boston Brahmin.[206]

In turning from the historiography of the first thirty years after World War II to the outpouring of scholarship on the Revolution in the last twenty years, I find several qualities striking—its sheer volume and diversity, the way the issue of transformation has moved to a central place, the attention scholars have given to groups left out by almost all previous schools, and the new syntheses that are emerging. If few young scholars now read J. Franklin Jameson, many take it for granted that they should consider the social dimensions of the American Revolution. The Revolution that is emerging is more many-sided and more perplexing—at once more radical and more conservative than anything Jameson or his critics envisioned.

The volume and diversity of the scholarship. It is not only that the Institute's selected bibliography of books about early America, which in 1970 had about 650 titles, had more than triple that number by 1989. Both listings embraced the colonial era as well as the Revolution, yet in the second list an even larger proportion of the titles would be relevant to a scholar seeking to understand the social themes of the Revolution. It took fourteen scholars to write the bibliographic essays for a volume covering colonial social and economic history, and by choice they only went up to but did not include the Revolution. Bibliographic essays, once the stock in trade of the profession, cannot keep up with the pace of scholarship about the

---

[206] William R. Taylor, "Francis Parkman," in Marcus Cunliffe and Robin W. Winks, eds., *Pastmasters: Some Essays on American Historians* (New York, 1969), pp. 1–38; Francis Jennings, "Francis Parkman: A Brahmin among Untouchables," *William and Mary Quarterly*, 3d ser. 42 (1985):305–28.

Revolution. But if the field is daunting, it is also exhilarating.[207]

The diversity is most apparent in the new fields that have come into being. Historians have been doing so many "new" histories that one wonders how they dealt with the majority of the people before. There is the new African-American history, which studies slaves and free blacks who, on the eve of the Revolution, numbered 500,000 in a population of 2,500,000; the new labor history, which deals with artisans in the skilled trades (masters, journeymen, and apprentices, the latter the most numerous group of workers in the cities), seamen (the largest group of wageworkers in colonial times), and indentured servants (the largest group of immigrants); the new agrarian history, which encompasses farmers of all conditions (slaveholding planters, yeomen, tenants, and the rural landless); the new women's history, which attempts to embrace women in all classes, as well as a new Indian history, which deals with Native Americans (more than 150,000 of whom lived east of the Mississippi) and the complex interactions of a multitude of diverse tribal societies with Anglo-Americans.

Diversity is also apparent in the geographic areas of the country now receiving scholarly energies. Chesapeake area studies may be overtaking New England, and historians are going back to the frontier, off to the West Indies, and outside Anglo-America to Hispanic America and the many worlds of Native Americans. Ethnicity is under scrutiny as are the varia-

---

[207] Institute of Early American History and Culture, *Books about Early America: A Selected Bibliography*, 4th ed. (Williamsburg, Va., 1970); compare to Ammerman and Morgan, comps., *Books about Early America: 2001 Titles*; Greene and Pole, eds., *Colonial British America*, in which the following essays are germane: Richard S. Dunn (labor); T. H. Breen (peoples and cultures); Gary B. Nash (social development); James A. Henretta (wealth and social structure); Joyce Oldham Appleby (value and society); Richard L. Bushman (vernacular cultures); Ronald L. Gephart, comp., *Revolutionary America, 1763–1789: A Bibliography*, 2 vols. (Washington, D.C., 1984), has 14,810 entries of books, articles, and primary sources, many with multiple titles; for the best recent bibliographic essays see James A. Henretta and Gregory H. Nobles, *Evolution and Revolution: American Society, 1600–1820* (Lexington, Mass., 1987), and Edward Countryman, *The American Revolution* (New York, 1985).

tions in the cultures of English migrants.[208] Diversity is also apparent in the kinds of history being done. Intellectual history, which once flaunted its divorce from social history, may be cohabiting with its old mate. There is a "new" political history as well, probing political culture. The shelves of biographies and "papers" of the Founding Fathers, groaning ever since the 1950s, are now joined by studies of Founding Mothers and unknown and lesser-known men and women, based on long neglected diaries, memoirs, and letters.[209] And most important, there is no longer one dominant interpretation—if there ever was—but many competing points of view and among younger scholars a wariness of overarching interpretations that try to squeeze this bulging diversity into the confines of a single container.

This diversity owes much, in the first place, to the explosion of American higher education that began in the 1960s. There were more universities granting the doctorate in history (some 132 in 1972) and more doctorates granted in history (one thousand a year through the 1970s, 600 or so in the 1980s). And there were more jobs for historians, especially as early American history—pronounced "a neglected field" in 1947 by Carl Bridenbaugh, the first director of the Institute of Early American History and Culture (1945–50)—came into

[208] Jack P. Greene, "Interpretive Frameworks: The Quest for Intellectual Order in Early American History," *William and Mary Quarterly*, 3d ser. 48 (1991):515–30; Bernard Bailyn, *The Peopling of British North America: An Introduction* (New York, 1986); Bailyn and Philip D. Morgan, eds., *Strangers within the Realm: Cultural Margins of the First British Empire* (Chapel Hill, 1991); David Hackett Fischer, *Albion's Seed: Four British Folkways in America* (New York, 1989); Jack P. Greene, *Pursuits of Happiness: The Social Development of Early Modern British Colonies and the Formation of American Culture* (Chapel Hill, 1988).

[209] Laurel Thatcher Ulrich, *A Midwife's Tale: The Life of Martha Ballard, Based on Her Diary, 1785–1812* (New York, 1990); Barbara Clark Smith, *After the Revolution: The Smithsonian History of Everyday Life in the Eighteenth Century* (New York, 1985); Barbara E. Lacey, "The World of Hannah Heaton: The Autobiography of an Eighteenth-Century Connecticut Farm Woman," *William and Mary Quarterly*, 3d ser. 45 (1988):280–304; Joy Day Buel and Richard Buel, Jr., *The Way of Duty: A Woman and Her Family in Revolutionary America* (New York, 1984); Young, "George Robert Twelves Hewes."

its own, in part due to the efforts of the Institute. The circulation of the *William and Mary Quarterly*, published by the Institute, went from 777 in 1947 to 2,469 in 1965 to 3,589 in 1985. Jameson's "convivium historicum" could not survive the polycentrism of a profession with many graduate departments, multiple research centers, the geographic decentralization of source materials made possible by new microform technologies, and the expanded outlets for publication in university presses and new specialized journals. As a consequence, historians can now analyze the decline of deference, a perennial subject of inquiry in early American history, among themselves.[210]

As expansion changed the social composition of the profession, Carl Bridenbaugh's worst dreams came true. In his presidential address to the AHA in 1962, he complained of the "environmental deficiency" of the rising generation of historians. "Urban bred" and "products of lower middle-class or foreign origins," they lacked the "understanding . . . vouchsafed to historians who were raised in the countryside or in the small town." "Their emotions," said Bridenbaugh, "not infrequently get in the way of their historical reconstructions. They find themselves in a very real sense outsiders on our past and feel themselves shut out." Soon the "environmental deficiencies" included gender; in 1980 one in four new history doctorates was a woman, in 1990 one in three. And had Parkman's ghost visited the D'Arcy McNickle Center for the Study of the American Indian at the Newberry Library, it

---

[210] For recent statistics, see Nell Irvin Painter, "The Academic Marketplace and Affirmative Action," *Perspectives* 31 (1993):7–11, tables 2 and 3; for the changes in technology, see Lawrence W. Towner, *Past Imperfect: Essays on History, Libraries, and the Humanities*, ed. Robert W. Karrow and Alfred F. Young (Chicago, 1993), chaps. 8–9; for the overall social social changes, see Novick, *That Noble Dream*, chap. 12; for the changes in the field, see Joyce Oldham Appleby, "A Different Kind of Independence: The Postwar Restructuring of the Historical Study of Early America," *William and Mary Quarterly*, 3d ser. 50 (1993):245–67; for the Institute, see Frederika J. Teute, "A Conversation with Thad Tate," *William and Mary Quarterly*, 3d ser. 50 (1993):268–97; statistics on the circulation of the *Quarterly* provided by Ronald Hoffman, director of the Institute of Early American History and Culture.

might have encountered scholars of Native American descent as well as outsiders of many stripes.[211]

The political coloring of early American historians also changed. There was something to Edmund Morgan's observation that "there is a sort of self-selecting process" in which "politically oriented" students were not drawn to early American history. But his retort to his interviewer in 1985—"colonial history, seventeenth- and eighteenth-century history is pretty safe (laughs). People may be drawn to it as a safe subject"—might not have been echoed in New York, Princeton, Philadelphia, Washington, Williamsburg, Durham, Chicago, DeKalb, Madison, Berkeley, or Los Angeles, or any number of places where, as Linda Kerber of the University of Iowa has put it, "a new generation of historians" was helping to "restore *rebellion*" to the histories of the Revolution. Anathemas against "present-mindedness" and "presentism," in any case, had lost the power of excommunication; there were too many churches. Anti-Marxism lost its sting, what with Bailyn proclaiming, "We are all Marxists," and Morgan saying that he "admires immensely" the writings of E. P. Thompson, a "sophisticated" Marxist.[212]

Transformation as a central concern. Scholars have been giving more and more attention to the results of the Revolution. We have long known about North America "before" (at least along the eastern seaboard); we are learning much more about North America "after" the Revolution. This shift can be measured in a number of ways—in the themes addressed from a wide range of views in the annual conferences on the Revolution sponsored by the United States Capitol Historical Society under the direction of Ronald Hoffman: the economy,

[211] Carl Bridenbaugh, "The Great Mutation," *American Historical Review* 68 (1963):322–23, 328; see also the entries under anti-Semitism, anti-Catholicism, Catholics, and Jews in the index to Novick, *That Noble Dream*, p. 633; for the changing character of scholars awarded fellowships by the Institute, see the essays by former fellows of the Institute in "Forum: The Future of Early American History," *William and Mary Quarterly*, 3d ser. 50 (1993):299–424.

[212] Courtwright, "Interview with Morgan," p. 355; Bailyn, "Challenge of Modern Historiography," p. 6.

internal civil wars, African-Americans, women, religion, American Indians, the Jameson thesis;[213] in the focus of scholars exploring radicalism in the 1993 successor to my 1976 volume of essays;[214] in the scholarship about the Revolutionary War, long neglected for its social and political dimensions;[215] in the burst of books on the internal history of Indian societies and the subject of Indian-white relations, which shows promise of breaking into the consciousness of nonspecialists.[216]

Why this shift of scholarly attention? It may be part of a worldwide trend among historians of revolutions who have responded to what Eric Hobsbawm calls "the neglected problem of how and when revolutions finished," poignant even before the collapse of communism and the unforeseen paths

[213] The following volumes are in the series Perspectives on the American Revolution: Ira Berlin and Ronald Hoffman, eds., *Slavery and Freedom in the Age of the American Revolution* (Charlottesville, Va., 1983); Hoffman et al., eds., *The Economy of Early America: The Revolutionary Period, 1763–1790* (Charlottesville, Va., 1988); Hoffman and Peter J. Albert, eds., *Women in the Age of the American Revolution* (Charlottesville, Va., 1989); Hoffman and Albert, eds., *Religion in a Revolutionary Age* (Charlottesville, Va., 1994); Hoffman and Albert, eds., *"The Transforming Hand of Revolution": Reconsidering the American Revolution as a Social Movement* (Charlottesville, Va., 1995); Hoffman, Fred Hoxie, and Albert, eds., *Native Americans and the Early Republic* (forthcoming).

[214] Alfred F. Young, ed., *Beyond the American Revolution: Explorations in the History of American Radicalism* (DeKalb, Ill., 1993).

[215] Hoffman and Albert, eds., *Arms and Independence: The Military Character of the American Revolution* (Charlottesville, Va., 1984); Don C. Higginbotham, "The Early American Way of War: Reconnaissance and Appraisal," *William and Mary Quarterly*, 3d ser. 44 (1987):230–73; Charles Royster, *A Revolutionary People at War: The Continental Army and American Character, 1775–1783* (Chapel Hill, 1979).

[216] For surveys of the literature, see James Axtell, "The Ethnohistory of Early America: A Review Essay," *William and Mary Quarterly*, 3d ser. 35 (1978):110–44, and T. H. Breen, "Creative Adaptations: Peoples and Cultures," in Greene and Pole, eds., *Colonial British America*, pp. 195–232; for a critique of the failure to integrate Indian history, see James Merrill, "Some Thoughts on Colonial Historians and American Indians," *William and Mary Quarterly*, 3d ser. 46 (1989):94–119; Daniel K. Richter, "Whose Indian History?" *William and Mary Quarterly*, 3d ser. 50 (1993):379–93.

of victorious colonial revolutions.[217] In part it is the influence of the *Annales* school, in part the stimulus of social historians working in the nineteenth century inspiring inquiries into the eighteenth. In good part it stems from asking what is the significance of the Revolution to African-Americans and women, a question that can only be answered at the point of outcomes. Without being conscious of it, scholars are overcoming an occupational fallacy of historians that a major event can be explained only by its "causes."

The centrality of transformation can be measured in books on single themes and in the shifting themes of area studies, long the staple of the field. I have risked singling out six books. Take, for example, two recent books dealing with land and religion, issues central to Jameson. Lee Soltow's unassuming monograph, *The Distribution of Wealth and Income in the United States in 1798*, tests Jameson's hypotheses head on. Analyzing the little-used returns from the federal direct tax of 1798 on dwellings and buildings coupled with the census of 1800, Soltow calculated 433,000 owners of land in a country with 877,000 adult white males. Comparing this to data assembled by Alice Hanson Jones for 1774, Soltow concluded that inequality may have decreased but that Jameson's claims for the impact of the forfeiture of loyalist estates, the ending of entail and primogeniture, and the opening of the West are difficult to measure. The thrust of his conclusion is that "inequality has been found to be substantial in 1798. It was not as extreme as in Europe, nor was it as egalitarian perhaps as Tocqueville suggested. But it was considerable."[218]

Nathan Hatch in his prize-willing study of "the wave of popular religious movements that broke upon the United States in the half century after Independence" between 1780 and 1830, posited that the American Revolution was "the most crucial event in American history" because it "dramati-

---

[217] Eric Hobsbawm, "Revolution," in Roy Porter and Mikulas Teich, eds., *Revolution in History* (Cambridge, 1986), pp. 6–46, quotation p. 6. This essay is based on a report Hobsbawm gave in 1975.

[218] Lee Soltow, *The Distribution of Wealth and Income in the United States in 1798* (Pittsburgh, 1989), p. 252; for Jameson, ibid., pp. 141, 145, 148, 240.

cally expanded the circle of people who considered themselves capable of thinking for themselves about issues of
freedom, equality, sovereignty, and representation." His
study of the Methodists, Baptists, black churches, and Mor-
mons reversed the negative value judgments of the Second
Great Awakening and religious populism in general, put
down in fear by Richard Hofstadter in the era of McCarthyite
anti-intellectualism. To Hatch, religious populism, "leadership that is deliberate in championing the interests of the
common people against professional expertise and elite institutions," has been "a residual agent of change in America over
the last two centuries."[219]

Transformation has also been the theme of area studies,
which have moved from the unit of the New England town
before the Revolution to larger units before and after the Revolution. This trend is exemplified by four prize-winning
books by Edward Countryman, Rhys Isaac, Allan Kulikoff,
and John Brooke.

Countryman's study of New York and Isaac's study of Virginia make transformation central in the Revolutionary era
per se. "How different was New York in 1790 from 1760?"
is Countryman's question. Organizing his study around the
concept of "political society," he is interested in "the changes
that took place . . . between power wielders and people affected by power." He finds "an explosion of political participation" by new groups, especially mechanics, farmers, and
"expectant small capitalists," all of whom made gains as a defensive ruling class accommodated them. On the other hand,
"neither blacks, Indians, nor women took part as a group in
the revolutionary coalition, and none of them got much that
they wanted out of its radicalism." The Revolution was successful in "laying the foundations of a liberal bourgeois society."[220]

Isaac attempted to portray "half a century of religious and
political revolution" in Virginia between 1740 and 1790,
which he called a "double revolution." He offered a series of

[219] Nathan Hatch, *The Democratization of American Christianity* (New Haven, 1989).

[220] Countryman, *A People in Revolution*.

tableaux interpreting physical landscapes—the great plantation house and the Anglican church—and the symbolic rituals
of court day, militia muster, the horse race, and cockfight that
bound together a consensual society. In the Revolution the
ruling slaveholding gentry were confronted by the challenges
of an evangelical upsurge of Baptists and the popular mobilization the war required. In this framework the successful disestablishment of the Anglican church—an old Jameson
theme—became a major result, leaving a landscape of "broken down" Anglican churches amidst the "rude and unadorned chapels" of the Baptists and Methodists. The gentry
also had to confront republicanism as "a vehicle of popular
assertion among the yeomanry" and "the consolidation of a
communal pattern" among slaves—in all, "a polarized
world."[221]

By contrast, two more recent books, Kulikoff's study of the
Chesapeake region from 1680 to 1800 and Brooke's study of
Worcester County, Massachusetts between 1712 and 1861
were framed over the *longue durée*, Kulikoff aspiring to "a
grand thesis in the French style" and Brooke to a kind of "total history." Yet unlike eventless modernization history, both
assigned a role to the Revolution as a transforming event and
to what Brooke calls "political insurgencies." Kulikoff's goal
was to describe and explain the "processes of class formation"
that emerged in Virginia and Maryland on the basis of a political economy of tobacco. In place of Isaac's graphics and tableaux he offered proof via maps, figures, and tables in an
uncommon effort to synthesize the historians' findings of demographic and family patterns with the findings of Isaac,
Hoffman, and Morgan on political and cultural developments. During the Revolution, according to Kulikoff, the gentry class that held political power in the 1760s confronted a
triple crisis—a popular movement that transformed politics,
the Dissenters who threatened the Anglican establishment,
and the surge for freedom among slaves. In Virginia large
planters consolidated their rule by accommodating yeomen
with land and a voice in government, Dissenters with religious
liberty, and African-Americans for a short time with manumis-

---

[221] Isaac, *Transformation of Virginia.*

sion and over a longer time with space for the development of their own institutions and culture within the confines of slavery. Kulikoff thus located in time the origins of the antebellum Old South.[222]

Brooke set the Revolution geographically in Worcester County, a vast domain in central Massachusetts, and conceptually in the framework of an inquiry into the competing "worldviews" of republican and liberal ideologies. His effort "to bridge the gap between social experience and intellectual discourse" presented the committee that bestowed on it the Merle Curti Award with the happy dilemma of deciding whether the book was intellectual or social history. Unlike other studies in which ideology appeared as an independent variable, Brooke placed his conflict of ideologies in the context of "rapid economic change [that] spawned a dramatic and unique concentration of political insurgencies between the 1730's and the 1850's." A new social order evolved during and after the war led by "the Popular Whig gentry" amidst the struggle of Baptists for religious liberty, Shays's Regulation, which divided farmer loyalties, and a deep populist fear that the Constitution of 1787 would, as the Worcester farmer Amos Singletary put it, permit "the moneyed men" to "swallow up all us little folks." Through these conflicts alternate visions of Lockean liberalism and Harringtonian republicanism competed.[223]

[222] Allan Kulifkoff, *Tobacco and Slaves: The Development of Southern Cultures in the Chesapeake, 1680–1800* (Chapel Hill, 1986).

[223] John L. Brooke, *The Heart of the Commonwealth: Society and Political Culture in Worcester County, Massachusetts, 1713–1861* (Amherst, Mass., 1989); for other localized studies dealing with transformation: Richard R. Beeman, *The Evolution of the Southern Backcountry: A Case Study of Lunenburg County, Virginia, 1746–1832* (Philadelphia, 1984); Gregory H. Nobles, *Divisions throughout the Whole: Politics and Society in Hampshire County, Massachusetts, 1740–1775* (New York, 1983); Nobles, "'Yet the Old Republicans Still Persevere': Samuel Adams, John Hancock, and the Crisis of Popular Leadership in Revolutionary Massachusetts, 1775–1790," in this volume; Rachel N. Klein, *Unification of a Slave State: The Rise of the Planter Class in the South Carolina Backcountry, 1760–1808* (Chapel Hill, 1990); Jean B. Lee, "Lessons in Humility: The Revolutionary Transformation of the Governing Elite of Charles County, Maryland," in this volume.

Attention given to groups left out. The outsider historians—and
a good many insiders—are doing the history of the outsiders.
It is remarkable how much the new histories—of the laboring
classes, farmers, African-Americans, and women—have not
only made transformation central but are forcing historians
to reconsider the Revolution as a whole. These new histories
have some traits in common. Some take the new social history's path of quantitative measurement of condition, but more
take paths opened by the New Left to deal with agency and
consciousness; some combine both. They are generally less
vulnerable to the strictures about "history with the politics left
out" leveled earlier against Schlesinger's old social history,
echoed in the mid-1970s against the new social history by the
Marxists Eugene Genovese and Elizabeth Fox-Genovese.[224]

The new history of the laboring classes, for example, has
recovered the agency of mechanics in the making of the Revolution and the shaping of political culture, especially in the
seaboard cities, Philadelphia, New York, and Boston. The urban crowd is being placed in historical perspective. From the
mid-eighteenth through the early nineteenth century, there is
a sense of an artisan presence as well as of a conflict emerging
between journeymen and masters and apprentices and masters.[225] Lemisch's seamen have been taken out to sea in an
earlier era by Marcus Rediker and then back to land where
they are a source of transatlantic radicalism. In the quantita-

---

[224] Elizabeth Fox-Genovese and Eugene D. Genovese, "The Political Crisis of Social History: A Marxian Perspective," *Journal of Social History* 10
(1976):205–20, reprinted in Fox-Genovese and Genovese, *Fruits of Merchant
Capital: Slavery and Bourgeois Property in the Rise and Expansion of Capitalism*
(New York, 1983), chap.7.

[225] For surveys of the literature, see Sean Wilentz, "The Rise of the American Working Class, 1776–1877," in J. Carroll Moody and Alice Kessler-
Harris, eds., *Perspectives on American Labor History: The Problem of Synthesis*
(DeKalb, Ill., 1989), pp. 83–90, and Gary J. Kornblith, "The Artisanal Response to Capitalist Transformation," *Journal of the Early Republic* 10
(1990):315–21. For a synthesis, the titles by Nash are cited in n. 248, below;
for the early nineteenth century, see Wilentz, *Chants Democratic: New York
City and the Rise of the American Working Class, 1788–1850* (New York, 1984),
and Christopher L. Tomlins, *Law, Labor, and Ideology in the Early American
Republic* (Cambridge, 1993).

tive tradition, other scholars have provided vivid collective portraits of "the lower sort" of tradesmen, of indentured servants, and of the vast prewar migration of the poor from the British Isles.[226]

The pattern in the new agrarian history is similar. Scholars in the *Annales* tradition have described a wide array of rural communities and opened a fruitful debate about agrarian *mentalité* that others pursue as "moral economy" or "vernacular culture." We are getting a sense of the fear of debt and dependency and of the importance of acquiring and keeping land as the underpinning of the agrarian response to public issues.[227] To the long history of agrarian insurrections in the late colonial period, recent studies of Shays's Rebellion of the 1780s, the Whiskey Rebellion of the 1790s, and agrarian protest in northern New England in the 1800s and other backcountries suggest a pattern of continuing and widespread rural protest.[228] We are also rediscovering plebeian agrarian

[226] Marcus Rediker, *Between the Devil and the Deep Blue Sea: Merchant Seamen, Pirates, and the Anglo-American Maritime World, 1700–1750* (New York, 1987); Rediker, "A Motley Crew of Rebels: Sailors, Slaves, and the Coming of the American Revolution," in this volume; Daniel Vickers, "Beyond Jack Tar," *William and Mary Quarterly*, 3d ser. 50 (1993):418–24; Sharon V. Salinger, *"To Serve Well and Faithfully": Labor and Indentured Servants in Pennsylvania, 1682–1800* (Cambridge, 1987); Billy G. Smith, *The "Lower Sort": Philadelphia's Laboring People, 1750–1800* (Ithaca, N.Y., 1990); Bernard Bailyn, *Voyagers to the West: A Passage in the Peopling of America on the Eve of the Revolution* (New York, 1986); Jean B. Russo, "Chesapeake Artisans in the Aftermath of the Revolution," in this volume.

[227] James A. Henretta, "Families and Farms: *Mentalité* in Pre-Industrial America," *William and Mary Quarterly*, 3d ser. 35 (1978):3–32; Allan Kulikoff, *The Agrarian Origins of American Capitalism* (Charlottesville, Va., 1992), chap. 1, sums up the debate; Richard L. Bushman, *King and People in Provincial Massachusetts* (Chapel Hill, 1985), chap. 5; Barbara Clark Smith, "Social Visions of the American Resistance Movement," in this volume.

[228] David P. Szatmary, *Shays' Rebellion: The Making of an Agrarian Insurrection* (Amherst, Mass., 1980); Thomas P. Slaughter, *The Whiskey Rebellion: Frontier Epilogue to the American Revolution* (New York, 1986); Robert A. Gross, ed., *In Debt to Shays: The Bicentennial of an Agrarian Rebellion* (Charlottesville, Va., 1993); Gross, "White Hats and Hemlocks: Daniel Shays and the Legacy of the Revolution," in this volume; Alan Taylor, *Liberty Men and Great Proprietors: The Revolutionary Settlement on the Maine Frontier, 1760–1820* (Chapel Hill, 1990); Taylor, "'To Man Their Rights': The Frontier Revolu-

thinkers like William Manning, the radical millennialist Hermon Husband, and other religious Dissenters who often led agrarian movements.[229]

The new history of African-Americans in the Revolution is the culmination of the rediscovery that slaves had a history in the years before the period from 1830 to 1860, which had long dominated the modern study of slavery. As recently as 1976, Herbert Gutman wrote that "most slave communities had their start in the eighteenth century but no aspect of African-American history has received so little attention as the eighteenth-century social and cultural processes by which enslaved Africans became Afro-American slaves." For the second half of the eighteenth century, historians have begun to recover the slave family, slave religion, the slave community, and the retention of African culture and its influence in Anglo-American culture.[230] And for the Revolution they have located the agency of slaves in the wave of insurrections that peaked in 1775, in the triangular struggle during the war among slaves, whig patriots, and the British, in the pressures by slaves for greater autonomy in the labor system, and in the rebellions that erupted in 1800–1802.[231] Postwar emancipa-

---

tion," in this volume; Michael A. Bellesiles, *Revolutionary Outlaws: Ethan Allen and the Struggle for Independence on the Early American Frontier* (Charlottesville, Va., 1993).

[229] Michael Merrill and Sean Wilentz, eds., *The Key of Liberty: The Life and Democratic Writings of William Manning, "A Laborer," 1747–1814* (Cambridge, Mass., 1993); Ruth H. Bloch, *Visionary Republic: Millennial Themes in American Thought, 1756–1800* (Cambridge, 1985); Mark Jones, "The Western 'New Jerusalem': Hermon Husband's Utopian Vision," unpublished manuscript.

[230] Herbert G. Gutman, *The Black Family in Slavery and Freedom, 1750–1925* (New York, 1976), p. 327; for surveys of the scholarship, see Wood, "'I Did the Best I Could,'" pp. 185–225; Peter H. Wood, *Black Majority: Negroes in Colonial South Carolina from 1670 through the Stono Rebellion* (New York, 1974); Berlin and Hoffman, eds., *Slavery and Freedom;* Mechal Sobel, *The World They Made Together: Black and White Values in Eighteenth-Century Virginia* (Princeton, 1987).

[231] Peter H. Wood, "'Liberty Is Sweet': African-American Freedom Struggles in the Years before White Independence," in Young, ed., *Beyond the American Revolution,* pp. 149–84; Sylvia R. Frey, *Water from the Rock: Black Resistance in a Revolutionary Age* (Princeton, 1991); Philip D. Morgan, "Black

tion studies show how blacks shaped their own emancipation and their own free black communities. Meanwhile, the scholarship of slavery as an issue in national affairs continues to remind us forcefully of the incompleteness of the Revolution.[232]

The modern historical study of women in the era of the Revolution is even more recent than African-American history. "Until the mid-1970s, historians of the American Revolution largely ignored women," Mary Beth Norton writes, "and historians of women largely ignored the Revolution." Joan Hoff Wilson's argument in 1976, based on modernization analysis, that the Revolution produced only the "illusion of change," has been challenged since 1980 by the pathbreaking books by Norton and Linda K. Kerber that emphasized changes in women's consciousness, especially as a result of their experiences during the war and the opening of postwar educational opportunity. These contributed to the accommodations of "matrimonial republicanism" (a contemporary term) and what Kerber called "republican motherhood."[233] Since then one line of scholarship has reinforced a picture of changing consciousness expressed, for example, in rising literacy, the creation of a women's reading public, and the rise of the American novel, while another has stressed the institutional conservatism of the Revolution, measured by laws on inheritance and women's property rights, and demographic

---

Society in the Low Country, 1760–1810," in Berlin and Hoffman, eds., *Slavery and Freedom*, pp. 83–142; Douglas R. Edgerton, *Gabriel's Rebellion: The Virginia Slave Conspiracies of 1800 and 1802* (Chapel Hill, 1993); Billy G. Smith, "Runaway Slaves in the Mid-Atlantic Region during the Revolutionary Era," in this volume.

[232] For a summary of the literature, see Shane White, *Somewhat More Independent: The End of Slavery in New York City, 1770–1810* (Athens, Ga., 1991), pp. 211–14.

[233] Mary Beth Norton, "Reflections on Women in the Age of the American Revolution," in Hoffman and Albert, eds., *Women in the Age of the American Revolution*, pp. 479–93; Wilson, "Illusion of Change"; Norton, *Liberty's Daughters: The Revolutionary Experience of American Women, 1750–1800* (Boston, 1980); Linda K. Kerber, *Women of the Republic: Intellect and Ideology in Revolutionary America* (Chapel Hill, 1980).

patterns.[234] Still other scholars are stitching together patterns of women's exercise of citizenship.[235] Synthesizing essays proffer long lists of unstudied subjects, especially of non-middle-class nonwhite women, while the appearance of biographical studies of women offers some prospect of resolving competing claims.

XII. TOWARD A NEW SYNTHESIS?

The recovery of all the new histories has been both a major challenge and a stumbling block to synthesis from any point of view. The old political question about "who shall rule at home" posed by Becker and refined by Jensen has been more or less resolved for all but the first generation of Counterprogressives. There were two concurrent struggles; whether one was more important than the other is a red herring; how to fit them together remains a problem. As to the outcome of the internal conflict, Robert R. Palmer's analysis of the American Revolution as both radical and conservative has more resonance now than before. There seems to be a consensus that a republican system emerged with strong democratic currents.

[234] For analyses of the scholarship, see Norton, "The Evolution of White Women's Experience in Early America," *American Historical Review* 89 (1984):593–619, and Linda K. Kerber, "Separate Spheres, Female Worlds, Woman's Place: The Rhetoric of Women's History," *Journal of American History* 75 (1988):9–39; Cathy Davidson, *Revolution and the Word: The Rise of the Novel in America* (New York, 1986); William J. Gilmore, *Reading Becomes a Necessity of Life: Material and Cultural Life in Rural New England, 1780–1835* (Knoxville, Tenn., 1989); for the limitations of reform see the essays by Daniel Scott Smith, Carole Shammas, and Marylynn Salmon in Hoffman and Albert, eds., *Women in the Age of the American Revolution.*

[235] Alfred F. Young, "The Women of Boston: 'Persons of Consequence' in the Making of the Revolution," and Linda K. Kerber, "'I Have Don . . . Much to Carrey on the Warr': Women and the Shaping of Republican Ideology after the American Revolution," in Harriet B. Applewhite and Darlene G. Levy, eds., *Women and Politics in the Age of the Democratic Revolution* (Ann Arbor, Mich., 1990), pp. 181–259; Elaine Forman Crane, ed., *The Diary of Elizabeth Drinker,* 3 vols. (Boston, 1991); Susan Branson, "Politics and Gender: The Political Consciousness of Philadelphia Women in the 1790s," Ph.D. diss., Northern Illinois University, 1992.

On the other hand the new social histories have forced a reformulation of the question of the Revolution as a social movement offered with such artful openness by Jameson. The question no longer is *whether* there was social change but *how much* change occurred and especially how much in the direction of equality. And the corollary question—because we know there were such disparities—is how do we explain the so-called contradictions in the results of the Revolution?

Wherever one turns to examine social consequences of the Revolution, one finds scholars struggling to make sense of opposites. By 1820 the number of free blacks had grown to almost 250,000 and the number of slaves to 1.5 million. The Revolution, in Ira Berlin's words, "was not only a stride forward in the expansion of black liberty, [but it] strengthened the plantation regime and slavery grew as never before, spreading across a continent. Thus if the Revolution marked a new birth of freedom, it also launched a great expansion of slavery." When and if "a new narrative" of the Revolution integrates gender, Linda Kerber writes, it "will be understood to be more deeply radical than we have hitherto perceived it because its shock reached into the deepest and most private human relations." But it will also be understood to be "more deeply conservative . . . purchasing political stability at the price of backing away from the implications of the sexual politics implied in its own manifestos." For free white men the contrasts in the achievement of personal independence present similar dilemmas. Soltow's finding that in 1800 less than half the adult white males were propertyholders, even when adjusted for variations in the life cycle, raises the question of whether the glass was half full or half empty. Sean Wilentz's analysis of artisans in the 1790s and early 1800s reveals contrasts between prospering entrepreneurial masters threatened by merchant capitalists and impoverished journeymen shoemakers driven to strikes. The new Indian histories churn up even greater challenges of irreconcilable opposites between Anglo-Americans and Native Americans as well as within tribal societies divided over how to resist.[236]

[236] Berlin and Hoffman, eds., *Slavery and Freedom*, p. xv; Linda K. Kerber, "'History Can Do It No Justice': Women and the Reinterpretation of the

To understand these contradictions, historians have moved toward analyses in which inequalities and exploitation are inherent either in the social system or in the ideologies. "The American colonists were not trapped in an accidental contradiction between slavery and freedom," David Brion Davis writes. As they emerged from the Revolution, "slavery was of central importance to both the southern and national economies and thus to the viability of 'the American system.'" The continuing subordination of women seems implicit in the values of republicanism, if not in the exploitation of the labor of women in a patriarchal system. Personal independence, the goal of every Tom, Dick, and Harry, whether farmer, mechanic, or merchant, was defined by the dependence of his wife and children. Independence, Joan Gunderson writes, "was a condition arrived at by exclusion, by not being dependent or enslaved." The decline of the independent artisan was a concomitant of a developing commercial capitalism. The displacement and disruption of Indian tribal societies was a consequence of a system of landed expansion that met the needs of would-be settlers, land speculators, southern slaveholders, and the suppositions of ethnocentrism, racism, and an ideology of expansion that envisioned, among the most benevolent expansionists, in Jefferson's words, an "empire for liberty."[237]

I have suggested elsewhere that the concept of conflict, negotiation, and accommodation may help us to reconcile the seemingly contradictory results in the multiple facets of the Revolution. In my own efforts at synthesis I have attempted to draw attention to the impact of popular movements on elites.

American Revolution," in Hoffman and Albert, eds., *Women in the Age of the American Revolution*, p. 10; Wilentz, *Chants Democratic;* Hoffman, Hoxie, and Albert, eds., *Native Americans and the Early Republic* (forthcoming), will bring together major trends in the new scholarship.

[237] Davis, *The Problem of Slavery in the Age of Revolution*, pp. 256, 259, 262; Joan B. Gunderson, "Independence, Citizenship, and the American Revolution," *Signs* 13 (1987):59–77; see also Ruth H. Bloch, "The Gendered Meanings of Virtue in Revolutionary America," *Signs* 13 (1987):37–58; James Merrill, "Declarations of Independence: Indian-White Relations in the New Nation," in Greene, ed., *American Revolution*, pp. 197–223.

There were many radicalisms in the Revolutionary era: a radicalism born of hope epitomized by Thomas Paine's *Common Sense,* whose millennialist plea that the "birthday of a new world is at hand" was appropriated by unequals in the society; a radicalism born of experience during the war among soldiers, seamen, and slaves who learned how to cast off deference; and a radicalism born of frustration, especially in the 1780s and 1790s, of promises unfulfilled.

Such radicalisms constantly shaped elites, would-be ruling classes trying to create or stabilize a system. Some turned to coercion, some to accommodation, learning how to "yield to the torrent if they hoped to direct its course," as Robert R. Livingston put it; some did both. At a crisis in the "political system" in 1787, Madison led elites at the Constitutional Convention to shape a government "intended for the ages" that would conform to "the genius of the people," including the Shaysite farmers and Paineite mechanics who were a presence even if they were not present.[238]

In 1976, in my afterword to my collection of essays on radicalism in the era, I thought that while farmers and artisans became a force to be reckoned with, the outsiders—African-Americans, women, American Indians—had little effect in pressuring elites. As I reflect on scholarship since then, it is apparent that historians are now working out similar processes of negotiation with the so-called outsiders. This is a hallmark of recent scholarship on slavery—the processes of negotiation by which slaves won "space" for themselves within an oppressive system. After the Revolution, as slavery grew and expanded, Ira Berlin finds central "continued renegotiations of the terms under which slaves worked for their masters." "We are ready to ask," Linda Kerber writes, "whether and how the social relations of the sexes were renegotiated in the crucible of the Revolution." James Merrill portrays Anglo-American elites oscillating between coercion and accommoda-

---

[238] Young, "Conservatives"; idem, "The Framers of the Constitution"; idem, afterword to Young, ed., *The American Revolution;* idem, "How Radical Was the American Revolution?" in Young, ed., *Beyond the American Revolution;* Young and Terry Fife with Mary Janzen, *We the People: Voices and Images of the New Nation* (Philadelphia, 1993).

tion of Indians. The alternatives Americans offered to Indians—"civilization or extinction," as Merrill writes—were "alternative routes to obliteration," but they were in response to resistance by tribal societies.[239]

How do historians attempting syntheses of the Revolution deal with these opposites? The deans of the Counterprogressive school, Edmund S. Morgan and Bernard Bailyn, judging by the most recent editions of their books, stand pat with their earlier interpretations. James A. Henretta, who in 1973 presented a new social history synthesis in the framework of modernization, in a recent revision in collaboration with Gregory H. Nobles, puts more emphasis on the "actions of thousands of 'unheeded' and obscure men and women" and on the "contradictions" in the results posed by the inequality of blacks and women and the displacement of the Indians. The framework, however, remains modernization with stress on the "transition to capitalism," a theme that is drawing the attention of many scholars.[240]

The first New Left synthesis since Staughton Lynd's has a different emphasis. In 1985 Edward Countryman drew together the new history that has "explored the experience, the consciousness, and the purposes of artisans, farmers, militiamen, blacks, and women." For Countryman the Revolutionary movement was a complex "series of coalitions that formed, dissolved, and re-formed as people considered what

[239] Ira Berlin, "Rethinking Afro-American Slavery in Mainland North America" (Paper presented at the Fifty-seventh Annual Meeting of the Southern Historical Association, Ft. Worth, Texas, November 1991); Kerber, "'History Can Do It No Justice,'" p. 10; Merrill, "Declarations of Independence," pp. 197–223.

[240] Henretta and Nobles, *Evolution and Revolution*, chap. 10; Henretta, "The Transition to Capitalism in America," in Henretta, Kammen, and Katz eds., *Transformation of Early American History*, pp. 218–38; Henretta, "The War for Independence and American Economic Development," in Hoffman et al., eds., *Economy of Early America*, pp. 45–87, the latter two reprinted in Henretta, *The Origins of American Capitalism: Collected Essays* (Boston, 1992); Joyce Oldham Appleby, *Capitalism and a New Social Order: The Republican Vision of the 1790s* (New York, 1984); for reflections on this theme, see Allan Kulikoff, "Was the American Revolution a Bourgeois Revolution?" in this volume.

they needed and what they believed." They lived through "a massive, disruptive, immensely confusing but popular Revolution" in which there was a "grand transformation that bound together many separate changes." Ordinary people, if they did not find equality, "found their own voices." "But change did begin. Like artisans and farmers of the revolutionary era, women and blacks would have to go through a long painful struggle to win their freedom."[241]

The contrast in interpretations of transformation in the Revolution is best represented in the work of two senior scholars, Gary B. Nash and Gordon S. Wood. Nash has produced the largest and most multifaceted body of scholarship on the era of the Revolution of any scholar in the new social history. Wood, identified with the republican ideological interpretation and intellectual history, has produced the first synthesis to embrace the Revolution as a whole. The two stand at opposite poles of the current debate on the Revolution.

That Gary Nash (1933–) has been perceived differently is a sign that over the last quarter of a century he has crossed boundaries within as well as among schools. I "am sometimes called a 'neo-progressive,'" he wrote in 1986, "a label that pleases me because I hope my work has some utility in wrestling with the awesome problems of contemporary American life." He was happy to give the first Merrill Jensen lectures at Wisconsin. When his multicultural textbook for the elementary schools was the subject of public hearings in California, he found himself the target of attack by ethnic nationalists who accused him of tokenism and Eurocentrism. He found this odd, he said, because "I spent my whole career trying to get rid of Eurocentric teaching and catching it from conservatives at the university level who think my work is too left-of-

---

[241] Countryman, *American Revolution;* Countryman, "'To Secure the Blessings of Liberty': Language, the Revolution, and American Capitalism," in Young, ed., *Beyond the American Revolution,* pp. 123–48. For a variant synthesis, see American Social History Project, *Who Built America? Working People and the Nation's Economy, Politics, Culture, and Society,* 2 vols. (New York, 1989); Alfred F. Young and Eric Foner were the consulting editors for volume one, for which the first drafts of the early American history chapters were written by Dorothy Fennell and Bruce Levine, and the revisions by Edward Countryman and Marcus Rediker.

center." He is most comfortable defining himself as a social historian; he is unique in attempting to bring together the two traditions of social history analyzed by James Henretta that stem from the *Annales* school and English revisionist Marxism and adding to it a third, the ethnohistory of American Indians and African-Americans.[242]

The evolution of his interests and methods suggests the way his own ideas are rooted in experience—a theme of his scholarship. As a senior at Princeton in 1954, to Richard S. Dunn, then a teaching assistant, Nash was "a sandy-haired, clean cut youth who wore his snappy Naval ROTC uniform to class and seemed from my jaundiced graduate school perspective to be designed by God for a military career." After three years on a destroyer in the Mediterranean, he returned to Princeton where he was an assistant to the dean of the graduate school and then a student. He did a thesis under Wesley Frank Craven on the divisions among elites in early eighteenth-century Pennsylvania politics. In 1966, when he moved from teaching at Princeton to UCLA, he "became deeply involved in the Civil Rights movement" and "at the same time," he writes, "I found that my students were far more diverse than in the East—diverse in terms of race, class, sex, age, and cultural background. My course in the history of colonial and revolutionary America began to change under this dual influence." In this environment his scholarship turned in two new directions—to the triracial character of colonial society, encapsulated in the title of a book that evolved from his teaching, *Red, White, and Black: The Peoples of Early America,* and to the study of social stratification, which made him one of the pioneers we have discussed in the first wave of the new social history.[243]

In the mid-1960s this trajectory from political history of elites to quantitative social history from the bottom up was

---

[242] Gary B. Nash, preface, *Race, Class, and Politics: Essays on American Colonial and Revolutionary Society* (Urbana, Ill., 1986), p. xix; David L. Kirp, "The Battle of the Books," *San Francisco Examiner Sunday Image,* Feb. 24, 1991, pp. 17–25, Nash quotation p. 19.

[243] Richard S. Dunn, foreword to Nash, *Race, Class, and Politics,* p. xiii; Nash, preface to "Social Change," p. 4; Meier and Rudwick, *Black History,* pp. 198–99; Nash, *Red, White, and Black,* 3d ed. (1991); Nash, *Quakers and Politics: Pennsylvania, 1681–1826* (Princeton, 1968).

not unique for scholars in his cohort. What was unusual was that he was interested in social class as a matrix to probe the origins of the Revolution. He collected his essays from 1963 to 1983 under the title *Race, Class, and Politics.* In focusing on the common people, he was as much interested in their agency, for which he reexamined traditional literary sources, as in analyzing their underlying life conditions, for which he quantified mute aggregates of sources. That he could carry on this research in California (with research trips to the East) is testimony to the decentralization of primary sources made possible by the microform revolution.[244] *The Urban Crucible* (1979) brought together the two methods. Later, when he moved from the origins to the results of the Revolution, as did other scholars, he focused on the experiences of African-Americans. His synthesis has appeared in works intended for a general audience—a college text, a series of elementary school texts, a museum exhibit on the history of Philadelphia, and a project to establish national standards in the teaching of history in the public schools. In this concern for reaching a larger public, the "new" social history is akin to the "new" history of Beard, Becker, and Curti in the interwar years.[245]

[244] Nash and Lemon, "Distribution of Wealth"; Nash, *Class and Society;* idem, *Red, White, and Black;* idem, "Up from the Bottom"; idem, "Urban Wealth and Poverty." For Nash's analysis of this scholarship, see his "Social Development," in Greene and Pole, eds., *Colonial British America,* pp. 233–61; for a response to a critic, see Nash, Billy G. Smith, and Dirk Hoerder, "Laboring Americans and the American Revolution," *Labor History* 24 (1983):414–39.

[245] For the permanent exhibit "Finding Philadelphia's Past: Visions and Revisions" at the Historical Society of Philadelphia, see Nash, "Behind the Velvet Curtain: Academic History, Historical Societies, and the Presentation of the Past," *Pennsylvania Magazine of History and Biography* 114 (1990):3–26. The texts are known as the Houghton Mifflin Social Studies series, 10 vols. (Boston, 1991), each volume with a different title; *America Will Be* goes through the Civil War; for the controversy over adoption of the texts, see Robert Reinhold, "Class Struggle, California's Textbook Debate," *New York Times Magazine,* Sept. 29, 1991, pp. 26–29, 46–47, 53. Nash is project director, with Charlotte Crabtree, of the National Center for History in the Schools whose report *National Standards for United States History: Exploring the American Experience* (Los Angeles, 1994) was sponsored by the United States Department of Education and the National Endowment for the Humanities; see Nash, "History for a Democratic Society: The Work of All People,"

Nash revealed the assumptions that guide his study of subordinate classes in *Red, White, and Black*. He was concerned with rescuing groups blotted out by American "historical amnesia" but not in portraying them as victims of exploitation or aggression. His focus was "the dynamic process of interaction" that shaped the history of American Indians, Europeans, and Africans in North America that included cultural exchange and the mixing of peoples as well as conflict and conquest. He rejected both the Gramscian notion of hegemonic domination of subordinate classes and the celebration of the masses. In introducing a collection of biographies of obscure individuals among colonial Spanish Americans, American Indians, and Anglo-Americans, Nash (and his co-editor David Sweet) wanted to avoid "Horatio Alger stories about individuals triumphing against adversity" as well as "Howard Fast stories about people triumphing against oppression." He has used biography of unknown and lesser known figures to explore both agency and ideology.[246]

The Urban Crucible, his magnum opus, rooted politics in the "social morphology" of the cities (in the *Annales* tradition) and in class relations, defining class (as did E. P. Thompson) as the product of conflict. Portraying the three major seaboard cities, Boston, New York, and Philadelphia on a broad canvas from 1690 to 1775, it was the richest single book to set the Revolution in the context of social change and prior internal conflicts. Nash placed his social analysis in the framework of a political narrative that integrated changing patterns of economic growth and the concentration of wealth with the Great Awakening, colonial wars, and factional conflict, building the variations among the three cities into his story. His thesis is that from the 1760s to 1776 the Revolution "was accompa-

---

in Paul Gagnon, ed., *Historical Literacy: The Case for History in American Education* (New York, 1989), pp. 234–48.

[246] Nash, *Red, White, and Black;* Nash and David Sweet eds., *Struggle and Survival in Colonial America* (Berkeley, 1981), pp. 1–13; for biographies, see Nash, "Thomas Peters: Millwright and Deliverer," in Nash and Sweet, eds., *Struggle and Survival*, pp. 69–85, and Nash, "'To Arise Out of the Dust'": Absalom Jones and the African Church of Philadelhpia, 1785–95,"in Nash, *Race, Class, and Politics*, pp. 323–55.

nied by a profound social upheaval" but not a "social revolution." The agency was clear: the Revolution "could not have unfolded when or in the manner it did without the self-conscious action of laboring people, both those at the bottom and those in the middle." Ideology was more problematic. Nash saw a division between "two broad ideologies"—whigs, whom he divided between conservatives and liberals, who "embraced the bourgeois spirit of commercial life," and evangelicals, who "clung to traditional ideals of moral economy" and an "egalitarian and communalistic ethos." There was "no perfect crystallization of class or class consciousness" and clearly "no unified ideology among the laboring classes."[247]

Nash has explored the results of the Revolution primarily in the social experiences of artisans and African-Americans in the cities and around the national issue of race. For artisans the decades from the close of the Revolution to the 1820s were a time of "momentous transformation" that "created permanent fissures in the structure of the mechanical arts." While mechanics became a political force in urban politics, masters and journeymen were in increasing conflict. The long-standing tension among artisans saw a "capitalistic mentality" winning out over the "older communalistic ethos."[248]

For African-Americans in the northern cities, Nash portrayed a dual theme of "triumph and tragedy." In his book on African-Americans in post-Revolutionary Philadelphia, the fullest study of the "inner history" of one of the first free black communities, the tragedy lay in the relatively harmonious race relations of the postwar years turning into growing discrimination and blatant racism; the triumph lay in blacks forging their own churches, societies, and fraternal orders. Analyzing ideology, Nash found evidence for W. E. B. Dubois's "two warring ideals" between African and American

[247] Nash, *Urban Crucible*, chap. 13, "Revolution."

[248] Nash, "Artisans and Politics in Eighteenth-Century Philadelphia," in Jacob and Jacob, eds., *Origins of Anglo-American Radicalism*, pp. 258–78; Nash, "A Historical Perspective on Early American Artisans," in Michael Conforti and William Puig, eds., *The American Craftsman and the European Tradition, 1620–1820* (Amherst, Mass., 1989), pp. 1–16; Nash, "The Social Evolution of Preindustrial American Cities, 1700–1820: Reflections on New Directions," *Journal of Urban History* 13 (1987):115–45.

identities. The alternative institutions cultivated by the first generation of free blacks, especially the autonomous African-American churches, enabled them to maintain "the dialectical existence" of this "double consciousness."[249]

In his analysis of race as an issue in the post-Revolutionary era, he focused on the failure of abolitionism, a question raised in the late 1960s by Lynd, Jordan, and Davis. He attributed this not to the intransigence of the lower South and the political fragility of the national union but to white northerners who "lost the abolitionist fire in their bellies." They failed to respond to liberal southern plans for compensated emancipation and succumbed to "a rampaging racism." Examining how slavery ended in Pennsylvania, Nash found "a tug of war between ideological commitment and economic interests."[250]

In Nash's way of thinking, ideology is rooted in experience. "All Americans could agree on many elements of the republican ideology," but "continuing debate over the meaning of republicanism lay at the center of the Revolutionary experience." Skeptical of the pervasiveness of a single ideology, he has variously portrayed alternative ideologies among white laboring people as "evangelical" or as a "small producer" ideology centering on equality or a "moral economy." He sees this outlook as "more traditional than modern," which "does not fit comfortably within the bounds of classical republican thought" posited by Gordon Wood or the liberalism posited by Joyce Appleby. And among the "outsiders," he finds evidence for ways of thinking that hardly fit into any frames.[251]

[249] Nash, *Forging Freedom: The Formation of Philadelphia's Black Community, 1720–1840* (Cambridge, Mass., 1988), pp. 6–7; Nash, *Race and Revolution*, p. 72; Nash, "Forging Freedom: The Emancipation Experience in the Northern Seaport Cities, 1775–1820," in Berlin and Hoffman, eds., *Slavery and Freedom*, pp. 3–48; Nash, "The Forgotten Experience: Indians, Blacks, and the American Revolution," in William F. Fowler, ed., *The American Revolution: Changing Perspectives* (Boston, 1981), pp. 27–46.

[250] Nash, *Race and Revolution*, chaps. 1–2; Nash and Jean R. Soderlund, preface, *Freedom by Degrees: Emancipation in Pennsylvania and Its Aftermath* (New York, 1991).

[251] For Nash's approach to ideology, see "Also There at the Creation: Going beyond Gordon Wood," *William and Mary Quarterly*, 3d ser. 44 (1987):602–11.

Nash's vision of transformation in the Revolution stresses the agency of the common people and their conflict with their betters. "In the course of resisting English policy" from 1765 to 1776, "many previously inactive groups entered public life to challenge gentry control of political affairs. Often occupying the most radical ground in the opposition to England, they simultaneously challenged the concentration of economic and political power in their own communities." Then, ordinary people "elbowing their way into a political system in which they had never been centrally involved . . . shaped the Revolutionary process in vital ways." The war "transformed the lives of all Americans" but had "different consequences for men than for women, for black slaves than for white masters, for Native Americans than for frontier settlers, for overseas merchants than for urban workers." "Outsiders," defined as black slaves, Native Americans, and white loyalists, "suffered the effects but reaped few of its rewards." American Indians suffered "both betrayal and defeat"; when peace came "the Indians' interests were totally ignored." The Revolution "changed many aspects of American life," but "changes did not come easily" as "people struggled with each other for political power and the ability to influence what government did."[252]

Criticism of Nash's work spans a range. Gordon Wood, characterizing Nash as someone who "has devoted his career to writing about the weak and dispossessed," expresses a debt "for uncovering the experience of these neglected groups." But Wood argues that Nash "sentimentalizes" the traditionalism and moral economy of popular majorities; small producers, he insists, were "entrepreneurial minded." Among social historians, Nash receives the kind of criticism often directed at scholars who open up a field: incompleteness. At a panel devoted to race and class in his work, Nash pleaded guilty to Jean Soderlund's charge that he subordinated gender analysis to race and class. "Historians can do double axels quite gracefully these days," he quipped, "and perhaps they will

[252] Nash et al., *The American People: Creating a Nation and Society* (1986), 2d ed., 2 vols. (New York, 1990), vol. 1, chaps. 5–7, generalizations pp. 159, 164, 188, 191, 196, 200, 205, 211, 228. Several chapters in this section of the book were written in collaboration with John R. Howe.

catch up with Olympic figure skaters and be able to do triple axels without falling." Accepting Allan Kulikoff's criticism that his work lacks "a systematic theoretical analysis of class relations," Nash suggests this may be a possible advantage. He is intensely aware of the problem of establishing unifying themes in ethno-history to avoid the pitfalls of "cameo history." After several years on the combat lines synthesizing the new histories in fifth, eighth, and eleventh grade textbooks and drawing up national standards, Nash expects to return to the challenge of synthesis in the era of the Revolution by exploring Indians and taking *Red, White, and Black* through the Revolution, which will enable him to attempt a general social history of the Revolution.[253]

Gordon S. Wood, in his recent work of synthesis, *The Radicalism of the American Revolution*, entered the door he left open to the Jameson thesis at the conclusion of his first book, *The Creation of the American Republic, 1776–1787*, in 1969. Indeed, in the 1990s, he has rattled Jameson's dry bones with such provocative and extravagant claims that one wonders whether the exacting Jameson, his predecessor at Brown University in the 1890s, might ask: "Has Gordon Wood *over*considered the American Revolution as a social movement?"

Wood's formulations are nothing if not bold. "Measured by the amount of social change that actually took place—by transformations in the relationships that bound people to each other," he writes, the Revolution was "not conservative at all; on the contrary: it was as radical and as revolutionary as any in history," and it was "as radical and social as any revolution in history." "It was the Revolution, more than any other single event, that made America into the most liberal, democratic, and modern nation in the world." "The idea of equality . . . the most radical and most powerful ideological force [was] let loose in the Revolution. Once invoked, the idea of equality

---

[253] Gordon S. Wood, "Ideology and the Origins of Liberal America," *William and Mary Quarterly*, 3d ser. 44 (1987):635–40; Nash, "Response to Commentaries," at the panel "Race and Class in the Work of Gary B. Nash" (Eighty-fifth Annual Meeting of the Organization of American Historians, Chicago, April 1992). The commentators were Jean R. Soderlund, Richard White, Douglas Greenberg, and Allan Kulikoff.

could not be stopped." Wood speaks of the "social transformation" and the "social radicalism" of the Revolution.[254]

The Radicalism of the American Revolution is a very different
book from *The Creation of the American Republic,* and the
changes reflect Wood's response in the intervening years to
changes in the landscape of scholarship. Wood (1933–) was
born in West Acton, near Concord, where, a recent interviewer reports, "his family had a chicken farm. His voice still
carries traces of a blue-collar Massachusetts accent." He received an undergraduate degree from nearby Tufts, and after
three years as a lieutenant in the Air Force (1955–58), did his
Ph.D. at Harvard where, if it needs to be said, as a student of
Bernard Bailyn he became an unexpected enthusiast of early
American history. He completed *Creation of the American Republic* on a fellowship at the Institute of Early American History and Culture (1964–66), taught at Harvard and the
University of Michigan, and has been at Brown University
since 1969. Wood has never been accused of being a populariz-
izer. *Creation* was a meticulously argued, very long book that
my graduate students made me feel I inflicted on them. Wood
has published articles for fellow historians, reviews for intellectuals in the *New York Review of Books* and the *New Republic,*
and given invited lectures in academic settings. The text he
coauthored with Bailyn, Davis, and three other distinguished
historians in its first edition proved too intellectual and too
sophisticated for its college audience. He has also never been
accused of political partisanship. He takes pride in what his
interviewer called his refusal to pick sides. "People have said
to me," he said "'I never know whether you're for the federalists or for the anti-federalists. Are you for the elites, or are
you for the common people?' I think I would have been one
of those people on the fence, the mugwump, I guess."[255]

This seeming diffidence notwithstanding, there is a passion

[254] Gordon S. Wood, introduction, *The Radicalism of the American Revolution* (New York, 1992), pp. 3–8, quotations pp. 5, 7, 232 ("idea of equality").
"An early version of the book was presented in 1986 as the Anson G. Phelps
lectures at New York University," p. ix.

[255] Missy Daniel, "A Radical History," *Brown Alumni Monthly* 93
(1993):23–27; Gordon S. Wood, "Curriculum Vitae," kindly provided by
Wood.

of a crusader in his new book which takes on meaning in the context of the critical reaction to his own scholarship and the Republican "school" he feels he is overidentified with and to what he has called a "crisis" in the field of intellectual history. From the publication of his first article in 1966 challenging his mentor to deal with the reality that underlay the rhetoric, through his 1969 book devoted to conflict rather than consensus, to his festschrift essay of 1991 interpreting Bailyn as a social historian who had for a time lost his way, Wood has established his independence of judgment. In the parlance of eighteenth-century artisans who passed from apprentice to journeymen to master, he became "a man on his own." But, by staking out a middle position between a so-called idealist or intellectual approach on the one hand and the so-called realists or materialists on the other, it was inevitable that he should be criticized by both and leave others bewildered. Bailyn was criticized by eminent intellectual historians because he "tend[ed] to exaggerate the autonomous power of ideas" (David Brion Davis) or because he "elevated ideology to causal preeminence" (Joyce Appleby). Wood has not escaped such criticism, although it has been muted. I, for one, never thought it was true of *Creation of the American Republic,* a book I welcomed at the time as an exploration of the ideology of the debate over the Constitution that restored conflict to the era and not as an ideological interpretation.[256]

Over the years Wood has staked out his position. He has disassociated himself from Bailyn's "aversion" to anything that smacks of a social analysis and from those who saw in Bailyn's emphasis on conspiracy a paranoid psychological interpretation of history; such a belief, Wood argues, was quite rational in the eighteenth century. He has also separated himself from "the so-called republican synthesis" of the 1970s and 1980s as "something of a monster that has threatened to devour us all." And in the 1980s he explored the terrain of "in-

---

[256] Wood, "Rhetoric and Reality"; idem, *Creation of the American Repbulic;* idem, "Democratization of the Mind"; idem, "Creative Imagination"; Davis, *The Problem of Slavery in the Age of Revolution,* p. 274n (his reference is to Jordan and Bailyn); Appleby, "A Different Kind of Independence," p. 261; Alfred F. Young, review of Wood, *Creation of the American Republic,* New-York *Historical Society Quarterly* 55 (1971):391–92.

terests" in the 1780s that he had bypassed earlier. Focusing, for example, on William Findley, the Irish-born former weaver, a self-made politician in western Pennsylvania, he concluded that the Antifederalists were spokesmen for "middling aspirations, middling achievements, and middling resentments."[257]

Twenty years after its publication, for all the recognition *Creation of the American Republic* received, Wood was put on the defensive about it. It is the only book the *William and Mary Quarterly* honored as a "modern classic," with a symposium in 1987 in which a dozen historians participated. Wood had to reply to a wide range of critics. On the one hand were those who faulted him for an "overly intellectual approach" to ideology (Jack N. Rakove) or for neglecting such other ideologies as liberalism or evangelical religion (Ruth H. Bloch, John Howe) or the seminal role of Thomas Paine (Pauline Maier). On the other he had to reply to historians who deal with the nitty gritty of interest politics like Jackson Turner Main or the role of capitalism like Edward Countryman or the agency of popular movements like Gary Nash. Nash, not surprisingly, finds Wood's version of 1776 to 1787 "too homogeneous, too static, and too shallowly rooted in the soil of social experience."[258]

Wood secondly has confronted the impasse in intellectual history as a field. In the post–World War II years, young historians who had entered the field at Harvard under Perry Miller or at Wisconsin under Merle Curti felt intellectual history was their crusade. "I taught, wrote, and believed in intellectual history," writes Henry F. May, at Harvard in the late 1930s. "When I came to Berkeley, [after the war] intellectual history was a satisfying radical cause," and then in the 1950s

---

[257] Wood, "Conspiracy and the Paranoid Style: Causality and Deceit in the Eighteenth Century," *William and Mary Quarterly*, 3d ser. 39 (1982):401–41; Wood, postscript to "Rhetoric and Reality," in *In Search of Early America*, pp. 76–77 ("something of a monster"); Wood, "Interests and Disinterestedness in the Making of the Constitution," in Beeman et al., eds., *Beyond Confederation*, pp. 69–109.

[258] "*The Creation of the American Republic, 1776–1787:* A Symposium of Views and Reviews," *William and Mary Quarterly*, 3d ser. 44 (1987):550–627, including Wood's rejoinder, pp. 628–40.

"my kind of history became for a short and heady few years, the rising fashion." The 1960s, of course, started the era of the new social history. By 1977, when Wood, like Bailyn an admirer of Perry Miller, spoke to fellow scholars at a conference called by John Higham, Curti's student, to address the crisis in the field, he felt the need to save intellectual history from being relegated to "the backwaters of the historical profession." "We have not made many people believe that ideas can 'cause' something like a revolution," he said. Speaking to the fear among historians of ideas that the new social history would once again reduce ideas to being simply the consequences of behavior, he pleaded with them to address "the larger cultural world, the system of values and conventions, in which historical actors lived—what historians have called 'traditions,' 'climates of opinion,' or 'habits of thought,'" especially if they wished to recover the mind of ordinary people.[259]

This is what Wood has tried to do in *The Radicalism of the American Revolution*. The spirit of J. Franklin Jameson hovers over the book. Jameson, Wood writes, "was at least right about one thing: 'the stream of revolution once started, could not be confined within narrow banks, but spread abroad upon the land.'" Wood's metaphor trumps Jameson's: "The revolution resembled the breaking of a dam, releasing thousands upon thousands of pent-up pressures." He found proof for Jameson's claims about the importance of the displacement of the loyalists and the destruction of feudal land forms, but these were minor matters. Regardless of his intention, Wood expanded the arguments in all four Jameson lectures—the status of persons, the land, commerce, thought and feel-

---

[259] Henry F. May, *Coming to Terms: A Study in Memory and History* (Berkeley, 1987), pp. 307 and 231–32 (Miller). May was at Harvard in the late 1930s and got his Ph.D. in 1947; Wood, "Intellectual History and the Social Sciences," in John Higham and Paul K. Conklin, eds., *New Directions in American Intellectual History* (Baltimore, 1979), pp. 27–41. The paper was given at the Wingspread Conference, 1977, Racine, Wis., in honor of Merle Curti in the year of his eightieth birthday; Higham, introduction to Higham and Conklin, eds., *New Directions*, pp. xi-xix; for the state of the field see Higham, *Writing American History*, chaps. 1–3, and Robert Darnton, "Intellectual and Cultural History," in Michael G. Kammen, ed., *The Past Before Us: Contemporary Historical Writing in the United States* (Ithaca, N.Y., 1980), pp. 327–53.

ing. But in his claims for the "social radicalism" of the Revolution, Wood makes Jameson look like a piker.[260]

Wood continues to write history in which a central idea, "the spirit of equality," is the principal engine of change—equality, "the single most powerful and radical ideological force in all of American history."[261] He has organized his book under three rubrics—"Monarchy," which gives way to "Republicanism," which gives way to "Democracy"—in which he explores the impact of ideas thematically; one will search in vain for familiar events of the Revolution. And he continues, in the consensus mode, to generalize frequently about what "all Americans," "the colonists," or "the revolutionary generation" thought, as if equality made its way with the agreement of Virginia slaveholding planters, Hudson Valley estate holders, Philadelphia merchant princes, and wealthy land proprietors on the frontiers.

But his causal framework is more complex. He recognizes that "a broader revolution," modernization, was underway but argues that it and the American Revolution were "inextricably bound together." "Perhaps the social transformation would have happened 'in any case,' but we will never know. It was in fact linked to the Revolution; they occurred together." He sees a third dynamic factor in migration into the interior: "This demographic explosion, this gigantic movement of people, was the most basic and most liberating force working on American society during the latter half of the eighteenth century."[262] And in capitalism he finds a fourth. America in the early republic "may have been still largely rural, still largely agricultural, but now it was also largely commercial, perhaps the most thoroughly commercialized nation in the world." By 1812 Benjamin Rush thought "we are indeed a bebanked, bewhiskied, and a bedollared nation," and

---

[260] Wood, *Radicalism of the Revolution*, pp. 5–6 (Jameson), 230 ("dam"), 175–76 (loyalists), and chap. 10, "Revolution."

[261] Ibid., p. 200.

[262] Ibid., pp. 7, 133, 306–7, chap. 8, "Loosening the Bands of Society," and chap. 17, "A World Within."

Wood agrees.[263] And if these four dynamics—the idea of equality, modernization, westward explosion, and capitalism—are not enough, Wood finds another in "the rise of popular evangelical Christianity. . . . As the Republic became democratized, it became evangelized."[264] Together these transformed American society after the war. "By every measure there was a sudden bursting forth, an explosion—not only of geographical movement, but of entrepreneurial energy, of religious passion, and of pecuniary desires."[265] As Wood describes changes as late as the 1820s and 1830s, puzzled readers are left to their own devices to disentangle the effects of the Revolution from the effects of these five dynamic factors. What Wood seemingly has done is to absorb under the umbrella of the ideological force of equality rival historical interpretations that stressed either modernization, the alternative ideology of liberalism, the development of capitalism, and, (is it possible?) Frederick Jackson Turner's frontier thesis.[266]

Wood has also introduced agency, but his notion of agency is highly selective. Ordinary people challenge deference, and in the cities there is clearly an urban artisan presence. We hear especially about "a new breed of popular leader[s]" risen from below asserting their "interestedness" and of acquisitive capitalists (often same men). We hear strong democratic voices of William Findley, Matthew Lyon, Abraham Bishop, Abraham Clark, and William Manning lambasting aristocracy, voices we did not hear in *Creation*.[267] Yet Wood writes a history of radicalism in which one often has to search for familiar radicals. There is equality but not the egalitarian Thomas Paine of *Common Sense* or *The Rights of Man*, millennialism but no

[263] Ibid., pp. 309–10, 364 (Rush), and chap. 18, "The Celebration of Commerce."

[264] Ibid., pp. 328–32.

[265] Ibid., p. 230; see also pp. 356, 366.

[266] Ibid., p. 308.

[267] Ibid., chap. 14, "Interests," and chap. 15, "The Assault on Aristocracy," an outstanding chapter.

Hermon Husband, religious dissent but no Isaac Backus. And while there is an explosion of population onto numerous frontiers, there are no explosions of Regulators, Shaysites, Whiskey Rebels, Green Mountain men, or Maine's Liberty Boys.

Wood's world is built around binary opposites: dependence-independence; inequality-equality. Yet it is a world free from paradoxes or contradictions. The book is remarkable for the scholarship of the last twenty years it does not synthesize. The unequals at the bottom of white male society are silent. There seem to be no seamen, apprentices, indentured servants, landless farmers, or angry impoverished veterans. Nor are the outsiders a presence. Slavery is important only as a concept defining utter dependence that everyone wanted to avoid. Well aware that the Revolution did not bring freedom for blacks or equality for women, Wood argues, as did Bailyn and Morgan before him, that the Revolution "made possible the anti-slavery and women's rights movements of the nineteenth century and in fact all our current egalitarian thinking." He claims that "in effect [it] set in motion ideological forces that doomed the institution of slavery in the North and led inexorably to the Civil War."[268] This is whig history, evading the historian's responsibility to explain by pointing to later progress; one could argue as easily that the failure of the Revolutionary generation to destroy slavery made the Civil War inevitable. Understandably, therefore, the voices of African-Americans who sought freedom or of free blacks who sought equality, Phyllis Wheatley, Thomas Allan, Absalom Jones, Prince Hall, James Forten, Paul Cuffe, Gabriel Prosser, Denmark Vesey—all, by the way, the subject of recent scholarship—are missing. One would have thought that an examination of the failure to achieve racial equality in the era—a theme that has occupied some of the best minds in the profession—would have illuminated the character of equality.

Wood recognizes that women who were subordinated in the colonial era (perhaps, Laurel Thatcher Ulrich might say, less than he thinks) gained after the war when the family was

---

[268] Ibid., pp. 7–8 ("made possible"), 186 ("set in motion").

"republicanized" (perhaps much less than Linda Kerber might claim). But in a book with so many new male voices, the voices of women are missing. John Adams writes to Abigail Adams, but strangely we never hear Abigail reply, and in a book heavy with New Englanders, we do not hear Mercy Otis Warren, Sarah Osborn, or Judith Sargeant Murray speak to the inequality of their sex, much less other women who speak in the privacy of their diaries or letters.[269]

Perhaps more striking for a narrative in which "it is impossible to exaggerate the significance of the westward movement" there are no Indians, not even for their impact on frontiersmen, which might come as a surprise to the generals who acquired fame in the early republic removing them, Andrew Jackson and William Henry Harrison. We do not hear the voices of Neolin or Pontiac, Joseph Brant or Alexander McGillivray, Tecumseh or The Prophet; but, then again, we rarely hear them in the pages of most historians.[270]

Wood's book is resonant of Alexis de Tocqueville's. Indeed Wood projects the themes of the French traveler of the 1830s back to the half century before. Wood's book has the sweep, insights, and enthusiasm of Tocqueville. It also shares many of the blind spots of the Frenchman's celebration of America. It is a synthesis so protective of the achievements of equality that it seems unwilling to come to grips with inequality. It is as if to allow all these voices to speak at the table would spoil the celebration.

Wood's book has been bepraised, beprized, and beleaguered. To those who can still follow the cast of historians in this essay's benumbing account of the last half century of scholarship, the critical response to Wood's book may even augur a redrawing of lines of debate over the Revolution. Edmund Morgan, the consistent holdout against social transformation, despite his reservations about Wood's "exaggerations" and "the overstatement of his case," finds "that case is still convincing." But Pauline Maier, Wood's fellow shaper of the republican interpretation, after warm praise, chides him for failing to do justice to the radical *politi-*

[269] Ibid., pp. 147, 182–83, 354–55, 357–58.

[270] Ibid., p. 355, about efforts to "civilize" the Creeks and Cherokees.

cal implications of republicanism, wondering whether he has fallen into "a time-bound assumption—the modern conviction that real revolutions are fundamentally social."[271] Joyce Appleby, the most trenchant critic of the failure of the republican interpretation to integrate economic liberalism, is dismayed at Wood "reducing democratic values to crass material striving and competitive individualism." She thinks the book reifies the radicalism of the Revolution "so that it could have been written by George Bancroft—if he had only read Clifford Geertz." On the left some historians have welcomed the book, as has Sean Wilentz, as "a powerful repudiation of the Revolution as a consensual, conservative, legalistic event" or, as has Edward Countryman, for describing "what amounts to a bourgeois revolution." But they and others along a wide spectrum have been skeptical for reasons my analysis anticipated: the utter failure of Wood's celebration of capitalism and hosannah to American equality to come to grips with inequality. I suspect many historians will agree with Michael Zuckerman's criticism that the book "denies class at every turn. It disregards race, gender, and ethnicity almost entirely. It is oblivious to region." Wood "has shrunk America to a country without slaves, women, families, or the South." Whether the book has clarified the streams overflowing J. Franklin Jameson's banks or muddied the waters remains to be seen.[272]

Is there a future to considering the American Revolution as a social movement? Yes, I would argue, as long as Americans

[271] Morgan, "Second American Revolution," pp. 23–24; Pauline Maier, "It Was Never the Same after Them," *New York Times Book Review* (Mar. 1, 1992), p. 34; see also Drew R. McCoy, review, *Journal of American History* 79 (1993):1563–65.

[272] Joyce Appleby, "The Radical Recreation of the American Republic," Barbara Clark Smith, "The Adequate Revolution," Michael Zuckerman, "Rhetoric, Reality, and the Revolution: The Genteel Radicalism of Gordon Wood," Gordon S. Wood, "Equality and Social Conflict in the American Revolution," *William and Mary Quarterly,* 3d ser. 51 (1994):679–83, 684–92, 693–702, and 703–16, respectively; Sean Wilentz, "The Power of the Powerless," *New Republic,* Dec. 23 and 30, 1991, pp. 32–40; Edward Countryman, "Revolution, Radicalism, and the American Way," *Reviews in American*

seek to fulfill the promise of the Declaration of Independence, the Constitution, and Bill of Rights. And yes, as long as young scholars have the skepticism to challenge received wisdom and a passion about what they discover.

They do, judging by the fellows of the Institute of Early American History and Culture who responded in 1993 to the Institute's plea on its fiftieth anniversary to "look forward to the next half-century and project lines of vision and revision for the field."[273] I do not wish to homogenize the views of these diverse, individualistic scholars (and I am very likely reading my own biases into their essays). But their responses are encouraging. Those for whom the Revolutionary era is central to their research confront issues of transformation whether the dawn of the penitentiary or the "plebeian populism" of the anti-Federalists.[274] And others whose fields are African-American, Native American, and women's history call for rewriting the "master narrative" of American history. To a scholar of African-American history, "it is not simply a matter of fitting non-European voices into an existing narrative as another stitch in the fabric while the fabric retains its basic pattern." To a scholar of Native American history the prime need is to overcome come the "cameo theory of history" and notions of "victimization" and explore the "middle ground" between cultures. Kathleen M. Brown asks not merely that we continue to add women's lives but that we confront "the centrality of gender history."[275] A scholar of maritime history asks that we go "beyond Jack Tar" in the spirit of Jesse Lemisch. A scholar of agrarian history struggles with the transfor-

---

History 20 (1992):480–85. Wood's book won the Pulitzer Prize in History and the Ralph Waldo Emerson Award of Phi Beta Kappa.

[273] "Forum: The Future of Early American History," *William and Mary Quarterly*, 3d ser. 50 (1993):298–424, at p. 298.

[274] Michael Meranze, "Even the Dead Will Not Be Safe: An Ethics of Early American History," and Saul Cornell, "Early American History in a Postmodern Age," *William and Mary Quarterly*, 3d ser. 50 (1993):367–78, 329–41.

[275] Jon F. Sensbach, "Charting a Course in Early African-American History," Richter, "Whose Indian History?" and Kathleen M. Brown, "Brave New Worlds: Women's and Gender History," *William and Mary Quarterly*, 3d ser. 50 (1993):394–405, 379–93, 311–28.

mations among the yeomanry, the vast Anglo-American majority. A scholar of ideas calls for a "materialist intellectual history" to understand "the thinking class."[276] Given such passions, as these scholars confront the American Revolution, most would probably share Michael Meranze's tough-minded vision "that the accomplishments of the Revolution and of liberal society are inseparable from its repressions and exclusions."[277]

Shaking the scarecrow of "presentism" at these scholars will not deter them. Most of them would take for granted the observation of Thad Tate after his long tenure as director of the Institute: "I am unabashed in believing that historians chose to do their work in terms of what's going on around them."[278] Many I suspect would heed Meranze's plea for "a new presentism that blocks false identification with the past but still disrupts the security of the present," a plea for "a critical socially engaged historiography."[279] Thus there are good grounds to anticipate that this new generation of scholars will consider the social dimensions of the Revolution but in their own ways, ways that we can not yet imagine.

[276] Vickers, "Beyond Jack Tar," Allan Kulikoff, "Households and Markets: Toward a New Synthesis of American Agrarian History," and Darren Marcus Staloff, "Intellectual History Naturalized: Materialism and the 'Thinking Class,'" *William and Mary Quarterly*, 3d ser. 50 (1993):418–24, 342–55, 406–17

[277] Meranze, "An Ethics of Early American History," p. 378.

[278] Teute, "A Conversation with Thad Tate," p. 273.

[279] Meranze, "An Ethics of Early American History," p. 372.

Contributors
Index

Contributors

ROBERT A. GROSS is Forrest D. Murden, Jr., Professor of American Studies and Director of American Studies at the College of William and Mary. His first book, *The Minutemen and Their World* (1976), won the Bancroft Prize in American History. He has edited a volume on Shays's Rebellion, *In Debt to Shays: The Bicentennial of an Agrarian Rebellion* (1993) and published essays on New England social and cultural history from the Revolution through the late nineteenth century. His study of Concord, Massachusetts, during the era of Emerson and Thoreau will be published shortly as *The Transcendentalists and Their World*.

ALLAN KULIKOFF, professor of history at Northern Illinois University, is working on a three-volume history of small farmers in America from 1607 to 1930. His current writing emphasizes the development of yeoman class ideology, household formation, and community life in colonial America. His publications include *Tobacco and Slaves: The Development of Southern Cultures in the Chesapeake, 1680–1800* (1986) and *The Agrarian Origins of American Capitalism* (1992).

JEAN B. LEE is associate professor of history at the University of Wisconsin-Madison. A specialist in the American Revolution and in Chesapeake society, she published *The Price of Nationhood: The American Revolution in Charles County* in 1994. Her continuing research explores the Revolution's impact upon American society.

GREGORY H. NOBLES is associate dean for academic affairs and professor of history at Georgia Tech. His previous work on the Revolutionary era includes *Divisions throughout the Whole: Politics and Society in Hampshire County, Massachusetts, 1740–1775* (1983). His recent research also focuses on frontier regions, and he is completing a book entitled *From Contact to Conquest: Encounters on the North American Frontiers*.

495

MARCUS REDIKER is associate professor of history at the University of Pittsburgh. He is the author of *Between the Devil and the Deep Blue Sea: Merchant
Seamen, Pirates, and the Anglo-American Maritime World, 1700–1750* (1987)
and a contributing author of volume one of *Who Built America? Working
People and the Nation's Economy, Politics, Culture, and Society* (1989). He is
currently working with Peter Linebaugh on *The Many-Headed Hydra: The
Atlantic Working Class in the Seventeenth and Eighteenth Centuries.*

MOREY ROTHBERG was educated at the University of Maryland, College
Park, and at Brown University, where he received his doctorate in American Civilization in 1982. His dissertation is titled "Servant to History: A
Study of John Franklin Jameson, 1859–1937." He has published articles
on Jameson in the *American Historical Review* (1984), the *Public Historian*
(1986), the *Brown Alumni Monthly* (1987), and the *History Teacher* (1994).
He is a contributor to the *Historical Dictionary of the Progressive Era* (1988).
He was the J. Franklin Jameson Fellow in American History at the Library of Congress for 1983–84. He is director of the J. Franklin Jameson
Papers Project at the Library of Congress, coeditor (with Jacqueline
Goggin) of *John Franklin Jameson and the Development of Humanistic Scholarship in America*, volume one, *Selected Essays* (1993), and editor of volume
two, *The Years of Growth, 1859–1905* (1996).

JEAN B. RUSSO is director of research for the Historic Annapolis Foundation, Annapolis, Maryland. She is a coeditor of *Colonial Chesapeake Society*
and editor of *Unlocking the Secrets of Time: Maryland's Hidden Heritage.* Her
current research interests include nineteenth-century urban and
African-American history.

BARBARA CLARK SMITH is a curator in the Division of Social History at the
National Museum of American History, Smithsonian Institution. She is
curator of the permanent exhibition "After the Revolution: Life in
America, 1780–1800," and is the author of *After the Revolution: The Smithsonian History of Everyday Life in the Eighteenth Century* (1985). Her current
project explores popular politics during the American Revolution, focusing in particular on patriot nonimportation pacts, food riots, and
price control agreements as they reflected popular political forms and
popular ideas about the meaning of liberty.

BILLY G. SMITH is professor of history at Montana State University. He is
interested in issues of class, race, gender, and resistance in early America.
He has authored *The "Lower Sort": Philadelphia's Laboring People, 1750–
1800* (1990) and "Poverty in Early America" (1993), coedited *The Infortu-*

nate: The Voyage and Adventures of William Moraley, An Indentured Servant (1992), and edited *Life in Early Philadelphia: Documents from the Revolutionary and Early National Periods* (forthcoming). Currently he is engaged in writing a book about African-Americans who fled slavery in eighteenth-century America and in editing a volume of essays about the 1793 yellow fever epidemic in Philadelphia.

ALAN TAYLOR is professor of history at the University of California at Davis. He is the author of *Liberty Men and Great Proprietors: The Revolutionary Settlement on the Maine Frontier, 1760–1820* (1990) and *William Cooper's Town: Power and Persuasion on the Frontier of the Early American Republic* (1995). He continues to study the settler and native peoples of northeastern North America in the late eighteenth and early nineteenth centuries.

ALFRED F. YOUNG is senior research fellow at the Newberry Library and emeritus professor of history at Northern Illinois University. He reports on his scholarship in "An Outsider and the Progress of a Career in History" in the *William and Mary Quarterly* (1995). His most recent books are, with Terry Fife and Mary Janzen, *We the People: Voices and Images of the New Nation* (1993), as editor, *Beyond the American Revolution: Explorations in the History of American Radicalism* (1993), and, as editor with Robert Karrow, *Past Imperfect: Essays on History, Libraries, and the Humanities by Lawrence W. Towner* (1993). His study "George Robert Twelves Hewes (1742–1840): A Boston Shoemaker and the Memory of the American Revolution" was voted one of the eleven most significant articles in fifty years of the *William and Mary Quarterly*. He is currently writing *Artisans and the American Revolution* and *Masquerade: The Adventures of Deborah Samson Gannett in the American Revolution*.

Index